The Confident Consumer

Sally R. Campbell
Consumer Economics
Author and Consultant
Winnetka, Illinois

Publisher
The Goodheart-Willcox Company, Inc.
Tinley Park, Illinois

Manufactured in the United States of America.

Library of Congress Catalog Card Number 99-11552

International Standard Book Number 1-56637-635-1

2 3 4 5 6 7 8 9 00 06 05 04 03 02 01 00

Library of Congress Cataloging-in-Publication Data
Campbell, Sally R.
The confident consumer / Sally R. Campbell.
p. cm.
Includes index.
ISBN 1-56637-635-1
1. Finance, Personal. 2. Consumer education.
I. Title.
HG179.C32 1999
332.024—dc21 99-11552
CIP

Introduction

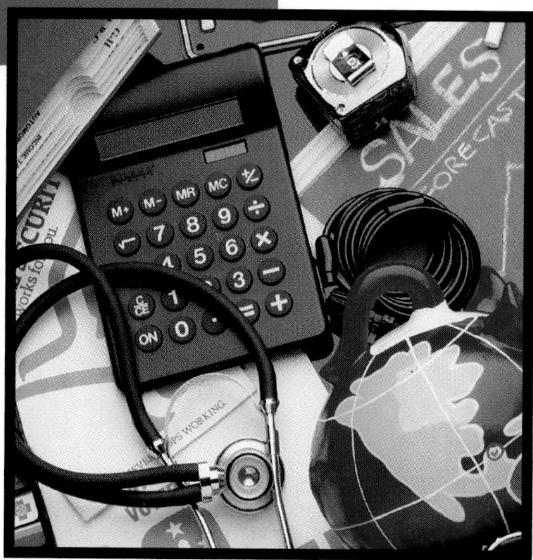

The Confident Consumer is designed to make you exactly that—a confident consumer. It will help you understand the economic system and how it affects you as a consumer, producer, and citizen. It will help you make the most of the opportunities that come your way in a market economy.

The text outlines the economic roles you play as worker, consumer, manager, and shopper. Mastering these decision-making functions lays the foundation for competence in the marketplace.

To be a confident consumer, you need to know what economic goals you want to achieve and how to achieve them. *The Confident Consumer* explains how to identify your most important needs and wants and how to manage your resources to reach your goals. It can help you make the best use of your money, credit, time, and other resources.

As you use this book, you will learn how to make decisions related to routine spending for food, clothing, and personal needs. You will learn where to find consumer information about products, services, government policies, and economic conditions. You will learn what to consider when making big spending decisions for items such as cars, housing, and home furnishings. You will learn what is important to know when you use credit, buy insurance, and invest your money.

Finally, you will look at your role as a citizen of the world. This includes your responsibilities as a citizen and taxpayer. The book also discusses your duties as a custodian of the environment and the world we share.

The Confident Consumer is straightforward and easy to read. Each chapter begins with learning objectives and new terms to understand. Each chapter ends with review questions, critical thinking questions, and activities to help you study effectively and organize what you learn. The case studies provided throughout the text will help you relate the material to real-life situations.

About the Author

Sally R. Campbell is currently a freelance writer and consultant in consumer econmics. She develops educational materials, including consumer information, publications, teacher's guides, curriculum guides, textbooks, and student activity materials. Her clients have included Household International, Insurance Information Institute, Kraft Foods, Sears Roebuck and Company, and Better Homes and Gardens.

She was formerly the editor and assistant director of the Money Management Institute of Household International where she wrote educational materials related to money management, consumer information, and financial planning. In this position, she carrried out research in all areas of personal finance and conducted consumer education workshops for teachers and the public.

Sally has a master's degree in education from St. Louis University and has completed the Certified Financial Planning Professional Education Program of the College for Financial Planning. She taught home economics and consumer education in the St. Louis public schools. She also served as an educational representative for the McCall Pattern Company where she presented educational programs, workshops, and demonstrations for teachers and students.

Contents

Unit 1 Economics

Unit 2 Making Decisions

Chapter 3 You, the Worker 63

Chapter 4 You, the Consumer 95

Chapter 5
You, the Manager 123

Chapter 6
You, the Shopper 149

Unit 3 Routine Spending

Chapter 7 The Grocery Cart 181

Chapter 8 The Shirt on Your Back 213

Chapter 9
How You Look and Feel 237

Unit 4 Big Spending

Chapter 10
Getting from Here to There 267

Chapter 11 Where You Live 301

Chapter 12 Inside Your Home 333

Unit 5 Finance

Chapter 13 Managing Credit 265

Chapter 14 Planning for Financial Security 389

Chapter 15 Using Financial Institutions and Services 409

Chapter 16 Investments and Life Insurance 437

Unit 6 Citizenship

Chapter 17 Your Role As a Citizen 465

Chapter 18 Your Role in the Environment 493

Glossary 519

Index 533

UNIT 1

Activity Growth
APPLE 0.50
MILK 1.00
FISH 1.50
INVEST
DOUBLE LETTER SCORE
DOUBLE WORD SCORE
TRIPLE WORD SCORE
by Milton Bradley

Economics

Chapter 1
Our Economic System

Chapter 2
You in Our Economy

Productive resources are turned into goods and services we use every day. This is done within the framework of our economic system. The role of government in our economy is to regulate businesses and enforce regulations to protect consumers. The government also creates fiscal and monetary policies to keep the economy stable. Competition for profits in our economic system leads to the development of new and improved products. Consumers, producers, and government all play vital roles in our economic system. International trade also plays an important role in our economic system.

You live in a market economy. Your economic activities, such as spending and voting, all make a difference. A command economy differs greatly from a market economy. In a command economy, a central authority, often the government, controls most of the economic activity. You are fortunate to live in a market economy with its freedom and many advantages. However, living in a market economy can present problems and challenges. Making wise choices and managing money carefully are important skills for consumers in the marketplace.

CHAPTER

SUPPLY
PROFIT
GROSS
NET

DEMAND
SCARCITY
BANK OF ENGLAND

SALES
FORECAST

Our Economic System

economy
producers
private ownership
public goods
productive resources
law of scarcity
law of supply and demand
economic competition
monopoly
antitrust laws
fiscal policy
gross domestic product (GDP)
consumer price index (CPI)
recession
inflation
monetary policy
reserve requirements
discount rate
open market operations
international trade
importing
exporting
balance of payments
trade deficit
protectionism
trade barrier
tariff
import quota
exchange rate
euro

After studying this chapter, you will be able to
- describe our economic system.
- explain how producers, consumers, and government interact with each other.
- define key economic terms.
- relate this information to real-life economic situations.
- cite examples of how international trade affects our economy.

You live in an economic world. Money changes hands every time you buy a hamburger, rent a movie, go to a concert, ride a bus, turn on a light, make a phone call, or see a doctor. Economic wheels turn to keep schools open, maintain streets and parks, and provide police and fire protection. Hundreds of times each day you use and depend on economic goods and services. ***Economy*** is the structure of production, distribution, and consumption of these goods and services.

Goods and services come to you largely through the economic activities of producers. ***Producers*** make and sell goods and services to satisfy consumer needs and wants. The exchange of goods and services takes place within the framework of an economic system. You need to understand the system in order to get the most out of it.

How Our Economy Works

Our economic system goes by many names: free enterprise, private enterprise, capitalism, a mixed economy, a consumer economy, and a market economy. Though these terms have slightly different meanings, they all describe a system based on the following four concepts.

❑ Private Ownership and Control of Productive Resources

Private ownership refers to property and resources individuals own and control as opposed to ***public goods*** owned and controlled by government. ***Productive resources*** include the labor, land, factories, machinery, capital, and management skills used to produce goods and services. In our economic system, citizens and businesses own and decide how to use these resources to produce goods and services.

❑ Free Economic Choices

Both citizens and businesses have the right to freely decide how they will earn, spend, save, invest, and produce. Their choices largely decide what the economy will produce, how much, and for whom.

❑ The Profit Motive

The desire for profit or money inspires businesses to produce the goods and services consumers want. See 1-1. The promise of earning money inspires the worker, shop owner, manufacturer, and investor to engage in worthwhile economic activity.

❑ Competition

Businesses compete with each other to win customers. Ideally, those who do the best job of producing quality goods and services at reasonable prices attract the most customers and earn the highest profits. Competition works in job markets, too, as workers compete with each other for jobs.

These key concepts come together to create a dynamic, ever-changing economy. You will explore how these concepts fit together in our economic system and how they affect you and your financial well-being.

1-1
The desire to fill the cash drawer motivates people to start a business and keep it going.

The Law of Scarcity

All economic systems attempt to resolve the problem of limited resources and unlimited needs and wants. This is the ***law of scarcity.*** Individuals, families, companies, and nations are all limited in the resources available to meet needs and wants. Resources are scarce, while the needs they must satisfy are never-ending. This makes it necessary to make choices in the use of resources and the needs to be met.

For example, your time, money, and other resources are limited. Consumers have unlimited needs and wants for a host of goods and services. These include food, clothes, compact discs, housing, medical care, cars, and spending money. Since resources are limited, while wants are unlimited, it is necessary to make decisions on which wants to satisfy. For example, you must choose between seeing a movie and going bowling if you haven't time for both. You choose either a new jacket or

Our Economy: Here's How It Works

The Profit Motive

Felipe Valdez is an 18-year-old high school senior. He has earned money running errands since he was in eighth grade. Several people in the apartment building where Felipe lives depend on him to run errands for them. Lately, the demand for his services has grown. Felipe now makes several trips per day. He goes further and further from home for pickups.

Felipe decides to make a real business of his delivery service. Over the years, he has saved several hundred dollars. Now seems like the perfect time to invest his savings and increase his earnings. The *desire to earn a profit* encourages Felipe to start his own business, or to become a real entrepreneur.

Felipe plans his new business venture carefully. He needs a car to reduce his traveling time. He needs an answering machine to take orders when he is not home. He also needs a way to advertise his services beyond the building where he lives.

In a local paper, Felipe finds an ad for a small used car at a good price. He takes it for a test drive. It runs well and doesn't use a lot of gas. The car is small enough to fit into tight parking spaces but large enough to carry his orders. Felipe then shops for a telephone answering machine. He chooses an inexpensive answering device that can be attached to his home phone. Finally, Felipe designs a folder to describe his delivery services. He has a neighborhood printer make 150 copies at a reasonable cost and distributes them to people in his neighborhood.

One major expense Felipe has overlooked is auto insurance. When he buys the car, he learns the law requires him to carry liability insurance. For young men, this insurance is expensive. By talking with the insurance agent, Felipe learns he can save on premiums by using his car only for business. This will also permit him to deduct all of his car expenses when he pays income tax. As his business grows, tax deductions will become more important.

Social Security tax is another expense Felipe underestimated. The Social Security tax is figured as a percentage of a person's income. The cost of the tax is shared by employees and their employers. Self-employed workers pay a higher tax rate because there is no employer to share the cost. Since Felipe is self-employed, he has to set aside a larger percentage of his earnings to pay Social Security taxes.

Even with all his expenses, Felipe feels confident. He is in business, and business is going well. Since there are no other neighborhood delivery services, he has little competition. He expects to earn a good income over the next few years. If all goes well, he will earn enough money for a reasonable profit after paying his investment and operating costs.

Case Review

1. How did the demand for delivery service influence Felipe to go into business?
2. What are some of the advantages and disadvantages of being self-employed?
3. What type of business do you see a need for in your neighborhood? Would you be willing to provide that service?
4. What are some of the obvious and hidden costs of starting your own business?

a pair of boots if you cannot afford both. You may choose between working 20 hours a week to earn more money or living with less money to have more time for study or fun. Families may choose between a new car and a family vacation, or between buying a home and starting a business. Economic choices are endless.

The law of scarcity applies to government in the same way. Government's resources are limited, and needs are unlimited. That's why it is necessary to make choices. Local governments may need to choose between building a public swimming pool and improving the streets, or between raising taxes and cutting services.

National resources are limited, while society's needs and wants are unlimited. No nation has the wealth and resources to meet all the wants of all its people. Major political and economic decisions center on how to divide limited national resources among unlimited needs. These needs may include crime control, health care, environmental protection, education, national defense, and aid to the poor and homeless.

The law of scarcity leads to three key economic problems common to all societies:

- What and how much to produce.
- How to use resources in producing goods and services.
- How to divide the goods and services that are produced.

Choices must be made. In our economic system, we address these questions largely through the forces of supply and demand operating in competitive markets.

The Law of Supply and Demand

Supply and demand are closely connected to the prices of goods and services in the marketplace. The ***law of supply and demand*** is that price and supply tend to follow demand. If demand for an item is steady, as it tends to be for items such as blue jeans, the price and supply of the item tend also to remain steady. If demand rises, such as with new and trendy items, prices will go up and suppliers will scurry to increase production. If demand falls, such as when trendy items become common, prices will fall and suppliers will cut production.

The demand for goods or services tends to fall when prices rise because fewer people are willing to pay the higher price. Demand may rise when prices fall because more can afford to buy at the lower prices. Consumers typically spend more when prices fall and less when prices rise. Supply tends to move in the opposite direction, falling when prices fall and rising when prices rise. This is because producers are willing to bring more goods to the market when they sell for high prices than when prices are low.

When the demand for an item is greater than the supply or when demand rises and supply remains the same, prices may rise sharply. For instance, airline ticket prices are highest during peak travel times. Seasonal foods become more expensive when the season ends and they become less plentiful. Food prices also rise when crops are lost to severe weather. If the supply of fuel oil is reduced or cut off by foreign suppliers, the price of oil rises.

To a large extent, demand in the marketplace determines *what and how much is produced*. Demand is expressed by spending choices of consumers, businesses, and governments. In our economy, the collective choices of individual consumers make the greatest impact. Consumers decide what to buy, where to buy, and how much to pay. They decide to use cash or credit, to spend or to save. These choices, to a large degree, determine what and how much producers will bring to the marketplace. In many cases, consumer demand leads to new product development and improvement. It was a major factor in the development of the consumer market in the computer industry.

Businesses generally own and control productive resources. They determine *how to produce* when they create the supply of products and services to meet consumer demands. Producers decide how to use resources of labor, land, equipment, and capital most efficiently in producing goods and services. See 1-2.

The forces of supply and demand in the job market largely determine *how to divide the goods and services produced.* Those who can offer the skills, knowledge, materials, or capital needed for production receive income or profits. In job markets, those who have the qualifications to perform the work most in demand generally earn higher incomes and can buy the goods and services they need. This determines how production is divided, 1-3.

USDA

1-2
Farmers still make key decisions on how to use land, labor, equipment, and capital in producing the nation's food supply.

DeVry Institute of Technology

1-3
Demand in the job market changes over time. Today those trained in high-tech fields are in great demand.

Profits in Our Economy

Without profits, our economic system could not move ahead. The desire for profit drives both individuals and businesses to produce. Individuals sell their productive resources, such as skills, labor, ideas, land, and capital. In return, they receive profit in the form of income or a return on their investments. This is what brings people into the workforce and investors into the stock market.

The desire for profit drives businesses to produce goods and services to meet consumer demands. Without the prodding of profits, our economy would falter. Individuals would not be motivated to work. Investors would not invest in businesses and provide the money needed to turn resources into goods and services. Businesses would not grow and try to increase sales. All businesses, from the corner grocery to a worldwide corporation, depend on profits.

The Need for Competition

Economic competition occurs when two or more sellers offer similar goods and services for sale in the marketplace. Each seller tries to do a better job than the other in order to attract more customers, make more sales, and earn more profits. For this reason, competition encourages competence and efficiency in the production and sale of goods and services.

Businesses compete with each other in many ways. They compete in the areas of price, quality, features, service, and new product development. Most often, the companies that provide the best products and services at the lowest prices achieve the highest sales and profits. Ideally, this results in better products and services at lower prices.

Competition can also be seen in the job market. The highest incomes go

Our Economy: Here's How It Works

Consumer Choice

Mrs. Casey, a 62-year-old widow, was one of Felipe's first customers. He picks up her groceries and runs other errands for her three times a week. Before Felipe turned his service into a real business, his fee was $1.00 per call. He gave regular customers like Mrs. Casey a special rate of $2.00 per week for three trips. Now that he is advertising, business is growing quickly. Felipe has more calls than he can handle. He decides to increase his fee to $1.50 per call and to charge Mrs. Casey $3.00 per week.

Because of the higher price, some of his customers begin using his service less often. Others stop calling altogether. When Felipe asks Mrs. Casey to pay $3.00 per week, she decides not to use his service anymore. He is sorry to lose Mrs. Casey, but business is still going well.

Mrs. Casey decides to look for a less expensive delivery service. When she can't find one in the neighborhood, Mrs. Casey calls together several of her friends who want occasional deliveries. They decide to ask someone else to run a delivery service for their group. They ask Darlene Adams, a high school senior who lives in their neighborhood. Darlene thinks Mrs. Casey's group has a good idea. She decides to go into the delivery service. Because free consumer choice creates a demand, a new business is born.

Case Review

1. What influence did Mrs. Casey have on the delivery service in her neighborhood?
2. How might Mrs. Casey's actions affect Felipe's business?
3. Why do you think free consumer choice is important?

to the most educated and skilled workers who produce the goods and services in greatest demand. In recent years, there has been a growing demand for such products as cellular phones, electronic games, and computers. This demand increases the competition among workers in the electronics industry. Workers try to update their skills and education to be qualified to earn higher incomes and better benefits. See 1-4. This, in turn, improves production, technology, and service in the electronic industry.

Competition in our economic system, as in sports, tends to keep everyone in top form. It helps bring out the best efforts and performance from business and labor. Another way to look at the value of competition is to consider the marketplace without it. A monopoly is the best example. A ***monopoly*** occurs when only one seller offers a given product or service for sale. The one seller controls the entire supply and has no competition. You can easily imagine the results. For instance, if there were only one car manufacturer, consumers would have no choice but to buy the car at the price set by the manufacturer. What would motivate that manufacturer to improve the car, lower prices, change models, or develop better safety and performance features?

The Role of Government

Our system is often called private enterprise because individual citizens own and operate businesses for the purpose of making profits. However, government plays an ever-growing role in the operation of our economy. Government influences economic decisions in three key areas:

- regulation
- taxation and spending
- economic policy.

1-4
These young people are learning computer skills so they will be ready to compete in the job market.

DeVry Institute of Technology

Our Economy: Here's How It Works

Competition

Darlene's father owns a grocery store. His customers often ask for deliveries, but Mr. Adams has never offered this service. He did not think the cost of buying a car and hiring someone to make deliveries would be profitable. However, when Darlene talks to her father about running a delivery service, he is willing to listen. They discuss the possibilities and come up with a plan.

Mr. Adams offers to let Darlene use the family car for her business. Since offering this service could bring more customers into the store, Mr. Adams suggests they keep the delivery charge low. They decide that Darlene should charge customers $1.00 for each grocery delivery from his store and $1.50 for each delivery from other stores.

To advertise this new service, Darlene designs a poster to display in the store and a folder to hand out to customers. She makes copies of the folder on a duplicating machine in the store. Like Felipe, Darlene must have auto insurance to use the family car. However, the insurance rate for Darlene is lower because she is a female. Statistically, teenage females are not as great an insurance risk as teenage males. Unlike Felipe, Darlene has an employer (her father). Thus, she pays less Social Security tax.

When all business expenses are totaled, Darlene's initial investment and operating expenses are much lower than Felipe's. By operating out of her father's store, using the store phone and the family car, Darlene can start and run her business at a much lower cost. She makes a fine profit, charging less than Felipe for deliveries.

To meet his new competition, Felipe decides to expand his business and hire some help. He contacts merchants in the area about making local deliveries for their stores. Five stores accept his delivery service plan. Through this plan, he will earn $2.50 for each delivery, $1.00 from the store and $1.50 from the customer. To handle the extra workload, he hires two helpers. With the merchants' business plus his regular customers, Felipe has as many orders as he can handle, in spite of the competition.

Now, consumers in the area can get delivery services from several stores at reasonable costs. Deliveries are made at almost any hour during the day and evening. Because Darlene and Felipe are competing with each other, they both try harder to please their customers.

Case Review

1. What advantages does Darlene have over Felipe?
2. What are some advantages and disadvantages of Felipe hiring extra help?
3. How did the competition between Felipe and Darlene affect the delivery service in their area?

Government Regulations

Government laws and regulations have a major impact on the economy. The earliest regulations were drafted mainly to promote fair competition and to ensure public well-being and safety. A look at these two areas will introduce you to the regulatory activities of government.

The ***antitrust laws*** were passed to promote competition and fair trade and to prevent monopolies and other trade restraints. The best known of these laws are:

- The Sherman Antitrust Act of 1890 prohibiting monopolies.
- The Clayton Antitrust Act of 1914 prohibiting price fixing and other unfair trade practices.
- The Federal Trade Commission Act of 1914 creating the Federal Trade Commission. This commission was given the power to investigate and issue orders preventing unfair or deceptive trade practices.

Government regulations that ensure public well-being and safety include laws in the areas of

- equal opportunity
- fair labor practices
- industrial safety standards
- environmental protection
- pure foods, drugs, and cosmetics
- product safety standards
- truth in advertising, lending, and labeling.

The Food and Drug Administration, the Environmental Protection Agency, the Consumer Product Safety Commission, and many other government agencies administer these regulations. These laws and their impact on business and the economy are discussed more fully in later chapters.

Taxation and Government Spending

Government taxing and spending decisions determine how much taxes individuals and businesses will pay. These policies also determine what services government will provide in return. Tax revenues pay for government operations. This includes expenses connected with Congress, the court system, presidential offices, law enforcement, and a host of federal agencies and commissions. Taxes also pay for public goods and services that private citizens and businesses cannot or do not produce. At the federal level, these include national defense, social welfare programs, education, highways, transit systems, and certain areas of research and development.

At the local and state levels, tax revenues pay for government operations and for services closer to home. These include schools, libraries, hospitals, roads, airports, parks, and fire and police protection. Citizens and businesses "buy" these goods and services from government with tax dollars.

When government taxes those who have money to provide for those who have little, it redistributes income. One way to achieve this goal is through a *progressive tax*. This means that those with higher incomes are taxed at a higher rate than those with lower incomes. The federal income tax system is progressive. The revenues are used to provide transfer payments for the needy. *Transfer payments* are income and benefits, which the needy receive in the form of social programs, such as food stamps, medical care, and welfare payments. These benefits are paid for largely by taxing those who do not receive them.

The Economic Policies of Government

Government economic policies are designed to regulate and control the ups and downs in the economy. Policy decisions affect the flow of economic activity in a variety of ways in an attempt to promote stability and prosperity. The government makes both fiscal and monetary policy decisions, 1-5.

Fiscal Policy

Fiscal policy refers to the federal government's taxing and spending decisions. Government often uses fiscal policy to stimulate the economy in periods of recession and high unemployment. Fiscal policy can also slow economic activity in periods of inflation or rising prices. Fiscal policy decisions are driven by certain economic indicators and analysis of the economy.

Two key measurements used to describe the state of the economy and the movement of prices are the gross domestic product and the consumer price index. The ***gross domestic product (GDP)*** is the total dollar value of final goods and services produced within the country in one year. It measures only final goods as they come to the consumer or end user. It does not include goods or services that go into producing finished products such as the flour in bread or the fabric in jeans. GDP does not include the value of any products or income produced by U.S. companies outside the country as well. When the GDP falls or fails to rise at an acceptable rate, the economy is said to be in recession. Rising figures indicate a healthy economy or the beginning of a recovery from recession.

The ***consumer price index (CPI)*** is a measure of the average change in prices over time for selected goods and services. It is based on prices in seven categories:

- food
- housing
- apparel and its upkeep
- transportation
- medical care
- entertainment
- other goods and services, such as fuel and utilities, consumers buy on a regular basis

Here is how the CPI works. The base period, currently 1982 through 1984, has an index number of 100. Price movements are stated as a percentage change from that base index number. For example, the 1997 CPI for all items

United Airlines

A

United Airlines

B

1-5
Lawmakers debate and propose federal legislation in the Capitol in Washington, DC (A). Laws are then presented to the President who signs them into law often in the Oval Office of the White House (B).

came to 160. This means you would need $1.60 in 1997 to buy what would have cost $1.00 in 1983. The CPI measures price changes and cost of living figures but does not include prices of stocks, bonds, real estate, or taxes paid by individuals and business. It is used also to adjust wages for workers covered by collective bargaining agreements and social security and pension benefits.

Fiscal Policy During Periods of Recession and Inflation

A ***recession*** is a slowing of economic activity marked by high unemployment, a decline in retail sales, lowered personal incomes, decreases in consumer spending, and less spending by business on plant equipment and expansion. Overall economic activity declines. During a recession, you may find it difficult to get or keep a job, to obtain a mortgage for building or buying a home, or to start a new business or keep one going.

To stimulate demand for goods and services during a recession, government may lower taxes and increase its own spending. These actions increase the amount of money in the marketplace. With more money in circulation, economic activity tends to expand. Government spending increases demand. Lower taxes leave more for consumers and businesses to spend, which also increases demand. Business expands to meet the increased demand. Economic growth and expansion result.

Inflation, or rising prices, occurs when spending increases at a faster rate than supply. One description of inflation is that too much money chases too few goods. This drives up the prices of limited supplies. In periods of inflation, government may increase taxes and reduce its own spending. This takes money out of circulation, reduces demand, and slows economic activity. Such action should help control inflation and bring prices down.

Unfortunately, government action can also make both inflation and recession worse. This happens when government spends more than it collects in tax revenues. This is called *deficit spending*. It tends to worsen inflation. When government borrows to cover its spending, less credit is available for business growth and expansion. This deepens a recession. When deficit spending continues over the years, it increases the *national debt* which is the total amount the government owes at a given time. The interest on this debt is often one of the largest expense items in the federal budget. It comes to billions of dollars that cannot be spent on other needs and programs. You and other taxpayers end up paying for this cost.

> ***"As soon as you start spending federal money in large amounts, it looks like free money."***
>
> *Dwight D. Eisenhower*

Monetary Policy

Monetary policy refers to actions the Federal Reserve Board takes to change the supply of money and credit. The Federal Reserve System, called the Fed, regulates the nation's monetary and banking system. See 1-6. It uses three tools to manage the supply of money and credit: reserve requirements, the discount rate, and open market operations.

- ***Reserve requirements***, set by the Fed, refer to the amount of cash that banks and other financial institutions must hold in reserve as a percent of their deposits. These reserves are amounts financial institutions must set aside rather than lend to customers. For example, if a bank has $10 million on deposit and the reserve requirement is

Official United States Mint Photograph

1-6
The United States Mint makes the nation's coinage, which is distributed through the Federal Reserve banks.

10 percent, it could only lend $9 million. The other million must stay on deposit. High reserve requirements reduce the amount of money available for lending. As a result, the supply of money and credit falls. Low reserve requirements have the opposite results.

- The ***discount rate*** is the interest rate Federal Reserve Banks charge commercial banks for credit when they borrow. A high discount rate discourages bank borrowing and reduces lending activities. This lowers the amount of money in circulation. Low discount rates have the opposite effect.
- ***Open market operations*** refers to the Fed's buying or selling of Treasury securities and other government debt instruments in the market place. When Federal Reserve Banks buy securities, the money supply increases. When they sell government securities, the money supply shrinks because the dollars paid for these securities are no longer in circulation.

When the Fed follows an "easy" monetary policy, interest rates are relatively low. Money and credit are readily available. Under these conditions, consumers and businesses tend to spend more than they would if under a "tight" monetary policy. For example, consumers tend to buy or build more homes when interest rates for home mortgages are lower. Companies borrow more capital for expanding their businesses. Farmers borrow to buy machinery and land to produce more crops. All of these activities stimulate the economy and create jobs. However, if too much money is pumped into the economy through Federal Reserve policies, inflation may result.

In times of inflation, the Fed will turn to policies that decrease the supply of money and credit. It will increase reserve requirements, raise the discount rate, and sell government securities. These actions will reduce the money supply and discourage the use of credit. As economic activity slows, prices tend to level off or fall.

It may sound simple for the Fed to speed up or slow down the economy, but maintaining a balance between supply and demand is no easy task. This is because all the parts in the puzzle are constantly changing. The changes follow a pattern called the *business cycle.* Every business expansion is followed by a contraction, which is followed by another expansion. Simply stated, "what goes up must come down." The actions of the government through fiscal and monetary policies serve to stretch, lengthen, shorten,and regulate the ups and downs in the cycle. In recent years, the result of government action seems to be less severe downturns and upswings in the economy.

Inflation is marked by rising prices and it carries the seeds of a follow-up recession. The government's attempts to control recession and inflation are outlined in 1-7.

Economic Concepts in Action

In a market economy, business successes and failures are a result of the forces of supply and demand, free economic choices, the profit motive, and competition. Government involvement and current economic conditions are also factors. One example that illustrates these concepts in action is the growth of the personal computer industry in recent years. The economic activities of consumers, producers, and government brought about the development and growth of this industry.

The Role of Consumers

Consumers provide the demand for goods and services they want at prices they can afford to pay. They do this by buying goods and services they want and by refusing to buy what they do not want or cannot afford. To be an active force in the economy, consumers must have:

- ❑ An awareness of goods and services available.
- ❑ Dollars to spend.
- ❑ Free choice of what, when, and where to buy.

Fiscal and Monetary Policies

Economic Conditions	Likely Fiscal Policy Taxation/Spending	Likely Monetary Policy Money and Credit Supply	Expected Results
Inflation–A period of rising prices.	❑ Increase tax rates leaving consumers and business with less to spend. ❑ Reduce goverment spending to cut the amount of cash flowing into the system.	❑ Raise reserve requirements so less money and less credit are available. ❑ Increase discount rate making credit more expensive ❑ Sell government securities, drawing money out of circulation.	❑ Lower credit availability. ❑ Less money in circulation. ❑ Reduced spending. ❑ Lower demand. ❑ Falling production. ❑ Slowing economy.
Recession–A period of economic slowdown and unemployment.	❑ Lower taxes giving consumers and business more money to spend. ❑ Raise government spending to pump more money into the economy.	❑ Lower reserve requirements permitting banks to lend more money. ❑ Lower discount rate making credit more affordable. ❑ Buy government securities pumping money into the economy.	❑ Increase availability of money and credit, which increases spending, which increases demand, which increases production, which leads to business expansion and jobs.

1-7
The government uses fiscal and monetary policies to alter economic conditions.

Consumer Demand and the Personal Computer Industry

Computerized devices were first developed to meet military, medical, and business needs. They were used in such fields as defense, medicine, and communications. Since consumers had little knowledge of computer technology in its early stages, there was no consumer demand for personal computers.

Digital watches and pocket calculators were among the first computerized products to enter the marketplace. They sold well, and consumers became interested in computer technology. Electronic games were next in the lineup of computerized products to hit the market. These games became popular and consumers began to demand computer software and accessories for home use, 1-8. As people grew familiar with the computer, they learned of its potential for household and personal business uses.

Radio Shack, A Division of Tandy Corporation

1-8
The consumers' use of home computers for pleasure, study, and work helped create mass demand for this product.

The first personal computers were developed and introduced for home use in the mid- to late-seventies. Soon consumers were demanding both computers and software packages. Manufacturers began to create software to teach a variety of subjects including foreign languages, geography, history, and math. Programs for financial planning, record keeping, and word processing became more and more popular. Consumer demand for computer hardware and software grew quickly. Sales of personal computers grew from slightly over six million in 1985 to well over 34 million in 1998. Revenues for the same period grew from nearly $12 billion to almost $82 billion. Since 1995, the number of U. S. households online has increased from just over nine million to 28 million. Software sales and computer services are increasing at a similar pace. Consumer demand is playing a major role.

The Role of Producers

Producers provide the supply of goods and services to meet consumer demands. This group includes all of those involved in bringing a product to the consumer—investors, entrepreneurs, researchers, managers, laborers, technicians, advertisers, and sellers. To succeed in a market economy, producers must have:

- An awareness of consumer demand.
- Productive resources, such as labor, land, money, tools, equipment, and other means to produce goods and services.
- Free choice in using productive resources to meet consumer demand.

Producers and the Personal Computer Industry

When producers saw the consumer demand for personal computers, they moved quickly to develop hardware and software for home use. At first, only two manufacturers produced personal computers and few companies produced software. After a few years, dozens of manufacturers produced personal computers with interchangeable parts and accessories. Hundreds of companies began producing software programs. As a result, a wide selection of both hardware and software became available to consumers.

As the market grew, producers began to compete with each other. Each created computers with new features and accessories to allow more memory, better color graphics, and faster work. Software was developed on a greater number of subjects with better graphics and more applications. Today, computer products are available in a variety of price ranges and quality levels to meet different consumer needs and compete for a larger share of the market, 1-9.

Zenith Electronics Corp.

1-9
More and more consumers are buying computers for home use, creating a demand for both hardware and software.

The Role of Government

In our economy, government affects every industry, including the personal computer market. Since the government is the nation's largest single consumer, it helps create demand in the marketplace. Government uses computer technology in a number of vital areas including communication systems, medical research, and national defense. Government demand for computer technology was a key factor in the early development of computers and software.

The government also supports research and product development in a variety of fields through grants and loans to universities and private businesses. Its support of technology in the consumer industry paid for much of the early development before a consumer market became established. Without the aid of government funding, the technology and the market for personal computers would have developed much more slowly.

Government economic policies were also a positive factor in the mid- to late-seventies when the technology for personal computers was developing. At that time, relatively low corporate tax rates made it possible for businesses to invest in expansion, research, and product development. At the same time, low interest rates encouraged the use of credit for expansion. Relatively low taxes and low interest rates, together with new technology, set the stage for the growth of the computer industry. As a result, many companies began to develop and sell personal computers and software.

Competing for Profits

Whenever there is a large demand for a product, there is a potential for profit. Investors who saw the rising demand for personal computers and software also saw the promise of profits. They invested their money in the computer industry expecting to receive a good return on their investments. Companies who saw the rising demand for personal computers expanded production to meet consumer demands.

Competing for these profits encouraged the development of new and better personal computers. Companies began producing a greater variety of computer features and software. They improved the quality of their products and lowered the prices. Our market economy worked, and both consumers and producers benefited.

International Trade and Our Economy

Our economy does not operate in a vacuum. The United States is the world's largest exporter, importer, and investor in world markets. It is dramatically affected by economic conditions and trade around the world. ***International trade*** is the buying and selling of products and services between nations. It involves ***importing*** or buying from other nations and ***exporting*** or selling to other nations. International trade occurs because nations cannot efficiently produce all the goods and services they need. At the same time, many nations produce more than they need of certain goods and services. Therefore, nations depend on each other to buy what they need and to sell what they produce beyond their own needs.

> ***"Not many Americans have been around the world, but their money sure has."***
>
> *Walter Slezak*

Today's world seems to be growing smaller because of advances in telecommunications and information technology. Nations are becoming increasingly interdependent economically, politically, and culturally. For this reason, international trade exerts a major impact on every nation. It influences supply and demand, profits, competition, consumer choice, and government policies. It influences job opportunities and living standards. Both consumers and producers operate in world markets. This is why it is important to understand the role of international trade in your economic life.

> ***"The real wealth of a nation resides in its farms and factories and the people who man them. A dynamic economy producing goods competitively priced in world markets will maintain the strength of the dollar."***
>
> *John F. Kennedy*

Imports and Exports

Nations trade products and services for many reasons. They tend to import goods and services they are not able to produce efficiently because they may lack natural resources or because of relatively high labor costs. In America, close to 90 percent of what we consume is produced here in the U.S. However, we import certain products and services we cannot provide for ourselves in sufficient quantity or quality. Coffee and cocoa are two imported commodities we do not grow. We import crude oil and petroleum products because we cannot produce these in quantities to meet consumer and business demand for them. Shoes and clothing are labor-intensive products we frequently import because it is cheaper to make them where labor costs are lower.

In some cases, we import products to meet consumer preferences for style and performance qualities of foreign-made products. This has been the case in high fashion clothing from European designers, high-performance automobiles from Japan and Germany, and a variety of electronic products primarily from Japan. Our chief imports in recent years include office machines, clothing, crude oil, electronics, and motor vehicles.

Generally nations export products and services they can produce in abundance as a result of natural resources, efficiencies in production, low-cost labor, technological advances, or national specialties. The United States, with less than 5 percent of the world's population, produces over 20 percent of all the world's output. We need foreign markets to sell goods and services we produce. Other nations buy over half of U.S. computers, cotton, aircraft, and wheat, 1-10. They buy more than one-third of our construction machinery, semiconductors and machine tools. Over one-quarter of our farm machinery, flat glass, and corn are sold to other nations. Financial and telecommunication services are also among top U.S. exports. America's "pop" culture can be found in every corner of the globe in the form of music, television, movies, books, and magazines. All of these services are exported by American companies and represent dollars coming into the country.

Effects of International Trade on Our Economy

What happens in international markets affects you—as citizen, as consumer, and as producer or worker. International trade affects you as a citizen because it helps define the role of the United States in the global economy and in related interactions among nations of the world. For example, countries that are trading partners have strong incentives to maintain friendly relations. When other nations need and want goods and services produced in the United States and we want goods and services produced in other nations, we come to depend upon each other. Trade can help bring about peaceful alliances between nations and stimulate economic growth.

International trade affects you as a worker because it influences the

USDA

1-10
The United States exports wheat to countries with less plentiful wheat crops.

supply of and demand for both domestic and imported goods and services. This, in turn, influences job creation and opportunities or the lack thereof. Increased exports mean growth, and growth means jobs. For example, when an American company gains access to foreign markets and can compete successfully in the sale of its products and services, the company will grow and expand. It will need more workers. There will be more jobs. Declining exports, which we experience when other nations go through economic crisis or when our products are not competitive in world markets, can lead to slowed growth and loss of job opportunities. Foreign competition may also lead to a loss of jobs for U.S. workers when companies cannot compete successfully with imports, as happened with the auto market in the early 1990s. Layoffs created hardships for American auto workers at that time. In recent years, U.S. auto companies have become more competitive.

International trade affects you as a consumer because it influences what goods and services will be available at different prices. Each country exports what it produces most efficiently with its available resources. Each country imports the goods and services it wants from other nations. When nations trade with each other, consumers gain more choices in the marketplace. This stimulates competition and, ideally, results in better products and lower prices for consumers.

Balance of Payments

To understand international trade, you need to know the meaning of the ***balance of payments,*** which is basically an account of the flow of goods, services, and money coming into and going out of the country. Two key pieces of the balance of payments accounts are merchandise imports and exports and services imports and exports. *Merchandise* refers to products and goods we buy or sell in world markets. *Services* refers to service items we buy and sell such as insurance, tourism, shipping, and technology. When we buy more products than we sell, a ***trade deficit*** develops. The United States has run a substantial trade deficit since 1976. To balance our account or to make up for the trade deficit, we can sell more services than we buy, which we do. However, our service surplus does not come close to balancing the merchandise trade deficit. To make up the remaining deficit, we sell shares of U.S. businesses, real estate, and securities to buyers in other nations. This brings enough money into the country to balance what goes out in the purchase of foreign goods.

While investments in the U.S. by foreigners are necessary to balance our trade deficit, many feel that in the long run this is not a healthy situation. They feel that trade deficits weaken our economy and threaten jobs of U.S. workers. ***Protectionism*** has been one answer to concerns about trade balances. It is a policy of discouraging imports through trade barriers such as tariffs or import quotas, in order to protect American businesses and jobs from foreign competition and to reduce the trade deficit. A ***trade barrier*** is any action taken to control or limit imports. A ***tariff*** is a tax on imports that makes them more expensive to consumers. It is intended to make U.S. products more cost competitive. An ***import quota*** is a limitation on the number or quantity of imports allowed into the country.

Because most governments believe that fair and open trade among nations benefits all, most nations participate in the *General Agreement on Tariffs and Trade (GATT)*. This is an international agreement that promotes free trade among nations and attempts to reduce the use of tariffs, quotas, and other trade restrictions.

The World Trade Organization was created to mediate trade disputes among nations and establish trade practices that are acceptable and fair to all nations. Trade disputes arise over certain policies and practices that create unfair competition. One of these, *dumping*, is the sale of products in foreign markets at low prices in order to eliminate the competition. Once the importer dominates the market for the product, the importer increases the price. For example, a company from another country produces TV sets to sell in the United States. It ships the sets here and sells them for less than cost. U.S. manufacturers cannot afford to meet the low selling price. Eventually, the majority of customers buys the cheaper import and the U.S. companies go out of business. Then the importer raises prices because there is no more competition.

Restricting access to markets is another unfair practice. This involves limiting opportunities for foreign companies to sell their products or services on an equal footing with domestic companies. At present the U.S. markets are open to other nations with relatively few restrictions. However, other countries often do not offer similar open markets for American goods and services. Restricted markets in Japan are a major concern both because our trade deficit with Japan is so high and because Japan is one of the world's largest markets. Disputes with Japan over access to markets have been brought before the World Trade Organization to be resolved. While there is still much to be done to reach the goal of fair and open trade among nations, global markets and interdependence make it important to try.

Exchange Rates

An ***exchange rate*** is the value of one currency compared to another. For example, the exchange rate will tell you how much you must pay in dollars to buy a unit of foreign currency. The value of a nation's currency goes up and down with the demand for it in other countries or in world markets. When a U.S. company sells a product or service in another nation, that nation must buy dollars to pay for it. When the value of U.S. dollars is high compared to the other nation's currency, the U.S. product costs more for the foreign buyer. When the value of the dollar is low, the product is cheaper. A strong dollar can dampen foreign demand for U.S. exports. At the same time, a strong dollar will buy more foreign goods and services for less. This could increase the demand for imported goods and services. A strong dollar is an advantage to you when buying imported goods and services and when traveling in countries where currencies are weak compared to the dollar. It means your dollars will go further.

When you travel to other countries, you exchange U.S. dollars for the currency used wherever you are traveling. When the value of the dollar is high compared to the currency you are buying, you get more for your money. Chart 1-11 shows the values of

Exchange Rates

In July of 1998, one U.S. dollar equaled

Canada	1.37 dollar
Mexico	7.75 peso
Japan	135.81 yen
Britain	.59 pound
France	5.87 Franc
Germany	1.76 mark
Italy	1,727.00 lira
Spain	148.65 peseta

1-11
Exchange rates change constantly. Check newspapers or the Internet to find out current exchange rates.

different currencies compared to the dollar as of July, 1998. Exchange rates change daily. They are published regularly and can be found in travel sections as well as the financial pages of most major newspapers.

The Euro

In 1999, a new currency called the ***euro*** was launched in Europe for noncash transactions such as credit cards, checks, and electronic transfers. This is the beginning of a common currency among the 11 nations participating in the *European and Monetary Union (EMU).* The initial 11 participating nations are Austria, Belgium, Finland, France, Germany, Italy, Ireland, Luxembourg, the Netherlands, Portugal, and Spain. This bloc of nations is called *Euroland.* Other nations are expected to join the EMU as it becomes established and as they can meet the economic criteria for membership.

Until the year 2002, the euro will be used only for noncash transactions. Euro bills and coins will begin to circulate in 2002. Until then, bank customers in euro countries can keep their accounts in either the euro or the national currency. If you visit one of the EMU nations, your cash transactions will still be in the local currency, while your credit card and bank transactions will be in euros, 1-12. Prices are likely to be posted in both the national currency and in the euro.

The gradual transition to a single currency is being managed by the European Central Bank (ECB) based in Frankfurt, Germany. This central bank is similar to our Federal Reserve System. Exchange rates for the euro will change from day-to-day against the U.S. dollar and other nonmember currencies. The desired outcomes of the EMU include political and economic stability among the participating nations and a competitive advantage in the global economy.

1-12
A variety of currencies are used throughout the world. Many countries in Europe are shifting to using the euro.

Summary

An economic system is the framework in which productive resources are turned into goods and services. In this market, the law of supply and demand serves to answer the problem of scarcity. In the act of balancing supply and demand, our system determines what to produce, how, and for whom. Consumers play an important role in creating demand. Businesses strive to meet that demand while earning a profit.

Government plays an ever-increasing role in the economy. Government regulates business in order to keep the marketplace fair and the products safe for consumers. Government agencies enforce regulations to protect consumers. Taxes are used to pay for government operations and public services. Finally, the fiscal and monetary policies of government help keep our economy stable.

Consumers, producers, and government all play important roles in our economic system. Consumers create demand for goods and services at reasonable prices. Producers meet these demands through production. Government plays multiple roles, including consumer and regulator. The competition for profits in this system leads to the development of new and improved products.

International trade also plays an essential role in our economic system. Responsible nations, through the General Agreement on Tariffs and Trade, strive to establish trade practices that will work to the advantage of all countries in world markets.

To Review

1. What are the four basic concepts that drive our economy?
2. Describe the law of scarcity and how it applies to individuals, families, and government.
3. What are the three economic problems common to all societies?
4. How does the law of supply and demand relate to the prices of goods and services in the marketplace?
5. How do profits and competition fit into our economic system?
6. In what three major ways does the government influence the economy?
7. What is the purpose of antitrus laws?
8. Explain how a progressive tax works.
9. How do government taxing and spending decisions affect the economy?
10. What is fiscal policy and how can it be used to stimulate or slow down the economy?
11. What is monetary policy and how can it be used to stimulate or slow down the economy?
12. Compare recession and inflation and explain how government attempts to deal with each.
13. Name three items a producer must have to be successful in a market economy.
14. What is international trade and how does it affect you as a citizen, consumer, and producer? How does it affect our economy?

To Think Critically

1. What can you gain by learning more about our economic system?

2. What productive resources do you and your family possess and how can you use them?
3. How do you and your family decide what needs and wants to satisfy?
4. What choices has your community made in recent years in the use of public funds or tax revenues to meet public needs and wants for such services as education, police protection, street repairs, parks, and recreation?
5. How do you and other consumers affect supply and demand?
6. In your state, how much sales tax do you pay for every dollar you spend? How does the government use this money?
7. How did consumer demand change the computer industry?
8. How do nations benefit from international trade?
9. What is the balance of payments? How can trade deficits be balanced?
10. Explain currency exchange rates.

To Do

1. Demonstrate the law of scarcity in your own life. Make a list of items you want and need over the next five years of your life. Include food, clothing, housing, sound equipment, car, education or training, medical care, travel, and vacations. What resources will you use to get what you want and need? Will you be able to satisfy all your wants? What compromises or choices will you have to make?
2. Make an appointment to visit a local government official at your village or city hall. Find out how local taxes are assessed in your community and what services they provide. If you do not live in a village or city limits, visit one near your home.
3. At your local library, look up information about the many agencies of the federal government. Look through the U.S. Government Manual for information or ask the librarian for other available resources. Make a list of key federal government agencies you find listed. Then research one agency in detail; look into its services, purpose, and budget. Report your findings to the class.
4. Invite an economist or another qualified authority to speak on one or more of the following topics:
   - Current events in international trade and their effects on the United States economy.
   - The impact of the federal deficit on the overall economy, on taxpayers, and on international trade.
   - The role of profits and competition in our economy.
   - The role of government in our economy.
   - Functions of the Federal Reserve.
5. Create a bulletin board of newspaper and magazine articles and advertisements which illustrate different economic concepts in action.
6. Make up a glossary of the terms listed at the beginning of the chapter with complete definitions.
7. Refer to at least four sources for information on international trade and present arguments for and against open markets. Discuss some of the problems and disputes that have arisen between nations over trade policies.

8. Find out the current value of the U.S. dollar related to the:
   - ❑ British pound
   - ❑ Japanese yen
   - ❑ German mark
   - ❑ Canadian dollar
   - ❑ Italian lira
   - ❑ French franc
   - ❑ Mexican peso
   - ❑ Spanish peseta

9. Go to the library or online for current information on the EMU and the euro. Try to find out and report on:
   - ❑ how it has succeeded in Euroland
   - ❑ how it affects American tourists and businesses
   - ❑ what impact it has in global markets
   - ❑ what problems have been experienced in converting to a single currency

Radio Shack, A Division of Tandy Corporation

In a market economy, producers compete for sales and profits by offering consumers a variety of similar products.

CHAPTER 2

Productivity Growth
Worker Produ
SCRABBLE
CONSUMER
CREDIT
SAVE
INVEST
EARN
CROSSWORD GAME by Milton Bradley
APPLE 0.50
MILK 1.00
FISH 1.50

You in Our Economy

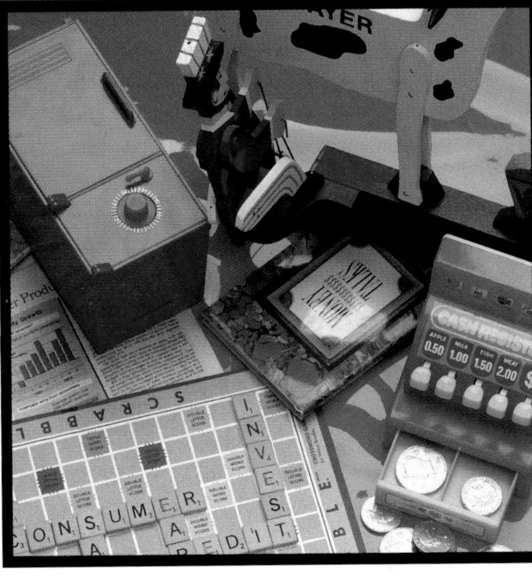

market economy
command economy
standard of living
productivity
durable goods
insurance
premium
indemnifies
claim

After studying this chapter, you will be able to

- ❑ describe a market economy.
- ❑ explain the economic activities and problems of consumers in a market economy.
- ❑ describe a command economy.
- ❑ compare the major differences between a market and a command economy.

A ***market economy*** is a system in which individuals and businesses respond freely to the forces of supply and demand in the marketplace. These responses determine economic activity. In a way, it is like our democratic form of government that responds to its citizens and their votes. A market economy is designed to respond to the people and reflect their decisions and choices. That is why consumers are important in our system. That is why your economic decisions and activities affect the way you live and the way our economy works.

A ***command economy*** is a system in which the state or some other central authority controls economic activities and consumer choices are limited. Often a command economy goes with a socialist or communist form of government. The central authority decides who will produce what. It decides how much to produce and sets the prices of goods and services. The needs and wants of consumers generally are not foremost in the decision making of the central authority. Consumers in a command economy often do not have freedom of choice and the opportunity to decide for themselves how to earn and spend income.

Learning how consumers live and work in a command economy is one way to better understand and appreciate our own economic system. Throughout this chapter, case studies describe experiences that are typical of consumers living in a command economy. Although the names in the case studies are made up, the experiences are based on factual information.

As you read about our market economy in this chapter, contrast this with the case studies that describe a command economy.

In the United States and other countries with a market economy, consumers are free to make many choices. They choose how they want to earn and spend money. They decide how they want to use their resources and how they want to live. Businesses respond to consumer choices by producing and selling the goods and services consumers want. In many ways, consumers can make an important difference in a market economy.

To play your role in our market economy, it is necessary to understand how the economic activities and problems of consumers fit into the overall economy. See 2-1.

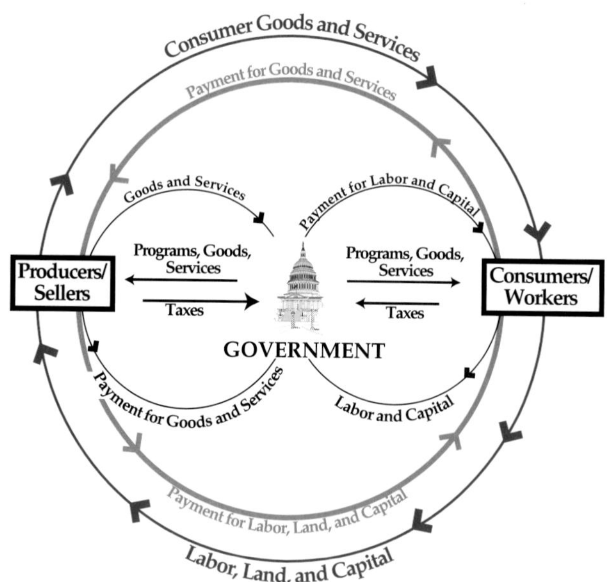

2-1
A circular flow of goods, services, and money takes place within the economy.
The outer purple circle shows the flow of consumer goods and services from producers/sellers to consumers and the flow of labor, land, and capital from consumers/workers to producer/sellers.
The red circle shows the flow of payments for goods and services from consumers to producers/sellers and payment for labor, land, and capital from producers/sellers to consumer/workers.
The inner circles, in black, show how government participates in the flow of goods and services and money. Producer/sellers provide goods and services to government and receive payment in return. Consumer/workers provide labor and capital for government and receive payment in return. Producer/sellers and consumer/workers receive programs, goods and services from government for which they pay taxes.

Living in a Command Economy

Mariya's and Sasha's Apartment

Mariya and Sasha were in their early twenties and planned to be married as soon as they found a place to live. Mariya lived in a two-room apartment with her mother and grandmother. They shared a kitchen and bath with another family living on the same floor. Mariya worked in a factory an hour away from her home. Sasha worked in the same factory but he lived an hour away in another direction in a small apartment with his mother, father, and sister.

Mariya and Sasha spent their Sunday afternoons together in an old section of town. Many people gathered there to make apartment switches and to find living space. Hundreds of people carried handmade signs advertising living quarters to trade or living space wanted.

Housing trades and agreements were often made among the people. However, no agreement was legal until approved by the city authorities. To get approval, the parties involved had to show their registration cards. The cards proved they had permission to live in their country. In addition, the agreement could not violate living space restrictions for different categories of people.

Mariya and Sasha both had valid registration cards. Since they had no children, they qualified for no more than a one-room apartment. However, if they could get it, Mariya and Sasha would be delighted with one room. That would be better than moving in with either of their families as so many of their married friends had done.

After several months of searching, they made an agreement with an older gentleman. The man planned to move from town to the country. He was offering a one-room apartment for a cash payment rather than an exchange for other living space. Mariya and Sasha agreed to pay him the U.S. equivalent of $300 to get the apartment. This was most of their savings, but they considered it a bargain.

They did not see the apartment until later, but they did know it was in a fairly new building not far from their work. More important, it would be theirs. For this, they were willing to overlook any undesirable characteristics of their new home.

Case Review

1. How might a severe housing shortage affect you now and during the next 10 years?
2. Housing costs in command economies are controlled by the state and are very low compared to those in the United States. To what extent would you be willing to sacrifice privacy, quality, and availability of housing to cut housing costs by 70 to 80 percent?
3. Why is housing likely to be more limited in a command economy than in a market economy?
4. In a market economy, what would happen to housing costs if housing were in short supply? How would this affect the productive resources used in housing construction?

Economic Activities of Consumers

In a market economy, consumers perform economic activities every day. They earn, spend, and save. They borrow money and charge purchases. They invest their dollars. They share financial risks through insurance. They pay taxes and vote on economic issues. The way consumers perform these activities determines how well they live and how well the economic system works.

Earning Your Way

A market economy permits individuals to choose the fields in which they wish to work. That choice determines to a large degree a person's job opportunities and earning power. Your ability to find employment and your performance on the job help determine how much you will earn. Your ***standard of living,*** the total amount and quality of goods and services you can afford, is directly related to your earning power.

Generally, the ability to find employment depends on job skills, experience, and education. It also depends on career choice and the demand for workers in the chosen field. Demand in job markets is ever changing. The *Occupational Outlook Handbook*, published by the U.S. Department of Labor, can help people identify careers with promising futures. Classified help-wanted sections of local newspapers can help people find jobs in a given area. One example of great demand in the current job market is the electronics field. Qualified people who want to work in this field are likely to find employment and earn fairly high incomes, 2-2.

Your job performance helps determine how far and how fast you will advance on the job. As you advance, income increases. Job performance is also one measure of your ***productivity,*** which is the amount of goods and services created for each hour on the job. Top-performing workers using efficient tools and equipment increase the nation's productivity, push up the gross domestic product, and increase wealth for themselves and the nation. The gross domestic product (GDP) measures the total output of goods and services created by all of the factors of production (labor, property, capital) within the country.

Your earning activities contribute both to your personal wealth and to the nation's wealth. At the same time, the state of the economy affects your earning potential. Economic conditions influence the number of jobs that are available, the type of work in demand, and salary levels. The link between the earnings of individual workers and the national economy is significant. It establishes personal standards of living as well as the national standard of living.

Your *personal standard of living* refers to the goods and services you can afford and that you consider essential for living. The *national standard of living* refers to the goods and services the majority of people in the nation can afford and consider essential for living. Depending on your income, your personal standard of living may differ from the national standard. As your income increases, your standard of living normally rises if prices do not rise faster than incomes.

© Randy Brown for AT&T Professional Development Center

2-2
Many companies run training programs in their fields to create a pool of qualified workers.

Spending What You Earn

A market economy permits individuals to make their own spending choices. The way you make those choices determines how much value you get for your money. Getting the most satisfaction for the dollars you spend requires careful choices in the marketplace.

Your spending decisions help create a demand for the goods and services you buy. You contribute to the profit and success of the businesses from which you buy. Your individual spending may not be major in creating a demand for specific products or in supporting one business over another. However, as a group, you and other consumers do determine the success or failure of specific goods, services, and businesses.

Overall consumer spending also affects the state of the economy. When consumers are confident, they tend to spend more. This creates a greater demand for goods and services. Businesses expand to meet the increased demand. As they expand, they create more jobs. The economy is in a state of prosperity or recovery.

When consumers are doubtful about the economic future, they tend to spend less and save more. This lowers the demand for goods and services. Businesses slow down because sales decline. Jobs become harder to find. Workers may be laid off. In this condition, the economy is described as *lagging* or in recession.

Saving Your Money

People generally think of savings as money put aside in a special savings account for later use. In its broadest sense, anything that improves your financial position is saving. This includes the cash in your wallet as well as the money in your checking account. It includes the contributions to the retirement fund you will collect someday and the cash value of your life insurance policy. House payments, home improvements, and the purchase of durable goods are also forms of savings. Furniture, appliances, and cars are called ***durable goods*** because they have lasting value. "Savings" such as these increase your financial welfare and security.

In a market economy, the money people save or deposit in financial institutions is pumped back into the economic system. See 2-3. The money you and other consumers deposit in savings accounts or certificates is loaned to businesses and other consumers. Your savings pay for business growth, building construction, and the purchases of homes. Savings invested this way generate more jobs, greater productivity, and a growing economy. Therefore, the health of the economy is closely related to the savings rate or amount of money people save that is pumped back into the system.

Borrowing to Spend

Each time you use a credit card, buy something on an installment plan, or take out a cash loan, you are

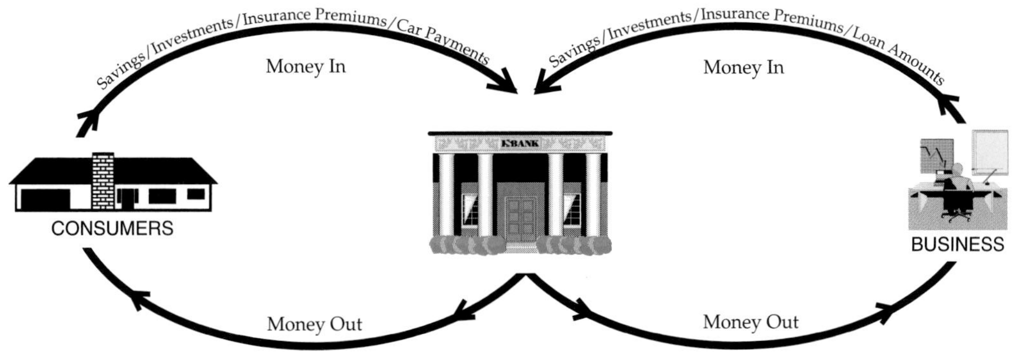

2-3
This diagram shows the flow of money in and out of financial institutions—banks, credit unions, savings and loan associations, and insurance companies.

borrowing. These forms of credit let you buy now and pay later. In most cases, you pay a finance charge for using credit. This means buying with credit costs more than paying cash.

Credit is costly in another way, too. When you use credit, you are spending future income. This means part of what you earn in the future must be used to pay what you owe. The use of credit reduces future income.

With credit, you can buy costly goods and services as you need them and pay for them over a period of time. Borrowing is sometimes the only way consumers can pay for major purchases, such as a house, car, or college education. Getting together enough cash to pay for these large expenditures all at once is difficult.

Consumer borrowing has two important impacts on the economy. It increases the amount of money in circulation, and increases the demand for consumer goods and services. For example, when you borrow, you have more money to spend. As you and other consumers use borrowed money, you increase consumer demand in the marketplace. When the economy is in a recession, the use of credit can help increase consumer demand. Consumer spending whether with cash or with credit stimulates productive activities. This is why the Federal Reserve System may lower interest rates and encourage the use of credit during a recession. It helps stimulate growth.

When inflation is the problem, borrowing can make it worse. Credit increases the amount of money consumers have to spend. When the supply of money increases faster than the supply of goods and services, prices rise. Inflation worsens. This is one reason the Federal Reserve System is likely to raise interest rates and follow a "tight" monetary policy during periods of inflation. It helps control spending.

Another reason for the cautious use of credit is its long-term effect. Unfortunately, the use of credit carries the seeds of an eventual economic downturn because the credit used today must be repaid with tomorrow's dollars. That means that tomorrow's dollars will be paying today's bills rather than supporting future demand. Using credit increases immediate demand, but it decreases future demand because a portion of future income must be used to pay debts.

Sharing Financial Risks Through Insurance

Insurance is a way to protect yourself against certain financial losses by paying a fee called a ***premium***. The insurance company ***indemnifies*** you, which means that it will pay either the actual cash value of a loss or an amount that will return you to your financial position before the loss, whichever is less. Basically, this means that the insurance will make up for your loss, but will not make you richer than you were prior to the loss.

When you buy insurance, you and other purchasers share financial risks related to life, health, and property. For example, you and 5,000 others buy health insurance. If you must go to the hospital for an illness, the insurance premiums or payments of those who do not need to be hospitalized will help pay your expenses. The premiums you and other policyholders pay for insurance are put together and invested by insurance companies. These premiums and their earnings are used to pay the claims of policyholders who suffer financial losses that are covered by their insurance. A ***claim*** is a formal demand for payment of a loss covered under the terms of an insurance policy. The number who make claims at any given time is much smaller than the number in the insurance pool.

Living in a Command Economy

Ivan and His Automobile

Ivan, 32 years old, lived in a command economy and worked as a chemist earning the equivalent of around $300 per month. Ivan rented a one-room apartment and had no family.

Since Ivan's living expenses were low, he was able to save enough money to buy the smallest, least expensive car on the market. The car sold for about $15,000 in American money. Ivan was on a waiting list for his car for almost five years.

When the car arrived, Ivan used his savings to pay for it with cash. Credit was not available. Ivan had hoped for a red car with a sun roof and one or two other features. He made no complaint, however, when the car turned out to be black with no extras. After waiting five years, extras seemed unimportant.

As Ivan drove away, he was very conscious of being one of the "elite." Few men in his country had the chance to own a car. Ivan was elated. His pleasure, however, ended three months later when the car broke down. The problem was not serious, but replacement parts were needed to repair it. Ivan had to wait three months. A short time after the car was repaired, the windshield wipers were stolen. It took six weeks to get new ones.

Over the years, Ivan had many problems keeping his car in running condition. For weeks and months at a time, he was unable to drive it. Still, he felt lucky to own the car. It was his most treasured possession.

Case Review

1. How was buying and owning a car different for Ivan in a command economy than it might be for you in our economy? How do you explain the differences?
2. What are some advantages of limiting the production and private ownership of cars? Do you think that Americans need as many cars as our economy produces? What do you think would be the consequences of a central authority limiting the production and ownership of private automobiles in the United States?
3. If public transportation were more convenient and less expensive, would you want to own a car? Do you feel that you have a right to decide for yourself whether or not to buy a car? Why?

Life insurance protects families against financial losses that result from death. Most often life insurance covers the wage-earning members of a family. If a wage earner dies, income is still available from the insurance company. *Health insurance* protects against the cost of illness and injury, 2-4. *Property insurance* covers the loss of, or damage to, property. You can buy it for personal possessions, a car, or a home. *Liability insurance* protects against financial losses that can result if you are responsible for injury to other people or for damage to the property of others. For example, it protects you if you have an accident injuring someone else and you are sued for damages.

Insurance not only protects the insured parties, it also contributes to overall economic stability. It spreads financial risks and it stabilizes income in the face of serious financial losses. Social insurance, such as unemployment compensation, Social Security, and medicare, contributes to financial stability for thousands of covered individuals. In addition, the premiums paid for insurance amount to billions of dollars each year. These dollars are invested by insurance companies in

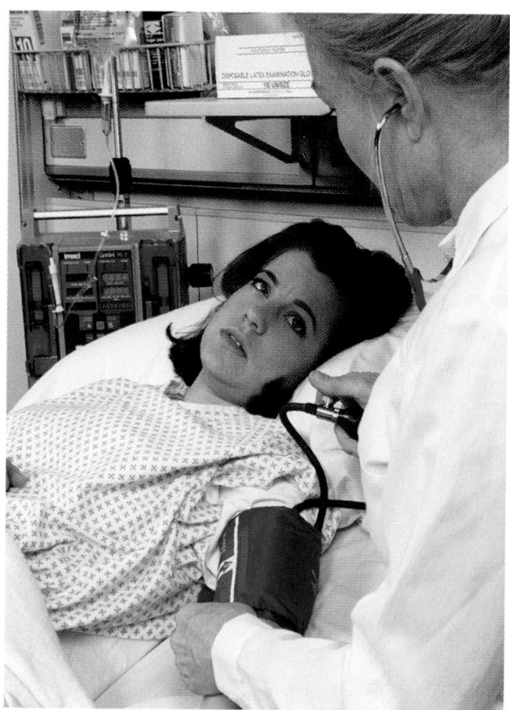

2-4
Health insurance will help pay this patient's medical bills.

business enterprises, which contribute significantly to the strength of the economy.

Investing for the Future

Consumers invest money primarily to improve their financial position and increase their economic security. Investments include real estate, stocks, bonds, business ownership, and valuable items, such as antiques or art. Generally, investments offer a greater return on money than savings accounts. However, the risk of loss is greater for investments than for savings accounts. The desire for profit motivates people to invest.

When you deposit money in a savings account, you expect to get it back with interest. When you invest in stocks or bonds, you expect to get back more than you invested. You hope to eventually sell your investments at a higher price than you paid for them.

The money you and other consumers invest pays for a large share of business growth and activity. Businesses look to investors for funds to help pay for new plants and equipment. Investments also help pay for the research and development of new technology and materials and the marketing of new products and services. Economic development and growth are directly related to the investments and the savings of individuals as described in the following example.

If an airline company needs new jet planes, it can issue new stock for sale to the public. When investors buy the stock, the company gets the money to pay for its new planes. Building the planes creates jobs. Operating the planes creates more jobs, better service for consumers, and a profit for the company. If the company continues to make a good profit, the price of the stock may rise. This would encourage more investors to buy stock in the company with the hope of making a profit. Investors make money on the investment, workers receive more job opportunities, the company makes money on the new planes, and the consumer benefits from more flights and better service. Investment dollars start this type of chain reaction in businesses of all types. See 2-5.

Paying Taxes for Services from Government

Your tax dollars pay for government operations and services. Local, state, and federal governments levy different types of taxes, such as *income tax* on the earnings of individuals and corporations, *sales tax* added to the price of goods and services you buy, and *property tax* on real estate owned by individuals and corporations. Tax revenues generally pay for the goods and services that citizens need and want from the government. (Taxes are discussed more in depth in Chapter 17.)

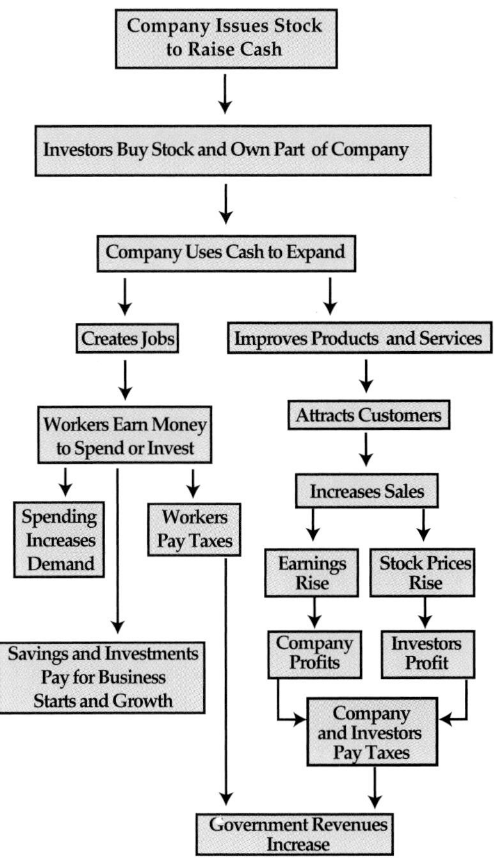

2-5
This diagram shows how consumers and business work together through consumer investments to keep the economy going.

In our system, the people decide indirectly what they want to "buy" from government and how much they will pay with tax dollars for their purchases. While you may think no one would willingly decide to pay more taxes, it happens all the time. For example, citizens vote for more taxes every time they vote for a new school, more police, or a new highway. They vote for higher taxes every time they vote for a candidate who promises new government programs without reductions in government spending. Furthermore, citizens allow tax increases every time they accept massive deficits in the federal budget.

The federal debt and deficit spending have become major tax issues in recent years. The federal debt is the total amount government owes. In 1998, the federal debt came to over 5 ½ trillion dollars which is more than $20,000 per citizen. Deficit spending is the amount the government spends each year over and above the amount it receives in revenues. The deficit is added to the debt yearly. The deficit spending for 1998 was expected to exceed $58 billion. The national debt must be paid off primarily through taxes.

The government raises money by borrowing, which it does by selling Treasury bonds and savings bonds. This means that the government goes into debt to cover current expenses. Excessive borrowing by government, just as for individuals and families, can lead to economic disaster. In 1998 the interest alone on the national debt came to over $248 billion and was the third largest annual expense in the federal budget. This does not include the expenditures and borrowing of state and local governments, which can also be very large. The money spent on interest cannot pay for health care, education, environmental protection, highways, defense, or a host of other public needs.

A growing concern over increasing government debt and rising tax rates has caused a number of groups to work for limitations on both. Taxpayers can decide what services they want from the government and how much they are willing to pay by

- ❑ Voting intelligently for candidates for public office and on government policies that are put to a vote.
- ❑ Becoming involved in government at local, state, and federal levels.
- ❑ Supporting organizations that watch government spending and promote limitations on spending and taxes.
- ❑ Communicating their views effectively to government officials and elected representatives.

Living in a Command Economy

Olga Shopping for Food

Olga was 25, married, and the mother of two preschool children. As a full-time secretary, she worked eight to ten hours a day outside her home. Her husband was an engineer working the same long hours each day, six days a week. Together, they earned the American equivalent to almost $750 per month. This was considered a very good income, but they had to spend almost half of it for food.

Olga's day began at 5:30 a.m. She got up, dressed, and went shopping for food. She had to shop daily because food was always in short supply and her refrigerator space was limited. By choice, Olga shopped before work. The stores often were out of the foods she wanted by the time her office closed.

Each morning Olga went to three or four stores. She went to a bakery, a butcher shop, a store for cheese and eggs, and another shop for fresh fruits and vegetables when they were available. The shopping took at least an hour each morning. Olga had to stand in three separate lines in each store. In one line, she selected and ordered what she wanted. In another line, she paid and got a receipt. In the third line, she picked up her purchases and turned in the receipt. Olga then hurried home to fix breakfast for her family. After feeding and dressing the children, she took them to the child-care center on her way to work.

At noon, Olga often spent her lunch hour at the central market in town. She bought the foods that were not available in the stores near her home. She and several other women in the office shared noontime shopping. Each took a day so that no one had to shop every day.

After work, Olga went home and prepared dinner for her family. She had to make everything from scratch. Few convenience foods (foods that are partially prepared or ready-to-eat) were available. Olga spent so much time shopping and cooking that it seemed like a second full-time job to her.

Case Review

1. How much time each week do members of your family spend shopping for food? How would the way you live change if shopping required one to two hours out of each day?
2. What are the advantages of small specialty shops over large supermarkets? What are the advantages of supermarkets?
3. How often does your family eat convenience foods? How would your eating habits change if these foods were not available?
4. In what ways is feeding Olga's family different from feeding your family?
5. Many foods Americans buy routinely are scarce in other parts of the world. How might scarcity of basic items affect your shopping habits? Why do you think scarcity is generally uncommon in a free-market economy?

1—*Reflect:* How would you feel about shopping for food the way Olga shops?

A government described in the Gettysburg Address by Abraham Lincoln as "of, for, and by the people" can be made to deliver what the people want *if* the people stand strong and speak clearly.

Taxation plays another role in the overall economy. The government's spending of tax dollars creates demands for goods and services. These demands are usually met by private businesses. For example, government pays for public schools with tax dollars. The schools are built by private contractors with materials produced by private industries. In this way, government spending for public goods and services stimulates the economy. It feeds money into the system, creates demands for goods and services, sparks business activity, and creates jobs.

During periods of inflation, government spending has a negative impact on the economy. When the combined demands of government and consumers are greater than the economy's capacity to produce, prices go up. This is why reductions in government spending help fight inflation by reducing demand.

Voting and Participation

Votes in the ballot box give consumers a voice in government just as their spending decisions give them a voice in the marketplace. The economy responds to the demand consumers create with their spending. Likewise, the government and elected representatives respond to the votes consumers cast on election day. The votes you cast in elections decide who will represent you and make policy decisions in government. By voting, you can influence economic policies and government activities.

Being informed and active in community organizations can also give consumers influence over government operations and activities. For instance, a citizen who is concerned about the quality of education in the local schools can make a difference by getting involved. This may mean joining the PTA, attending school board meetings, running for election to the school board, or doing volunteer work in the schools. Through such activities, citizens often can voice their opinions and influence policies.

Economic Problems of Consumers

A market economy offers you, the consumer, both the privilege and the challenge of making free economic choices. You are free to choose how to earn a living and what to do with your money. You can choose to pay cash or use credit. You can decide to spend or to save. These freedoms allow you to get personal satisfaction from your income.

Market Characteristics and Consumer Problems

Free choice, however, does not guarantee satisfaction. Certain characteristics of a market economy can complicate choices. For example, a market economy encourages businesses to compete with each other. As a result, the same or similar goods and services are sold by a wide variety of outlets. These include supermarkets, specialty shops, department stores, discount stores, catalog order houses, and door-to-door sellers. Choosing a reliable seller and finding the best product for the best price is a challenge and sometimes a problem. To meet the challenge of complex markets, it is necessary to learn something about the sellers as well as the products and services you buy. Following are some characteristics that can complicate choices in a market economy.

Confusing Variety of Products

A market system supports the development of new products and ideas. The system rewards producers who give consumers what they want. As a result, the variety of goods and services found in our marketplace is astonishing. Consider all the fabrics and clothing styles you can buy. See 2-6. Consider the many sizes, models, and features of cars. Count the specialties in medical care and the number of choices in home furnishings. Think of the many forms of consumer credit, types of insurance, and ways to save and invest money. Even the many flavors of ice cream can make it difficult to choose.

The many choices open to consumers make it a challenge to choose intelligently. Just keeping up with what's new is a full-time job. Choosing from so many alternatives presents a challenge for most consumers at one time or another. Careful comparison shopping,

2-6
A market economy presents consumers with many choices, which can sometimes be confusing.

particularly for costly purchases, is one way to reduce the confusion that can come with so much variety.

Questionable Selling Methods

In a system where the survival of a business depends largely on attracting consumer dollars, selling plays an important role. Every business wants to sell as much as possible at the best prices possible. With this goal in mind, most businesses advertise and market their goods and services aggressively.

Some businesses may use questionable selling methods to increase their sales and profits. Techniques, such as high pressure selling, less-than-truthful advertising, contests, and "free" offers, can encourage consumers to buy for the wrong reasons. Too often, factual information is not part of a sales pitch. Consumers must focus on what is important to them for each purchase.

Keep in mind that deliberately deceptive advertising and other dishonest business practices are illegal. *Bait and switch* is a prime example of a fraudulent sales technique. It involves advertising the "bait," which may be a 19-inch color TV for $98. This attractive offer is designed to bring you, the customer, into the store. Upon your arrival, the bait item is either sold out or is totally undesirable. The salesperson "switches" to another "much better" offer that also is more expensive. Bait and switch advertising is illegal.

If you question the ethics of a store or selling method, contact the local Better Business Bureau, the chamber of commerce, and the nearest office of the Federal Trade Commission. You have the power through these agencies to fight dishonest and deceptive merchants and illegal sales practices.

> ***"One man's wage rise is another man's price increase."***
>
> ***Harold Wilson***

Conflict of Interest

To a certain extent, buyers and sellers want different things. Suppose you are in the business of selling tape recorders. You want to sell as many tape recorders as you can at the highest price you can get. You want to be able to pay your business expenses and make a good profit. When you are buying a tape recorder, you want the best recorder you can get at the lowest possible price. You want to have money left over to spend for other items. In other words, sellers want the highest price they can get so they can earn a profit. Consumers want the best quality at the lowest price so they can buy more with their money.

In a market economy, both wages paid to the seller and the prices paid by the buyer are tied to the forces of supply and demand. We depend on these forces to achieve the proper balance between

Living in a Command Economy

Yuri's Vacation

Yuri was 23. Yuri had been on the job for three years. He worked hard and rarely was late or absent.

Yuri's good work record earned him a highly coveted vacation pass. It entitled him to spend 24 days at a country rest home. The cost of the vacation was only $125 in American money. This covered all of his expenses except the train fare, which cost $37.

Yuri was assigned to take his vacation the first few weeks in May. He felt fortunate because May was one of the best times to go for good weather. In the past years, he was assigned time in December and February.

Although Yuri always wanted to vacation in Paris, he took the vacation pass anyway because he did not have permission to leave the country.

When Yuri arrived at the rest home, he found his vacation well planned for him. He was given a daily schedule and a diet. The rest home, like many others across the country, was scientifically planned for health, rest, comfort, and relaxation.

Yuri's day started at 7:30 a.m. and officially ended at 10:00 p.m. with lights out and doors locked at 11:00 p.m. During the day, activities followed a planned time schedule. The activities included early morning exercises, medical conferences, and three meals plus afternoon tea. Also included were one quiet hour in his room, one free hour, a walk on the beach, and cultural activities. The exercise program and medical conferences were different for each person, but all the other activities were the same for everyone.

This was not exactly the type of vacation Yuri would have planned for himself. However, he did come back well rested and healthy. The vacation cost him only $162 for the full 24 days.

Case Review

1. This type of vacation cost little because it is subsidized by the government. What do you think are the advantages of this vacation system? How does it differ from typical vacations for Americans?
2. Family vacations often are difficult to arrange in a command economy. Both husband and wife work in most families, and they rarely are assigned the same vacation time. As a result, children are sent to camps run by the government, and the husband and wife take separate vacations. How would this arrangement work out for your family? In what ways is it a good idea? What would you dislike about this vacation system?
3. To what extent would you be willing to give up free-choice vacationing for low-cost vacationing?

wages and prices. The free-market system helps resolve the conflict of interest between sellers and buyers. The system strives to create a supply of goods and services to meet demand at prices that will keep the producer in business and the buyer able to buy.

Consumer Mistakes Leading to Problems

For a variety of reasons, consumers sometimes make poor choices. These choices can be a major cause of consumer economic problems. Following are some consumer mistakes that can lead to less than satisfying choices in the marketplace.

Lack of Planning

"Economy is too late at the bottom of the purse"
Seneca

Some of the worst consumer economic problems are caused by lack of planning. When consumers fail to plan ahead, they lack direction for their spending. They do not set up goals for the use of income or build up savings for future needs. Lack of planning also makes it difficult to control the use of credit. Without planning, each month's expenses and bills come as an unhappy surprise.

Consumers who do not plan ahead often have trouble paying routine monthly bills. Without some pre-planning it is difficult even to get to the supermarket and back with the food needed to put nutritious meals on the table at reasonable prices. Clothing buys that fit into one's wardrobe require planning. Buying a car to meet needs for transportation and fit the budget requires planning. Having money available for occasional expenses, such as birthday gifts, insurance premiums, vacations, and taxes, calls for planning, 2-7.

Poor planners often find it difficult to save enough for big expenses, such as a car, a home, education, or retirement. They often end up making purchases that do not meet needs and wants. Planning is the only way most consumers can pay their bills without running out of money. Careful monthly and yearly planning is especially important to reach long-term goals. It

Living in a Command Economy

Tania in the Department Store

Tania was 21. She lived in an apartment with her parents and older brother. She worked in an office close to her home.

Tania was always on the lookout for fashionable clothes and fabrics and attractive, comfortable shoes. At the major department store in her country, daily fashion shows featured the latest clothing styles. However, only the patterns and fabrics were available for sale, not the actual clothes. Stylish ready-to-wear clothes were hard to find. Good shoes and boots also were difficult to get.

Like most of her friends, Tania carried extra cash in case she would see something to buy. There were no charge accounts or credit cards. Since consumer goods often were in short supply, people tried to carry extra cash so they could buy on the spot when scarce goods were unpacked in the stores.

Each lunch hour, Tania went to the department store. She hoped to find fabrics, boots, handbags, or other choice items for herself and her friends. The other women at work did the same for her.

One lucky day, Tania found some beautiful Spanish shoes. When she saw people lined up at the shoe counter, she knew something "good" had just been unpacked. Fortunately, the line had just formed. Only nine or ten others were ahead of her. She bought not one, but three pairs of shoes—one for herself, one for her mother, and one for a woman in her office.

Often 80 to 100 shoppers lined up for scarce items. At times, people formed a line not even knowing what was being sold at the other end. Sometimes Tania waited an hour in a line only to see the last item sold shortly before her turn.

For Tania, successful shopping was being at the right place at the right time with enough cash to buy rarely available goods.

Case Review

1. When have you had trouble finding what you wanted to buy in the stores? Why do you think you had trouble?
2. How would you explain the shortage of consumer goods in a command economy?
3. What economic goals, if any, do you think are more important than the goal of satisfying consumer wants? How do you think those goals could be met in a market economy?
4. How does Tania's experience compare with the confusing variety of available goods and services in a market economy? How would you explain the differences?

Club Med

2-7
With proper financial planning, you will not only be able to afford a vacation but also relax and enjoy the time away.

allows people to match the highs and lows of expenses with the highs and lows of income over a lifetime.

Failure to Use Information

Uninformed choices cause problems for consumers every day. For example, a young man buys a second-hand car because the price is right. Later, he learns he cannot drive it because the insurance costs as much as the car, and he cannot afford it.

A young woman signs up for an $800 correspondence course in communications. She doesn't finish the course because the assignments take more time and hard work than she expected, and it is difficult to get help from the school except by mail or phone lines that are always busy. She loses her $800.

A young couple takes a $1,200 package trip to Mexico. When they arrive in Mexico, they learn that it is the rainy season. Their hotel isn't near anything they want to see and do. The meals are not included in the vacation package as they had thought. It turns out to be a miserable trip and they have spent both their money and their vacation time.

All of these situations could have been avoided by using *available* information. Reliable facts abound for almost every product and service consumers can buy. Sources of information include product labels, instruction booklets, warranties, magazine and newspaper articles, advertisements, government publications, and a number of consumer and trade organizations.

People can offer reliable product information, too. Salespeople and consumers who have had firsthand experience with specific products and services can be helpful. The fastest and easiest way to get information is to ask questions. Make it your rule to ask first and buy later. Getting the facts first is especially important where health, safety, or large amounts of money are involved. Making uninformed choices can be costly, disappointing, and even dangerous.

Impulse Spending

Even informed consumers sometimes indulge in impulse or thoughtless spending. Look at these examples.

> ***"He who buys what he does not need steals from himself."***
>
> *Swedish Proverb*

Ginny buys a pair of red shoes because they are on sale. They are the right size, the right price, comfortable, and good looking—but she has nothing in her wardrobe to wear with them. Rafael goes to the grocery store for a loaf of bread and ends up spending $12 for groceries he did not intend to buy. Althea sees a TV commercial for an exercise machine and dials the toll-free number. When the machine is delivered, she has lost interest and sticks it in the closet.

Most consumers at one time or another do a little impulse spending or choose by habit rather than thinking. When done regularly, this type of spending can eat up a sizable amount of money. Careful spending will leave more dollars for the needs and wants that are truly important.

Poor Communication

Consumers have much to gain by communicating effectively with producers and sellers. Most businesses want to know the likes, dislikes, wants, needs, and problems of their customers. Failure to speak up, ask questions, and complain when necessary can be costly. An open line of communication can lead to greater satisfaction with products, services, and sellers. Consider the following examples.

Shirley buys a $25 calculator at an office supply store. After using it for a week, the plus (+) lever jams, and the calculator doesn't work. Shirley is furious and throws the calculator away. She vows never to go back to that store.

Toward the end of winter, Mario buys a pair of skis for $150 on a Wednesday. The following Saturday, the day before Mario plans to go skiing, the same skis go on sale for half price. Mario is really mad at himself for not waiting for the sale.

Charlene calls to request servicing for her television. She is told that a repair person could service it on Monday afternoon. Since Charlene works during the week, she takes Monday afternoon off to let the repair person into her apartment. She is docked $20 from her paycheck. Later she learns that the repair could have been done on Saturday or in the evening.

In each of these situations, better communication would have saved money. Shirley could have received a refund or a new calculator if she had returned to the store and explained the problem. If Mario had asked, he might have been told of the upcoming ski sale. If Charlene had requested it, she could have had her TV repaired in the evening or on Saturday.

Summary

You live in a market economy in which your freedom, spending power, job choices, and participation all make a difference. You and other consumers carry out economic activities every day. These activities range from spending money to voting on government policies.

A command economy differs greatly from a market economy. A command economy pays little attention to the voice of consumers. A central authority, usually government, controls most of the economic activity. Planners decide what products are produced, how, and for whom.

While a market economy offers freedom and many advantages to consumers, it also presents problems and challenges. For example, the vast array of goods and services available in the marketplace can make it difficult to choose. Selling methods of merchants often create pressures to buy what you do not need. There is a natural conflict of interests between the seller who wants to make a profit and the buyer who wants to get the most for money spent.

In many instances, consumers create their own problems in the marketplace. For example, lack of planning can result in faulty buying decisions and poor money management. Consumers should be careful to avoid such common mistakes.

To Review

1. In what way is a market economy like our democratic form of government?
2. Name the eight economic activities of consumers.
3. How can a person's income affect his or her personal standard of living?
4. How does consumer spending affect the state of the economy?
5. How does the use of credit affect immediate and future consumer demand?
6. How does consumer and government use of credit impact on the economy?
7. What role do consumer savings and investments play in the overall economy?
8. What questionable selling methods do some businesses use to increase their sales and profits?
9. Explain the conflict of interest between consumers and sellers in a market economy.
10. Name four common ways consumers create problems for themselves in a market economy.
11. Name five reliable sources of consumer information.
12. Describe how poor communication can result in problems for consumers.

To Think Critically

1. What industries suffer most when consumer spending is down? For example, what happens to the housing and construction industry? What related industries are likely to suffer? What industries seem to suffer the least during a recession?
2. How does the money consumers save and invest support business growth and expansion?
3. How do you go about registering to vote in local, state, and federal elections?
4. How and with whom would you communicate if:
   a. You buy a radio and it stops working in a short time?
   b. You try a new cosmetic and it causes a serious skin rash?
   c. You receive prompt, competent service in an auto repair center?

   d. You buy a product because of an advertisement and find that it does not live up to the advertising claims?
5. What consumer problems do you consider most serious? What do you think can be done about them?
6. What are several ways a command economy differs from the market economy of the United States?
7. What are some of the problems of changing over from a command to a market economy?

To Do

1. List five economic activities that you and/or your family have done in the past few weeks. How might these activities have been different in a command economy? Record the differences and discuss them with the class.
2. Explain how savings, investments, and insurance premiums serve as the source of credit for consumers and businesses. Illustrate your explanation with a chart or drawing. Show the flow of money from the consumer through the financial institution, insurance company, or stock market and on to other consumers and businesses.
3. Using travel guides, books, and encyclopedias, make a chart comparing our economy with the economy of another country. Include information on:
   a. Living conditions in the country.
   b. Price comparisons for similar goods and services.
   c. Restrictions on economic activities or travel.
   d. "Good buys" according to shopping guides.
4. Using an encyclopedia or recent almanac as a source compare the U.S. economy with that of one of the following nations: Japan, Germany, Mexico, Canada, Great Britain or another nation of your choice. Compare:
   - type of government
   - gross domestic product (GDP) figures
   - income per capita
   - natural resources
   - growth and inflation rates
   - export and import figures
   - cost of living figures
5. Find at least five articles in recent newspapers or news magazines that cover the transition in Russia from a command economy to a free market economy. Pick out the key points in each article and present them to the class for discussion.

In a market economy, consumer demand affects the price of goods.

Ace Hardware

UNIT 2

Jobs
and holding a job
volatile market
Carol Kleiman
Jobs
LE CHEF
Tips For Finding the Right Job
ARMY
OPPORTUNITIES FOR WOMEN
ARMY
COLLEGE LOAN REPAYMENT
CASH REGISTER
APPLE 0.50
MILK 1.00
FISH 1.50
MEAT 2.00
$
MONEY TALKS
EXPENSES PERSONAL RECORD
Pay Bills

Making Decisions

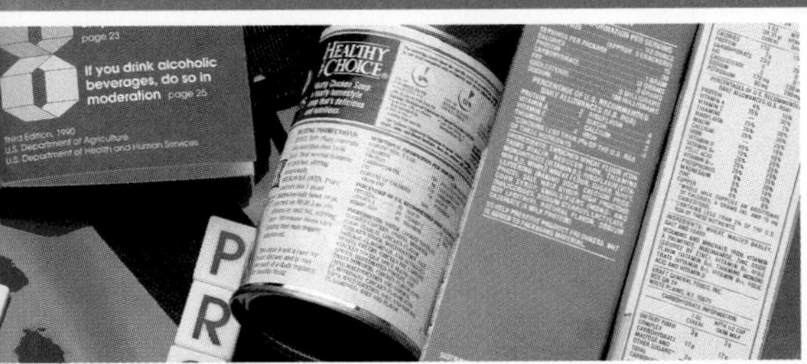

Chapter 3
You, the Worker

Chapter 4
You, the Consumer

Chapter 5
You, the Manager

Chapter 6
You, the Shopper

In the years to come, you will be making many choices—as a worker, as a consumer, as a manager, and as a shopper. Mastering these decision-making functions lays the foundation for competence in the marketplace.

Now is the time to begin planning for the training and education you will need to open doors to future opportunities. The career choices you make should fit the way you want to live.

As a consumer, you enjoy certain rights and carry certain responsibilities. Intelligent choices made in the marketplace are based upon your personal needs and wants—on the values and goals that are most important to you.

As a manager, you use resources to reach goals. By planning, acting, and evaluating, you can manage your money to create an effective money management plan.

As a shopper, you want your money to go far in the marketplace. Smart shopping skills involve knowing where to shop, rational decision making, and using a personal spending plan.

CHAPTER 3

Departure goes tongues wagging
Workplace solutions
Jobs
and holding a job
volatile market
Carol Kleiman
Jobs
LE CHEF
Tips For Finding the Right Job
High School
ARMY
COLLEGE LOAN REPAYMENT
OPPORTUN
From School to Work
APPLICATION FOR EMPLOYMENT - WISCONSIN
PLEASE READ CAREFULLY
PLEASE PRINT IN INK
PERSONAL AND GENERAL HISTORY

You, the Worker

aptitudes
abilities
values
goals
Internet
internship
apprenticeship
resume
reference
interview
entrepreneur
wages
minimum wage
salary
piecework income
commissions
tips
bonuses
fringe benefits
gross pay
net pay
deductions

After studying this chapter, you will be able to

- ❑ identify interests, aptitudes, abilities, and personality traits that influence career decisions.
- ❑ list sources of career information.
- ❑ identify employment trends.
- ❑ describe careers in family and consumer economics.
- ❑ plan for future job training and education.
- ❑ write a resume and cover letter.
- ❑ complete an application form correctly.
- ❑ list important points to remember during an interview.
- ❑ define terms used in the world of work.
- ❑ list advantages and disadvantages of becoming an entrepreneur.

Most Americans enter the workforce at some point in their lives. People work primarily to earn money for life's necessities and a few extras. Most people begin working during their teens or early 20s and continue to retirement age. Because you will likely be working for many years, it pays to get the training and education that will lead to good jobs and good pay.

If you are like most young people, entering the world of work will be a major step. It calls for thoughtful

> *"He who loves money must labor."*
>
> *African Proverb*

choices. You will spend about one-third of your waking hours at the occupation you choose. Therefore, it pays to find work you can do well and enjoy. Finding it is a challenge.

Some people seem to know from an early age what they want to do with their lives. Most have to search out jobs that will bring adequate income and job satisfaction. For high school students who plan to go on to college or enter a training program after graduation, the world of work may seem far away. However, it is not too early to begin thinking about future employment.

Making a Career Plan

It may be too soon to choose a lifetime career path, but it's not too early to begin thinking about what you would like to do in the world of work. Career planning begins with a careful look at yourself—at what is important to you, what you like to do, what you do well, how you see yourself both now and as an adult. Your interests, aptitudes, skills, and abilities will determine, to a large degree, what type of career will be right for you. Your values and goals will also be important indicators of the type of work that will bring you satisfaction.

Even if college stands between you and the work world, a little self-knowledge can be helpful at this point in your life. It will help you select courses of study, identify part-time job opportunities, and find a promising career path.

Identify Your Interests

Your *interests* can include activities you enjoy, subjects you like, ideas that fascinate you, sports you play, or hobbies you follow. Some of your interests may be key to choosing work you will enjoy. Very often, identifying your interests can start with a look at the past. What have you enjoyed in your life so far? What are your favorite hobbies, subjects, and extracurricular activities?

Projecting yourself into the work world can include a look at you in the present school setting. Consider subjects you have taken. List those you like most. List also the hobbies, activities, and part-time jobs you have pursued outside of school. Which of these interested you the most?

Consider the ways school and nonschool interests could carry over into a job or career. See 3-1. For example, if you are a member of a school athletic team, what skills and learning might you develop that would make you a better employee? If you write for the school newspaper, are great with numbers, or are really at home in the science lab, how might these experiences and talents help you find a job? If you are president of the student council, act in the school play, or play in the band, what might you learn that will help you in the work

3-1
These teens are learning valuable lessons in cooperation and teamwork. Athletic experience can often help prepare a person for future job situations.

Career Choices

George Goes from School to His Favorite Hobby

For George, graduation will be a real celebration. He will be finished with school and can give himself totally to his favorite pastime—the computer. Since fifth grade, he has been experimenting and playing games on the family computer and, when necessary, doing his homework on it, too.

George has a real knack for computer technology, and even the instructor in the computer class at school respects George's expertise. He works part-time at a nearby Compumart where he has experience in sales, service, and training. Because George is a natural and shows so much promise, the Compumart manager has invited him to join the staff full-time. He will go through a training program and then work in sales and service. The money will be good and he already knows a lot about the business. The best part is an opportunity to help develop new programs and to work with the latest equipment. Eventually, George thinks he may become a computer programmer or possibly a systems analyst. That will require more schooling, so for the moment he just plans to enjoy his job.

Case Review

1. What are the advantages of being able to move right into the job you want from high school? Do you see any disadvantages for George?
2. What other hobbies or activities can you think of that could lead to satisfying full-time employment?
3. Under what circumstances would George be smart to delay his computer job and go to college or enroll in an advanced training program?
4. What are some of the occupations that are open to high school graduates?

world? What part-time jobs have you held? Has part-time work given you any insight into what you do or do not want to do with your future?

Identify Your Aptitudes and Abilities

A look at your strengths and weaknesses, your talents, and your skills is key to self-knowledge. ***Aptitudes*** refer to natural physical and mental talents. For example, if you score high in verbal aptitude, you may find it relatively easy to learn language arts. You may be well suited for work in written or oral communications. If you do well in math, you may find work with numbers satisfying. The General Aptitude Test Battery (GATB) is a series of tests that measures nine aptitude areas, 3-2. It may be possible to take these tests through your school guidance department.

Abilities refer to physical and mental skills developed through learning, training, and practice. You are born with certain aptitudes, but your abilities are learned.

When aptitude and ability go together, you are likely to learn quickly and well. For example, if you are highly coordinated and athletic, you could learn a sport quickly and play relatively well. If you are interested in playing tennis but do not have athletic aptitude, you might overcome a lack of coordination with hard work and practice. When you can put interests, aptitudes, and abilities together into a job choice, you are likely to be successful on the job.

Try to picture yourself at work. If you have a burning desire to paint, act, dance, protect the environment, practice medicine or law, teach, swim, or coach, find out what jobs will let you follow your dream. Take the path that leads to your ultimate goal.

If you enjoy a number of activities but are not clear on a career path, you will need to keep your options open. It might help to consider job categories in

General Learning Ability: The ability to understand instructions and underlying principles, to reason, and make judgments.

Verbal Aptitude: The ability to understand the meanings of words and to use words effectively.

Numerical Aptitude: The ability to perform arithmetic operations quickly and accurately.

Spatial Aptitude: The ability to think visually of geometric forms and comprehend the two-dimensional representation of three-dimensional objects.

Form Perception: The ability to perceive detail in objects, pictures, or graphics and to make visual comparisons and discriminations of shapes and shadings of figures and widths and lengths of lines.

Clerical Perception: The ability to perceive detail in verbal or tabular material.

Motor Coordination: The ability to coordinate eyes and hands or fingers rapidly and accurately in making precise movements with speed.

Finger Dexterity: The ability to move the fingers and manipulate small objects with the fingers rapidly or accurately.

Manual Dexterity: The ability to move the hands easily and skillfully and to work with the hands in placing and turning motions.

3-2
Taking the GATB series of tests can help you identify and evaluate your aptitudes in eight different areas.

terms of what you do well and what you like doing. For example, try completing this sentence: "I like working with _____." (Possible answers might be words, numbers, people, animals, plants, machinery, computers, books, ideas, cars, artistic concepts, or whatever else you really enjoy.) List your options, then try to rank them in order of importance. Start with what you like the most and work down to what you like least.

Assess your strengths by completing another sentence: "I am particularly good at _____." (Possible answers might include communicating with people, selling, research, acting, painting, design, dance, sports, problem solving, math, science, making people laugh, helping people, working on a team, or whatever else you see as your strong points.) Again, list your strengths, then rank them starting with your greatest strength.

Look at Your Personality

Personality traits also provide a clue to the type of work you can do well and enjoy doing. Seeing yourself as others see you is not always easy, but it is a useful exercise when trying to match yourself to a job. Think about the type of person you are. For example, would others describe you as quiet or talkative, shy or outgoing, tense or easygoing? Are you an energetic self-starter or do you often need a push to get going? Are you quick to try new things or are you more comfortable with the familiar? Are you cautious or are you willing to take risks?

Try to write a paragraph describing your personality. Pretend you are writing to a prospective employer for a job you really want. Which of the adjectives in 3-3 would you use?

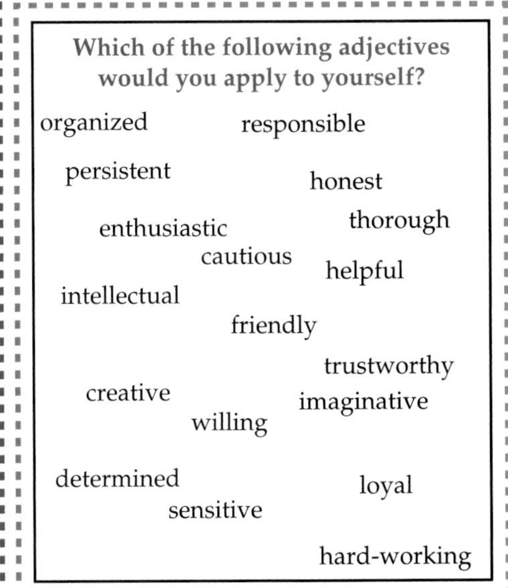

3-3
These are just a few of the many terms that can be used to describe personality.

Assess Your Values and Goals

Finally, consider what you want to do with your life. This will be closely connected with your values and goals. ***Values*** are the ideals and principles that are important to you. ***Goals*** are the specific achievements or objectives you want to reach. The two generally are related. For example, if you place a high *value* on a clean and safe environment, a related work *goal* may be a job that involves environmental research and protection, waste management, and conservation.

Analyzing personal values and goals can help you make the most appropriate career and job choices. What is really important to you? What contribution do you want to make? Most people need to feel the work they do has value and meaning. What job or career will make you feel you are making a difference?

Many people find satisfaction in jobs that serve others. It is possible to serve others in almost any career. However, there are more opportunities in such fields as social work, health care, education, the ministry, and other services to the public. See 3-4.

Identify Future Roles

The career goals you set for yourself may one day overlap marriage, parenting, and other life goals. Identifying your personal life goals can help you make wiser decisions about your future career. Keep in mind your work can determine where you live, how much you earn, how much free time you have, whether and how often you travel on the job or change locations, what kind of job security you can expect, and other important aspects of your personal life. Consider how your career will fit in with your life goals.

Since many young people plan to marry and have a family, discussing both marriage and career goals is important. If you and your spouse plan to have careers outside the home and raise a family, you will be part of a *dual-career family.* This means managing the demands of a career as well as family responsibilities.

Success in managing the dual roles of career and family depends on the

Radio Shack, A Division of Tandy Corporation

3-4
You can pursue an interest in working with children by becoming a teacher.

attitudes of both partners. If one partner does not want the other to work, friction may arise in the marriage. It is important for engaged couples to talk through their career and parenting goals before marriage. They need to discuss the options available if both need or want to continue their employment after they have children. They need to measure the risks and rewards of dual careers against the quality of family life they desire.

The way family members manage their multiple roles at home and at work varies from one household to the next. In some families, the woman still ends up with more responsibility for child care and household management. In other families, husbands and wives share these responsibilities on an equal basis. Men are becoming more and more involved as fathers in recent years.

Child care generally is the most critical issue for working parents to resolve. Many arrange for child care in their own home or in a neighboring home. Others use child care centers where children are cared for in small groups by qualified child care providers.

Some employers offer assistance to employees with children. They may offer flexible work schedules that permit parents to have more time at home with the children. Some companies provide part-time positions for working parents. Others offer flextime. Flextime allows employees to set their own work schedule, within certain limits. Parents with school-age children could benefit by starting work earlier and arriving home by the end of the school day.

A few companies offer on-site child care facilities to help parents arrange for child supervision, 3-5. In some cases, it may be possible for one spouse to set up a business that he or she can operate out of the home in order to be there for the children.

The Family and Medical Leave Act requires employers with more than 50 workers to provide employees up to 12 weeks unpaid leave per year for care of a new baby, sick relative, or for personal medical needs. This leave may be taken with assurance the same or an equivalent job would be available on return.

3-5
Child care facilities at this bank simplify finding desirable child care for employees' children.

The Northern Trust Company

In addition to child care concerns, dual-career couples must find ways to manage household responsibilities. They may need to set priorities and lower their housekeeping standards. By doing this, couples can complete household tasks and have time left over to relax. Outside help can make an important contribution in completing some tasks. If all family members support the dual-career arrangement, they will find ways to manage child care and household responsibilities and spend quality time together as well.

Study the Job Market

Knowing a few basic facts about different jobs and careers can help you make the right choices in the work world. Study the job market as you make career decisions.

Job and Career Information

It is vital to learn what you can about the occupations and work fields that interest you. You will want to look for job areas that offer the most and best opportunities for the future. Early planning can help you find the courses and experiences that will open career doors for you later. Many sources of information are readily available.

Career Guides

The U. S. Department of Labor issues a variety of career information publications including:

- The *Occupational Outlook Handbook,* published every two years, profiles 250 jobs. For each, it describes work activities, earnings, education and training requirements, personal qualifications, and outlook for employment. The Handbook is available in most public libraries.
- The *Employment Outlook: 1994-2005* covers Bureau of Labor Statistics projections related to employment and job growth.
- *Occupational Outlook Quarterly* includes practical, up-to-date information about job choices for today and tomorrow.

Internet

The ***Internet*** is a network that allows access to millions of different resources around the globe. It is an incredible tool for researching colleges, jobs, career information, and employment opportunities. Most colleges and universities have Web sites that provide information on the school, courses of study, tuition, financial aid, scholarships, and other details. You may even be able to take certain courses online.

> *"Education is the first step in preparing yourself for a job."*
>
> *Coleman Young*

You can also conduct a widespread job search on the Internet. It allows you to post your resume, locate job listings and related information, research individual companies, explore career opportunities and employment trends. You may even be able to apply for some jobs online.

If you are connected to the Internet, you can do your research right at home. If not, you may be able to go online at school or at your public library. Ask for any assistance you need. At some point, ideally in high school, it's a good idea to take a course or two in the computer lab to become familiar with commonly used software and with the use of the Internet. This will be increasingly important both in many occupations and in managing your personal life as well.

School Guidance Counselors

School counselors may offer a wealth of job information. They can help you determine the areas best suited to your aptitudes and abilities. The guidance department at your school may provide files of information on education, training, and careers. Counselors may also help you evaluate your options, direct you to more information, and guide you in the choice of a college or training program. Check out the guidance department in your school to find out what services it offers.

Libraries

School and community libraries also offer a host of information. Some libraries may have an education and employment section containing a variety of books and publications. When searching the card catalog, look under headings such as careers, colleges and universities, jobs, and occupations. Also check other headings of specific career fields that interest you.

Career Events

Special career days at school and career fairs in the community can provide up-to-date information on jobs, education, and training. In addition, college or business representatives often visit high schools to speak with interested students. It is a good idea to take advantage of both. You can learn firsthand about opportunities in the work world. It is also helpful to talk to people who work in fields that interest you. Ask about job training, experience and qualifications needed, and opportunities in the field.

Employment Trends

In job markets, it is very possible that today's opportunity will become tomorrow's dead end. It is important stay abreast of new technology and to follow the trends in industry. Consider where the best jobs are likely to surface given current trends and developments. The *Occupational Outlook Handbook* can help you keep up with

Career Choices

Reba Is a Mass of Indecision

Reba is entering her senior year of high school without the slightest idea of what she wants to do after graduation. She half-heartedly applied to college last year and was accepted at the state university, but she really doesn't want to go. Reba is a reasonably good student, but she is sick of school. There is nothing she wants to study or pursue with any energy at all. She figures the parties and social life at the university might be fun, but she isn't sure it would be worth it to spend that much time going to classes.

Reba and Tim have been seriously dating for two years and have talked of getting married. They both agree with their families that it is too soon to think of marriage and a lifelong commitment. Besides, Tim's uncle is an optician and has almost convinced Tim to enter an apprenticeship in that field. This would take him to another city for two to five years.

As Reba considers her future, she often wishes graduation wasn't approaching so fast. High school has been fun and not too demanding. Now she has hard choices to make and not much notion of what she wants. Should she go ahead and go to college like many of her friends? Should she look for a job and try to earn enough money to live on her own? Should she just wait and see what the future brings? Should she move across the country and live with her aunt for a year or so just for the experience? Maybe she should just go to a cosmetology or secretarial school so she would be trained for something.

Case Review

1. How would you advise Reba?
2. If you were undecided and unfocused, what would you do?
3. Do you think it is a good idea to go to college even if you aren't interested in going? Why?
4. Where might Reba go for advice on planning her future?
5. What choices do you see for Reba? for yourself?

these changes. Following the news and relating it to the work world will also give you timely clues to upcoming opportunities.

New technology requires highly trained and skilled workers in a variety of fields. Untrained workers will either be unemployed or remain at bottom-level, low-paying jobs. Not only is initial training important, the willingness to retrain over the years is equally important. Technology makes dramatic and sometimes sudden changes. These changes often lead to a demand for workers with different types of skills and training. You need to learn and relearn work skills over a lifetime.

The emphasis on jobs in service fields continues to grow faster than manufacturing. By the year 2005, the service sector is expected to account for four of every five jobs. This means more opportunities in industries such as health service, business services, education, social services, retailing, finance, transportation, and communications. See 3-6. You are likely to find fewer opportunities in manufacturing.

Economic factors, both at home and around the world, can seriously affect employment in different fields. Recession, inflation, tax policies, and international trade all have an impact on what and how many jobs are available and what qualifications workers will need to find employment. For example, when unemployment is high and jobs are hard to find, training, education, and competence become even more important in finding and keeping a job. When taxes and interest rates are high, there may be fewer jobs because businesses are less likely to expand and are more likely to cut back on hiring.

Economic conditions can vary around the world and from one part of the country to another. It pays to look at opportunities in different areas when you are searching for employment. Supply and demand in the job market varies greatly from one field of employment to another and from one area to another.

Think long and hard about your career goals. The work you choose will affect the way you live, the people you meet, the money you earn, and the satisfaction you get out of work and life. Try to decide what will be the best preparation for the work you want. Will you need a college degree or occupational training? Will the job require an internship, an apprenticeship, or previous work experience? Will you need a combination of these to achieve your career goals?

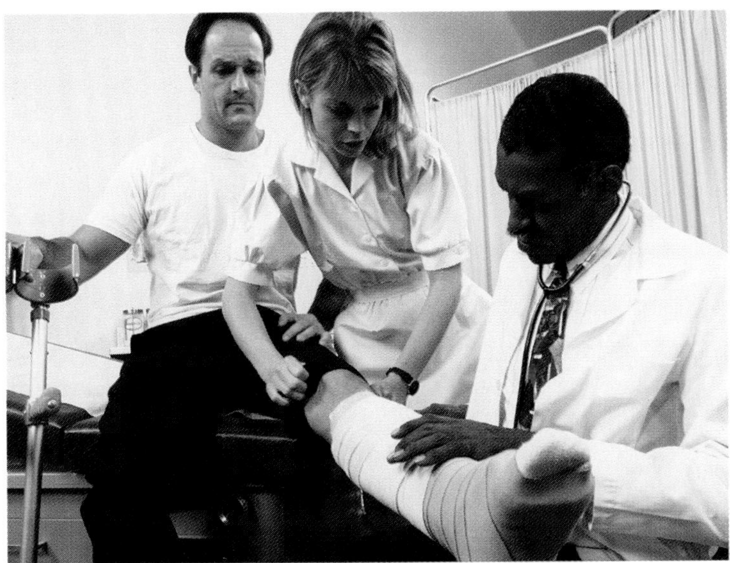

3-6
Demand for trained health care providers continues to grow.

Careers in Family and Consumer Economics

As you think about plans for the future, you may want to consider a career in family and consumer economics. If you are interested in helping people with consumer decisions and problems, a career in this field may interest you. Following are some areas of job opportunities in consumer economics and related areas.

- **Business.** Many corporations, companies, and public utilities have consumer relations or customer service departments to serve the buying public. They offer opportunities to work with customers on problems related to the products and services sold. Companies may also produce educational publications for customers.
- **Government.** Federal, state, and local government departments and agencies offer a variety of services, protection, and information related to consumer interests and needs. Areas covered include nutrition, sanitation, child development, health care, product safety, environmental protection, advertising, sales and trade practices, safety standards, product labeling, housing, employment, etc. Government agencies that serve consumers are listed in Chapter 4. They offer employment opportunities related to consumer economics.
- **Education.** Courses on consumer education, economics, and related topics are taught across the country in junior and senior high schools and in colleges. Opportunities exist in this field for qualified teachers and educators, 3-7.

Deere & Company

3-7
Teaching consumer economics can be a rewarding career.

- **Political action.** A number of consumer organizations, such as the Consumers Union and the Consumer Federation of America, hire individuals with backgrounds in consumer economics to carry out lobbying activities, conduct research, and inform the public on current issues related to consumers. Similar positions may be available with the staffs of members of congress and senators, as well as with environmental protection groups.
- **Finance.** Many positions in the financial field are related to consumer economics. These include financial planners and advisers, credit and debt counselors, money management consultants, and financial writers and broadcasters.
- **Associations.** Many organizations, associations, and professional groups hire consumer specialists to inform and educate the public on the purchase, use, care, and disposal of consumer products and services. Work includes research, writing, customer

relations, public appearances, and political action. Such groups include the American Bankers Association, Better Business Bureaus, medical associations, and other business and professional groups.

- ❑ **Research.** Businesses, government agencies, and private organizations offer jobs in research. Employees test and rate products for safety, efficiency, and reliability.
- ❑ **Communications.** Jobs are available with newspapers, magazines, radio and television stations, as well as business and government agencies. Writers and broadcasters cover a wide range of consumer and economic issues and interests.
- ❑ **Social work.** Agencies employ social workers to serve individuals and families. Jobs exist in the areas of consumer and financial matters, particularly money and credit management.
- ❑ **Entrepreneurship.** Those who wish to be self-employed will find many opportunities to freelance or start their own businesses in the fields described above. Opportunities are available in financial planning, credit counseling, writing, and consulting.

Plan the Training and Education You Need

A college education or occupational training is required for many jobs, and it is an advantage in almost all occupations. Preparation for the work you want will normally pay off in the form of higher earning power, better job opportunities, greater job satisfaction, and security. It can enrich your life in other ways as well.

> *"One by one the solid scholars get the degrees, the jobs, the dollars."*
>
> *W. D. Snodgrass*

Following high school, you will find many opportunities for further education and training. Your choices will depend largely on the career path you want to pursue. The following pages describe several options that may work for you.

College or University Education

Higher education will be the first choice for many high school students. It can be the most costly single investment of a lifetime. It can also bring the best return in higher earnings, better job opportunities, and a fuller life. If college is in your plans for the future, start planning now. See 3-8. There are many factors to consider in choosing a school and field of study.

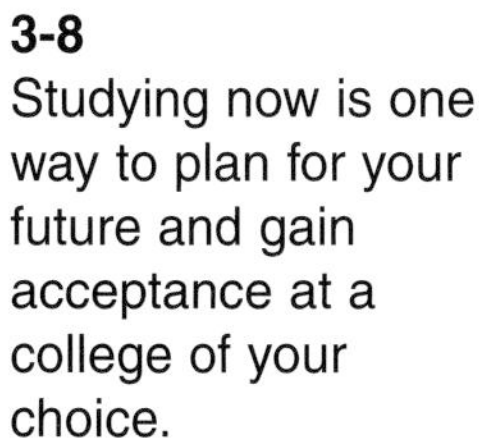

3-8
Studying now is one way to plan for your future and gain acceptance at a college of your choice.

Personal Goals

Take a look at your reasons for going to college. Are you interested in a specific field of study? Do you want to learn more in broad areas to help you decide what you want to pursue in greater depth? Is your primary goal to learn and broaden your horizons or to qualify for a particular career? Answers to these questions can help you choose a school.

Personal Preferences

Consider whether a small or large school appeals more to you. Do you want to be near home or far away? What part of the country attracts you most? Weigh the pros and cons of an urban versus a rural setting, and private versus state schools.

Your Record and Performance

Colleges look at grades, test scores, class rank, activities, special talents, and other achievements of prospective students. Some schools are more competitive than others. However, if you have a reasonably good record and really want to go to college, there will be a school for you. Prepare a resume and outline your strongest points to present to the admissions office of the schools that interest you.

College Choices Open to You

Schools differ greatly. No doubt several will meet your needs and accept you as a student. When looking at colleges, compare the following:

- ❑ *Programs of study.* Look at the courses offered in different fields, special programs of foreign study opportunities, work-study, student-designed majors, and exchange programs with other schools.
- ❑ *Faculty.* Consider the number of doctorates, faculty/student

Career Choices

Yolanda Wants to Change the World

Yolanda is a junior at Sherman High School. She is an outstanding student involved in everything, especially student government. She is a serious young woman already committed to specific plans for her future. She has been a class officer since fifth grade and she constantly is marching and demonstrating for one cause or another. Among the causes she actively supports are animal rights, aid to the homeless, conservation, adult literacy, and gun control.

When she was a freshman, Yolanda was named "Teen Volunteer of the Year" for organizing a food and clothing drive for the homeless. During the summer before her junior year, Yolanda worked as a runner for the local Better Government Association. More than anything else she wants to make the world a better place, and she is no idle dreamer. Her plans for the future are well thought out and practical.

Yolanda knows she will need both education and experience to get to a position where she can bring about change. She intends to go to the best college she can get into. With her academic and extra-curricular records, she will have a choice of several fine colleges. She expects to do well in college and then go on to law school. Then Yolanda wants to find a job or an internship in Washington where she can get experience and learn more about the way government works. Finally, she wants to run for office—the Congress, Senate and, perhaps, even the White House.

Case Review

1. What do you think of Yolanda's plan of action?
2. How might Yolanda's activities and accomplishments to this point help her reach her ultimate goals?
3. In what ways do you think Yolanda is unusual?
4. What future goals and objectives are important enough to you that you would work and sacrifice now in order to achieve them?

ratio, and the academic reputation of the school. Focus particularly in the field of study you want to pursue.

- *Facilities.* Check out the library, science labs, computer labs, athletic facilities, fitness programs, and other items of special interest to you. Also find out about the availability of these facilities.
- *Environment.* Find out about dormitories and living quarters, the makeup of the student body, extracurricular activities, campus size and setting, existence and importance of fraternities and sororities, and other services offered by the school.
- *Cost.* Determine the total amount of tuition, room and board, fees, books, and overall cost of living in the area and on campus.
- *Financial aid.* Investigate loans, scholarships, grants, part-time job opportunities, and work-study programs available to students. See 3-9.

To learn more about specific schools, see the guidance or career counselor at your high school. Check out publications on colleges and universities from your library. *Barrons' Profiles of American Colleges* and *Peterson's Guides* are among the most comprehensive guides. If you use a computer in your search for the right college or training program, you will find a variety of software programs and CD-ROMS dealing with this topic. In addition, most colleges operate Web sites that provide detailed information on courses of study, housing, tuition, fees, and other facts you want to know about the school. You can find almost unlimited sources of information online. Other sources include:

- catalogs and printed material from schools that interest you
- college and career orientation programs and fairs
- college representatives who visit your school or community
- students and graduates of schools that interest you.

Occupational Training

Preparing for employment in a specific field may be a smart move for you. Generally, this type of education costs less money and takes less time than a college education. Occupational training may be a good choice for you if

- You have specific skills and talents that you want to put to practical use.

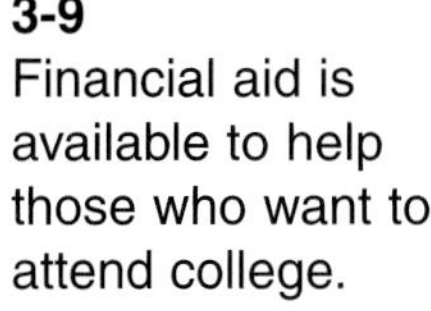
3-9
Financial aid is available to help those who want to attend college.

Jack Klasey

- ❑ You have narrowed your work goals to one specific field or occupation.
- ❑ You need to complete formal training as soon as possible so you can begin working and earning your own way.

Occupational training is available through a variety of schools and programs. If you are interested in this type of job preparation, consider the following sources.

Occupational Schools

Occupational schools, usually privately owned, depend on satisfying students for their continued success. Training, equipment, facilities, and qualifications of instructors vary greatly. Check thoroughly before enrolling.

Community Colleges

Community colleges usually are two-year schools offering both academic and occupational courses. It may be possible to transfer credits from a community college to a four-year college degree program.

Adult Education Programs

Adult education programs usually include both academic and occupational courses offered in a "night school" setting. They may be an extension of a nearby college or university, offered through the local board of education, or sponsored by a YMCA or YWCA. Course offerings vary greatly in different areas.

Correspondence or Home-Study Programs

Both colleges and private correspondence schools offer a variety of home-study courses. Students fulfill the course requirements at home and mail their work to the school for evaluation and credit. Successful home-study requires both determination and independence since there is no face-to-face teacher or classroom contact to assist and motivate students to complete work.

Career Choices

Janna Knows What She Wants

Janna also sees graduation as an opportunity to move on to a training program and then a job she really wants. Her plan is to enter the emergency medical technician (EMT) course offered at the community hospital. She plans to complete the course work and experience needed to become a full-fledged paramedic.

Janna has been hooked on emergency and police TV shows since she was a little kid. She always pictured herself taking charge in a crisis. In her family, she has done just that. It was Janna who drove the family dog to the vet when he was hit by a car. It was Janna who called the paramedics when her grandfather fell down a flight of steps. It was Janna who rushed the six-year-old she was babysitting to the emergency room. The child had acute appendicitis.

While becoming a paramedic is Janna's first interest, she may train to become a firefighter as well. She knows the job outlook and the pay is much better for the combination of paramedic and firefighter. Fire departments pay the highest salaries for paramedics. In addition to the job security she will have with her training, Janna likes the idea of knowing what to do in an emergency.

Case Review

1. What do you think of Janna's plan for the future?
2. With her interest in medicine, what advantages or disadvantages might there be for her in considering nursing or college and medical school rather than the paramedics courses?
3. What advantages and disadvantages do you see in Janna's plan?

Employer-Sponsored Training

Large companies may offer courses or training for new employees to teach them how to operate equipment or perform certain job skills.

Since the quality and content of occupational education varies greatly, it pays to investigate carefully before enrolling in a program or course of study. Question school representatives about course offerings, qualifications of faculty members, class sizes, and entrance requirements. Ask also about the number of students employed at the end of their training. To check the reputation of the school and the quality of the education and training offered, look for

- ❑ Qualified, experienced instructors.
- ❑ Adequate, up-to-date equipment and facilities.
- ❑ State licensing or accreditation from industry or educational agencies.
- ❑ Recommendations from prospective employers and former students.

Know what you will be getting for your money. Find out about the costs of tuition, equipment, supplies, fees, and other charges. Take a look at classrooms to be sure equipment and facilities are up-to-date and adequate, 3-10.

Occupational training programs can run from a few weeks to a year or more. Find out about the length of time needed to complete training as well as the amount of time you will need to give to class attendance and homework. Check policies on transferring credits and on refunds for noncompleted courses. Find out what type of degree or certificate you will receive and what it will qualify you to do in the workplace. Finally, be sure you understand all the terms of any agreement or enrollment contract before you sign it.

Note that local TV stations may offer both academic and occupational courses for credit or certification. This can be an effective and relatively inexpensive way to learn. Check program listings in your area for courses offered. The Internet may also offer courses and training possibilities with outstanding visual presentations.

Internships

On-the-job training and experience can be very helpful in getting started in a career. An ***internship*** is a short-term position with a sponsoring organization to gain experience in a certain field of study. They are available in a variety

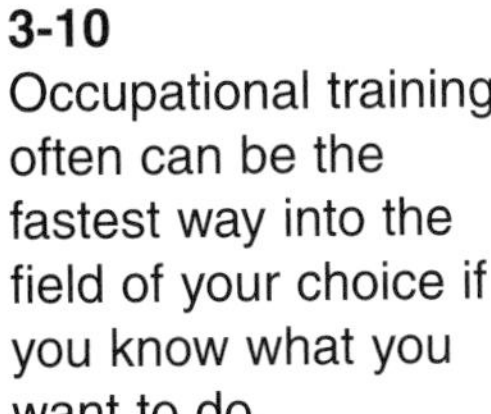

3-10
Occupational training often can be the fastest way into the field of your choice if you know what you want to do.

of career areas. They are designed to give the intern an introduction to his or her chosen field of study. Many internships lead to full-time employment with the sponsoring organization or assistance in finding work with other organizations in the field.

Peterson's Guide to Internships is updated annually and offers the most comprehensive listing of opportunities for internships. It describes over 50,000 short-term job opportunities in 22 career areas.

Internships can be an excellent way to learn more about a career field as well as a way to enter the field of your choice. They often lead to permanent placement.

Apprenticeships

An ***apprenticeship*** is a combination of on-the-job training, work experience, and classroom-type instruction. This can be a very practical way to start a job. About 350 apprenticeships are registered with the Bureau of Apprenticeship and Training, a division of the U.S. Department of Labor. Over 800 occupations fall into the apprentice category. These are largely jobs that are learned through a structured program of on-the-job training. They are clearly identified and recognized throughout an industry. The occupations involve manual, mechanical, or technical skills. They

Career Choices

Raul Looks to Internships

Raul is 17, a junior at Washington High, and second of seven children. He has always been small and slight for his age, which put him at a disadvantage in team sports over the years. However, he is a reasonably good student and is well-known among both students and faculty for his artistic talent. Raul's paintings have won awards in several local art exhibits. Two summers ago, he participated in a community project of painting murals on an exterior wall of the city hall. His technique and use of bright color brought him recognition from several established artists in the area.

With his senior year approaching, Raul worries about his future. He is not really interested in, nor can he afford, four years of college for a degree. What he wants most is to pursue his art, but everyone knows that most beginning artists make no money. His family cannot give Raul much help with five children still at home to feed and educate.

In a conference with the college counselor at his school, Raul learns of the internship path to the world of art. While an internship would not pay Raul well, it would open doors to the future in the field he wants to enter. If he can find part-time work together with the stipend paid to interns, he may just be able to pursue his painting and support himself in the process.

Raul checked the latest edition of *Peterson's Guide to Internships*, which described some 200 to 300 on-the-job training opportunities in creative arts. He found several internships that would give a chance both to paint and to learn more about job opportunities in the art world. With the help of his counselor, Raul obtained application forms and sent them off to 11 of the organizations listed in the directory.

Case Review

1. What advantages does an internship offer someone like Raul?
2. What disadvantages do you see in internship programs?
3. What are some factors to consider when applying for and choosing an internship program?
4. What might internships offer for the college graduate?

require a minimum of 2,000 hours of on-the-job work experience along with classroom or other types of learning.

An apprenticeship program may be a good choice if you need to learn a specific craft or skill for your job choice. Advantages of apprenticeships include:

- Pay and job benefits while you learn.
- Training and instruction from experienced tradespeople.
- Certification of apprenticeship completion.
- Improved opportunities for employment, advancement on the job, self-employment, and higher earnings.

For more information on apprenticeship opportunities and possibilities, contact the nearest regional or state office of the Bureau of Apprenticeship and Training.

The Armed Forces

Training and educational opportunities in the military are available through both recruitment service and the Reserve Officers' Training Corps (ROTC). The armed forces generally offer a wide range of educational opportunities at little or no cost. Possibilities include both occupational training and college credits.

The ROTC program is coordinated with academic courses of study offered at most colleges and universities. See 3-11. It involves taking ROTC courses and training while attending college then entering the service as an officer upon graduation. The service commitment varies. It will usually involve several years of active service followed by a period of time in the reserves. Each branch of the military also offers a service academy where students can earn tuition-free college degrees. Competition for these schools is stiff and standards are high.

In addition to educational opportunities, those who enter the military normally receive good salaries and generous benefits. These benefits include health care, housing, travel opportunities, social and athletic facilities, and PX privileges. (The PX or Post Exchange is a store on a military base that sells products to service personnel at low prices.) A number of the benefits, such as medical care and insurance, continue after leaving the military or retiring.

3-11
These three young people are studying the course offerings available to them through ROTC.

U.S.A. ROTC

A disadvantage of turning to the military for education and training is the possibility of being called to active duty during times of war or danger. There also is very little room for individuality. Those in the military wear what they are told, do what they are told, and go where they are told. They must accept transfers whenever they come and go wherever they are sent.

Once a member of the service, a person must serve out the entire term of his or her contract—two, four, or six years. It is not possible to resign or quit. Still, the advantages of the military may outweigh the disadvantages for those who:

- Do not know what they want to do and are willing to accept life in the service for a few years.
- Work well with others.
- Can take orders and conform to routine.
- Want education and training beyond high school but cannot afford to pay for it.
- Feel a need for outside direction and discipline.

Paying for Training and Education

When you invest, you have to spend money to make money. Education is an investment in yourself. A college education and some job training programs can cost thousands of dollars. Deciding how much you can afford to invest and how you will pay for it requires careful thought. Here are a few steps to guide you in financing your education.

- Estimate the cost of attending the colleges or occupational schools you are seriously considering.
- Estimate the resources available to you including savings, investments, student earnings, and family income.
- Measure estimated costs against estimated resources to determine how much additional money you need.
- Consider ways to cut costs without sacrificing important goals and objectives for your future.
- Search for additional resources—scholarships, grants, loans, and earnings—to help pay for your education.

> *"Without education, you are not going anywhere in this world."*
>
> *Malcolm X*

Getting Where You Want to Go

Whether you are going from school to a training program, a college, or a job, there are several skills you will want to master. These include writing a resume and a cover letter, filling out an application form, and interviewing. These are likely to turn up more than once in your lifetime. It will benefit you to learn how to put your best foot forward for each of them.

The Resume

A ***resume*** basically outlines what you have to offer a prospective employer, school, or organization. See 3-12. You may need to tailor your resume for different purposes, but the basic information and general format will be the same. It should be keystroked and include the following:

1. Identifying information—your name, address, and phone number.
2. Goals and objectives—a specific statement of what you expect to bring to and learn from the school, program, or job you want.
3. Education—schools attended, dates, degrees earned, class rank, major and minor areas of study, and courses completed.
4. Work experience—a listing of jobs held with names and addresses of employers, dates, and brief descriptions of responsibilities. Be

Mary R. Poston

1036 Spring Street
Milwaukee, Wisconsin 53172
(414) 555-3214

JOB OBJECTIVE	Entry-level job as a receptionist or secretary leading to a position as an executive secretary.
EDUCATION	Washington High School, Milwaukee Graduating June, 20XX. Emphasis on business training. Skilled in keyboarding, shorthand, and bookkeeping. Can operate computer, calculator, and copying machine.
WORK EXPERIENCE 20XX-20XX	Secretarial Assistant, Watkins Insurance Agency, Milwaukee As a cooperative education student employee, I filed and operated the computer, telephone and office machines. I also handled some correspondence for the office manager.
Summer 20XX	Grill Crewperson, McDonald's Restaurant, Milwaukee Responsible for cooking and preparing food and keeping the work area clean.
HONORS AND ACTIVITIES	Member of the Office Education Association for two years. Secretary during senior year. Member of the Student Council during junior year. Member of the high school marching band for four years. 4-H member for eight years. Recipient of the Washington Achiever Award.
HOBBIES	Bicycling, tennis, reading.
REFERENCES	Available upon request.

3-12
Your resume will be one of the first things that introduces you to a prospective employer. It pays to give it careful, detailed attention.

sure to include both paid and volunteer positions that give a true picture of your previous experience.

5. Activities and honors—names of school or community activities and organizations in which you have participated. Describe any offices held and honors received. Mention any specific skills and talents you possess if they would be assets on the job.
6. References—on the resume state, "References available upon request." A ***reference*** is a person who is qualified and willing to speak on your behalf. References may include former teachers, employers, counselors, or others with knowledge of your character and qualifications. Always ask permission from anyone you wish to use as a reference. If a prospective employer wishes to contact your references, provide the employer with the name, title, address, and phone number of the reference.

The Cover Letter

This letter introduces you and your resume to the reader. It also gives you an opportunity to expand on material in the resume or to include other experiences and qualifications. See 3-13. Keystroke your letter on good quality paper taking care to use correct spelling and punctuation. It should include the following:

- ❑ Your name, address, and phone number.
- ❑ The date.
- ❑ Name, title, and address of the person receiving it.
- ❑ The purpose of the letter—to go with your resume, to ask for an interview, to inquire about a position.
- ❑ A brief statement of your interest in the school, job, or program for which you are applying.
- ❑ Highlights from your resume along with other pertinent information on your experience or qualifications.
- ❑ Mention of follow-up steps you plan to take, such as calling to arrange for an interview or to inquire further. Also include how and where you can be reached for an interview or more information.
- ❑ A thank you.

The Application Form

It pays to master this document because it will come up in one way or another throughout your life. You may have to complete application forms for jobs, schools, credit, apartments, mortgages, or insurance. See 3-14. Following are some pointers to help you complete a typical application form.

- ❑ If possible, make a copy of the form to work on before completing the form you will submit.
- ❑ Read the entire form before filling in any spaces. Be sure you understand each question before trying to answer it.
- ❑ Follow directions for completing the form with care, making sure to write clearly and spell correctly.
- ❑ Complete all of the questions that apply to you on the front and back of the form. For those that do not apply, write "Not applicable" or "NA" to show that you read the question.
- ❑ Give factual, accurate, and positive answers to questions about your education, work history, and past experience.
- ❑ Include names, titles, addresses, and phone numbers of former employers and any references you submit.

Mary Poston
1036 Spring St.
Milwaukee, WI 53172
(414) 555-3214

April 25, 20XX

Mr. Robert Drake
Personnel Manager
Whitaker Publishing Company
1822 W. Meridian St.
Milwaukee, WI 53172

Dear Mr. Drake:

Mr. James Mitchell, Cooperative Education Coordinator at Washington High School, informed me that your company plans to hire a full-time secretary in June. I would like to apply for this position.

The enclosed resume outlines my office skills. I have successfully completed a number of business courses in high school. As a cooperative education student at Washington High, I am presently gaining on-the-job experience as a secretarial assistant with Watkins Insurance Agency. I feel that my education and work experience have prepared me to perform well as a secretary for your company.

I will call you early next week to discuss the possibility of an interview for this position.

Sincerely,

Mary Poston

Mary Poston

3-13
A cover letter gives you another opportunity to make a positive impression.

APPLICATION FOR EMPLOYMENT

WPC

Whitaker Publishing Company
1822 W. Meridian Street
Milwaukee, WI 53172

PERSONAL INFORMATION

Date__________ Social Security Number____________________

Name____
Last First Middle

Present Address ______________________________________
Street City State Zip

Permanent Address_____________________________________
Street City State Zip

Phone No. ____

If related to anyone in our employ, state name and department

____

Referred by

____

EMPLOYMENT DESIRED

Position Date you can start Salary desired

Are you employed now? If so, may we inquire of your present employer?

Ever applied to this company before? Where When

EDUCATION

	Name and Location of School	Years Completed	Subjects Studied
Grammar School			
School School			
College			
Trade, Business or Correspondence School			

Subject of special study or research work____________________

____

3-14
Most job application forms will call for the information that appears in this form.

(Continued)

U.S. Military or Naval service ______ Rank ______ Present membership in National Guard or Reserves ______

Activities other than religious (civic, athletic, fraternal, etc.) ______

Exclude organizations the name or character of which indicates the race, creed, color, or national origin of its members.

FORMER EMPLOYERS List below last two employers starting with last one first.

Date Month and Year	Name, Address, and Phone Number of Employer	Salary	Position	Reason for Leaving
From To				
From To				
From To				

REFERENCES Give below the names of two persons not related to you, whom you have known at least one year.

	Name	Address/Phone	Job Title	Years Acquainted
1				
2				

PHYSICAL RECORD

In case of emergency notify ______
Name Address Phone No.

I authorize investigation of all statements contained in this application. I understand that misrepresentation or omission of facts called for is cause for dismissal.

Date ______ Signature ______

3-14
(Continued)

The Interview

Basically an ***interview*** is a talk between you and the admissions officer of a school or a prospective employer. This is an important talk and calls for careful preparation. Following are some tips for putting your best foot forward in an interview situation.

Learn Important Background Information

Find out as much as you can about the school, company, or program for which you are applying. Be informed also about your field of interest, if it is established at this point.

Anticipate What Questions Might Be Asked of You

These may include: Why do you want to go to school here, work for our company, apply for this position? What can you contribute to our school or organization? What are your strengths and weaknesses with respect to academics, work experience, and special qualifications? What are your educational and professional goals?

Prepare a List of Questions to Ask During the Interview

Ask specific questions about job responsibilities, opportunities for advancement, courses of study, and other items that fit the situation for which you are being interviewed. Practice answering these questions with someone before the interview.

Collect and Bring with You Any Material You May Need

Materials you will need to bring with you include copies of your resume, application form, correspondence, references, transcripts, etc. Be ready with your Social Security number, class rank or grade point average, and other facts that may be requested.

Look to Your Appearance and the Impression You Make

Pluses here include appropriate clothing, prompt arrival, a firm handshake, eye contact, direct answers to questions, intelligent questions of your own, and a confident manner.

Thank the Interviewer and Clarify the Follow-Up You Can Expect

Will you be contacted or should you call to learn the results of the interview? Should you send additional information or materials? Where and when can the interviewer contact you?

Follow Up Each Interview with a Thank-You Letter

If necessary, call to inquire about results or decisions if you do not receive a response within a reasonable time.

Entrepreneurship

Becoming an ***entrepreneur***, owning and operating your own business, is another way to become employed. It involves investing your money and your talents for profit and income. Creating a business of your own can take three basic forms: a *sole proprietorship*, meaning a single owner; a *partnership*, meaning two or more owners; and a *corporation*, meaning a separate entity created and owned by the founder and shareholders.

Another way to go into business is through a franchise. A *franchise* is an agreement that permits the franchisee to market and sell goods and services in a given area that the franchiser provides. Fast-food outlets, car rentals, and cleaning services are among the many franchise businesses.

You may think "big business" dominates the marketplace, but small businesses are the backbone of the U. S. economy. Since the mid-1970s, over two-thirds of the new jobs in the nation were created by small businesses. Small firms employ approximately 60 percent of the nongovernment workforce. Approximately 21 million small businesses exist in America today and account for 98 percent of all business establishments. Over half of the small business firms employ fewer than five workers and 90 percent employ fewer than 20 workers. For those who like to be their own boss, the entrepreneur route may be the answer. See 3-15.

However, starting a business can be risky. Thousands of small businesses fail each year. To succeed in a business of your own, it is a good idea to have previous work experience with the service or product you plan to sell or produce. You need to know how to manage a business, sell your goods and services, and deal with customers and suppliers. You need to keep financial records accurately and know the legalities involved in running a business. You also need enough money to get started and to operate until the business begins to pay for itself.

To establish your own business, you will need to work long and hard. Unfortunately, there is no sure income, no assurance of success, and very little financial security when you begin. However, for those who do succeed, the rewards are great. They include not only income and profits, but also independence and personal satisfaction.

Small Business Innovations

air conditioning
airplanes
insulin
lasers
optical scanners
pacemakers
personal computers
turbojet engines
xerography

3-15
Entrepreneurs running small businesses have brought us some of our most valuable inventions.

Language of the Work World

Your first job search may well introduce you to a whole new language that you will need to understand as you move through the world of work. You will learn that income for the work you do can come in different forms. Take-home pay can be much less than you expected. You will also learn that various deductions from income can amount to a considerable sum.

Income, the money you earn, can come in any of the following forms or a combination of them. You should understand the differences.

Wages refer to income paid by the hour. An hourly wage is a set amount paid for each hour worked. The amount depends on the type of work, the skill or experience of the worker, the demand for workers, and the employer. Many unskilled and beginning workers are paid the ***minimum wage***, which is the lowest hourly wage an employer can pay workers according to the Fair Labor Standards Act (FLSA). The federal minimum wage as of 1997 is $5.15 per hour. The minimum for employees who receive tips is $2.13 per hour, however, if that wage plus tips received do not amount to $5.15 per hour, the employer is required to pay the difference.

Some states require higher minimum wages. Generally, when workers put in more than 40 hours per week they receive overtime pay, which is 1½ or 2 times their hourly rate.

The term ***salary*** refers to income paid as a set amount for a period of time. This is usually an annual figure. The income may be paid weekly, every two weeks, or monthly. Salaried workers, such as teachers, managers, supervisors, and professionals, are paid an annual salary. They are expected to put in as much time as it takes to do the job. Generally salaried employees are not paid overtime.

Piecework income refers to money paid per piece of work done. For example, garment workers may be paid by the number of garments completed. The more they finish, the more they are paid. They must, however, receive at least the applicable minimum wage.

Commissions refer to income paid as a percentage of sales made by a salesperson. The more salespersons sell, the more they earn. People in sales may earn a commission only or a combination of base salary plus commission. A good salesperson can earn far more in commissions than in salary.

Tips, or gratuities, refer to income in the form of money customers give to workers for services provided. This form of income is common for waiters in restaurants, taxi drivers, bellhops, barbers, and others in service industries. Tips can come to a considerable sum, but they are voluntary and not a set amount the worker can rely on as income.

Bonuses refer to an amount added to base pay either as a reward for performance or as a share of business profits. Bonus income usually is based on the worker's sales, length of time with the company, or company profits.

Fringe benefits refer to non-wage compensation that offers important financial advantages to workers. Such benefits include paid vacations and holidays, life and health insurance, child care facilities or allowances, advanced training or tuition credits, and other extras depending on the company and type of work. While these are not dollar income items, they contribute significantly to financial stability for workers. Recent studies indicate that fringe benefits often account for close to 30 percent of total compensation.

"Take-home" pay is another concept you need to understand. On your first job, you may be offered an hourly wage of $5.50 and a work week of 40 hours. At the end of the week, you expect to bring home $220. Not so. Your ***gross pay*** will be $220, or the amount you earn before deductions. Your ***net pay***, or amount you have left after deductions, is the amount you bring home. ***Deductions*** are the amounts subtracted from your gross pay for the following:

- ❑ Social Security or FICA (Federal Insurance Contributions Act), which comes to 7.65 percent of earnings up to $53,400.
- ❑ Federal withholding tax, which will vary with the amount you earn and the exemptions you claim.
- ❑ State withholding tax, which will vary with earnings and from state to state.
- ❑ Other benefits or insurance you buy through your employer.

Deductions from gross income can run as much as 20 percent or more for various forms of taxes and benefits you pay for through your employer, 3-16. Some of these, such as Social Security and withholding taxes, are required by law. These are discussed in greater detail later in the text.

As a job seeker, it is important to remember that the gross pay you earn will be reduced considerably by various deductions. Your net income is the amount you will actually have to spend.

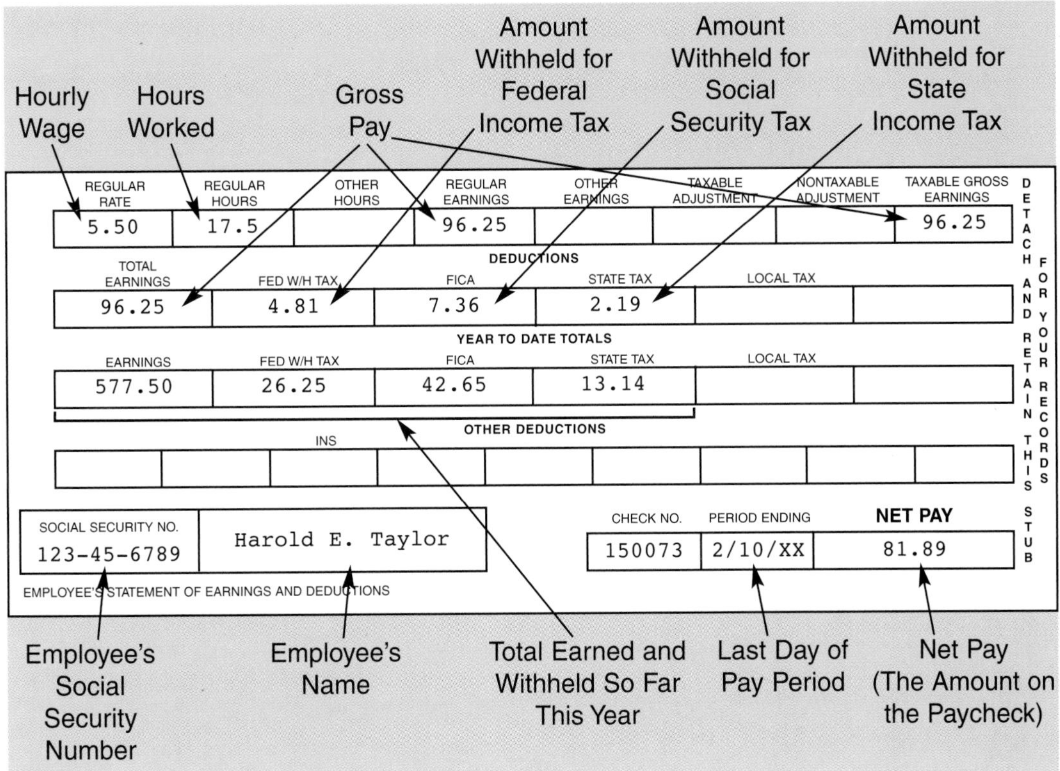

3-16
This paycheck stub shows some of the common deductions from income.

Summary

You will spend almost one-third of your waking hours at whatever job you choose. Finding work you can do well and enjoy is important. It requires an objective assessment of your interests, aptitudes, and abilities. It calls for insight into your personality, your values and goals, and your expectations for the future. In planning, it will be important to make work choices that fit the way you want to live.

Some basic, up-to-date knowledge of the job market is necessary to make intelligent career choices. Once you narrow down your interests, you need to learn what qualifications, training, and education are required for the areas you want to pursue. As you search out employment opportunities, look to reliable sources of career information. These include government publications, the Internet, school guidance counselors, and public libraries. Career days and exhibits can also offer reliable information and guidance. When making career choices, you may want to look into the field of family and consumer sciences.

Now is the time to begin planning for the training and education you will need. Explore the opportunities open to you including college, junior college, and occupational training. Internships and apprenticeships may open doors in certain fields. The Armed Forces also offer job training and college courses.

Paying for training and education after high school requires advance planning for most families. It begins with estimates of costs and of resources with plans to cover the difference. Financial aid may be available to some. Scholarships and other forms of assistance exist as well.

Certain tools help open doors to future opportunities. These include resumes, application forms, interviews, and correspondence with possible employers. You will want to learn to use each of these to your advantage. At some point, you may want to consider a business of your own. Take a careful look at the advantages and disadvantages.

Finally, you will need to learn the language of the work world. For example, what exactly is take-home pay? What are fringe benefits? What is the difference between wages, salaries, and commissions? What are payroll deductions and how much of your income will they take?

What you do now to prepare for the world of work can help you in the years ahead. One thing is clear. Job markets are competitive, and the workers with the best training, education, and experience will have the edge.

To Review

1. How do interests, aptitudes, and abilities apply to education and career choices?
2. Give an example of how values and goals affect career choices.
3. List two major challenges of managing the dual roles of career and family.
4. Describe two ways that families manage the challenges of dual roles.
5. List three reliable sources of information on job and career opportunities.
6. Give two ways that employment trends in industry and technology affect job markets.
7. List and describe three areas of job opportunities in family and consumer economics.

8. What are four factors to consider when choosing a college?
9. Name three sources of occupational training.
10. Where can you find detailed information about internships and apprenticeships?
11. What are two advantages and two disadvantages of receiving training and education through the Armed Forces?
12. Name two advantages and two disadvantages of being an entrepreneur.
13. What is the difference between gross pay and net pay?

To Discuss

1. Discuss the key advantages and disadvantages of going from high school to each of the following:
   - ❑ College
   - ❑ Occupational training
   - ❑ An internship
   - ❑ An apprenticeship
   - ❑ The Armed Forces
2. What are the pros and cons of going to college when you do not really want to go and have no special field you wish to study?
3. Discuss key factors to consider in evaluating career choices and job offers.
4. What personal characteristics do you think an employer would look for when filling a job opening?
5. What types of experiences and activities in high school do you feel would be helpful in getting full-time employment? Explain.
6. What career fields or job areas are of particular interest to you? How might you pursue these interests?
7. What types of training and education do you think would be required to obtain the type of employment and position you want to achieve?
8. Discuss pointers you can give for selling yourself through a resume, an interview, and an application form.
9. If you owned a business, what characteristics would you look for in persons you hire to work for you?

To Do

1. Develop charts to use in assessing yourself and assessing job or career choices.
2. Develop an annotated bibliography of informative sources on college choices, occupational training programs, internship opportunities, and apprenticeships.
3. Prepare a resume and complete an application form with information that applies to your personal situation as a high school graduate. You can obtain job application forms from local business firms.
4. If you plan to go to college, obtain and study financial aid forms and college application forms. These may be available from the guidance office at your school, at the public library, or online. Complete forms that apply to your situation.
5. Interview an entrepreneur in your community to learn about the challenges and rewards of being in business for yourself. Also interview an employee of a large company to learn about the challenges and rewards of working for an employer. Compare the advantages and disadvantages of being an entrepreneur versus working for an employer.
6. Review the help wanted section of the local paper and pick at least three jobs you would like. Discuss the reasons these jobs appeal to you. Write a letter that you could use to request an interview for one of the positions.

7. Working in small groups, make a checklist of personal qualities a successful entrepreneur needs.
8. An entrepreneur is a person who starts and manages his or her own business and assumes all the risks this involves. Interview an entrepreneur in your community regarding following:
   - ❑ What motivated the person to start a business?
   - ❑ What risks are involved?
   - ❑ What are the advantages and disadvantages of being self-employed versus working for an employer who takes most of the risks?
   - ❑ What advice would the person offer to someone who wants to start a business?
9. Using the Internet, research and outline your findings in one of the following areas. (If you are not online at home, arrange to go online at school or at the public library to complete this assignment.):
   - ❑ Finding a college—check out at least three schools
   - ❑ Apprenticeship and internship opportunities
   - ❑ Conducting a job search
   - ❑ Occupational outlook for the next decade and beyond.

Attending college classes can help you prepare for your career goals.

CHAPTER 4

Use sugars only in moderation
page 21
Use salt and sodium only in moderation
page 23
If you drink alcoholic beverages, do so in moderation page 25
Third Edition, 1990
U.S. Department of Agriculture
U.S. Department of Health and Human Services
HEALTHY CHOICE
Hearty Chicken Soup: a hearty homestyle soup that's delicious and nutritious.
DISTRIBUTED BY:
NABISCO FOODS
EAST HANOVER, NJ 07936
MADE IN U.S.A.
REG. PENNA. DEPT. AGR. (IFE)
© 1992 NABISCO FOODS, INC.
WHEN WRITING TO US, PLEASE ENCLOSE THE
EASY-TAB FLAP, OR CALL 1-800-932-7800,
WEEKDAYS, 9:00 AM-7:30 PM, EST
PROOF OF PURCHASE
VOICE
PROTECTION
CHOICE
SAFETY
National
Insurance
Consumer

You, the Consumer

consumer advocates
binding arbitration
small claims court
class action lawsuit
needs
wants
priorities
value system
standards
family life cycle

After studying this chapter, you will be able to

- ❑ describe the rights and responsibilities of consumers.
- ❑ identify government regulations and agencies that protect consumer interests.
- ❑ write an effective letter about a consumer problem.
- ❑ identify reliable sources of consumer information.
- ❑ explain how needs, wants, values, goals, and standards serve as guides to consumer decisions.
- ❑ describe how a family's goals, values, and standards affect family economics.

There are many types of consumers. Some seem to know what they want. They find goods and services they need at prices they can afford. They seem to manage their resources well and avoid costly mistakes. Others often make the wrong choices. They are often "taken in" by unscrupulous merchants. They sometimes take on too much debt. They never seem to be in control of their finances.

Most people probably fall somewhere in between the confident, competent consumer and the uncertain, inexperienced "victim." You can be either type. However, confidence and competence pay big dividends in the marketplace.

To be a confident, competent consumer, you need to know your rights and responsibilities in the marketplace. You need to know how the government protects your interests. You need to learn where to find reliable information about products and services, consumer legislation, and economic conditions. You need to master the steps involved in making complaints and finding solutions to consumer problems. You need to understand the personal aspects of managing money and how they influence your consumer decisions.

Consumer Rights and Responsibilities

In a message to Congress in 1962, President John F. Kennedy outlined four basic consumer rights: the right to safety, the right to be informed, the right to choose, and the right to be heard. Since 1962, four more rights have been added: the right to satisfaction of basic needs, the right to redress, the right to education, and the right to a healthy environment. Today, these eight consumer rights have been endorsed by the United Nations and affirmed by Consumers International, a worldwide consumer organization. Each of these rights carries responsibilities. Together they form the basis for fairness in meeting consumer needs. Following is a brief discussion of consumer rights and the responsibilities they entail.

Safety: Rights and Responsibilities

The right to safety means protection against the sale and distribution of dangerous goods and services. You should not have to worry about the safety of items you buy. The government plays an important role in protecting consumers against the sale of dangerous or hazardous products and services.

Responsibilities for safety rest also with consumers when they buy and use products and services. For example, it is up to the consumer to read and follow directions that come with a product. This is really important for items that can present hazards with misuse such as electric and gas appliances, household chemicals, yard equipment, etc. Care in the safe use, storage, and disposal of potentially dangerous products is a key responsibility of consumers. See 4-1.

When product-related safety problems occur, consumers have a responsibility to report them promptly to the seller and the manufacturer. If a product presents a serious health or safety hazard, consumers also should inform the proper government agency. This agency can take prompt action to prevent an injury or accident. For example, in the case of shock from an electric product or allergic reaction to a cosmetic, notify the appropriate

4-1
These labels are required on products containing hazardous substances.

government agency. This could prevent similar mishaps for other consumers. The Consumer Products Safety Commission handles hazardous products. The Food and Drug Administration deals with food, drug, and cosmetic products.

Truthful Information: Rights and Responsibilities

The right to know calls for accurate information on which to base buying decisions. This includes product information, labeling requirements, and protection against false or misleading advertising. The facts you need to know about products and services depend on what you are buying and how you plan to use them.

The most common sources of consumer information include advertising, product labels, warranties, articles in newspapers and magazines, salespeople, and other consumers. Advertising is one of the most available sources, but not always the most reliable. Its main purpose is to sell, so only favorable information on a product or service is likely to appear in an ad or commercial. However, the law prohibits advertisers from giving false and misleading information. It protects consumers against false advertising, fraud, illegal sales schemes, and other unfair trade practices.

With this right comes the responsibilities of seeking, evaluating, and using available information on products, services, and sellers. This involves checking out not only merchandise and services, but also sellers. Before you buy, investigate a seller's policies on sales, returns, and exchanges. It also pays to check a store's reputation for honesty and fair play, to evaluate claims and performance, and to compare quality and prices. In other words, research *before* buying.

Choice: Rights and Responsibilities

The right to choose means the opportunity to select the goods and services you want to buy and the places you want to shop. To make free choices, you need a number of sellers offering a variety of goods and services at competitive prices. This variety exists and is protected by laws that prohibit monopolies and encourage competition. Healthy competition results in a greater selection of products and services at different price levels. Without a number of sellers and a variety of offerings, there can be no free choice in the marketplace.

Responsibilities go with the right to choose from a variety of goods, services, and sellers. Consumers have the responsibility to choose with care those products and services that will best meet their needs at prices they can pay. This calls for informed and careful decisions. Choosing is not always an easy matter. The average supermarket alone carries over 10,000 items with a wide variety in almost every product category. See 4-2.

The responsibilities of choice go beyond the goods and services you buy. Consumers also have an

4-2
Piggly Wiggly
Consumer choice in a market economy is well illustrated in the modern supermarket. Each department offers a host of choices.

obligation to deal only with reliable, reputable businesses. This is for their own protection and for the overall good of the marketplace.

Besides looking to their own needs when exercising the right to choose, consumers send a message by their choices. Every buying choice expresses approval of the purchase and the seller. Consumers need to be aware of the message they send with their free choices and their dollars.

A Voice: Rights and Responsibilities

When consumers have problems or concerns, they have the right to speak up, to be heard, and to expect results. Their legitimate interests, comments, and complaints should be heard and appropriate action taken. This requires that both business and government respond to the voice of the consumer.

In order to exercise their right to be heard, consumers must learn to express their concerns to business and government representatives. This means learning how to communicate. It means using appropriate and effective means of getting the message where it needs to go. Unless consumers communicate, their needs and wants are likely to remain unknown and unmet. To make their voices heard, consumers need to speak out on the issues that concern them. They need to develop the ability to compliment and complain. Let businesses know what you like and want, as well as what you dislike.

Satisfaction of Basic Needs: Rights and Responsibilities

The right to satisfaction of basic needs means access to essential goods and services including adequate food, shelter, clothing, health care, education, and sanitation. These basics should be available to all consumers. To satisfy basic needs, you need both enough income to purchase essentials and a marketplace that provides them. Governments play a major role both in defining basic needs and ensuring that citizens are able to satisfy these needs. Public housing and social programs, medicare and medicaid, Social Security, tax-supported schools and hospitals, and sewer and sanitation systems are some of the ways governments ensure that basic needs are available to all.

Responsibilities for satisfaction of basic needs rest also with consumers themselves. For example, it is up to the consumer to put essential needs ahead of other needs and wants in allocating income and planning spending. It is the consumer's responsibility to learn about and take advantage of basic services provided by government.

Redress: Rights and Responsibilities

The right to redress means the consumer's right to receive a fair settlement of disputes, including some form of compensation for misrepresentation, shoddy goods, or unsatisfactory services. Here again, consumers share some of the responsibilities connected with redress. They need to present their disputes clearly to the appropriate authorities and make their demands reasonable. It also helps to avoid problems, when possible, by trading only with reliable sellers and service providers and by thoughtful choices in the marketplace. Methods of achieving redress are discussed in this chapter.

Consumer Education: Rights and Responsibilities

The right to consumer education refers to the consumer's right to some form of training and mastery of the knowledge and skills needed to make informed, confident choices in the marketplace and to achieve an awareness of basic consumer rights and responsibilities. You are fulfilling a part of the responsibility related to this right by taking a consumer education course and reading this book. There are many opportunities for consumers to learn the skills they need to function to their own advantage in the marketplace. Sources of consumer education and information are discussed in this chapter.

Healthy Environment: Rights and Responsibilities

The right to a healthy environment refers to consumers' rights to live and work in an environment that is nonthreatening to the well-being of present and future generations.

This right calls for pure water and air, safe and responsible waste disposal, preservation of essential natural resources, conservation measures, and respect for the earth and overall environment we all share. Chapter 18 outlines environmental concerns along with consumer rights and responsibilities connected to environmental issues.

Consumer Protection by Government

Every society has its laws. Thomas Jefferson said, "Laws and institutions must go hand in hand with the progress of the human mind." If this is true, the human mind must be making great progress in this country. The United States has countless laws and regulations governing our nation. These laws affect every phase of life.

Government Regulation of Business

Almost every phase of business and economic activity falls under some form of government regulation. For instance, the simple hamburger sold in fast-food outlets across the nation is subject to more than 40,000 state and federal regulations. Rules cover everything—fat content of the meat, ingredients in the catsup, advertising slogans, hiring practices, wages, restaurant inspections, disposal of trash, etc.

Charge accounts, credit cards, and loans also are subject to countless controls. Government regulates finance charges and terms of credit contracts. It determines what must be stated in a credit agreement and how credit terms may be advertised. It sets requirements for credit application forms, agreements, and monthly statements. Laws govern procedures for processing credit applications, granting credit, handling billing errors, and collecting overdue bills.

Every phase of the auto industry is regulated by government, from the manufacturer to your garage. Federally mandated safety features and pollution controls alone add hundreds of dollars to the price of a new car. Other regulations cover plant working conditions, employee benefits, car warranties, auto servicing, registration and licensing, insurance, and advertising.

Federal laws are passed by Congress in the U.S. Capitol, and signed into law by the President, 4-3. As the number of regulations and regulatory agencies increases, so does the cost to government, business, and ultimately

> ***"The United States is the greatest law factory the world has ever known."***
>
> ***Charles Evans Hughes***

4-3
Legislators present bills to be enacted in the Capitol where they are voted upon by Congress and Senate and then presented to the President to be signed into law.

consumers. The scope of regulations and the paperwork they require also add to the cost of regulating. Historically, government regulations were directed at a specific product or industry. Today, laws, such as the Occupational Safety and Health Act (OSHA) and the Consumer Product Safety Act (CPSA), apply to almost every existing business and product. Many recent regulations also require more record keeping and paperwork than in the past.

Over-regulation can contribute to serious economic problems. The impact of both inflation and recession becomes greater in an atmosphere of excessive regulations that cut into productivity and add to the cost of doing business. The case study about Jake illustrates the impact of regulations on business.

Government Agencies Serving Consumers

Government agencies assist consumers in a variety of ways at the local, state, and federal levels. They administer and enforce laws and regulations. These agencies set standards for and provide information about many products and services. They protect consumers from unsafe products and unethical business practices. They represent consumer interests in many areas.

Government agencies at the local and state levels provide information, protection, and a number of other services for consumers. In most communities and states, laws exist to protect the health, safety, and rights of citizens. These laws regulate food standards and sanitation practices, credit and insurance transactions, and business and trade practices. They also govern the licensing and certification of medical professionals, hospitals, nursing homes, funeral homes, lawyers, and others who serve the public.

Local laws and agencies vary widely among different communities and states. In addition, many federal government agencies operate local and state offices to serve citizens where they live. Investigate government agencies and services in your area so you know where to go for information, protection, and assistance.

Consumer Decisions

Government Regulation: Jake's Bread Factory

Jake worked for many years in a large bakery making bread. He managed to save a few thousand dollars and to borrow several thousand more to open a business of his own. He called it, "The Bread Factory" and baked only top quality breads and rolls. The business was very successful and soon it was impossible to meet the demand for bread.

Jake wanted to expand and hire more help, but doing so would make his business subject to more government regulations and significantly increase his costs. Here are some of the requirements Jake must meet if he expands in order to comply with local, state, and federal regulations:

- Mandatory safety equipment and materials
- Employee health and retirement benefits
- New content and nutritional labeling
- Packaging specifications
- More detailed record keeping
- More inspections by the city health department
- Additional record keeping connected with these regulations

Jake wants to enlarge his plant, buy improved equipment, and hire more help to increase his production. Unfortunately, the cost of meeting government requirements does not leave Jake enough money to do so.

If Jake proceeds with his expansion, he will be forced to raise his prices to cover the expenses of complying with government regulations. These expenses do not improve his productivity. Increasing prices without increasing productivity is inflationary. Jake's business by itself will not contribute greatly to inflation, but Jake is not alone. Thousands of businesses across the country face similar circumstances. The costs of record keeping and meeting government requirements do not increase productivity, but they do increase business costs significantly. Higher prices result.

If Jake decides not to expand, the jobs he would have created and the increased productivity will not happen. When the costs of regulation become too heavy for businesses already suffering in a recession, they may close shop altogether. This deepens the recession.

Case Review

1. Obviously, some regulation is needed to ensure that Jake uses wholesome ingredients in his bread and that he is fair and honest with employees and customers. How much and what type of regulation do you feel is necessary to achieve these goals?
2. Some people argue for more regulations, stronger consumer protection, and broader government powers. How do you feel about this position? What evidence can you find in support of or opposition to this position?
3. Critics of government regulations claim that the cost is too high. They argue that the money spent to comply with regulations reduces the amount available for capital improvements. The cost is ultimately passed on to consumers in the form of higher prices. How do you feel about this argument? What evidence can you find to support or oppose it?
4. How have government regulations improved or complicated your life in the recent past? Give at least two examples of each.

Over 80 federal government agencies and departments exist to serve consumers in one way or another. Following is a list of several key agencies with a brief description of their primary functions in the area of consumer protection and interests.

The *Department of Agriculture (USDA)* is one of the largest federal agencies. Its various departments and services relate to farming, economics, environment, and international trade. In the interests of consumers, the USDA supervises food safety and inspection services, sets standards of quality for the food supply, administers a nutrition information service, and manages food programs for the needy. See 4-4.

The *Department of Labor* promotes the welfare of wage earners, improves working conditions, and advances employment opportunities. This department enforces labor laws that include minimum wage, child labor, anti-discrimination, maximum working hours, and safety and health regulations. It also administers the Bureau of Labor Statistics and the Occupational Safety and Health Administration (OSHA).

The *Department of Health and Human Services (HHS)* attempts to serve the health and human needs of citizens from birth to old age through a variety of programs and assistance. It administers financial aid programs, promotes public health, and works to control drug and alcohol abuse. HHS supervises and coordinates the work of a number of agencies including the Administration for Children and Families, Food and Drug Administration, Public Health Service, Social Security Administration, National Institute of Health, and the Center for Disease Control.

The *Food and Drug Administration (FDA)* works to protect the public against impure and unsafe foods, drugs, cosmetics, and certain other potential hazards. It operates national centers for drug evaluation and research, food safety and applied nutrition, veterinary medicine, radiological health, and toxicological research.

The *Department of Housing and Urban Development (HUD)* supervises programs related to housing needs, fair housing opportunities, and community development. It administers mortgage insurance to promote home ownership, rental assistance for low and moderate income families, housing safety standards, urban renewal programs, and federal real estate laws.

The *Consumer Product Safety Commission (CPSC)* protects the public against risk of injury from consumer products, sets safety standards for consumer products, and promotes research into the causes and prevention of product-related injuries and deaths.

The *Federal Trade Commission (FTC)* promotes free and fair competition by preventing deceptive practices, false advertising, and unfair trade practices in the marketplace. It enforces consumer protection legislation in a variety of

USDA

A

USDA

B

4-4
The USDA is an enormous government agency. It has many departments that serve a variety of consumer interests (A). One of these departments is responsible for the school lunch and nutrition program (B).

areas including consumer credit transactions, packaging and labeling, product warranties, and truth in advertising.

The *Securities and Exchange Commission (SEC)* provides for fair and full disclosure of financial data about securities being offered for sale. The SEC also protects investors against fraud when buying or selling securities. It regulates security exchanges and associations, investment companies, brokers, dealers, and investment counselors.

Descriptions of other government agencies serving consumer and citizen interests are featured in other sections of this book.

Specific Laws Protecting Consumers

In addition to the many agencies that serve and protect consumers, a host of federal, state, and local laws addresses consumer issues and protection. A few of the many federal laws that protect you and all consumers in the marketplace are described in 4-5.

Consumer Self-Defense

Looking after your own interests is an essential consumer skill. It involves taking the proper steps when products and services do not meet your expectations or the sellers' claims. It calls for settling differences with sellers and seeking the help of third-party consumer advocates when necessary. ***Consumer advocates*** are individuals or groups who promote consumer interests in areas such as health and safety, education, redress, truthful advertising, fairness in the marketplace, and environmental protection. Finally, consumer self-defense may require legal action when all else fails.

Successful Complaining

Self-defense begins with addressing problems with goods and services directly with sellers. What do you do when a product fails, when you are overcharged because of a billing error, when you pay for car repairs but the car isn't fixed, or when a salesperson is rude? To address any of these problems, you need to complain to the right person in the right way. The art of complaining is an essential self-defense tool. Simple exchanges and returns of unsatisfactory merchandise can often be handled by taking purchases back where you bought them and explaining your dissatisfaction. Most reliable merchants will take care of simple matters on the spot at the point of sale. Here are a few suggestions for success when problems are more involved or complicated:

Put It in Writing

When you complain about anything serious, it is wise to put it in writing. Make every effort to explain the problem clearly, rationally, and briefly. Include important facts, figures, and dates along with copies of receipts. See 4-6.

Be Prompt

Don't wait weeks or months to act. If you know you have a problem, put your case in writing right away. When mailing a complaint letter, you may want to use registered mail so you have a record of its delivery. The receiver must sign for a registered letter, and the sender receives a receipt showing that it was delivered.

Address the Right Source

Direct your complaint to the right person and place. A few inquiries by phone should let you know where to send your letter. Routine problems can often be handled by salespeople or customer service employees. If an adjustment requires approval from higher up, the department or store manager is the person to see. For billing errors and other credit problems, contact the credit department.

Federal Legislation for Protection of Consumers

1887 Interstate Commerce Act
Establishes federal regulation of railroads.

1890 Sherman Anti-Trust Act
Prohibits price fixing, monopolies, and other restraint of free trade.

1906 Pure Food and Drug Act
Provides for federal supervision of interstate sales of food and drugs.

1906 Meat Inspection Act
Provides for federal inspection of meat sold across state lines.

1914 Federal Trade Commission Act
Established the Federal Trade Commission to control concentrations of economic power and to protect business from unfair competition and trade practices.

1933 Federal Reserve Act
Established Federal Deposit Insurance Corporation to provide insurance coverage of bank deposits.

1934 Communications Act
Created the Federal Communications Commission to regulate interstate and foreign communications in the public interest.

1934 Securities Exchange Act
Created the Securities Exchange Commission to enforce federal securities laws written to protect investors and to maintain fair and honest securities markets.

1934 Federal Food, Drug and Cosmetics Act
Requires presale testing of drugs and gives the FDA authority to protect the public against impure and unsafe foods, drugs, cosmetics and other potential hazards.

1934 Wheeler-Lea Amendment
Gives the FTC authority to protect consumers against deceptive advertising and unfair trade practices.

1953 Flammable Fabrics Act
Sets mandatory flammability standards for clothing sold across state lines.

1960 Federal Hazardous Act
Requires warning labels on toxic substances and household chemicals.

1962 Kefauver-Harris Drug Amendment
Requires that drugs be proved safe and effective before marketing.

1965 Cigarette Labeling Act
Requires health warning labels on cigarette packages.

1966 Child Safety Act
Bans the sale of any chemical so "dangerous that no warning could make its use safe."

1966 Fair Packaging and Labeling Act
Requires packaged foods to be labeled with net weight, ingredients, and manufacturer's name and address.

1966 Motor Vehicle Safety Act
Establishes motor vehicle safety standards.

1967 Wholesome Meat Act
Requires state inspection of meat products.

1968 Truth in Lending Act
Requires full disclosure of credit costs of installment sales and loans.

1969 Child Protection and Toy Safety Act
Bans the sale across state lines of toys with electrical, mechanical, or thermal hazards.

1970 Poison Prevention Packaging Act
Sets standards for child-resistant packaging.

1970 Credit Card Liability Act
Limits consumer liability for credit cards and prohibits issuing unsolicited credit cards.

1971 Fair Credit Reporting Act
Requires credit reporting agencies to provide consumers with a summary of credit reports and to correct any inaccurate information on reports.

1972 Consumer Product Safety Act
Established the Consumer Product Safety Commission to protect the public against unreasonable risks of injury from consumer products, to aid consumers in judging the safety of products, to develop safety standards for consumer products, and to promote research into the causes and prevention of product related death, accident, and injury.

1973 Health Maintenance Organization Act
Provides grants to medical care groups and encouraged formation of HMOs.

1973 Toxic Substances Control Act
Requires premarket testing of all new chemical substances.

1974 Fair Credit Billing Act
Requires creditors to correct billing errors and to credit payments promptly, and allows consumers to withhold credit card payments on defective products.

1974 Equal Credit Opportunity Act
Prohibits discrimination in granting credit on the basis of sex or marital status.

1975 Magnuson-Moss Warranty Act
Requires certain disclosure statements on product warranties.

1976 Equal Credit Opportunity Act Amendments
Prohibits credit granting discrimination on the basis of age, creed, race, national origin, or receipt of public assistance.

1976 Cosmetic Labeling Rule
Requires ingredient labeling on cosmetic products.

1977 Fair Debt Collection Practices Act
Eliminates abusive tactics and harassment in collection of debts.

1980 Depository Institutions Deregulation and Monetary Control Act
Permits nonbank financial institutions to offer checking accounts and other financial services previously limited to banks. Also lifts restrictions on interest paid on deposited savings.

1980 Electronic Fund Transfer Act
Establishes procedures to follow in using electronic fund accounts and resolving any errors on EFT statements.

1990 Safe Medical Devices Act
Regulates safety, effectiveness, and labeling of medical devices.

1990 Nutrition Labeling and Education Act
Improves the quality and type of nutrition information provided on food product labels.

1991 Americans with Disabilities Act
Prohibits discrimination against people with disabilities and requires accessibility to public accommodations, such as stores, schools, museums, theaters, restaurants, wash rooms, and telecommunications.

4-5 *(Continued)*
These are some of the many federal laws that protect consumers from the confusion of the marketplace, from careless and dishonest business practices, and in many cases from themselves. This listing does not include the countless state and local laws and ordinances that also protect consumers in a wide variety of areas.

Federal Legislation for Protection of Consumers

1991 Truth in Savings Act
Provides for clear disclosure of interest rates and conditions on savings accounts.

1991 Telephone Consumer Protection Act
Establishes rules concerning telemarketing and permits consumers to sue telemarketers who violate the rules.

1992 Cable Deregulation Act
Regulates basic cable television rates and services.

1993 Child Safety Protection Act
Requires toy products manufactured in or imported into the United States to comply with Child Safety Protection Act standards.

1993 Family and Medical Leave Act
Requires employers who employ 50 or more people to provide employees up to 12 weeks unpaid continuous or intermittent leave per year with continuing health benefits and assurance upon return of being restored to the same or an equivalent position.

1996 Food Quality Protection Act
Establishes strong health-based safety standard for pesticide residues in foods.

1996 Personal Responsibility and Work Opportunity Reconciliation Act
A welfare reform plan which requires work in exchange for time-limited assistance.

1996 Health Insurance Portability and Accountability Act
Protects health insurance coverage for workers and their families when they change or lose their jobs.

1996 Telecommunications Act
Promotes competition, encourages speedy use of new telecommunication technologies, and reduces regulation in the hope of securing lower prices and improved services for telecommunications consumers.

4-5 (continued)

(Your Address)
(Your City, State, Zip Code)
(Date)

(Name of Contact Person)
(Title)
(Company Name)
(Street Address)
(City, State, Zip Code)

(Dear Contact Person):

On (date), I purchased (or had repaired) a (name of the product with serial or model number or service performed). I made this purchase at (location, date, and other important details of the transaction).

Unfortunately, your product (or service) has not performed well (or the service was inadequate) because (state the problem).

Therefore, to resolve the problem, I would appreciate your (state what you want—repair, replacement, refund, apology, etc.). Enclosed are copies (copies, NOT originals) of my records (receipts, guarantees, warranties, canceled checks, contracts, model and serial numbers, and any other documents).

I look forward to your reply and a resolution to my problem, and will wait (set a time limit) before seeking third-party assistance. Please contact me at the above address or by phone at (home or office numbers with area codes).

Sincerely,

(your name)
(your account number)

4-6
This sample complaint letter shows what information to include when writing about a consumer problem with a product or service.

Complaining to the top management of a company is usually the final step when a problem is not solved at lower levels. However, if a problem is so serious that you feel the top people should be told, contact top management first. For names and addresses of local businesses and organizations, check your local phone book. Look for toll-free numbers in the directory. To find the names of officers of large business firms, use *Standard and Poor's Register of Corporations*. This book is available in most public libraries. This information is also available online.

Be Specific and Factual

When writing a complaint, clearly identify the product or service in question and describe the problem. Include the date and place of purchase, the product name and model number, and the purchase price. Include your credit card or account number if the purchase was charged.

Be Reasonable

You are more likely to get a satisfactory response if you state your problem reasonably. It also helps to sympathize with the person who will receive your letter. For example, you might say, "I realize it takes time to correct a computer error, but . . ." or, "I know it must be difficult to give one-day service on appliances, but . . ." Threatening or sarcastic letters rarely promote a satisfactory solution to problems. It pays to enlist the understanding and support of the person who handles consumer problems.

Suggest a Solution

Even a well-presented complaint can leave the reader confused unless you spell out what you want. Do you expect repair, replacement, refund, an apology? You may not always get your way, but it helps to outline the solution you are seeking.

Be Businesslike

Put your grievances and transactions with business firms in writing. When you communicate or inquire by phone, keep a written record of phone conversations with the date, the name of the person who talked with you, and promises made or action to be taken. Keep important receipts and records together. Sometimes you may need to furnish papers or documents such as sales slips, bills, receipts, warranties, and previous correspondence. If you do, send copies of these papers and keep the originals in case you need to refer to them again.

Be Persistent

Most problems can be solved with one letter directed to the right person. However, if you don't get the desired results, write a second, or even a third letter.

When you send follow-up letters, enclose a copy of earlier correspondence. Indicate a date by which you expect some action. If a third letter is necessary, include copies of the previous letters and the names of persons you intend to contact if the matter is not settled by a certain date.

Consumer Advocates

If you cannot settle differences directly with sellers, it is often helpful to contact an outside party or organization, such as a consumer advocate. Government agencies that offer consumer assistance and services were listed earlier in this chapter. When you are dealing with dishonest and fraudulent business practices, contact the appropriate government regulatory agency. Most federal agencies will have local or regional offices. In addition, local and state governments provide regulatory and law enforcement functions to deal with fraud in the marketplace. Check your telephone book for names and numbers of consumer advocacy agencies that assist consumers. Most major city phone books provide a separate listing of government services.

Nongovernment consumer advocacy comes from a variety of sources and offers a range of services to consumers. Some, like the Better Business Bureau, you will recognize. Others may not be as familiar. The advocacy groups fall primarily into the following categories:

- *Better Business Bureaus (BBBs).* These are nonprofit organizations supported largely by local businesses across the country. They promote ethical business practices and in some cases, offer dispute resolution programs. Call a local BBB to learn what assistance and services it offers consumers.
- *National Consumer Organizations.* Consumer interest groups across the nation offer a variety of services including advocacy of consumer causes, educational materials, and information on products and services. Many of these groups work actively for better consumer protection and services. Among the well known consumer organizations are the American Association of Retired Persons (AARP), Consumer Federation of America (CFA), Consumers Union which publishes Consumer Reports, the National Consumers League, The National Foundation for Consumer Credit, Inc., which sponsors Consumer Credit Counseling Services, the National Fraud Information Center which operates a hot line for consumer complaints and inquiries related to telemarketing and Internet problems.
- *Trade Associations and Dispute Resolution Programs.* Companies that produce or sell the same types of goods and services to consumers may belong to industry associations made up of firms with similar business interests. These associations act on behalf of the industry and often act as a go-between for the companies they represent and consumers. They often provide consumer information on products and services and may offer dispute settlement programs.
- *Corporate Consumer Departments.* Many companies operate consumer affairs departments with the responsibility of dealing with consumer concerns, hearing complaints and resolving disputes. When you have a problem with a product you have purchased and you cannot get satisfaction where you bought it, you may find satisfaction through the consumer affairs department at the company headquarters. Very often these departments publish toll-free numbers for your convenience.

Difficult Cases

Problems beyond the help of consumer-oriented organizations or government agencies may require some form of legal action. Depending on the nature of the problem and the amount of money involved, your choices may include binding arbitration, small claims court, a class action lawsuit, or a full-fledged lawsuit. Because legal action is costly and time consuming, most consumers consider it only as a last resort.

Binding arbitration is a method of settling disagreements through an objective third party. Once both parties agree to arbitrate, each presents his or her case to the arbitrator who decides how the dispute will be solved. The arbitrator's decision is final and legally binding. Arbitrators are chosen from a pool of volunteers or professionals depending on the program. Advantages of this type of dispute settlement include speedy resolution of differences at relatively low cost. It is a simple, informal process.

Small claims court offers a simple, inexpensive way to settle minor differences involving small amounts of money. The small claims court follows relatively relaxed procedures. Consumers normally represent themselves without a lawyer. Maximum claims that can be brought up to this forum are limited to $1,200 in some states and up to $5,000 in others. Procedures vary from state to state. Check out this method through your local courthouse. This method offers simple, prompt settlements for a small fee. It does involve putting your case together with all of the available documentation and evidence available.

Class action lawsuits are legal actions in courts of law brought by a group of individuals who have been similarly wronged. In these cases, the courts permit members of a common class, such as consumers who have been similarly harmed or defrauded, to pool their grievances and sue for damages on behalf of the entire class or group. Laws governing this type of lawsuit vary from state to state.

> *"Knowledge is of two kinds: we know a subject ourselves, or we know where we can find information upon it."*
>
> *Samuel Johnson*

The Informed Consumer

Wouldn't it be nice to learn one set of facts that would make you an informed consumer forever? Unfortunately, the information you need to know as a consumer is made up of constantly changing facts and figures. Products, services, laws, and economic conditions change a great deal from year to year. It is to your advantage to stay up-to-date.

Community Resources

To be an informed consumer, you need to know what sources of facts and figures are available to you. Chart 4-7 lists some of the resources available in most communities. The people, places, and organizations listed can provide valuable information related to consumer needs and interests. From these resources, you can build a foundation of knowledge to help you make wise economic decisions in the marketplace.

A valuable resource that is sometimes overlooked is the newspaper. Almost every daily and weekly newspaper offers articles and advertisements related to consumer issues. Chart 4-8 lists the types of consumer information you can find in different sections of most newspapers.

The Internet

The Internet opens a whole new world of consumer information and resources. (A working Internet vocabulary list is given in 4-9.) You can find product information, the latest on consumer laws and protection, comparison shopping data, credit and financial information, health and medical news, and a variety of other helpful data. You also can go online to buy almost anything you can buy in stores or out of catalogs. You can do your banking and trade securities online, and, in some areas, you can arrange a home mortgage. **Caution:** When using the Internet for information or shopping or personal business, take care to check the reliability of sources and sites. In a

Community Resources

People
- Automotive technicians
- Bankers
- Business people
- Car dealers
- Credit managers
- Customer service managers
- Financial advisers and planners
- Government officials and representatives
- Healthcare providers
- Insurance agents
- Journalists
- Lawyers
- Real estate brokers
- Stockbrokers
- Teachers
- Other consumers

Places
- Brokerage houses
- Broadcasting stations
- Colleges and universities
- Consumer service or education departments of companies
- Courthouses
- Department stores
- Financial institutions
- Government agencies
- Insurance companies
- Libraries
- Main offices of major corporations
- Model homes or apartments
- Newspaper offices
- Real estate firms
- Small claims court
- Supermarkets

Organizations
- Bankers Association
- Bar Association
- Better Business Bureau
- Chamber of Commerce
- Community Action Groups
- Consumer Organizations
- Legal Aid Society
- Medical Associations
- Trade Associations
- Urban League

Government Agencies*
- Consumer Information Center
- Consumer Protection Agencies
- Department of Agriculture
- Department of Energy
- Department of Health and Human Services
- Department of Transportation
- Environmental Protection Agency
- Extension Service
- Federal Communications Commission
- Federal Trade Commission
- Food and Drug Administration
- Housing and Urban Development
- Internal Revenue Service
- Postal Service
- Social Security Administration
- State Departments of Education

*Most of these agencies can be accessed online.

4-7
Knowing and using the resources available in your community will help you make intelligent consumer decisions.

sense, you need to be your own security guard. See 4-10 for a few of the many Web sites offering consumer information and protection you can access on the Internet.

Evaluating Consumer Information

After identifying reliable sources of information, you may want to begin a consumer information file. This will put the latest facts and figures at your fingertips when you need them. You can then use material in your file to make intelligent decisions when you buy, spend, use credit, save, and so forth.

Data you can use is available in such large quantities that you couldn't possibly file all the material that comes your way. You will need to evaluate articles and booklets to see what is worth keeping. When evaluating materials, keep the following guidelines in mind:

Use a Reliable and Informed Source for the Type of Information You Need

A reliable source on one subject may not be the best place for facts on other topics. For example, a banker

Dissecting a Newspaper

Section	Information Related to Consumer Education
Financial News	Stock market reports, government regulations affecting business, prices, taxes, company earning reports, new products and developments, business planning, economic conditions, international trade, and political developments.
News: Local, Regional, National, and International	Events and personalities in business and government that affect consumers and the economy.
Editorials	Comment on current issues in business, employment, politics, government, the economy, and other items affecting consumers.
Fashion	New trends, pointers on clothing selection, wardrobe planning, tips on sewing and clothing care, sales, clearances, and special events.
Food	Weekly specials in grocery stores, seasonal buys, menu planning, budget meals, shopping guides, recipe ideas, nutrition, diet, and labeling.
Home	Trends and ideas in home furnishings and decorating, pointers on shopping and caring for furniture and home furnishings, and notice of sales and special events.
Advertisements	Prices, features, new products, coupons, use and care information on products, special offers, information on company policies that affect consumers, sales, and clearances.
Classified Ads Jobs	Job opportunities, pay schedules, working conditions, training and educational requirements, and qualifications.
Housing	Homes and apartments for rent or sale in different areas, purchase and rental costs in current markets, and availability of different types of housing.
TV and Radio	Programs related to consumer interests, the economy, and world markets.
Cartoons	Humorous side of various topics related to money management, consumer education, and economics.
Transportation	New car models, features, costs, automotive news, safety and mileage data, auto care and maintenance, sales, rebates, and special offers.

4-8
The newspaper can be a valuable consumer resource.

Working Internet Vocabulary

Baud - the speed at which data is transmitted.

Browser - software that lets you travel the World Wide Web and access documents.

CD-ROM - Compact Disc Read-Only Memory, designed to be played by a computer. It contains graphics, text, video-like movies and sound. One disc can hold an entire library.

Cyberspace - slang for Internet.

Download - to receive files from another computer over phone lines, through your modem, into your computer.

E-mail - electronic mail messages sent and received via the Internet.

Hardware - the computer with its wires, cables, printer, disk drive, modem, etc.

HTML - Hypertext Markup Language used to write pages for the World Wide Web.

HTTP - Hypertext Transfer Protocol, a common system used to request and send HTML documents on the World Wide Web.

Hypertext - a system of displaying text which allows it to be linked to related documents online. It usually is underlined or highlighted and if you point and click, it will take you to other related documents and files.

Internet - the largest system of interconnected computer networks with worldwide connections for exchanging messages and documents.

Modem - a device that connects computers to each other over phone lines.

Monitor - a video display terminal.

Search engine - specialized software made available by companies on the Internet that lets you look for material on the Internet.

Service provider - an organization that provides access to the Internet.

Software - computer programs or applications that make the computer usable.

Surfing - exploring the Internet.

World Wide Web (WWW) - a system of hypertext-based documents linked across the Internet. Its connections are an unrestricted, nonlinear, and seemingly endless Weblinking information from one resource to another.

4-9
Being familiar with these terms can help you to navigate the Internet.

Consumer Information Center www.pueblo.gsa.gov

Consumer World www.consumerworld.org

National Fraud Information Center www.fraud.org

Federal Trade Commission www.ftc.gov

Consumer Product Safety Commission www.cpsc.gov

National Highway Safety Commission www.dot.gov/affairs/

Project OPEN (National Consumer League) www.isa.net/project-open

Council on Economic Priorities www.accesspt.com/cep

Consumer Alert www.consumeralert.org

Better Business Bureau www.bbb.org

U.S. Department of Justice www.usdoj.gov

4-10
The following Web sites offer information of interest to consumers.

may give sound financial advice, but know nothing about buying furniture. A medical association can tell you how to find a doctor, but not how to buy a car. The Food and Drug Administration can tell you how to read a nutrition label, but not how to judge auto repair services.

Determine the Primary Purpose of the Information

Is it intended to inform the buyer or to sell a product, service, or idea? Both news articles and advertisements can offer helpful information, but advertisements generally present only positive facts. While ads and commercials can provide important data, it is wise to remember that their primary goal is to sell.

Evaluate the Usefulness of the Information

Look for material that is up-to-date and easy to understand. Read to see if recent developments on the product or subject are discussed. Consider whether the data is complete. Does it tell what you need to know about products, services, features, quality, performance, warranties, and prices?

Once you begin collecting consumer materials, you will need to organize the information for easy use. Find a drawer or box large enough to hold all of the materials you collect. Then sort according to subject matter. As you gather new materials, add them to your file. Periodically, review what you have filed and discard information that is no longer current or useful.

Personal Aspects of Consumer Choices

Some people always seem to know what they want and where they are going. They seem to know what is important and what is not worth serious attention. This sense of direction and purpose often is a key factor separating the people who achieve what they want from those who don't. Developing this sense of direction and purpose requires a clear understanding of personal needs, wants, values, goals, and standards.

Needs and Wants

Needs are those items you must have to survive. They can be physical or psychological. Food, clothing, and shelter are basic physical needs. Psychological needs include feelings of safety, security, love, acceptance, approval, and success.

Wants are items that you would like to have, but that are not essential for life. For instance, you may want to buy a CD player, to take a vacation, or to star in the school play. However, you no doubt will survive without achieving these wants.

Sometimes distinguishing between needs and wants is difficult. For instance, generally speaking, a car is not necessary for survival. Therefore, it is not a true need. On the other hand, you may require a car to get to work. If you cannot get to work, you cannot earn the money to pay for food and shelter. In this case, a car can become a necessity.

In most situations, it is desirable to satisfy needs before wants. It also is important to determine the point at which needs become wants or vice versa. Basic transportation can be a need while a fancy sports car is a want. A reliable used car with few features would meet the need for basic transportation at a reasonable price. The good looks and great performance of the sports car are expensive features that go beyond basic transportation. Of course, there is nothing wrong with buying a sports car—if you take care of essentials first.

Values and Goals

Values are the beliefs and principles that are important to you. They influence the way you live and think, your actions and behavior, the friends you choose, the way you spend your money, and almost everything you do. Values differ for different people and they may change over the years. Among the important values for many people are family, friends, good health, career, success, financial security, romance, adventure, education, material possessions, money, and religion. Each person's list would be different.

Values govern your life whether or not you are aware of them. To gain a sense of control, it is necessary to identify and choose the values that will direct your life. Make a list of items that are important to you and examine it thoughtfully. Why do you consider these items important? When you give it some thought, you no doubt will find that your family, friends, education, and life experiences all influence the items on your list of values. As you meet new people and have new experiences, what is important to you may change. As life unfolds, your values may change, too. Some will become more important and others less.

Goals are the objectives you want to attain. Usually they are closely related to values. For example, if health and fitness rank high on your list of values, you may set goals to establish a personal fitness program, avoid drugs, and eat nutritious foods. If you rank education high, a college degree could become an important goal. This might motivate you to begin a savings program to pay for college. You might also commit extra hours to homework in preparation for further schooling.

You can set goals for almost anything in life. You may set "to be" goals, "to do" goals, and "to have" goals. "To be" goals are related to personality and character. You might want to be knowledgeable, popular, entertaining, reliable, laid-back, or competitive. This group of goals also includes career choices. You may want to be a teacher, doctor, salesperson, musician, or an artist. See 4-11.

"To do" goals cover the endless list of things you might want to accomplish. You may want to learn to play the piano or speak a foreign language. You may decide to go to college, travel, or get a job as soon as possible.

"To have" goals are easy to identify and they continually change. It usually takes very little time to come up with a wish list of items you would like to have. You may want a watch, a car, your own phone, a new wardrobe, or concert tickets. This covers the endless list of routine purchases as well as specific items for which you need to plan and save.

It is helpful not only to identify your goals, but also to rank them in order of importance. This helps you direct your time, energy, and money to the goals that are most important to you. As you set and rank your goals, ask yourself the following key questions:

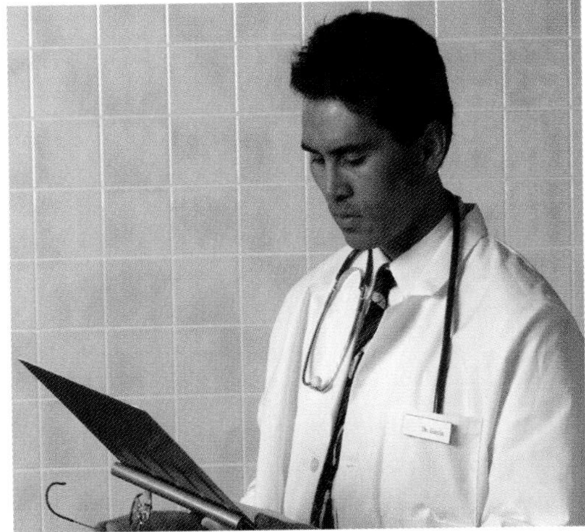

4-11
Career choices, such as becoming a doctor, are "to be" goals.

Is the Goal Realistic and Possible?

Getting all A's is a realistic goal for some, not for others. Buying a new car in six months is possible for some, not for others. Make an effort to set realistic and possible goals for yourself.

What Will the Goal Cost in Time, Money, and Effort?

After thinking it through, you may decide that some objectives are not worth what it takes to achieve them. For example, if you want to become a doctor, a long look at the education and training required—college, medical school, internship, residency—may change your mind.

Will You Still Want a Specific Goal by the Time You Are Able to Reach It?

For instance, a high school senior may want a moped for getting to and from school. If it requires a year or more of savings, the need may vanish by the time the money is available.

It pays to think seriously about setting worthwhile, realistic goals. Attaining them can give you a sense of satisfaction and accomplishment. On the other hand, working toward unrealistic goals can cause frustration, as Shanae's story shows.

Goals have different time schedules. Some are *immediate.* These are goals that you can achieve today or tomorrow, such as finishing your homework before your favorite TV show tonight. *Short-range goals* are those that you want to reach within the next few weeks or months or in the near future. For instance, saving enough money to buy an airline ticket may take several months. *Long-range goals*, such as completing school, starting a career, getting married, or buying a house, may take years to achieve, 4-12.

Many goals are interdependent. Sometimes you have to achieve one goal in order to reach another. For instance, you need to finish high school before you go to college; you need to complete training before starting a career; you need to complete driver education before you get a driver's license.

Consumer Decisions

The Impossible Dream

Robert is a high school senior. He is in love with Shanae who is also a senior. Robert dreams of marrying Shanae. All he thinks about is Shanae, their wedding, and their life together. What he really wants more than anything is to marry her right after graduation.

Shanae has other ideas. Although she likes Robert, she plans to go to college and then to medical school. She also wants to travel and see more of the world before getting married. In fact, Shanae is not sure she will ever marry. Certainly, she isn't considering marriage for several more years.

As graduation draws closer, Shanae talks about her plans for the future. Robert begins to realize that marrying Shanae is out of the question, at least for the near future. Now, he must start thinking of his own future, without Shanae at the top of his list.

This is an unhappy time for Robert. Getting over his disappointment is painful. Eventually, Robert enrolls in a nearby community college. He decides to follow a general course of study until he can set career and life goals for himself.

Case Review

1. How would you handle a situation similar to Robert's?
2. What are some other examples of impossible dreams?
3. What specific steps would you take to replace impossible goals with realistic goals?
4. How would you determine whether or not a goal is realistic?
5. Why are unrealistic goals unproductive?

4-12
Graduating from college is a long-range goal.

Sometimes goals can conflict with each other. For example, Alfonso has $800. He wants to buy a used car, take a vacation, and go to summer school. He doesn't have enough money for all three. Alfonso must decide what he values most among these conflicting goals.

Judy also has conflicting goals. She wants to be on the girl's basketball team, which practices each day after school. At the same time, she wants to keep her part-time job after school. Judy can't reach both her goals. She must decide which is more important to her.

When goals are in conflict, you have to consider your priorities to choose the goals that will direct you toward whatever is most important to you. In the following case study, Maurice learns that he must reexamine his priorities.

Establishing Priorities

Priorities refer to the importance you place on different values and goals. It is helpful not only to identify what is important to you but also to rank the most to the least important. This helps you direct your time, energy, and money to the things you most want to achieve—your priorities. Whenever you decide one thing is more important than another, you are making a priority judgment. For example, you may decide that comfort is more important than appearance and wear old shoes. If you think looking and feeling good is more important than relaxing, you may choose to exercise rather than watch TV. If you think it is important to really like what you do, you may choose a job you like over a higher paying job that doesn't really appeal to you.

As you continually make these types of decisions, you eventually create a value system. A ***value system*** guides your behavior and provides a sense of direction in your life. For example, your value system may place school performance high. If so, you will make an effort to participate in class, complete your homework, and prepare for exams. You will become a conscientious student. If loyalty to friends is high in your system, you will try to be with your friends when they need you. If popularity ranks higher than loyalty, you may be tempted to do whatever pleases others. It may be difficult for you to stand by an unpopular person or cause.

Some values are related to money and financial matters. These can have a

Consumer Decisions

A Matter of Priorities

Maurice wants the male lead in the school play. He has been in school productions before and shows real talent on the stage. Thus, getting the lead is a very possible goal for Maurice.

The problem is that play practice is held for two hours every weekday afternoon for three months before the play. If Maurice gets the lead, he would have to quit his job after school. Even though he is not crazy about his job at a service station, the pay is good and after-school jobs are hard to find. If Maurice quits now, the station manager would have to hire a replacement. The manager would probably not hire Maurice back for full-time summer work that he really needs.

Maurice's sister has just had costly major surgery. His family needs every penny it can earn to pay the medical bills. Maurice doesn't see how he can quit his job because he wants to help his family.

On the other hand, he really wants to be in the play. Since he is a senior, this is his last chance to be in a high school production. Maurice also knows that the best actors in the spring play are sometimes chosen for summer theater. Summer theater often leads to a career in drama, which Maurice has always wanted.

Maurice takes a hard look at his situation. He tries to establish his priorities and determine what decision he should make.

Case Review

1. What will Maurice lose if he keeps his job?
2. What will he sacrifice if he decides in favor of the play?
3. What other alternatives might Maurice have?
4. How would you resolve Maurice's goal conflict if this were your decision?
5. What goal conflicts have you experienced? How did you resolve them? What did you consider in determining your priorities?
6. When goal conflicts involve other people, how might priorities be affected?

major impact on the choices people make in the marketplace and in their personal life. The case studies about Carla, Terrence, and Carlos present three different viewpoints about the importance of money. Reading them may help you understand how values, goals, and priorities affect behavior.

Standards of Quality and Excellence

Standards are established measures of quality or excellence. You have probably heard the word standard used in many different ways. Electrical products must meet certain safety standards before they receive a seal of approval. People in professions like law and medicine must meet certain educational and performance standards before they can practice their professions. To earn good grades, students must meet the learning standards set by teachers.

A nation's standard of living refers to the goods and services the majority of citizens consider essential for living. Individuals develop their own personal standards of living. For some, fur coats, Broadway plays, and dinners at fancy restaurants symbolize the "good life." Other people's standard of living may be based on blue jeans, TV shows, and fast-food stops.

You set standards for the way you want to live, what you want to do, and the goods and services you choose to buy. These will depend on your values and goals. Standards will vary from situation to situation. For instance, if clear, sound reproduction is a top priority when you are buying a CD system, you may settle only for the best

Consumer Decisions

What's Important to You?

Carla, Terrence, and Carlos have three very different views on what's important in life. They have different priorities. As you read about their goals and values, think about what you consider most important in your life.

Carla Wants Money

Carla, a 15-year-old sophomore, is the third of five children in her family. As long as she can remember, the family has been short of money. Carla has food to eat and clothes to wear, but she rarely gets any of the extras her friends enjoy. Except for the money she earns baby-sitting, Carla has no money of her own. Most of her clothes come from her older sister. Her bike once belonged to her older brother. Carla jokes about being "secondhand Rose," but she really doesn't think it is funny.

Carla believes that having money is just about the most important thing in life. She intends to have plenty of it when she grows older. Even now, Carla dates only the boys who have lots of cash to spend. She also tries to be part of the "rich crowd" at school. Although she won't admit it, Carla thinks people who have money are really better than people who don't.

Terrence Does Not Care

Terrence is a 17-year-old junior. After high school graduation, he expects to attend one of the better universities in the country. His grades are good, and his family has money. Being accepted at the school he wants will be no problem. But Terrence hasn't decided which school that will be. In fact, he isn't crazy about going to college at all. Still, he knows it will be easier to go than to fight his family.

Terrence's father is a very successful business executive and his family always has had plenty of money. Terrence has enjoyed most of the wants that money could satisfy. His father enjoys making money almost as much as spending it. When he asks Terrence, "What are you going to do with your life?" he really means, "How are you going to make your fortune?"

Terrence has little use for fortunes. He has always had money, but somehow, money isn't enough. Terrence believes there are more important things in life, but he doesn't know where to search for them. One thing he does know is that money is not the key to happiness. The family gardener is the happiest man Terrence knows, and he doesn't even own a car.

Carlos Cannot Decide

Carlos is 25 and single. He works in a service station—a job he likes as well as any. He comes from a family that has never had much money, but his home has always been a happy place. Carlos' needs and wants are simple. He has never felt any pressure to earn a great income. But that's beginning to change.

Carlos met Angelique a few months ago. Now, he finds himself in love for the first time. Angelique and Carlos want to get married. When they tell Angelique's family, her father begins to ask Carlos about his finances and future plans. "What are your job prospects? Are you moving ahead professionally? How much money have you saved? Where will you and Angelique live?" Her father tells Carlos that Angelique is accustomed to having what she wants. He wonders if Carlos' income is adequate for the two of them and for children if they start a family. He wonders if Carlos is ready for the financial responsibilities of marriage.

These questions trouble Carlos because he doesn't know how he feels about money in his own life. Also, he hasn't given much thought to money in marriage. He loves Angelique. She loves him. In his mind, that is enough.

Money has never been important to Carlos, but what about Angelique? She always wears beautiful clothes. She has her own car, and her family lives in a big house. She claims that money isn't such a big deal, but now Carlos wonders. Can she be happy without all the luxuries she has always enjoyed? Should he and Angelique give the simple life a try? Should he think about finding a better-paying job, or should he just forget Angelique and find someone with a background like his own?

Case Review

1. What does Carla consider most important? What about Terrence? What about Carlos?
2. How does each one's view of money influence behavior and attitudes?
3. In what ways do you think Carla, Terrence, and Carlos might change their views about money in the future?
4. How do their views differ from your own? To what extent do you agree with each of them?

on the market. Your standards for a CD system would be high. When it comes to buying a car, you may settle for anything that runs well enough to get you from here to there. You may place little value on the car's appearance or special features. Thus, your standards for cars would not call for the best.

What degree of quality do you seek as you work toward your goals? Do you strive for A's and B's in school, or are you satisfied with C's? Do you practice a piece of music until you can play it without a single mistake, or are you satisfied playing it reasonably well? Do you always have to look your best? How do you feel about the appearance of your room at home? As you answer these questions, you will become aware of some of your standards. A clear understanding of your standards, priorities, and goals will help you make wise decisions about consumer issues and other aspects of your life.

Consumers in the Family

As you grow older, many of your needs and wants, values and goals, and priorities and standards may change. This is true not only for individuals, but for families, too.

As families grow and change, they go through stages known as the ***family life cycle***. The life cycle consists of five stages: beginning, expanding, developing, launching, and aging. The stages are defined according to the events taking place and the ages of the children in the family. Each stage brings significant changes in consumer needs, wants, priorities, and spending patterns. Chapter 14 gives a detailed discussion of consumer and financial changes during the stages of the life cycle.

At each stage in the family life cycle, key expenses will be slightly different. The amount of money available to meet expenses depends on several factors. The number of members working to contribute income to the family will affect the amount of money available. The types of work family members do and the levels of advancement they have attained will also affect earnings.

Values, goals, and standards also affect family economics. For instance, a family that puts a high priority on education may save money for college tuition for the children. This would give the family less money to spend for lower priority items. A family that sets a goal to buy a boat might not be willing to spend money on vacations until they get their boat. A family may have a higher standard for the appearance of their home than for the appearance of their car. This family may find it more important to remodel the kitchen than to buy a new car.

Family income usually must accommodate both the family unit and the individuals within the unit. This calls for establishing some method of dividing money to arrive at what is fair for all. Each family will decide differently how to allocate family income to individual needs as well as meeting the needs of the group as a whole. When there are two or more earners, pooling resources and making these decisions can become even more complicated. It is an important issue to resolve.

Summary

As a consumer, you enjoy certain rights and carry certain responsibilities. For example, you are entitled to safety in the marketplace—safe products and services. However, you are responsible for using products as directed and for heeding safety precautions and warnings.

Government protects your consumer interests and rights in countless ways. Specific laws cover almost every possible type of consumer product and transaction. Government agencies and departments serve and protect consumers at federal, state, and local levels. Government regulates everything from the purity of your food and water, to the air you breathe, and the money you borrow. As a consumer, learn about the laws written to protect your interests and the government agencies serving you.

Knowing how to complain effectively is an essential consumer skill. Getting results involves stating your case and presenting important details to the appropriate person in a business-like manner. Learning the key sources of reliable product information is also key to being a competent, confident consumer. It pays to keep a well-organized file of useful data to look at when making choices in the marketplace.

Knowing yourself may be the most important requirement when it comes to making intelligent choices. Competent consumers base decisions on personal needs and wants—on the values and goals that are most important to them. Goals for spending and well-established priorities can guide you to choices that will give lasting satisfaction.

To Review

1. Name and describe the four consumer rights as defined by President John F. Kennedy.
2. Name six government agencies that serve and protect consumers.
3. Name six laws that protect consumer interests and describe the purpose of each.
4. List three reasons why a consumer complaint may go unanswered.
5. List five guidelines to follow when making a complaint.
6. Where can you find the names of officers of large business firms?
7. List three guidelines to follow when evaluating consumer information.
8. Why might ads and commercials not be the best sources of consumer information?
9. Discuss how consumer choices and behavior are affected by:
   A. needs and wants
   B. values and goals
   C. priorities
   D. standards of quality
10. Name and describe the three types of goals that differ by the amount of time it takes to reach them. Give an example of each.
11. How are standards related to values and goals?
12. Give an example of how a family's goals and values would affect family economics.

To Think Critically

1. How do laws that prohibit monopolies protect the consumer's right to choose?
2. When have you or your family complained about a product or service? What was the problem? How did you resolve it?
3. What course of action would you take if you could not get a consumer problem solved by the seller or manufacturer?
4. How many of the consumer resources listed in 4-7 are available in your community or county?
5. What points should you consider when evaluating consumer information?

6. What are the personal aspects of making consumer choices?
7. Why are values and goals different for different people?
8. Why and how are values and goals likely to change as you enter the adult world and move on through life?
9. List several goals. In a class discussion, identify each as a "to be," "to do," or "to have" goal.
10. Why is it important to establish priorities to guide your consumer and life choices?
11. Why do a person's standards vary from situation to situation?

To Do

1. Start collecting material for a personal consumer information file. Concentrate on collecting information that applies directly to you as a consumer and to products and services you buy.
2. Research a consumer issue of your choice on the Internet, or shop for a specific product online. Report findings to the class. (If you do not have access to the Internet at home, try the school computer lab or public library.)
3. Write a letter to a manufacturer either to complain about or to praise a product you own. If you currently have a problem with a product or service, use this letter as a step in problem solving.
4. List several goals you might want to achieve over the next five years. Identify each goal as immediate, short-range, or long-range. Outline steps you can take to reach these goals.
5. Make a chart illustrating how family financial planning might change at each stage of the family life cycle.
6. Make up details for a serious consumer problem involving an amount of at least $2,000 and a seller who refuses to cooperate in settling the complaint. Investigate and outline steps you would need to take if you were to solve it through each of the following:
   A. binding arbitration
   B. small claims court
   C. a lawsuit

Needs, wants, values, goals, and standards serve as guides to consumer decisions.

CHAPTER
5

EXPENSES
PERSONAL RECORD
Management Series®
CASH
Macintosh
PowerBook 170
Pay Bills

You, the Manager

management
resources
human resources
nonhuman resources
opportunity costs
budget
fixed expense
flexible expense
occasional expenses
financial statement
assets
liabilities
net worth

After studying this chapter, you will be able to

- ❑ identify and plan the use of resources available to you.
- ❑ describe the process of making rational decisions.
- ❑ explain how to use the principles of management to achieve important goals.
- ❑ prepare a personal money management plan or budget.
- ❑ prepare a personal financial statement.
- ❑ list important financial and legal documents that should be kept.

Management is the art of using what you have to get what you want. It is the skill that puts your resources to work for you. ***Resources*** are any and all of the things you can use to reach your goals. Money is just one of your many resources.

No one has enough resources to reach all his or her goals at one time. However, you can get the most out of your resources by planning how and when you will use them. This will help you gain more control over your life.

Management involves identifying and using resources, making decisions, and solving problems. By managing your money resources, you can control the dollars that pass through your hands every year. Developing good management skills and a simple financial plan can help put you in the driver's seat.

Identifying and Using Resources

Resources are tools you can use to reach goals. There are two types of resources—human and nonhuman.

Human resources are those resources you have within yourself. They include energy, knowledge, experience, skills, and talents. Motivation, imagination, and determination also are valuable human resources. See 5-1.

Nonhuman resources are external, such as money, time, and equipment, 5-2. It is easy to overlook some of these. People often do not see their possessions as resources or as a means to achieving goals.

Everyone has different amounts and types of resources. To be a good manager, you need to identify your resources. List your human and nonhuman resources. Then analyze your list. Which resources are in short supply? Which are plentiful? As you consider how to use your resources, keep the following tips in mind:

Resources Are Limited

The amount of available time, energy, money, land, and other resources is limited. Planning is necessary to make the most of them.

Chevron

5-1
One of the most valuable human resources is the ability to be creative.

Nonhuman Resources
Financial Resources—cash, credit, savings, investments
Tools, Equipment and Technology—carpentry tools, computer, fax, lawn equipment, sewing machine, freezer, range, washer, drier, telephone, television, computer Internet
Property—home, auto, furnishings, clothing
Natural Resources—air, water, wood, coal, land, plant life
Community Facilities and Services—schools, libraries, hospitals, parks, roads and streets, public transit, fire and police protection, museums, churches, temples
Businesses and Industry—stores, the marketplace of goods and services, factories, theaters, financial institutions
National Facilities and Services—federal government departments and agencies, highway systems, communication systems, Social Security system, park system, environmental protection

5-2
The nonhuman resources available to you are almost endless.

Resources Are Manageable

You can manage resources to meet specific goals. For example, saving money over time or using credit lets you buy costly items you cannot purchase out of a single paycheck.

Resources Are Related to Each Other

You can often combine several resources to reach a specific goal. For example, you might use both savings and credit to buy a big ticket item, such as a car. In addition, one resource may be needed to produce or make use of another. You could use your talent and skills to get a job and earn money. Finally, you can use one resource to make up for the lack of another. For example, if you have plenty of time and not much money, you can use the time to check several stores for the best values.

As you plan the use of resources, there will be questions to consider. Which resources are plentiful and which are scarce? What are your strengths and weaknesses in terms of human resources? Can you combine several resources for more effective use of each? How can you use what you have to make up for what you are missing? Managing resources well will help you reach your goals. See 5-3.

Holbrook

5-3
The telephone becomes an important resource at an early age.

Making Decisions and Solving Problems

Every day you make countless decisions—big, small, important, unimportant, careful, and thoughtless decisions. Some are so routine you hardly know you are deciding. Think back on today. Before you left home, you decided what time to get up, how to greet the day, what to wear, what to eat, what time to leave home, and how to get to school.

Every day you face big and little problems. You make a promise and can't keep it. You are supposed to be in two places at the same time. You run out of money before payday. You want to go to college but don't know which college to choose. All of these situations require decision making.

Making decisions and solving problems are essential parts of management. People arrive at decisions in different ways. Many choices are made by accident or circumstance rather than by deliberate choice. Have you ever made a decision:

- ❑ To please someone else? Would you go to a movie you've seen because your friend wants to see it? Would you take piano lessons to please a parent? Would you buy a certain brand of jeans because everyone else wears them?
- ❑ Out of habit? Do you automatically have cereal and orange juice for breakfast every day? Do you sit with the same group for lunch? Do you shop in the same stores all the time?
- ❑ On impulse? Do you ever forget your diet and order a shake and fries? Did you ever bring home a pet because it was cute, even though you had no room to keep it? Did you ever buy a pair of shoes on sale, even if they didn't really fit? Did you ever go to a movie you didn't care to see just because there was nothing else to do?

- ❑ By failing to act? Have you settled for unemployment by not applying for summer jobs until they were all taken? Have you earned a poor grade by not studying for an exam? Have you been broke when you needed money because you failed to save?

You have probably made decisions in all of these ways at one time or another. For some choices, these methods work just fine. However, some decisions in your life carry lasting benefits or consequences.

Making Rational Decisions

When deciding on important matters and big problems, rational decision making can help you choose wisely. Rational decision making involves five steps, 5-4.

Steps in Rational Decision Making

Step	Key Word	Approach
1	Problem	Define the problem
2	Goals	Set specific goals or objectives
3	Resources	Identify available resources
4	Alternatives	Determine and analyze the alternatives
5	Decision	Make a decision and act upon it

5-4
The five steps to rational decision making can help you solve problems effectively.

1. **Define the problem to be solved.** A clear idea of the challenge before you is essential to finding the best solution. Start by answering, "What is the problem?" For example, if you never have enough time for what you need and want to do, identifying this problem can lead to a solution. Failing to do so may just leave you feeling rushed and tired.
2. **Establish specific goals**. What do you want to achieve? Using time shortage as an example, you might decide to manage your time better. A specific goal could be to allow an extra two hours each day for important things you never have time to do. In many situations, there will be more than one goal. Knowing what you want to achieve aids in planning.
3. **Identify the resources available to you.** What do you have to help you? For instance, to manage your time better, a key resource may be the willpower to turn off the TV or unplug the phone. Make a list of the resources you can use to arrive at the best answers to the problem.
4. **Consider the alternatives.** What choices are open to you? Identify the various approaches you can follow and analyze each to determine which will best serve your needs. Using the time example again, there will be many alternatives to consider. You might find various ways to rearrange your schedule to allow time for the things that are most important to you.
5. **Make your decision.** What is the best choice? After considering all the options, choose the best solution. Though it is the last step, the decision involves some ongoing responsibility. You must carry out your plan and evaluate as you go along. Sometimes you will need to make adjustments. The evaluation process helps you stay on track,

and it may help you in making future decisions. In the case studies throughout this chapter, you will see how each person solves his or her problem by using this decision-making process.

The Art of Management: Using Resources to Reach Goals

Management can make the difference between hitting and missing the targets in your life. Whether you run a big corporation, an average household, a ball team, or your own personal affairs, management is the tool that gets things done. It keeps you moving forward toward important goals. Management skills put you in control. You make the decisions. You carry them out. You benefit from the right choices, and occasionally suffer from the mistakes.

Management is an ongoing process you can use in countless ways. Decision making is an important part of management. However, management involves more than making decisions and solving problems. Management is a three-part process: planning, acting, and evaluating.

The Planning Phase

A job well-planned is a job half done. This familiar saying points out the importance of the planning phase of management. Whether you want to reach a career goal or decide what clothes to wear, some forethought or planning helps. Deciding what to wear to school may involve very little conscious planning. Choosing what to wear to a wedding or a job interview may take more thought. Building an appropriate wardrobe for your lifestyle can be a major planning challenge.

As defined earlier, management is the art of using what you have to get what you want. The planning phase of management involves identifying goals, obstacles, and resources. Start by establishing your goals. What do you want to get or achieve? Next, consider the obstacles. What stands between you and your goals? What must you overcome? Then list your resources. What can you use to overcome the obstacles and reach your goals? Put some thought into your list of resources. To reach your goals, you may need to combine resources or substitute one for another. This is the time to make full use of personal resources, such as energy, creativity, determination, special skills, and talents.

Three management plans are shown in 5-5. Listed under each goal are the obstacles and resources related to it.

The Action Phase

Planning is of little value without action. The action phase of management involves putting your resources to work to overcome the obstacles that stand between you and your goals. Success in this phase depends on two key characteristics—determination and flexibility.

Determination helps you get off to a good start, keep an eye on the final goal, and stick with the project to the end. Very often it is easy to get started with a new plan. The difficult part is staying with it when the new becomes old. It is important to check your progress as you go along. Be sure you are still moving forward.

> ***"Never put off till tomorrow that which you can do today."***
>
> ***Benjamin Franklin***

You may find that plans do not work as you expected or something happens to change your plans. This is when determination is necessary. For instance, you plan to write a term paper at home, but your brother invites friends over for a party when you wanted to work. Determination will take you to the

Goal	Obstacles	Available Resources
To complete an English assignment on time.	Time limitations, lack of interest in the topic, difficulty getting started, tough grading by the English teacher.	Two hours after school each day, the public library reference room, knowledge of the topic and where to go for information, detailed instructions from the English teacher, writing and typing skills, the family word processor, need of a high mark to maintain grade point average, determination to finish on time.
To build a spectacular wardrobe with a limited budget.	Small amount of money for clothing, frequent changes in fashion trends, stong desire to wear the latest fashions, high cost of trendy clothing.	$15 weekly from part-time job; four hours weekly to sew; excellent fashion sense and good taste in clothes; knowledge of figure type, fabrics, fashions, and wardrobe needs; sewing machine and tools; sewing skills; time and energy to plan and shop for clothes and fabrics; conveniently located fabric shop; fashion magazines and books from the library.
To become president of the student body.	The popularity of the other candidates, difficulty in contacting all the voters, limited time before the election, lack of organization among the supporters.	Knowledge of the job and its demands, experience in student government, organizational skills, public speaking skills, reputation for leadership, energy and enthusiasm for planning and running the campaign, knowledge of what the voters want, broad support from both student body and faculty, friends who are willing to help run the campaign, use of school art department and copying machine, the desire to win.

5-5
Listing your goals, obstacles, and resources will give you perspective on what you can accomplish.

library and keep you on track. Maybe you plan to save $10 per week for a mountain bike, but your mother's birthday comes up. You need to buy her a present with the $10. Determination will make you baby-sit, run errands, or work extra hours to restore your savings.

Flexibility helps you adjust to new and unexpected situations. When your plans are interrupted as in the examples above, flexibility helps you find new ways to cope and continue to move toward your goals. It can be helpful even when your plans are working. Once you are headed toward your goals, you may find a way to revise and improve your plan.

A good manager takes advantage of opportunities when they arise. For instance, you have two goals for the weekend. One is to earn spending money for next week's camping trip. The other is to write a book report that is due Monday morning. You estimate that you need five hours Saturday to earn money baby-sitting and three hours Sunday to write the book report. When you are called to baby-sit from seven to midnight Saturday, you revise your plans. You decide to write the report during the last three hours of baby-sitting when the children are asleep. This gives you time to do something else on Sunday.

The Evaluation Phase

The purposes of evaluation are to assess your progress as you go along and to improve management skills for future projects. Evaluation is a continuous function. It applies to all stages of the management process. Ongoing evaluation can help you develop better ways of using resources to reach goals, 5-6.

Money Management

According to statistics, the average worker can expect to earn around one million dollars or more over a lifetime with an eighth grade education, just over one million with a high school diploma, and more than two million with a college degree. With or without a formal education, thousands of dollars will pass through your hands over the years. To make the most of these dollars, you need to know how to manage them.

The Process of Evaluation

Evaluating Plans	Evaluating Actions	Evaluating Results
What are the goals? What obstacles stand in the way? What resources are needed? Are the needed resources available? Are the goals realistic, given the obstacles and resources? Are the goals worth the effort and resources required to attain them?	Is the plan working? Is there steady progress toward the goals? Are resources being used to their best advantage? Are top priority goals getting top priority attention? Is there room for improvement in the original plans? What adjustments can be made? Have new or unexpected developments created the need to change the original plans? What changes are needed?	Were the goals achieved? Was achieving the goals worth the effort and resources used? Are results satisfactory? What key factors contributed to reaching or failing to reach the goals? What were the weaknesses in the plans and actions? What were the strengths? How can future plans be improved?

5-6
Evaluation is an important part of effective management.

Solving Problems Through Decision Making

Russell Needs a Job

Russell will graduate from high school at the end of the month. He is not a top student and has no desire to spend more time in school. Russell is the oldest of four children and his family cannot afford to support him. He needs to find a job as soon as possible.

The Problem

Russell's problem is to find the right job. Since he probably will be working the rest of his life, he doesn't want just any job. His father worked 20 miserable years at a job he didn't like. Russell isn't about to make the same mistake. He wants to find work he can enjoy with good wages and a chance to learn and grow on the job.

Russell needs a full-time job that does not require more than a high school diploma. Since he does not have a car, he wants to work within walking distance of public transportation.

Russell hopes to find a job working with animals. Through the years, he has had a number of pets, including three dogs, two cats, and several rabbits. He also has cared for snakes, turtles, squirrels, a talking parrot, sick birds, and a lame raccoon. Once he even nursed a wounded fox back to health.

The Goals

A counselor at the school suggested that Russell make a list of the things he wants most in a job. The counselor instructed him to arrange the items on his list in order of importance. Russell made the following list of job requirements or goals:

- ❑ Full-time work.
- ❑ Work with animals.
- ❑ Job satisfaction.
- ❑ Good wages and job security.
- ❑ Opportunity to learn on the job.
- ❑ Possibility of getting to and from work without driving.
- ❑ Agreeable coworkers and superiors.

The Resources

The counselor also suggested that Russell list the resources he can use to find the job he wants. His list is as follows:

- ❑ A high school diploma with reasonable grades and a good attendance record.
- ❑ A reputation for being honest, reliable, and responsible.
- ❑ Work experience on three part-time jobs during high school.
- ❑ Experience and competence in handling animals.
- ❑ Good recommendations from teachers, counselors, and former employers.
- ❑ Willingness to work long hours, weekends, and evenings.
- ❑ Willingness to start at the bottom if there is an opportunity for job advancement.

The Alternatives

With his goals and resources outlined, Russell begins his search with the telephone book. He turns to the classified pages in the phone book. He finds many listings and referrals under Animal Shelters, Pet Shops, Dog Kennels, Animal Hospitals, and Veterinarians. He also looks under "Zoo" for employment possibilities. Russell makes a list of the most likely places to find a job. He then tries to learn as much as he can about each possible employer.

Through phone calls and interviews, Russell learns of several job opportunities. He follows through on every lead and compares each job opening with his list of job goals. Following a number of interviews, Russell is offered four jobs. After weighing the pros and cons of each, he makes a decision.

The Decision

Russell decides to work as an assistant in a nearby veterinarian's office. He is hired as a full-time, permanent employee. Here, he will have the opportunity to learn more about animals and their care. Russell will also be given more responsibility as he learns the office routine.

Case Review

1. How did Russell's list of job goals help him make a final decision?
2. How did Russell's list of resources help him reach his job goals? How could you use a similar list to sell yourself during a job interview?
3. What might have happened if Russell went on a random job search rather than following the steps of rational decision making?
4. What did you learn from Russell's job searching experience to help you make rational decisions?

Economic Concepts That Affect Money Management

Several key economic concepts apply to personal money management and budgeting just as they apply to the operation of the economy. One of these concepts is the *law of scarcity*. This means your unlimited wants all fight for a piece of your limited resources. To satisfy your most important wants with the money you have to spend, you must make careful choices.

The need to make choices involves another important economic concept—***opportunity costs***. This is the resource you use to satisfy one goal that cannot be used for another. In other words, the price of meeting one goal is the inability to meet another goal. For example, if you have $5 to spend Friday night, you can buy food or go to a movie. If you choose the food, it not only costs $5, it also costs you the opportunity of going to the movie or doing something else with the $5. The fact is, every time you spend money for one thing, you give up the opportunity to spend it for something else.

Opportunity costs apply to time also. The hour you spend on the phone cannot be spent on working out or doing homework. Thinking of opportunity cost as well as the dollar cost of a purchase helps you direct your spending and time to those goods and services you most want.

Inflation (a period of rising prices) is another economic concept that relates to personal money management. As prices go up, the value of your dollars goes down. If your income does not rise at the same rate prices rise, your buying power will be reduced. You will not be able to buy as much or save as much. Although you cannot stop rising prices, being aware of the effects of inflation can help you plan for the future.

Recession (a period of slowed economic growth) can have a major impact on personal money management for those who are out of work or whose incomes are reduced because of overall economic conditions. It tends to spread a blanket of uncertainty over others as well. During a recession, consumers generally have less confidence in the future. They will spend less and save more if possible.

Tailoring a Budget to Income and Needs

Regardless of the economic climate, a simple money management plan, or budget, can help you make the most of your money and avoid financial problems. A ***budget*** is a plan for the use or management of money. Creating a simple, workable budget involves seven basic steps.

Establish Financial Goals

Decide what you want your money to do for you. Determine what style of living you wish to achieve. Then decide what you can afford, what goods and services you want to buy, and when you expect to make major purchases. Well-thought-out goals can help you direct your dollars to those things you consider most important. See 5-7.

Include immediate, short-range, and long-term goals so you can be ready for them when the time comes. For example, money for a concert this Friday night is fairly immediate. If you do not have the money on hand, you may have to forego the pleasure. Saving enough money for a ski weekend in two months is short-range, and careful planning between now and then may get you there. A new car, a summer vacation, or college in a year or two are long-term goals that require savings over a period of time.

Keep in mind that financial goals change over the years. At this moment, your goals may include money for a sound system, a car, travel, or college.

Solving Problems Through Decision Making

David Wants a Car

For the past two summers, David has worked with three friends painting houses. When one friend goes to school and the other two move to another city, David decides to continue the painting business alone. He needs a car to carry all of his supplies and equipment. The car will be David's first major investment in his business. He wants to make the right choice.

The Problem

David wants to find a car that will fulfill his business and personal needs. He needs to find a good used car since he can't afford to buy a new one. It must be large enough to haul all of his paint and equipment.

The Goals

Before shopping, David makes the following list of his needs and goals in a car:

- ❑ Used, but in good condition.
- ❑ Large enough to carry paint, supplies, and equipment.
- ❑ Useful for personal driving as well as on-the-job driving.
- ❑ Fuel efficient.
- ❑ Sold by a reliable dealer or private seller.
- ❑ Equipped with good tires, air conditioning, a radio, and a luggage rack.

The Resources

With his list of goals in mind, David considers the resources he can use to get the right car. They include:

- ❑ $1,500 cash.
- ❑ Time to shop.
- ❑ Knowledge of cars in general and of his particular car needs.
- ❑ Flexibility in choice of brand and model.
- ❑ Internet auto mart.

The Alternatives

To begin his car search, David reads the classified ads in the local paper. This gives him an idea of what cars are available at what prices from individuals selling their own cars. He makes a few phone calls in answer to some of the ads. He follows through on two ads by going to look at the cars.

Next, David visits several used car dealers to price their cars and to ask about warranties and servicing. In addition to cars, David looks at vans and small trucks.

After test-driving many vehicles, David narrows his choices to three. One is a five-year-old van in good condition but missing some of the features he wants. It would be perfect for his job needs but awkward for personal use.

Another choice is a four-year-old station wagon. It is not in the best condition, but it costs only $1,000. This would leave him $500 to make improvements. The wagon is adequate for both job and personal use, and it includes all of the features he wants. However, it is being sold by a private party without a warranty. If the car falls apart the day after the sale, it will be David's tough luck.

The third choice is a small wagon, priced at $1,400. A reliable dealer is selling the car with a very good used-car warranty. The car has the features he wants and gets good gas mileage. The only drawback is its size. It is fine for personal driving but a little small for business. However, David can carry his extension ladder on the car's luggage rack, and he can squeeze everything else inside.

The Decision

After much debating, David decides to buy the small wagon. It comes the closest to meeting most of his work and personal transportation needs.

Case Review

1. How do you think rational decision making helped David make a good choice?
2. How did David's list of goals help him make a decision?
3. What goals would you have if you were in the market for a car?
4. How do you think having a list of goals would help you shop for cars and talk with car dealers?

Financial Goals				
Financial Goals	**When Wanted**	**Estimated Cost**	**Amount I Have**	**Amount Needed**
Immediate Goals (within six months)				
Concert Tickets	______	$ ______	$ ______	$ ______
Boots	______	$ ______	$ ______	$ ______
Short-Range Goals (six months to 1 year)				
Summer Trip	______	$ ______	$ ______	$ ______
Birthday Gift	______	$ ______	$ ______	$ ______
Long-Range Goals (one to 5 years)				
Used Car	______	$ ______	$ ______	$ ______
Training Course	______	$ ______	$ ______	$ ______

5-7
Organizing your goals on a chart similar to this can help direct your spending and saving to whatever is most important to you at a given time.

As you go from high school to college, work, marriage, and parenthood, and as you change jobs or move, your financial goals will change. Consider, for example, your goals at this time compared to those of your parents or grandparents.

Estimate and Total Income

Add up your earnings and the money you receive from other sources, such as allowance, gifts, bonuses, and interest on savings. See 5-8. Try to come up with a total income figure for the budget period you will use weekly, biweekly, monthly. Figure out how much money you can count on for each budget period. Your time period will depend on when you get your money. If you receive a weekly income or allowance, it makes sense to budget on a weekly basis. When you earn a steady income and pay monthly bills, it may be easier to work with monthly figures. You will also need yearly estimates and records. These will help you make long-range plans and figure your income taxes.

Estimate and Total Expenses

The next step in preparing a budget is to estimate your expenses. List all of your spending under three headings: fixed, flexible, and occasional. See 5-9.

A ***fixed expense*** is a set amount of money due on a set date. Rent, tuition, insurance premiums, organization dues, and installment payments are examples of fixed expenses. They tend to increase as you move into adult years. You may want to include a set amount of savings each week or month in your fixed expenses. This will help make sure you are moving toward important financial goals. As a rule, fixed expenses must be paid when due. Therefore, it is important to list them

Estimating Income		
Week or Month of ____________		
Income Sources	**Estimated**	**Actual**
Jobs		
Baby-sitting	$ ________	$ ________
Yard Work	$ ________	$ ________
Part-Time at Pizza Parlor	$ ________	$ ________
Allowance	$ ________	$ ________
Gifts	$ ________	$ ________
Interest	$ ________	$ ________
Total Income	$ ________	$ ________

5-8
Use a form similar to this one to estimate expected income. Unless you have a steady job, it may be difficult to estimate future income accurately. Review your estimates and fill in with actual figures to stay up-to-date on the amount you have to spend and save.

first when estimating expenses in your budget. There generally is not a lot of room to play with fixed costs.

Flexible expenses come up regularly but in varying amounts. Food, clothing, and entertainment are examples. Teenagers who receive the basic necessities from their families are likely to spend most of their money for other items, such as CDs, magazines, snacks, clothes, and movies. Because these items are flexible, you often can reduce or shift them about to fit the amount of cash available and to save money for important goals.

Occasional expenses come up only now and then. Examples include taxes, vacations, and gifts. Although these expenses often vary in amount, they usually are predictable. It is a good idea to plan ahead for major occasional expenses. Save a small amount regularly in a special fund so you will have cash available when they arise.

To prepare for a specific occasional expense, such as a two-week camping trip, estimate how much money you need and the date you need it. If the trip costs $360 and you plan to go in five months, divide $360 by 5 and save $75 each month until it is time to go. If it is easier to save by the week, divide $360 by 20 and save $18 each week. You can use this method to plan for any expense if you know the approximate amount you need and when you need it.

When you first estimate expenses, you may be off target. It is a good idea to keep a detailed record of your spending for a few weeks. This will show exactly where your money goes. Then you can estimate future expenses more accurately and control spending.

Estimating Expenses

Week or Month of ______________			
Expense Items	**Due Dates**	**Estimates**	**Actual**
Fixed Expenses			
Bus Pass	______	$ ______	$ ______
Lunches	______	$ ______	$ ______
Savings	______	$ ______	$ ______
Flexible Expenses			
Snacks	______	$ ______	$ ______
Movies/Concets/Events	______	$ ______	$ ______
Clothes	______	$ ______	$ ______
Tapes/CDs	______	$ ______	$ ______
Magazines	______	$ ______	$ ______
Grooming Aids	______	$ ______	$ ______
Occasional Expenses			
Gifts	______	$ ______	$ ______
Taxes	______	$ ______	$ ______
Insurance	______	$ ______	$ ______
Total Expenses	______	$ ______	$ ______

5-9
Fixed expense items normally run the same from budget period to budget period. Flexible expenses will vary. Make adjustments to your flexible expenses when you are short of cash. It may be necessary to save in advance to cover large occasional expenses. It helps to know when they will occur.

Solving Problems Through Decision Making

Nirmala Picks a College

Nirmala will graduate from high school with honors at the end of next year. She wants to go to college and become an engineer. Nirmala's father, aunt, and two brothers are all engineers. She wants to carry on the family tradition. Her chief interest is the development of new energy sources. She plans to specialize in that branch of engineering.

The Problem

Selecting the right college is Nirmala's problem. She has chosen her career. Now she must select the best college for pursuing that career. Nirmala's grades are outstanding so getting into a good school will be no problem. However, she is one of seven children and the family cannot afford to send all of them to expensive schools. This means Nirmala will need to consider expenses carefully. Finding the right school is a major decision.

The Goals

Nirmala begins by writing down what she needs from a college. To become an engineer and pay for her schooling, Nirmala needs to go to a school that offers

(Continued)

- ❑ ***Accreditation.*** She wants an accredited college that maintains high standards to qualify graduates for professional jobs and admission to graduate school.
- ❑ ***A strong engineering department.*** Nirmala wants to go to a school where engineering is an important part of the curriculum offerings and the engineering professors are highly qualified.
- ❑ ***Equal opportunities for female students.*** Nirmala does not want to be stuck in a school where women are not taken seriously.
- ❑ ***Low tuition, part-time work opportunities or financial aid possibilities.*** Nirmala's money for college is limited and she needs to consider money if she expects to finish in four years.
- ❑ ***Decent, safe, low-cost housing on or near the campus.*** Nirmala can save on living expenses by locating near campus in inexpensive housing.

Nirmala discusses her college goals with her parents and her school guidance counselor. They all approve. Her next step is to decide what resources she can use to get into a school that will meet her needs.

The Resources

Nirmala thinks carefully about what she has that can help her get into a good school. She makes a list of her resources:

- ❑ An excellent scholastic record.
- ❑ Well-stated college and career goals.
- ❑ Participation in extracurricular school activities, including those connected with ecology and environment.
- ❑ Family background and interest in engineering.
- ❑ High test scores that show an aptitude for science and math.
- ❑ Enough money to pay college costs in a state school or a private school with financial aid.
- ❑ Internet college search.

The Alternatives

Nirmala now knows what she wants in a school and what resources will help her get into the school of her choice. She begins her search for colleges in the local library with well-known college directories. These books describe many schools and their entrance requirements and course offerings. She writes to several schools that sound promising for a catalog and application form. In a few weeks, Nirmala receives information from a number of colleges. After reading through the college catalogs, Nirmala compares the pros and cons of each college.

In the process of matching her goals to possible schools, Nirmala eliminates several colleges. One college has a poor reputation for placing female graduates in engineering jobs. Another is a private school with high tuition that offers very limited financial aid. She eliminates a third school because living expenses on or near campus are too high.

Finally, Nirmala narrows her choices to three schools that meet her most important goals. She applies to all three. She hopes her high school record and other resources will help her get at least one letter of acceptance.

The Decision

Nirmala is accepted by two of the three schools. Once again, she compares her list of goals to the characteristics of the two colleges. She chooses the college that meets most of her goals and has the fewest drawbacks.

Case Review

1. How did Nirmala's list of goals help her select a college?
2. How did Nirmala's resources help her?
3. What are the advantages of using rational decision making to choose a college? What disadvantages might surface if a person fails to follow a rational procedure in making such an important decision?
4. How can you use this approach to make a similar decision for yourself?
5. How might Nirmala's approach and results differ if
   a. She had not already decided on a particular field of study?
   b. Her scholastic record and test scores had been only average?
   c. She had no financial resources for a college education?

Analyze Current Income and Spending

Taking a close look at your record of income and spending is an important step in money management. It is easy to overestimate income and underestimate expenses. A detailed record of spending almost always turns up some surprises and some unnecessary expenses. Inspect your record of income and expenses. Are your income figures accurate? Subtract your expenses from your income for each budget period. Do you come out even? Do you have money left over for goals? If you have nothing left or if you are in the hole, consider ways to increase income or cut expenses. This will allow you to balance your books and have something left for items you want most from your money.

To increase income, explore these possibilities: Can you negotiate an increase in allowance or wages? Can you earn extra money by taking on more responsibilities at home or at work? Have you overlooked job opportunities? Can you work longer hours without sacrificing time you need for schoolwork and other important activities?

To reduce spending, look carefully at your record of expenses. Does it reflect your priorities and goals? Can you identify wasteful spending and unnecessary items on your list of expenditures? Can you reduce some expenses? Can you omit some entirely? Make your money buy what is really important to you. Increasing income and reducing expenditures are ways to increase financial resources. When you get a little money ahead, saving and investing can add to your resources. These methods of making your money grow are discussed fully in Chapters 15 and 16. The use of credit to meet your goals and manage the peaks and valleys of income and expenses is discussed in Chapter 13.

Prepare a Trial Budget

At this point, it is time to bring together your goals, income, and expenses into some form of a plan. The purpose of a budget is to take control of your money and spending. A plan reduces the temptation to spend carelessly. The form in 5-10 illustrates one way to organize a budget. You may wish to draft a similar form for your own financial planning. It is helpful to keep these records over a period of time so you can review your financial situation now and then. The important thing is to put your budget in writing and keep it up-to-date as you go along. The tips in 5-11 can make a budget work better.

Put Your Budget in Action and Keep Organized Records

Once your budget is set up, you need to spend and save according to plan. Keeping organized records can help you stay within your budget and make adjustments as needed. You may also may need financial records to prepare income tax returns.

A good record-keeping system will be simple and convenient to use. It should contain financial records related to your income, spending, and savings as well as credit, investments, taxes, and insurance. Income records to keep include paycheck stubs, statements of interest earned on savings accounts, records of dividends, and amounts of cash gifts, tips, and bonuses you receive. If you receive cash for a job, such as lawn work or baby-sitting, keep a written account of what you have been paid.

Spending records include canceled checks, receipts from bills paid, statements from credit accounts, and cash register receipts. These are especially important for fixed expenses, such as rent or loan payments, and for major purchases, such as a sound system. Receipts for these items serve as proof of payment. They may be needed for warranty services or settling disputes.

Trial Budget

Week or Month of ____________________

	Planned	Actual
Income		
Jobs	$ ________	$ ________
Allowance	$ ________	$ ________
Gifts	$ ________	$ ________
Other	$ ________	$ ________
Total Income	$ ________	$ ________
Expenses		
Fixed Expense	$ ________	$ ________
Flexible Expense	$ ________	$ ________
Occasional Expense	$ ________	$ ________
Total Expenditures	$ ________	$ ________

5-10
You could use a form similar to this for your trial budget. Use your estimates of income and expenses, financial goals, and record of spending in making up your trial budget.

Quick Tips to Better Budgeting

1. Keep it simple.
2. Write it down.
3. Be specific.
4. Be flexible.
5. Be disciplined.
6. Keep it all together.
7. Be prepared for the unexpected.

5-11
When planning a budget, keep these tips in mind.

You need not save receipts for minor purchases, such as cosmetics or movie tickets. However, if you have trouble staying within your budget, you may want to keep a record of all your spending for a while. Then you will have a better idea of where your money goes.

It is also important to keep receipts for any purchases you may need to return, exchange, or take in for servicing. Proof of purchase is often required for these after-purchase transactions.

As you earn more money, other financial records will become an important part of your money management, 5-12. Use a simple filing system to keep these records organized. You may use a desk drawer, file cabinet, or box to keep records gathered in one place. You may want to keep original documents, such as insurance policies or stock certificates, in a safety deposit box at a financial institution with copies in your files. Also, keep your budget with other money management material. Then you will have all the information needed when you want to evaluate and make necessary revisions to your budget.

5-12
When two people marry, money management changes substantially for both of them. It is important to work together on new goals, spending and saving choices, and a budget.

Evaluate Your Budget and Financial Planning Periodically

Finances, like everything else, change. From time to time, it pays to review your money management plan to be sure that it is working for you. Whenever your income, expenses, or goals change significantly, review your budget to see if you need to make any changes. You can expect your financial plans to change with significant events in your life. These include graduation, going to college, starting a new job, leaving home, getting married, having children, or changing jobs, 5-13.

Consider these questions as you evaluate your budget. Is your financial plan working? Is your money doing what you want it to do? Are you reaching important goals? As you achieve goals, do you set new ones? Are you controlling spending? Has your income or pattern of spending changed significantly? Are there changes in your life that call for adjustments in your financial planning?

When revisions are needed, make the necessary changes and write up a new budget. Recheck in a week or two to see if the new entries are an improvement. If you keep a handle on your finances month by month, your income will work well for you over the years.

5-13
The arrival of children will call for another careful adjustment in financial planning.

Money Management in Your Future

As you enter the adult world, your money management activities will expand. You will not only find personal finances more involved, but you will discover that the world around you will affect your economic life as well. This is a good time to take a look at what the future holds for you.

Adjusting to the World in Which You Will Live

To some degree, the way you manage money in the years ahead will depend on where you fit into the overall social and economic landscape. Socioeconomic values and realities tend to change over the years. This affects the way people live and manage their affairs. For example, families are changing. Today, couples tend to marry at a later age. The average age at the time of their first marriage was 26.8 for males and 25 for women in 1997, compared to 24.7 for males and 22 for women in 1980. There are more two-income families. Over 60 percent of married couples earn two incomes. The number of single-parent families is increasing. Almost 26 percent of births are to unmarried women and 28 percent of children under 18 lived with only one parent. Divorce rates are higher. Ten percent of the adult population is divorced compared to just over six percent in 1980. More people are living alone—over 25 million or approximately 25 percent of all households.

People tend to live longer, and the population as a whole is aging. The over 65 population jumped from 25.5 million in 1980 to almost 34 million in 1997. This affects both personal spending and the federal budget. For example, the costs of Social Security and medicare continue to climb, leaving fewer federal dollars for other needs. Advances in biotechnology and medicine may mean that you will live a longer, healthier life. At the same time, rising health care costs and managed care policies may make it difficult to obtain some of the latest treatments and medications. Research findings on healthful lifestyles, including fitness routines, nutritious diets, and stress reduction let people know how to improve their own quality of life.

These trends in family structure and lifespans may change the way you think about your future and the way you spend, save, and manage money. Earning levels will also have an impact on your personal finances. Average incomes are increasing—up from $10,000 per person in 1980 to $26,000 in 1998. At the same time, 13.7 percent of families live below the poverty line, almost the same as in 1980. While advanced technology is creating new job opportunities, the better jobs require higher levels of education and training. Education has never paid off more than in today's economy.

Technology brings other changes in the way you live and deal with financial matters. The World Wide Web may alter the way you buy goods and services. You can buy everything from groceries to autos on the Internet. You can do your banking online and follow your investments minute-by-minute. Information technology can bring you the latest information from around the world about consumer products, services, and issues.

Technological advancements and global economics are changing both job and consumer markets. These developments create new job opportunities. The Internet brings an international marketplace into the home. The world is growing smaller thanks to instant communication, travel, and interdependence among nations. Economic and political events in Japan, Brazil, Russia, Germany, France, and throughout the world can affect prices, markets, jobs, and daily life in your home town. Successful money management in your future will require keeping up with the world in which you live.

Evaluating Your Personal Finances

As you earn more income and assume more financial obligations, your budget will become more detailed. In addition to preparing a budget and keeping necessary records, it's a good idea to evaluate your total financial situation. A financial or net worth statement will help you do this accurately. This may not seem important now, but you will be surprised at how fast your circumstances can change and how complicated keeping track or your finances can become.

A ***financial statement*** is a written record of your current financial situation. It tells you what you are worth at a given time. As you revise this declaration each year, it helps you see the progress you are making toward your goals.

On a financial statement, you list assets and liabilities to determine net worth. See 5-14. ***Assets*** are items that a

Financial Statement

Assets

Liquid Assets:

Cash on hand	$_____	
Cash in savings, checking, and money market accounts	_____	
Cash value of insurance	_____	
Other	_____	
Total Liquid Assets		$ _____

Investment Assets:

Stocks and bonds	$_____	
Mutual funds	_____	
Individual Retirement Accounts	_____	
Other	_____	
Total Investment Assets		$ _____

Use Assets: (market values)

Auto	$_____	
Home	_____	
Furniture and equipment	_____	
Clothing	_____	
Other	_____	
Total Use Assets		$ _____

Total Assets . . . . $ _____

Liabilities

Current Liabilities:

Credit cards and charge account balances due	$_____	
Taxes due	_____	
Other	_____	
Total Current Liabilities		$ _____

Long-term Liabilities:

Auto loan	$_____	
Home mortgage	_____	
Other	_____	
Total Long-term Liabilities		$ _____

Total Liabilities . . . . $ _____

Net Worth (total assets less total liabilities) . . . . $_____

5-14
A financial statement helps you determine your net worth at a given point in time.

person owns, such as cash, stocks, bonds, real estate, and personal possessions. Assets are divided into three categories. *Liquid assets* include cash and savings that can quickly and easily be converted to cash. *Investment assets* include securities and invested funds that are set aside for long-range goals, such as the education of children or retirement needs. *Use assets* include home, auto, personal possessions, and other durable goods that enrich your life through use. Because assets tend to change in value from year to year, it is recommended you list them at market value. This is their estimated worth at the time you are making up your financial statement.

Liabilities are amounts a person owes, such as unpaid bills, credit card charges, personal loans, and taxes. These are divided into current and long-term. *Current liabilities* include items due soon, usually within the year, such as medical bills, taxes, and outstanding bills from credit cards and charge accounts. *Long-term liabilities* include obligations to be paid over a long period of time, such as the unpaid amount of a home mortgage or auto loan.

Your ***net worth*** is the difference between total assets and total liabilities. Subtract liabilities from assets to arrive at your net worth. If it is a plus figure, the surplus can be invested or applied to reaching your financial goals. If it is a negative figure, you will need to look to ways of reducing expenses or increasing income to put yourself on sound financial footing.

Avoiding Financial Difficulties

Avoiding financial problems is usually much easier than solving them. The warning signals in 5-15 can help you see trouble coming before it arrives. As you read the questions, let each yes answer serve as a note of caution. If you answer yes to several questions, you will need to make some serious changes in your financial planning.

Warning Signals

1. Do you often wonder where your money goes?
2. Do you fail to set aside cash for emergencies?
3. Do you dip into savings or reserves for nonemergencies?
4. Do you fail to save for important goals?
5. Do you frequently use credit as a substitute for cash?
6. Are you financially standing still or falling behind?
7. Do you often use money intended for one thing to pay for another?
8. Do you ever receive overdue notices on bills?
9. Do you ever overdraw your checking account?
10. Do you overestimate income and underestimate expenses?
11. Do you find it difficult to keep up with routine expenses?
12. Do you let tomorrow take care of itself rather than plan for the financial future?

5-15
Check these warning signals from time to time to avoid slipping into financial trouble.

Keeping Financial and Legal Documents

As you enter the world of work and adult responsibilities, certain documents and papers will become important in managing your affairs. It is helpful to set up a system for keeping these items so you can find them when they are needed, 5-16. Find a safe place to file important documents.

Uses of Documents and Papers

You will need these documents for a variety of financial and legal transactions and purposes. You may refer to your file of records when:

Documents and Records You May Need:

Personal
- ❑ Birth/Marriage/Death certificates
- ❑ Passports
- ❑ Adoption and custody papers
- ❑ Military papers
- ❑ Separation agreements
- ❑ Divorce decree
- ❑ Social Security card
- ❑ Citizenship papers

Employment
- ❑ Resumes
- ❑ Copies of completed job applications
- ❑ Employment contracts
- ❑ Letters of recommendation.
- ❑ Employment benefit information and documents
- ❑ College transcripts and training certificates

Finances
- ❑ Budget
- ❑ Financial statements
- ❑ Bank statements
- ❑ Canceled checks
- ❑ Credit card and charge account statements and records of payments
- ❑ Loan papers and receipts of payments

Insurance
- ❑ Original policies
- ❑ List of premium amounts and due date
- ❑ Claims information
- ❑ List of policies, numbers, company names, and types of coverage
- ❑ List of beneficiaries and amounts of expected benefits
- ❑ Medical history with names of physicians and record of current prescriptions

Taxes
- ❑ Copies of past tax returns
- ❑ Record and receipts of deductible expenses
- ❑ Record of taxable income
- ❑ Paycheck stubs
- ❑ W-2 Forms

Property
- ❑ Lease/Mortgage papers
- ❑ Property tax statements and receipts of payments
- ❑ Deeds and title papers to property
- ❑ Inventory of personal possessions with purchase prices, estimated value, and photos of valuables
- ❑ Warranties and instruction manuals
- ❑ Service and repair records
- ❑ Bills of sale and receipts of payments for valuable purchases
- ❑ Receipts for improvements of real estate property
- ❑ Appraisals of real estate and valuables

Savings and Investments
- ❑ Purchase and sale records for stocks, bonds, and mutual funds
- ❑ Investment certificates
- ❑ Savings account records

Estate Planning
- ❑ Will (original and copies)
- ❑ Individual Retirement Account (IRA) statements
- ❑ Pension information
- ❑ Social Security records
- ❑ Retirement plan documents

Account Statements
- ❑ Pension information
- ❑ Social Security records
- ❑ Retirement plan documents

Records

5-16
Keeping these documents organized and handy will help you to be a better manager.

- ❑ Applying for jobs.
- ❑ Making budget and financial planning decisions.
- ❑ Preparing and filing income tax returns.
- ❑ Making loss estimates and insurance claims.
- ❑ Documenting or proving bill payments, tax deductions, insurance claims, and property ownership.
- ❑ Filing for employee or Social Security benefits.
- ❑ Making savings and investment decisions.
- ❑ Working on retirement and estate planning.
- ❑ Settling an estate.

Key Lists to Keep Current and Available

Along with important documents and records, you should keep several lists handy for your own convenience and in managing your financial affairs. Also, in the event of your absence, disability, or death, important information should be readily available to the person who would handle your financial and legal affairs. The following lists, kept in one place, will guide anyone who takes over for you.

- ❑ Savings and checking accounts with account numbers, names on each account, name of financial institution where each account is located.
- ❑ Credit card and charge accounts with account numbers, name of issuer, expiration dates, names of persons authorized to use each account.
- ❑ Securities and investments including stocks, bonds, mutual funds with identifying numbers, names of issuers, estimated values, purchase prices and dates, names of brokers, location of certificates.
- ❑ Locations of wills and trusts, insurance policies with claims information, mortgage papers, other loan contracts, tax records, securities and investment records, property deeds and titles, pension plans and employee benefit documents, Social Security and medicare records.
- ❑ Names, addresses, and phone numbers for lawyers, investment brokers, physicians, insurance agents, financial advisers and consultants, executors and guardians named in will, business partners or co-owners, real estate brokers, and any others who should be consulted in the management of your legal and financial affairs.
- ❑ Property, possessions, and valuables with their location, estimated market value, appraisals, details of their purchase, and intentions for their disposition.
- ❑ Instructions for the management of your affairs, care and provisions for your dependents, disposal of your property and possessions, and other wishes you want carried out.

You will need to keep many of these records and lists readily available in a home file. Others may call for the extra security of a safe deposit box at a financial institution. It is also helpful to have certain types of information at your fingertips. This will be more important as you find yourself dealing with the details of adult life.

Summary

Management is the art of using what you have to get what you want. It starts with identifying and using available resources. There are two types of resources—human and nonhuman. Resources are limited, manageable, and related to each other. Management involves using resources (what you have) to reach goals (what you want).

The art of management also requires making decisions and solving problems. When aiming at specific goals, rational decision making helps consumers make intelligent choices. It is a five-step process. Making the best use of resources in management is a three-step process. It calls for planning, acting, and evaluating.

Managing money follows the same process as the management of other resources. Certain economic concepts apply to the use of money and affect the money management process. The law of scarcity refers to unlimited wants fighting for limited resources. This requires choice. Consumers must also consider the opportunity costs of certain resources. The time or money spent on one item cannot be spent on another.

Inflation is a period of rising prices or too many dollars chasing too few goods. It results when demand in the marketplace is greater than supply. Rising prices affect personal budgeting. Recession is a period of economic decline or slow growth. It is often characterized by high unemployment, low wages, business failures, and uncertainty. This also affects personal money management.

A budget tailored to income and needs can guide consumers through the maze of financial decisions over a lifetime. The seven steps to tailoring a money management plan include: establish financial goals, estimate total income, estimate total expenses, analyze current income and spending patterns, prepare a trial budget, put the plan in action, and periodically evaluate making changes as necessary.

The money management process expands as income increases. Periodic financial statements that help chart progress will be an important tool. Attention to warning signals can help consumers avoid serious financial problems.

It also becomes increasingly important to develop a system for keeping necessary financial and legal documents. Knowing what to keep and where to file different papers can be a significant help in managing your financial and legal affairs.

To Review

1. List five human resources and five nonhuman resources.
2. What are the three parts to the management process?
3. What four factors should be identified in the planning phase of management?
4. Success in the action phase of management is determined by what two key characteristics?
5. What are the two purposes of evaluation in management?
6. What four key economic concepts influence personal money management?
7. Give three examples of each kind of expense: fixed, flexible, and occasional.
8. Name three events in life that call for a change in financial plans.
9. What financial facts are included in a net worth statement?
10. What are three types of assets?
11. Name two types of liabilities.
12. List and describe three situations where you might have to refer to financial or legal documents.

To Think Critically

1. What are your most important and valuable human and nonhuman resources?
2. Give examples of decisions people make
   A. just to please someone else.
   B. on impulse.
   C. on the spur of the moment.
   D. by failing to act.
3. What are some advantages of using the rational decision-making process to solve a problem or make a decision? When is rational decision making most important?
4. How might rational decision making help in
   A. making family or group decisions?
   B. establishing government policies?
   C. solving business problems?
5. How can good management help people achieve specific goals?
6. What are some steps people can take to
   A. increase income?
   B. reduce unnecessary spending?
   C. increase resources for goals?
7. Discuss ways you could use each of the following resources to save money and time.
   A. telephone
   B. newspaper
   C. car
   D. library
   E. credit card
   F. computer
   G. the Internet

To Do

1. Apply the rational decision-making process to an important decision you expect to face within a year or two. Write down the problem, your goals, your resources for reaching the goals, the alternatives, and the decision you would make. What are the pros and cons of rational decision making?
2. Where does your money go? Can you account for the money you have spent over the past few weeks? In a small notebook, keep a record of all the money you receive and spend over the next two weeks. Account for every penny. Are you satisfied with the way you use your money? How could you better control spending and manage your money in the future?
3. Develop a bulletin board that explains how to organize a record-keeping system. Include samples of documents a person should keep.
4. Set up a money management plan based on your financial goals, income, and expenses. Follow the plan for a month and then evaluate. What are its strengths and weaknesses? How can you improve the plan?
5. Project your money management plan into the future for two, five, and ten years. How do you expect it to change and what events and circumstances are likely to bring about changes in your financial planning?
6. What are some of the adjustments people need to make in financial planning and decisions when they marry? Draw up a list of financial topics couples should discuss and resolve before marriage.
7. Set up a filing system for important documents and papers according to categories used in the chart in 5-16.

Careful budgeting can help people plan for such costly expenses as family vacations.

CHAPTER 6

BEST BUY
Scotch
BX/90
Normal Bias
Polarisation normale
CONSUMER'S
RESOURCE HANDBOOK
$158
Striped twill shirt, International Male.
White twill jacket, J. Crew.
Red and white pajama top, Brooks Brothers.
Red lambswool cardigan, J. Crew.
AUTOMATIC FOR THE PEOPLE
R.E.M.
genesis
STEVIE WONDER
MUSIC FROM THE MOVIE
Canon
CANON LENS

You, the Shopper

retail stores
nonstore sellers
consumer cooperatives
buying incentives
loss leader
rebate
bait and switch
pyramid schemes
clearance sale
closeout sale
going-out-of-business sale
introductory offer
liquidation
warranty
full warranty
limited warranty
implied merchantability
implied fitness
generic products

After studying this chapter, you will be able to

- ❑ identify various types of sellers in the marketplace.
- ❑ explain how shoppers can recognize and take advantage of various selling methods.
- ❑ identify reliable sources of shopping information.
- ❑ identify shopping tools for consumers.
- ❑ list guidelines for making rational shopping decisions.

Shopping skills can help you make $50 seem like $100. You can buy far more for your dollars than an unskilled buyer who spends the same amount of money. As a smart shopper, you will get greater satisfaction for your dollars. Your shopping experiences will be rewarding rather than frustrating.

Shopping smart is largely a matter of understanding the marketplace, knowing what you want, using reliable consumer information, and making sound decisions. In our economic system, there are countless places to shop and items to buy. High-powered selling methods can tempt you to buy what you do not really need or want. Knowing what you want and seeking out reliable consumer information can help you make the right buying decisions.

Understanding the Marketplace

The marketplace is an arena where buyers and sellers meet to exchange goods, services, and money. In a free enterprise economy, the marketplace has certain characteristics that set it apart from markets in other economies. It is characterized by free economic choice, the profit motive, and competition. Within the framework of these three characteristics, the forces of supply and demand create a vast arena of sellers and buyers. To make your way through the marketplace, you need to know something about the many places you can shop. You should also know about the methods sellers use to encourage customers to buy.

Places to Shop

The marketplace is made up of many sellers and places to shop. Store locations include neighborhoods, shopping centers, and downtown areas. Each presents different types of stores, goods, and services.

Neighborhood stores may offer convenience and personal service, but selection often is limited by size and space. Prices may be higher because of the small sales volume and the high cost of operating a small business. The small stores in your immediate area are a good choice when you are in a hurry or you want personal service. You may also feel some sense of loyalty to these stores because you know the owners and sales staff. In addition, they depend heavily on your business. They may go out of the way to take care of your needs. See 6-1.

Shopping centers range from small strip centers with eight or ten stores to huge malls with several major department stores and a variety of specialty shops. Advantages of these centers include a broad selection of goods and services selling at competitive prices. In the larger malls, it is possible to shop for a wide variety of goods and services at one time and often under one roof. Many malls offer special attractions and promotions to bring in more customers. Easy parking is a plus at most shopping centers.

Downtown shopping areas offer some of the same advantages of shopping centers. However, stores are usually more spread out, and it is not

6-1
Neighborhood stores frequently offer friendly service and a personal touch.

as easy to go from one to another. In most major cities, parking is a challenge, but public transportation is readily available. Leading department stores are a big draw for city shoppers. Cultural and sporting events, hospitals, clinics, and professional offices and services are often located in the area. This makes it possible to combine shopping with other activities. For those who work in the city, it may be one of the more convenient places to shop.

Types of Sellers

The marketplace is made up of sellers who do business in different ways. It includes different types of retail stores and a variety of nonstore sellers such as door-to-door sellers, catalogs, telemarketers, electronic sales via television and the Internet, and consumer cooperatives.

Retail stores. ***Retail stores*** sell goods and services directly at their place of business. Retailers include department stores, specialty shops, superstores, warehouse clubs, discount stores, factory outlets, and resale shops. Stores may be independently owned and centered in local areas, or they may be chain stores located across the country. Some of these retailers also operate active catalog and Internet businesses.

Department stores sell a wide variety of goods and services in a single store. Merchandise is divided into departments that seem like small shops within the larger store. Sections include clothing that is divided into mens, womens, juniors, boys, girls, and childrens. Cosmetics, linens, furniture, home furnishings, housewares, shoes, lingerie, jewelry, and home appliances are some of the other departments. These stores offer the convenience of one-stop shopping and may offer a variety of customer services.

Specialty stores sell a specific type of merchandise or services such as shoes, toys, health foods, books, or gifts. Stationers, pharmacies, barber shops, and beauty salons also are examples. Generally, the sales staff in these stores are fairly well informed about the products or services offered. See 6-2.

Superstores and *warehouse clubs* offer advantages to consumers, but they threaten local neighborhood stores who cannot compete with their pricing or wide selection of merchandise. These stores generally are located in shopping malls or on the outskirts of town. They have large parking lots. Most are open every day and many have extended hours. They sell great quantities of whatever merchandise they offer. Some superstores specialize

6-2
This specialty store sells only computers and computer accessories. The salespeople know the merchandise and can answer customers' questions intelligently.

LDI Corporation

in specific products such as books, CDs, sporting goods, foods, household items, or building and office products. Others sell a wide variety of merchandise similar to the department stores. The warehouse clubs sell memberships to customers who want buying privileges. They usually offer a wide variety of merchandise, often including food products and prescription drugs, at discount prices.

Discount stores sell certain lines of merchandise at lower prices than other stores. They can afford to do this because they buy in large quantities and limit customer services such as deliveries, credit, and returns. Most discount stores are self-serve operations with few salespeople. They may offer real bargains on some items, but it pays to compare prices because they do not always offer the best buys on all of the merchandise they sell.

Factory outlets generally are owned by the manufacturer or distributor of the merchandise they offer. They sell directly to the consumer rather than through wholesalers or other retailers. Very often, a variety of factory outlets locate in an outlet mall usually in an outlying area. Shoppers come from long distances in hope of finding bargains. Merchandise featured at the outlets may include overstocks and items that did not sell in other stores. Factory outlet prices usually are lower than prices for the same merchandise in other retail stores.

Resale shops sell used merchandise at greatly reduced prices. Extras such as warranties or guarantees, exchanges, credit privileges often will be limited, but prices are likely to be exceptionally low. Since merchandise is used, it is important to inspect it carefully to be sure items are in good condition. Clothing, household items, and furniture are among the items typically sold in resale shops. *Resale shops* generally refer to shops that buy merchandise from individuals and sell it to customers. *Thrift shops* are operated by churches, hospitals, or charitable organizations for the benefit of those they serve. *Consignment shops* accept merchandise to sell and pay the owners a percentage when the items are sold.

Nonstore sellers. ***Nonstore sellers,*** also called direct marketers, sell goods and services in different ways and from different locations. They include door-to-door salespersons, catalogs, telemarketers, electronic sales via television or Internet, consumer cooperatives, and vending machines. These methods of selling goods and services offer advantages, but it is important to check out the reliability and legitimacy of the seller before buying. It can be difficult to locate a distant seller if there are problems after the sale.

Door-to-door salespersons are sellers who come to your door and offer the convenience of buying at home. It can also be a plus to see certain products such as home furnishings or decorating items in the home before buying. Before opening your door to a seller who comes to your home, ask to see his or her identification, selling permit or license, and a company connection. If you buy, obtain a written copy of all of the details of the sale such as delivery dates, model numbers, price, warranties, credit terms, etc., and a contact name and number for after sale follow-up if there are any problems with the purchase.

Catalogs allow you to order goods and services. It is another way to shop at home. You can buy almost anything through catalogs. It is important to check out the reliability of the seller before buying and to understand the policies for return or exchange of purchases. Also consider shipping costs both for orders and possible returns. Add any costs involved to the purchase price.

Peapod

6-3
Shoppers can shop for anything online. This shopping page allows consumers to shop for food.

Telemarketing is a form of selling that generally involves the seller calling you on the telephone to sell goods or services. You can buy everything from toys to insurance to burial plots by telephone in the comfort of your own home. Generally, you can shop by phone 24 hours a day, seven days a week. However, telemarketers may call you at inconvenient times with offers that do not interest you. Consumer protection laws require telemarketers to clearly state both company and caller name, the purpose of the call, and the type of goods or services being offered. Telemarketers are not allowed to call again once you ask them not to call, to call before 8:00 a.m. or after 9:00 p.m., or to misrepresent their offer or the goods and services offered.

Electronic shopping allows you to shop electronically via television or the Internet. Television marketers present merchandise on specific marketing channels, or you may simply see a product advertised on TV with a phone number to call for more information or to purchase. Either way, you can see the product, order by phone, usually pay by credit card, and have purchases delivered to your home.

Shopping on the Internet, also called E-commerce or E-shopping, is growing fast. In 1998, online sellers reached approximately eight million households. In the future, they are expected to serve over 16 million. You can access more than 100,000 World Wide Web-based retail sites online. The surge in this form of retailing is likely to bring some of your favorite stores to the Internet, allowing you to buy from retailers you know online in the comfort and convenience of your own home. Offerings range from books and CDs to clothing, food, furniture, vacation and business travel, automobiles, investments, cosmetics, and prescription drugs. Almost anything you can buy offline can be bought online. The variety of merchandise and services available is almost unlimited. A typical online shopping page is shown in 6-3.

The Internet offers not only buying opportunities, but also a convenient and thorough way to learn about products and do comparison shopping. Online brokers offer shopping robots called "bots" that search the Web for the best values for different products. You select a category and then type in the name of the product to find comparative prices and features. The Internet mall offers a great many features and advantages.

Consumer cooperatives are nonretail associations owned and operated by a group of members for their own benefit rather than for profit. Members contribute services and dues to participate in the association. Goods and services usually sell at lower prices than retail stores. However, selection of goods and services and customer services will be limited to what the membership can provide.

Vending machines started primarily as places to buy snacks and soft drinks. Today, a large variety of merchandise is available through vending machines, including a wide selection of food items as well as cosmetics, clothing items, grooming supplies, and jewelry. They offer the advantages of easy, fast purchases and often are available 24 hours, seven days a week. However, since the actual vendor or seller is not present, dissatisfaction with items purchased from a vending machine can be difficult to resolve.

Dealing with Sellers

To make the most of shopping with any nonstore or direct marketer, follow these guidelines:

- ❑ ***Know the seller.*** Find out the name and physical location of the company. Before you buy, ask questions about the company and the products and services it offers. If you have doubts about the company or the products, check with the organizations listed in 6-4.
- ❑ ***Understand what you are buying, from whom you are buying, and all of the details of the sale.*** Use the checklist in 6-5 to mark off what you need to know before completing a purchase through the telephone, Internet, television, catalog, or salesperson at your door. Get any information in writing so you have a record of the transaction if you need it.
- ❑ ***Maintain online security when buying online.*** Do not give your account *password* to anyone. This is the personal code you use to access your online account. Check a Web site's *privacy policy* before

6-4
These agencies and organizations offer information and assistance with consumer problems and complaints.

Sources of Consumer Information and Assistance

The Better Business Bureau where companies are located.	Your state Attorney General or consumer protection agency Consumer Response Center Federal Trade Commission 6th and Pennsylvania Avenue, NW Washington, D. C. 20580
National Fraud Information Center (NFIC) Consumer hotline at 800-876-7060 or www.fraud.org	
Federal Communications Commission Consumer Protection Branch Common Carrier Bureau Washington, D. C. 20554	Consumer Services Department or Mail Order Action Line (MOAL) Direct Marketing Association 1111 19th Street, NW, Suite 1100 Washington, D. C. 20036

Jack Klasey

6-5
There are literally thousands of mail and phone order companies. You can buy almost any product by mail or phone.

giving personal and financial information such as a Social Security or credit card numbers. The privacy policy is a statement on a Web site that tells what information about you the site collects and how it is used.

- ❑ ***Do not provide any personal or financial information*** such as credit card numbers, social security number, telephone number, or mailing address unless the information is necessary for the transaction and you know the company or seller requesting information is legitimate and reliable.
- ❑ ***Pay by credit card.*** Credit cards offer the advantages of easier returns and exchanges, convenience in resolving problems, and the protection of consumer credit laws.
- ❑ ***Know your rights.*** Consumer protection laws apply to online transactions. Contact the appropriate law enforcement agency if you have problems. See 6-6.
- ❑ ***Take your time.*** Do not let sellers rush you into a buying decision particularly for costly items. Study the offer. Discuss it with a person you trust if you have any doubts or questions.
- ❑ ***Don't fall for the unbelievable.*** If an offer sounds too good to be true, it probably is not true. Check out "good deals" before you buy.

Regardless of what you are buying, deal only with reputable sellers who are fair and honest with customers.

6-6
Use a checklist/form similar to this one before you buy.

Consumer Checklist

__Name of the salesperson ____________________
__Name, address, and phone number of the company ____________________
____
__Description of the product or service ____________________
____
__Identifying model and order numbers ____________________
__Purchase price __________ Sales tax _____
__Cost of handling and shipping _________
__Total cost _________
__Delivery date___________ Delivery method ____________
__Seller's policies regarding returns, exchanges, refunds ________
____
__Terms of any warranties ____________________
____
__Terms of any credit agreement____________________
____
__Customer service contract_________ Phone number __________

This is the only way you can protect your interests in the marketplace. The checklist in 6-7 can help you evaluate the many places to shop.

Selling Methods

When you enter the marketplace to buy goods and services, remember that businesses are there to sell and make a reasonable profit. You enter to buy at the best price. The purpose of the market is to arrive at a transaction and price that is acceptable to both seller and buyer.

To increase sales and profits, businesses use a number of selling methods. Advertising, a trained sales staff, buying incentives, special sales, and available credit all are designed to encourage consumers to buy. You can make these selling methods work for you as long as you understand that their main purpose is to sell goods and services.

Evaluating Sellers

1. Are policies concerning returns, exchanges, and refunds reasonable?
2. Is advertising believable? Are goods and services available at advertised prices?
3. Are salespeople helpful without being pushy?
4. Can you get straight answers to questions about products, services, and store policies?
5. Does the seller belong to the local chamber of commerce, Better Business Bureau, or other associations that set standards for fair business practices?
6. Do prices and services compare favorably with those of other sellers?
7. Have people you know had favorable experiences dealing with the seller?
8. Do you get prompt, courteous attention when you have questions, problems, or complaints?
9. Does management accept responsibility for the actions of salespeople and other employees?
10. Does the seller have a good reputation in the community?

6-7
These questions can help you evaluate the reliability and fairness of sellers. Several no answers should warn you away from a seller.

Advertising: Getting the Message to You

Businesses advertise to sell goods, services, ideas, and images. They spend close to $130 billion annually to put their messages before you. These messages are in newspapers and magazines, on television, in direct mail, on the radio, in the yellow pages, and on billboards. Every day you are exposed over and over again to advertising in its many forms.

Through advertising, sellers tell you about their products and services. Keep in mind that the primary purpose of advertising is to sell. Only positive information about a product or service is likely to appear in an ad or commercial.

Although false and misleading advertising is prohibited by law, you still should expect some exaggerated claims. It pays to develop a healthy skepticism when it comes to analyzing advertisements. There is an art to reading an ad or hearing a commercial. Look for the following information:

- ❑ Descriptions of the products or services offered for sale.
- ❑ Listing and demonstration of special product features and qualities.
- ❑ Statement of differences between advertised items and similar goods and services on the market.
- ❑ Details on prices, availability, places to buy, special offers, and terms of sale.

Words that should alert you to possible deception are: "free," "one

Winners and Losers

Food Choices

Conetta and Lenard have been married for three months. They both work full-time, so they must do their shopping in the evenings or on weekends. Although they share household responsibilities, Conetta does most of the food shopping.

Before shopping, Conetta reads the weekly food pages and ads in the newspaper. She compares advertised food prices in nearby supermarkets and saves money by taking advantage of advertised specials.

The newspaper food section tells Conetta what foods are plentiful at good prices. It also gives her ideas for meals and helps her plan menus. By knowing how to read the food pages and ads, Conetta saves time planning meals and saves money buying food. Conetta is a winner.

Tybrell has a weight problem. He simply cannot pass up a chocolate fudge sundae, an order of fries, or a plate of doughnuts. He seems to be eating all the time. His extra weight makes him self-conscious and disgusted with himself. The more he worries about his problem, the more he eats.

One day Tybrell sees an ad titled, "Eat your way slim and trim." The product is Weight Losers Chocolate. The ad says to eat one chocolate bar before meals and whenever the urge to snack strikes. Tybrell thinks this is the perfect answer to his weight problem. He goes to the nearest drugstore and buys a large supply of the miracle candy. What does he have to lose besides his unwanted weight?

Tybrell becomes a loser all right. The candy doesn't taste like candy, hot fudge sundaes, or anything else Tybrell likes. For a few days, he makes himself eat the diet snack, but it doesn't satisfy his craving for a tasty treat. Soon the candy finds its way into the trash can. Tybrell loses money, not pounds.

Case Review

1. How did advertising influence consumer demand for goods and services in Conetta's case? In Tybrell's case?
2. How did Conetta use advertising to her own advantage? How was Tybrell's approach different?
3. What makes an ad misleading, false, deceptive, or unfair? How can consumers protect themselves from this type of advertising? What does the government do? What can reputable businesses do?
4. What advertisements have you seen that would help you make a rational buying decision? What ads can you name that make false or misleading promises? What are some ways to tell the difference between the two?

time offer," and "valued at." When an offer sounds too good to be true, you can be almost sure that it is. The Better Business Bureau publishes a Code of Advertising. This booklet sets standards for advertising. Businesses that belong to the Better Business Bureau should follow this code. A copy of the booklet is available from your local bureau.

Sellers use several techniques in advertising to get you to buy their products. *Sex appeal*, using attractive models, is common. This is used in all types of advertising—from soda commercials to insurance ads. Sellers also use the *bandwagon* technique to convince the public that a product is fashionable or trendy—that everyone is buying it. *Puffery* is a term used to describe exaggerated claims that advertisers sometimes make about a product or service. Advertisers also use *testimonials*. These are "real people" recommending a product or service. These people are usually paid actors. Sometimes a company may hire a famous personality to promote their product. This is called an *endorsement*.

Sellers try to show their products and services in the best light possible. They do this by telling you only the good things about what they want to sell. If you remember this, advertising can help you as well as the seller. You win when you look for useful information in ads. You lose when you let ads persuade you to buy what you do not want, do not need, or cannot afford.

Buying Incentives

Buying incentives are offered by sellers to help sell goods and services. Trading stamps, coupons, contests and games, rebates, premiums, and prizes all are forms of buying incentives. They are often found in magazines or newspapers. Sometimes these incentives come with the purchase of goods and services. Their primary purpose is to sell. You benefit from this form of selling as long as you limit purchases to the goods and services you would ordinarily buy or try. You lose if you buy something you do not really want just to get stamps, use a coupon, or win a "free" prize.

Two-for-one offers, cents off, bargain buys, and other forms of special pricing are also buying incentives. Some sellers offer loss leaders to bring customers into the store. A ***loss leader*** is an item priced at or below cost to attract buyers who will then purchase other merchandise. Another type of buying incentive, usually used for big ticket items, is the rebate. A ***rebate*** is a deduction in price that is returned after a product has been purchased. Manufacturers holding large inventories of appliances or autos may offer cash back to buyers. For example, a seller may advertise a $75 rebate on the purchase of a $600 television set. The buyer sends the proof-of-purchase to the manufacturer and receives the $75 rebate.

Various buying incentives can offer real savings to alert shoppers. These shoppers know when price reductions are real. They refuse to be sidetracked into buying merchandise they do not need or want.

Deceptive Selling Techniques

Certain selling methods, though illegal, are still relatively common in the marketplace. These include bait and switch selling and pyramid schemes. Both are against the law. If you encounter any of these practices, contact the nearest Federal Trade Commission office or your state consumer fraud agency.

Bait and switch is a technique that involves advertising an item at a very attractive price to attract customers. When the customer comes to buy, the seller claims to be out of that item. Instead, the seller presents a more expensive substitute.

Pyramid schemes are scams calling for each participant to buy into the plan for a given amount of money and to sign up a certain number of additional participants to do the same. The only way you can move up the pyramid and collect the promised profits is to recruit new participants who in return will recruit other participants. The many at the bottom of the pyramid end up paying money to the few at the top. The promises almost always are exaggerated and false.

Special Sales and Promotions

Businesses hold special sales and promotions to attract customers and increase sales. Because price reductions and promotions increase sales and profits, they benefit the seller. When you buy goods and services you need on sale, you benefit as well. However, if you let reduced prices persuade you to buy what you do not need, you lose. To take advantage of sales and promotions, shoppers need to:

- ❑ Know what they need and want with or without sales.

Winners and Losers

Cosmetics Coupons

Anita has been wanting to try a new creamy lipstick marketed by a well-known cosmetic company. To introduce its new product to consumers, the company runs ads in a number of magazines and newspapers. The ads include a 50 cent coupon that can be redeemed with the purchase of one of the new lipsticks. Anita cuts out the coupon and receives 50 cents off on a purchase she had planned to make anyway. She wins the coupon game.

Another cosmetic firm decides to promote its new Masculine Scents with a contest. Prizes include $500 cash, five graphite tennis rackets, and 50 free bottles of Masculine Scents. To enter the contest, all you have to do is complete the sentence, "What I like best about Masculine Scents is. . . ." Along with the entry, you must include a label from a bottle of the cologne.

Although Larry does not use men's cologne, he buys a bottle of Masculine Scents just to enter the contest. He buys something he doesn't want and will never use just to enter a contest that he doesn't win. Not only does he lose the contest, he also loses the $9.50 he spent on the cologne. In this case, Larry is a two-time loser.

Case Review

1. What value do you see in buying incentives such as coupons, trading stamps, contests, and prizes?
2. What experience have you had with incentives that encouraged you to buy specific products or services?
3. What are the pros and cons of buying incentives from the seller's point of view and from the buyer's point of view?
4. What key differences do you see between Anita's and Larry's approach to buying incentives?

- Stay within preset price limits for given items, buying only what they can afford.
- Stick to an overall spending plan. They should not be sidetracked by price reductions, especially for major purchases.
- Anticipate reduced prices on products and services they intend to buy. For example, stores usually offer both pre-season specials and end-of-season sales for a wide range of goods and services. Also, with products such as appliances, autos, and computers, manufacturers bring out new models each year. The current product will be reduced just prior to the introduction of the new model. Waiting for predictable price cuts can save substantial amounts, particularly for major purchases. See 6-8.
- Control the urge to respond to sales and promotions without specific savings in mind in hopes of getting "something for nothing."

It is in your best interest to know the meaning of the following terms frequently used to attract customers and sell merchandise.

- ***Clearance sale***—indicates a reduction from previous prices on merchandise the seller wants to "clear" or sell, usually to make room for new merchandise.
- ***Closeout sale***—refers to products that are no longer being produced, that have been discontinued by the supplier or manufacturer.
- ***Going-out-of-business sale***—refers to sellers who actually are closing their business and are selling goods at reduced prices to hasten the closing.

6-8
It's always a plus if you can buy what you want on sale.

Caution: "going-out-of-business" is a phrase often used just to get you into the store.

- *Introductory offer*—indicates new merchandise selling at a price that will increase after the initial offer.
- *Liquidation*—refers to the sale of merchandise at reduced prices in order to aid in converting stock to cash. This is another term that is often misused.

Packaging and Display

Tools of the seller include packaging and display. Take a walk through a large supermarket or drug store. Study the packages and product displays. Note how many items seem strategically placed to attract your attention. What eye-catching techniques are used?

Studies indicate that items placed at floor level attract the least buyer notice. When the same products are raised to waist level, sales increase by almost 60 percent. At eye level, they jump almost 80 percent.

Products you are likely to buy on impulse usually will be placed in spots near the check-out counter. These may also be in display racks in the aisles where you can pick them up with ease. Staples in the supermarket, such as dairy products, breads, meat, poultry, and produce, will be located well into the store. Nonessentials will be near the front. This way, you are drawn into and through the store. Then you are apt to see and buy more products than you intended.

Packaging can be a powerful selling tool. Notice the color, shape, size, and labels on the packages that attract you most in your walk through the store. You will feel the urge to reach for some products more than others. See if you can figure out what draws you to different packages. In addition to appearance, packages may sell for their convenience features or their ecological claims. Ecological selling terms include *recyclable* and *earth friendly*. Convenience innovations include "boil-in-the-bag" foods, squeezable bottles and tubes, pull-tab cans, spray containers, designer containers, and reusable containers.

Consumer Credit

Businesses often offer credit to make it easier for customers to buy more and higher priced goods and services. See 6-9. Credit is good for sellers because it increases sales. It can be good for consumers, too, when they use it with forethought and planning. Credit is a curse for consumers who use it to buy more than they can afford. The case studies show a few examples of winners and losers in the use of credit as a shopping tool. More on the pros, cons, and intelligent use of credit appears in Chapter 13.

Winners and Losers

It's in the Bag

Morrie needs to replace the sleeping bag he received as a gift for his tenth birthday. He and a friend are planning a cross-country camping trip right after their high school graduation.

In the Sunday paper, Morrie sees an ad for down sleeping bags at one-third off the regular price. The next day he makes a trip to the sports shop that ran the ad where he finds a good selection of sleeping bags at reduced prices. He decides to buy a $150 down sleeping bag which is marked down to $100. Morrie wins with this bargain that saved him $50.

Susan sees the same ad. She has never been camping, but she thinks it might be fun. Several of her friends go on family camping trips every spring. She has been invited two or three times but has always been busy doing something else. Susan figures she will go camping someday and will need a sleeping bag. She has heard that down sleeping bags are the best.

The day after seeing the ad, Susan picks up her paycheck and heads for the sports shop. She spends most of her paycheck for a down sleeping bag. It is a $120 bag reduced to $80. Susan doesn't see how she can go wrong with a bargain like this. Susan never does go camping. The sleeping bag sits in her closet for years in its original wrapping. She loses $80.

Case Review

1. What advantages do sales and promotions offer shoppers?
2. What experiences have you had buying goods and services during special promotions and sales?
3. Why was the purchase of a sleeping bag on sale a bargain for Steve and a costly mistake for Susan?
4. Why are people so often tempted to buy at a sale even if the goods and services do not meet real needs?

Shopping Information

There is no substitute for reliable information when you go shopping. As goods, services, and markets become more varied and complex, knowledge becomes more important. Consumer information on a wide variety of topics comes from the sources outlined and discussed in Chapter 4. Common sources of shopping information on specific goods and services include advertisements, labels and hangtags, product rating and testing

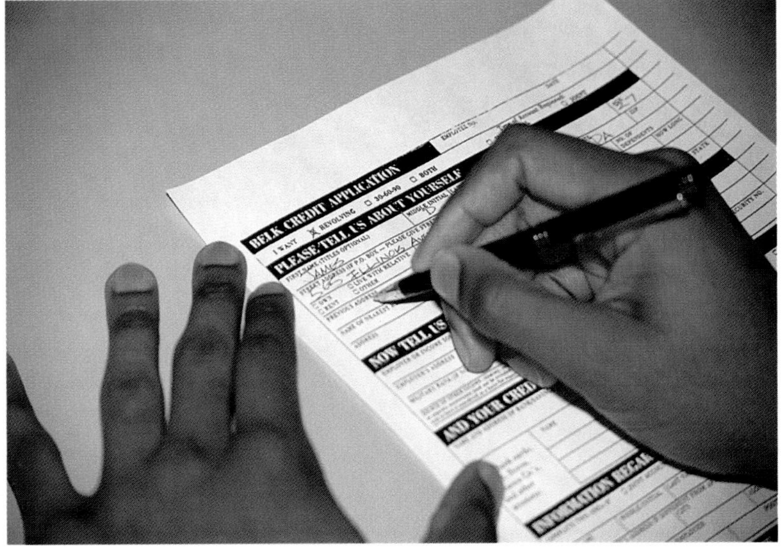

6-9
Shoppers often favor stores where they have charge accounts. Credit privileges can increase sales.

Jack Klasey

organizations, warranties, and salespeople. Knowing how to find, evaluate, and use available information can help you become a smarter shopper.

Advertisements

Advertising is probably the most readily available source of information about goods, services, and sellers. Although ads and commercials vary in format, most contain some useful information. Specifically, you generally can count on advertising to introduce new products and services, keep you up-to-date on existing products, give changing price information, and tell where to find advertised items. To make the best use of ads and commercials, concentrate on the facts. Look and listen for specifics on brands, features, warranties, and prices.

Winners and Losers

The Credit Game

Lewauna graduated from college recently and moved into a place of her own. For the first time in her life, she has a steady job and a fairly good income. One of her first official acts as an independent working person is to apply for a credit card. She wants the convenience of being able to charge her purchases.

Having a credit card makes Lewauna feel more like a complete adult than her job does. She loses no time in using the new card. Her first purchases are mostly clothes and little extras she has always wanted but could not afford before she had a job.

At the end of the first month, Lewauna's credit card bill comes to almost $400. It is a real shocker. Since Lewauna did not keep a record of her charges, she can't believe that she has spent so much. Her paycheck is only $735 a month after deductions. By the time Lewauna pays her rent and other expenses, she has just $60 left to pay on her credit account. Already she is well into debt.

Looking back, Lewauna really doesn't have much to show for the $400 she spent. She could have done without most of the purchases. It takes Lewauna five months to pay off her credit card debt. She also pays over $25 in finance charges. Lewauna is a credit card loser.

Jeff looks at credit as a useful but dangerous tool. He too is on his own for the first time with his first credit card. He realizes the importance of establishing credit so he can get loans in the future. Besides, he doesn't think it is realistic to buy everything with cash.

Although Jeff is happy to have his credit card, he is a little afraid of it. His family had some debt problems when he was younger. Jeff doesn't remember the details, but he does remember "doing without" while the family worked its way out of debt.

Jeff decides to use his credit card sparingly and to keep track of his charges. He plans to limit his overall debt to an amount he can repay with ease. He also plans to use credit only for things he really needs. His first big charge is for a raincoat he buys on sale, $20 off the regular price. Jeff uses his credit card because he doesn't have enough cash before payday. If he waited until payday, the coat would no longer be on sale. By using credit wisely, Jeff saves $20. Over the years, his careful use of credit makes him a winner.

Case Review

1. How does the availability of credit influence consumer demand?
2. How does offering credit work in the interest of sellers?
3. How can the use of credit work for consumers? How can it create problems?
4. What advice would you give Lewauna for the future use of credit? What did you learn from Jeff's example?
5. What can consumers do to enjoy the benefits and avoid the problems of using credit?

Labels and Hangtags

Information on labels and hangtags tells you about the content, quality, performance, care, and maintenance of products, 6-10. This information helps you select, use, and care for products.

Some laws require specific facts to appear on the labels of certain products. For example, the Federal Trade Commission issued the Care Labeling Rule. This rule requires that all clothing labels give clear and complete instructions for care and maintenance.

When reading labels and hangtags, you will find the brand name of the product and the name and address of its manufacturer. Look for information about materials and quality work used in the product, the size or quantity of the product, and how to use and care for it.

For food products, note the ingredients, nutritive values, grade and quality levels, expiration dates, and storage instructions. Drugs and cosmetics will be labeled with ingredients, directions for use, and cautions against misuse. Home appliances should include labels and owners manuals with care and operating instructions and energy efficiency ratings. Laundry supplies, household cleaning agents, pesticides, and herbicides all should be labeled with directions for use and safe disposal. They should contain cautions or warnings against hazards of misuse.

Jack Klasey

6-10
This label gives useful product information.

Obviously, the information on labels and hangtags and in owner manuals will depend on the product. Many products will carry label information required by law. Food packages, for example, must carry a list of ingredients, the name and address of the manufacturer, quantity by weight, number of servings, and specific nutritional information. Clothing and textile products must be labeled with fiber content, identification of the manufacturer and country of origin, plus detailed care instructions. Hazardous products must carry warning labels. New cars must be labeled with certain price information. In addition, many manufacturers voluntarily provide useful information on labels, such as recipes and serving suggestions on food packages. Regardless of the product you are buying, its label can be an important source of practical, reliable information.

Testing and Rating Services

The testing and rating of consumer goods and services provides valuable guides for shopping. Consumers can use testing and rating information to evaluate features and compare different models and brands of products and services. This helps consumers make purchase decisions that will best meet their needs. Two common forms of testing and rating results are seals of approval or certification and ratings in consumer publications.

Seals usually rate products as "certified," "approved," "tested," or "commended." The same organizations that test products issue seals for the products that meet their standards. A common seal is shown and explained in 6-11. Green marketing seals, indicating products' environmental impacts, are described in Chapter 18.

Consumer Reports and *Consumers Research Magazine* carry ratings of tested products and services. Both of these provide comparative buying information to help consumers shop wisely. To use testing and rating information from these and other sources wisely, you need answers to the following questions:

Who Sponsored or Conducted the Testing?

Consider the qualifications, interests, and intentions of the testing organization. Can you expect the ratings to be honest and objective, or are they designed to help promote the product?

What Features and Performance Standards Were Tested?

Be sure features and performance standards that are most important to you are included in the testing and rating.

Under What Conditions Were Tests Run, and What Test Methods Were Used?

Check to see if products were tested for the type of use you will give them. For example, suppose TV reception was tested under ideal laboratory conditions and you live where there is a lot of interference. The test results may not be the best guide for you.

What Do the Test Results Mean?

Read explanations of seals and ratings carefully to find out exactly what they mean.

When Were Products Tested and Which Models Were Included?

Products tested one year could improve or become less desirable the next year, particularly in product lines where research brings about frequent changes. If you use test results and ratings as a guide, be sure they include the actual models you are considering.

What Factors Are Important to You That Are Not Included in Testing?

Consider price, availability, credit terms, delivery, installation, and reputation of the seller. None of these will be covered by product testing and rating services. Smart shoppers will weigh all the important factors before buying.

Written Warranties

A written ***warranty*** guarantees that a product will meet certain performance and quality standards.

The Seal	Where It Is Found	What It Means
UL® Underwriters Laboratories, Inc.	On appliances, equipment, and materials that could be hazardous and on products used to detect or extinguish fires.	Products have passed original laboratory tests and periodic factory tests and examination in accordance with UL Standards for Safety.

6-11
This seal indicates that an appliance meets specific performance and safety standards.

The warranty provides for specific remedies if the product does not live up to stated promises. The basic types of written warranties are full and limited. According to law, a ***full warranty*** must provide the following:

- ❑ Free repair or replacement of defective products or parts.
- ❑ Repair or replacement within a reasonable time.
- ❑ No unreasonable demands on the customer as a condition of receiving repairs or replacement.
- ❑ Replacement if a number of attempts at repair fail.
- ❑ Transfer of coverage to a new owner if the product changes hands during the warranty period.

A ***limited warranty*** may require the customer to pay labor costs or handling charges. It may cover repairs only and not replacement. It may also require return of the product to the seller or authorized service center for warranty servicing.

Most warranties cover warranted products for a stated period of time, such as 90 days or one year. A product may carry a full warranty on certain parts and a limited warranty on other parts. Warranties do not protect against failure caused by customer misuse of a product. The law requires a warranty to clearly state the following:

- ❑ Whether it is full or limited.
- ❑ How coverage is limited (if it is not a full warranty).
- ❑ What it covers—the entire product or only certain characteristics or parts.
- ❑ What will be done if the product fails.
- ❑ How long coverage lasts.
- ❑ How to get warranty benefits with names, addresses, and details needed to request warranty action.
- ❑ What the buyer must do to obtain coverage.

In addition to the written warranty, most products carry unwritten implied warranties of merchantability and fitness. ***Implied merchantability*** means that a product is what it is called and does what its name implies. A toaster must toast bread; a heater must produce heat. The product must be in working order. ***Implied fitness*** means that a product must be fit for any performance or purpose promised by the seller. If a salesperson or hangtag suggests roller skates for outdoor use, they must be fit for outdoor skating. Implied warranties apply to the condition of a product at the point of sale. They cover defects that are present but may not be obvious at the time of purchase.

You may need a proof of purchase to receive warranty service, so be sure to keep the sales slip, warranty, and model number of the products you buy. To make the best use of a product warranty, read it carefully. Is it full or limited? Does it cover the entire product or only parts of the product? What performance and characteristics are guaranteed? Is the labor to repair the product included? Find out who is responsible for carrying out warranty promises. Also be sure you understand what you must do to receive warranty benefits. Warranties are a form of consumer protection. However, they protect you only if you do your part.

Salespersons

Good salespeople often can be one of your best sources of information on the products and services they sell. They should know how different brands and models compare and what features are most important. They should also know when new merchandise is expected, when sales are scheduled, and a host of other facts that can help you make sound buying decisions. Of course, not all salespeople are well informed, helpful, and conscientious. Their job is to sell the merchandise as well as to please the customer. Some do a better job than others.

Be fair and considerate with salespeople, especially in stores where you shop regularly. You are likely to get better service and more reliable information. For example, a salesperson who likes you may tell you of an upcoming sale, call you when new merchandise arrives, or give you a straight answer when you need an opinion about a product.

Making Shopping Decisions

Smart shopping depends on rational decision making. To be a smart shopper, you need well-defined goals and a clear view of your resources. Review the section on rational decision making in Chapter 5. Apply this process to shopping for goods and services. Then you can evaluate alternatives and make rational decisions when you shop.

A spending plan based on rational decisions works to your advantage both for routine shopping and big purchases. Spending plans need to fit into an overall budget tailored to your specific income and needs. This type of planning can help you avoid impulse buying and guide you in major decisions. A clear picture of your needs can also help you choose the best quality level for different purchases. See 6-12. Finally, planning can help you buy within price ranges you can afford. The case studies throughout the rest of this chapter point out the importance of planning purchases and making rational decisions when shopping.

You need a variety of shopping skills to carry you through the marketplace with confidence. Certain guides apply to shopping in general and others apply specifically to buying goods or products, shopping for services, and shopping at sales.

Best quality	Medium quality	Lower quality
Top of the line. Upper price range. The most and best features.	Medium price range. Standard features. Adequate standards for materials, design, workmanship, and performance.	Lowest price range. Very few features. Minimum standards for design, workmanship, and performance.
Buy when:	**Buy when:**	**Buy when:**
Top quality and performance are needed for your purpose. The item will be used a long time. You can afford the best and owning it is worth the cost.	Medium quality suits your purpose. Medium quality sells at the best price for your budget. The best is not necessary for the way you will use the product. Durability, practicality, and reasonable price are important. Extra features are not necessary.	Lower quality suits your purpose. The item will be used only occasionally or temporarily. The item will be outdated or outgrown soon.

6-12
The way you will use a product and your budget will determine what quality level to buy for different products.

General Shopping Tips

Whether you are shopping for goods or services at regular prices or on sale, here are some general shopping guides to help you get value for your dollars.

- Deal only with reputable, reliable businesses, sellers, service people, and professionals. Countless consumer problems arise each year as a result of trading with dishonest, disreputable sellers and being taken in by shady selling schemes. It pays to know who you are dealing with when you spend your money, particularly for major purchases.
- Compare products, services, and places to shop. Check prices, quality, performance, and anything else that is important to you for a specific purchase. Find out about the sellers operating policies concerning returns, exchanges, credit, and customer satisfaction. Check warranties, too, especially for products that are likely to need servicing.
- Consider the value of time and energy as well as money. For example, suppose the price of a product is lower in a shopping center than in a neighborhood store. The neighborhood store is just around the corner. The shopping center is 15 minutes away by car. Getting to the shopping center would take more time, energy, and gasoline. When you weigh these disadvantages against your savings, is it worth it? You will face many judgments like this one as you shop. You can save time and energy by planning and combining shopping trips. Try to make one trip to a store or shopping center rather than several.
- Do your homework before buying expensive goods and services. If you are unfamiliar with a product or service, take time to learn more about it before you shop. Basic knowledge of prices, ratings, and features of products and services can help you make informed decisions.
- Report unfair or dishonest business practices to appropriate organizations and authorities. Places to look for action or assistance, include Better Business Bureaus, chambers of commerce, the Federal Trade Commission, the Food and Drug Administration, or the post office. Consumer protection offices of local and state governments and the state attorney general's office can also help resolve customer-seller conflicts. In some cases, law enforcement agencies depend on the help of citizens to track down wrongdoers in the marketplace. By contacting the proper authorities, you can help put dishonest sellers out of business.
- Handle money with care whether you shop with cash or credit. When paying cash, keep receipts and sales slips for possible returns or exchanges. When using credit, be sure to keep track of purchases and limit total charges to an amount you can pay on time with ease. When paying by mail, send a check or money order, never cash. This is safer and it gives you a record of the payment. Take care to keep track of both cash and credit cards as you shop. Lost cash is gone and a

Shopping Solutions

Planning Is the Key

Sheri and John have been married six months. Random spending has been a drain on their income. They both tend to make snap buying decisions. They have never seriously discussed their goals and set up a buying plan.

They both want a long list of things for their new apartment including blankets, towels, lamps, pots and pans, pictures, and furniture. Each time John and Sheri walk through a store, they see something to buy.

In the first month or two of their marriage, Sheri and John bought randomly. They made some foolish purchases. They also bought items they could have postponed. Now they must do without some things they really need. Because of random spending, Sheri and John have an electric knife but no toaster. They have lots of nice sofa pillows but a cheap lumpy mattress for their bed. They also have furniture that doesn't go well together. Sheri bought a green flowered chair the same day John bought a blue plaid sofa.

As Sheri and John look closely at their finances and their apartment, they begin to see their mistakes. They decide to change their situation by reviewing their needs and setting goals. They plan key purchases for the year by deciding which items are most important. They also estimate the cost of each purchase. This plan serves as an overall guide to shopping and spending. Sheri and John find that financial planning helps them make sound shopping decisions.

Case Review

1. How can random spending create money problems?
2. How can well-established goals help people make better shopping decisions?
3. How might your goals for the next three to five years influence your shopping decisions?
4. It is easy to see the value of a spending plan for major purchases. How can an overall plan improve shopping skills for small purchases and routine spending?

lost credit card in the wrong hands can cost you even more. If you lose a credit card, report it to the issuer immediately by phone and follow up with a written notice.

- Deal fairly and honestly with others in the marketplace. Look to the guidelines in 6-13 as you come in contact with various businesses, salespeople, professionals, and other shoppers. You will get more respect and better service by being honest, courteous, and fair.

The Right of Refusal

You can be a winner in most of your shopping experiences. Simply exercise the "right of refusal" when sellers offer items you do not need, do not want, or cannot afford. As long as the economic system guarantees free economic choice, no one can make you buy what you do not need or want. You always have the ultimate right of refusal. Use this right to protect your financial interests.

On a larger scale, consumers need the right of refusal to maintain control of demand in the marketplace. Consumers have the power to strengthen the demand for what they buy and to weaken the demand for what they refuse. Thus, the economic system, as well as your own financial welfare, depends on the intelligent use of the power of refusal.

Shopping for Goods

Making the best selections from a wide variety of products is not always easy. Today, choices are almost unlimited. The average supermarket alone

Fairness Guide

With Salespeople	With Professionals
Show courtesy to salespeople and others who serve you in the marketplace. Wait your turn when stores are crowded and salespeople are busy. Avoid shopping just before closing time. Ask for salespeople who have been helpful in the past, and thank them for their help. Handle merchandise with care to avoid soiling or damaging it. Return merchandise to its proper place after you handle it. Inform salespeople if you come across damaged or broken products. Be as free with compliments for good service as you are with complaints for poor service.	Respect the expertise, training, and education a professional person offers. Understand that professionals are selling their time; do not waste it. Be on time for appointments or give plenty of notice if you must be late or cancel. Pay promptly for professional services unless you have made credit arrangements. Call during office hours except when emergencies require off-hour calling. Remember, in most cases, you are in partnership with the professionals who serve you. Working together is the best way to achieve mutual goals.
With Other Shoppers	**With Businesses**
Wait your turn when several shoppers want help at the same time. Avoid pushing, shoving, raising your voice, and blocking aisles or doorways. Control children, pets, and shopping carts. Respect the needs and belongings of other shoppers.	Let merchants and manufacturers know what you like or dislike about their products, services, and policies. Make necessary returns and exchanges promptly, particularly when merchandise is seasonal. Be businesslike about handling problems and registering complaints. Avoid damaging merchandise or making unfair returns, exchanges, or demands.

6-13
Fairness in the marketplace is a two-way street that both businesses and consumers travel.

carries over 15,000 items for sale. Imagine the number of products for sale in a large shopping mall!

When you buy merchandise, as opposed to services, you can inspect it before you buy. Look products over carefully. Read labels, hangtags, seals, instruction manuals, and warranties. Look for information about the price, quality, and performance features. Also consider any extra costs for the delivery, installation, upkeep, and servicing of goods. Be sure to find out what you are buying and the quality you are getting. See 6-14.

For certain goods, it may pay to buy in quantity. For example, soap at three bars for a dollar is a better buy than 40 cents each. When buying in large quantities, make sure the merchandise will keep. Only buy what you can conveniently store. Also be certain that you will use the entire amount. If you have to throw away part of your purchase, you will not have saved much money.

As you shop for goods, remember the options available to you. Compare different stores as well as products to find the best values. You may be able to save a lot of money by comparison shopping. For example, the cost of identical products can vary greatly from store to store. You also may choose to buy generic brand products rather than brand name. ***Generic products*** are items that do not carry brand names or trademarks. They come in plain packaging and usually sell for less than similar, brand name products.

In some cases, you can meet your needs with used instead of new products. For example, an apartment can be furnished with used furniture for a small fraction of the price you would pay for new. Secondhand stores, auctions, army surplus stores, garage sales, and classified ads all offer opportunities for buying used items in good condition.

To make shopping for goods easier, determine what characteristics and features are important to you in different products. When shopping for products with a variety of features, make a list of the features that are most important to you. Knowing what features, performance requirements, quality, and price range you want gives direction to your shopping. It will also help you evaluate quality and performance.

6-14
Being able to inspect products before buying is especially important for major purchases.

Shopping for Services

Buying services is different from buying goods. When you buy a product, you can see it, inspect it, try it on, or handle it. After using a product once, you can usually expect it to be the same each time you buy it.

When buying a service, you don't really know what you are getting until after you receive it. For the most part, you buy on faith. Therefore, it is important to check the reputation of any business or person who offers a service. Try to talk with former customers. Find out if they have been satisfied with the service they received.

Some services require special knowledge or skills. These services include dental and medical care, auto and household repairs, and legal and financial advice. When buying such services, carefully investigate the person's qualifications and reputation. Check out the person's education and training, experience, and membership in professional organizations. Choose only qualified professionals whom you can trust to do a good job. See 6-15.

Ask questions when you shop for services. Find out who performs the service, how long it takes, how much it costs, and what the price includes. For expensive services, such as auto repairs and home improvements, get several written estimates from different sources. Compare estimates carefully, reading all the details. Look for reasonable price estimates along with

The Service MASTER Company

6-15
When shopping for services it is important to investigate thoroughly and ask questions before buying.

assurance the job will be done right, on time, and with appropriate guarantees.

Also give a clear and complete description of the service you want. For example, when you get a haircut, describe the type of cut you want or bring a picture of the style. If you don't know what you want, ask for advice. Professionals who know their fields can give you valuable information.

Shopping at Sales

All of the smart shopping guides also apply to buying at sales. However, there are a few special tips for sale time. One important point to remember: do not let price reductions tempt you to buy what you do not want or will not use. For example, a $289 sewing machine on sale for $119 is no bargain if you don't sew. A $90 jacket on sale for $35 is no bargain if it doesn't fit. A half-price banana split is no bargain if you are on a diet.

When shopping at a sale, examine the sale merchandise carefully. Very often you cannot return or exchange sale items. If a product is marked "second," "irregular," or "as is," it probably is flawed in some way. Look for possible flaws and see if they will affect your use of the product.

Compare the sale prices to the original prices to see how much you are saving. If sale items are soiled or damaged, add to the sale price any cleaning or repair costs. For example, suppose a $150 white coat is marked down to $110 but is soiled and needs dry cleaning. Add the cost of dry cleaning to the sale price before figuring your bargain.

> *"Price, for all its importance, is only one of the terms of the bargain."*
>
> ***Walton Hamilton***

Before you buy a sale item, find out store policies on sales. Does the store allow refunds and exchanges on sale items? Some stores may not allow returns on sale items.

Try to plan your purchases to match the timing of sales. Seasonal sales usually offer the best buys. Midsummer is the best time to buy summer clothes and sporting goods at reduced prices. After Christmas, decorations, gift items, and toys go on sale. Most stores have holiday sales every year. Knowing when to expect price cuts on certain products and services can help you plan

Shopping Solutions

A Shopping List Saves the Day

Pamela is 16. She agrees to do the grocery shopping for her family since both of her parents have full-time jobs. When Pamela first assumes this responsibility, she often forgets important items, and she sometimes ends up with a number of foods she didn't intend to buy. The money she has to spend for food each week doesn't go as far as it did when her father did the shopping. Soon the family starts complaining. They say that Pamela spends too much money and doesn't buy the things everyone likes.

One day Pamela comes home with a dozen artichokes, but she forgets the milk and the meat. Pamela loves artichokes and they were on sale. Unfortunately, no one else in the family will touch one. The family makes such a fuss that Pamela agrees to pay for the artichokes with her own money which really bites into her budget.

Pamela decides there must be a better way. Her first step toward smarter shopping is to prepare a shopping list to help her remember all the things she needs. It should also help her control impulse spending. She will think twice before buying items that are not on her list.

Within a few weeks, Pamela is shopping in the supermarket like a pro. She knows what she wants and buys it. She now comes home with three bags of groceries for the same price she was paying for two. Pamela also notices that less food is wasted. The family is beginning to praise her shopping skills.

Pamela's shopping list is the main reason for her improved skills. She keeps her list in a handy place in the kitchen. When she is almost out of something, she adds that item to the list. Before going to the store, she checks the food pages of the local paper for advertised specials. She adds low-priced items to her list when they fit into her meal plans.

Once in the store, Pamela sticks to her list. She makes exceptions only when she finds:

- ❑ A good substitute for something on her list. For example, she might buy pork chops instead of chicken breasts when pork is a better buy.
- ❑ Foods selling at special prices. Pamela strays from her list for low prices only when she is sure the foods will fit her meal plans and family tastes.
- ❑ Nonperishable staples at low prices. Pamela knows she can save in the long run by buying staples such as canned foods, paper goods, or cleaning supplies at low prices and storing them until they are needed.
- ❑ Shopping with a list saves Pamela both time and money.

Case Review

1. What experience have you had shopping in a supermarket with or without a list?
2. How do you think a shopping list would help you make shopping decisions
   A. In a supermarket?
   B. For Christmas presents?
   C. At the drugstore?
   D. In a department store or shopping center?
3. How might the information on a shopping list differ for different types of purchases such as food, clothing, gifts, a car, or an apartment?

your purchases to get the best values for your dollars. Chart 6-16 gives a general monthly guide for sales shopping, but the schedule may vary from area to area and store to store. Check newspaper ads and store mailings to know what's on sale in your area.

Shopping Guide for Seasonal Sales

January	February	March
Watch for: postholiday sales preinventory sales January "white" sales Best buys: winter clothing coats, furs, bedding, linens furniture and floor coverings	Watch for: Lincoln's and Washington's birthday sales Valentine's Day specials Best buys: china, silverware, glassware rugs and floor coverings TVs and sound equipment sportswear and equipment furniture and home furnishings housewares used cars	Watch for: Spring and Easter promotionals Best buys: china and glassware garden supplies housewares laundry equipment
April	**May**	**June**
Best buys: fabrics lingerie and hosiery sleepwear ladies shoes spring cleaning, painting, and repair supplies	Watch for: Mother's Day sales Memorial Day specials Best buys: outdoor furniture luggage jewelry auto tires and accessories	Watch for: Father's Day sales bridal and graduation gift specials Best buys: floor coverings bedding lingerie and hosiery sleepwear men's and boys' clothing women's shoes
July	**August**	**September**
Watch for: 4th of July sales Best buys: fabric furniture furs summer clothes sportswear and equipment	Watch for: summer clearances back-to-school sales Best buys: sports equipment white goods furniture outdoor furniture and garden supplies furs	Watch for: back-to-school specials Best buys: outgoing year's car models auto accessories china and glassware fall fashions housewares
October	**November**	**December**
Watch for: Columbus Day specials Best buys: major appliances furniture women's coats fall/winter sportswear last of outgoing year's car models	Watch for: Election, Veterans Day, and Thanksgiving Day specials Best buys: shoes blankets white goods major appliances china and glassware holiday gifts and toys	Watch for: Holiday gift and toy promotions postholiday sales Best buys: used cars resort and cruise wear children's wear men's and boys' wear coats

Household International

6-16
This shopping calendar can help you time purchases to get the best sale prices.

Shopping Solutions

The Purpose Guides the Choice

Tony is captain of his high school tennis team. He hopes to go to college on a tennis scholarship. Tony's tennis racket cracked during practice yesterday, so he needs to replace it. Selecting a new racket is an important purchase for him.

Tony needs a racket with the right grip, weight, balance, and flexibility. He also wants a racket that will last a long time. Tony is willing to shop carefully and pay the price for a good racket. He knows exactly what features he wants.

After looking at rackets in several stores, Tony buys a top-of-the-line racket from a tennis pro. The pro checks the grip for Tony and strings the racket with just the right tension. The racket is expensive, but Tony knows he is getting his money's worth. He is paying for the best because he needs it for his level of the game.

Catina is 15. She wants to play tennis because some of her friends play. She needs a racket, but it doesn't have to be the best. Catina doesn't know if she will like the game or how much she will play. She doesn't want to spend a lot of money for a racket.

Catina goes to a reliable store that sells sporting goods. She asks to see an inexpensive racket that will be good enough for learning the game. She buys a medium quality racket for a reasonable price. The racket works very well for her.

Case Review

1. How do you think price is related to quality and features in a product?
2. What quality and price factors might influence your choice of a
   A. Winter coat?
   B. Computer?
   C. CD player?
   D. Suntan lotion?
   E. Musical instrument?
   F. Car?
3. What are some consequences of failing to consider how you will use a product when you make a buying choice?

Summary

Shopping skills make money go further in the marketplace. Smart shopping is a skill almost anyone can develop. It involves knowing about different places to shop and different types of sellers. For example, there are advantages and disadvantages to shopping in neighborhood stores, in shopping centers, and in downtown stores. Both retail stores and nonstore sellers, such as catalogs, television, and the Internet, offer places for consumers to buy goods and services and do some comparison shopping. Various types of sellers offer different types of merchandise, prices, and customer services.

Sellers use a variety of methods to encourage consumers to buy. Customers who understand selling methods can use them to their advantage. For example, advertising provides information of use to consumers. Buying incentives may offer unique opportunities to try new products at special prices. Sales and promotions offer price reductions. Credit offers a way to buy now and pay later. This can be helpful to consumers who keep it under firm control.

Consumers need reliable information on goods and services to make intelligent buying decisions. Key sources of information include advertisements, labels and hangtags, product testing services, and salespersons. Warranties are promises that a product will meet certain performance and quality standards. They can guide consumers both in the purchase of products and in later need for service and satisfaction. Other consumers can be an important source of information on products and services they have purchased. Collecting, evaluating, and using information as it applies to different purchases is part of smart shopping.

Smart shopping depends on rational decision making and on a personal spending plan. A variety of shopping skills is also important. For example, general shopping tips apply to all kinds of buying situations. Specific suggestions apply to buying products and others apply to buying services. Shopping at sales calls for another set of techniques to get the best bargains.

To Review

1. Name three common locations where you can buy goods and services.
2. Name four types of sellers.
3. What are some advantages and disadvantages of buying from a door-to-door seller?
4. Distinguish between shopping through television and shopping online. How do the two differ? What are some advantages and disadvantages of this type of shopping?
5. How do consumer cooperatives differ from retail stores and other nonstore sellers? Name one advantage and one disadvantage of joining a consumer cooperative.
6. What is the primary purpose of advertising?
7. Name and describe three advertising techniques.
8. Name three questions you should answer before using testing and rating information.
9. When you buy a product with a warranty, what information do you need to keep with the warranty?
10. Describe the major difference between buying products and buying services.

To Think Critically

1. Where do you do most of your shopping? Do you shop at different places for different types of goods, such as clothes, grooming supplies, sporting goods, snacks, and groceries? Why?
2. How can you use the selling methods of businesses to your own advantage? Give several examples.
3. How can a shopping list help you save money and time?
4. What sources of information have you found most helpful when buying goods and services? Why were they helpful?
5. How do you decide what to buy? How do needs, prices, and quality affect your shopping decisions?
6. How can well-established needs and goals help you make sound decisions as you shop?
7. Describe your most successful shopping experience. Describe your most disappointing shopping experience. Why was one successful and the other disappointing?

To Do

1. Look at the advertisements in a number of magazines and newspapers. How much useful information can you find among the ads? Which ads give little or no information but appeal to your emotions? Find five examples of informative ads and five that appeal primarily to the emotions.
2. List at least five products that you expect to buy in the near future. According to the monthly buying guide, what month of the year would you most likely find the best price for each item?
3. From your product list above, choose one that costs $100 or more. Make a list of the characteristics and features you want this product to have. Then check brand names and prices for this product at three or more stores. What differences do you find in quality and prices from one brand to another and from one store to the other?
4. Explore shopping possibilities online. Develop a list of guidelines to follow when shopping for products or services online.

Shopping skills are the keys to shopping smart.

UNIT

3

1/2 PRICE
Pyramid
Food Choices
PERDUE
BETTER FABRICS
MORE BODY

Routine Spending

Chapter 7
The Grocery Cart

Chapter 8
The Shirt on Your Back

Chapter 9
How You Look and Feel

As a consumer, you make decisions every day related to routine spending for food, clothing, and personal needs. Knowing where to find consumer information about products, services, government policies, and economic conditions can help you to make wise decisions.

A sizable share of income is spent on food in grocery stores and restaurants. Establishing a food budget and planning purchases will help you get more for your money.

Putting together a wardrobe that fits your lifestyle takes planning. Setting up a clothing budget, comparison shopping, judging quality, and having a sense of fashion can help you to get the most from your clothing dollars.

Good looks and good health involve using consumer skills to purchase grooming aids and cosmetics and choosing health care options. It also involves managing time and money to spend on fun, travel, and entertainment.

CHAPTER 7

1/2 PRICE
Washington Red or Golden Delicious Apples
99¢
Perdue. Bird-Watcher. Thermometer
OVEN STUFFER
PERDUE
FRESH
Whole Roaster
Pyramid
Food Choices
Ohio Valley Vegetable Soup
A PRODUCT OF THE FLORIDA SUNSHINE TREE

The Grocery Cart

nutrients
Recommended Dietary Allowances (RDA)
Dietary Guidelines for Americans
convenience foods
impulse spending
point-of-sale
universal product code (UPC)
standard of identity
unit price
open dates
pull date
freshness date
expiration date
pack date
inspection stamps
food grades

After studying this chapter, you will be able to

- ❑ identify nutritional needs and the best food sources of essential nutrients.
- ❑ plan nutritious, appetizing meals and snacks.
- ❑ establish a food budget based on individual needs and resources.
- ❑ evaluate food stores to determine where to shop for the best prices, selection, and quality.
- ❑ apply guidelines for buying specific foods.
- ❑ explain the use of food labels, unit pricing, open dating, and government grading.
- ❑ store different foods properly to maintain quality, flavor, and nutritive value and to ensure safety.
- ❑ list guidelines for choosing and eating at restaurants.

On average, families in the United States spend slightly over 13 percent of their income in food stores and restaurants. Low income families may spend as much as 40 percent and upper income families as little as 9 percent of total income. Regardless of the percentage, over a lifetime you will spend thousands of dollars feeding yourself and your family. It will help to learn the basics of smart food shopping early in life.

The food you eat affects the way you look, feel, and perform. Eating the right foods can help you stay healthier and live longer. Learning to plan nutritious meals and to shop for the best food values can have a positive effect on both your health and your budget.

Planning Nutritious Meals and Snacks

To plan nutritious meals and snacks, you need to be aware of the foods and nutrients your body needs. Then you can select nutritious foods with confidence.

Nutrients You Need

Nutrients are chemical substances found in foods. They furnish energy, build and maintain body tissues, and regulate body processes. You need six types of nutrients: proteins, fats, carbohydrates, vitamins, minerals, and water. Chart 7-1 lists the functions and sources of these key nutrients.

Fiber is also essential for proper nutrition. It is the indigestible or partially indigestible part of foods you eat. It helps move food and digestive byproducts through the large intestine and promotes healthy digestion. Whole grains, fruits, and vegetables are particularly good sources of fiber.

The ***Recommended Dietary Allowances (RDA)*** can help you decide the amount of each nutrient you need each day. These guidelines are set by the Food and Nutrition Board of the National Academy of Sciences. The RDA contains detailed dietary recommendations for people of different sexes, ages, and weights.

The Food Guide Pyramid

The RDA can be used to plan a well-balanced diet, but few people want to use this complex guide. Luckily, there is an easier way. The Department of Agriculture's Food Guide Pyramid is a simple guide to proper nutrition, 7-2. It can be used by anyone who is not on a special diet for medical reasons. You should eat the suggested number of servings from each group in the Pyramid and use fats, oils, and sweets sparingly. This is a simple way to get all the nutrients your body needs each day.

> ***"The history of the world is the record of man in quest of his daily bread and butter."***
>
> ***Hendrik Willem Van Loon***

The Pyramid includes five basic food groups:

- ❑ Bread, cereal, rice, and pasta.
- ❑ Vegetables.
- ❑ Fruits.
- ❑ Milk, yogurt, and cheese.
- ❑ Meat, poultry, fish, dry beans, eggs, and nuts.

You can combine items from several groups of the Pyramid into one tempting meal, 7-3.

The Bread, Cereal, Rice, and Pasta Group

Whole grain and enriched breads, hot and cold cereals, rice, crackers, pancakes, and pastas are among the many foods in this group. The chief nutrients in these foods are carbohydrates, B-vitamins, and iron. Carbohydrates are the body's main source of energy. Whole grain products also provide needed fiber. Six to eleven servings each day are recommended from this group.

The Vegetable Group

Foods in this group are a major source of vitamins A and C. They also provide other vitamins, minerals, and fiber. You need 3 to 5 servings from the vegetable group each day. For appetite appeal and nutrition, eat a variety of vegetables.

The Fruit Group

This group includes fresh, canned, frozen, and dried fruits and fruit juices. They are important lowfat sources of vitamins, minerals, and fiber. Citrus fruits are particularly rich sources of vitamin C. You need 2 to 4 servings from this group each day.

7-1
A well-balanced diet provides the body with the six types of nutrients: vitamins, proteins, fats, carbohydrates, minerals, and water.

Key Nutrients

Nutrient	Functions	Sources
Vitamins **Vitamin A**	Helps keep skin clear and smooth. Helps keep mucous membranes healthy. Helps prevent night blindness. Helps promote growth.	Liver, egg yolk, dark green and yellow fruits and vegetables, butter, whole milk, cream, fortified margarine, ice cream, cheddar-type cheese.
Thiamin (Vitamin B-1)	Helps promote normal appetite and digestion. Helps keep nervous system healthy. Helps body release energy from food.	Pork, other meats, poultry, fish, eggs, enriched or whole grain breads and cereals, dried beans, brewer's yeast.
Riboflavin (Vitamin B-2)	Helps cells use oxygen. Helps keep skin, tongue, and lips normal. Helps prevent scaly, greasy areas around mouth and nose. Aids digestion.	Milk, all kind of cheese, ice cream, liver, other meats, fish, poultry, eggs, dark leafy green vegetables.
Niacin (a B-vitamin)	Helps keep nervous system healthy. Helps keep skin, mouth, tongue, and digestive tract healthy. Helps cells use other nutrients.	Meat, fish, poultry, milk, enriched or whole grain breads and cereals, peanuts, peanut butter, dried beans and peas.
Vitamin C	Helps wound heal and broken bones mend. Helps body fight infection. Helps make cementing materials that hold body cells together.	Citrus fruits, strawberries, cantaloupe, broccoli, green peppers, raw cabbage, tomatoes, green leafy vegetables, potatoes and sweet potatoes cooked in the skin.
Vitamin D	Helps build strong bones and teeth. Helps maintain bone density.	Fortified milk, butter and margarine, fish liver oils, liver, sardines, tuna, egg yolk, and the sun.
Vitamin E	Acts as an antioxidant although exact functions are not known.	Liver and other variety meats, eggs, leafy green vegetables, whole grain cereals, salad oils, shortenings, and other fats and oils.
Vitamin K	Helps blood clot.	Organ meats, leafy green vegetables, cauliflower, other vegetables, egg yolk.

(Continued)

Key Nutrients (Continued)

Nutrient	Functions	Sources
Protein	Builds and repairs tissues. Helps make antibodies, enzymes, hormones, and some vitamins. Regulates fluid balance in the cells. Regulates many body processes. Supplies energy, when needed.	High quality proteins: Meat, poultry, fish, eggs, milk and other dairy products, peanuts, peanut butter, lentils. Low quality proteins: Cereals, grains, vegetables.
Fat	Supplies energy. Carries fat-soluble vitamins. Protects vital organs. Insulates the body from shock and temperature changes. Adds flavor to foods.	Butter, margarine, cream, cheese, marbling in meats, nuts, whole milk, olives, chocolate, egg yolks, bacon, salad oils, and dressings.
Carbohydrate	Supplies energy. Provides bulk and fiber in the form of cellulose (needed for good digestion). Helps the body digest fats efficiently.	Sugar: Honey, jam, jelly, sugar, molasses. Fiber: Fresh fruits and vegetables, whole grain cereals, and breads. Starch: Breads, cereals, corn, peas, beans, potatoes, pasta.
Minerals **Calcium**	Helps build bones and teeth. Helps blood clot. Helps muscles and nerves function properly. Helps regulate the use of other minerals in the body.	Milk, cheese, other dairy products, leafy green vegetables and fish eaten with the bones.
Phosphorous	Helps build strong bones and teeth. Helps regulate many body processes. Aids metabolism.	Protein and calcium food sources.
Iron	Combines with protein to make hemoglobin. Helps cells use oxygen. Aids metabolism.	Liver, lean meats, egg yolk, dried beans and peas, leafy green vegetables, dried fruits, enriched and whole grain breads and cereals.
Water	Is a basic part of blood and tissue fluid. Helps carry nutrients to cells. Helps carry waste products from cells. Helps control body temperature.	Water, beverages, soups, and most foods.

7-1
(Continued)

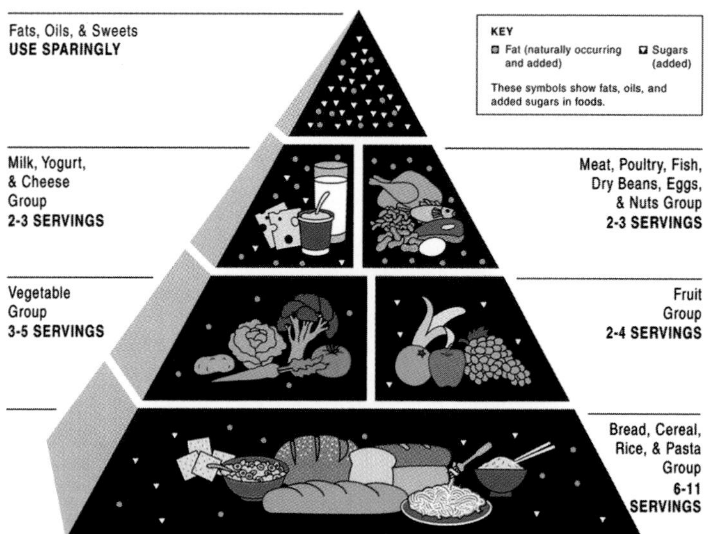

7-2
The Food Guide Pyramid makes it simple to choose the nutrients you need each day.

7-3
Eating well-balanced meals and nutritious snacks is a basic good health practice.

The Milk, Yogurt, and Cheese Group

Milk and milk products provide calcium, riboflavin, phosphorus, protein, and many other nutrients. If milk has been fortified, it is a major source of vitamin D. Choosing lowfat dairy foods will give you the recommended nutrients with fewer calories.

Calcium is the most important nutrient found in this food group. Everyone needs calcium for healthy bones and teeth. The recommended number of daily servings from this group is 2 for children and adults. Teens, young adults, and pregnant or nursing women need 3 servings from this group each day.

The Meat, Poultry, Fish, Dry Beans, Eggs, and Nuts Group

Beef, pork, veal, lamb, poultry, fish, seafood, dry beans, eggs, and nuts belong to this group. All of these foods provide the same important nutrient—protein. Protein is needed for the growth and repair of body tissues. Foods in this group also provide other important vitamins and minerals, including B-vitamins and iron.

The body needs 2 or more servings from this group daily. One serving equals 2 to 3 ounces of lean, boneless, cooked meat, poultry, or fish. Vegetarians should take special care to include dry beans, legumes, nuts, and other sources of protein in the diet.

Fats, Oils, and Sweets

Candy, salad dressings, butter, margarine, jellies, syrups, and soft drinks are some of the foods that do not fit into the basic five groups. They are made from fats, oils, sugars, and other food substances that provide energy but little else. These foods do, however, complement other foods and add flavor and variety to meals. For example, most people like syrup with pancakes, butter on toast, and dressing on salads. Since fats, oils, and sugars are high in calories and low in nutritive value, it is recommended that they be used sparingly.

Dietary Guidelines for Americans

In 1990, the U. S. Department of Agriculture developed the ***Dietary Guidelines for Americans.*** These guidelines offer seven suggestions for healthy eating, 7-4.

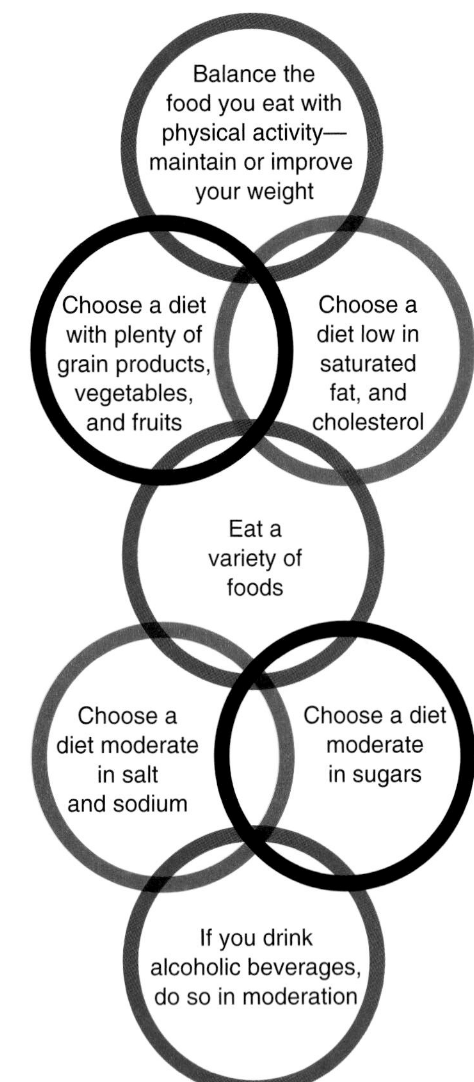

7-4
These easy to follow guidelines will lead to a well-balanced diet.

Eat a variety of foods.

Choose an assortment of foods from each of the five groups pictured in the pyramid. For good health, you need over 40 different nutrients. No single food can provide all the nutrients in the amounts you need. For a well-balanced diet, you need a variety of foods.

Balance the food you eat with physical activity—maintain or improve your weight.

Find out the recommended weight for your height, body type, sex, and activity level. Strive to reach and maintain that weight through proper eating habits and exercise. Remember that a "healthy" weight depends on how much of your weight is fat, where in your body the fat is located, and whether you have weight-related medical problems.

Choose a diet low in fat, saturated fat, and cholesterol.

Use fats and oils sparingly. Select lean meats, fish, and poultry without skin. Eat lowfat dairy products. Nutrition information labels can help you find lowfat, low-cholesterol foods. See 7-5.

Choose a diet with plenty of grain products, vegetables, and fruits.

All of these foods provide essential nutrients and fiber. Look for at least one good source of vitamin C each day and a good source of vitamin A every other day.

Choose a diet moderate in sugars.

Sweets generally supply calories but few nutrients. They sometimes are called "empty calories." Foods containing sugars should be eaten sparingly, particularly by anyone concerned with weight control.

Fat Facts on Food Labels

fat free—contains less than 0.5 gram of fat per serving
lean—contains less than 4 grams of saturated fat and less than 95 milligrams of cholesterol per serving
extra lean—contains less than 5 grams total fat with less than 2 grams saturated and less than 95 milligrams of cholesterol per serving
light or lite—contains one-third fewer calories or half the fat contained in a regular version of the same product
low calorie—contains 40 calories or less per serving
low fat—contains 3 grams or less of total fat per serving
low saturated fat—contains 1 gram or less of saturated fat per serving
low cholesterol—contains less than 20 milligrams of fat per serving and 2 grams or less of saturated fat per serving
reduced or less fat—contains at least 25 percent less fat and 2 grams or less of saturated fat per serving than that contained in a regular version of the same product

7-5
This chart defines the terms used in fat fact labeling.

Choose a diet moderate in salt and sodium.

Salt is a primary source of sodium in your diet. It is also present in many food additives, condiments, and seasonings. You may be able to reduce the risk of high blood pressure by reducing salt intake and limiting foods containing salt and sodium.

If you drink alcoholic beverages, do so in moderation.

The use of alcohol is associated with several health problems, accidents, and addiction.

In addition to proper eating habits, you can improve your physical and emotional health with less stress, more fun, enough sleep, plenty of exercise, and routine medical checkups.

Before You Shop for Food

Some knowledge of the factors that affect food prices can help you stretch food dollars. It can help you anticipate price trends and plan ahead to take full advantage of good buys.

A food budget can also be an important shopping guide. It helps you remember what you need to buy and prevents impulse buying and overspending. It is easy to buy too much in a supermarket.

Finally, a plan for meals and snacks with some ideas for leftovers can make you a better shopper. It gives direction to your choices and reduces waste and costly mistakes.

Factors Affecting Food Prices

Basically, the food price story is a lesson in economics. It begins and ends with supply and demand. When supply of food is greater than demand, prices fall. When demand is greater than supply, prices rise. Rising prices tend to speed up production and increase supply, thus lowering demand. Falling prices tend to slow production and decrease supply, thus increasing demand. Prices tend to go up and down until a price equilibrium is reached. That occurs when supply and demand for a given product at a given price are in balance.

A look at the supply and demand for beef illustrates the relationship between supply, demand, and prices. Suppose the supply of sirloin steak at $3.00 per pound is met by a demand for sirloin steak at $3.00 per pound. If the supply at that price becomes greater than the demand, prices will fall. They will continue to fall until the low prices encourage more consumers to buy more sirloin. Eventually this increasing demand will meet the supply. If the demand increases so much that it becomes larger than the supply, steak prices will rise. They will continue to rise until the high prices encourage producers to increase the supply. Eventually the increasing supply will meet the demand.

Now let's examine some issues that might affect supply and demand. Following is a list of several factors that would affect the price of sirloin.

- *Increased grain exports reduce the supply of grain in the United States.* This increases the price of grain for cattle producers, 7-6. High grain prices increase the price of feed and the cost of raising cattle. To cover increased costs, cattle producers hold out for higher prices when they bring cattle to market. Ultimately, the price consumers must pay for sirloin increases.
- *Flooding in cattle states reduces crop production and increases feed prices for livestock.* This increases the cattle producers' costs and may reduce the supply of cattle, 7-7. With increased production costs and limited supplies, the price consumers pay for sirloin rises.
- *Cattle producers refuse to bring beef to market because they feel the price is too low.* This boycott lowers the supply of sirloin and increases the price of existing supplies. A meat packers' strike also reduces the supply of sirloin and increases its price. If the strike is settled by higher wages, another hike in the price of sirloin would occur to cover increased labor costs.

7-6
Heavy exports of wheat and corn tend to reduce supplies for domestic use. This in turn increases the cost of grain and of feeding cattle.

USDA

7-7
Flooding can severely damage crops and reduce production, driving up prices for all types of food.

- *Nutritionists praise the value of poultry and fish over red meat.* This lowers the demand for sirloin and its price will fall. The same news is likely to bring about a rise in the price of poultry and fish. Demand for these foods might increase with nutritional awareness.

- *Consumers boycott beef.* This decreases the demand for sirloin. As a result, the price will eventually fall. But if demand continues to drop so producers can't make a profit, supply will decrease, too. Then, when the boycott ends, demand will be high and supply will be low. Prices will be high until the supply catches up with the demand.
- *The price of poultry decreases.* A reduction in the price of poultry would also affect the price of sirloin. With lower poultry prices, a portion of the consumer demand for sirloin would shift to poultry. Lower demand would cause the price of sirloin to fall.
- *The minimum wage is increased.* An increased minimum wage would increase the cost of raising, butchering, and delivering sirloin to consumers. The price of sirloin, and most other products, would go up to cover increased labor costs.
- *Increases in personal income tax reduce the amount of money consumers have to spend for food.* The demand for sirloin would drop and eventually its price would fall as well. Reducing the price of sirloin would bring the demand and supply of sirloin into balance.
- *Personal income tax is reduced.* Reducing personal income tax increases the amount of money consumers have to spend. This could increase the demand for sirloin and its price would rise. Prices would remain higher until the supply of sirloin meets the demand.

The factors that affect the supply and demand for food include weather conditions, transportation and labor costs, and a host of other things. The price of farmland and machinery is also a major factor in the ultimate price you pay for food, 7-8. By reading newspapers and keeping up with current events, you can anticipate changes in supply and demand. When you understand how prices respond to supply and demand, you can often anticipate changes in food prices. You can often find out which food prices will change in local food stores and when you can get the best buys.

Establishing a Food Budget

Individuals and families spend different amounts for food. How much

7-8
The costs of labor, farmland, and machinery are reflected in the price of food and almost all other products.

you spend depends on your income, living expenses, food needs, and personal preferences. Generally, higher income families spend a relatively small portion of total income for food—around 10 to 15 percent. Low income families sometimes spend as much as 30 to 40 percent of income for food.

When planning a food budget, consider nutritional needs, resources, and preferences. To determine a reasonable amount of money to allow for food, answer the questions below.

- *Who eats in your household?* The amount of food you need depends on the number of family members, their ages, and their activities. For example, a family of four with two athletic teenage boys may eat twice as much as a family of four with two toddlers.
- *What special dietary needs must be met?* Weight control, infant feeding, illness, pregnancy, and special diets for medical reasons influence food choices and costs. Consider special needs in your family when making a food budget.
- *What personal and family tastes and preferences will affect food choices?* Eating habits, cultural or ethnic traditions, and food likes and dislikes all need to be considered when planning menus and shopping for food. Depending on your needs and where you live, special foods may be hard to find and expensive.
- *How much do you entertain and eat away from home?* The type and amount of entertaining you do will affect the amount you spend for food. Eating away from home may cut grocery store bills, but it will probably increase overall food spending. Meals away from home almost always cost more than similar meals prepared at home.
- *Where do you normally shop?* Food prices vary from store to store. As a rule, small neighborhood stores and convenience marts have a low sales volume and must pay relatively high prices for the foods they sell. Therefore, they charge higher prices than large supermarkets. Large markets and chain stores buy in large volume because they have high-volume sales. This means the larger stores can charge lower prices and still make a reasonable profit. It pays to compare prices at several stores over a period of time to find out which stores offer the best values.
- *How skilled are you at food shopping and preparation?* Experienced, skilled shoppers usually get far more from food dollars than uninformed, inexperienced shoppers. Consumers who have the time and skill to prepare foods at home can use these resources to save money. Consumers with little time and skill for food shopping and preparation will probably spend more money feeding their families. These consumers are likely to use more ***convenience foods,*** which are partially prepared or ready-to-eat foods. These foods tend to be expensive.

Since food is a flexible expense, you can often adjust the amount you spend on food to the amount of money available. You can eat lobster, go to your favorite restaurant, or throw a party when your pockets are full. You can stay home and eat canned tuna or tacos when you need money for car repairs, medical bills, or other pressing expenses.

Before you go to the store, plan your food purchases. Shop with a grocery list and a set amount of money in mind. Try to keep track of what you actually spend each week. If your spending exceeds the amount you planned without a good reason, you will need to adjust your food choices and control impulse buys.

Planning Food Purchases

Planning what to buy before shopping helps you get what you want and avoid costly impulse spending. ***Impulse spending*** refers to unplanned or "spur of the moment" purchases. Experienced shoppers may plan meals mentally. Beginners usually need to sketch weekly menus and snack plans on paper. All shoppers will do better with a written shopping list. Here are some tips for effective planning.

- ❑ Check food pages and ads in local papers for prices, specials, and menu ideas that use foods that are in season or on sale.
- ❑ Outline meal, snack, and left-over plans for the week.
- ❑ Refer to cookbooks for ideas and ingredients you will need.
- ❑ Keep a running shopping list. Add items as you run short. Include foods you need for planned meals and specials you want to buy.
- ❑ Clip coupons from newspapers, magazines, food pages, and stores. Use them to save on products you intend to buy.

All of this planning is designed to guide you purposefully through the store. It is not meant to be constraining. When you come across good buys that are not on your list, don't be afraid to revise your plans on the spot. Substitute beef for pork when beef is cheaper. Buy pears instead of the apples you planned if the pears look better. Buy a new product you have been wanting to try if the price is right.

When You Shop

Knowing how to shop for food can help stretch food dollars. With a little knowledge, an alert shopper can buy three bags of groceries for the same amount an uninformed or careless shopper spends for one bag.

There are many sources of information that lead to values and quality in food stores. Knowing how to use this information can help you make wise choices and control spending. Point-of-sale information is available in stores. Newspaper pages and ads, nutrition labels, cookbooks, and food magazines all provide information you can use when planning meals for your family.

The Food Store

Prices, selection, and quality of foods, as well as customer services, vary from store to store. Finding grocery stores with good buys may take a little comparison shopping. Answering the questions in 7-9 can help you compare places to shop for food.

After trying a number of food stores, differences in quality and selection may become obvious to you. You may realize that one store carries better quality meats than another. Still another store may have a better selection of fresh fruits and vegetables. Therefore, you may decide to shop at certain stores for certain items. If your time is limited, you may choose to do most of your shopping in a supermarket that features many departments in one store. See 7-10. In some regions, farmers' markets and seasonal roadside stands are popular, 7-11. Shopping around and reading food ads can help you choose places to shop.

Generally speaking, the fewer times you shop, the less money you spend. Going into a food store to buy one or two items may tempt you to

Choosing Where to Shop for Groceries

1. Do regular food prices and specials compare favorably with prices and specials at other stores?
2. Are fresh foods, such as dairy products, meats, fish, poultry, produce, bakery products, and deli foods, delivered or prepared daily?
   Do they appear fresh, clean, and wholesome?
3. Is the frozen food section kept well below freezing?
4. Does the overall selection of foods and groceries suit your needs and preferences?
5. Is it easy to find the foods that you want?
   Are staples usually in stock?
6. Are there convenient stores within the store, such as a delicatessen, bakery, pharmacy, newsstand, or film-processing center?
7. Are employees generally helpful, knowledgeable, and pleasant?
8. Does the store offer the services you want, such as check cashing, an ATM for cash cards, credit, deliveries, recycling, coupon exchanges, unit pricing, open dating of perishables, and express checkout?
9. Does the store follow fair policies, such as rain checks for specials that run out, replacements or refunds for purchases that are not satisfactory?
10. Is the store clean, attractive, and well mainatined?
11. Is the store conveniently located and open during the hours you want to shop?
12. Is the overall atmosphere inviting and acceptable to you?

7-9
This questionnaire can help you choose a reliable store to shop for groceries.

Piggly Wiggly

7-10
This store offers a flower shop, deli, and fish market as well as many sections all under one roof.

7-11
Farmers' markets generally offer a fine selection of fresh seasonal fruits and vegetables.

buy many more. To save both time and money, try to make one major food marketing trip a week. It is best to do your weekly shopping at a time when you can go alone and when you are not hungry. You will probably save even more money.

For the bulk of your food buying, it is a good idea to shop in the same two or three stores most of the time. You will get to know the store and stock well enough to find what you want quickly. You can compare prices of items from week to week. The store employees will get to know you. They may be more likely to make a special effort to keep you a satisfied customer.

When shopping, don't be afraid to ask for what you want and to return what isn't satisfactory. For example, if a meat cut you want isn't in the meat case, ask to have it cut for you. If fresh tomatoes are packaged in groups of six and you only need one or two, ask to have the package opened. If you arrive home from the grocery store with sour milk or stale bread, take it back for credit or exchange. Since food stores want your business, they will usually try to keep you satisfied. You'll be a welcomed customer wherever you shop when you follow the guidelines outlined in 7-12.

Point-of-Sale Shopping Aids

As you shop, look for aids that can save you time and money and help you make appropriate selections. These are called ***point-of-sale*** shopping aids. In-store information to assist consumers includes the universal product code, generic sections, food labels, unit pricing, open dating, and government inspection and grading information. Each of these offers advantages to the consumers who understand how to use them.

Universal Product Code

The ***universal product code,*** or ***UPC,*** is part of a computer checkout system used in many stores today. The UPC is designed to save time and labor costs. It shortens checkout lines and may reduce grocery prices since it cuts costs for retailers. As you shop, you will see the UPC symbol. It is the series of black and white lines, bars, and numbers that appears on products and items for sale in stores. See 7-13.

Supermarket Shopping Code

1. Handle carts with care to avoid bumping into other shoppers and displays.
2. Keep aisles clear.
3. Avoid unnecessary handling of fresh fruits and vegetables.
4. Notify management of accidental spills and breakage so they may be properly cleaned up.
5. Complete shopping before entering a checkout line.
6. Follow posted express line rules.
7. Present cents off coupons for credit only for the items actually purchased.
8. Have cash, check, I.D. card, and coupons ready when entering the checkout line to avoid delays and inconvenience to other customers.
9. Return bottles and plastics for recycling to designated areas.
10. After placing bags in the car, return grocery carts to the store or designated area for empty carts.

7-12
Simple courtesy helps take the hassle out of grocery shopping.

7-13
Most supermarkets use UPC symbols to check out grocery items by computer.

In stores that are equipped to use the UPC, the checkout clerk passes each item over a computer scanner. From the UPC symbol, the computer identifies the name and size of the item and records the information in a computer terminal. Then the computer transmits the price to the cash register. The price and description of the item are printed on the customer's receipt.

The UPC speeds up the checkout process and reduces the chance of errors by checkout clerks. It also helps stores keep more accurate inventories. Store managers can easily tell which products sell best and determine when they need to reorder.

This computer checkout system eliminates the need to mark the price on every item. Instead, prices appear on the shelves where items are displayed. A change in the price of a product can simply be entered into the computer. This reduces labor costs. By reducing costs and making food stores more efficient, the UPC should help to hold down food prices.

For consumers, the main drawback to the UPC is the difficulty in comparing prices both in the store and from week to week. For example, if you buy peanut butter this week and again in two or three weeks, it will be difficult to compare the prices when the item itself is not marked. As a result, you may not be aware of price changes. It is also harder to compare the price of fresh, frozen, and canned items in different sections of the store when prices only appear on the shelves. Finally, it may be difficult to read the prices on the highest and lowest shelves in the store.

Generic Products

Generic products come in plain packages without pictures or brand names. A generic label lists the name of the product, ingredients, net weight or contents, name and address of the manufacturer or packer, and nutrition facts.

These products cost less than national and store brands because less money is spent on packaging and advertising. However, generic products may be of lower quality. For example, generic paper products may be lighter in weight and less absorbent than brand name paper products. Generic foods are just as wholesome and nutritious as brand name foods, but they may be irregular in appearance or less flavorful. Canned fruits, for instance, may have uneven sizes and shapes.

In deciding whether generic products will meet your needs, compare products and think about how you are going to use them. If you like the taste of generic green beans but not their appearance, you may want to use them in a casserole where appearance is less important. When serving plain green beans, you may decide to use a higher quality national or store brand.

Food Labels

Food labels tell you exactly what you are buying. Some information on food labels is required by law. Other information, such as cooking directions and recipe ideas, is given voluntarily by food manufacturers to help consumers use and enjoy their products. Following is the information required by law on every food label:

- The common name of the food and its form (whole, chopped, diced, etc.).
- The net contents or net weight.
- The name and address of the manufacturer, packer, or distributor.

A list of the ingredients must also be included in descending order of amounts present. For example, a listing for canned tomato sauce may read, "Ingredients: tomatoes, salt, dextrose, spices, onion powder, and garlic powder." The tomatoes are present in the largest amount by weight and garlic powder in the least amount by weight. Any additives used in the food must be listed and the word "artificial" must be stated if flavors are artificial.

A number of common food products are made according to a ***standard of identity*** set by the FDA. These foods contain ingredients in preset amounts. They have standard names, such as ice cream, ketchup, and mayonnaise. In the past, standardized foods did not have to carry a list of ingredients. Since 1993, all ingredients in these foods must be listed.

Most food products are required to carry a label. This label must include certain information listed in a certain order. See 7-14. The nutrition facts panel must list:

- Serving size in both household and metric measures.
- Servings per container.
- Calories per serving and calories from fat.
- Percent of Daily Values in grams or milligrams for:
  - Total fat and saturated fat.
  - Cholesterol.
  - Sodium.
  - Total carbohydrate including dietary fiber and sugars.
  - Protein.
  - Percentages of Daily Values for vitamin A, vitamin C, calcium, and iron per serving. Amounts of other vitamins and minerals may also be listed.

Unit Pricing

Consumers can use unit pricing in comparing similar items to find the best buy. The ***unit price*** of a product is based on the cost per unit, weight, or measure. A product's unit price is usually listed on the shelf label where the product is displayed.

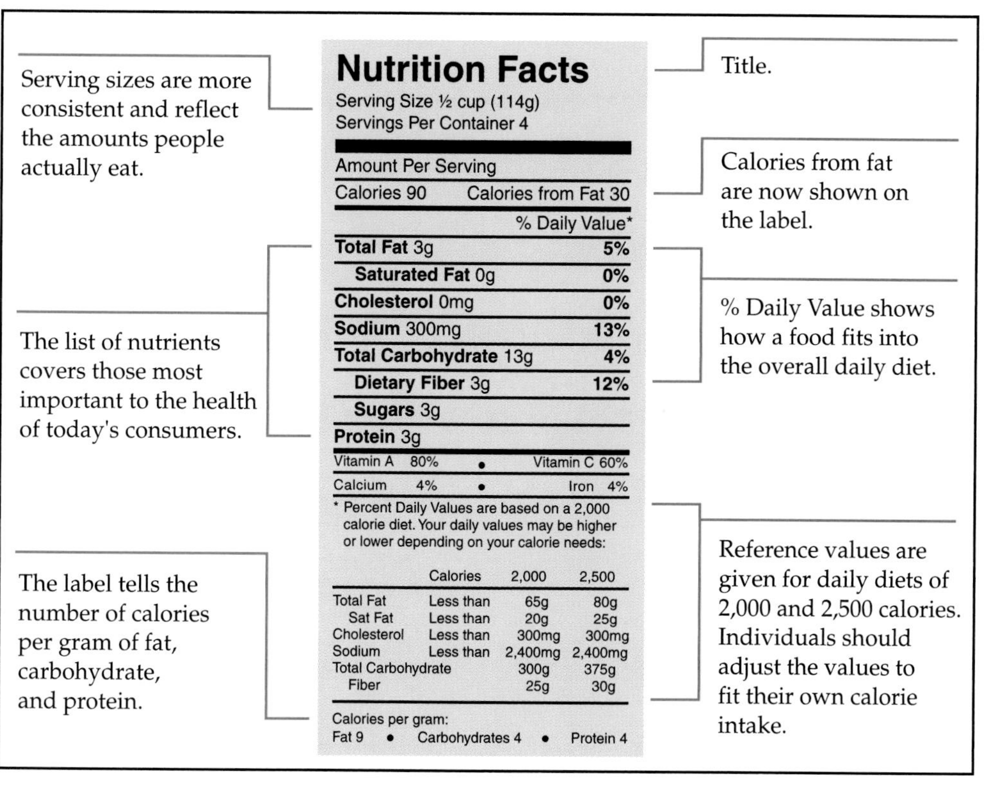

7-14
This format is required for nutrition labels. The diagram shows the types of information labels carry.

This type of pricing lets you compare food prices at a glance. To make use of unit pricing when shopping, remember to:

- Compare the price per unit of a product to different brands and sizes of the same product.
- Compare the price per unit of different forms of a product. For example, compare the price of canned corn to frozen corn.
- Compare the price per unit of a product to different brands and sizes of similar products. For example, compare the price of canned peaches, pears, and pineapple to find the best buy in canned fruit.
- Consider personal preferences for quality, flavor, convenience, and container size as well as price.
- Determine how much more you pay when you choose not to buy the item with the lowest unit price. For example, suppose you buy a 16-ounce can of your favorite sliced peaches at 4.6 cents per ounce when another brand is selling at 4.2 cents per ounce. If you multiply the .4 cents per ounce difference by the total 16 ounces, you will find that your preference is costing you 6.4 cents.

Illustration 7-15 shows a comparison of different sizes of grape juice. The unit prices tell you the cost per ounce of grape juice in a small jar is 4.63 cents. The cost per ounce of juice in a larger jar is 4.05 cents. The larger size jar is the best buy.

Open Dating

Open dating helps consumers select fresh and wholesome foods. ***Open dates*** indicate when the foods should be used for best quality, flavor, and nutritive value. Many food manufacturers date perishable and semi-perishable foods.

The dates on food items most often refer to the pull or sell date. The ***pull date*** is the last day a product should be sold. This date allows some time for safe home use and storage. For example, if a milk carton is dated Jan. 15, you should be able to keep it refrigerated at home a few days beyond January 15. Dairy products, meats, and poultry are often stamped with pull dates.

Products may carry other dates. A ***freshness date*** is the last day you can expect a product to be of peak quality. This date usually appears on bakery products, such as breads, rolls, doughnuts, and cakes. Sometimes these foods are sold at reduced prices after they pass the freshness date. Foods are safe to eat for a few days beyond their freshness date, but they will not be at peak quality.

Other food items may be stamped with an expiration date or a pack date. An ***expiration date*** refers to the last day a product should be used. Baby formula and yeast often carry expiration dates. The ***pack date*** is the day the product was processed or packaged. Canned foods are often marked with a pack date.

When you are not sure what the date on a food package means, ask a few questions. Food store employees should be able to explain dating codes.

7-15
Unit pricing helps shoppers compare costs of different quantities and brands of food.

To benefit from open dating:

- ❑ Determine whether the date on food products is the pull, freshness, expiration, or pack date.
- ❑ Buy only the products you can use before the expiration date or within a few days of the pull or freshness date.
- ❑ Notify store management when you find items on the shelves after their pull date.
- ❑ Store foods properly at home and use them within a reasonable period of time.

Government Inspection and Grading Programs

The United States Department of Agriculture (USDA) regulates the inspection and grading of foods you buy. ***Inspection stamps*** tell you the foods are wholesome and safe to eat. This means they have been processed and packaged under sanitary conditions. ***Food grades*** indicate the quality of foods.

Although most government inspection programs and all grading programs are voluntary, many food manufacturers and packers have their foods inspected and graded. Certain foods, such as meat and poultry, must be federally inspected before they can be sold and shipped across state lines.

Foods that have not been inspected or graded may be just as fresh and wholesome as the foods that have been government approved and graded. However, inspection and grade markings guarantee the safety and quality of food.

Buying Specific Foods

Knowing how to judge the quality and nutritional value of specific foods is essential to getting your money's worth in the supermarket. Following are some general guides to follow when shopping in different departments within the food store.

Dairy Products

Dairy products, because of their high nutritional value, are among the best food buys. In addition to being one of the best sources of calcium, dairy products are excellent sources of other essential nutrients. These include protein, phosphorus, and vitamins A, B-2, and D. It is safe and economical to substitute dairy products for more expensive protein sources in meals and snacks. You can choose from a wide variety of dairy foods, such as milk, cheese, ice cream, and yogurt.

Most milk and milk products are pasteurized and homogenized. During *pasteurization,* milk is heated to a specific temperature to destroy any harmful bacteria. It is *homogenized* to break up the fat particles and distribute them evenly throughout the milk. When milk is not homogenized, fat particles rise to the surface and form cream. Milk products may also be *fortified* with extra vitamins and minerals. Vitamins D and A and extra calcium are among the nutrients frequently added.

Milk and milk products are available in many forms, 7-16. Fresh milk is

Dean Foods Company

7-16
You can choose from a wide variety of dairy products in the supermarket.

most popular for drinking and many other uses. You can buy it whole, lowfat, or fat free with the primary difference being the fat content. Labels state fat content, calories per serving, and nutritional information. Flavored milk drinks are also available. Cultured buttermilk and yogurt are other milk products found in the dairy section of food stores.

Canned and dried milk products are concentrated by removing the water content of fresh milk. These include canned evaporated milk. This can be diluted with water and used for drinking and cooking. Its nutritional value is the same as fresh milk. Sweetened condensed milk is made by diluting the water content and adding a sweetener to whole or fat free milk. It is most often used in recipes. It does not substitute for either evaporated or fresh milk and should be used only in recipes that call for sweetened condensed milk. Dried milk may be whole or nonfat. It is often used in baby formulas, baking, and by adding water, as fresh, fluid milk. It costs from one-half to two-thirds less than fresh milk.

When shopping for milk, compare prices of its different forms. Generally, the higher the fat content in a milk product, the higher its cost will be. Fresh lowfat and fresh fat free milks cost less than fresh whole milk. Evaporated milk and dry milk cost less than fresh milk. Flavored milk, buttermilk, sweetened condensed milk, and yogurt cost more because they require special processing. You will also want to compare unit prices for milk products. Ounce-for-ounce, products sold in larger containers are usually less expensive than the same product sold in small containers.

Cream and ice cream are also milk products. Cream is available with different fat content and includes light or coffee cream, whipping cream, and half-and-half as well as sour cream and sour half-and-half. Ice cream is a frozen mixture that contains milk fat. Like milk, creams and ice creams with higher fat contents generally are more expensive and contain more calories. Read the labels carefully for nutrition information on these products.

Cheese is a dairy food that is made from a concentrated form of milk or cream. Hundreds of cheese varieties can be made by using different kinds of milk and different processing steps. Nutrients, color, texture, aroma, flavor, and cost vary with each variety. Labels tell the story.

The more steps, time, and special ingredients involved in making a cheese, the more expensive it will be. Ripened cheese (cheese stored at a specific temperature to develop texture and flavor) is generally more expensive than unripened cheese. Cheeses with added ingredients cost more than plain cheeses.

When buying cheese, compare the prices of various forms of the same type of cheese. For example, cheese that has been sliced, cubed, shredded, or grated for convenience usually costs more than the same quantity of cheese sold in a solid piece.

Butter is another dairy product. It is made from the fat or cream of milk. The cost of butter is influenced by how it is packaged. Butter packaged in "sticks" or small amounts costs more than bulk butter. Whipped butter costs more than regular butter. National brands and higher grades cost more than house brands and lower grades of butter.

Margarine, though not a dairy product, is a widely used butter substitute. It is made from vegetable oils, animal fats, or a combination of both. The type of oil or fat used to make the margarine helps determine its market price. Pure vegetable oil margarines generally cost more. Whipped margarine packaged in tubs usually costs more than regular margarine packaged in quarters or "sticks."

When selecting butter or margarine, consider price, dietary needs, and taste preferences. Butter usually is more expensive than margarine. However, if you prefer the taste of butter, you may be willing to pay more. Most margarines are cholesterol free and will be your best choice if you need to reduce your cholesterol intake. Labels will state nutrition facts you need to meet special dietary requirements.

When buying dairy products, look at the labels for nutrition information, check unit prices for the best buys, and look for the dates indicating freshness. The form of the food, its packaging, and the brand all influence price. Careful shopping and comparisons will help you find the products that best meet your needs.

Eggs

Eggs are high in protein and can be served as an inexpensive substitute for meat. They are a complete protein and also provide B vitamins, iron, phosphorus, and vitamins A and D. However, egg yolks are high in cholesterol and may need to be limited by persons with high cholesterol readings.

A variety of egg products are now available at most food stores. They are similar to whole eggs in nutrients they provide. These can be found in the dairy section near whole eggs.

The price of eggs depends on their grade and size. Higher grades and larger sizes are more expensive. Most eggs in the supermarket have been government graded for quality. Grades are based on the appearance of the egg yolk, white, and shell. The three grades are: U.S. Grade AA, U.S. Grade A, and U.S. Grade B.

Many stores sell only Grade AA or A eggs. Grade AA eggs are of the highest quality and are well suited to frying and poaching since they hold their shape well. Grade A eggs can be used for all purposes. Grade B eggs have the same nutritional value as Grade AA and A eggs, but they have thinner whites and yolks. They are used for baking and cooking where appearance of the egg is not important. Grade B eggs are rarely seen in supermarkets. They are sold mainly to bakeries and food service operations.

Eggs are sized according to their weight per dozen. For example, one dozen large eggs weighs at least 24 ounces. One dozen medium eggs weighs at least 21 ounces. Extra large, large, and medium are the egg sizes most commonly sold in food stores. Most recipes are based on large size eggs.

When shopping, select eggs with clean, uncracked shells. Cracked shells are an open invitation to bacteria. Do not be influenced by the color of the shell. Shell color has nothing to do with the quality, nutritive value, or flavor of eggs. Shell color just indicates the breed of the laying hen.

Meats

Meats have traditionally been a staple in the diets of most Americans. Beef, veal, pork, and lamb are the most commonly chosen meats. All are high in protein as well as phosphorus, iron, copper, and the B vitamins. Each type of animal is sold in different cuts that vary in tenderness, size, shape, and amount of fat and bone. Becoming familiar with the various cuts of meat can help you shop for meat and prepare it correctly.

The amount of meat you need to buy depends on the cut and the number of people you plan to serve. Between 2 and 3 ounces of cooked lean meat is considered one serving. Boneless, fat-trimmed meat cuts yield more servings than cuts containing bones and fat. Ask in the meat department where you shop for advice on the amount to buy of different cuts for the number of servings you need. You may also be able to get expert advice on ways to prepare different cuts of meat. When shopping for meats:

- ❑ *Look for government inspection and grading.* The "U.S. Inspected and Passed" stamp indicates that meat is wholesome and produced under sanitary conditions. Meat grades indicate quality and such characteristics as flavor, juiciness, and tenderness. Prime, Choice, and Select are the grades most commonly found in retail stores for beef, veal, and lamb. Pork, because it is considered tender, does not carry grade markings. All three grades of meat are comparable nutritionally. Prime is considered top grade and is sold primarily to hotels and fine restaurants. Choice meats are the better quality available in supermarkets. Select meats will be a bit less flavorful and tender.
- ❑ *Select firm, moist, fine-grained, and well-marbled meat. Marbling* refers to the small flecks of fat throughout the lean that help make meat tender. Veal has little fat and little marbling. High quality beef is bright red in color; veal is light pink; pork is grayish-pink; and lamb is pinkish-red.
- ❑ *Compare different meat cuts and prices.* Although one pound of meat with bones may cost less than a pound of boneless meat, it will not yield the same number of servings. That's why it is important to compare meat prices on the basis of cost per serving rather than cost per pound. You can also save money by buying large cuts of meat and cutting them into smaller cuts yourself.
- ❑ *Consider variety meats, such as liver, kidney, heart, and tongue.* These are highly nutritious and are usually priced lower than other meats.
- ❑ *Compare the quality and taste of canned and processed meats.* Processed ham, bacon, corned beef, sausage, and luncheon meats may vary in quality because of brand, processing method, or the ingredients used. Compare ingredients and experiment to determine which processed meat brands you prefer.

Poultry

Poultry includes chicken, turkey, duck, goose, and Rock Cornish hens. All of these, if sold across state lines, are federally inspected and marked for wholesomeness. Poultry may also be graded for quality. The highest grades go to the meatiest birds with the least pinfeathers and skin defects.

The age of a bird, not its grade, determines how tender it will be. Young birds are more tender than mature birds. Young chickens are labeled broiler, fryer, capon, roaster, or Rock Cornish hens. Young turkeys and ducks are labeled "young." Since mature birds are less tender, they are best when stewed, steamed, or pressure-cooked. Mature chickens are labeled hen, fowl, and stewing chicken. Other older birds are labeled "mature" or "old."

Almost all poultry on the market has been cleaned and readied for cooking. When shopping for poultry, buy birds that have been inspected and graded. Choose clean, moist, plump birds with meaty breasts, legs, and thighs. Remember to select young, tender birds for frying, roasting, and broiling and mature birds for steaming and stewing.

About 3 ounces of cooked poultry is one serving. You can buy poultry whole, halved, or cut up. Larger birds usually cost less per pound than smaller birds. Whole chicken is less expensive than chicken cut into pieces. Boned chicken is less expensive than deboned.

Poultry is also available canned and frozen in whole, cut up, boned, or rolled forms. Usually, canned poultry is more expensive than fresh or frozen poultry, but there is no waste.

Fish

Fish may be either finfish with fins and backbones or shellfish with shells and no backbones. Both have been in great demand in recent years partly because of studies indicating their nutritional value. People are also becoming more familiar with different types of seafood, 7-17.

Fresh fish is usually sold by the pound. Generally about 3 ounces of cooked boneless fish will serve one person. When buying fresh products, the salesperson can usually advise you on the amount to buy and on the recommended ways to prepare different fresh fish and shellfish. Check the labels on packaged, canned, and frozen products to determine the amount of fish or shellfish to purchase for the number of servings you need.

Burhop's Seafood

7-17
This market features a variety of fish and seafood along with information on selection, preparation, and nutritional values.

Inspection and grading of fish is not mandatory. However, the National Marine Fisheries Service provides a voluntary inspection program for the fish industry. Since not all fish are inspected or graded, careful selection is especially important. Look for firm flesh, tight, shiny scales, and bright, bulging eyes. The fish should look and smell clean. Fresh fish and shellfish should always be refrigerated or on ice in the marketplace and transferred promptly after purchase to refrigeration at home.

You can buy fish in a variety of forms. Whole fish is sold as it comes from the water. Dressed fish has head, fins, scales, and tail removed. Fish fillets are the sides of the fish cut lengthwise. Fillets have few or no bones and are ready to cook. Fish steaks are cross-sectional slices of a dressed fish with one large central bone. Steaks are also ready to cook.

Fruits and Vegetables

Fruits and vegetables are available in a variety of forms—fresh, canned, frozen, and dried. Fresh fruits and vegetables are called *produce.* The price you pay for produce and other forms of fruits and vegetables depends on the time of year, the growing conditions, and the quality.

Most fruits and vegetables are high in vitamins and minerals and generally are low in fat and calories. They provide fiber, which aids in digestion. Several servings from these two food groups should be included in the diet each day.

The best time to buy fresh fruits and vegetables is during their season. When supplies are plentiful, you usually have a better selection to choose from at lower prices. When selecting, consider the degree of ripeness. If you select very ripe fruits and vegetables, make sure you'll be able to use them before they spoil. Look for undamaged produce and avoid shriveled, wilted, bruised, or decayed pieces. Use the chart in 7-18 to help you select quality fresh fruits and vegetables.

When you shop for produce, consider size and weight, freshness and ripeness, shape, and appearance. The way you intend to use fruits and vegetables can influence your choice. For example, there is no need to buy top quality tomatoes for spaghetti sauce or perfectly formed peaches for a pie. Unless the best quality is of great importance, consider lower-quality produce or canned, frozen, or dried fruits and vegetables. These are offered at lower prices. The nutritive value will be the same.

Compare prices of fresh, frozen, and canned fruits and vegetables. Usually frozen fruits and vegetables cost less than fresh produce. Canned foods cost less than frozen or fresh. You may also want to compare prices of different forms and brands of fruits and vegetables. Canned or frozen fruits and vegetables that are chopped, sliced, or cut cost less than whole pieces. Different brands of the same food may also vary in cost and the most expensive is not necessarily the best. Lower-priced brands may be satisfactory. Experiment to find the brands you like best.

Grain Products

Grain products include breads, cereals, rice, and pastas. Whole grain products contribute valuable nutrients and fiber to the diet and provide the body with energy. Refined grain products provide fewer nutrients unless they are enriched. *Enriched* products contain added thiamin, niacin, riboflavin, and iron. The law requires that certain refined products be enriched. Compared to many other foods, most breads and cereals are inexpensive, well liked, and easy to include in meal plans.

Wheat, barley, corn, oats, rice, and rye are the grains from which most breads and cereals are made. Flour is the basic grain product that is used to make breads and bakery products. Most flour is made from wheat although you can also buy rye, potato, rice, and buckwheat flours.

All-purpose, self-rising, cake, and instant flours are the more common flours in food stores. All-purpose and self-rising flours are suitable for most cooking and baking. The difference between the two is that self-rising flour has baking powder, baking soda, and salt added to it. Cake flour is finely textured and often used to make pastries and cakes. It is the most expensive of the four flours. While most flours come bagged, instant flour usually comes in a pour container. It blends well with liquids and is used to make gravies and sauces. It is more expensive than all-purpose and self-rising flours.

Cereals made from any and all of the grains come in a variety of forms, flavors, and nutritive values. Many are sugar-coated, most have sugar added, and a few contain no sugar. Other ingredients often added to cereals include nuts and dried fruits. Ready-to-eat and instant cereals are more convenient and more costly than cereals that require cooking. Small boxes and individual serving size boxes of cereal cost more per serving than the same cereal in a larger box. Most cereal products are enriched. The labels on cereals tell a complete nutrition story and it pays to compare nutritional values when shopping.

Pasta usually has a slight nutty taste and comes in different shapes and sizes. Although a relatively inexpensive food, pasta is a favorite in a variety of recipes among consumers of all income levels.

Buying Fresh Fruits and Vegetables

Fruit	Look for	Avoid
Apples	Firm, well-colored.	Bruised, overripe, shriveled apples.
Bananas	Firm, brightly colored, free of bruises or defects.	Bruised, overripe, or discolored bananas.
Berries	Firm, plump, brightly colored, free from defects.	Soft, spongy, shriveled leaky berries.
Cantaloupes	Thick veined cantaloupes with a yellowish rind and pleasant aroma.	Cantaloupes with soft spots.
Citrus fruits	Brightly colored, firm well-shaped limes, oranges, tangerines, and grapefruits, heavy for size.	Dull and shriveled skin.
Grapes	Brightly colored, plump.	Soft, shriveled, leaky grapes.
Peaches	Slightly firm flesh, just becoming soft.	Very firm, immature peaches and soft, overripe bruised peaches.
Pears	Firm with good color.	Very hard, immature pears and soft, overripe bruised pears.
Pineapples	Plump, firm, yellowish-orange with a pleasant aroma.	Dry, dull, yellowish-green skin.
Watermelons	Smooth with bright red, firm juicy flesh.	Pale-colored, dry or watery flesh.
Vegetables	**Look for**	**Avoid**
Asparagus	Rich green color, firm but tender stalks, and closed, compact tips.	Open, moldy tips; discolored, shriveled stalks.
Beans (snap)	Brightly colored, tender beans with crisp pods.	Thick, tough, dry pods and blemishes.
Beets	Smooth, round bulbs with a rich red color.	Wilted with brown scaly patches.
Broccoli	Deep green color, tight flower clusters, and stems that are not too thick or tough.	Open buds; yellow color; soft, spongy, wilted stalks.
Cabbage	Firm, bright red or green cabbage head, heavy for its size.	Wilted, decayed, yellow outer leaves.

(Continued)

7-18
Select fresh fruits and vegetables according to their color, appearance, and ripeness.

Buying Fresh Fruits and Vegetables (Continued)

Vegetables	Look for	Avoid
Carrots	Firm, smooth, bright orange skin.	Limp, discolored carrots.
Cauliflower	White color and tight flower clusters.	Discolored cauliflower.
Celery	Smooth, rigid stalks with a bright color.	Limp, discolored stalks.
Corn	Fresh green husks and plump kernels.	Wilted husks and small kernels.
Cucumbers	Firm, well-colored cucumbers.	Soft, yellowing cucumbers.
Lettuce	Brightly colored, crisp leaves; heavy for its size.	Irregular heads with brown or soft spots.
Onions	Smooth, firm onions with a papery outer covering.	Soft, wet or damp skins.
Peppers	Firm brightly colored peppers with a glossy sheen.	Punctured peppers with soft or decayed spots.
Potatoes	Smooth, firm, well-shaped potatoes, free from blemishes.	Large cuts, bruises, green spots, and potatoes that show signs of sprouting.
Tomatoes	Smooth, firm, bright red tomatoes.	Soft, bruised, and cracked tomatoes.

7-18
(Continued)

Rice is also marketed in many forms and many varieties. The special rice varieties, such as wild rice, seasoned rice, and the instant rice brands, tend to cost more than regular white rice that require cooking. Chinese fried rice and other seasoned and flavored rices are available canned or frozen, ready to heat and serve. These forms of rice cost more because of the additional processing required.

Bakery items include breads, rolls, cakes, and pastries. Their cost depends partly on convenience. Ready-to-serve products cost more than home baked or those requiring some preparation. Fresh bakery goods usually cost more than refrigerated or frozen goods. Often, ready-baked goods will cost more than the same items baked at home. However, the time and energy saved is often worth the extra cost. Many large supermarkets contain a bakery section of freshly baked breads and desserts. These foods usually will cost more than the prepackaged varieties of the same foods. However, the freshness, aroma, and taste can be very tempting.

After You Shop

What you do with food at home is the key to enjoying all that you have carefully purchased at the grocery store. Proper storage is necessary to maintain food quality, flavor, and nutritive value and ensure safety. Using skill and originality as you prepare and serve food can make meals more appetizing, nutritious, and enjoyable.

Food Storage

Different foods require different types of storage. Basically, there are three places to store foods—on the shelf, in the refrigerator, and in the freezer. Packaged foods usually will give storage suggestions on the labels. Certain foods, such as bread, that you intend to use soon, may stay fresh on the shelf at room temperature. However, they keep for longer periods of time in the refrigerator or freezer, 7-19. Other items, such as meat or casserole dishes, keep one to three days in the refrigerator, but should be stored in the freezer for longer periods.

Food Preparation

Planning and preparing food in an attractive, appetizing way increases mealtime pleasure. Preparation also can affect the nutritive value, appearance, and taste of different foods. You can get more satisfaction from food dollars if you learn to prepare foods that appeal to the people you are feeding.

General Electric Company

7-19
Refrigerator or freezer storage is recommended for many perishable foods. This refrigerator-freezer makes proper storage easy.

When planning meals, consider food contrasts. Try to serve a colorful combination of hot and cold foods, sweet and tart flavors, and crisp and soft textures. Also consider food combinations. Hot dogs and baked beans seem to go together, while hot dogs and creamed peas don't. Try to combine foods that complement each other.

Appearance and temperature are two important factors to consider in meal planning. When food looks good, it seems to taste better. Try to preserve natural colors and textures of food. Work to achieve the right consistency in gravies, sauces, and other combination dishes. Time the meal so when you serve, the hot foods are hot, and the cold foods are cold. No one wants to eat cold french fries or warm coleslaw.

> *"Food does not become nutrition until it passes the lips."*
>
> *Ronald M. Deutsch*

When preparing meals, remember individual and family food preferences. Try to include one or two known favorites in each meal. It is also fun occasionally to try new and different foods and combinations. Fresh recipes and menus add interest and variety to mealtime.

It is a good idea to find one or two good, basic cookbooks to guide you in planning and preparing meals. A pinch of this and a handful of that may work for experienced cooks and simple meals, but recipes are more reliable for beginners and more difficult dishes, 7-20. Don't be afraid to experiment with recipes to find the tastes that appeal to you and the people you serve. Adding just the right amount of herbs, spices, or seasonings can wake up the flavor of many ordinary foods.

Before serving meals, think about the atmosphere and the setting in which a meal is served. Not every meal calls for candlelight and flowers. However, even a quick breakfast can taste better if you eat at a clean, uncluttered table. For parties and special occasions, you can create a festive atmosphere with flowers, decorations, table settings, and music.

Zenith Electronics Corporation

7-20
Learning to prepare foods properly can start at any age.

Eating Out

Americans spend over 40 percent of their food dollars in restaurants. Whether you spend more or less than the national average, you are likely to spend a considerable amount of money eating out. You may eat meals in fast-food outlets or bring them home from "carry outs." Over the years, you will spend a great deal of money in cafes ranging from hot dog stands to fancy restaurants. Whether eating away from home is a necessity or a pleasure, you will want to get good food and pleasant dining for your money.

Selecting a Restaurant

Before choosing a restaurant, it is a good idea to find out about the types of foods served and the prices. A phone call before you leave home or a few questions before you are seated may save you time, money, and embarrassment. If you do your homework, you will never need to order a meal you don't want at a price you can't afford.

By calling the restaurant ahead of time, you can also find out if

Dining Out

An Even Split

Egon is a college freshman. He has a part-time job on campus and gets a little spending money from his parents each month. He finds that his cash goes pretty fast now that he lives and eats away from home. Egon has $10 to stretch over three more days until he gets paid again.

Egon and four friends are eating at the Macho Taco. Egon orders very carefully, trying to keep his tab under $3. He manages to get two tacos and a lemonade for $2.75. Egon is congratulating himself on his cheap meal while the other guys order big meals.

The waitress puts all the orders on the same bill. When they are ready to leave, Sam takes the check and divides the total by five instead of trying to figure out who had what. Egon's share comes to $5.25.

Sam is a "big deal" on campus. Everyone looks up to him, and nobody crosses him. Egon doesn't have the nerve to speak up and say his share is really only $2.75. He is afraid of looking cheap.

Case Review

1. How could Egon have avoided this problem?
2. What would you have done if you were Egon?
3. How can you prevent similar experiences from happening to you?

Dining Out

Leroy and His Date

Leroy is 23 years old and working at his first full-time job as a computer programmer. He met Patty at work and has been wanting to date her for a long time. Finally, he worked up the courage to ask her out and she accepted. They have a date Saturday night. Leroy plans to take her to dinner and a movie.

Leroy eats out a lot but never any place very special. For this occasion, he wants to find a nice restaurant with a little atmosphere. He has heard commercials for a new place called Le Chateau. The commercials describe the restaurant as a "romantic, candle-lit dining spot for special evenings." This is just what Leroy has in mind.

The evening proves to be unforgettable! Leroy picks up Patty at six o'clock. They drive to Le Chateau and join a crowd of 30 to 40 people waiting for a table. Leroy didn't know they needed reservations. After waiting almost 45 minutes, Leroy and Patty are seated at a small table wedged between the doors to the kitchen. It is a noisy, cramped spot, anything but romantic.

Leroy is already embarrassed about the evening—waiting 45 minutes for a table between the kitchen doors. He just hopes the evening will get better, but things seem to get worse.

A waiter with a French accent brings them a menu that is printed in French. Neither Leroy nor Patty understands the names of the foods, but the prices are clear enough. Leroy orders the least expensive item on the menu. Even that is more than he can easily afford. Patty senses that Leroy is over his head and orders the same thing.

When the food comes, they learn that "oeufs perigourdino" is a baked egg dish with finely ground goose liver. It is not a dish either of them ever wants to try again. They both eat quickly with very little conversation and not much appetite.

When the check comes, it is twice the amount Leroy had planned to spend. Luckily, he has enough money with him to pay. All he has to do now is figure out what to do with the rest of the evening. He has no money left for a movie.

Case Review

1. How could Leroy have avoided this unforgettable evening at Le Chateau?
2. What might Leroy have done once they arrived at Le Chateau and he realized that it was not what he expected?
3. How would you plan a dinner at a restaurant you have never tried before?

reservations are required or accepted; if a certain type of clothing, such as tie or jacket, is required; and if credit cards are honored. If you go to a restaurant and find it is not what you expect or want, it is a good idea to leave quietly and find a place you can enjoy.

Restaurant reviews in local papers and magazines can be very helpful. They describe the types of food served, the house specialties, the atmosphere, and the service. They tell the price range and the hours the restaurant is open. You can also find up-to-date restaurant guides and information online.

Sometimes you can find bargains as well as atmosphere at ethnic restaurants. See 7-21. In metropolitan areas you can find food from many lands. Italian, Greek, Asian, Mexican, and German are among the more common and popular ethnic restaurants. They usually serve a variety of foods and dishes you may not normally prepare at home. Prices are often reasonable, too.

If you want to try a more expensive restaurant, consider going for lunch rather than dinner. The same food, atmosphere, and service often cost less at noon than in the evening.

When you eat out, remember that you are paying for more than just the food. You are paying for someone to buy, prepare, cook, and serve the food.

7-21
A casual night out at a local pizzeria can be fun with friends, family, or a date.

Even at inexpensive fast-food operations, meals usually cost more than similar foods you prepare at home. Consider how much and how often you are willing to pay someone else to shop and cook for you.

If you are eating out with friends, decide ahead of time how you want to pay. Ask for separate checks when each person is paying his or her own way. Separate checks save figuring and hassling when the bill comes.

Tipping

Don't forget to add tips when you figure the cost of eating out. Fast-food, self-serve places do not call for tips. In most other restaurants, those who serve you should be tipped. In fact, servers rely on tips for a good portion of their incomes.

Be prepared to leave 15 to 20 percent of the bill for a tip. Many restaurants will automatically add the tip to the bill when there are six or more people in a party. When you're in a smaller group, however, you will have to figure the tip yourself. For a total food bill of $4.00, a 15 percent tip comes to 60 cents and a 20 percent tip comes to 80 cents. A 20 percent or slightly higher tip is appropriate in more expensive restaurants and for exceptionally good service. A 15 percent tip is adequate in less costly, casual restaurants. When eating at a buffet or cafeteria-type restaurant,

Dining Out

All for the Price of a Tip

Lynette is 20, working at her first job, and living in her first apartment away from home. Recently, she won a dinner for two at a very nice, expensive restaurant. She invites Marcel, a neighbor and frequent date, to join her for the free meal.

The restaurant is a big step above the neighborhood cafe and fast-food spots where Lynette and Marcel usually eat. In fact, neither of them feels entirely comfortable with the fancy surroundings and the hovering waiters. The menu itself is intimidating. After studying the expensive selections, they finally settle on the house specialty—rack of lamb for two. Without the winning coupon, the dinner would have cost $50.

Although the meal is free, the tip is not included. Lynette and Marcel usually eat in places where little or no tip is expected. It is clear to them their waiter expects a healthy amount. In fact, the waiter has earned it. The service has been excellent.

Quietly, Lynette and Marcel try to decide how much tip they should leave the waiter. The total bill comes to $65. This includes appetizers, the rack of lamb, dessert, and coffee. Since the meal was free and the service was excellent, they decide to leave a $10 tip. The waiter does not seem overly pleased.

Case Review

1. How much do you think Lynette and Marcel should have tipped?
2. What are some guidelines to help you decide how much to leave for a tip in restaurants?
3. When are you justified in leaving no tip at all?
4. What do you think makes people under tip or over tip?
5. What experience have you had with tipping in restaurants?

a 10 percent tip is considered to be adequate. No tip, along with a complaint to the management, is appropriate if service is rude or very incompetent.

The more you eat out, the easier it will become for you to choose eating places to match your mood and your budget. Sometimes you may just want a casual spot for a soft drink. Other occasions may call for a fancy meal with plenty of atmosphere. Most people agree that experience is a powerful teacher.

Summary

Food is an important item both in your budget and in your overall health and well-being. A sizable share of income is spent on food in grocery stores and restaurants. The food you eat will affect the way you look, feel, and perform.

Smart eating begins with nutritious meals and snacks. There are several reliable guides to nutrition. The Recommended Daily Allowances specify the amount of nutrients you need each day. The Food Guide Pyramid is one of the simplest guides to proper nutrition. The Dietary Guidelines for Americans offer suggestions for healthful eating.

To get the most for your dollars when shopping for food, you should understand how supply and demand affect food prices. When demand is greater than the supply of food, prices will rise. When food is plentiful, prices will fall. Many factors affect supply and demand, such as weather, transportation and labor costs, crop failures, and strikes.

Establishing a food budget will help you control spending and get more for your money. Consider who eats in your household, any special dietary needs, and your family's food preferences. Your budget will also depend on how much you entertain and eat out, where you shop, and how skilled you are as a food shopper.

Planning purchases is one key to smart shopping. Food pages of local papers can give you ideas for menus. Using a list helps you remember all the items you need and gives direction to your shopping. Certain shopping aids in grocery stores can help you find the best buys. The labels on food products will be one of your most reliable guides. By law, labels are required to provide certain types of information.

It is also important to know what to look for when buying specific foods. Each type of food has different characteristics that determine quality and freshness. Follow guidelines for buying each type of food.

Once you bring home your groceries, food storage and preparation become important. Storing foods properly is a key factor in preserving flavor, freshness, and quality. The type of storage will depend on the food and how soon you intend to use it. Preparation of foods is a vital part to enjoying meals and snacks. Planning ahead and serving meals attractively will make food more enjoyable.

There are several factors to consider when eating in restaurants. Call ahead when choosing a new place to eat so you will know what to expect. Ask about reservations, prices, types of food served, dress requirements, etc. When going out with friends, decide ahead of time how you will pay. Be prepared to leave a tip for the wait persons in most restaurants—usually 15 to 20 percent of the bill.

To Review

1. How many daily servings are recommended from each of the groups in the Food Guide Pyramid?
2. List three of the Dietary Guidelines for Americans.
3. Name five questions that can help you establish a food budget.
4. How can planning food purchases make consumers better food shoppers?
5. Name three reasons for shopping in the same one or two stores for routine marketing.
6. List three ways the UPC system can affect food shopping.
7. What information is required on nutrition facts panels?
8. How can you use unit pricing to save money?
9. The last day a product should be sold is called the:
   A. Freshness date.
   B. Pack date.
   C. Expiration date.
   D. Pull date.

10. True or false. Inspection stamps on foods help you judge the quality of foods.
11. Which milk product usually costs the most: lowfat milk, fat free milk, or whole milk? Why?
12. True or false. When buying poultry, remember to select mature birds for frying, roasting, and broiling.
13. Why is it a good idea to call a restaurant ahead of time if you have never eaten there before?

To Think Critically

1. Name three good food sources for each of the six nutrients the body needs.
2. How many servings from each group in the Food Guide Pyramid do you usually eat? Is your diet supplying you with the right amount of the nutrients you need?
3. How can the Pyramid help you plan meals and shop for foods?
4. What are some of the factors that can affect food prices?
5. What can you do to be a better meal planner and food shopper?
6. How would you decide where to shop for food?
7. Do you or your family use unit pricing when food shopping?
8. Why is proper food storage and food preparation important to successful food budgeting?
9. How would you choose a restaurant for a special occasion or celebration?

To Do

1. Bring to class news items from newspapers and magazines that describe events that could affect the supply and demand of food. In class, discuss how food prices could be affected.
2. Evaluate three food stores in your community using the questionnaire "Choosing Where to Shop for Groceries" in 7-9. Report to the class which one of the three stores you prefer and why.
3. Collect 15 to 20 labels from different foods to study and compare. Check to see if the information on each label includes the common name of the food, the net contents, and the name and address of the manufacturer, packer, or distributor. If nutrition information is given, check to see if the required information is included in the specified order. What other information do you find on these food labels?
4. Take responsibility for the food planning and marketing for your family for one week. Using the Food Guide Pyramid, outline nutritional menus and snacks for the week and make up a shopping list of the foods you will need. Refer to newspaper food pages for ideas and specials. Then do the actual food shopping. (If this is not possible, go to the store and write down the prices of the items on your list.) Remember to look at unit pricing, open dating, inspection marks and grades, and food labels. Prepare a three-minute oral report on your experience telling what foods you bought, how much money you spent, and how you would improve your plan if you were to do it again.
5. Conduct some research to learn what foods need to be included in a vegetarian diet to meet basic nutritional needs. Plan several meals including these foods.
6. Conduct an experiment to evaluate the effects of improper food storage by placing bread in a variety of favorable and unfavorable storage situations.
7. For two weeks, keep track of the food that becomes waste in your home. Report to the class what types of foods were wasted, why the food was wasted, and how much money was lost.

CHAPTER 8

Cotton Knit Dresses
BETTER FABRICS
give our Turtleneck Dresses
MORE BODY
THE NEW YORK TIMES
ON THE STREET
Christmas
delivery
guaranteed

The Shirt on Your Back

wardrobe inventory
fads
natural fibers
manufactured fibers
blend
woven fabrics
knit fabrics
nonwoven fabrics
fabric finish

After studying this chapter, you will be able to

- ❑ explain how clothes influence the way other people see you.
- ❑ explain how clothes can reflect your personality.
- ❑ identify wardrobe needs.
- ❑ establish a clothing budget.
- ❑ evaluate construction features, fabrics, fit, and appearance of garments when shopping.
- ❑ list guidelines for proper care of clothing.

Since the first animal skin was used to cover a human figure, the question of what to wear has occupied the minds of men and women around the world. "What will I wear?" "I have nothing to wear." "What is everyone else wearing?" These are familiar concerns in every household.

Most people want clothes that look nice and feel comfortable. They want a wardrobe that will be right for where they go and what they do. Having the right clothes for all seasons and all places calls for careful planning and buying. Knowing how to analyze your wardrobe, shop for clothing, and care for clothes properly can help you achieve the look you want at a price you can afford.

> *"The fashion wears out more apparel than the man."*
>
> *Shakespeare*

First Impressions

When you meet someone for the first time, what do you notice first? Most people notice the way a person looks. People tend to form first impressions about others based on appearance. Clothes are an important part of the image you create. That's why it pays to put some thought into the way you dress. The clothes you wear make a statement to other people and influence the way people see you. See 8-1.

First impressions can be important as you meet new people, start a training program, enter college, or apply for a job. Think for a moment about impressions you make on others. Did you ever meet someone important to you when you were looking your absolute worst? Have you ever gone to a party or school activity wearing clothes totally different than those others were wearing? Have you ever been caught looking grubby when you wanted to look your best? How did these experiences make you feel? Think back on your impressions of others. Have you ever formed an opinion of someone you do not know strictly on what they were wearing and how they looked? Do you often find your first impressions wrong?

8-1
What could you tell about someone wearing these clothes? For what occasions might these garments be appropriate?

Clothes and Your Personality

Clothes do more than just cover and protect the body. The clothes you wear express your personality. They can show your desire to conform or to be different. They can show your concern for status or your indifference to it. They also express your individuality, imagination, and creativity. See 8-2.

8-2
Creating an outfit involves giving attention to detail, color coordination, and style. Where might you wear these clothes?

Clothes not only express your personality to others, they also influence the way you feel about yourself. Your clothes can make a difference in the way you act in different situations. If you are unhappy with the clothes you are wearing, you may not feel confident. A lack of confidence usually is reflected in behavior. On the other hand, if you feel appropriately dressed, it will add to your comfort and confidence. This is true for all types of occasions, from parties to job interviews.

No matter how you dress, you are expressing yourself to others. Do you give much thought to your appearance? What do you think your clothes say about you? What do you want your appearance to say?

A Wardrobe for All Seasons

At one time or another, you have probably complained, "I have nothing to wear." You may have been staring at a closet full of clothes when you said it. At the time, you probably thought the clothes you had were not right for the occasion or your mood.

By developing a wardrobe plan, you can gradually collect the clothes and accessories you need for different occasions. A good wardrobe plan involves three major steps—taking a wardrobe inventory, clearing out clothes you never wear, and adding the clothes you need. The wardrobe additions you make will depend on the

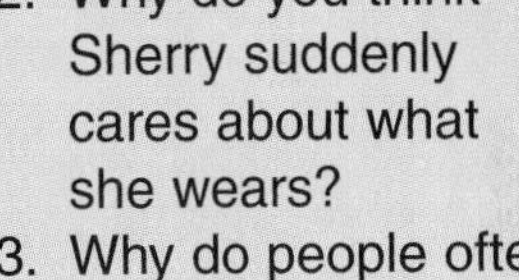

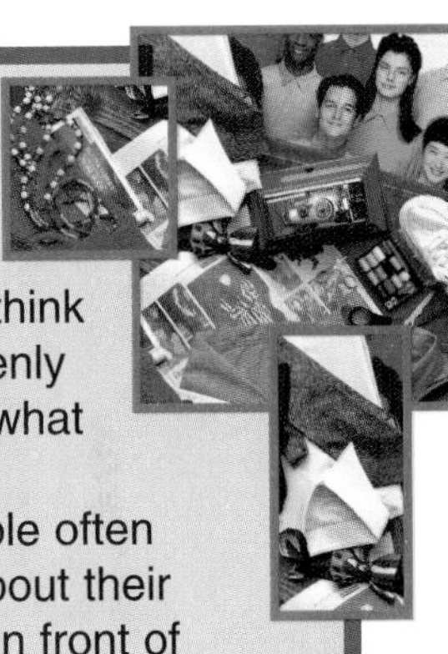

Clothing Speaks

A First Look at Clothes

Thirteen-year-old Sherry is the only sister of four older brothers. She and her family have an active lifestyle. They go camping, water skiing, and hiking often. With seven family members, someone is coming or going all the time. Sherry's home seems to be a center of never-ending activity.

Sherry's closet is full of jeans, shirts, and sweaters passed down to her by her older brothers. She has worn hand-me-downs most of her life and has felt comfortable doing so. As the younger sister of four athletic brothers, Sherry is known and accepted by almost everyone in town. Regardless of what she wears, Sherry is always well liked. Until now, Sherry has been too busy to be very interested in clothes.

This year Sherry's social life will change. She is going to a new community high school. For the first time, Sherry will be surrounded by lots of unfamiliar faces. Although she has never given much thought to her clothes, Sherry knows that her brothers' worn shirts and jeans won't be right for high school. She also knows that the wrong clothes could make it harder for her to meet new friends and be accepted at school.

For the first time, Sherry is thinking of clothes as a way of communicating something about herself. She wants to say, "I'm okay. I am comfortable with myself. I am interested in lots of activities and people. I like to have fun. I know what to wear and what to do."

Case Review

1. What types of clothes do you think Sherry should wear to say what she wants to say about herself?
2. Why do you think Sherry suddenly cares about what she wears?
3. Why do people often care more about their appearance in front of strangers than among friends?
4. When are you most concerned about the way you look?
5. When do you most want to wear what others are wearing?
6. How do you feel about people whose clothes are very different?
7. How would you feel in a situation where your clothes and appearance seemed totally wrong?

amount of money you can spend. Your shopping skills will determine how much you get for your money.

The Inventory

A ***wardrobe inventory*** is a list of all the clothes, shoes, and accessories you own. Accessories are items designed to go with an outfit. They include belts, ties, scarves, hats, gloves, purses, and jewelry. Taking an inventory each season can help you decide what you need for all occasions.

When making an inventory, list all the clothes you have according to their type (jackets, slacks, shirts, etc.). Consider where and how you would wear different items. See 8-3. Include sleepwear, undergarments, shoes, and accessories on your inventory. Also list any special clothes or uniforms you wear for work, sports, and other activities.

> *"Be not the first by whom the new are tried, nor yet the last to lay the old aside."*
>
> *Alexander Pope*

The Clearance

One purpose of an inventory is to clear out items from your closet you no longer wear, need, or want. When deciding which clothes to keep and what to give away, ask yourself the following questions about any items that are questionable:

- ❑ Does it fit well and comfortably?
- ❑ Is it fashionable and flattering?
- ❑ Does it go with other clothes you own?
- ❑ Is it in wearable condition or can you make it wearable?
- ❑ Is it right for where you go and what you do?
- ❑ Will you really wear it in the future?

8-3
Casual clothes are right for camping, picnics, knocking about, and active leisure time (A). Certain jobs and activities call for more formal clothing, such as a nice shirt and tie (B). Comfort often is the most important feature in clothes for around home and dorm (C).

A

B

C

U.S. West, Inc.

Clothing Speaks

The Scene Changes

Carl has just graduated from high school. In school, Carl was known and liked by almost everyone. He was the star of the football team and had the lead in the senior play.

Until Carl graduated, he had never thought much about the clothes he wore. Everyone in school dressed pretty much alike. It was simple to wear the "right" clothes. Now Carl is more concerned about his appearance. He is wondering what clothes he will need for a summer job and for college in the fall. Carl wants to make the right clothing choices so he won't have to worry about the way he looks.

Case Review

1. What do you think Carl should wear for job interviews? How do you think the way he looks might influence possible employers?
2. What do you think Carl should wear if he worked at the following jobs?
   A. Stock clerk at a super market.
   B. Clerk in a clothing store.
   C. Aide at a hospital.
   D. Little League coach.
   E. Door-to-door salesperson.
   F. File clerk in an office.
3. What type of wardrobe do you think Carl will need at college? How can he find out what he needs before buying?

If clothes need laundering, mending, or altering, set aside a time to do the necessary work. Don't miss wearing a skirt or pair of jeans just because you didn't take the time to shorten, launder, or put on a missing button.

Sometimes clothes that are too small or out of style can be recycled or altered. *Recycling clothing* means finding ways and methods of extending the use of garments. For example, you can make a jeans skirt or cut-offs out of a pair of jeans that are too short. Jeans that are too small can become a tote bag. Taper pants with legs that are too wide. Shorten skirts that are too long.

When you come across garments you really do not or cannot wear, clear them out of your closet and drawers. You may want to give wearable clothes to persons or organizations that can use them or pass them along to others. Your giveaways may become someone else's favorite outfits.

The Additions

The final step in wardrobe planning is to complete your wardrobe with well-planned additions. Using your current inventory as a guide, identify the gaps. Make a list of the clothes and accessories you need to fill those gaps.

Before you buy anything, study the current fashions. Look through fashion magazines. Walk through clothing stores. Look at the colors and styles of clothes and at the accessories used with them. How would the colors look with your skin and hair coloring? Would the lines and textures be flattering to your body shape? Can you coordinate new fashions with clothes and accessories you already have? Would the latest fashions fill the gaps in your wardrobe?

Consider how long the new fashions are likely to stay in style. This is especially important for expensive items. ***Fads*** are fashion styles that stay popular for only a short time. More conservative or classic styles tend to last for many seasons. It has been so through the ages. For example, if you buy a flared-leg, striped pair of pants featured in magazines this year, they will probably be "out" next year. If you buy a good pair of jeans, you probably can wear them as long as they hold together.

While you look at magazines or store windows, make a note of the prices of the new clothes and accessories you want to buy. Also consider the time and money involved in caring for the clothes. If your money and time are limited, look for easy-care garments. If you choose clothes that need dry cleaning, estimate how often they will need cleaning and how much it will cost.

> *"Every generation laughs at the old fashions, but follows religiously the new."*
>
> *Thoreau*

Clothing Dollars

Once you have an idea of what you want to add to your wardrobe, it's time to look seriously at dollars and cents. What you buy will depend largely on how much money you have to spend. Try to establish priorities and identify your most critical needs to guide you in making new purchases. If you have enough casual clothing, don't buy another casual shirt just because it is new or different or on sale. Look for the clothes that will fill the gaps in your wardrobe. The wardrobe analysis chart in 8-4 can help you organize the clothes you own and decide what to buy.

Since wardrobe planning is often done each season, you may want to set up your clothing budget on a seasonal basis. To plan a clothing budget, consider:

- ❑ The total amount you have to spend.
- ❑ The total amount of your essential non-clothing expenses.
- ❑ The importance of clothing and personal appearance to you.
- ❑ The amount you can allow for your wardrobe after meeting other essential needs.

Compare the amount you can spend to the prices of clothing you need. If you can afford everything you want, start buying! If you can't afford everything on your list, start thinking. Decide which wardrobe additions are most important, and buy those first. If you sew, you may want to make some of the clothes you need. Sewing skills can cut wardrobe costs substantially.

Bargain hunting and comparative shopping can help you save money if you know how to judge quality and style. Clothes and accessories are sold at low prices at clothing warehouses, factory outlets, surplus stores, resale shops, and discount stores. Check the yellow pages in your phone book to see if there are any such stores in your area. Look also for specials and pre-season sales at clothing stores in your area. Allow yourself plenty of time when you go bargain hunting. Before you buy, check quality, colors, fit, and care requirements, as well as return and exchange policies. Sometimes a low price signals a real bargain. Other times it signals poor quality or outdated fashions. It's important to know the difference.

When you can wait, end-of-season sales offer some of the best savings. In early and mid-July, swimwear and summer clothing is often reduced by 30 to 50 percent to make room for fall clothing. By August, what is left of summer items will be marked down even more. You may be able to save as much as 50 to 70 percent by waiting for sales.

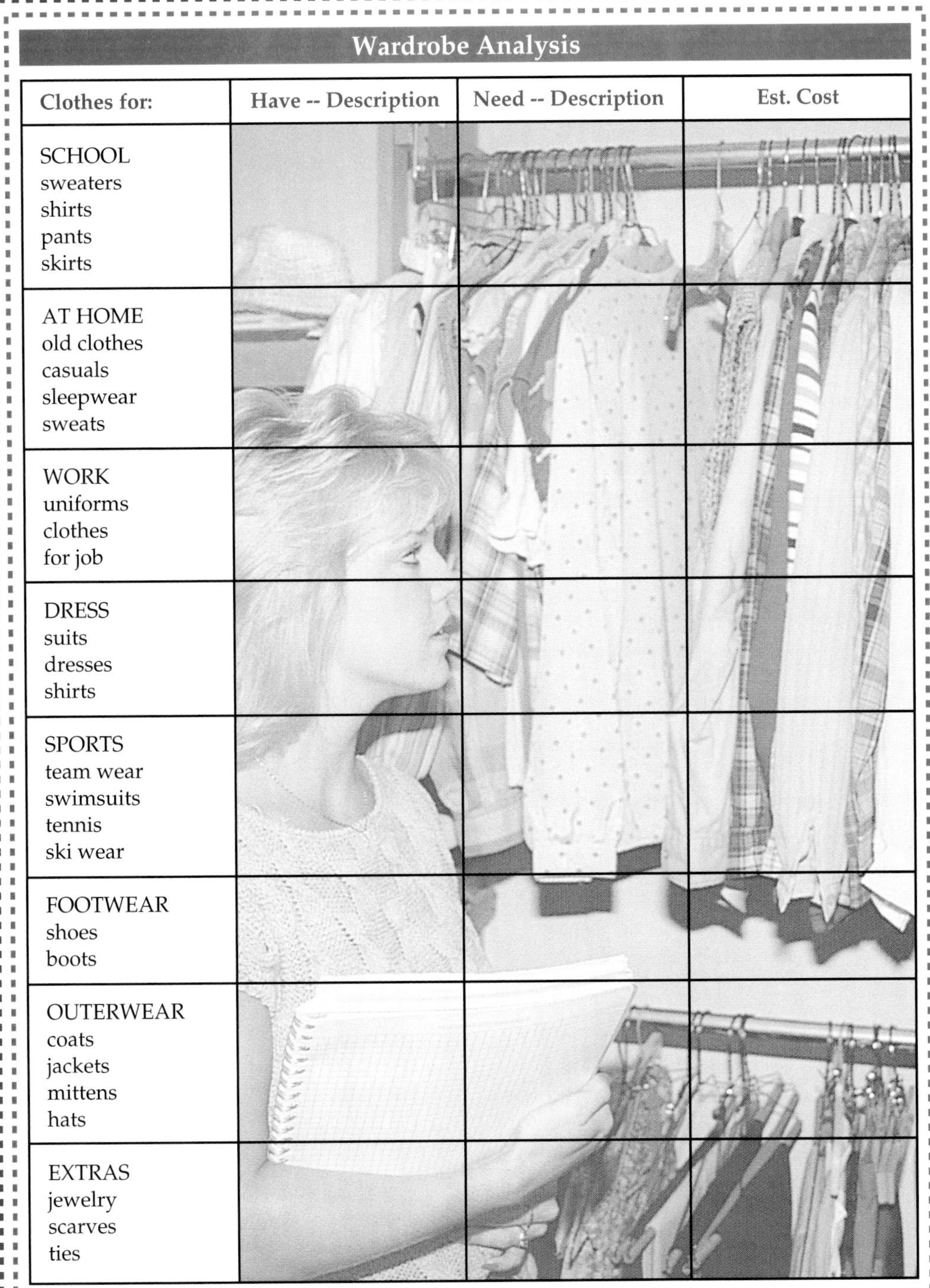

Wardrobe Analysis

Clothes for:	Have -- Description	Need -- Description	Est. Cost
SCHOOL sweaters shirts pants skirts			
AT HOME old clothes casuals sleepwear sweats			
WORK uniforms clothes for job			
DRESS suits dresses shirts			
SPORTS team wear swimsuits tennis ski wear			
FOOTWEAR shoes boots			
OUTERWEAR coats jackets mittens hats			
EXTRAS jewelry scarves ties			

8-4
Go through your wardrobe and identify the gaps and needs with estimated costs. This can help you make the best choices when shopping.

The Shopping Scene

Tina Buys a Mistake

Tina is searching her closet for something to wear to a school party. Normally, she gives little thought to clothes, but she is excited about this party because Tom has asked her to go with him. It is Tina's first date, and she wants to look her best. Nothing in her closet is right. Tina decides she must have a new outfit. She has $65 saved from last year's paper route. With money in hand, Tina goes shopping.

In the store where Tina usually buys clothes, she tries on several outfits, but none appeal to her. She goes to another store where she has never shopped before. The clothes in this store cost more than Tina normally spends. However, she sees some beautiful things. A smiling salesclerk asks Tina what type of outfit she wants, but Tina really isn't sure. She tells the clerk she will know it when she sees it. The clerk brings out several dresses, all of which cost more than Tina can afford. Since the salesclerk is so persistent, Tina feels obliged to try on at least one or two of the dresses.

One dress of lightweight wool in deep purple with black velvet trim seems to be made for Tina. It is truly lovely. The salesclerk insists that Tina must have it. Not knowing how to say no to the woman, Tina agrees to buy the $85 dress. It takes all of her $65 plus another $20. The store agrees to let her pay the remaining $20 over the next two months.

When Tina arrives home with her costly purchase, she is almost sick. Her only coat is much too casual to go well with the dress and it doesn't look right with any of her shoes either. To make matters worse, she learns that everyone else plans to wear more casual clothes to the party.

Case Review

1. Have you ever let a salesclerk talk you into buying something you really did not want to buy?
2. How might Tina have avoided her expensive mistake?
3. What information would you want to know about a store before buying something from that store?
4. Where could Tina have found information and ideas that might have helped her make a better choice?
5. What can Tina do about her mistake?

Shopping for Clothes

Shopping for clothes is much like shopping for anything else. You need a list or plan of what to buy. You need to know how to judge quality and what quality level will best serve different purposes. You need a firm estimate of how much you can spend. You need to know where to shop for different items. Shopping for clothes also requires some special knowledge and skills. Before you buy, it is important to:

- ❑ Check the construction.
- ❑ See what fibers, fabrics, and finishes have been used.
- ❑ Consider how they will affect fit, comfort, and appearance.
- ❑ Evaluate the fit and appearance.
- ❑ Read labels and tags for use and care information.

Clothing Construction

The way garments are put together can affect appearance, fit, and durability. Poorly made garments look worn and unattractive quickly. Better quality clothes are usually more expensive, but they may be better buys. With proper care, they will look attractive much longer.

Judge the quality of construction. Check important sewing and finishing details on the seams, linings, hems, collars, lapels, buttonholes, zippers, and pockets. Chart 8-5 describes how these and other construction features should look in well-made clothing. Look also for buttons and trims that are suited to the garment and to its care requirements.

Judging Quality

Construction Features	Quality Indicators
Cut and Fabric Allowance	❑ Garment pieces cut with the grain.* ❑ Generous allowances for seams, hems, pleats, lapels, and fitting ease. ❑ Stripes, plaids, checks, and other designs matched at seams.
Seams	❑ Flat, even in width, wide enough to withstand strain and permit alterations. ❑ Double row stitching to reinforce stress points, such as armpits, crotch, waist, neckline. ❑ Smooth outside seams and darts.
Stitching	❑ Short, continuous, and straight. ❑ Securely fastened at the ends. ❑ Thread of the right weight, color, and fiber for the fabric.
Reinforcements	❑ Extra stitching, bar tacks, metal rivits, or tape at points of strain. ❑ Reinforced underarm seams, openings, slits, pockets, knees and elbows in work clothes, sportswear, and children's play clothes.
Hems	❑ Flat, even in width, invisible on the right side. ❑ Carefully finished and evenly stitched on inside. ❑ Even in length.
Buttonholes	❑ Smooth and properly placed. ❑ Right size and type for the garment. ❑ Firmly stitched and trimmed with no loose threads or frayed edges. ❑ Evenly spaced with reinforced corners.
Buttons, Hooks and Eyes, Snaps	❑ Firmly attached and properly spaced. ❑ Right size and type for garment. ❑ Extra buttons often included for high quality clothes.
Trim and Decoration	❑ Suited to the garment, well placed, and firmly attached. ❑ Same care requirements as garment.
Zippers and Closures	❑ Smooth, flat, securely stitched. ❑ Right size, type, strength, and color for garment. ❑ Smooth sliding zippers and easy to operate closures.
Linings	❑ Smooth, properly inserted. ❑ Right weight and texture for garment with same care requirements.
Interfacing**	❑ Properly placed and inserted. ❑ Made of materials right for the garment and its care requirements.
Shoulder Pads	❑ Soft, lightweight, smoothly shaped. ❑ Smooth fitting. ❑ May be attached with velcro for easy removal.
Pockets	❑ Flat, smooth, and properly matched to garment. ❑ Reinforced corners and firmly woven linings.
Collars and Lapels	❑ Collar points neatly finished. ❑ Collar top slightly turned over undercollar around seam edges. ❑ Lapels lying flat to the chest with graceful roll and smooth edge. ❑ "V" formed by lapels ending in soft roll at top button.

*Grain is the direction of lengthwise and crosswise yarns woven together in making fabric. When the yarns are at right angles, fabric is "grain perfect." A garment cut on-grain is grain perfect with pattern pieces running parallet to the lengthwise or crosswise yarns. Garments cut on-grain hang better and hold shape longer than clothing cut off-grain.
**Interfacings are extra layers of fabric inside neck facings, cuffs, lapels, and collars and often under buttons and buttonholes to provide extra strength, body, and a smooth finish.

8-5
The ability to judge quality is essential in getting value for the dollars you spend on clothes.

Fibers, Fabrics, and Finishes

Fiber content, construction methods, and finishes affect the way a fabric looks and feels, its performance and care, and its price. Knowing how fabrics are made can help you make informed clothing choices.

Fiber Content

Most fabrics are made from natural or manufactured fibers. Cotton, linen, silk, wool, and other hair fibers, such as camel's hair and cashmere, are ***natural fibers.*** They come from plants and animals. ***Manufactured fibers*** include polyester, nylon, rayon, acrylic, acetate, and a host of others. Most manufactured fibers are made from chemicals. Charts 8-6 and 8-7 outline the major advantages, disadvantages, and uses of the natural and manufactured fibers commonly used for clothing.

A ***blend*** is made by combining two or more fibers. Blends usually have the best characteristics of the different fibers used. For example, cotton/polyester is a very common and popular blend. It combines absorbent and comfort properties of cotton with the wrinkle-resistant, easy-care properties of polyester.

Fabric Construction

The way fibers are made into fabric affects appearance and performance. Weaving and knitting are the two most common methods of fabric construction. ***Woven fabrics*** are made by interlacing two or more sets of yarns at right angles. A number of weaving variations can be used to achieve special effects. Generally, weaving produces durable fabrics that hold their shape well.

Knit fabrics are made by looping yarns together. Depending on the knitting methods and fibers used, fabrics can vary greatly in appearance and texture. Most knit fabrics offer natural stretch that makes them wrinkle-resistant and comfortable to wear. Fabrics that are closely woven or knitted tend to hold their shape better than those that are loosely woven or knitted.

Cloth made from construction methods other than weaving or knitting includes ***nonwoven fabrics,*** such as felt and artificial suedes, bonded fabrics, quilted fabrics, lace, and net.

Finishes

A ***fabric finish*** is a treatment applied to a fabric to achieve certain characteristics. Finishes affect the appearance, comfort, durability, performance, and care of fabrics.

Finishes can affect the appearance of fabric by improving its color and dyeability. They can also improve the luster, texture, and drapability of fabrics.

Certain finishes make clothing more comfortable to wear because they provide greater insulation, reduce static cling, resist water, and soften fabrics.

Other fabric finishes provide resistance to moths and mildew. They can prevent shrinking, fading, and staining. Certain finishes make cloth flame-retardant and water-resistant. Finishes also can help fabrics resist wrinkles, hold pleats and creases, and release soil.

Before buying a garment, find out if it has been treated with a finish. Some finishes require special care when being cleaned. Be sure you know how to care for the garment before you buy it. Also check the durability of the finish. Will it last the life of the garment? Will it have to be renewed after laundering or dry cleaning? Read labels and tags to know just what you are buying and how to care for it.

Natural Fibers

	Advantages	Disadvantages	Uses
Cotton	Absorbent. Comfortable and cool to wear. Easy to dye and print. Does not generate static electricity. Withstands high temperatures. Combines easily with other fibers.	Wrinkles easily unless treated with special finish. Shrinks in hot water, unless treated. Mildews if stored in damp area or put away damp. Weakened by wrinkle-resistant finishes and prolonged exposure to sunlight. Highly flammable unless treated with flame-retardant finish.	Underwear and outerwear, socks, jeans, shirts, dresses, blouses, coats, etc.
Linen	Strongest of natural fibers. Cool to wear—absorbs moisture from skin and dries quickly. Looks smooth and lustrous. Withstands high temperatures. Durable—withstands frequent laundering.	Wrinkles and creases easily unless treated. Shines if ironed on right side. Expensive if of good quality. Poor resistance to mildew and perspiration.	Dresses, suits, blouses, coats, jackets, trousers, handkerchiefs.
Silk	Looks and feels smooth and luxurious. Very absorbent. Strong but lightweight. Combines well with other fibers. Resists wrinkling. Resists soil.	Requires dry cleaning unless labeled washable. Yellows with age. Weakened by detergents, perspiration, and long exposure to sunlight. Attacked by insects such as silverfish. Spotted by water unless specially treated. Expensive.	Evening gowns, dresses, blouses, suits, trousers, scarves, lingerie, neckties.
Wool	Warmest of all fibers. Combines well with other fibers. Highly absorbent—absorbs moisture without feeling wet. Resists wrinkles. Retains shape well. Creases well. Durable.	Will shrink and mat when moisture and heat are applied. Usually requires dry cleaning unless labeled washable. Burns easily. Attracts moths and carpet beetles. Expensive if of good quality.	Suits, sweaters, coats, skirts, socks, outerwear.

8-6
Fabrics made from natural fibers generally are attractive and comfortable to wear. They may also be more expensive than manufactured fibers and blends.

Five Common Manufactured Fibers

	Advantages	Disadvantages	Uses
Polyester	Strong and durable. Easy to dye. Colorfast. Retains shape well. Resists wrinkles, stretching, shrinking, moths, and mildew.	Nonabsorbent. Generates static electricity. Subject to oily stains, soil, and pilling.	Shirts, blouses, dresses, slacks, suits, lingerie, children's wear, insulated garments, and permanent press garments.
Nylon	Strong and durable. Lightweight and lustrous. Easy to dye. Drapes well. Retains shape well. Dries quickly. Resists moths, mildew, and oily stains.	Nonabsorbent. Generates static electricity. Subject to soil and pilling.	Hosiery, lingerie, underwear, dresses, raincoats, and ski wear.
Rayon	Resembles cotton. Soft and comfortable. Absorbent. Easy to dye. Colorfast. Drapes well. Resists moths and pilling.	Wrinkles easily unless treated with a special finish. Shrinks in hot water unless treated. Highly flammable unless treated.	Blouses, shirts, skirts, slacks, dresses, suits, coats, jackets, lingerie, and ties.
Acrylic	Resembles wool. Soft, warm, and lightweight. Colorfast. Retains shape well. Resists wrinkles, chemicals, moths, mildew, and sunlight.	Nonabsorbent. Generates static electricity. Subject to abrasion, pilling, stretching, and soil.	Sweaters, dresses, infant wear, slacks, ski wear, and socks.
Acetate	Looks and feels soft and luxurious. Easy to dye. Drapes well, resists pilling, moths, and mildew.	Nonabsorbent. Usually requires dry cleaning. Melts under high heat.	Blouses, shirts, skirts, slacks, dresses, sportswear, lingerie, linings, and robes.

8-7
Fabrics made from manufactured fibers generally are strong, wrinkle resistant, and easy to launder or clean.

Following are some of the finishes commonly applied to fabrics along with their functions.

- *Antistatic.* This finish prevents the buildup of static electricity so garments will not cling to the body.
- *Durable-press.* This is also called permanent press. It helps fabric retain its original shape and resist wrinkling after washing and drying.
- *Flame-resistance.* Fabrics treated with this finish resist supporting a flame. It works by cutting off the oxygen supply. The Flammable Fabrics Act requires that this finish be applied to flammable fabrics used in children's sleepwear and other clothing and household items.
- *Mercerization.* This finish is used most often on cotton, linen, and

rayon fabrics. It increases luster, strength, and dyeability.

- *Mildew-resistance.* This helps prevent mildew from forming on fabrics.
- *Moth-resistance.* This finish is added to wool fibers to inhibit attacks by moths and carpet beetles.
- *Preshrinking.* With this finish, fabrics are shrunk by a heat and moisture process to prevent further shrinkage. When a garment is labeled preshrunk, the consumer is guaranteed that it will not shrink more than three percent.
- *Sanforized®.* This finish guarantees the consumer that a fabric will not shrink more than one percent in either length or width.
- *Scotchgard®.* This creates resistance to water and oil stains.
- *Soil-release.* A soil-release finish makes it possible to remove oily stains from durable-press fabrics. It makes water-resistant fibers more absorbent so detergents can release soil.
- *Waterproof.* A fabric treated with a waterproofing finish is completely resistant to water and air passage. Fabrics with this finish can be uncomfortable to wear.
- *Water-repellent.* This finish makes a fabric resistant to wetting but does not make it waterproof or resistant to heavy rain. The finish must be renewed after several launderings.

Fit and Appearance

Clothing that looks great on the hanger or a model in a magazine may not look so terrific on you. A dress or suit that is just right on one person may be all wrong for another. The only way to know which garments do the most for you is to try them on. Check the fit, style, and appearance. When possible, try on clothes with the shoes, accessories, and other garments you plan to wear with them. It is particularly important to check skirt lengths and pant cuffs with the shoes you will wear. It also helps to try out accessories you plan to use with new garments.

Stand, sit, move, and stretch to check comfort and fit of new garments. Inspect your overall appearance in a full length mirror from the front, side, and rear. If clothing fits well, it will not bind, wrinkle, or pucker.

The Shopping Scene

Lupe Is in a Hurry

Lupe is always busy. Besides classes, she has play practice, band practice, homework, and a part-time job. She never has much time for shopping, so she takes shortcuts whenever possible.

Last month, Lupe bought an expensive raincoat on sale at 30 percent off. As usual, she was in a hurry. She slipped the coat on over the jeans she was wearing. It seemed to fit and the price was right, so she bought the coat.

A week later Lupe was dressing for a special date. When she put on her new raincoat, she realized the coat was much shorter than her dress. The mismatched hem lengths looked awful, but there was nothing Lupe could do. The dress was the right length, and the coat could not be lengthened.

Case Review

1. How could Lupe have avoided this problem?
2. What are some precautions to keep in mind when buying clothes on sale?
3. What are some practical shortcuts you can take when you don't have much time to shop for clothes?

The way a garment looks on you is just as important as the way it fits. Select colors, lines, styles, and textures that flatter your figure type and coloring. You can use color, line, and texture to look thinner or heavier and shorter or taller. These elements can also call attention to your positive features and away from negative features. Chart 8-8 can help you find the lines, colors, and textures to create the look you want. See 8-9.

Labels and Legislation

The labels and tags on clothes provide important information. Most labels will identify the manufacturer, designer, or seller; the name of the country where the garment was made; and the fiber content. If a special finish has been applied to the fabric, it is usually listed. Labels also give care instructions and size information.

Much of the data listed on labels of clothing and other textile products is required by law. Some facts are provided voluntarily by manufacturers or sellers. Four of the most important laws and regulations that govern the labeling, marketing, and safety of clothing and textile products are described in 8-10.

Create the Look You Want Through Color, Line, and Texture

Look thinner with:	Look heavier with:
❑ Cool colors (colors related to blue and green). ❑ Dark, subtle colors. ❑ Vertical lines. ❑ Smooth, nonlustrous, medium weight textures. ❑ Subtle prints, checks, and plaids. ❑ Clothes that skim the body and don't fit tight. ❑ Simple, uncluttered styles. ❑ Thin shapes and narrow widths in coats, sleeves, collars, trousers, and belts.	❑ Warm colors (colors related to red, orange, and yellow). ❑ Bright, light colors. ❑ Horizontal lines. ❑ Nubby, bulky, or stiff textures with surface interest. ❑ Bold prints, checks, and plaids. ❑ Full sleeves, wide-leg trousers, large pleats, and gathers. ❑ Wide contrasting belts.
Look taller with:	**Look shorter with:**
❑ One color or related color tones head to foot. ❑ Vertical lines. ❑ Designs, lines, and trims that lead the eye up instead of down. ❑ Narrow, uncuffed trousers. ❑ Emphasis at or above the neckline.	❑ Bright, contrasting colors. ❑ Horizontal lines. ❑ Designs, lines, or trims that lead the eye down instead of up. ❑ Wide-cuffed trousers. ❑ Emphasis below the waist or at the feet.
Accentuate positive features with:	**De-emphasize negative features with:**
❑ Warm, bright, light colors. ❑ Lines and designs that lead the eye to your best features. ❑ Fabrics and textures that emphasize your best features.	❑ Cool, dark, subtle colors. ❑ Lines that lead the eye away from poor features. ❑ Styles, fabrics, and textures that hide or cover poor features.

8-8
Color, line, and texture in clothing can help you highlight attractive features and de-emphasize negative features.

Buying Footwear

Comfort is the key word when buying footwear. The best looking, well-made shoes are worthless if they don't fit. The right fit not only adds to your comfort, it can help you avoid aching feet and serious foot problems.

Do not rely only on sizes when buying footwear. Sizes often vary with different styles or brands. Try shoes on to check fit. The entire shoe should fit snugly without being tight. The widest part of the shoe should fit the widest part of your foot. Shoes should not slip or pinch your feet when you stand or walk. If you can't move your toes freely, try a different size, width, or style. Check fit with the socks or hose you plan to wear with footwear.

Before buying shoes or boots, examine the construction, 8-11. Are they stitched well and lined smoothly? Are the shoes made of soft, durable, flexible materials?

The materials used to make shoes can also affect comfort. Feet need to "breathe" inside a shoe to keep dry and comfortable. Open shoes and footwear made of leather allow air to circulate around the foot. Plastic, vinyl, and rubber materials do not allow feet to breathe well.

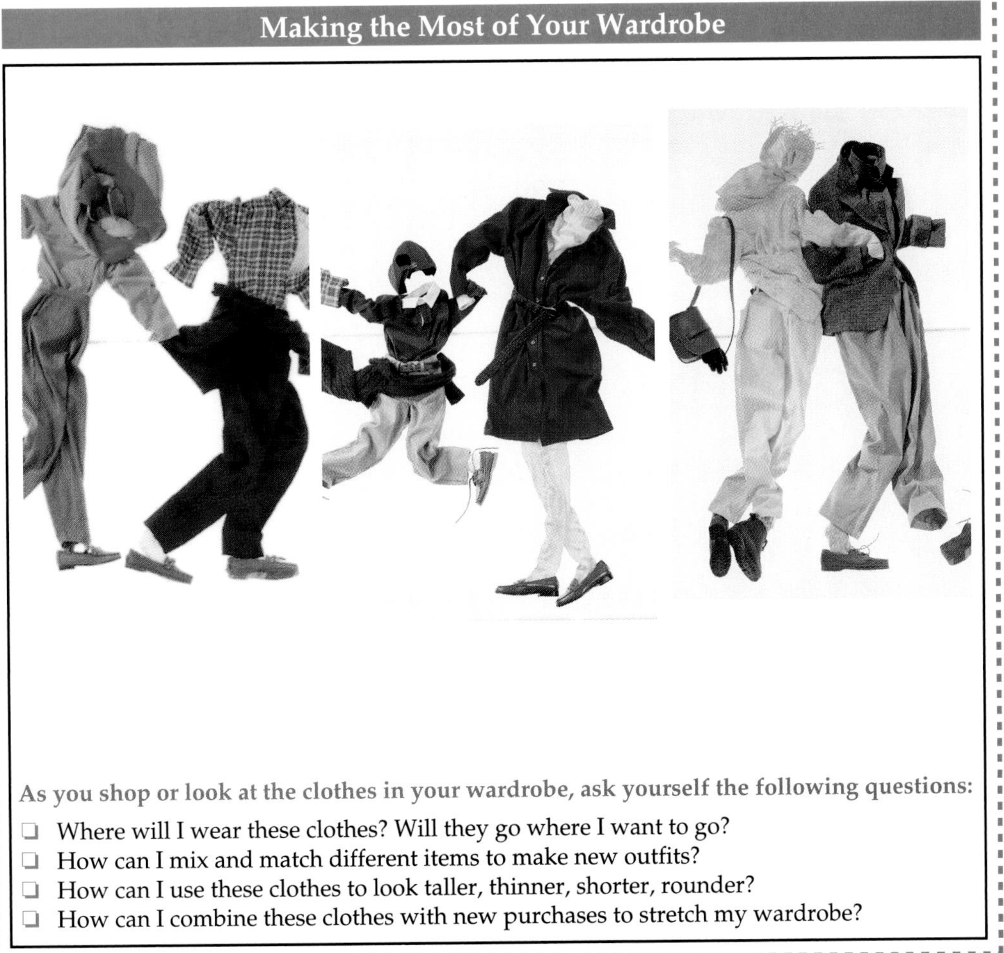

8-9
You can mix and match clothes to help you create the look you want.

Regulations Governing Clothing and Textile Products	
Wool Products Labeling Act	This act requires products containing wool to be labeled with the percentage and type of fibers used—new or virgin wool, reprocessed or reused wool. This act is enforced by the Federal Trade Commission.
Textiles Fiber Products Identification Act	This act requires textile products to be labeled with the generic name, fibers used, and the percentage of each fiber present by weight. The name or identification of the manufacturer and the country of origin, if the item is imported, must also be listed. This is required for wearing apparel, accessories, and textile products used in the home such as draperies, upholstered furniture, linens, and bedding. This act is enforced by the Federal Trade Commission.
Permanent Care Labeling Rule	This rule requires manufacturers to attach permanent care labels to apparel explaining the best way to clean a garment including methods and temperatures for laundering, drying, ironing, and dry cleaning. Fabrics, draperies, curtains, slipcovers, upholstered furniture, carpets, and rugs must also be labeled with care instructions. This rule is enforced by the Federal Trade Commission.
Flammable Fabrics Act	This act sets flammability standards for children's sleepwear, general wearing apparel, carpets, rugs, and mattresses to protect consumers from unreasonable fire risks.This act is enforced by the Consumer Product Safety Commission.

8-10
These laws regulate the labeling, marketing, and safety of clothing and textile products.

Men's Fashion Institute

8-11
When buying shoes, fit is particularly important.

Different activities call for different shoes. For example, tennis, hiking, running, basketball, and other sports require shoes that provide adequate support and that will stand up to heavy-duty action. When buying athletic shoes, you need the best fit, comfort, and support. Athletic shoes should be well made, durable shoes that can take the pressure. These shoes can be very expensive. Cost is not always the best guide to quality. It pays to shop carefully for good values.

As a rule, buy the best quality footwear you can afford. In addition to comfort and quality, consider the style. Choose colors and designs that look well on your feet and fit into your wardrobe. Look also for shoes that are easy to clean and maintain.

Buying Accessories

Accessories add color, variety, and interest to an outfit. Sometimes a new necktie, a different belt, or a bright scarf can create a whole new look.

Before buying accessories, consider your wardrobe needs. Think about the color, size, and style of the accessories you need to complement the different clothes you wear. Choose items that are appropriate for the style of clothing you wear. For example, a woven leather belt usually looks right with casual clothes. A velvet, jewel-trimmed belt goes best with dressy clothes.

Buy a few accessories of high quality rather than a number of inexpensive items. This will be more economical. For example, buying a fine leather belt in a basic color and style may be better than buying several low-quality belts.

Fashion is another important consideration when buying accessories. Are narrow or wide neckties in style? Is jewelry big and gaudy or subtle and delicate? Are wide belts in or out? While fashion is important, don't compromise your appearance just to be fashionable. If wide belts are "in" but are not right for your figure, buy a narrow belt.

Accessories also need to be in scale with your size and shape to look well. A small person can be overpowered by large, bulky jewelry. A short, narrow tie may seem lost on a large man. A long, flowing scarf or a dramatic cape could look just right on a tall, thin woman, but would be too much for a short, stout person. A careful look in a full-length mirror is the best way to judge the scale or proportion of accessories.

Caring for Clothes

Proper clothing care keeps clothes looking better and makes them last longer. Clean, pressed, and mended garments will also enhance your appearance. Spending a few dollars on clothing care can help you get more out of the many dollars you spend on clothing purchases.

Routine Care

Caring for clothes on a routine basis will keep clothes and accessories in good condition and ready to wear. Simple things, like dressing and undressing carefully, can help you avoid snagging, ripping, or stretching garments. After wearing clothes, check to see if they need cleaning, spotting, pressing, or mending before you put them away. You may only need to brush garments to remove lint and dust. Air your clothes in an open room before returning them to the closet or drawer.

Remember to protect clothes with aprons or napkins when you are cooking or eating. Wear old clothes for tough, dirty jobs to avoid ruining good garments. Also avoid overstuffing pockets or handbags. This can cause them to become unstitched or stretched out of shape.

Storing Clothes

Proper storage is an important part of clothing care. Make it a habit to hang clothes straight on sturdy hangers. Close zippers and fasten buttons. Fold sweaters and knit garments neatly and store them in drawers. Avoid overcrowding closets and drawers so clothes will not be crushed or wrinkled.

Periodically, clean and organize closets and drawers. This will help you keep track of the clothes you own and make them easy to find. Make a clothing inventory at the beginning of each season. This is also a good time for sorting, repairing, and cleaning garments and footwear.

> ***"Fashion is made to become unfashionable."***
>
> *Coco Chanel*

Before storing out-of-season clothes, always clean and mend them. Remember to check and empty pockets. Clothing needs to be stored in clean, dry places. Avoid damp areas, such as basements, where fabrics could mildew or become musty. If storage space is a problem, you may want to store out-of-season clothing with a local dry cleaner. They very often offer this service at a relatively low cost.

Plastic bags, garment bags, and cardboard boxes are good to use for storing clothes. Try to avoid crowding items into bags or boxes. You may want to spray woolens with moth repellents or store them with mothballs to prevent moth damage.

Laundering

Learning how to clean clothes properly is simply a matter of reading. If you follow the directions on clothing care labels, laundry products, and washers and dryers, clothes can continue to look nice after many washings. See 8-12.

Preparing items to be washed is the first step in home laundering. Empty all pockets, fasten closures, make necessary repairs, and remove any non-washable trims. Also remove stains and pretreat heavily soiled clothes before washing.

Sorting comes next. The purpose of sorting is to separate items that could damage other clothes. Wash together those items that call for the same water temperature, wash speed, and other treatment. For best results, wash similar colors and fabrics together. For example, wash dark clothes with dark colors, whites with whites, and delicates with delicates.

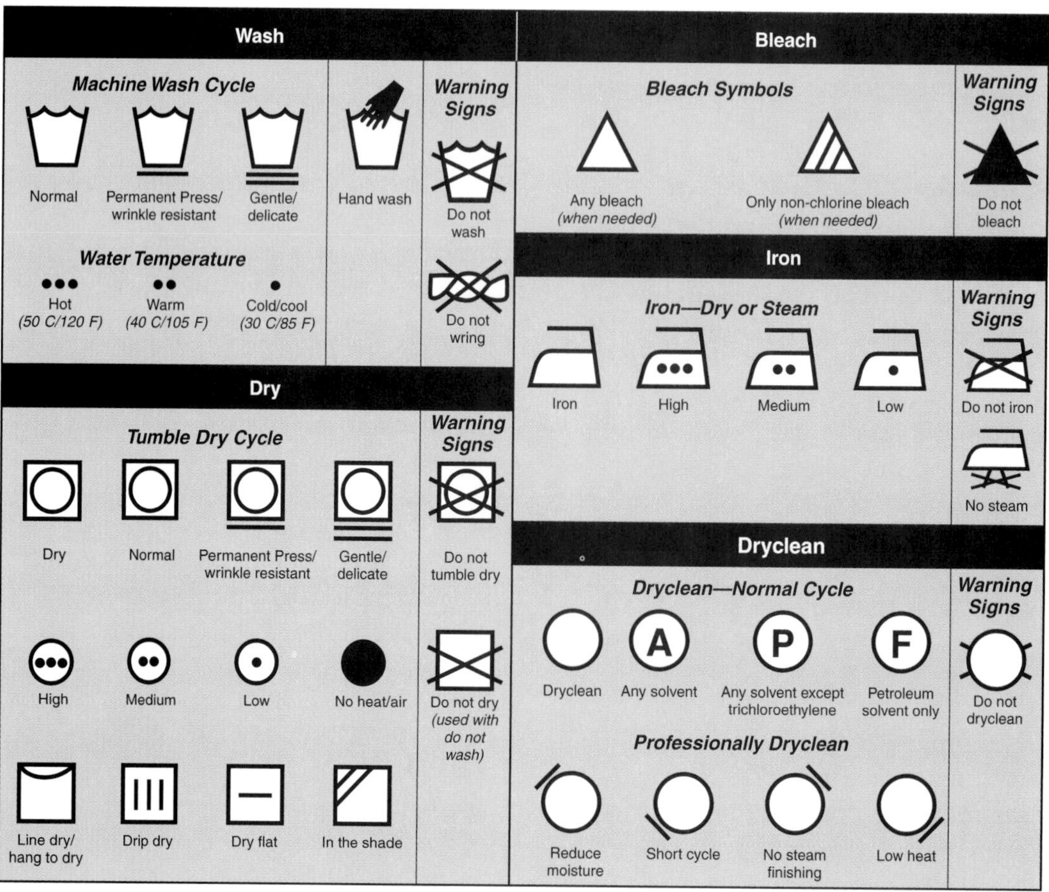

8-12
Proper clothing care increases wear life and improves appearance of garments. These symbols are your guide to clothing care.

As you may have noticed in stores, there are many kinds of laundry products. Choose only the products you need, and follow the package directions carefully. Liquid or powder soaps and detergents are the basic laundry products. Bleaches may be used to remove stains or to whiten and brighten clothes. Since chlorine bleaches are made of strong chemicals, they should not be used on all garments. Items that cannot withstand bleaching should be labeled "No Bleach."

Fabric softeners may be added to the rinse cycle to make fabrics soft and to reduce wrinkles and static electricity. Again, follow the directions when using these products. Sheet fabric softeners are available to use in the dryer.

Before washing clothes, make sure you select a wash cycle that is suitable for the clothes you are washing. Wash delicate items on a delicate or gentle cycle. Wash permanent press on the permanent press cycle. Most other items can be washed on the normal cycle. Select water temperature as directed on the care labels.

When drying clothes in an automatic dryer, select the cycle that will be best for the clothes you are drying. If you do not know which cycle to use, read the directions that came with the dryer and the care labels on clothing. Whatever cycle you use, remove clothes as soon as they are dry to prevent wrinkling.

Some care labels may recommend other drying methods, such as drip-drying on a hanger or flat drying on a towel. Be sure to use the correct method for all the clothes you wash.

Dry Cleaning

Clothes that require dry cleaning may be done in a coin-operated dry cleaning center or by a professional dry cleaner. Coin-operated machines often are available at laundromats. Using these machines is less expensive than professional dry cleaning. However, dry cleaning clothes yourself takes more time and effort. It also does not include the advantages of professional spotting, pressing, and other services dry cleaning establishments may offer.

Professional dry cleaners do all the work for you. They can often remove spots and stains that you may have difficulty removing. They can add sizing to a garment to give it more body. They can also restore a water-repellent finish after cleaning. Dry cleaners may offer additional services, such as alterations, pickups, and deliveries.

Summary

Your clothes and personal appearance can make a difference in the way others see you and in the way you feel about yourself. Most people want appropriate clothes for the way they live and places they go.

Putting together a wardrobe that fits your lifestyle takes planning. It means learning what colors and styles look best on you. It means building a wardrobe of clothes that will be right for you and your activities. You also need to find clothes and accessories that go well together.

Wardrobe planning usually begins with an inventory of clothes on hand. It involves taking a close look at what is wearable and clearing out what you no longer can use. Identifying the gaps in your wardrobe will serve as a guide to making new purchases.

Once you know what you want, it pays to do a little pre-shopping in magazines and stores to find current fashions that will work well for you. This will also give you a good idea of the prices you will need to pay for different items.

Setting up a clothing budget will help you afford what you want and avoid overspending. Bargain hunting and comparison shopping can help you stretch the amount you have to spend on clothes. End-of-season sales can make dollars go farther, too.

When it comes to shopping, you should know how to judge clothing construction and have a sense of fashion. Fabric is a key factor in the look and feel of clothes. Fabric type will affect performance, price, and care. Information you need on fabric finishes will appear on labels. Reading labels will provide information on fiber content and care of fabrics.

Buying footwear is a major part of dressing well. Here comfort is particularly important. Trying shoes on with the socks you will wear with them is vital. Mistakes can cause serious foot problems. Select appropriate shoes for appearance and for the way you will wear them.

Accessories add the touches of individual flair to the way you dress. A scarf, belt, gloves, and jewelry can change the look of an outfit and offer a way to express your own style. The key to shopping for accessories lies in finding items that will go well with the clothes you wear.

Proper clothing care is the secret to a ready-to-go wardrobe of clothes that look and wear well. Laundering clothes requires reading labels and following directions. Care labels in garments and labels on laundry products tell how to use the products for different types of laundering. The user's manual that comes with washers and dryers will also provide important information. Dry cleaning will be necessary for certain types of fabrics and clothing. Keeping clothes clean and in good condition will make them look better and last longer.

To Review

1. What are the three major steps involved in wardrobe planning?
2. Give four examples of accessories.
3. List five items a wardrobe inventory should include.
4. Describe two ways you could recycle clothes you have outgrown or that have gone out of style.
5. What four things do you need to consider when establishing a wardrobe budget?
6. Where are some places to buy clothes and accessories at low prices?
7. List two examples of nonwoven fabrics.
8. What is the difference between a waterproof finish and a water-repellent finish?

9. Why is it important to try on clothes before you buy them?
10. What is the purpose of permanent care labels on clothes?
11. True or false. As a rule, always buy the best quality footwear you can afford.
12. What are some important factors to consider when buying accessories?
13. List four routine clothing care tasks.
14. Describe three sources of clothing care information.

To Think Critically

1. Discuss how clothing can express your personality.
2. How can the clothes you wear influence a person's first impression of you?
3. How does the way people dress relate to
   A. The way they feel about themselves?
   B. The way others feel about them?
   C. Their popularity?
   D. Their success on the job?
4. What clothes or outfits do you like most in your wardrobe? What is it you particularly like about each favorite item of clothing? How can you apply this knowledge to future purchases?
5. What are the advantages of identifying your wardrobe needs and establishing a clothing budget before shopping for clothes?
6. What do you need to consider before making additions to your wardrobe?
7. What colors, lines, and textures look best on you? What clothes should you wear to flatter your body shape and accentuate your positive features?
8. How fashion-conscious are you? How much importance do you place on fashion when buying clothes?
9. How important is quality clothing construction to you? Would you rather have fewer clothes of very good quality or more clothes of lesser quality? Why?
10. Before buying, what should you find out about a fabric or a garment that has been treated with a special finish, such as soil-release?
11. What do you need to consider when buying footwear?
12. What are some tips to remember when storing out-of-season clothes?
13. What problems have you had with clothing care? What did you do to solve these problems?

To Do

1. Plan two trips to the same store to shop for the same item in the same department. Shop at a store where you are not known and at a time when stores will not be crowded. On one shopping trip, wear your most presentable street clothes and try to look your best. On the other trip, dress in old, mismatched, soiled clothing and make an effort to look messy and poorly groomed. Compare the two experiences. What differences did you notice in the way you felt? What differences did you notice in the way salespeople and other shoppers treated you? How might this experience work in other situations, such as a job interview, a date, or a day at school?
2. Select five different items of clothing for comparison shopping. Shop for each of the five items in different outlets—clothing stores, discount stores, department stores, and catalogs. Compare the price, quality, selection, and styles of like items. Also compare the services and policies of the places you shopped. In a short oral report, tell

the class which places offered the best price, quality, selection, styles, services, and business policies.

3. Compare the cost of buying a shirt at a store where you usually shop to the cost of making a similar shirt yourself. What is the cost difference? How much time would you spend shopping for the shirt compared to the time you would spend shopping for the fabric and making it?
4. Find out the cost difference between taking three shirts to a professional dry cleaner and washing and ironing them at home.
5. At a time when stores are not too busy, interview an experienced salesperson in a clothing department of a store where you shop. Ask the following questions:
   A. What clothing is selling best at the present time?
   B. What is new in fabrics, styles, patterns, and colors?
   C. What fashion changes do you notice from year to year?
   D. What trends are expected for the upcoming season?
   E. What type of customers do you most like to serve? Which do you find most disagreeable?

When shopping for clothes, evaluate construction features, fabrics, fit and appearance.

CHAPTER 9

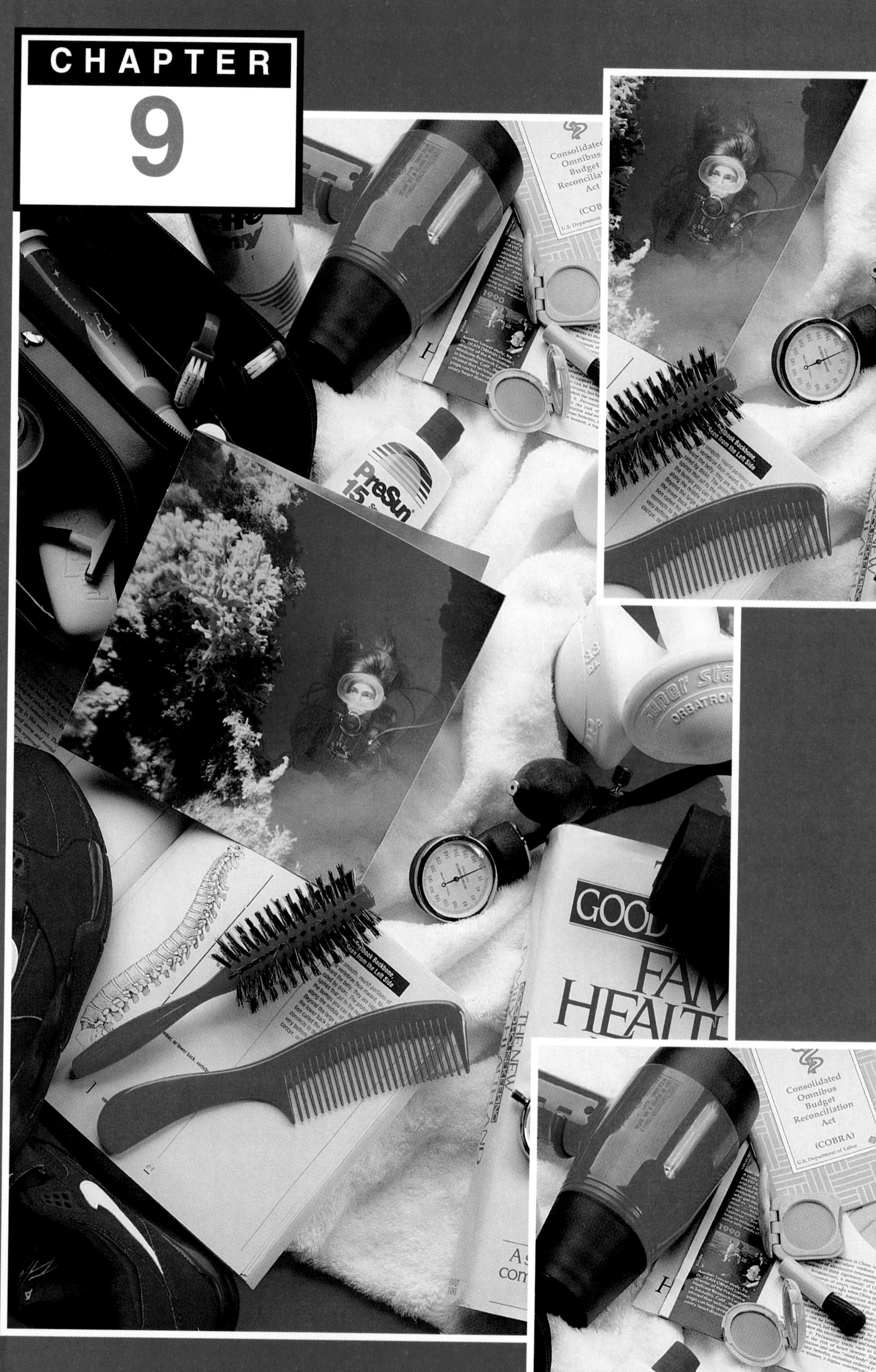

PreSun 15
Consolidated Omnibus Budget Reconciliation Act
(COBRA)
U.S. Department of Labor

How You Look and Feel

hypoallergenic
primary care physician
specialist
osteopathic medicine
prescription drug
over-the-counter drug
generic drug
medicare
medicaid
deductible
co-payment
medigap insurance
fee-for-service
managed care plans
health maintenance organization (HMO)
preferred provider organization (PPO)
point of service (POS) plan
co-insurance

After studying this chapter, you will be able to

- ❑ evaluate and select appropriate grooming aids, appliances, and services.
- ❑ select qualified health care professionals and evaluate the quality of care provided in health care facilities.
- ❑ evaluate the health care delivery services available to you.
- ❑ explain the two types of government-funded health insurance programs—medicare and medicaid.
- ❑ outline the different types of private health insurance coverage.
- ❑ manage money and time in pursuing fun and leisure-time activities.

When you look and feel your best, you get more out of life. Developing good grooming and health habits is the first step in improving the way you look and feel. Getting your fair share of fun helps, too.

It is difficult to separate the way you look from the way you feel. When you look good, you feel better. When you feel in top shape, you look better. It is also difficult to separate a "good looks" program from a "good health" program.

Keys to looking and feeling great at every stage of your life are listed in 9-1. It is nearly impossible to look and feel your best without a balanced

Keys to Looking and Feeling Your Best at Every Stage of Life

- ❑ Adequate sleep, rest, relaxation
- ❑ Regular exercise and physical activity
- ❑ A well balanced, nutritious diet
- ❑ Maintaining healthy weight
- ❑ Competent medical and dental care
- ❑ Attention to known safety precautions
- ❑ Attention to posture and grooming
- ❑ Challenge, achievement, involvement
- ❑ Positive mental attitude
- ❑ Family, friendship, and support
- ❑ Effective control of stress
- ❑ Avoidance of tobacco and drugs

9-1
This chart outlines the keys to good health and good looks.

9-2
Regular exercise is part of a well-rounded approach to looking and feeling good.

approach in these areas. See 9-2. Still, thousands of people routinely ignore one or more of these basics. At the same time, they spend billions of dollars on products that promise effortless beauty and health. Not all of these dollars are wasted. Many products are helpful, and some are even necessary. However, consumers should consider the way they live as well as the money and effort they invest in these products.

Each year, Americans spend over $40 billion dollars on personal care needs including cosmetics, grooming aids, and personal care services. As a nation, we spend over one trillion dollars annually on health care. This came to an average of almost $3,800 per person in 1996. Compare this to an average of $1700 in 1985. The way you look and feel can cost big dollars. For many, this heavy spending is not combined with the best health practices. A national health survey showed that, of all persons interviewed,

22 percent sleep less than six hours nightly;
24 percent never eat breakfast;
16 percent get inadequate physical exercise;
37 percent drink five or more alcoholic beverages per day;
25 percent smoke (35 percent of teenagers smoke);
35 percent are above a healthy weight.

The Way You Look

Teenagers typically spend a large percentage of income on personal care products. Have you ever totaled the dollars you spend to improve your looks and enhance nature's work? An inventory of personal care products will show how much you have invested. Think of all the different products you use, their prices, and effectiveness. Do you feel you are getting your money's worth? Which products are giving you the most and least satisfaction? Your inventory can be your guide for future purchases.

Selecting Grooming Aids

Cosmetics or grooming aids are items used to cleanse, beautify, or alter the appearance of the body. They do not alter body structure or functions. Certain cosmetics are also drugs. That is, they are intended to treat or prevent disease or to affect the functions of the body. These include fluoride in toothpaste, hormone creams, sunscreens, antiperspirants, and anti-dandruff shampoos. Cosmetics and drug products must be labeled with the "active ingredients" and must meet FDA standards for safety and effectiveness.

When you buy a cosmetic or grooming aid, keep in mind these four questions: Is it safe to use? Will it work? Is it a good buy? Do I need it? As you shop, read labels to compare the contents and prices of different products and brands. Often, salespersons can help you make the best choices, 9-3. Read directions on how to use products before you buy and before you use them.

Walgreen Co.

9-3
The choices of grooming products are almost unlimited. Read labels and ask questions when you shop.

For Your Health

What's in a Face?

Gloria spends an hour and a half getting ready for school every day. She starts with her hair. She shampoos, blow-dries, and styles it every morning. Next comes the face—moisturizer, foundation, blush, eye shadow, mascara, and lipstick. The top of her dresser is covered with bottles, jars, and tubes of cosmetics. She tries every sample offer and keeps a full stock of her favorites.

Gloria and her best friend, Allie, recently went out on a double date. Allie went over to Gloria's before the date so the two girls could get ready together. Since Gloria had a great selection of cosmetics, Allie did not bring her own. The girls passed jars and bottles of cosmetics from one to the other to see how they could change their looks.

The girls looked great that night, and had an enjoyable double date. Shortly after the date, both girls developed a skin infection. Neither of them could wear any makeup until the infection cleared. For Gloria, no makeup was like a death sentence. On top of that, she had to get rid of all her cosmetics. They became contaminated when she shared them and failed to replace the tops on several of the containers. Gloria has had to spend a lot of time and money replacing all her cosmetics.

Case Review

1. How do you feel about Gloria's love of cosmetics and grooming?
2. How much do you think Gloria spends each month to maintain her storehouse of cosmetics?
3. How could Gloria and Allie have avoided the skin infection?
4. How would you describe a balanced approach to buying and using cosmetics and grooming appliances?

Cosmetics, Safety, and the Law

Though it is not required by law, reputable cosmetic manufacturers test products thoroughly before marketing. They test for safety, effectiveness, and customer appeal, 9-4. Many manufacturers also voluntarily register their formulas with the Food and Drug Administration (FDA). They may make safety data available before marketing a product.

The FDA is the government agency that looks to the safety and labeling of cosmetics. The FDA requires manufacturers who do not test a product for safety to place a warning on the label. The warning reads, "The safety of this product has not been determined." The FDA can also ban unsafe or misbranded cosmetics. However, the agency must first prove that the product is unsafe or misbranded.

Product labels can be helpful buying guides. The Federal Food, Drug, and Cosmetic Act requires labels on cosmetic products to state

- ❑ The name of the product.
- ❑ A description of the nature or use of the product.
- ❑ Ingredients in descending order of predominance.
- ❑ Net quantity of contents by weight, measure, or count.
- ❑ Name and address of the firm marketing the product.
- ❑ Name of the manufacturer if different from the distributor.
- ❑ Country of origin if imported.

Labels must also carry warnings and adequate directions for safe use on any products that may be hazardous to consumers if misused. In addition to labeling requirements, tamper-resistant packaging is required for certain cosmetic products. These include liquid oral hygiene products, vaginal products, eyedrops, and contact lens preparations.

Keep in mind that cosmetics labeled hypoallergenic are not necessarily safe for persons with allergies. A product that is ***hypoallergenic*** is one that does not contain ingredients that are likely to cause allergic reactions. There is no way of producing a cosmetic that is totally nonallergenic for all users.

For your own safety, keep a record of any harmful reactions you experience from cosmetic products. Avoid buying anything that irritates your skin. If you have a serious reaction to a specific product, contact both the manufacturer and the FDA. Manufacturers should know of adverse reactions caused by their products. They can then take steps to modify the product and address the problem. The FDA investigates products that cause unusual reactions and will take corrective action if necessary.

Dean Foods Company

9-4
Most major cosmetic, chemical, pharmaceutical, and food companies operate sophisticated testing laboratories.

Buying Tips

Choose personal care products according to your skin and hair type and the results you want to achieve. See 9-5. For example, if you know you have oily skin, buy products that are made for oily skin. If dandruff is a

9-5
When you choose grooming products that are right for your skin type and coloring, you will look and feel better.

problem, consider shampoos with ingredients that fight or control it. Try to identify the colors that are most flattering as well. Many department stores and pharmacies offer demonstrations on the use of different cosmetics. This may be an opportunity to learn more about products before buying.

Look for special prices and sales on products you have tried and want to use again. Usually it is best to avoid buying sets of makeup, colognes, and other grooming aids unless you plan to use every product in the set. For products you have never used before, it is a good idea to buy a small, sample size to see if you will like using it.

If you are dissatisfied with a product or it does not meet specific advertising claims, return it. Some products have a money-back guarantee and most retailers will allow reasonable returns.

Certainly, it would make no sense for reputable, established companies to take chances with consumer safety. Unfortunately, there are some fly-by-night companies that make exaggerated claims for untested cosmetics in an attempt to make quick sales and profits. By the time their products are found unsafe or ineffective, the companies no longer exist. To protect yourself, learn what you can about the manufacturer as well as the product before you buy.

Although the FDA tries to keep unsafe cosmetics off the market, you will need to assume some responsibility for your own safety. Most cosmetics are safe for most people. However, adverse reactions to cosmetics are not uncommon. You can increase your margin of safety by reading product labels and by choosing and using cosmetics carefully, 9-6.

Selecting Grooming Appliances

In addition to cosmetics and grooming aids, consumers buy many personal care appliances. These include blow-dryers, curling irons, electric curlers, electric shavers, electric toothbrushes, lighted makeup mirrors, and a host of other products. There are many brand names, features, and prices for each appliance. The money you spend on these products will bring you greater satisfaction if you know how to make the best choices for your wants and needs.

Before buying an appliance, make sure you really need it and will use it. Check to see if you have enough space to use and store it. Storage space near an electrical outlet makes appliances more convenient to use. When shopping for personal care equipment, look closely at the product features. Don't pay extra for features you won't use. Also, make sure you can use the appliance with ease. For example, if you are buying a blow-dryer, check its weight and size. Buy a dryer you can handle and operate easily.

Look for the manufacturer's name. Make sure the appliance is made by a reputable company and sold by a reliable retailer. Any electric appliance

Use Cosmetics Safely

1. Read labels for information on ingredients, purposes, and uses of product.
2. Follow the use and care directions exactly.
3. Stop using any cosmetic that causes irritation. If irritation continues or becomes serious, see a doctor and take the cosmetic with you.
4. Don't use eye cosmetics if you have an eye infection.
5. Keep cosmetic products and containers clean. Wash your hands throughly before applying cosmetics.
6. Finish using one container of a cosmetic before opening a new container. Throw away cosmetics if they change color or an odor develops.
7. Do not share or borrow cosmetics. Another person's bacteria may be harmful to you.
8. Avoid using cosmetics on irritated or infected areas unless it is a medicated product intended to aid healing.
9. Never add any liquid to a cosmetic product, especially saliva. Bacteria is saliva may contaminate the product and cause infection.
10. Be sure to do a "patch test" according to directins when products call for one. This is especially important for harie coloring products.
11. Tightly close cosmetic containers after each use to prevent contamination.
12. Promptly report any serious reactions caused by a cosmetic to the FDA and to the manufacturer.
13. Keep cosmetics away from small children. Misuse of cosmetics may be hazardous.
14. Never apply cosmetics while driving.

9-6
These guidelines can help you use and store cosmetic products safely.

produced by a reputable manufacturer should carry the Underwriters Laboratories symbol. This symbol tells you that the product meets standards for electrical safety.

As you shop, it is important to read product warranties carefully. Find out exactly what is guaranteed, how long it is guaranteed, and what you must do to get service. Also ask if service, parts, or replacements for the appliance will be available after the warranty period.

Of course, price is an important factor to consider. Compare prices of similar appliances that have the same features. It also pays to compare prices at several stores. The cost of the same product can vary greatly from one retailer to another.

> ***"When it comes to your health, I recommend frequent doses of that rare commodity among Americans—common sense."***
>
> *Vincent Askey*

Once you buy a grooming appliance, look to your own safety in using it. Read and carefully follow directions for use, care, and storage of products. See 9-7.

Buying Grooming Services

Beauty and grooming services include haircuts, hair coloring, hair removal, permanents, facials, body massages, manicures, pedicures, tanning, and other procedures. Buying a service is different from buying a cosmetic product or grooming appliance because you can't really see what you are getting until you get it.

To avoid disappointments, make it a practice to check the qualifications and experience of persons performing services for you. Ask other customers if they were satisfied with the services they received.

Try to find persons who will provide the grooming services you

For Your Health

Girl Pleaser

Fifteen-year-old Bijal is in love at last–not with a girl but with all girls! He thinks females are awesome. With his new interest in the opposite sex, Bijal is giving more time and attention to the way he looks. His collection of grooming aids is growing. He has a number of toothpastes, mouthwashes, hair styling products, shampoos, and deodorants. He just bought a blow dryer with styling combs and brushes. This will help him keep his new, expensive haircut looking stylish. He is getting in shape at the local fitness center, too.

Frankly, Bijal is looking pretty good. When a few girls start noticing him, Bijal feels it is the start of something terrific. All of this makes Bijal game for the "girl pleaser" ads selling Lion's Lure cologne. This cologne is guaranteed to attract girls, so Bijal rushes out to buy a bottle.

Unfortunately, the more Lion's Lure Bijal uses, the weaker his drawing power becomes. The girls do not exactly flock to Bijal's side. In fact, many of them seem to move a few steps away when he comes close.

Case Review

1. To what extent do you think Bijal's use of grooming aids made him more attractive to girls?
2. What part do you think cosmetics and grooming aids play in making people attractive to the opposite sex?
3. How do you think perfumes and colognes can help or hinder success with the opposite sex?
4. Why do you think advertisers often use a sex appeal approach when selling cosmetics and grooming aids? Do you think this type of advertising is misleading? Is it effective in selling products? Is it believable? Why?

Use Appliances Safely

1. Read the manufacturer's use and care instructions before using an appliance. Follow the directions carefully.
2. Use and store electrical appliances away from water.
3. Turn off appliances before connecting or disconnecting them. Disconnect by pulling the plug—not the cord.
4. Disconnect any appliance that gives a shock. Have it checked and repaired before using it again.
5. Keep electrical cord and plugs in good repair. Avoid coiling cords tightly.
6. Do not loop or coil cords to shorten them. Buy shorter cords instead.
7. Check the wattage rating stamped on appliances. Avoid connecting more than 1600 watts on any single electrical circuit.

9-7
Follow these guidelines to safe use of grooming appliances.

want at prices you can afford. When you do find someone who cuts your hair just right or does other services to your satisfaction, it's a good idea to stick with that person.

When deciding where to get a haircut or any type of service, consider the location of the shop and its business hours. You want to find a place that is convenient to reach during hours that work well for you. Also consider promptness, cleanliness, and any other factors that may be important to you.

Be sure to ask about prices ahead of time and find out what the prices include. For example, does the cost of a haircut include a shampoo and styling? Will you be expected to leave a tip? Find out all the details to avoid any surprises.

Staying Healthy

Taking care of yourself is the key to staying healthy and avoiding many health problems. Quality self-care involves the right eating habits, adequate rest and exercise, good grooming practices, and workable ways to deal with life's stressful situations. Medical attention when you need it is also important.

Regular physical and dental checkups may help you avoid serious illnesses or at least identify them in their early stages. Knowing how to select health care professionals and to evaluate hospitals and medical facilities can help you get adequate health care when you need it.

> *"The healthy, the strong individual is the one who asks for help when he needs it. Whether he's got an abscess on his knee or on his soul."*
>
> *Rona Barret*

Selecting Health Care Providers

The best time to choose a physician, dentist, or specialist is when you are healthy. Most people go to a ***primary care physician*** for most health care needs. This is a physician who is trained to diagnose and treat a variety of illnesses in all phases of medicine. This doctor oversees general treatment for most patients. When a specific health problem arises, your *primary care physician* may refer you to a specialist.

A ***specialist*** is a physician who has had further education and training in a specific branch of medicine. Chart 9-8 describes some of the many medical and dental specialists. These specialists are fully qualified and licensed to practice general medicine or dentistry, but they focus on care within their specialties.

A physician or specialist is a doctor of medicine, or M.D. The M.D. is also called an allopathic physician. In your search for a physician, you may also come across a doctor of osteopathy, or D.O. Both M.D.'s and D.O.'s are qualified to provide complete medical care. Both may decide to go beyond basic medical education into a chosen specialty. Both must pass comparable state licensing exams. Both practice in accredited, licensed hospitals and other care facilities.

Osteopathic medicine emphasizes the relationship among nerves, muscles, bones, and organs in treating the whole person. Osteopaths also receive training in manipulative therapy. It pays to be sure that the doctor you choose has hospital privileges in your area. Osteopathic hospitals are scarce in some parts of the country, but some osteopaths have hospital privileges at allopathic hospitals.

One way to find qualified health care providers is to ask friends, relatives, employers, and coworkers for advice. When someone you know and trust is satisfied with a physician or dentist, that can be a good reference. If you move to a new area, your former doctor may be able to refer you to a new physician. If medical or dental schools are located in the area, administrators there can provide you with a list of faculty doctors and graduates who practice in the area. National and state medical associations operate referral services. Local hospitals can also be good sources of information.

If you receive care through a managed care program, you may be required to choose a physician or hospital or other care provider that participates in the plan. Before you make a final decision about a doctor,

Health Care Specialists		
Medical	Cardiologist	Treats diseases of the heart.
	Dermatologist	Treats diseases of the skin, hair, and nails.
	Gynecologist	Deals with the diseases and hygiene of women.
	Internist	Diagnoses and treats physical diseases, particularly those of inner organs.
	Neurologist	Treats disorders of the brain, spinal cord, and nervous system.
	Obstetrician	Provides medical care for women during pregnancy and birth.
	Oncologist	Diagnoses and treats tumors.
	Ophthamologist	Provides care for the eyes.
	Orthopedist	Treats fractures, deformities, and disease of the skeletal system.
	Otolaryngoloist	Treats diseases and disorders of the ear, nose, and throat.
	Pediatrician	Deals with the development and care of children and treats children's diseases.
	Psychiatrist	Diagnoses and treats mental and emotional disorders.
	Surgeon	Performs operations to diagnose or treat a variety of diseases or physical conditions.
	Urologist	Deals with the urinary tract and the male reproductive system.
Dental	Oral surgeon	Performs operations to extract teeth and to treat injuries and defects of the jaw and mouth.
	Orthodontist	Corrects irregularities and deformities of the teeth, usually with braces.

9-8
Certain health care needs call for the attention of a medical or dental specialist.

find out what services are performed in the office. Some doctors' offices are equipped to take X rays and perform other tests that require special equipment. Tests performed in the office can save you a trip to the lab, hospital, or clinic. Ask in advance about charges and fees for routine office visits, a complete physical, and other services you may need.

You may also want to consider the location of the office, the office hours, and the backup staff available in the doctor's absence. If you have any special medical needs, make sure the doctor or group practice you choose can meet them.

Chiropractors, optometrists, podiatrists, and psychologists provide limited medical services. (Coverage of these services varies with insurance and managed care plans.) A chiropractor treats certain illnesses related to abnormal nerve functions.

Chiropractors practice by manipulating parts of the body, particularly the spinal column. An optometrist tests eyes for vision defects and prescribes corrective glasses and contact lenses. A podiatrist diagnoses and treats minor foot ailments. A psychologist diagnoses and treats mental and emotional problems and learning difficulties. Licensing requirements for these fields vary from state to state. Do not rely on these health care providers for medical advice beyond their limited fields.

When choosing health care professionals, select well-qualified persons who are graduates of approved medical or dental schools. They should be licensed to practice in your state. Look also for membership in one or more local, state, and national professional societies and associations. Look for doctors who are well established in their practice with a good reputation among both patients and fellow professionals. Once you find a primary care physician and a dentist, make every effort to work with them in your own best interests.

Evaluating Hospitals and Medical Facilities

If you need hospital care, your doctor normally will arrange for your hospitalization. Consider where physicians have hospital privileges when choosing a doctor. You will want to evaluate the facilities that provide care as well as the health care professionals who supervise your hospital stays. Again, your choice may be limited or designated if you received medical services through a managed health care plan. The following questions can help you assess health care facilities.

Is the hospital accredited by the Joint Commission on Accreditation of Health Care Organizations or by the American Osteopathic Association? An accredited hospital must meet certain quality standards in providing health care.

Who owns or finances the hospital? A *nonprofit hospital* is supported by patient fees, contributions, and endowments. A *proprietary hospital* is owned by individuals or stockholders and operated for profit. A *government-supported hospital* is operated with local, state, or federal funds. Ownership can make a difference in the eligibility for treatment, the services offered, and the charges.

Is it a teaching hospital? Hospitals and clinics affiliated with a medical or nursing school generally provide a high level of training for students. As a result, they are likely to provide high-quality medical services.

Does the hospital employ an adequate, qualified staff of physicians, specialists, nurses, therapists, and technicians? If a hospital is understaffed or if the staff is underqualified, you may not receive the quality of medical care you need.

What type of facilities are located at the hospital or clinic? Is there an intensive care unit? Is the emergency room well equipped and staffed? Look for the up-to-date equipment and facilities required to provide quality care.

What type of care and services are provided? An *acute care facility* diagnoses and treats a broad range of illnesses and emergencies. A *special disease facility* diagnoses and treats a special illness or group of diseases. A *chronic disease facility* provides continuing care for ongoing illnesses. If you have specific medical needs, choose a hospital accordingly.

Does the hospital enjoy a good reputation in the area? If both medical professionals and patients speak highly of a hospital, that's a sign of quality health care.

How sensitive is the staff to patients' private and special needs? Patients and their families are concerned with privacy. They want complete and honest information on diagnosis and treatment. They are also concerned with the attitude of nurses and others who deal directly with patients. Look for sensitivity to patients' comfort and special needs.

Ask questions and find out all you can about health care facilities and hospitals where you may end up with serious illness or injury. Keep in mind the hospital or clinic where you go for treatment may be determined by your choice of a primary care physician or your health care plan. It pays to check out emergency room and ambulance services in the area before you are in an emergency situation, 9-9. Knowing you are being treated in a facility that provides quality medical care can have a positive effect on your mental and physical health.

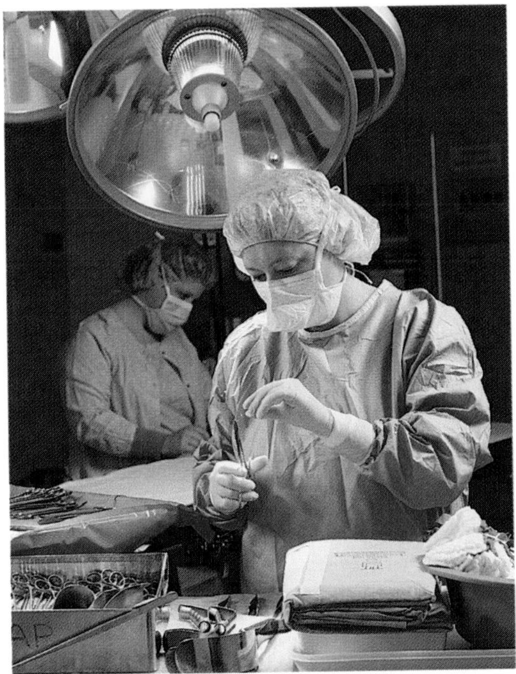

Baxter Health Care Corporation

9-9
A ready emergency room can be important for serious accidents and injuries or for sudden illness, such as a heart attack or appendicitis.

Drugs and Medicines

Drugs and medicines eat up a sizable portion of the health care dollar. Drugs fall into two major groups—prescription drugs and over-the-counter drugs. ***Prescription drugs*** are medications prescribed by a doctor and available only by prescription. ***Over-the-counter drugs*** are nonprescription medications considered safe for consumers to use by following label directions and warnings. These include more than 300,000 different drugs. Painkillers, antacids, cough medicine, antihistamines, and vitamins are examples.

The cost of prescription drugs and medicines often is only partially covered by insurance and managed care plans. You will pay a percentage or a set fee per prescription. You also pay the total cost of nonprescription or over-the-counter medications.

Most drugs are available either by generic names or by trade and brand names. A ***generic drug*** is sold by its common name, chemical composition, or class. Usually it costs considerably less than a similar brand-name drug. All prescription and over-the-counter drugs meet the same federal standards. Generic drugs are required to have the same active ingredients and effects as their brand-name equivalents.

When your physician prescribes a medication by brand name, ask if the generic equivalent may be substituted. If so, ask the doctor to write this on the prescription. Many health management and insurance plans call for the use of generic equivalents for brand name medications or they increase the patient's share of the payment for medication.

With the ever-rising costs of drugs, consumers are asking more questions about what their doctors prescribe. They should also become better informed about the many over-the-counter drugs available without prescription, 9-10. Labels on over-the-counter drugs serve as keys to choosing products and comparing generics with brand names. Information on these labels must include:

- ❑ Name and address of the manufacturer, packer, or distributor.
- ❑ Quantity of contents in weight, measure, or count.
- ❑ Purpose of the medication.
- ❑ Directions for use and storage.
- ❑ Recommended dosages for different purposes, ages, and conditions.
- ❑ Number of times and length of time the medication may be used.
- ❑ Conditions under which the drug should not be used.
- ❑ Adequate warnings and precautions related to use, possible side effects, and interactions with other drugs.
- ❑ List of active ingredients and the quantity of each per dosage.
- ❑ List of all other ingredients including the name and quantity of any habit-forming drug contained in the product.
- ❑ An expiration date after which the product should not be used.

Prescription drug labels dispensed by doctors or pharmacists are exempt from certain labeling requirements. These labels state the pharmacist's name and address, the number and date of the prescription, the name of the prescriber and patient, directions for use, and any cautionary statements contained in the prescription. They also will tell you if the prescription may be renewed and give an expiration date. Many pharmacies also provide leaflets with more complete information on prescription drugs, including a description of possible side effects, detailed instructions on when and how to use the medication, what to avoid while taking the drug, etc. Be cautious with both over-the-counter and prescription drug interactions with other drugs, alcohol, and various foods. Consult your doctor or pharmacist for information on drug interactions.

To be an informed partner in your own health care, ask the following questions when your doctor prescribes medicines for you:

- ❑ What is the brand name and the generic name of the drug?
- ❑ What is it intended to do? Is it really necessary for you to take it?
- ❑ How much of this drug should you take, at what time of day, and for how many days?

Walgreen Co.

9-10
Over-the-counter drugs are available on open shelves and do not require a prescription.

- ❑ Is the medication habit-forming?
- ❑ What, if any, side effects should you expect?
- ❑ What activities, other drugs, foods, or beverages should you avoid while taking the drug?
- ❑ Is this a generic drug? If not, is there a generic equivalent that is as effective at a lower cost?

Health Care Delivery Systems

Today, approximately 19 percent of health care costs are paid by individual patients, 33 percent by private insurance that usually is sponsored by employers, and 47 percent by government through medicare or medicaid. The continuing high cost of health care has brought about significant changes in health care delivery systems over the past few years. Among the developments designed to help control health care costs are managed care programs that include health care maintenance organizations (HMOs) and preferred provider organizations (PPOs). These health care delivery systems are discussed in this chapter. Here are some ways you can control health care costs in your own budget:

- ❑ Stay as well as possible. Follow a balanced approach to diet, exercise, sleep, stress control, and accident prevention.
- ❑ Find out what free or low-cost health services and programs are available through your school, employer or union, community, and government.
- ❑ Protect yourself against major medical and hospital costs by getting adequate health insurance or joining a managed care program.
- ❑ Know exactly what expenses your health insurance covers, keep accurate records, and file claims promptly for covered expenses.
- ❑ Discuss fees and prices with doctors, dentists, hospitals, and pharmacists. Cost-conscious patients can often avoid unnecessary expenses and obtain essential treatment and drugs for less.
- ❑ Minimize hospital costs by asking for outpatient care, if possible, and keeping hospital stays as short as possible.
- ❑ Get a second opinion before agreeing to nonemergency surgery or other costly treatments.
- ❑ Obtain necessary authorizations prior to receiving treatments to be sure your insurance provider or managed care system will pay for them.

Government Health Care Programs

Federal, state, and local governments pay for over 47 percent of personal health care costs. Medicare and medicaid are the two major health care programs funded by government. ***Medicare*** is a federal government health insurance program serving people 65 and older and certain disabled individuals under 65. Current information and applications for medicare are available at local Social Security offices. ***Medicaid*** is a medical assistance program administered and financed by the states with matching funds from the federal government. It is designed to pay the cost of certain health care services for low-income persons. Medicaid applications are available at local public aid offices.

The Medicare Program

Medicare provides two types of coverage—hospital insurance and medical insurance. The medicare hospital insurance is a compulsory program that is paid for along with

Social Security taxes. Employers and employees each pay half of the premium. In 1999, this came to 1.65 percent each for a total of 3.3 percent of cash wages earned during the year. Self-employed individuals pay the full 3.3 percent.

This program covers inpatient hospital services and skilled nursing facility care for up to 90 days. Medicare hospital insurance pays for all covered services provided during hospital stays of up to 61 days after the patient pays the deductible. A ***deductible*** is the amount the policyholder must pay before insurance makes any payments. Under certain conditions, it also helps pay for home health services and hospice care.

If the patient stays in a medical facility more than 60 days, the insurance calls for co-payments. A ***co-payment*** is a stated amount the policyholder will have to pay for certain expenses. This means patients pay part of the daily costs from day 61 to day 90. The amounts of the deductible and the co-payments change annually. A local Social Security office can provide current figures.

Medicare medical insurance is a voluntary program financed jointly by monthly premiums of those who choose to enroll and by general government revenues. The premium in 1998 was $43.80 per month. Patients must also pay an annual deductible for medical expenses each year before insurance coverage begins.

The insurance pays 80 percent of the fees for covered health care services the patient receives for the rest of the year. The patient must cover the remaining 20 percent. Medicare medical insurance helps pay for a variety of health care costs, such as doctors' fees, outpatient hospital services, and home health visits. Both the premium and the deductible change periodically. The nearest Social Security office can provide the latest figures.

Most medicare recipients buy supplemental insurance coverage, often called ***medigap insurance***, to pay for health care not covered by medicare such as deductibles, co-payments, and other out-of-pocket costs. This type of protection is sold by insurance companies—not by the government. It is available in 10 standard benefit packages that provide varying degrees of coverage. The broader the coverage the higher the premium will be. Each benefit package is standard in terms of the coverage it provides, but servicing of the policy may vary with different insurers. It pays to shop carefully for a reputable, reliable insurance company with a good record of customer service.

The Medicaid Program

Medicaid is a medical assistance program. The program was established in 1965 as part of the Social Security Act. It is financed by the federal government together with state and local taxes. Medicaid is administered by the states. It pays the cost of specified basic health care services for blind, disabled, and eligible low-income persons.

Patients apply for medicaid in the state where they live. The services provided vary from state to state. Most medicaid programs pay for inpatient and outpatient hospital services, clinic care, X rays, and laboratory services. Some states also pay for family planning, home health care services, dental and eye care, and other medical needs. In some states, prescription drugs, dental services, and eyeglasses are covered by medicaid.

Nongovernment Health Care Programs

Approximately one-third of personal health care expenditures in the U. S. are paid for through some form of insurance plan or managed care program, 9-11. Most of these are employer-sponsored plans. In some cases, employees pay a portion of the

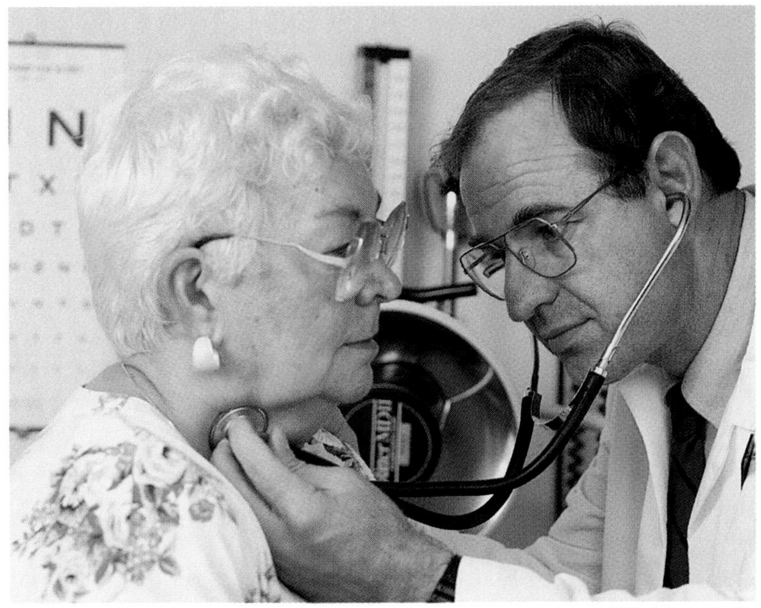

Bristol-Myers Squibb

9-11
A major portion of health care expenditures is paid for by some type of insurance plan.

premiums plus some deductible and co-payment amounts. Many employer-sponsored plans offer workers a choice of fee-for-service or managed care coverages.

Fee-for-service plans, also called indemnity insurance, pay their share of covered medical services after treatment is provided. As a plan participant, you generally can go to any licensed health care provider or accredited hospital of your choice. These plans call for a deductible amount you must pay annually in medical costs before the insurer begins to pay. You are also responsible for a co-payment for services up to a set amount. The co-pay amount usually is 20 percent. These plans normally pay for medical tests and prescription drugs as well as doctor and hospital fees. Usually fee-for-service plans offer a wide choice of health care providers, including primary care doctors, specialists, hospitals, therapists, and clinics.

Managed care plans contract with specific doctors and other health care providers, hospitals, and clinics to provide a range of medical services and preventive care to members of the plan at reduced cost. Generally, your choice of service providers will be limited to those who participate in the plan except for necessary referrals to specialists who are not part of the plan. You and/or your employer pay a set amount in monthly premiums that pay for the services covered by the plan. Three forms of managed care are *health maintenance organizations (HMOs), preferred provider organizations (PP0s),* and *point-of-service (POS) plans.*

Health maintenance organizations (HMOs) provide a list of participating doctors from which you may choose a primary care doctor. This doctor will coordinate your health care and carry out routine exams and treatments. Normally, you must go through your primary care doctor for a referral if you require treatments, consultations, or procedures from specialists. Your primary care doctor and a referral specialist decide what care you may need from specialists. The plan normally covers only treatment provided by doctors who participate in the plan. If you go outside the plan for care, you pay the bill.

Preferred provider organizations (PPOs) arrange with specific doctors, hospitals, and other caregivers to provide services at reduced cost to plan members. You receive services at lower cost by going to participating care givers, but you may go outside the plan if you are willing to pay the extra cost. For example, the plan may pay 80 percent of the cost of care within the plan and only 60 percent of services provided by caregivers outside the plan. This offers you more choice, but at a higher cost than you pay in an HMO.

Point-of-service (POS) plans connect you with a primary care doctor who participates in the plan. That doctor supervises your care and makes referrals as necessary to participating or nonparticipating specialists. You may choose specialists outside the plan on your own as well. However, as in PPOs, you will pay more for nonparticipating physicians if the referral does not come from your primary care doctor.

Fee-for-service and managed care plans often share certain features. Both charge *premiums,* or the amount you or your employer pay monthly to cover health care services. Both plans often call for ***co-insurance*** which is the amount or share of the costs you must pay for services. Usually this will be 20 percent up to a stated annual maximum, after which the plan pays in full. There normally will be an annual *deductible* you will be required to pay before the plan pays for any services. For example, if you have a deductible of $250 annually, you must pay for services until you reach a total of $250 at which time, the plan will begin paying. Plans also may require *preauthorization* and *utilization reviews* for certain services. A preauthorization is a requirement to obtain approval from the plan in advance of receiving certain procedures and treatments. A utilization review is an assessment of appropriateness and necessity of specific medical treatments and procedures. The following are other terms you may encounter:

- ❑ *Pre-existing conditions* are illnesses or injuries you have at the time you sign up for a health care plan. These frequently will not be covered by a new plan for a stated period of time, if at all.
- ❑ *Renewability* refers to your right to renew coverage annually. Even guaranteed renewable policies may charge higher premiums for renewals.
- ❑ *Maximum benefits* refer to limits on benefits such as the maximum amount that will be paid for specific types of treatment or the maximum number of days of care covered. For example, payment for mental health care may be limited to $1,000 annually; the number of days in a hospital may be limited as well.
- ❑ *Open enrollment period* refers to open sign-up periods for managed care plans during which you can enroll in the plan or change your coverage options.
- ❑ *Exclusions* refer to medical services that are not covered. These may include certain medical services such as mental health care, dental care, or treatment of pre-existing conditions.

Most employed Americans and their families receive their health care plans through their employers. This type of group coverage provides several advantages over individual coverage. It generally provides broader coverage, with fewer exclusions at lower cost. See 9-12. To make the most of group plans you need to know:

- ❑ How much coverage you receive.
- ❑ What choices are open to you in terms of benefit packages and care providers.
- ❑ What share of premiums and charges you must pay and the amount of the deductible.
- ❑ What uncovered health costs you should be prepared to pay.

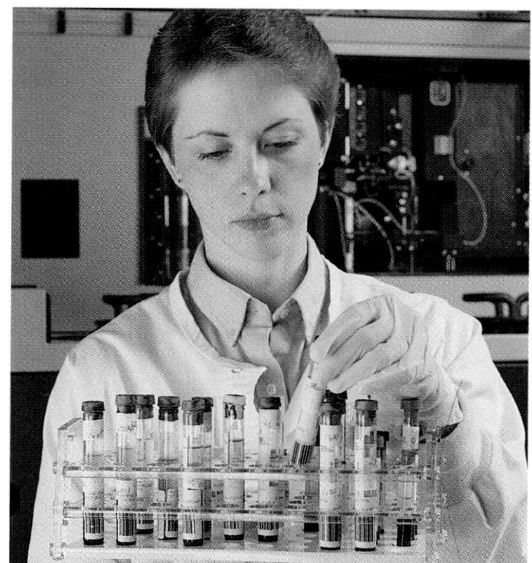
Baxter Health Care Corporation

9-12
If you have medical tests run, your health insurance may cover the costs.

- ❑ Whether and under what conditions you can covert coverage to an individual plan if you leave the group.

If you are covered by an employer-sponsored group plan and leave your job, you are likely to lose your health care coverage. In this case, you may be entitled to continue your health benefits under the Consolidated Omnibus Budget Reconciliation Act (COBRA). This law gives qualified workers the right to continue their group coverage at group rates for up to 18 months, provided they pay the premiums. For information on COBRA and its possible benefits, contact the nearest U. S. Department of Labor office.

Choosing a Health Care Plan

Many employers will give you a choice of health care plans. Here are some points to consider as you compare health care programs and your alternatives. Look carefully at medical services that are covered. No plan will pay for all your medical expenses or cover all the services you may need. Look for coverage of the services that are most important to you. These may include the following:

- ❑ Inpatient hospital services
- ❑ Outpatient surgery
- ❑ Preventive care and screenings
- ❑ Doctor visits in the hospital
- ❑ Office visits
- ❑ Medical tests and X-rays
- ❑ Dental care
- ❑ Physical therapy
- ❑ Mental health services
- ❑ Prescription drugs
- ❑ Speech therapy
- ❑ Maternity care
- ❑ Well-baby care
- ❑ Home health care
- ❑ Drug and alcohol abuse treatment.

Find out what preauthorizations and utilization reviews are required by any plan you are considering. Check out any exclusions, service limitations, or restrictions on pre-existing conditions that may apply to you.

You will also want to consider cost factors. What portion of premiums will you pay? What deductible amount is applied to your coverage? Very often you can reduce monthly premiums by paying a higher deductible. This can save you money if you typically require only routine health care services. What portion of charges must you co-pay? Co-payments may apply to any medical service you receive or only to specific items such as office visits, prescription drugs, and screening or preventive care services. In a managed care program, find out whether co-payments are higher if you go outside your health care plan for treatment. Figure out the total cost of the amount of the premiums you pay together with your deductible.

Finally, consider choice. How important is it to you to choose your own doctor and hospital? How important is it to be able to change doctors without prior approval if you are dissatisfied with your primary care physician? Are you willing and can you afford to see a specialist of your own choice without prior approval by your primary doctor? Choice in these matters may be very limited in some managed care plans.

Regardless of the health care coverage you have, a certain degree of organization on your part will be necessary to make the most of it. Read your copy of the plan carefully and keep it in a safe place. If you have fee-for-service coverage, learn how to file claims and file them promptly. Keep the name and phone number of your plan handy together with identifying membership numbers and other information you may need to receive services or payments.

Emergency Health Care

Emergency health care has become a specialty in recent years. This type of health care is often provided by emergency medical technicians, or EMTs, who staff ambulances and rescue squads. These people are trained to make an immediate, accurate diagnosis and provide temporary treatment. Emergency care can mean the difference between life and death in many situations. You should go to a hospital emergency room or an emergency care center if you have an injury or sudden illness that requires immediate attention. When you go for emergency care be ready to give:

- ❑ Your name, address, and phone number.
- ❑ Information on your injury or illness.
- ❑ Your managed care or insurance card or identifying data.
- ❑ Information on any current medication you take or allergies you have.

Medic Alert™

Medic Alert™ is a program that alerts paramedics and emergency care staffs to hidden medical problems.

For Your Health

It's Negotiable

Maurice has just been elected to represent his union at the bargaining table. In three months, negotiations will begin for a new contract. The members of the union are unified in their demands. One of their demands is complete health care benefits covering union members and their families at no cost to themselves.

The company has made it clear it will not negotiate a health benefit program unless union members pay a share of the costs. Carmela, a company spokesperson, argues that "free" health care would be abused. She says that workers would flock to doctors' offices with every hangnail and hiccup if they didn't have to pay for it. She says the costs to the company would run into the millions. To make it worse, the costs would be unpredictable and uncontrollable.

This issue will have to be negotiated. Compromises will have to be made. If you were Maurice, what arguments would you make in favor of the union's demand? If you were Carmela, what arguments would you make on the company's behalf?

Case Review

1. To what extent do you think companies should be financially responsible for the health care of employees and their families?
2. To what extent should employees be responsible for paying a portion of their own health care costs?
3. What types of problems might occur in an employer-sponsored health program?
4. How might health care programs differ for large and small companies?
5. What health care provisions should employees be aware of in case they lose or change their jobs?

Medic Alert™ bracelets and necklaces are signals of medical conditions needing attention in emergencies. Persons who wear Medic Alert™ tags also carry a card with additional medical information in their wallets. The Medic Alert™ tags identify wearers of contact lenses and persons with allergies, diabetes, heart disease, epilepsy, and blood problems. The tags also carry the phone numbers of Medic Alert™ emergency answering services where detailed medical information is available 24 hours per day.

Keeping Health and Medical Records

Up-to-date health and medical records are valuable for many reasons. This information will be needed if you switch doctors or health care plans to give your new care providers a thorough knowledge of your medical background. It will also be required if you are admitted to a hospital. Health and medical records can help doctors with the diagnosis and treatment of illnesses as well as with the prevention of certain diseases. Having health facts readily available is very important for anyone with health conditions that would require special treatment in an emergency.

Data from health histories is also helpful when filling out school records and insurance forms. Organized receipts for paid medical bills and the purchase of medications are needed for filing insurance claims and tax forms.

The list in Chart 9-13 includes types of information to keep in personal and family medical records. You may want to write some of this information on a card to carry with you. You may receive a medical identification card to carry with you. This card will identify the insurance company or managed care plan that covers your medical services and give the necessary information to confirm your coverage.

Having Fun

Very few people have all the time and money they want to spend for fun. Getting more fun out of your limited recreation hours and dollars calls for careful planning. Knowing what you enjoy is the first step toward having more fun.

Some people put every free moment into a favorite hobby, sport, or activity. Others are always saying "There's nothing to do," or "I'm so bored," or "I'm so sick of doing the same old thing all the time." Silly as it sounds, lots of people miss out on fun because they don't know what they enjoy. What do you do when you have nothing to do? What do you really enjoy? Making a list of what you enjoy can help you zero in on what interests you, and it may lead to new ways to have fun.

To avoid that "nothing to do" syndrome, you might try making a list of the activities that you enjoy. Include active and spectator sports, social activities, hobbies, and fitness programs. You may also want to make a list of books you want to read and movies to see. Next, set priorities. Put the items that bring you the most pleasure at the top of your list. It's a good idea to plan a variety of free-time activities. You may also want to work toward a balance of physical and mental activities and to occasionally spend time alone as well as with friends.

To pursue the activities you like most, plan the use of both time and money, 9-14. As you consider the resources available to you for fun and entertainment, think how you want to use the hours and dollars. Remember each hour or dollar you spend on something you do not enjoy is not available for something fun. Once you set aside a reasonable amount of time and money for a good time, enjoy it.

Personal Medical Records

- ❑ Name, address, date and place of birth, height, weight, occupation, and blood type.
- ❑ Persons to notify in an emergency with addresses, phone numbers, and relationship.
- ❑ Personal physicians and health care providers with names, addresses, and phone numbers.
- ❑ Allergies.
- ❑ Medications with dosages, prescription numbers, prescribing physician, and pharmacies.
- ❑ Chronic illnesses with important details on history, medication, and treatment.
- ❑ Visual or hearing defects and other disabilities.
- ❑ Immunizations, screening tests and results, and dates for follow-up.
- ❑ Infections and childhood diseases with important details.
- ❑ Hospitalizations, injuries, and surgeries with dates and details.
- ❑ Physical checkups and laboratory tests with dates and details.
- ❑ Social Security, medicare, and medicaid numbers.
- ❑ Details of employer-sponsored or individual health insurance or managed care plans including names, addresses, and phone numbers of plan managers or claims officers, medical services covered, policy and membership numbers, premium amounts and due dates, claims records, agent or contact person, and related membership data.
- ❑ Dental treatment records.
- ❑ A copy of *advance directives,* if any. This is a legal document describing the types of treatments and life sustaining measures you do and do not want in the event of an inability to communicate or to function without the aid of life support.

9-13
Record this type of medical information for each family member.

Selecting Sports and Hobby Equipment

The money you spend for pleasure will include the equipment, supplies, and special clothes needed for these activities. It may also include lessons or coaching. Costs will depend on the activities you choose. Below is a list of guidelines to follow as you shop for equipment, supplies, or clothes.

Anticipate Costs

Before becoming involved in a sport or hobby, find out how much it will cost. When money is limited, you may want to choose less costly activities. Unless you already have the equipment, sports and hobbies may be expensive. Golf, skiing, sailing, and photography require expensive equipment. Other sports and activites may be less costly, 9-15.

Do Your Homework

Before making any major purchases, check product ratings in *Consumer Bulletin* and *Consumer Reports.* Also look for information in specialized sports and hobby magazines and from manufacturers and retailers.

9-14
Hiking can be a great low-cost and high-pleasure choice.

Seek Advice

Talk with people who have experience in the sport or hobby that interests you. Coaches, pros, and instructors as well as experienced sales persons can offer good advice on the purchase or rental of hobby and sports equipment. You can also find information on individual sports and hobbies online. Find out what kinds of equipment are recommended and how much you should pay.

Learn to Judge Quality and Performance

Find out the important quality and performance features of a piece of equipment before you spend your money. For example, suppose you want to buy a tennis racquet. What size racquet would you choose? Would you want a racquet made of wood, graphite, or some other material? What kind of strings would you choose? Buy the equipment that best suits your ability, interests, and budget.

Club Med

9-15
If you like skiing, set aside the time and money you need to enjoy it.

For Your Health

Finding Time for Fun

Greg is a freshman in a big high school. He is finding the schoolwork a little tough. He brings books home every night. In addition to schoolwork, Greg is involved in many other activities. He is on the football team, in the band, and a member of the debate team. He also likes to jog, read, and watch TV. He finds there just isn't enough time to do everything.

Greg is beginning to feel the pressure. Whether he is working or playing, he always worries about everything else he is supposed to be doing. Some of the activities he started for pleasure are becoming boring. He is falling behind in his classes, and nothing is fun anymore.

Sixteen-year-old Brenda has lots of interests, but she never seems to have time for any of them. She sleeps late and barely arrives at school on time. Her first class is at 8:30. She has five classes, an activity period, a study hall, and a lunch period each day.

Brenda usually eats with friends and relaxes during her 45-minute lunch break. During study hall, she often works on club activities or looks at fashion magazines in the library. School is out at 3:15. Brenda arrives home around 3:30 unless she stops for something to eat with friends. Then she gets home about 4:30.

Once at home, Brenda usually watches TV even though the late afternoon programs are boring. Soon it's time for dinner. After dinner, Brenda's favorite TV shows come on and her friends start calling on the phone.

Brenda, however, never has time to talk to her friends or to watch her favorite TV shows. It's all because of homework. Her parents won't let her do anything after dinner until her homework is done. It's a real problem. She just doesn't have time to do any of the things she really likes.

Case Review

1. Have you ever signed up to do more than you could handle?
2. How might Greg deal with his problem? How might he have avoided it in the first place?
3. Do you know someone with a problem like Brenda's?
4. What time-wasters do you see in Brenda's day?
5. How do you think Brenda might solve her problem?
6. What time-wasters rob you of hours for fun?
7. Do you often feel like you have too much to do and not enough time? If so, what can you do about it?

Try Rental

If you are not sure what equipment to buy or if you are not sure of your interest in a new sport or hobby, try renting equipment first. Sometimes rental fees can be applied toward the purchase of equipment if you later decide to buy. Ski equipment and musical instruments are often rented first and bought later.

Look for Money Savers

When you need expensive costly equipment, you may want to consider buying used equipment. Other ways to save are to check discount stores for good buys or to wait for end-of-season sales. Skis, for example, will sell for less in April than in November.

Travel and Vacation Planning

Americans are on the move. Each year, consumers spend billions of dollars on travel within the United States and abroad. For most people, however, time and money for travel and vacation are limited. It takes careful planning to get the most fun and satisfaction out of these limited resources.

Smart travelers begin their vacation planning at the library or online. They check out articles, books, and Web sites on areas they want to visit and the special activities they like, such as biking, rafting, and skiing. Chart 9-16 lists a few reliable sources of travel and vacation information. Before

Reliable Sources of Travel and Vacation Information

- ❑ Airlines, railways, bus lines, and cruise lines.
- ❑ Automobile clubs.
- ❑ Travel agencies.
- ❑ Convention and visitor's bureaus.
- ❑ Travel books, magazines, and sections in newspapers.
- ❑ Internet.
- ❑ Hotels, resorts, and tourist offices in vacation areas.
- ❑ Passport offices and customs services.
- ❑ Friends who have been where you plan to travel.

9-16
Check these sources for information when planning vacations and travel.

you make travel or vacation plans, ask yourself the following questions.

When and where do you want to go? What time of the year do you want to travel? Do you want sun or snow, city or resort, water or mountains, sports or sights to see?

How will you get there? Will you go by car, bus, plane, train, or ship? Check on reservations, time schedules, and fares. The transportation you choose will depend on where you are traveling and how much you have to spend. Be sure to make reservations early when traveling in peak seasons. This can often mean big savings on airfares. Lower-fare tickets must be purchased in advance and travel may be restricted to certain days. There may also be penalties for later changes or cancellations. Some tickets are nonrefundable and may not be changed for any reason short of serious illness or death in the family.

Where will you stay? Investigate choices of hotels, motels, resorts, youth hostels, and campgrounds. Find out about reservations and rates. Rooms will be easier to get and rates will be lower during off-season months. When you make reservations, ask what will be included for the price you pay. For example, will your hotel room have TV and air conditioning? Will you have access to a swimming pool, restaurants, and tennis courts? Be sure to reserve several months ahead for peak seasons and popular places.

What are the special things to see and do where you are going? Are there seasonal festivals, sight-seeing tours, athletic events, or historical sites? Check to see if you need advance tickets for any special events.

How much will it cost? Make a list of estimated expenses for transportation, lodging, and meals. Also figure in the amount of other charges and fees for such items as equipment rental, sports activities, and sight-seeing. It is a good idea to include an allowance for souvenirs and a little impulse vacation spending. Check your estimates against your budget. Will you have enough money to cover your costs? If not, are there ways to reduce expenses or increase your spending money?

Package Tours and Trips

Throughout the year, travel agencies and resorts offer many vacation packages and group tours at special rates. Look through the travel ads carefully. You may be able to find your dream vacation at a reasonable price. However, before you sign up for a package trip, find out exactly what you are getting. For example, know the

- ❑ Length of the trip and dates of departure and return.
- ❑ Type and quality of accommodations.
- ❑ Meals and other items that are included in the price.
- ❑ Total costs itemized.
- ❑ Available options.
- ❑ Penalties for cancellations.
- ❑ Size and makeup of the tour group.

For Your Health

Having Fun with Hobbies

Spending Top Dollar

Last summer, 15-year-old Bill moved to Chicago from a small town in Texas. As the hockey season approached, Bill started looking forward to joining a hockey team. The sport fascinated him. He hadn't missed a game on TV in five years. Just before the season started, Bill talked his parents into buying him all the gear he would need to play hockey. They bought very good (and very expensive) equipment at a local sports shop.

The following week, one of the area schools held its annual Winter Sports Equipment Exchange. Good, used gear was sold there for a fraction of its original price. Unfortunately, Bill hadn't seen the notice about the exchange that was posted at school.

The next month, Bill dropped hockey. His ankles were weak, he didn't skate very well, and the hockey schedule left no time for anything else. Bill decided hockey was more fun to watch than to play.

Fun but Costly

Teresa was given a camera for her tenth birthday and immediately started taking pictures. She has photo albums full of snapshots taken during the last five years. She has become the official photographer in her family and among her friends.

Last summer, Teresa decided she wanted to begin using better equipment and learning more about photography. From a summer photography course, Teresa learned more about taking photos and developing her own film. She bought a good camera and set up a darkroom in her basement. Now Teresa is one of the photographers for the school paper. She is entering photo contests and has already won a few prizes.

Photography is a hobby that Teresa will enjoy throughout her life. Unfortunately, it is a costly hobby. Over the years, she plans to invest several hundred dollars in equipment. Each month she will also spend money for film and darkroom supplies.

A Musical Note

Gordon plays the piano for the school chorus. He really is very good. He started picking out tunes on the family piano when he was about seven years old. Since Gordon seemed to have an ear for music and a good sense of rhythm, his family encouraged him to take piano lessons.

After eight years of lessons, Gordon took off on his own. He organized a small group of friends into a band. For months, they held jam sessions every Friday after school. Later, the group started playing for a few parties and dances. Now their band is in great demand. Over the summer, they will earn about $600 each and have fun doing it.

Except for the piano lessons, Gordon and his family have spent very little money for Gordon's music. Now, he can continue learning on his own and earn a little cash besides. Gordon has a hobby that he will be able to enjoy through the years.

Case Review

1. Do you think Bill would have done anything differently if he had been spending his own money?
2. What are some ways Teresa might enjoy photography without spending as much money?
3. How could Gordon's hobby turn into a career?
4. What are your thoughts and feelings about expensive hobbies?
5. How can you make a hobby pay for itself?
6. What are some relatively inexpensive hobbies?
7. What hobbies might be a source of income?

Deal only with a reliable travel agency or tour company. If possible, talk with other travelers who have dealt with the agency or company and find out if they were satisfied with their travel arrangements.

If you are planning a trip to another country, you need to be familiar with the terms in 9-17. Take the time to learn the meanings of these words before you travel far from home. It is also a good idea to read a few articles and books about your destination before leaving home. Study the maps and learn about the currency and exchange rates for countries you plan to visit. An ATM card can be an advantage in obtaining currency in foreign countries almost anywhere in the world. This is a card you use in automated teller machines to obtain cash or make deposits. Foreign travel can introduce you to different cultures and customs. The world at large is very different from your small corner of it.

The Traveler's Vocabulary

- ❑ Customs—the government agency responsible for processing travelers into and out of the country, collecting customs duties on imported merchandise, inspecting luggage, and seizing contraband, such as narcotics and illegal drugs.
- ❑ Duty—a tax paid on items purchased in foreign countries.
- ❑ Exchange rate—the price at which one country's currency or money can be converted into another country's currency.
- ❑ Free port—a place where products of different countries can be bought without paying a duty.
- ❑ Hostel—low-cost lodging, usually for young travelers, sometimes call youth hostels.
- ❑ Inoculation—a shot, given to create immunity to certain diseases, that may be required before entering certain countries.
- ❑ Itinerary—a schedule or program of travel plans including dates, times, reservations, accommodations, events, and activities.
- ❑ Passport—an official government authorization to travel to foreign countries that also serves as proof of identity and citizenship while traveling.
- ❑ Rail pass—a permit that allows train travel at reduced rates; passes are available in Europe, the United States, Canada, Japan, and other countries.
- ❑ Traveler's checks—checks that can be cashed around the world and are safer than carrying cash because they can be replaced if lost or stolen.
- ❑ U.S. Consulate—the official U.S. representative in a foreign country who looks to the protection and welfare of U.S. citizens traveling abroad.
- ❑ Visa—an authorization to travel to a specific country or to stay for a specific length of time.

9-17
Learn the meaning of these terms before you leave the country on vacation.

Summary

Good looks and good health often work together. Both call for a wholesome lifestyle, attention to personal appearance, and health care, along with fun and relaxation. This means using consumer skills to purchase and use grooming aids and cosmetics. It calls for careful choices among available health care options. It also requires managing time and money to spend on fun, travel, and entertainment.

Tending to the way you look often involves the use of grooming aids and appliances. Use these products safely. Study the labels on cosmetics and follow the directions for use. Check out the qualifications of persons offering grooming services. Find out about prices and what they include.

Staying healthy starts with taking care of yourself. Routine checkups and appropriate health care as needed are also important. The key to getting the care you need is finding experienced and qualified health care providers. It is equally important to check out health care facilities in your area. When taking any type of drug, read and follow the directions on the label.

You no doubt will share the cost of your health care with an employer-sponsored program or your personal insurance plan or managed care program. Medicare and medicaid are the two government-sponsored health care programs. To make the most of health insurance or managed care, it is important to keep accurate records of treatments and claims.

Having fun begins with knowing what you enjoy and then planning the use of time and money in pursuing fun and recreation. Choosing and shopping for sports and hobby equipment are important consumer skills. Both used and rental equipment can save money for beginners in various sports and hobbies. Travel and vacation planning skills will also lead to good times.

To Review

1. What government agency regulates the safety of cosmetics?
2. What information must be listed on cosmetic products?
3. What symbol should you look for on electric appliances? What does this symbol mean?
4. Name four characteristics that M.D.s and D.O.s have in common.
5. What are the types of hospital ownership? List three ways that ownership can affect the way a hospital operates.
6. True or false. Generic drugs are more expensive than brand name drugs.
7. Name four ways you can keep personal health care costs down.
8. What are the major health care programs funded by government? Who is eligible for each program?
9. How do fee-for-service and managed care plans differ?
10. How do HMOs and PPOs differ?
11. Give four reasons it is important to keep family health and medical records.
12. List four guidelines that can help you shop for sports or hobby equipment, supplies, and clothes.
13. List four details that you should know before signing up for a package tour.

To Think Critically

1. What risks are connected with careless, unsanitary use of cosmetics?
2. How many grooming appliances do you and your family own? Do you use every appliance on a regular basis? What appliances could you do without? What more do you need?
3. What should you consider when selecting a physician or dentist?
4. What should you consider when choosing a hospital?

5. What questions should you ask your doctor or pharmacist about prescribed drugs?
6. What are the advantages and disadvantages of fee-for-service versus managed care plans?
7. Do you know anyone that has a Medic Alert™ bracelet? Why is it important for people who have a special health condition to identify it by wearing an identification tag?
8. What problems have you had finding the money and the time for the leisure activities you enjoy the most?
9. Have you or your friends ever rented sports equipment? What are some advantages of renting equipment rather than buying it?
10. What should you find out before you make vacation plans with a travel agency?

To Do

1. Make a list of the cosmetics and grooming aids you own. Estimate the total amount you spend on these items monthly. Draw a line through items you do not use and determine how much you could have saved by not buying them.
2. Make a list of five grooming aids or appliances you use regularly. Comparison shop and find the price of each item in five different stores. If you were buying all five items from the same store, which store would charge you the least amount?
3. Write a research report on the laboratory methods used to test cosmetics for safety. Cosmetic manufacturers and the FDA should be good sources of information on this project.
4. Find out what type of health care protection you and your family have. What does the protection include? Can you identify any serious gaps in the coverage?
5. As a class, collect several health insurance policies or managed care plan booklets to study. Review each to learn:
   - ❑ what medical services and benefits are included.
   - ❑ how premiums, deductibles and co-pay amounts compare.
   - ❑ what limitations and exclusions apply to benefits.
   - ❑ how much choice each allows of care providers and treatments.
   - ❑ Underline any words or phrases in the plans that you do not understand and find out the meanings. Then discuss the underlined words in class.
6. Check to see if your family keeps health and medical records. If so, make sure the records are up-to-date and well-organized. If records have not been kept, begin keeping them now. Include a list of names and phone numbers for doctors, specialists, dentists, hospitals, and clinics that you and your family use.
7. Conduct a survey and develop a descriptive directory of health care services and facilities in your area.
8. Investigate and report on recent health care reform proposals. Outline methods of payment, benefits and limitations, supervision and control over services and charges, options or choices within the plans, and impact on individuals and employers.
9. Plan a three-day weekend for you and your family. Outline where you would go, how you would travel, where you would stay, and what you would see and do. Estimate the cost of the trip including the cost of travel, accommodations, food, and entertainment. Call or visit travel agencies, airlines, bus lines, travel bureaus, and libraries, or go online to obtain travel ideas and cost estimates.

UNIT 4

Big Spending

Chapter 10
Getting from Here to There

Chapter 11
Where You Live

Chapter 12
Inside Your Home

Most consumers face some big spending decisions. These involve choosing transportation, housing, and home furnishings. Factors such as financing and insurance must also be considered.

There are many transportation possibilities from which to choose. Buying a car or choosing other forms of transportation calls for careful analysis of your transportation needs and finances.

Finding a place to live can be an exciting adventure. Your choice will depend on the amount you can spend and your housing needs.

Furnishing your home involves many decisions. As you make decorating decisions, consider the ways you use space, the items you like around you, the resources you can use, and your needs. As you choose appliances and consumer electronics, consider performance, operating and safety features, energy efficiency, warranties, and servicing.

CHAPTER 10

Getting from Here to There

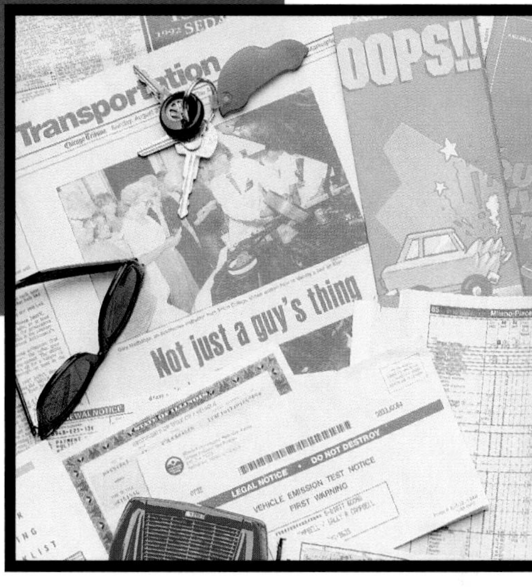

lease
depreciation
options
collateral
Truth in Lending Law
finance charges
annual percentage rate (APR)
financial responsibility laws
compulsory auto insurance laws
premiums
deductible

After studying this chapter, you will be able to

- ❑ explain the advantages and disadvantages of different forms of transportation.
- ❑ identify the pros and cons of buying versus leasing a car.
- ❑ identify the pros and cons of buying a used car versus a new car.
- ❑ evaluate car makes and models, features and options, dealers, and warranties.
- ❑ identify and use reliable car Web sites.
- ❑ compare finance charges and other credit terms of auto loans.
- ❑ describe the responsibilities of car ownership.
- ❑ select auto insurance coverage to meet individual needs.
- ❑ list factors to consider in the choice of a bicycle, moped, or motorcycle.

Whether you drive the family car, buy or lease your own car, or ride a bus, you will do a lot of traveling over the years. Americans spend billions of dollars each year on transportation. You personally will spend thousands of dollars transporting yourself in your lifetime.

In the United States, the car is the most widely used form of transportation. If you plan to own a car, you will face many decisions. This chapter presents information on choosing, paying for, insuring, and maintaining a car. Since cars aren't the answer to everyone's transportation needs, public transit, bicycles, mopeds, and motorcycles will also be covered.

Transportation Choices

The transportation choices open to you depend partly on where you live. In most urban and suburban communities, you will be able to choose from several forms of public and private transportation. You may have access to buses, trains, subways, and taxis. In rural areas, riding a bike or taking the school bus may be the only alternatives to driving a car. Whatever way you choose to get from here to there, it pays to look carefully at the advantages and disadvantages of each option.

Mass Transit

In major cities, mass transit is widely used, 10-1. It usually costs less than owning a car. However, the quality, cost, safety, and reliability of mass transit systems varies from city to city. One of the major advantages of traveling by bus, subway, or train is freedom from car owner responsibilities, 10-2.

> *"Nowadays everyone wants life, liberty, and an automobile in which to pursue happiness."*
>
> *Unknown*

There are several disadvantages to using mass transit for your transportation. It may be difficult to match your travel schedule with the transit schedule. Unless you plan carefully, you may waste a lot of time waiting for the bus or train. If public transit is not within walking distance, you may have to drive or be driven to it. You may also have to pay to park at the stop or station.

If you use mass transit during rush hours, it can be difficult to find space to sit. Unless you board at one of the first stops, you may have to stand for most of the ride. If you travel during off hours or late into the night, there may be safety concerns connected with using public transit.

Taxicabs

Taxicabs offer door-to-door service with no parking problems and no car owner responsibilities. Taking a cab also offers the convenience of coming and going as you please so long as cabs

PACE suburban bus agency

10-1
In many areas, buses offer an economical way to go from here to there.

10-2
Commuting and traveling by train can meet transportation needs in many situations.

Metra

are available. A disadvantage of cabs is their expense. Using taxis on a regular basis is very costly. It can also be difficult to find a taxi during rush hours or in bad weather. Therefore, taxis are not always a reliable, affordable form of transportation.

Owning or Leasing a Car

Owning or leasing a car is the most desirable answer to transportation needs for many Americans. See 10-3. When you drive your own car, you can come and go as you please. Many people take pride and pleasure in owning a car. If your work involves time on the road, owning or leasing a car may be an absolute necessity.

Although a car is a convenient and comfortable form of transportation, a car of your own is a major responsibility and expense. The purchase or lease price of a car is only the beginning. Other expenses include insurance, licensing, maintenance, fuel, and parking. In some urban areas, parking and traffic problems may rob you of the satisfaction and convenience of driving yourself.

A *carpool* is economical for people who come from and go to the same places at the same times. Carpooling

10-3
An automobile may be the best choice for transportation, particularly where public transportation does not exist or serve a broad area.

Oldsmobile

can save energy, minimize parking problems, and reduce traffic congestion. Many people enjoy the companionship of a carpool when it is made up of riders who get along well together. Others find carpooling inconvenient. Since the needs of other riders must always be considered, carpooling offers only limited flexibility. Also, it does not provide an answer to transportation needs outside the pooling situation.

Two-Wheelers

Two-wheelers may offer adequate transportation in many situations. Depending on your transportation needs, a motorcycle, moped, or bicycle may offer a convenient way of traveling. Compared to cars, two-wheelers are inexpensive forms of transportation. They conserve energy and require little parking space. They are also easy to maneuver in traffic.

A major disadvantage of two-wheelers is the high accident rate, particularly on highways and in heavy traffic. Riding a bike, motorcycle, or a moped safely requires special skill, constant attention, and appropriate safety equipment. This type of transportation is also uncomfortable in bad weather and inconvenient if you need to carry baggage or supplies.

Evaluating the Choices

One person's ideal means of getting around may not work at all for the next person. As you consider your transportation alternatives, follow these guidelines.

- ❑ ***Determine transportation needs.*** Where do you live? Where must you go? When and how often do you need to travel?
- ❑ ***Identify available choices.*** Do you have access to mass transit? Could you join or form a car pool? Do you own a bicycle, moped, or motorcycle you can use to get around? Can you walk to most of the places you need to go? Is a family car available to you? Would buying or leasing a car be a practical and affordable alternative?
- ❑ ***Compare costs.*** What are the daily, weekly, and monthly fares for public transportation? How much would it cost to drive and maintain a car? How much would it cost to car pool?
- ❑ ***Consider comfort and convenience.*** Is public transportation close to your home? Will it take you where you want to go? Is it reliable and safe? Does it run at convenient times? If you drive your own car, would there be a problem with traffic and parking? Would the weather permit you to ride a bicycle, moped, or motorcycle?
- ❑ ***Consider safety.*** What is the safety record of the mass transit system? Would you feel safe getting on and off or waiting at the transit stop during the hours you travel? If driving, would you have to travel on congested highways during rush hours? Is your car, bicycle, moped, or motorcycle equipped with important safety features?
- ❑ ***Consider personal preferences.*** Do you want a car of your own? Would you rather not have the responsibilities and expenses of car ownership? Do you prefer public transportation to driving your own car? Would you prefer biking or walking if possible?

Deciding how to get from here to there may be a big decision for many. The case studies throughout this chapter feature several people who must decide what method of

You Decide

Good News and Bad News

Marcus lives in Chicago. He goes to college part-time and works part-time. His apartment is close to campus, so he walks to all his classes. Concerning his job, Marcus has both good news and bad news. The good news is that he works for a law firm. The work is great experience for him since he is studying to become a paralegal. The bad news is the law firm is quite a distance from where he lives and goes to college.

If Marcus rides the bus, the trip takes an hour, and he has to transfer twice. On his way to work, shortly after noon, the bus is usually on schedule and rarely crowded. The ride home, during rush hour, is different. Marcus often has to wait as several full buses pass before one stops for passengers. When a bus does stop, it is usually so crowded he ends up standing most of the way home.

Since Marcus does not like taking a bus to and from work, he is considering other forms of transportation. Cabs are out of the question because of their cost. Besides, he would have trouble getting a cab during rush hour when he leaves work. Marcus could buy a used car, but he cannot afford the cost of owning a car and parking it at work and on campus. Plus, he has few transportation needs outside his job. He spends most of his nonworking time around the campus where he can walk.

Marcus has a bicycle, but the distance to work is too far to bike every day. He could afford a motorcycle, but he is not eager to drive it in city traffic and in winter weather. He would like to be in a car pool, but he doesn't know anyone who drives where and when he needs to go.

Case Review

1. If you were Marcus, what factors would you consider in making a transportation choice?
2. For Marcus, what would be the advantages and disadvantages of public transportation? A bicycle? A motorcycle? Car ownership? A car pool?
3. How could Marcus find out if there is a car pool he could join?

transportation will be best for them. Consider how you would choose in each situation.

Buying or Leasing a Car

If you decide that a car is the best way to meet your transportation needs, you can either buy or lease the car of your choice. In recent years, leasing has become a common way to acquire a car. Today, almost one-third of new cars are leased. Here's a look at the ways buying and leasing differ.

If you buy a car, you generally make a down payment and borrow the remainder, which you repay in monthly payments. You own the car, and it is totally yours when the loan is repaid. Under a ***lease***, you pay an initial cost, which usually includes the first monthly payment, a security deposit, and a *capitalized cost reduction.* The *capitalized cost* of a leased car is the price on which the lease is based. The *capitalized cost reduction* may include a down payment, trade-in allowance on a car you are trading, or rebates all of which lower the capitalized cost. There will also be fees for registration, licensing, and other charges for both buyer and lessee. Both people who buy a car and people who lease a car make monthly payments for a set period of time. Generally, the lessee's initial costs and monthly payments are less than those of the buyer. However, the lessee does not own the car at the end of the lease, though there may be an option to buy it.

You will sign a contract whether you finance (buy) or lease a car. Finance contracts are discussed later in this chapter. Here are some facts you should know before leasing and steps to follow in negotiating a lease. Words that make a difference include:

- ❑ *capitalized cost*–- the price for a leased car. Negotiate this just as you would the price of a new car. The lower this figure is, the lower your monthly payments will be.
- ❑ *capitalized cost reduction* — cash down payment, rebates, trade-in allowances, and other buying incentives that reduce the capitalized cost and, thus, lower your monthly payments.
- ❑ *residual value* — worth of a car at the end of the lease. The higher the residual value is, the lower your monthly payments will be.
- ❑ *money factor* — interest you pay usually stated as a small decimal such as .00265. To convert this to an annual interest rate multiply by 24 (.00265 x 24 = 6%). The money factor should be similar to or lower than new car loan rates.
- ❑ *lease term* — length of the lease — usually 24, 36 or 48 months. Try to limit the lease term to the length of the car warranty.

You also want to consider mileage limitations stated in the lease. Usually, you will be limited to 12,000 or 15,000 miles annually. Find out what you will pay if you go over the limit. It also is important to be aware of the penalties if you terminate the lease early. Try not to do this. It can be very costly. Consider "gap insurance" which covers you if the car should be stolen or totaled in an accident. It pays the difference between what you owe on the lease and what the car is worth. Finally, look for a fixed residual price option to buy at the end of the lease if you think you may want to own the vehicle rather than lease a new car. If you are going to lease:

- ❑ Just as in buying a car, a car lease can be negotiated. Shop carefully and negotiate all of the terms of the lease including the price of the car and the trade-in allowance if you are trading a car. Some items to consider when negotiating a car lease are listed in 10-4.
- ❑ Carefully review charges you must pay up front and at the termination of the lease.
- ❑ Check out any extra charges for excess mileage, wear and tear, early termination, etc.
- ❑ Get all of the figures and promises in writing.
- ❑ Review the warranty and be sure it is good for the entire term of the lease.
- ❑ Before you sign the contract, take it home and study it carefully. Get answers to any questions you have and be sure you understand all the terms of the agreement.

If you decide to buy or lease a car in the future, take care to make the right choice. Mistakes can be costly. Start with a thoughtful look at your needs and wants. Follow up with a

Items to Negotiate on a Car Lease

- ❑ capitalized cost or price of the car
- ❑ capitalized cost reduction
- ❑ residual value at the end of the lease
- ❑ mileage limitations
- ❑ turn back condition requirements
- ❑ car care packages, if any
- ❑ insurance and financing — compare lessor offers with your own sources.

10-4
When negotiating a car lease, keep these items in mind.

study of your financial situation. Then you will be ready to enter the market in search of a car that meets both your needs and your budget.

Your Needs and Wants

Think about why you want a car and how you will use it. Is a car primarily a necessity, a convenience, or a pleasure? Will you drive mostly on city streets, in heavy traffic, on highways, or on rugged country roads? See 10-5. Will you travel short or long distances? Will you drive frequently or only occasionally?

Consider how much space you will need for carrying passengers or cargo. Weigh the advantages and disadvantages of a new car versus a used car that meets your requirements. If you must park on city streets, you may want to look for a good used car rather than submit a new car to the weather and risks of vandalism or theft.

You may want to rank certain car characteristics from most to least important in meeting your needs. For example, consider the importance of the following items in evaluating a car for your own use:

- ❑ Size.
- ❑ Appearance and styling.
- ❑ Model or body type.
- ❑ Performance and handling.
- ❑ Features and options.
- ❑ Comfort.
- ❑ Purchase price.
- ❑ Safety record and features.
- ❑ Fuel economy.
- ❑ Warranty coverage.

Your Financial Situation

The initial cost of a car is only the beginning of car owner expenses. Auto costs will include a down payment, monthly payments, interest charges, insurance, licensing, registration, taxes, operating costs, maintenance, and possibly parking.

Before you make any commitments, it is important to be sure you can pay all the expenses associated with owning or leasing a car. The chart in 10-6 outlines some of those expenses. The figures will vary from car to car, owner to owner, and area to area. You will need to estimate how the figures are likely to play out for you and how much money you can spend on car ownership expenses.

Depreciation is a major cost of car ownership. ***Depreciation*** is a decrease in the value of property as a result of use and age. It represents the difference between the amount you pay for the car and the amount you get for it when

USDA

USDA

10-5
City streets and rural areas present very different transportation needs.

The Cost of Owning a Car

	Yearly Totals
Operating Costs	
Gas and oil per mile*	______
Number of miles driven	______
Cost per year (multiply miles driven by gas and oil per mile)	______
Maintenance (tune-ups and repairs)	______
Tires	______
TOTAL OPERATING COSTS	______
Ownership Costs	
Depreciation (divide by number of years of car ownership)**	______
Insurance Premiums	______
Taxes	______
License and Registration Fees	______
Finance Charge (if you took out a loan)	______
TOTAL OWNERSHIP COSTS	______
OTHER COSTS (car wash, repairs, and accessories)	______
TOTAL DRIVING COSTS PER YEAR	______
COST PER MILE (divide total costs by total miles driven)	______

***Gas and oil**—Start with a full tank of gasoline. Record the mileage on the odometer. From then on, note how many gallons of gasoline you buy, how much you pay, and the odometer reading.

Tank filled		odometer	8850
Buy 9.3 gallons	cost $11.36	odometer	9062
Buy 9.5 gallons	cost $11.61	odometer	9280
Buy 7.6 gallons	cost $ 9.29	odometer	9456
TOTAL			
26.4 gallons	cost $32.26	miles	9456
			-8850
			606

Miles per gallon: 606 ÷ 26.4 = 23
Cost of gas per mile: $32.26 ÷ 606 = 5 cents

Figure oil consumption the same way.
Remember to add the cost of every oil change.

****Depreciation**–To calculate depreciation—the difference in what you pay for your car and what you sell it for—subtract the projected trade-in value from its purchase price. Divide the difference by the number of years you plan to keep the car.

American Automobile Association

10-6
This worksheet can help drivers figure annual costs of owning a car.

You Decide

Transportation for Julie

Julie has her first full-time job. She is on an investigative reporting team for a large newspaper. Much of her research and investigation must be done on location. This means that Julie must be able to travel around the city quickly at any time of day.

Since Julie doesn't have a car, she relies mainly on city buses for transportation. However, buses run infrequently except during rush hours. Another problem is the difficulty in keeping track of all the bus routes and schedules to the many different places Julie travels.

Three other members of the reporting team have their own cars. When Julie goes on group assignments, one of them drives. When Julie goes on her own, she can sometimes borrow a car from one of the other reporters. Still, there are times when getting where she has to go is a problem.

Julie lives close enough to the office to walk in good weather, and she rides a bus in bad weather. Her apartment is close to stores and restaurants, so she can walk to most of the places she wants to go on her free time. Even so, Julie often feels that she needs her own transportation. Then she could get around the city conveniently when she is on assignment.

Case Review

1. What factors should Julie consider carefully before she makes a decision about transportation?
2. What are pros and cons of owning a car? A moped?
3. How would you solve Julie's transportation needs?

you sell or trade it in for another car. When you lease a car, the residual value at the end of the lease will be based on depreciation estimates. Although it is not an expense you actually pay, depreciation can represent a sizable amount of money, particularly if you buy a new car. For example, you buy a new car this year and plan to sell or trade it in three years. Its value is likely to drop by 30 percent the first year, 20 percent the second year, and just over 15 percent the third year. You lose less to depreciation if you buy a used car.

To determine how much you can afford to spend on a car, start with the amount of cash you have on hand for a down payment and initial costs. If you own a car you can sell or trade, add its value to the amount you can spend. You will also need cash up front for licensing, registration, taxes, and insurance. Next, determine how much you can spend each month to cover ongoing costs of car ownership. These will include fuel, maintenance, payments, insurance, parking, and an allowance for miscellaneous expenses.

Take a look at your overall income and expense picture. Total your monthly income after deductions and subtract your total monthly expenses. You will need to cover monthly car costs out of the amount left. To buy the car you want, it may be necessary to increase your income or cut your spending in other areas. (See Chapter 5 for details on managing money and expenses to reach important goals.)

The Automobile Marketplace

Finding a car to match your needs, wants, and budget can be a challenge. It helps to enter the marketplace knowing what you want and how much you can afford. A look at car size categories, models, and options may help you decide what type of car will best meet your needs. ***Options*** are features available at extra cost.

Cars come in a variety of standard sizes and styles, all with different options and features, 10-7. You can find compact, small, mid-size, and large cars in almost all styles and makes. Common styles or body types

10-7
The variety of car sizes and models makes it easier to meet individual needs for transportation.

Ford Motor Company

Ford Motor Company

Ford Motor Company

You Decide

To Own or Not to Own?

In one short month, Chris and Holly graduated from college, got married, and moved to their first city apartment. Both of them have full-time jobs. Holly is a nurse and Chris works at an ad agency. Their apartment is located in the heart of the city. It is close to their jobs, to shopping, and to most of the places they want to go.

Chris and Holly have a four-year-old car. They needed a car in college, but in the city, the car is a liability. With parking and traffic problems, trying to drive to work or anyplace else is frustrating. Owning a car is expensive. The rented parking space near their apartment is very costly, too.

The only time Chris and Holly use their car is on weekends when they go driving in the country. But days, even weeks, go by when they do not use the car at all. With the cost of parking and insurance, the car has become an expensive extra.

Chris and Holly discuss their alternatives. They could keep the car, paying for the convenience of having a car when they want one. They could ask Holly's family to keep the car for them. Then they would have the car for vacations. It also would be available if they needed it at a later time. Another choice would be to sell the car and rent a car when they need one.

Case Review

1. What are the advantages and disadvantages of having a car in a large city? Under what circumstances would you want to own a car in the city?
2. Can you think of other choices open to Chris and Holly?
3. What is the approximate cost of renting a car for a day, a week, or a month?
4. What would you do in Chris and Holly's situation? Why?

include 2- and 4-door sedans, station wagons, hatchbacks, convertibles, sport cars, pickups or light trucks, sport-utility vehicles (SUVs), mini-vans, and full-size vans. Light trucks and SUVs have been especially popular in recent years, accounting for almost half of new vehicle sales.

New car manufacturers are continually adding new options or features. Some options or features contribute to safety, performance, and economy. Others are primarily for appearance and convenience. Deciding which extras are important to you can be a major challenge. The chart in 10-8 outlines common features and categorizes them according to purpose. They may be standard or extra. *Standard options* or *features* come at no additional cost. Different makes and models come with different sets of standard options or features. *Extra options* or *features* can add significantly to the price of a car. Every year, manufacturers add to the available options or features on new cars. Very often, you will find *option packages* which are sets of features offered at special prices. Try not to pay for any options you do not really want and be sure you know the cost of each extra.

You will also need to choose between a domestic (American-made) and an imported (foreign-made) automobile. Determining whether a car is domestic or imported is not always easy. Engine and body parts may be made in two different countries, and assembly may take place in a third.

The American Automobile Labeling Act of 1992 was enacted to provide consumers with more information about domestic and foreign sources of car parts. This act requires car and light truck labels to list the country in which engine and transmission parts were manufactured.

Common Options or Features			
Safety Options or Features	❑ Air bags. ❑ Antilock brakes. ❑ Child restraint seats. ❑ Automatic restraint system. ❑ Alarm system. ❑ Rear wiper and defrost. ❑ Fog lights. ❑ Daytime running lights.	Convenience & Preference Options or Features	❑ Air conditioning. ❑ Sound system. ❑ Sun roof. ❑ Electronic instrument panel. ❑ Power seats. ❑ Intermittent windshield wipers. ❑ Rear wiper and defroster. ❑ Leather seats. ❑ Plush interior. ❑ Power mirror adjustment. ❑ Trip computer. ❑ Adjustable steering column. ❑ Adjustable ride control. ❑ Electronic vehicle monitor.
Performance Options or Features	❑ Automatic transmission. ❑ Power steering. ❑ Front-wheel or four-wheel drive. ❑ Large engine. ❑ Cruise control.		
Security Options or Features	❑ Antitheft alarm system. ❑ Power windows. ❑ Single switch lock. ❑ Cellular phone. ❑ Remote keyless entry.		

10-8
These options or features are usually available at additional cost, although a few of these may be standard equipment for certain cars.

The country in which the vehicle was assembled must be shown, too. Labels must state the overall percentage of parts that originated in the United States and Canada. Countries that contributed more than 15 percent of a vehicle's parts must also be listed.

There are both real and apparent differences between domestic and imported vehicles. For many years, foreign-made cars dominated the U.S. market. Today, the "buy American" sentiment and the lower cost and improved quality of domestic cars have helped to reverse this trend. More and more buyers want to give American products a chance.

Some consumers buy domestic in an effort to improve national employment figures and prosperity. The United States trade deficit puts the nation at a disadvantage in world markets. The deficit also reduces job opportunities at home. Therefore, many citizens feel it is both patriotic and in their own best interest to buy American-made products. When buying a car, you may want to consider the domestic versus foreign issue as well as the quality, value, and price of the car.

Most of the standard car models are available in different sizes, prices, and makes. They come with different features and options. They may be either imported or domestic. You will need to shop carefully to determine your preferences and match your car choice to your transportation needs and budget.

Used Car Choices

For first-time buyers, the used car market can be the best place to satisfy both budget and transportation needs. See 10-9. Used cars cost less to buy and

You Decide

To Buy or Be Sold

Bart is in the market for his first car. For Bart, owning a car is more than a dream come true, it is actually a necessity. He goes to college three hours away from his family's home. His part-time job is across town from campus, and mass transit is not available. A car is the only way he can get to all the places he needs to go.

Bart is excited about buying a car, but he is cautious enough to look carefully before choosing one. He will be spending his own money, and he wants to spend it wisely. Bart has always been interested in automobiles, and he is familiar with all the makes and models. He follows the new car ratings that appear in various magazines every year. This knowledge gives him a head start in shopping for a car of his own. He knows what make and model he wants and what features are important to him.

Bart also has decided to buy a new rather than a used car. Since he plans to drive the car for a long time, he decided the extra investment will be well spent. Bart has saved enough money for a large down payment. The income from his part-time job will take care of the monthly payments. Bart is ready to buy. All he has to do is find the best deal.

Bart begins his shopping at Moe's Motors, which is located near campus. Moe's ads claim the lowest priced cars around. As soon as Bart steps into the showroom, he knows it is going to be quite an experience. One of the many salespersons approaches Bart and says, "You look like a man who knows cars. Let me tell you, we make the best deals around. You can almost name your own price."

Although Bart says he is only looking, the salesperson is not discouraged. She introduces herself, "My name is Carla Mondez. Let me guide you through our showroom." She leads Bart away from the model he really wants to see and shows him a sports car with all the options. Carla tells Bart the car is priced at an all-time low because the new models will be delivered soon. The sales pitch sounds tempting–"You won't strike a better deal anywhere else. . . She runs like a dream. . . She can't be passed on the open road. . . She'll make you feel like a man."

The car is a beautiful machine–and well beyond his budget. However, before he knows what's happened, Bart finds himself behind the wheel taking the sporty car for a test drive.

Case Review

1. Do you think Bart should consider this car rather than the model he originally intended to buy? Why?
2. Do you think the deal is as good as it sounds? What are some ways Bart could find out for sure?
3. What does Bart need to do before making any decisions?
4. What would you do if you were Bart?

10-9
These young buyers are checking out possibilities at a used car lot.

Nicole LaMotte

to insure. They also depreciate more slowly. You can choose from a wide selection of makes, models, and sizes. Generally, it is a good idea to look for a two- to three-year-old car with low mileage and in good condition. It is a plus if the manufacturer's warranty is still in force.

The Federal Trade Commission's *Used Car Rule* requires a "Buyers Guide" sticker on the window of any used car sold by a dealer. This guide describes warranty coverage or lack of it. It directs the buyer to ask that all promises from the dealer be in writing. The sticker suggests the buyer ask to have the vehicle inspected by an independent automotive technician. It also lists some major defects that may occur in used cars.

Learn all you can about a used car before buying. Try to find out who owned it and how it was driven and maintained. Look up performance, safety, and service records for the make and model you are considering. In recent years, auto manufacturers, dealers, and superstores have begun to sell ***certified used cars.*** Certification means that a car has received a thorough mechanical and appearance inspection along with necessary repairs and replacements. Most certified vehicles meet age and mileage restrictions, pass inspections of 70 to 130 points that include checks for damage, top-off of fluids, and repair or replacement of damaged parts.

Once a vehicle passes this process, the dealer or manufacturer generally extends the existing warranty or issues a new 12-month/12,000-mile warranty.

Your best sources of information on a specific used car include the previous owner, if available, the dealer or seller, and any available service and other records on the car. You will find general information on the make, model, and year you are considering in the *Official Used Car Guide* from the National Automobile Dealers Association, the *Automotive Lease Guide* that lists the estimated residual values of leased cars, and the *Kelley Blue Book.* These publications may be available in local bookstores, libraries, or online. You can also get pricing and other used and new car information online at such

You Decide

Just Get Me to My Job on Time

Wendy is faced with a transportation problem that seems to have no answer except buying a car of her own. She has very little interest in cars, but now she needs one. She has just landed her first job teaching health and physical education at three schools. She has to spend time at each school every day. Driving is the only way she can get to work.

The only thing greater than Wendy's lack of interest in cars is her lack of knowledge about them. She doesn't know or care anything about them. All she wants is a reliable car to get her to work on time in all kinds of weather.

Wendy does know that a car will cost a lot of money, even if she buys a used one. She can afford a down payment and reasonable car payments, but Wendy doesn't want to spend any more than necessary on a car.

Case Review

1. What do you think Wendy needs to learn about cars before shopping? Before buying?
2. Where can Wendy get reliable information about car buying?
3. What type of car do you think Wendy needs? Why?
4. What will she need to know about owning and maintaining a car?
5. What factors related to the car and the dealer might be especially important to Wendy since she knows and cares so little about cars?

Web sites as, Autobytel, Edmunds, Intellichoice, SmartMoney Auto Guide, and individual car manufacturers. Safety data on various car models will be available from some of these sources, too, and from the National Highway Traffic Safety Administration's toll-free Auto Safety Hot Line listed in your local phone directory. Magazines, such as *Automobile Magazine, Car and Driver, Motor Trend* and the auto issue of *Consumer Reports, Consumer Research,* and *Kiplinger's Magazine,* all provide useful information on car buying, leasing, and ownership. It pays to learn as much as you can before you begin to shop. Well-informed customers get the best car deals.

Where to Buy

The way people acquire autos has changed dramatically the past few years. Today, over 30 percent of consumers lease their cars. Almost 25 percent of consumers look to car buying services or online sources for information and/or purchasing. Traditional auto dealerships have become more "user friendly" as a result of competition from auto superstores and the Internet. The result is a competitive market and a confusing array of ways and places to look for the car of your choice. All of this can work to your advantage.

You can buy or lease a new car from traditional auto dealers, the new auto superstores such as Carmax or AutoNation, or on the Web. If you don't want to do your own shopping and bargaining, car-buying services such as Auto-by-Tel and Autoweb will find and price the car you want online and put you in touch with a dealer near you. When you start to look at cars, decide right now to make several shopping trips before you buy. This will let you become familiar with different makes and models, compare prices, and check out options without falling prey to high-pressure salespersons. Online shopping is another way to gather the information you need before the actual moment of decision. Here is a rundown on places and ways to shop for a car.

- ❑ *Traditional dealerships* usually represent one or two manufacturers, sell new and some used cars, and may also lease new cars. Many dealerships sell certified used cars with full warranties. They will offer financing and take your car as a trade-in if you have one. As you shop, check out the service department. Is it well equipped and staffed with skilled, certified automotive technicians?
- ❑ *The Internet* provides both a source of information and a way to purchase or lease. You can find up-to-the-minute information on new and used vehicles, on leasing and financing, on insurance, and shopping, etc. Most manufacturers and many dealerships also have online services. You can use the Internet to find the car you want.
- ❑ *Auto superstores* such as AutoNation USA and Carmax sell both new and used vehicles that are inspected, serviced, and warranted. They typically carry huge used car inventories made up largely of leased vehicle returns. Most superstores are computerized. You can enter into the system the type of vehicle you want, price you are willing to pay, and other details, and the computer will locate cars in stock that meet your requirements. Prices are

normally fixed. Financing, insurance, and auto servicing can be arranged as well as trade-ins if you own a car to trade.

- *Private sellers or auctions* are other options if you are buying a used car. Normally, you receive no warranty coverage from private sellers unless the original warranty is still in force. Cars sold at auction are usually sold "as is" which offers no protection either, if you later have problems with the vehicle. See 10-10. In these cases, you want to make very careful inspections and have the vehicle checked by an independent, certified automotive technician.

Wherever you shop, whether you buy or lease, start the process with a low offer. Negotiate the cash price of the car first, then negotiate the trade-in allowance, if any. Don't be afraid to walk away if you aren't getting what you want. You always can come back. If you are looking at a used vehicle, ask to see the service record which will tell you how the vehicle has been maintained. Have an independent, certified automotive technician's inspection before you buy a pre-owned car. Be sure the title is in order and get all of the figures and quotes in writing when you are shopping. Take a day or two to think over the deal you are offered before committing yourself to a leasing or financing contract.

BILL OF SALE

I, Mark Smith ("Seller"), do hereby convey title and possession of my 19XX Volkswagon Golf, Vehicle Identification Number 1VWBA 0123GV012345, to John G. Canap ("Purchaser"), in exchange for consideration of $ 5000—.

FURTHERMORE, it is understood by the parties that the above vehicle is a used vehicle, has approximately 42,500 original miles on it, and it sold AS IS. It is further understood that SELLER MAKES NO WARRANTIES, EXPRESS OR IMPLIED, AS TO THE CONDITION OR FITNESS OF SAID VEHICLE.

FURTHERMORE, it is understood by the parties that the expense of transferring and registering the title and license of said vehicle shall be borne by the Purchaser.

WE THE PARTIES HEREBY ACKNOWLEDGE THAT WE HAVE READ THIS BILL OF SALE AND FULLY UNDERSTAND ITS CONTENTS.

Mark Smith
SELLER

John G. Canap
PURCHASER

Dated this 20th day of August, XXXX

10-10
This bill of sale shows the information you should receive if buying a used car from a private seller.

A Look at Warranties

Normally, new cars carry full warranty protection on some parts and limited protection on others. Items such as the air conditioner, radio, and tires carry separate warranties. When shopping for a car, study the warranties to learn just what they cover and what you must do to receive warranty coverage.

A full warranty generally provides for free repair or replacement of any defective part during the warranty period. Auto warranties usually run for one year or for the first 12,000 miles. A limited warranty offers less than full protection. Read it carefully to understand the limitations.

Most auto warranties set forth specific maintenance requirements the owner must meet during the warranty period. If the car needs any repairs during that time, they must be made by a factory-authorized service department to keep the warranty valid. However, routine maintenance may be done by an independent service center as long as the work and the parts meet specifications in the owner's manual.

The Final Four-Point Check

After answering the many questions about car buying or leasing, you may be ready to zero in on the car of your choice. However, before you part with your money, take time to check the car over carefully—in the driver's seat, on the road, under the hood, and on paper.

In the Driver's Seat

Sit in the driver's seat and see if you are within comfortable reach of the steering wheel, foot pedals, and controls. Also check for good visibility. Make sure you can see well out the front, side, and rear windows. Check seat position and adjustments for comfort.

On the Road

Test-drive the car to see how well it handles in traffic, on the open road, and when starting, stopping, turning, and parking. Is it comfortable and easy to drive? Also test all the equipment and controls, such as the emergency brake, turn signals, horn, radio, windshield wipers, and headlights.

You Decide

Experience Is the Best Teacher

Chuck and Carol Moore are twins. They will be 16 in two weeks. With two new drivers in the family, the Moores decide it's time for a second car. The twins understand the new car will be a family car, but they expect to drive it quite a bit.

Mr. and Mrs. Moore are busy people who believe in learning by doing. They decide to give Chuck and Carol the responsibility of researching the new car purchase and doing the initial shopping. This will save Mr. and Mrs. Moore time, and it will be an ideal learning experience for the twins.

Mr. and Mrs. Moore write down the following guidelines and turn the car research over to the twins.

Auto Shopping Guidelines:

- ❑ Review current Web sites, magazines, and books to learn about different makes, models, options, and list prices.
- ❑ Describe on paper the needs the family has for a car. List the types of cars that would meet those needs.
- ❑ Discuss the car purchase with experienced adults, such as the driver education teacher and friends who recently bought cars.
- ❑ Choose three or four car possibilities based on what you learn from research and investigation.
- ❑ Shop at several dealerships and online to compare cars, prices, warranties, and servicing.
- ❑ Present three recommendations, and give at least five supporting reasons for each recommendation.

Case Review

1. What do you think of Mr. and Mrs. Moore's guidelines?
2. Do you think Chuck and Carol will be able to do a good job of finding a family car by following the guidelines? Why?
3. What problems might Chuck and Carol have in carrying out this project?
4. How would you feel about accepting the responsibility of shopping for a family car?
5. What do you think Carol and Chuck will learn from this experience?

Under the Hood

A careful check of the engine and working parts of a car is particularly important when buying a used car. Unless you know all about cars, ask an independent, certified automotive technician to look under the hood with you. Take an overall look at the engine. Check the levels of all the fluids—oil, water, brake, transmission, and power steering. If fluid levels are low, it could be a sign of leakage or of poor maintenance. Also check the condition of the tires. Then start the engine. If you hear any strange noises, find out the cause. The car should idle smoothly and should not emit any burning odors. When buying a used car, it often pays to have it checked out by a reliable independent, certified technician.

On Paper

The checklist in 10-11 should help you evaluate the items that are important to you when buying a car. When the car you are considering passes the four-point check, you are ready to buy with confidence.

Financing a Car

Most purchases of new and used cars are financed. This means the buyer takes out a loan and pays for the car with monthly payments. Financing a car costs more than paying cash because you pay interest on the amount borrowed. By understanding the ins and outs of financing a car, you will be able to shop more intelligently for auto loans.

Sources of Financing

Car loans can be obtained from a variety of sources. Shop for the best deal on a loan just as you shop for the best deal on a car. Common sources of car loans include auto dealers, banks, credit unions, finance companies, and savings and loan associations.

Dealer financing is a convenient, on-the-spot source of financing. Rates may also be attractive when dealers are overstocked and need to sell cars to reduce their inventories. When asking a dealer about auto financing, be sure to insist on separate quotes for the car and the financing. This is the only way you can accurately compare finance charges and terms with other loan sources. Beware of a dealer who tries to package the car and the financing together. This can be a costly package. After looking at the dealer's credit terms, check financing terms from other sources. You can always come back to the dealer. You can also investigate financing sources online and compare rates and terms.

To obtain an auto loan, the borrower pledges the car as security or collateral. ***Collateral*** is something of value pledged as security for a loan. This means that the creditor will hold the title to the car until the loan is paid in full. If the borrower fails to repay the loan, the lender may legally take back or repossess the car and sell it.

The installment loan is the most common form of auto financing. It is repaid in monthly payments over a period of time. The size of the monthly payments and the length of the repayment period for installment loans vary greatly. This makes it relatively easy for car buyers to obtain loans they can afford to repay comfortably.

Costs of Financing

The overall cost of auto financing varies with the annual percentage rate, the amount borrowed, and the length of the repayment period. Consider these three variables carefully as you shop for a loan.

The higher the annual percentage rate is, the more money you will pay in interest. For example, the interest on a

Car Review Checklist

	O.K.	Not O.K.
Cost Factors		
Total Price including:		
base price	_____	_____
options	_____	_____
delivery, preparation, and other charges	_____	_____
Down payment requirement or capitalized cost reduction	_____	_____
Amount and number of monthly payments	_____	_____
Finance charge or money factor in a lease	_____	_____
Estimated cost of maintenance and service	_____	_____
Projected fuel economy	_____	_____
Warranty Coverage		
Number of miles and period of time	_____	_____
Parts covered	_____	_____
Labor covered	_____	_____
Owner responsibilities	_____	_____
Safety Features and Considerations		
Visibility	_____	_____
Acceleration speed	_____	_____
Braking speed	_____	_____
Ease of handling	_____	_____
Antilock brakes	_____	_____
Air bags	_____	_____
Automatic restraint system	_____	_____
Other features	_____	_____
Comfort and Convenience		
Smooth riding	_____	_____
Sound insulation	_____	_____
Passenger space and seating comfort	_____	_____
Ease of getting in and out	_____	_____
Luggage space	_____	_____
Air conditioning	_____	_____
Sound system	_____	_____
Other features	_____	_____
Seller		
Reputation of the dealership, superstore, or Web site	_____	_____
Service facilities and competence	_____	_____
Convenient location	_____	_____
Appearance of the Car		
Design	_____	_____
Model	_____	_____
Color	_____	_____
Interior	_____	_____

10-11
This checklist can help you run a final check on what is important to you in a car before buying or leasing.

$2,500 loan repaid in 12 monthly payments would be

$109.65 at 8 percent.

$165.50 at 12 percent.

$250.50 at 18 percent.

You pay less by shopping for the lowest rates available.

The more money you borrow, the more interest you pay. For example, the interest on a loan repaid in 12 monthly payments at an annual rate of 18 percent would be

$150.30 for a $1,500 loan.

$200.04 for a $2,000 loan.

$300.60 for a $3,000 loan.

You pay less by increasing the down payment and decreasing the size of the loan.

The longer the repayment period is, the more interest you will pay. For example, the interest on a $2,500 loan at an annual rate of 18 percent would be

$250.50 if repaid in 12 monthly payments.

$371.25 if repaid in 18 monthly payments.

$495.50 if repaid in 24 monthly payments.

$753.75 if repaid in 36 monthly payments.

You pay less by increasing the size of monthly payments and shortening the repayment period.

Finance Contracts

The ***Truth in Lending Law*** requires creditors to provide borrowers with a complete written account of credit terms and costs. According to this law, a loan contract must state:

- ❑ The amount borrowed or financed.
- ❑ The total amount to be repaid.
- ❑ The dollar cost of ***finance charges,*** which is the total amount paid for the use of credit, including interest charges and any other fees.
- ❑ The ***annual percentage rate*** or ***APR*** (rate of interest figured on a yearly basis).
- ❑ The date charges begin to apply.
- ❑ The number, amount, and due dates of installment payments.
- ❑ A list and explanation of any penalties for late payment, default, or prepayment.
- ❑ A description of the security pledged, which is usually the car.

If the agreement is with the dealer, the contract must also state:

- ❑ A full description of the car.
- ❑ The retail or cash price of the car.
- ❑ The deferred payment price (price with credit charges).
- ❑ The amount of the down payment.

For your own protection, before signing any car loan agreement, be sure to read it carefully. Ask questions if any part of the contract is unclear. Make sure there are no blank spaces or lines to be filled in later. Also, pay special attention to the creditor's legal rights in case of late payment, default, or prepayment. You should be aware of any possible consequences. Finally, review your financial situation one more time. Be sure you can carry out your responsibilities and make payments according to the terms set forth in the contract, 10-12.

Car Owner Responsibilities

A car of your own involves two major responsibilities. You are expected to carry adequate auto insurance and to operate and maintain your car properly and safely. Failing to carry out these responsibilities can endanger lives and financial resources of the car owner as well as passengers, other drivers, and pedestrians.

Auto Insurance Coverage

When you own or lease a car, you take certain personal and financial risks. If you are involved in a car accident, you may be required to pay thousands of dollars for injuries and

10-12
Put the financing figures through a final analysis before signing a car loan contract.

Ford Motor Company

property damage. If you are in an accident where you are at fault or claims are filed against you, it can cost thousands of dollars in legal fees as well as damages. This makes car insurance essential.

Practically no one can afford the financial risks of serious injury, death, or extensive property damage without insurance coverage. All 50 states have ***financial responsibility laws*** that require drivers to show proof of their ability to pay stated minimum amounts in damages after an accident. Most states have ***compulsory auto insurance laws*** that require proof of insurance prior to the occurrence of an accident. In these states it is illegal to drive a car without proof of insurance.

When you are ready to buy auto insurance, you will need to shop carefully to get the coverage you need at the best price. An auto insurance policy may include several types of coverage for the insured individual or family. Of the six basic types of auto insurance coverage, two are *liability coverages.* That means they pay losses of other parties caused by insured persons.

Liability Insurance

Bodily injury liability is the first type. This coverage protects insured persons when they are liable for an auto accident that injured or killed others. *Property damage liability* protects insured persons when they are liable for an auto accident where the property of others is damaged. These policies cover the policyholder, family members, and any person driving the car with the owner's permission. Both types of coverage pay the legal fees for settling claims. They also pay for damages assessed against the insured, up to limits stated in the policy. These damages include injuries to other parties or damage to property of others.

Basic Auto Insurance

Basic auto insurance coverages that pay for losses of the insured parties include the following:

- *Collision insurance* pays for damage to the insured person's car due to an auto accident.
- *Comprehensive physical damage insurance* pays for loss or damage to the insured's car that is not the result of collision. It covers auto damage or loss resulting from fire, theft, falling objects, explosion, earthquake, flood, riot, civil commotion, and collision with a bird or animal.
- *Uninsured motorist insurance* pays for injuries caused by an uninsured or hit-and-run driver.

It covers insured persons whether they be driving, riding, or walking. It also covers passengers in the insured person's car.

- *Medical payments coverage* pays for medical expenses of the insured persons resulting from a car accident, regardless of who is at fault. It covers the insured persons involved in an auto accident whether they were driving, riding, or walking. Any person injured in or by the insured's car is also covered. This coverage pays up to the limits stated in the policy.

Other Insurance Coverages

Personal injury protection (PIP) is a broader form of medical payments insurance. It varies from state to state. The broadest coverage pays for medical expenses, lost income, and services an injured person requires as a result of injuries sustained in an accident. This type of coverage is required in states that have no-fault insurance laws. It may also be available in other states.

No-fault auto insurance eliminates the faultfinding process in settling claims. When an accident occurs, each policyholder makes a claim to his or her own insurance company. Each company pays its own policyholder regardless of who is at fault.

No-fault insurance is designed to simplify and speed up payments to accident victims. It also acts to lower insurance rates by reducing costly court trials to determine fault. State legislators decide whether their state will adopt a no-fault insurance plan and what form it will take. Most states with a no-fault plan actually have a combination no-fault and liability insurance. The no-fault pays for claims up to a set amount called a *threshold.* However, in most states individuals can sue for additional damages when an accident involves severe injuries, death, or major medical bills. Liability insurance pays for damages over and above the threshold amount.

Auto replacement insurance covers the full cost of auto repairs or, if repair is not possible, the cost of a new car. Without this coverage you cannot collect more than the book value of the car for repairs or a new car.

Underinsured motorist insurance covers the difference between the liability coverage of an underinsured motorist and the amount of your losses. For example, if you suffer a $30,000 loss in an accident and the other driver carries only $10,000 in liability insurance, you can collect $10,000 from the other driver's policy plus $20,000 from your underinsured motorist policy.

Rental reimbursement covers the cost, up to limits in the policy, of renting a car while yours is being repaired.

Auto Insurance Costs

Auto insurance is a costly service. Coverage for young drivers is particularly high because statistically they have more accidents. Adding a teenage driver to a family policy may increase the insurance premium by as much as 75 percent. ***Premiums*** are periodic payments for an insurance policy. The cost of auto insurance depends on the following factors:

Driver Classification

Driver classification is determined by the age, sex, and marital status of the driver. Driving record and habits are also considered. Statistically, young, single males are involved in more serious accidents than other classes of drivers. Therefore, they tend to pay the highest insurance premiums. If a young man marries, his insurance costs may decrease because, statistically, married men have fewer serious accidents than single men. Rates for women, single and married, are lower than for males. A poor driving record tends to increase premiums as does a record of previous claims and costly settlements. When your driver classification changes, so might your insurance rates.

Where You Live

Insurance rates vary from state to state and in different areas of a state. The premium you pay will be determined by the number and amount of claims an insurance company processes in your rating territory. In areas where claims are frequent and high, such as big cities, premiums will be greater.

Eligibility for Premium Discounts

Some companies reduce premiums for those who successfully complete a driver education course. Discounts often are available for a variety of other conditions including safe driving records, good grades for students, nonsmokers, nondrinkers, antitheft devices, air bags, and people over a certain age. Premiums may also be discounted if you have two or more cars on a policy. Check with your insurance company about possible discounts.

The Year, Make, and Model of the Car

Cars that are costly to repair or that are favorite targets of thieves will cost more to insure. Premiums will be higher for luxury, sports, and new cars than for standard models and older cars, 10-13. For older cars, collision insurance may not even pay. Cars that require expensive repairs and parts generally cost more to insure. Sport utility vehicles and very popular models will cost more to insure than low profile, more ordinary cars.

Check the insurance costs for different models before buying a car. The Highway Loss Data Chart gives information on loss experience with different models and makes of cars. For a copy, write to the Insurance Institute for Highway Safety, 1005 North Glebe Road, Arlington, VA 22201 or go online.

The Amount of the Deductible

Most collision and comprehensive damage policies are written with a deductible clause. The ***deductible*** is the amount the insured person must pay before the insurance company pays on a claim. Premiums for collision and comprehensive damage coverage can be reduced by increasing the deductible amount. Increasing your deductible from $250 to $500 could save you 15 to 30 percent on your premium. The higher the deductible is, the lower the premium will be.

The Amount of Coverage

The more protection you buy, the higher the premium will be. However,

10-13
Insurance premiums will be higher for sportier model automobiles.

Ford Motor Company

the cost per dollar of coverage is usually less for larger policies. For example, a $100,000 policy costs less per dollar of coverage than a $50,000 policy. Just remember to buy the amount of coverage you need. A reliable agent can help you decide.

The Insurance Company

Premium rates and service for the same coverage may vary greatly from company to company. It pays to shop carefully. You may be able to save by combining different coverages into one policy rather than buying each separately.

After reading the guidelines in 10-14, you will be better prepared to select the automobile insurance you need for your particular car. To compare insurance costs, check the cost of coverage you need with several reliable insurance companies. Once you buy auto insurance, read your policy carefully and know what coverage you carry. It also is a good idea to keep the policy and records of premium payments and claims together in one place so you can find them as needed. See 10-15 for procedures to follow at the scene of an accident and in filing an insurance claim.

High Risk Drivers

It can be difficult for individuals with poor driving records to buy insurance. Insurers consider these drivers too great a risk. In such cases, it may be possible to obtain coverage through an assigned risk plan. This is a state-supervised program in which high-risk drivers are assigned to insurance companies. The companies are required to provide coverage, but premiums are considerably higher than for those with better driving records.

Suggestions for Buying Automobile Insurance

1. Decide on the types and amounts of coverage you need. If you now have a policy, review your coverage and its cost before renewal time.
2. Check with several reputable insurers. Keep in mind the least expensive coverage is not necessarily the best for you. Consider such things as the company's reliability and its reputation for service, including claims handling. If you're in doubt about a company, check with your state insurance department.
3. Consider the amount you would save by paying a higher deductible. You may find it pays in the long run to take care of small losses yourself.
4. Check with your agent regarding your eligibility for premium discounts for:
   - ❏ Safe driving.
   - ❏ Graduates of driver education courses.
   - ❏ Good students.
   - ❏ Drivers over a certain age.
   - ❏ Low annual usage.
   - ❏ Farmers.
   - ❏ Multicar families with all cars insured on the same policy.
   - ❏ Carpools.
5. Consider special coverages or higher policy limits if you frequently drive other commuters to work or groups of children to school or special events.
6. Consider reducing or dropping collision coverage as cars get older.

Insurance Information Institute

10-14
These guidelines can help you select auto insurance.

Auto Accidents and Insurance Claims

At the Scene of an Accident

- ❑ Stop your car safely beyond the accident and out of traffic. Turn on flasher or warning light.
- ❑ Assist the injured, but do not move anyone unless absolutely necessary, e.g. the car is burning or the victim is in the flow of traffic.
- ❑ Administer any first aid you are qualified and trained to provide.
- ❑ Stay calm and help others to do the same.
- ❑ Get help as fast as possible. Call or have someone call the police and an ambulance if needed.
- ❑ Provide police with information they request.
- ❑ Ask for a copy of the police report.
- ❑ Write down 1) names, addresses, and phone numbers of those involved in the accident and of any witnesses, 2) license number, make, and model of cars involved, 3) driver's license number of drivers involved, 4) insurance company and identification number of each driver involved, and 5) names and badge numbers of police officers and other emergency assistants.
- ❑ For a collision with an unattended or parked auto, try to find the owner. If unsuccessful, leave a note with your name, number, and address. Damages over a certain amount must be reported to the police in most states.

Filing an Insurance Claim

If your car is involved in an auto accident; if it is damaged by fire, flood, or vandalism; or if it is stolen, follow these steps in filing a claim for your losses.

- ❑ Phone your insurance agent or a local company representative as soon as possible to report the incident.
- ❑ Ask the agent how to proceed and what forms or documents will be needed to support your claim. These may include medical and auto repair bills and a copy of the police report.
- ❑ Obtain and provide the information the insurer requires. Cooperate fully with your insurance company in the investigation and settlement of claims.
- ❑ Turn over copies of any legal papers you receive in connection with the accident and losses you are claiming. If you are sued or claims are brought against you, the insurance company will provide legal representation for you.
- ❑ Keep copies of any paperwork and documents you submit with your insurance claim.
- ❑ Keep records of any expenses you incur as a result of an automobile accident. They may be reimbursed under the terms of your policy.

Note: It is unlawful to leave the scene of an accident in which you are involved without proper notification if there is injury, death, or property damage over a certain amount. Check the laws on reporting accidents in your state.

10-15
Follow these steps if you are involved in an auto accident and must file an insurance claim.

Operation and Maintenance

You have much to gain by operating and maintaining your car properly. You will be rewarded with better car performance, driving safety, and car reliability. You will also have fewer breakdowns and repairs, better fuel economy, less pollution, and greater trade-in value.

Operating Your Car

To operate your car competently and safely, you need to be familiar with the car and all of its features. Begin by reading the owner's manual. Understand the purpose of every gauge and switch on the dashboard and steering column. Learn how to read or operate each one properly. If a warning light flashes, stop and investigate the problem promptly.

Before starting your car, adjust the rearview mirror and side mirrors so you can see traffic behind and to the side of you. Buckle seat belts and shoulder harnesses securely. Place small children in approved safety seats in the backseat.

As you drive, start slowly and maintain a steady driving speed. Try to anticipate stops to avoid unnecessary braking and sudden stops except in emergencies. It is important to slow down for railroad crossings and bumps in the road. Drive slower under hazardous driving conditions such as heavy rain or snow, ice, fog, or where road construction is in progress.

For safe driving, anticipate and stay prepared for the unexpected. This means driving defensively. Watch traffic signs and try to maintain a sense of driving conditions and the flow of traffic. You need to give driving your full attention. Avoid reading maps, sightseeing, eating, drinking, or talking on the phone when you are behind the wheel. Though you've heard it a thousand times, once again: *do not ever drive under the influence of drugs or alcohol.*

Since rear-end collisions are the most common kind of accident, watch the car ahead and do not tailgate. To avoid being hit from the rear, signal well in advance your intentions to turn, stop, change lanes, or park.

Maintaining Your Car

Keeping your car in good driving condition is necessary for safety, economy, and performance. Just as you read the operating procedures for your car, study and follow the owner's manual for routine maintenance and service schedules. Manufacturer's instructions offer guidelines for lubrications, tune-ups, and other routine servicing. However, if you drive a car hard or under severe conditions, your car may need more frequent attention than indicated in the owner's manual.

One key to long car life is anticipating and avoiding potential problems. Listen to your car and investigate strange noises and sluggish performance. Pay attention to warning lights, gauge readings, and any leaks, drips, or unusual odors. Check out irregularities promptly. If you ignore little sounds and changes in performance, a small problem may become a big one. Discovering problems early gives you time to shop around for the best place to go for repairs and service. If you let problems go, your car may have to be towed or you may have to take the car to the nearest service station or repair shop. Then you may not get the best service at the best price. Early attention can save hundreds of dollars.

You also need to keep a close check on your tires. For safer driving and better fuel economy, keep the tire pressure at the recommended level. Replace worn tires with the proper size as recommended in the owner's manual. Tires also need to be rotated periodically.

Shopping for auto servicing can be a real challenge. Basically, you have three choices: a dealer, a chain auto service center, or an independent, certified automotive technician. For warranty servicing, it usually is necessary to go to the dealership. For routine repairs and maintenance, it pays to shop around. Evaluate service and repair centers according to the following guidelines.

Reputation

Look for membership in such organizations as the local chamber of commerce or Better Business Bureau. Also question several customers of the shop about their satisfaction with services and prices.

Competence

Look for experienced, well-trained automotive technicians. Certification is one indication of competence. ASE certified technicians have completed the training and passed the tests of the National Institute for Automotive Service Excellence, 10-16. Certified technicians receive credentials listing their areas of competence. They usually wear the blue and white ASE insignia. Where these technicians are employed, an ASE sign usually appears on the premises.

The sign may also appear in yellow page listings of auto repair shops. An endorsement by the American Automobile Association is another indicator of reliable servicing. Endorsed repair centers must meet the high standards of the Association.

10-16
Look for the blue and white symbol, as worn on the technician's arm, when shopping for auto servicing.

Facilities, Equipment, and Parts Inventory

Look for auto service shops and centers that are adequately equipped to care for your car and to perform the specific services required. Also ask about the availability of necessary parts.

Convenience

It pays to find servicing in convenient locations when you need to leave your car for service. Business hours that work well for you may also be important when dropping off or picking up your car. Before taking your car in for service, it is a good idea to call for an appointment. Also check in advance to see how long you can expect to be without your car.

Charges

Compare fees and charges for routine maintenance jobs, such as a lubrication, wheel alignment, and oil change. You can often make these comparisons on the telephone. Though it is not certain, it is likely that shops with reasonable charges for routine maintenance will be reasonable on bigger jobs as well.

Paperwork

It pays to get certain things in writing when you buy costly services. Be sure you receive written estimates, itemized bills, and written guarantees on the work performed. When you leave your car to be serviced, make it clear you want to be contacted before any unexpected major repairs or services are performed.

Two-wheelers

Whether you ride a one-speed bike, a motor scooter, or a motorcycle, two-wheelers are economical to drive, easy to maneuver, and easy to park. They offer environmental advantages, too. Bicycles are pollution-free, and powered cycles pollute far less than cars. Travel on a two-wheeler also saves fuel.

If you can satisfy part or all of your transportation needs with a two-wheeler, there are many choices to consider. Bicycles, scooters, and motorcycles come in many styles and sizes. Choose your two-wheeler according to how you will use it, what size and style you prefer, and how much money you have to spend.

Selecting Bicycles

There are over 100 million bikes in the United States today. In some countries, including China, India, and Japan, bicycle owners far outnumber car owners. Bicycles are the most energy efficient means of transportation and the least expensive. Biking rather than driving just for trips of three miles or less could save sizable amounts each year in fuel costs. It can cut down on pollution as well. With world-wide environmental concerns, many countries and some major cities in the U.S. are working to make cycling a convenient and safe alternative to the automobile. It also offers pleasure and fitness advantages, 10-17.

If you can use a bicycle for some or most of your transportation needs, finding the right bike is the first step. The many types and styles from which to choose can be overwhelming unless you know exactly what you want. The best bike for you will depend largely on how you plan to use it. For riding around your neighborhood and an occasional trip to the store, a sturdy one-speed model may do. For more frequent riding or commuting, you may want a mountain bike or all-terrain bike. Racing and touring bikes are also available, but carry performance and design features the average cyclist does not need. Consider the following factors when shopping for a bicycle.

Size

Bicycles come in many sizes. It is important both for comfort and safety to find the right fit. Frame sizes range from 13.5 to 28 inches. When straddling the bicycle, there should be approximately two inches between the crotch and the top tube. Once you find the right frame size, adjust other components, particularly seat and handlebar heights, for the best overall fit. A reputable bike shop can help you with size.

Weight

Most mountain bikes weigh around 30 pounds; touring or road bikes weigh slightly less. Generally, the heavier bikes will be sturdier. However, if you need to lift and transport your bike when you are not riding it, lighter weight may be important.

Wheels and Tires

The wider, knobby tires of the mountain and all-terrain bikes will stand up to fairly heavy-duty riding. The lighter, narrower wheels of a tour or racing bike are good for top speed but call for careful riding and upkeep. For riding comfort and pleasure, keep tires inflated at recommended pressure.

Gear Systems

Today, most bikes are multispeed models. For serious, long-distance cycling or commuting, you may want the 18 to 21 gear combinations of mountain or all-terrain bikes. Touring and racing cycles usually come in 10- to 15-speed models.

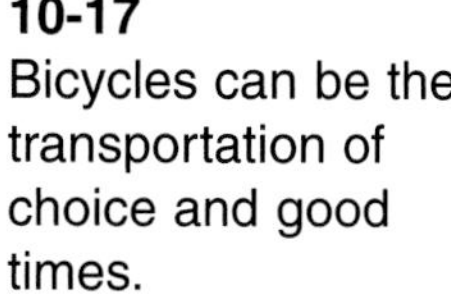

10-17
Bicycles can be the transportation of choice and good times.

Alumax

10-18
Motorcycles can meet transportation needs and give riding pleasure.

Harley-Davidson, Inc.

Brakes

Some models come with foot or coaster brakes that slow the bike by stopping the rear wheel. Most multi-speed all-terrain, racing and tour bikes come with hand or caliper brakes that brake both wheels. For greater braking power, bicycle standards require caliper brake pads to be ¾ inch by 2 inches.

New Developments

Recent innovations in bicycle design include two-wheel drive models that provide better traction, more stability, and better maneuverability. Advanced suspension systems take the shock out of curbs, potholes, and rough terrain. Hydraulic disc brakes provide superior stopping power. Each year brings improvements in performance and safety features.

If you plan to invest a sizable amount in a bicycle you hope to ride often and for many years, buy from a reliable bike or sports shop. Buy where you can count on knowledgeable salespersons, a wide selection of bikes, a service department for initial and follow-up maintenance, and a good selection of accessories. Most buyers need reliable help getting the proper fit and style for their riding needs. If you are already knowledgeable about bikes, you may want to shop for one at a department store, a discount house, in a mail-order catalog, or online.

In most areas, you can find used bikes for sale in classified ads, auctions, house sales, and bike shops. In some cities, police departments hold bike auctions annually to sell unclaimed bikes. If you buy a used bike, check it out carefully. A reconditioned bike from a bicycle shop may be your safest bet, especially if it carries a warranty. Test ride several bikes before you make a choice.

Finally, there are certain accessories you will need. A good helmet is a must for safety and it is required by law in some states. You also need a front headlight for night riding. Other items to consider include a water bottle, seat bag, lubricants, tool kit, and a sturdy lock. It pays to lock up. Each year, over 500,000 bicycles are reported stolen. These extras can add up and prices vary from dealer to dealer. Shop for the best deal on accessories.

Selecting Motorcycles

Some six million Americans choose a motorcycle for transportation and riding pleasure, 10-18. If this appeals to you, decide right now you will learn to ride before you even begin to shop for a motorcycle. The Motorcycle Safety Foundation offers training courses for both beginning and skilled riders. You can go online or check with a reliable motorcycle dealer to learn of courses in your area. After some formal training, you will know more about motorcycles and what you want in one.

There are several basic models, each designed for a different type of cycling. The best choice for you will depend on how you plan to use the bike. If you want to do off-road cycling, a dirt bike or trail bike may be right for you. For on-road and highway cycling, a sport bike, cruiser, or touring bike may meet your needs. Most manufacturers produce quality motorcycles. Your choice of make and model will depend on personal preferences and what you can afford. The Internet can be a good place to begin shopping. It gives volumes of information on selection, maintenance, insurance, safety, and related topics. *Cycle World* magazine is another good source. Visit several dealers and test drive different makes and models. You should feel comfortable and confident riding the bike you buy. Check noise, vibration, cruising speed, comfort, and ease of handling. Excessive noise and vibration can be very tiring on long trips.

The cost of a motorcycle can be substantial, ranging from $5,000 to $25,000. You may want to look for a good used motorcycle for your first buy. Check the "Financing a Car" section of this chapter if you plan to finance a bike. The process will be the same. A motorcycle averages 30 to 50 miles per gallon and costs very little to drive. However, insurance is essential and will be expensive. Since motorcycles are considered a greater risk to drive than cars, insurance companies charge higher premiums. The types of insurance coverage offered is similar to that provided by auto insurance. Talk to a reliable insurance agent about coverages and cost before you buy a motorcycle.

Motorcycle licensing, registration, and traffic laws vary from state to state. For example, some states require cycle drivers to wear helmets and other states do not. Check your state laws before driving or buying a motorcycle. A good helmet is a safety necessity whether required by law or not.

Remember, when shopping for a motorcycle, check out the dealers as you would car dealers. The Internet also is a good place to shop for a motorcycle and to find volumes of information on selection, maintenance, insurance, and related topics. Buy from a reputable dealer that has a reliable service department. If you are considering a used motorcycle, check it out with great care. Very often, mechanical problems occur two or three years after buying a motorcycle. Maintenance on motorcycles is important both for safety and performance. Follow the instructions in the owner's manual for periodic servicing. Pay particular attention to lubrication and proper tire pressure. The useful life of cycles is closely tied to proper maintenance. Before you go on the road or trail with a new cycle, practice operating it in an area with little or no traffic. Starting, shifting gears, braking, and gradual acceleration are important skills to master before you ride in traffic.

Summary

Most consumers can choose from a variety of transportation possibilities. These include mass transit, a car, or traveling on two wheels. The best choices will depend on personal needs, available options in the area, and the costs of different ways of getting around. Comfort, convenience, safety, and personal preferences are also important.

Most Americans at some point in time will own or lease a car. Buying an automobile calls for careful analysis of your transportation needs and finances. The cost of owning a car includes the purchase price and any finance charges if you buy on time. Leasing costs are similar. Insurance, licensing, registration, taxes, operating costs, maintenance, and parking are other expenses connected with a car of your own. It is important to estimate the total costs to be sure you can afford a car.

It helps to know your way around the automobile marketplace. Some knowledge of car sizes, models, and body types can help you pre-shop and appear knowledgeable when you visit the showroom. You also need to know about available features and options.

For many first-time buyers, a used car will be the best choice to satisfy both budget and transportation needs. A good used car will cost less to buy and insure than a similar new car. The Federal Trade Commission's *Used Car Rule* requires a "Buyer's Guide" sticker on the windows of used cars sold by dealers. Study this sticker carefully to learn about the car and its warranty coverage. Certified used cars have passed rigid mechanical and appearance inspections and carry a warranty. There is also a variety of publications that provide useful information on used cars.

Deciding where to buy can be a challenge. Dealerships, auto superstores, and the Internet are among the places you can shop for the car of your choice. Compare different cars and models, warranty coverages, service facilities, and prices. When you have narrowed down your choice, apply the four-point check—in the driver's seat, on the road, under the hood, and on paper.

Auto financing is available from several sources. These include auto dealers, banks, credit unions, finance companies, and savings and loan associations. It pays to shop for the financing at several sources and to read contracts carefully. Both finance charges and terms can vary greatly. Credit costs will depend largely on the percentage rate charged, the amount borrowed, and the length of the repayment period.

Carrying adequate auto insurance is a major responsibility of car owners. Different types of coverage protect against the different risks a person assumes as a car owner. The cost of insurance will depend on many factors, including driving record, where you live, and the type of car. It pays to shop carefully for the best coverage at the best price.

Proper operation and maintenance are also important for car owners. This means safe and sensible driving and timely car care and servicing. Finding a reliable service center is a key factor in auto maintenance and repairs.

Two-wheelers are a transportation choice for many consumers. There is a wide variety of bicycles and motorcycles to meet different needs and preferences. Two-wheelers often serve recreational and fitness purposes in addition to providing transportation. Do your homework before buying. Shop and compare at several reliable dealers to find the best buys. Warranty coverage is important, and safety equipment a must for this type of transportation.

To Review

1. Name two advantages and two disadvantages of mass transit.
2. What six factors should you consider when evaluating transportation choices?
3. List eight expenses involved in buying or leasing a car.
4. How does depreciation affect the price of a car?
5. Name two places you can find suggested prices of used cars.
6. What is a disadvantage of buying a used car from a private owner or at an auction?
7. What do most full car warranties provide?
8. True or false. Long-term loans cost more than short-terms loans.
9. What three factors influence the cost of financing a car?
10. List five factors that determine auto insurance costs.
11. Which type of insurance coverage pays for any damage your car causes to the property of others if you are responsible for the accident?
    A. Comprehensive physical damage.
    B. Uninsured motorist.
    C. Property damage liability.
    D. Bodily injury liability.
    E. Collision.
12. How can early attention to car problems save hundreds of dollars?
13. What are some advantages of two-wheeler transportation?
14. Name three new developments in bicycle design.
15. Why is it smart to take a training course in riding a motorcycle before shopping for or buying one?

To Think Critically

1. If you were to organize a car pool of four to six people to go to and from work or school, what rules or policies would you want to make clear to each rider?
2. How can you decide if you have enough money to buy, operate, and maintain a car?
3. What are some of the options that increase the price of a car? Which are important for safety, performance, and economy?
4. Why do finance charges vary with different sources of credit?
5. Why are auto insurance costs higher for some drivers than for others?
6. What kinds of auto insurance coverage do you or your family carry? How might the family coverage and costs change if you are added to the policy as a new driver?
7. What are some guidelines to follow when buying auto insurance?
8. How does no-fault auto insurance work?
9. What steps can car owners take to operate cars safely and smoothly?
10. What are some things a car owner can do to get reliable auto servicing?
11. What determines the price of a bicycle? What features add to the price of a bicycle? What are some of the necessary and desirable accessories for bike owners?
12. What are some factors to consider when buying a motorcycle?

To Do

1. Obtain copies of two or three new and used car warranties from dealers or from car owners in your family. Study the warranties and compare
   A. Parts and labor covered.
   B. Length of time or number of miles under warranty.
   C. Buyer responsibilities.
   D. Conditions for receiving warranty servicing and keeping the warranty in effect.

   How do used car warranties differ from new car warranties? Discuss your findings with the class.
2. Check at least four sources of auto financing in your area and compare credit costs and terms for:
   A. A two-year, $5,000 loan for a used car.
   B. A two-year, $10,000 loan for a new car.

   In a short written report, explain how the annual percentage rate, the amount of the loan, and the repayment period affect credit costs. Also explain why credit costs differ for used and new cars.
3. Design a bulletin board on buying a car. Include in your display copies of all the legal papers and documents related to car buying and ownership.
4. Arrange, as a class or individually, to visit at least three auto service and repair facilities. Take note of the
   A. Experience and qualifications of technicians.
   B. Equipment and facilities for servicing different cars.
   C. Guarantees on parts and servicing.
   D. Charges for routine jobs such as a tune-up or an oil change.
   E. Attitude of service people toward answering questions and complaints and satisfying customers.

   As a class, discuss how the three service facilities compare. Does one seem preferable to another? If so, why?
5. At three different insurance companies, compare insurance costs for motorcycles to insurance costs for used and new cars. Report to the class how car and motorcycle insurance differ in cost and coverage.
6. Obtain an auto insurance policy to study and analyze. Underline the most important phrases and circle any terms you do not understand. Discuss the policy in class, explain the coverage it provides, and define the circled terms.
7. Pick three new cars you would consider buying. Specify make, size, style, and features. Shop for these cars online. Use the Internet to locate the best buys on the cars you want in your area. Report your findings to the class.
8. Take a trip to a car dealership and to an auto superstore if there is one in your area. Compare the two. What type of selection did you find? Were salespeople helpful? Were prices competitive? How did the service center look? What guarantees and warranties were offered? Were there both new and used cars? Could you lease a car? Which place would you prefer if you wanted to buy?

Owning or leasing a car is the most convenient option for many consumers, but is is also the most costly.

CHAPTER 11

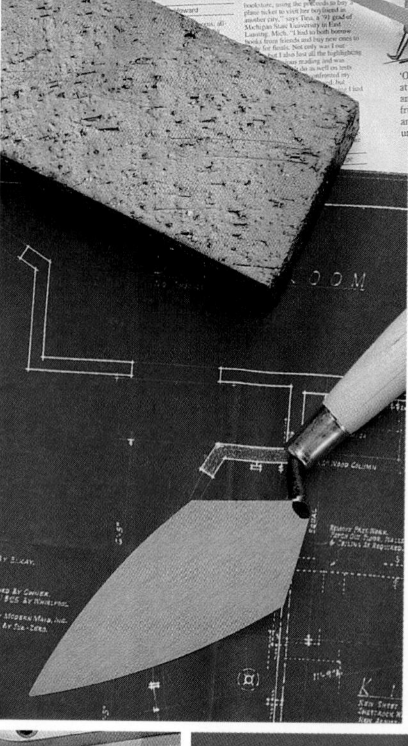

APARTMENT
FOR RENT
'I room with a girl. The problem is her boyfriend is the biggest pig I've ever met'.
'One of my roommates attached herself to me and wanted to be best friends. She wouldn't go anywhere or do anything unless I went with her'.
FOR SAL
THERE'S NO PLACE LIKE HOME
THE HOME-
KITCHEN

FOR SAL
THERE'S NO PLACE LIKE HOME
THE HOME-OWNER SURVI MANI
METROP HOME

Where You Live

condominium
cooperative
security deposit
lease
purchase agreement
title
abstract of title
survey
appraisal
mortgage
amortization
fixed-rate mortgage
adjustable rate mortgage
graduated payment mortgage
conventional home mortgage
FHA-insured loan
VA-guaranteed loan
points
mortgage lock-in
closing costs
cash value

After studying this chapter, you will be able to

- ❑ list key factors to consider when choosing a housing location.
- ❑ evaluate different types of housing.
- ❑ explain the steps to follow when looking for housing.
- ❑ describe and compare the responsibilities involved in renting versus buying a home.
- ❑ compare and shop for home financing terms.
- ❑ outline the key factors to consider when buying home insurance.

The word *home* has different meanings to different people at different times in their lives. To some, a home is a base of operations—a headquarters. To others, a home is a secure shelter from a threatening or unfriendly world. For many people, home brings to mind a warm feeling of being surrounded by family members. It conjures happy memories of times shared with loved ones. Home may be a place to go when there is nowhere else to go. It may be a place to relax and entertain. A home may mean all of this and more. It's whatever people make it.

> *"Home is the place where, when you go there, they have to take you in."*
>
> *Robert Frost*

In order to meet their need for shelter, people through the ages have lived in caves, huts, cabins, and tents. Today, you are more likely to meet your housing needs with an apartment, a condominium, or a house. You will probably spend a large portion of your income on a place to live. Consider the choices very carefully. The home you choose will influence the way you live, the people you meet, and your overall sense of well-being.

When making housing decisions, you need to consider location. You need to decide what type of housing you want and need. It will also be important to figure out how much you can spend on housing. Finally, you need to weigh the pros and cons of buying versus renting a home at different stages in your life.

Housing Location

The location of your first home away from home may be determined largely by what you are doing. Will you be working, going to school, or getting married? Very often a job or school will dictate in part where you live. Even so, you will be able to make some choices within existing limitations.

Consider how you like to live. Would you prefer living in the country, a small town, a city, or a suburb? Some people like the pace and excitement of city living. Others like rural areas with lots of open space, 11-1. Still others try to have both by living in the suburbs. There's more to choosing a location than deciding between city and country, though. Here are some other factors to consider.

Employment Opportunities

What types of jobs are available in the areas that appeal to you? Will you be able to find the type of work you want? How much money can you expect to earn if you work in the area? Local or state employment offices and chambers of commerce are places to check out employment opportunities in different areas. You can also find job listings and career opportunities for different areas and in different fields online.

Cost of Living

What is the average cost of housing in different areas? The Bureau of Labor Statistics publishes cost of living figures for different cities and parts of the country. Business and world almanacs also give cost of living and other economic information on different places. It will pay to find out the costs of food, housing, health care, transportation, and utilities for places

USDA

USDA

11-1
Some people like the excitement and fast pace of big city life while others prefer the peace and quiet of life in the country.

where you would like to live. What are the rates for home and car insurance? What are the sales, income, and real estate tax rates? The cost of maintaining similar lifestyles in different areas can vary greatly.

Climate

What type of weather do you like—warm, dry, wet, cold, or mild? Is a change of seasons important to you? Would you rather live near the desert, the mountains, or the ocean? A world almanac or the National Climatic Center of the U.S. Department of Commerce can provide weather statistics for different cities. These statistics include average high and low temperatures, rainfall and snowfall, humidity, and wind speed.

Lifestyle

Will you be living alone or with a roommate or spouse? Do you expect to have children? Young, single persons or childless couples may prefer living in the heart of a city. Families with young children often prefer to live in a suburb or small town where there is more space and a stronger sense of community.

Try to decide what is most important to you. Do you want to live close to your family or friends? Do you want to live near a college or university to further your education? Do you want to be close to the mountains so you can ski in the winter? Would you rather be near water so you can enjoy water sports? Your answers to these and similar questions will help guide your choice of location.

Neighborhood

Once you have narrowed your choices to a specific region, you can begin evaluating different neighborhoods. Appearance is one of the most obvious factors to consider in a neighborhood. Are the buildings attractive? Do the architectural styles offer both variety and harmony? Are both private and public areas well kept? Are the yards attractively landscaped with trees, bushes, and flowers? Is the street layout attractive and functional?

What is the overall character of the neighborhood? Does it appear residential, commercial, industrial, or mixed? What zoning laws and building codes apply to the neighborhood? Is the area relatively free of heavy traffic, noise, and air pollution? How would you assess property values now and in the future?

You may want to consider the ages, interests, occupations, and educational backgrounds of the people in the area. Is the overall income level similar to your own? Are most people living in the area single or married? Are there children in the neighborhood? Are there enough similarities to make life comfortable and enough differences to make it interesting?

How far is the neighborhood located from your work or school? Is there adequate space for parking? Would you have to drive to work and other places you travel? Could you take public transportation?

Community Facilities

Check out the community services and facilities that are available in the neighborhood. Are services convenient to use and reasonable in cost? Is fire and police protection adequate? What is the cost of water, electric power, and heating fuel? Does the community provide trash pickup, recycling, and snow removal? Are streets and other public areas well maintained? Learn what you can about health care in the area. Is public transportation convenient and reliable?

Look for services and activities that are important to you. For example, does the community sponsor athletic programs and cultural events? Are citizens actively involved in local government? Will you have access to a public library, churches, parks, and athletic facilities? See 11-2. Is there a variety of shops and stores?

Schools

The education system will be important if you have children of your own and also if you want to guarantee the value of your property. Find out whether the schools in the area are noted for quality education. What are teacher qualifications and pay scales? What is the average class size? Are textbooks and lab equipment up-to-date? Are special education programs offered for students who are disabled or exceptional? What extracurricular activities are offered?

11-2
Families with small children will probably prefer to live near a park or playground.

Landscape Structures, Inc.

Hunting for Housing

University Living

Lynn will be a freshman at a university in the fall. She is a good student and an excellent tennis player. She also is talented in music and drama. In spite of her talents, Lynn is shy and finds it hard to talk to new people. She is very close to her family and has never been away from home for more than a week.

Lynn has mixed feelings about going to college. She wants to continue her education, but she is worried about being far away from home. The university she has chosen is 1,400 miles from her hometown.

One of Lynn's major concerns is deciding where to live—on or off campus. If she lives on campus, should she choose a freshman dorm, an all-female dorm, or a coed dorm? Should she room with someone or ask for a private room? If she lives off campus, should she rent a room or an apartment? The housing choices outlined in the materials she received from the university are not helpful in making a decision.

Case Review

1. What are the advantages and disadvantages of each housing alternative?
2. Where do you think Lynn should live her freshman year? Why?
3. What choice would you make if you were in Lynn's position? Why?
4. How might your choice differ if you were a senior at the university?

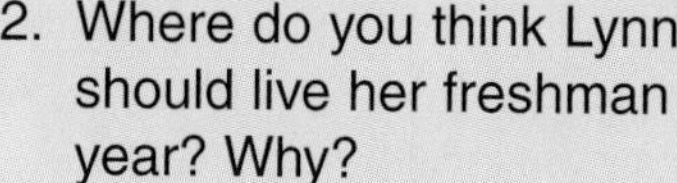

Sources of Information

Be sure to check out a location carefully before you settle. Moving into a place that doesn't suit you can be costly in terms of happiness, time, and money. The following sources can provide helpful information about specific regions and communities:

- ❑ Chambers of commerce.
- ❑ Local newspapers and magazines.
- ❑ Classified ad pages and local government listings in phone books.
- ❑ Long-time and new residents of an area.
- ❑ Travel books and almanacs.
- ❑ Community organizations in the area.
- ❑ Real estate brokers.
- ❑ Internet.

Types of Housing

At different times in your life, you will most likely choose different types and styles of housing. Your choices will probably be compromises based on what you need and want, what you can afford, and what is available. You may want a country mansion, while your budget calls for a suburban apartment. You may want a three-bedroom condominium, but there may be none available in your area. You may want a two-story colonial style house, when the only house for sale in the neighborhood is a ranch style. It may be a challenge to find a home you can live in happily. Some compromises must be made.

Once you know generally what type of housing you want and where you want to live, a real estate broker may be able to help you locate what you want. In most areas, you can go online to find listings of houses and apartments for rent and for sale. Often, you can find detailed information, including pictures and floor plans.

Apartments, Condominiums, and Cooperatives

Most rental apartments, condominiums, and cooperatives are multifamily dwellings. They are in buildings that house more than one family or living unit. Each unit has its own complete private living quarters. Residents share common areas, such as lobby, grounds, laundry facilities, and other building services.

Apartment buildings vary in the types of services and facilities they offer. They may or may not have laundry equipment, parking space, recreational facilities, and other extras. If you are considering apartment living, the checklist in 11-3 can help you evaluate different complexes.

The main difference that separates rental apartments from condominiums and cooperatives is ownership, 11-4. A person who lives in a rental apartment leases the apartment from the owner. A person who lives in a condominium or cooperative generally owns it. Condominium and cooperative ownership are somewhat similar. Buyers share common areas and have some voice in the management of the property. However, there are some distinct differences.

A ***condominium*** is a form of home ownership where a person owns the unit he or she occupies. The ownership of the surrounding building and grounds is shared. The owner pays a monthly assessment or maintenance fee to cover the costs of operating, maintaining, and repairing the shared property. The owners generally elect a board of managers to make policy and management decisions for the shared property.

In some ways, owning a condo is like owning a single-family house. Most people obtain a mortgage when buying a condo. They make mortgage payments and pay property taxes just as the owner of a house does. Condo

Checklist for Apartments, Condominiums, and Cooperatives

Building and Grounds

- ☐ Attractive, well-constructed building.
- ☐ Good maintenance and upkeep.
- ☐ Clean, well-lighted, and uncluttered halls, entrances, stairs.
- ☐ Reliable building management.
- ☐ Attractive landscaping with adequate outdoor space for tennants.
- ☐ Locked entrances, protected from outsiders.
- ☐ Clean, attractive lobby.

Services and Facilities

- ☐ Laundry equipment.
- ☐ Parking space (indoor or outdoor).
- ☐ Swimming pool.
- ☐ Tennis courts.
- ☐ Receiving room for packages.
- ☐ Convenient trash disposal.
- ☐ Adequate fire escapes.
- ☐ Storage lockers.
- ☐ Locked mailboxes.
- ☐ Elevators.
- ☐ Engineer on call for emergency repairs.
- ☐ Extras—window washing, decorating, maid service, shops.

Inside Living Space

- ☐ Adequate room sizes.
- ☐ Convenient floor plan.
- ☐ Suitable wall space for furniture.
- ☐ Soundproof.
- ☐ Attractive decorating and fixtures.
- ☐ Pleasant views.
- ☐ Windows located to provide enough air, light, and ventilation.
- ☐ Agreeable size, type, and placement of windows.
- ☐ Windows with blinds, shades, screens, and storm windows.
- ☐ Easy cleaning and maintenance.
- ☐ Attractive, easy-to-clean floors.
- ☐ Furnished appliances in good condition.
- ☐ Clean, effective heating, thermostatically controlled.
- ☐ Up-to-date wiring.
- ☐ Conveniently placed electric outlets.
- ☐ Well-fitted doors, casings, cabinets, and built-ins.
- ☐ Extras—air conditioning, carpeting, dishwasher, disposer, fireplace, patio.

Household International

11-3
This checklist can help you compare available apartments, condominiums, and cooperatives.

11-4
Buildings similar to this one are available as rental apartments, condominiums, or cooperatives.

owners have the same tax and equity benefits as the house owner. Another similarity is both condo and house owners can make their own decisions about redecorating, refinancing, or selling their homes.

A ***cooperative*** is a form of home ownership in which a person buys shares in a corporation that owns the property. In return, the buyer lives in a designated unit and becomes a member of the cooperative. Owners pay a monthly fee that covers their share of maintenance and service costs. The fee also covers the building mortgage and taxes. Usually it is necessary to obtain approval from an elected board of directors before selling or remodeling a unit.

Hunting for Housing

The Search Is On

Milt has just finished a training program in automotive technology. He has also just landed a job as an automotive technician in St. Louis. Now that he has a job, he must find a place to live. Milt is a man of action. He loads the car and sets out for St. Louis, thinking about a place of his own as he drives.

After a 10-hour drive, Milt arrives in St. Louis in a pouring rain, hungry and tired. He checks into a motel close to the center where he will begin working the next week. Milt knows he can't afford motel prices for long. He also knows he won't have much time to look for a place to live once he starts working. He figures he had better find a place of his own within the next three days.

Early the next morning, Milt begins his housing search. He has a few conditions in mind that must be met. He wants a one-bedroom apartment, not a studio. He also wants to be able to walk in and out of his apartment without taking an elevator. None of the high-rise buildings will do. He needs a place for his car. And he wants to be in an area where he can meet lots of people his age.

Milt's problem is that he doesn't know where to start looking. He studies the classified ads for apartments, but they aren't much help because he doesn't know the city. Finally, Milt sits down and thinks about what he should do next. Here are some of his options:

- ❑ Visit the chamber of commerce to get a map of the city and information on apartments in the area.
- ❑ Check out some of the apartments listed in the classified ads.
- ❑ Take a day or two to drive around St. Louis and get a feel for the city.

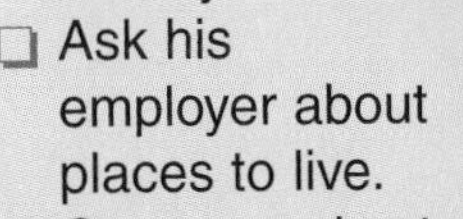

- ❑ Ask his employer about places to live.
- ❑ Go to a real estate agent for help in finding an apartment.
- ❑ Take a room at the YMCA for a few weeks until he is more familiar with the city.

Case Review

1. If you were Milt, how would you search for a place to live?
2. Which of the ideas from Milt's list might you use in your search for a place to live?
3. What should Milt consider before he chooses an apartment?
4. If Milt wanted to share an apartment with a roommate, how could he go about finding someone?

When buying a condominium or a cooperative, it is important to do some thorough homework. The soundness of this type of investment depends greatly on the management, restrictions, operating policies, and types of people involved in both ownership and management. Here are a few questions to answer before buying.

- ❑ How is the property managed, and by whom? What voice do owners have in management decisions?
- ❑ Are current residents generally satisfied with the management and the building?
- ❑ What is the financial status of the building? Is there a mortgage on the property? Are any major repairs or renovations anticipated? Does the appraised value compare favorably with the selling price?
- ❑ How much is the monthly maintenance fee or assessment? What does it cover? When and how can it be increased?
- ❑ What control do occupants have over their units? Are there restrictions on selling, remodeling, renting, or refinancing? Are pets permitted?
- ❑ How does the condominium or cooperative unit compare with similar units in other buildings and with other forms of available housing in the area?

Single-Family Houses

The single-family house is still the most popular type of housing, 11-5. If you decide to live in a house, you will face many decisions. A few people choose to build a house of their own. The majority rent or buy a house that is already built.

If you are planning to move into a single-family house, there are a number of factors to consider, 11-6. If you are buying, solid construction is of great importance. Be sure to check both outside and inside construction features. It pays to carefully evaluate the outside of the house, the yard, and the neighborhood as well as the inside living space. Choose a house that is conveniently designed for your lifestyle and housing needs. Looking at different types of houses can help you decide what you like best. If you are buying, it generally pays to hire an independent contractor to inspect the house and evaluate construction details you cannot judge.

If you decide to build or buy a home, there are many professionals who can help, 11-7. Become familiar with the various experts, what they do, and how they can help you make housing decisions. Single-family houses are built in a variety of ways.

Custom-Built Houses

Custom-built houses are usually designed by an architect to meet the specific needs and wishes of the person or family wanting to build. A contractor is hired to build the house according to the architect's plan. This can be a costly and lengthy project.

Tract Houses

Tract houses are built by a developer who, in a sense, creates a neighborhood by building many houses at once within a given area. These houses are built from similar plans in order to keep costs down. Most tract houses look alike and lack the individuality of custom-built houses. They are less expensive, however, and builders often will make minor alterations to meet individual buyers' needs.

Modular and Kit Houses

These houses are partially built in factories. They are then moved in sections to the home site for completion. These houses are relatively inexpensive. Quality depends on the manufacturer as well as the builder who puts the house together.

Town Houses

Town houses are single-family units that share one or both sidewalls with other town houses. The units are usually built at the same time from similar blueprints.

11-5
Both existing and new, single-family homes are available in a wide variety of sizes and styles. They are located in urban, suburban, and rural areas.

Checklist for Single-Family Houses

Outside House and Yard

- ☐ Attractive, well-designed house.
- ☐ Suited to natural surroundings.
- ☐ Lot of the right size and shape for house and garage.
- ☐ Suitable use of building materials.
- ☐ Compatible with houses in the area.
- ☐ Attractive landscaping.
- ☐ Good drainage of rain and moisture.
- ☐ Dry, firm soil around the house.
- ☐ Mature, healthy trees—placed to give shade in summer.
- ☐ Convenient, well-kept driveway, walks, patio, porch.
- ☐ Parking convenience—garage, carport, or street.
- ☐ Distance between houses for privacy.
- ☐ Sheltered entry—well-lighted and large enough for several to enter the house together.
- ☐ Convenient service entrance.

Outside Construction

- ☐ Durable siding materials—in good condition.
- ☐ Solid brick and masonry—free of cracks.
- ☐ Solid foundation walls.
- ☐ Weather-stripped windows and doors.
- ☐ Noncorrosive gutters and downspouts, connected to storm sewer or splash block to carry water away from house.
- ☐ Copper or aluminum flashing used over doors, windows, and joints on the roof.
- ☐ Screens and storm windows.

Inside Construction

- ☐ Sound, smooth walls with invisible nails and taping on dry wall surfaces.
- ☐ Well-done carpentry work with properly-fitted joints and moldings.
- ☐ Properly fitted, easy-to-operate windows.
- ☐ Level wood floors with smooth finish and no high edges, wide gaps, or squeaks.
- ☐ Well-fitted tile floors—no cracked or damaged tiles—no visible adhesive.
- ☐ Good possibilities for improvements, remodeling, expanding.
- ☐ Properly-fitted and easy-to-work doors and drawers in built-in cabinets.
- ☐ Dry basement floor with hard, smooth surface.
- ☐ Adequate basement drain.
- ☐ Sturdy stairways with railings, adequate head room—not too steep.
- ☐ Leakproof roof—in good condition.
- ☐ Adequate insulation for warmth and soundproofing.

Living Space

- ☐ Convenient floor plan and traffic patterns.
- ☐ Convenient entry with foyer and closet.
- ☐ Convenient work areas (kitchen, laundry, workshop) with adequate drawers, cabinets, lighting, workspace, electric power.
- ☐ Bedrooms located far enough from other parts of the house for privacy and quiet.
- ☐ Social areas (living and dining room, play space, yard, porch, or patio) convenient, comfortable, large enough for family and guests.
- ☐ Adequate storage—closets, cabinets, shelves, attic, basement, garage.
- ☐ Suitable wall space and room size for your furnishings.
- ☐ Outdoor space convenient to indoor space.
- ☐ Windows located to provide enough air, light, and ventilation.
- ☐ Agreeable type, size, and placement of windows.
- ☐ Usable attic and/or basement space.
- ☐ Attractive decorative features and fixtures.
- ☐ Extras—fireplace, air conditioning, porches, new kitchen and baths, built-in equipment.

Household International

11-6
This checklist can help you evaluate the appearance, construction, and living space of single-family homes.

The Experts

Who Are They?	What Do They Do?	When Do You Need One?
Real Estate Agents	Bring buyer/tenant and seller/landlord together and negotiate a deal acceptable to both. Provide helpful information on community tax rates, schools, services, shopping, property values, etc. Recommend lenders and help arrange financing for home purchase. Represent the seller in a sale and receive a commission for services—usually a percentage of the price.	When you need help finding the housing you want in an area you like at a price you can pay. When you are unfamiliar with an area and need facts to decide exactly where and what to buy or rent. When you need help finding professional services and home financing. When you want to sell a home at a fair price in a reasonable length of time.
Lawyers	Represent either buyer or seller in transferring real estate. Protect client's interests when selling, buying, building, or leasing a home. Draw up agreements for client and check agreements drawn by others before the client signs. Represent client at the closing of a real estate transaction.	When you buy or sell a home. When you have questions about a housing contract or lease. When you become involved in a dispute with a landlord, seller, builder, or buyer in a real estate transaction. Before you sign any contract or agreement involving more money or time than you can afford to sacrifice.
Architects	Draw up plans for building or remodeling. Choose suitable building materials. Help find a lot suited to the house design, or design a house suited to the lot. Hire and work with the contractor and supervise building.	When you want to build a house or do extensive remodeling. When you want a custom-designed home.
Contractors	Accept responsibility for building or remodeling a home. Order building materials. Hire and supervise workers. See that work is done according to specifications and terms in the contract.	When you want to build a home or make home improvements.

11-7
These experts can help you buy, sell, lease, build, or remodel a home.

Manufactured Homes

Manufactured homes (mobile homes) are another housing alternative. They generally cost considerably less than other types of housing with comparable living space and facilities. Maintenance costs are usually low, too. The fact that they can be moved with relative ease is an advantage for people who change locations frequently. Manufactured homes are located in manufactured home communities or on private lots.

Choose a manufactured home land-lease community or development carefully, too. See 11-8. As you shop for a lot, compare the costs involved in renting and buying. Look closely at the design and management of different communities. Find out what services

Manufactured Housing Institute

11-8
Today many manufactured homes have a permanent, high-quality appearance. Communities for manufactured homes should be well managed and well maintained with attractive landscaping and important services.

Hunting for Housing

Joining Forces

John and Susan met six months ago in the laundry room of their apartment building. Since that first meeting, neither of them has had much time for anything or anyone but each other. They plan to marry in two months and are looking for a new home. Both are tired of living in an apartment building, but they have different ideas about an ideal home.

John wants to live in the suburbs where there is more open space. He wants a two-story house with a basement and an attic. He wants space for a darkroom and his photography equipment. John also wants to move into an older house so he and Susan can have the challenge of fixing it up. Plus, he wants to make as large a down payment as they possibly can so they will pay less interest on the home loan.

Susan wants to be located in the heart of the city close to the theaters, the museums, and her work. She wants to live in a newly constructed condominium with modern appliances. She wants to make a small down payment on a condominium so they will have more cash for decorating, furnishings, and other needs.

John and Susan do agree on some points. Both want to buy rather than rent. They both want at least two bedrooms, some kind of outdoor space, and a garage. They also want plenty of storage space, space for entertaining, and a fireplace. They both want an easy commute to work.

Case Review

1. How might John and Susan resolve their differences concerning their first home?
2. What would be most important to you in a first home?

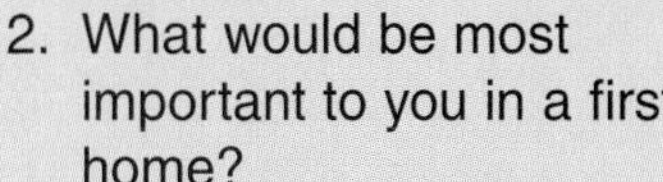

3. What pros and cons do you see in:
   A. City vs. suburban living?
   B. New vs. old construction?
   C. Apartment vs. house?
   D. Owning vs. renting?
4. How might a young couple's list of housing goals and needs change with:
   A. Infants and preschool children?
   B. School-age children?
   C. Teenagers?
   D. A live-in parent?
   E. Old age?

and facilities are available free or for a fee. Ask about the rules and regulations.

In 1976, the U.S. Department of Housing and Urban Development began enforcing the Manufactured Housing Construction and Safety Standards Code, called the HUD Code. As a result, these homes meet high quality and safety standards that make them a more attractive choice and easier to finance than in the past. Today, 18 million Americans live in some form of manufactured housing.

However, this type of housing still presents some disadvantages. Many municipalities restrict the location of manufactured home communities. This means that they often are not situated in the most desirable areas. However, it may be possible to erect a manufactured home on your own lot. Living and storage space can be limited in these homes. Frequent storm damage was a negative factor in the past. However, today's manufactured homes are safer than those of the past due to the federal safety standards. These standards regulate body and frame construction and plumbing, heating, and electrical systems. Before buying a manufactured home, consider the following guidelines.

Choose a Dealer Carefully

Check dealer reputation with local banks, businesses, the Better Business Bureau, chamber of commerce, and previous customers. Also find out if the dealer is a member of the state manufactured housing association.

Figure and Compare Total Costs

Find out what the purchase price does and does not include. Compare the costs of finance charges and insurance. Check the prices of a home lot, delivery to the lot, and installation.

Check Warranty Terms

Be sure to read the warranties on the manufactured home and on the appliances and equipment that come with it. Find out what is warranted, for how long, and what the owner must do to receive warranty benefits.

Check Features and Extras

Find out how the home is heated, cooled, insulated, and furnished. Also check the capacity of the hot water heater. Make sure the model you choose will provide basic comfort, convenience, and safety. Ask about available extras, too. You can choose anything from a wood-burning fireplace to a whirlpool to central air conditioning in manufactured homes today.

Budgeting for Housing

Before choosing a place to live, you will need to determine how much money you can spend on housing. The amount you can afford will depend on several factors. These include your income, other expenses and obligations, housing needs, and your expected future income. Since housing is generally a monthly expenditure, you may want to begin by figuring a reasonable monthly housing allowance. If you plan to buy a home, it also will be necessary to arrive at a purchase price and mortgage obligation you can handle over a long period of time.

Monthly Housing Costs

Most financial advisers suggest that total monthly housing costs come to no more than one-third of monthly take-home pay. Take-home pay is the amount of money you receive after taxes and other deductions are subtracted from your paycheck. Housing costs include not only rent or mortgage payments, but also utility costs, property taxes, and homeowner's or renter's insurance. The following steps can help you determine a monthly housing allowance.

1. Total the amount you have to spend each month. Include all income and earnings.

2. Total monthly nonhousing expenses. Include food, clothing, transportation, recreation, loans, insurance, and taxes.
3. Subtract total monthly nonhousing expenses from total monthly income. This is the amount you can spend for housing each month.
4. Adjust earnings, spending, and housing costs if necessary. If you don't have enough money for the home you want, you have three choices. You can try to increase your income, spend less on non-housing expenses, or choose a less expensive home.

Determining a Home Purchase Price

Most people can afford to spend approximately 2 ½ times their gross annual income for the purchase price of a home. Gross income is the amount of money you earn before taxes and other expenses are deducted. If your gross annual income is $20,000, you should be able to afford a $50,000 home.

This is a very general guideline. Mortgage lenders are more specific. You normally can qualify for a home mortgage that requires monthly payments of no more than 28 percent of your gross monthly income. This means the amount you can spend on a home will depend on the purchase price, the amount you can pay for a down payment, and current interest rates. For example, monthly payments on a $50,000, 30-year mortgage would be

- ❑ $367 at 8 percent.
- ❑ $439 at 10 percent.
- ❑ $514 at 12 percent.

Interest rates can vary greatly from year to year. If you buy when interest rates are high, you may have to look at lower priced homes. If you buy when interest rates are low, you may be able to afford a more expensive home.

The amount you can afford will also depend on other factors. You can probably spend more than the experts recommend on housing if most of the following statements apply to you: Your family is small. Living costs in the area are low. You expect income increases regularly for a number of years. Major increases in nonhousing expenses are not likely. You are willing to spend less on other goods and services to have the home you want. You have enough savings and insurance to cover emergencies and unexpected cash needs.

If you are buying a house, you may be able to spend the maximum that mortgage arrangements allow if the following statements apply to your situation: The house is in good condition and equipped with necessary appliances and equipment you need. You can take care of necessary maintenance, repair, and decorating jobs yourself. Property taxes are low and not expected to increase greatly. Interest rates are low. You can make a large down payment. You can arrange reasonable long-term financing.

You should probably spend less on housing in general under the following circumstances: Your income is irregular and not expected to increase. Your family is large. You have large nonhousing expenses or debts. Living costs in the area are high. You have no cash reserves or emergency funds. Interest rates are high. Housing is less important to you than other wants and needs.

If you are buying a house, you should probably look for a relatively low-priced home if the following statements apply to you: You buy an older house that needs many repairs. The house is poorly equipped or without the appliances. Property taxes are high and expected to increase. Home mortgage rates are high and terms are unfavorable. You can make only a small down payment. You have other long-term obligations.

Renting a Home

The primary financial responsibility of renting a place to live is to pay the stated rent each month. Normally, renters must also pay a security deposit and certain utility costs. A ***security deposit*** protects the landlord against financial losses in case the renter damages the dwelling or fails to pay rent. It usually must be paid to the landlord before moving into a rental unit. The amount of the security deposit generally comes to one month's rent. This will be returned when the lease expires, provided there is no damage to the property. The renter is also responsible for taking reasonable care of the rental unit and paying any utility bills that are not included in the rent.

Renting a home offers certain advantages over ownership. Renters are not responsible for major home repairs, improvements, or property taxes. They do not need to worry about property values. They do not need a large sum of money to make a down payment nor must they assume the burden of a home mortgage.

Another advantage of renting is the freedom to move easily. Renters usually commit by signing a lease for one year. After one year, they can move or continue to rent the same unit. Buyers make a long-term housing commitment. Selling a house is much more involved than ending a rental agreement.

Any type of housing can be rented, but apartments are the most common rental units. Rentals usually are leased for a set period of time, such as one year. Some may be available on a month-by-month basis.

Lease Terms

Most renters are asked to sign a lease when they begin renting. A written ***lease*** is a legal rental agreement between the tenant (lessee) and the landlord (lessor), 11-9. It outlines the terms and conditions under which the tenant occupies the property. The lease explains the rights and responsibilities of both the tenant and the landlord. Before signing a lease, read it carefully and know the answers to the following questions.

How much is the rent and when must it be paid? What are the penalties for late payment? Is a security deposit required? If so, how much is it? Will it draw interest? How do you get the deposit back? Under what circumstances may the landlord keep part or all of it?

What utilities are included in the rent? How much do the utilities generally run that are not included? Ask to see a record of previous billings. This will give you some idea of the amount you will pay for gas, electricity, phone service, etc. What furnishings and appliances are included? What building services and facilities are available? What is included in the rent and what costs extra?

What term or period of time does the lease cover? What are the beginning and ending dates of the lease? When do payments begin? When can you begin renting? When must you renew the lease or give notice that you will not renew?

What happens if you leave before the lease expires? Can you sublet or assign the lease to someone else? What are the conditions for doing so? What will be your responsibilities if the person taking over does not pay the rent?

What conditions rule your use of the space? Can you paint, wallpaper, and decorate? If you install shelving, carpet, or equipment, can you remove it later? Can you keep pets? Can you have a roommate?

Who is responsible for upkeep, maintenance, and repairs? What does the landlord maintain, and what must you maintain? What can either of you do if the other fails to carry out upkeep and maintenance responsibilities?

NO. L-17
JUNE 2000

CAUTION: Consult a lawyer before using or acting under this form. Neither the publisher nor the seller of this form makes any warranty with respect thereto, including any warranty of merchantability or fitness for a particular purpose.

IF UNHEATED, CHECK HERE: ______
(SEE PARAGRAPH 11)

APARTMENT LEASE

UNFURNISHED

DATE OF LEASE	TERM OF LEASE		MONTHLY RENT	SECURITY DEPOSIT*
	BEGINNING	ENDING		

* *IF NONE, WRITE "NONE". Paragraph 2 of this Lease then INAPPLICABLE.*

LESSEE

NAME •

APT. NO. •

ADDRESS OF PREMISES •

LESSOR

NAME •

BUSINESS ADDRESS •

In consideration of the mutual covenants and agreements herein stated, Lessor hereby leases to Lessee and Lessee hereby leases from Lessor for a private dwelling the apartment designated above (the "Premises"), together with the appurtenances thereto, for the above Term.

ADDITIONAL COVENANTS AND AGREEMENTS *(if any)*

LEASE COVENANTS AND AGREEMENTS

RENT

1. Lessee shall pay Lessor or Lessor's agent as rent for the Premises the sum stated above, monthly in advance, until termination of this lease, at Lessor's address stated above or such other address as Lessor may designate in writing.

SECURITY DEPOSIT

2. Lessee has deposited with Lessor the Security Deposit stated above for the performance of all covenants and agreements of Lessee hereunder. Lessor may apply all or any portion thereof in payment of any amounts due Lessor from Lessee, and upon Lessor's demand Lessee shall in such case during the term of the lease promptly deposit with Lessor such additional amounts as may then be required to bring the Security Deposit up to the full amount stated above. Upon termination of the lease and full performance of all matters and payment of all amounts due by Lessee, so much of the Security Deposit as remains unapplied shall be returned to Lessee. This deposit does not bear interest unless and except as required by law. Where all or a portion of the Security Deposit is applied by Lessor as compensation for property damage, Lessor when and as required by law shall provide to Lessee an itemized statement of such damage and of the estimated or actual cost of repairing same. If the building in which Premises are located (the "Building") is sold or otherwise transferred, Lessor may transfer or assign the Security Deposit to the purchaser or transferee of the Building, who shall thereupon be liable to Lessee for all of Lessor's obligations hereunder, and Lessee shall look thereafter solely to such purchaser or transferee for return of the Security Deposit and for other matters (including any interest or accounting) relating thereto.

CONDITION OF PREMISES; REDELIVERY TO LESSOR

3. Lessee has examined and knows the condition of Premises and has received the same in good order and repair except as herein otherwise specified, and no representations as to the condition or repair thereof have been made by Lessor or his agent prior to, or at the execution of this lease, that are not herein expressed or endorsed hereon; and upon the termination of this lease in any way, Lessee will immediately yield up Premises to Lessor in as good condition as when the same were entered upon by Lessee, ordinary wear and tear only excepted, and shall then return all keys to Lessor.

LIMITATION OF LIABILITY

4. Except as provided by state statute, Lessor shall not be liable for any damage occasioned by failure to keep Premises in repair, and shall not be liable for any damage done or occasioned by or from plumbing, gas, water, steam or other pipes, or sewerage, or the bursting, leaking or running of any cistern, tank, wash-stand, water-closet, or waste-pipe, in, above, upon or about the Building or Premises, nor for damage occasioned by water, snow or ice being upon or coming through the roof, skylight, trap-door or otherwise, nor for damages to Lessee or others claiming through Lessee for any loss or damage of or to property wherever located in or about the Building or Premises, nor for any damage arising from acts or neglect of co-tenants or other occupants of the Building, or of any owners or occupants of adjacent or contiguous property.

(Continued)

11-9
The lease clearly states the rights and responsibilities of both landlord (lessor) and tenant (lessee).

11-9 *(Continued)*

USE; SUBLET; ASSIGNMENT

5. Lessee will not allow Premises to be used for any purpose that will increase the rate of insurance thereon, nor for any purpose other than that hereinbefore specified, nor to be occupied in whole or in part by any other persons, and will not sublet the same, nor any part thereof, nor assign this lease, without in each case the written consent of the Lessor first had, and will not permit any transfer, by operation of law, of the interest in Premises acquired through this lease, and will not permit Premises to be used for any unlawful purpose or purpose that will injure the reputation of the same or of the Building or disturb the tenants of the Building or the neighborhood.

USE AND REPAIR

6. Lessee will take good care of the apartment demised and the fixtures therein, and will commit and suffer no waste therein; no changes or alterations of the Premises shall be made, nor partitions erected, nor walls papered, nor locks on doors installed or changed, without the consent in writing of Lessor; Lessee will make all repairs required to the walls, ceilings, paint, plastering, plumbing work, pipes and fixtures belonging to Premises, whenever damage or injury to the same shall have resulted from misuse or neglect; no furniture filled or to be filled wholly or partially with liquids shall be placed in the Premises without the consent in writing of Lessor; the Premises shall not be used as a "boarding" or "lodging" house, nor for a school, nor to give instructions in music, dancing or singing, and none of the rooms shall be offered for lease by placing notices on any door, window or wall of the Building, nor by advertising the same directly or indirectly, in any newspaper or otherwise, nor shall any signs be exhibited on or at any windows or exterior portions of the Premises or of the Building without the consent in writing of Lessor; there shall be no lounging, sitting upon, or unnecessary tarrying in or upon the front steps, the sidewalk, railing, stairways, halls, landing or other public places of the Building by Lessee, members of the family or others persons connected with the occupancy of Premises; no provisions, milk, ice, marketing, groceries, furniture, packages or merchandise shall be taken into the Premises through the front door of the Building except where there is no rear or service entrance; cooking shall be done only in the kitchen and in no event on porches or other exterior appurtenances; Lessee, and those occupying under Lessee, shall not interfere with the heating apparatus, or with the lights, electricity, gas, water or other utilities of the Building which are not within the apartment hereby demised, nor with the control of any of the public portions of the Building; use of any master television antenna hookup shall be strictly in accordance with regulations of Lessor or Lessor's agent; Lessee and those occupying under Lessee shall comply with and conform to all reasonable rules and regulations that Lessor or Lessor's agent may make for the protection of the Building or the general welfare and the comfort of the occupants thereof, and shall also comply with and conform to all applicable laws and governmental rules and regulations affecting the Premises and the use and occupancy thereof.

ACCESS

7. Lessee will allow Lessor free access to the Premises at all reasonable hours for the purpose of examining or exhibiting the same or to make any needful repairs which Lessor may deem fit to make for the benefit of or related to any part of the Building; also Lessee will allow Lessor to have placed upon the Premises, at all times, notice of "For Sale" and "To Rent," and will not interfere with the same.

RIGHT TO RELET

8. If Lessee shall abandon or vacate the Premises, the same may be re-let by Lessor for such rent and upon such terms as Lessor may see fit, subject to Illinois statute, and if a sufficient sum shall not thus be realized, after paying the expenses of such reletting and collecting, to satisfy the rent hereby reserved, Lessee agrees to satisfy and pay all deficiency.

HOLDING OVER

9. If the Lessee retains possession of the Premises or any part thereof after the termination of the term by lapse of time or otherwise, then the Lessor may at Lessor's option within thirty days after the termination of the term serve written notice upon Lessee that such holding over constitutes either (a) renewal of this lease for one year, and from year to year thereafter, at double the rental specified under Section1 for such period, or (b) creation of a month to month tenancy, upon the terms of this lease except at double the monthly rental specified under Section 1, or (c) creation of a tenancy at sufferance, at a rental of________________dollars per day for the time Lessee remains in possession. If no such written notice is served then a tenancy at sufferance with rental as stated at (c) shall have been created, and in such case if specific per diem rental shall not have been inserted herein at (c), such per diem rental shall be one-fifteenth of the monthly rental specified under Section 1 of this lease. Lessee shall also pay to Lessor all damages sustained by Lessor resulting from retention of possession by Lessee.

RESTRICTIONS ON USE

10. Lessee will not permit anything to be thrown out of the windows, or down the courts or light shafts in the Building; nothing shall be hung from the outside of the windows or placed on the outside window sills of any window in the Building; no parrot, dog or other animal shall be kept within or about the Premises; the front halls and stairways and the back porches shall not be used for the storage of carriages, furniture or other articles.

WATER AND HEAT

11. The provisions of subsection (a) only hereof shall be applicable and shall form a part of this lease unless this lease is made on an unheated basis and that fact is so indicated on the first page of this lease, in which case the provisions of subsection (b) only hereof shall be applicable and form a part of this lease.

(a) Lessor will supply hot and cold water to the Premises for the use of Lessee at all faucets and fixtures provided by Lessor therefor. Lessor will also supply heat, by means of the heating system and fixtures provided by Lessor, in reasonable amounts and at reasonable hours, when necessary, from October 1 to April 30, or otherwise as required by applicable municipal ordinance. Lessor shall not be liable or responsible to Lessee for failure to furnish water or heat when such failure shall result from causes beyond Lessor's control, nor during periods when the water and heating systems in the Building or any portion thereof are under repair.

(b) Lessor will supply cold water to the Premises for the use of Lessee at all faucets and fixtures provided by Lessor therefor. Lessor shall not be liable or responsible to Lessee for failure to furnish water when such failure shall result from causes beyond Lessor's control, nor during periods when the water system in the Building or any portion thereof is under repair. All water heating and all heating of the Premises shall be at the sole expense of Lessee. Any equipment provided by Lessee therefor shall comply with applicable municipal ordinances.

STORE ROOM

12. Lessor shall not be liable for any loss or damage of or to any property placed in any store room or any storage place in the Building, such store room or storage place being furnished gratuitously and not as part of the obligations of this lease.

DEFAULT BY LESSEE

13. If default be made in the payment of the above rent, or any part thereof, or in any of the covenants herein contained to be kept by the Lessee, Lessor may at any time thereafter at his election declare said term ended and reenter the Premises or any part thereof, with or (to the extent permitted by law) without notice or process of law, and remove Lessee or any persons occupying the same, without prejudice to any remedies which might otherwise be used for arrears of rent, and Lessor shall have at all times the right to distrain for rent due, and shall have a valid and first lien upon all personal property which Lessee now owns, or may hereafter acquire or have an interest in, which is by law subject to such distraint, as security for payment of the rent herein reserved.

NO RENT DEDUCTION OR SET OFF

14. Lessee's covenant to pay rent is and shall be independent of each and every other covenant of this lease. Lessee agrees that any claim by Lessee against Lessor shall not be deducted from rent nor set off against any claim for rent in any action.

RENT AFTER NOTICE OR SUIT

15. It is further agreed, by the parties hereto, that after the service of notice or the commencement of a suit or after final judgment for possession of the Premises, Lessor may receive and collect any rent due, and the payment of said rent shall not waive or affect said notice, said suit, or said judgment.

PAYMENT OF COSTS

16. Lessee will pay and discharge all reasonable costs, attorney's fees and expenses that shall be made and incurred by Lessor in enforcing the covenants and agreements of this lease.

RIGHTS CUMULATIVE

17. The rights and remedies of Lessor under this lease are cumulative. The exercise or use of any one or more thereof shall not bar Lessor from exercise or use of any other right or remedy provided herein or otherwise provided by law, nor shall exercise nor use of any right or remedy by Lessor waive any other right or remedy.

FIRE AND CASUALTY

18. In case the Premises shall be rendered untenantable during the term of this lease by fire or other casualty, Lessor at his option may terminate the lease or repair the Premises within 60 days thereafter. If Lessor elects to repair, this lease shall remain in effect provided such repairs are completed within said time. If Lessor shall not have repaired the Premises within said time, then at the end of such time the term hereby created shall terminate. If this lease is terminated by reason of fire or casualty as herein specified, rent shall be apportioned and paid to the day of such fire or other casualty.

(Continued)

11-9 *(Continued)*

SUBORDINATION 19. This lease is subordinate to all mortgages which may now or hereafter affect the real property of which Premises form a part.

PLURALS; SUCCESSORS 20. The words "Lessor" and "Lessee" wherever herein occurring and used shall be construed to mean "Lessors" and "Lessees" in case more than one person constitutes either party to this lease; and all the covenants and agreements herein contained shall be binding upon, and inure to, their respective successors, heirs, executors, administrators and assigns and be exercised by his or their attorney or agent.

SEVERABILITY 21. Wherever possible each provision of this lease shall be interpreted in such manner as to be effective and valid under applicable law, but if any provision of this lease shall be prohibited by or invalid under applicable law, such provision shall be ineffective to the extent of such prohibition or invalidity, without invalidating the remainder of such provision or the remaining provisions of this lease.

COMPLIANCE WITH LAWS, STATUTES AND ORDINANCES 22. The parties to this lease acknowledge that the terms of this lease may be inconsistent with the laws, statutes or ordinances of the jurisdiction in which the Premises are located, and where inconsistent, those terms may be superseded by the provisions of such laws, statutes or ordinances. To the extent the provisions of such laws, statutes or ordinances supersede the terms of this lease, such provisions are hereby incorporated into the terms of this lease by this reference, and the parties to this lease agree to be bound thereby. With respect to Premises located in the City of Chicago, the parties agree to refer to and, to the extent provided above, be bound by the provisions of the City of Chicago Residential Landlord and Tenant Ordinance, Chapter 193.1, Municipal Code of Chicago, as amended from time to time. A summary of such Ordinance is attached to this lease.

WITNESS the hands and seals of the parties hereto, as of the Date of Lease stated above.

LESSEE: LESSOR:

________________(seal) ________________(seal)

________________(seal) ________________(seal)

ASSIGNMENT BY LESSOR

On this ____________, 20____, for value received, Lessor hereby transfers, assigns and sets over to ________________, all right, title and interest in and to the above lease and the rent thereby reserved, except rent due and payable prior to ____________, 20____.

________________(seal)

________________(seal)

GUARANTEE

On this ____________, 20____, in consideration of Ten Dollars ($10.00) and other goods and valuable consideration, the receipt and sufficiency of which is hereby acknowledged, the undersigned Guarantor hereby guarantees the payment of rent and performance by Lessee, Lessee's heirs, executors, administrators, successors or assigns of all covenants and agreements of the above lease.

________________(seal)

________________(seal)

Associated Stationers

What legal remedies are available? What can you do if the landlord breaks the lease in some way, such as failing to make necessary repairs or to provide adequate heat? What can the landlord do if you break the lease by not paying the rent or failing to obey building rules? Does the lease outline ways, such as arbitration or legal action, to handle disagreements with the landlord? Who pays the legal costs of settling differences?

What other details are important? Are all spaces in the lease filled in accurately, including dates, dollar amounts, addresses, and names? Are all verbal agreements written into the lease? Where and how do you contact the landlord or rental agent with questions, problems, or complaints? Do you understand all clauses, obligations, and consequences?

If you have serious questions or doubts about signing the lease, you may want to get a lawyer's advice. It is also a good idea to talk with several tenants. There are some questions that only those who live in a building can answer accurately. For example, are apartments warm enough in winter and cool enough in summer? Are other tenants agreeable? Is the noise level acceptable and is privacy adequate? Find out if current tenants are satisfied with maintenance and repairs, building services and security, and the overall atmosphere.

> *"The fellow who owns his own home is always just coming out of the hardware store."*
>
> *Frank McKinney Hubbard*

Buying a Home

Over 58 percent of people in the United States choose to become homeowners at some point in their lives. For many people, owning a home gives a sense of permanence and financial security. It is a source of pride and satisfaction. Homeowners can decorate living space as they like and make any alterations they choose. Each improvement is an investment that promises a return when the home is sold.

Buying a home may be a smart financial move. When you buy real estate, you are making an investment. You are buying something you probably can resell for a profit. In addition, home mortgage interest and property tax on a home can be deducted from federal income tax. Renters do not enjoy these financial advantages.

On the other hand, buying a home involves more financial responsibilities than renting. There are many financial and legal details connected with buying and owning a home. Following are some of the documents associated with the purchase of real estate.

Purchase Agreement

When the buyer agrees to buy and the seller agrees to sell, they both sign a contract called a ***purchase agreement***. Sometimes this contract is called a sales agreement. It should include a description of the real estate, its location, the purchase price, and the possession date. The agreement should state all of the conditions and terms of the sale. For example, if the seller agrees to make any home repairs, these should be stated in the agreement. If the owner promises to leave the draperies, dishwasher, range, and refrigerator, these should also be listed and described.

When you sign a purchase agreement, you must deposit *earnest money* to show that your purchase offer is serious. This is usually a percentage of the home price. It will be applied toward the down payment at the closing of the sale. Buyers can lose the earnest money if they fail to go through with the agreement.

A home purchase agreement may contain a *contingency clause* that calls for certain requirements to be met before the contract is binding. For example, the validity of the agreement may depend upon obtaining a mortgage within a certain period of time or at a certain rate. It may be made contingent upon the sale of the buyer's current home.

Abstract of Title

A ***title*** is the right of ownership of a particular piece of property. An ***abstract of title*** is a summary of the public records or history of the ownership of a particular piece of property. Before buying a home, the buyer needs to make sure the seller is the legal owner of the property. The buyer should have an attorney or title insurance company review the abstract of title. This is necessary to be sure the property comes to the buyer free of debts or problems.

Survey

A property ***survey*** is a map of the property drawn by a surveyor to show measurements, boundaries, and characteristics of the property. A survey is often required by lenders to make sure the building is actually on the land according to its legal description. This is normally the seller's responsibility.

Appraisal

Before approving a mortgage loan, the lender will usually require the property be appraised. An ***appraisal*** is a written estimate of the value of the real estate. It helps the lender decide if the home is worth what the buyer is paying for it and if the mortgage is a good investment.

Home Mortgages

Since a home is such a large expense, most home buyers borrow to finance the purchase, 11-10. A home loan, called a ***mortgage,*** is a contract between a borrower and a lender. The lender is usually a bank, a savings and loan association, or a mortgage company. The borrower promises to repay the lender the loan amount plus interest. The mortgage is paid in monthly installments over a set number of years. If the borrower fails to pay according to the terms of the mortgage contract, the lender can repossess the home.

Amortization is the process by which loan payments are applied to the principle, or amount borrowed, as well as to the interest on the loan according to a set schedule. Most home mortgages are amortized. In the beginning, payments are applied largely to interest. As the loan is repaid, an increasing amount of each payment is applied to the principle. This means the borrower builds up equity, or ownership, in the property as the loan is repaid.

Types of Mortgages

For years, the long-term, ***fixed-rate mortgage*** was the most common way to finance a home purchase. It calls for a down payment and fixed monthly payments. The monthly payments include interest figured at a set rate throughout the life of the loan. These loans are normally written with 20-, 25-, or 30-year repayment periods.

Long-term, fixed-rate mortgages still account for the majority of home loans. However, in the late 1970s, climbing interest rates led to new ways of financing real estate purchases. Shorter term, fixed-rate loans were one alternative. Fifteen-year mortgages dramatically increased monthly payments, but brought an equally dramatic reduction in overall interest charges.

Home financing alternatives vary from state to state and lender to lender. Research all the options to find the method of financing that is best for you. Consult a lawyer before signing any home financing agreement. Small mistakes can have big consequences.

Several other forms of mortgage lending were developed in the early 1980s to meet the needs of both lenders and borrowers. These new developments included the adjustable rate

11-10
Most home buyers must secure a mortgage to finance their purchase.

mortgage (ARM) and the graduated payment mortgage. When shopping for home financing, you should be familiar with these mortgages.

The ***adjustable rate mortgage*** allows the interest rate to be adjusted up or down periodically. The adjustments are made according to a national rate index and other predetermined factors. This, in turn, causes monthly payments to increase or decrease.

The ***graduated payment mortgage*** allows the buyer to pay low monthly payments at first and higher payments in the future. The idea behind this type of mortgage is that the buyer's income will increase as the monthly payments increase. This type of repayment makes it possible for more young people to afford home mortgages. It has the advantage of low monthly payments in the early years of the loan. The main disadvantage is the slower build up of equity in the property and higher payments as time passes.

Conventional home mortgages are made by most lending institutions. The lender decides the maximum amount of the loan, the amount of the down payment, the interest rate, and other terms of the agreement. Most conventional loans call for a 10 percent down payment. Under certain circumstances, it may be as low as 5 percent if there is private mortgage insurance.

An ***FHA-insured loan*** is guaranteed by the Federal Housing Administration. This is a part of the U.S. Department of Housing and Urban Development (HUD). The FHA makes no loans, but it insures lenders against borrowers' possible default or failure to pay. The maximum loan amounts are determined by a formula based on average cost of homes in the area. Down payment requirements for FHA-insured loans can be as low as 3 percent. Borrowers can take up to 30 years to repay the loan. Interest rates may be lower than for conventional loans because the government insures the lender. Anyone can apply for an FHA loan through an approved lender institution. However, there is sometimes a long waiting period for processing an FHA loan. The home being bought and certain loan terms must meet FHA requirements and standards.

The ***VA-guaranteed loan*** is insured by the Veterans Administration, 11-11. Only veterans of the U.S. Armed Forces are eligible for these loans. They are long-term, fixed-rate mortgages. Rates are set by the Veterans Administration. There are no down payment requirements. Interest rates usually are lower than the current market rate. Borrowers can take up to 30 years to repay. The only disadvantage of a VA loan is the red tape involved. It can take a long time for the loan to be approved.

In deciding among different types of mortgages, it is important to consider how long you expect to live in the home. If you expect to move within a few years, it may be wise to look to the adjustable rate mortgage, which usually is available at lower rates than long-term, fixed-rate mortgages. For buyers who expect to live in a home for many years, the long-term, fixed-rate mortgage may be a good choice if rates are relatively low at the time of

Jack Klasey

11-11
Veterans of the U.S. Armed Forces are eligible for special VA-guaranteed loans.

purchase. A graduated payment mortgage can be a disadvantage for short-term ownership. Equity does not build up fast enough to help with the purchase of another home.

There are other ways to finance a home purchase besides a mortgage. Following are two common methods.

Entering a Contract Sale

This is a loan by the seller to the buyer for the purchase of the seller's property. This form of financing is used primarily when a buyer has trouble getting affordable financing. The seller agrees to make the loan in order to sell the home. During the period of the contract, the buyer makes payments to the seller. When the contract expires, the buyer secures other financing and pays the seller in full. Contract sales are not regulated by law. Therefore, these sales call for caution on the part of both buyer and seller.

Assuming an Existing Mortgage

This involves the transfer of the seller's mortgage to the buyer. The lender must approve the new buyer. Depending on the lender and circumstances, the buyer may be able to take over the mortgage at the same rate or an adjusted rate may be required. If the rate is adjusted, it usually will be higher than the original rate but lower than current rates. With this form of financing, the buyer usually has to make a large down payment to cover the difference between the remaining mortgage balance and the purchase price.

Shopping for a Mortgage

The only way to find the most favorable financing terms is to shop carefully and ask the right questions. Sources of home loans include commercial banks, savings and loan associations, savings banks, mortgage companies, and credit unions. It pays to be thorough. Shop at least three sources to compare rates and terms. It is a good idea to start with the financial institution where you save, borrow, and keep checking and saving accounts. You are likely to get prompt, serious attention where you are known.

Nationwide mortgage search services report on mortgage terms and availability in different localities. Quotes are also available online. These services or a licensed mortgage broker might help you. Using a computerized program, they can help find the best mortgage package for your situation.

When you apply for a mortgage, the lender will ask detailed questions related to your financial circumstances. You should be prepared with facts and figures, 11-12. Here are some points to consider as you shop for and compare different types of mortgage financing.

Down Payment

How much of your own money can you put down to get a loan? The more you put into the down payment, the less your monthly payments and total interest charges will be.

Size of Mortgage

How much do you need to borrow? What is the maximum size mortgage your income and resources

Items Lenders Require with an Application for a Mortgage Loan

- ❏ Income tax returns.
- ❏ Paycheck stubs.
- ❏ Employment information.
- ❏ Property listing with a legal description.
- ❏ Savings account records.
- ❏ Real estate sales contract.
- ❏ Debt history.
- ❏ Application fee.

11-12
This lists some of the information lenders will require to process a loan application.

will support? Lenders normally limit monthly payment commitments to no more than 28 percent of gross monthly income.

Repayment Period

How long can you take to repay? Are original terms in force for the life of the loan or must you renegotiate periodically?

Interest Rate

What is the annual percentage rate (APR) for the loan? How does it compare with the current market rate? Will it remain fixed, or will it change during the repayment period?

Points

Points are a one-time charge by lenders at closing. Most lenders charge one to four points. A point equals one percent of the mortgage amount. Four points on a $50,000 mortgage comes to $2,000. It maybe possible to negotiate for a lower rate of interest if you are willing to pay more points at the time of purchase. Find out how many points different lenders charge.

Mortgage Lock-Ins

When you shop for home financing, the terms you are quoted often apply only at the time you apply for the mortgage. These terms may change significantly by the time your mortgage is approved and you come to the settlement on the closing date. The ***mortgage lock-in***, sometimes called a rate-lock or rate commitment, is a promise from the lender to honor the quoted rates and terms while your application is being processed. Ask lenders about mortgage lock-ins when you shop for home financing. Examine the terms of the lock-in as well as the terms of the mortgage. Is it in writing? What exactly is guaranteed? How long is the lock-in valid? What options are offered?

Charges and Closing Costs

What do different lenders charge for loan application fees? How much will you pay in settlement charges? Many fees, called ***closing costs*** or settlement charges, must be paid before the sale of a home is final. The Real Estate Settlement Procedures Act requires lenders to provide home buyers with certain information. This includes a Good Faith Estimate of Settlement charges. This estimate will contain some or all of the following:

- ❑ Termite inspection.
- ❑ Loan discount or points.
- ❑ Appraisal fee.
- ❑ Tax stamps.
- ❑ Title examination.
- ❑ Title insurance.
- ❑ Attorney's fees.
- ❑ Recording fees.
- ❑ Credit report.
- ❑ Lender's loan origination fee.
- ❑ Reserves for insurance and property tax.

Monthly Payments

How much will you pay each month to cover mortgage interest and principle? How much will you pay for property insurance and taxes? Normally, all of these items will be included in the monthly payment to the lender. If property taxes or insurance increase, it will cause higher monthly payments. Is the monthly amount likely to change during the life of the loan? Will you have enough left for property maintenance, utilities, and other housing costs?

Special Features and Provisions

What are the provisions and penalties for prepayment if you sell or refinance? Can the mortgage be assumed by a new buyer if you sell? (Having an assumable mortgage may make it easier to sell a home.) What are the policies and penalties for late payments? How much and what type of insurance does the lender require?

Property Tax

Find out the property tax rates in the area and for the home you are buying. When and how can these rates be increased?

Home Insurance

Once you invest in or rent a home of your own, you will want to protect what is yours with homeowner's or renter's insurance. You will need to learn what type and amount of coverage to buy and how to make the most of the protection it provides.

Types of Home Insurance

Homeowner's insurance provides two basic types of coverage: property protection and liability protection, 11-13. *Property coverage* insures you against damage to or loss of dwelling and personal property and possessions, such as clothes and furnishings. It may also pay for additional living expenses if you should need to move out of your home because of damage to the property. The specific losses covered depend on the type of policy you buy.

Liability coverage protects you against financial loss if others are injured on or by your property. This coverage also protects you if you, your family, pets, or property accidentally damage the property of others. It pays for the legal costs of defending you if you are sued because of these injuries or damages. Limits on this coverage generally run around $100,000. You can buy additional coverage either in an umbrella policy or extended liability policy.

Renter's insurance provides similar protection for those who rent housing. However, the property protection for renters only covers damage or loss of personal property and possessions. The landlord will have coverage on the dwelling itself. The liability protection under the renter's policy is similar to the homeowner's policy. Policies are also available for condominium owners, older homes, and other special needs.

College students living in a dorm or renting an apartment may need renter's insurance, a floater, or an endorsement to protect their possessions. A *floater* is a form of insurance that covers specific items wherever you take them. It "floats" with your possessions. An *endorsement* is an attachment to existing insurance coverage to provide additional protection. Check out coverage provided by a family policy and take the necessary steps to protect possessions not covered. This is important for expensive items, such as computers and sound equipment.

11-13
Adequate insurance is the only way most people can recover from major losses, such as this one created by Hurricane Hugo.

Nationwide Insurance

Policy Forms

The various home insurance policies differ primarily in the risks they cover. Chart 11-14 outlines the key policy forms and the perils each covers. Note that homeowner's insurance policies do not cover flood damage. If you live in an area that is likely to be flooded, contact the Federal Insurance Administration to learn about the National Flood Insurance Program.

Amount of Coverage to Buy

It pays to obtain the right amount of home insurance. The first step in buying the right homeowner coverage is to find out how much it would cost to rebuild your home. This may be more or less than the price you paid for the home or the amount it would bring if you sold it today. The cost of rebuilding your home will depend on local building costs and the type of home you own. Your insurance agent may be able to help you calculate building costs, or you may need an appraisal. An *appraisal* is an estimate of the current value of property. An appraisal should be made by a qualified appraiser.

Once you arrive at an appraised value, buy enough insurance protection to cover the cost of replacing your home. Today most insurance companies recommend insuring for 100 percent of the cost of rebuilding. This will allow you to collect the full cost of insured property that is damaged or lost.

To keep insurance coverage up-to-date, inform your insurance agent of any major home improvements you make. You also may want to add an inflation guard clause to your policy. This will automatically adjust policy renewal coverage to reflect current rebuilding costs.

Policy Forms	
Basic Form ❑ Fire or lightning. ❑ Windstorm or hail. ❑ Explosion. ❑ Riot or civil commotion. ❑ Aircraft. ❑ Vehicles. ❑ Smoke. ❑ Vandalism or malicious mischief. ❑ Theft. ❑ Glass breakage. ❑ Volcanic eruption.	**Broad Form** Basic form risks plus: ❑ Falling objects. ❑ Weight of ice, snow, or sleet. ❑ Water or steam discharge. ❑ Tearing apart of air conditioning, heating, or plumbing systems or appliances. ❑ Freezing of above. ❑ Accidental damage from electric current.
Special Form Basic and broad form risks plus all others not specifically excluded. Typical exclusions include: ❑ Flood. ❑ Earthquake. ❑ War. ❑ Nuclear accidents.	**Tenant's Form** Tenant's Form covers personal possessions against risks covered by the basic and broad forms of homeowners' policies.

11-14
This chart explains the perils against which property is covered by different homeowners' policies.

Check out how much protection your policy provides for the contents of your home. Read the policy to learn what coverage is provided for personal possessions. It generally is limited to 50 percent of the amount of coverage on the home, but may be higher. Compare the contents limit with the total value of your possessions. If coverage is not adequate, talk to your insurance agent about increasing protection.

Knowing whether your personal property is insured for replacement cost or actual cash value is also important. ***Cash value*** is the replacement cost minus depreciation. *Depreciation* is a decrease in the value of property as a result of wear and tear or age. For example, a five-year-old TV set, even in good condition, is no longer worth what you paid for it, or what a new similar set would cost. If the set were stolen, cash value recovery would not pay for a new one. If it were insured for replacement value, you could recover the full cost of a new TV set of comparable quality. Obviously, it pays to insure possessions for replacement rather than cash value, though it costs from 10 to 15 percent more.

When insuring home and possessions, make a complete inventory of your belongings. Include the purchase date and price for costly items. It is a good idea to take photos of each room. This will help you remember the contents and establish your claims in case of major losses.

Cost of Home Insurance

The cost of protecting your home and personal possessions depends primarily on four major factors:

- *The type and amount of coverage.* The higher the amount of protection purchased and the more perils covered, the higher the premium will be. Replacement value coverage is more than cash or market value protection.
- *The size of the deductible.* The *deductible* is the amount a policyholder must pay toward loss or damage before insurance begins to pay. The higher the deductible is, the lower the insurance premium will be.
- *The risk factor where you live.* The type of home you own and its location influence premium rates. For example, you will pay more for fire protection on a frame house than on a brick house. You will pay more for protection against theft and vandalism in high crime areas than in low crime areas.
- *The insurance company.* The cost of insurance premiums varies from company to company. Be sure to call or visit with representatives from several companies to comparison shop before you buy insurance. Compare company reputations for honoring and prompt processing of claims as well as cost of premiums.

Check with your insurance agent to see if you qualify for premium reductions for more than one policy with the company such as home and auto coverage, for devices such as a smoke detector or burglar alarm, for nonsmoker policyholders, or for long-term policyholders. These discounts can reduce your home owner premiums considerably.

When you are ready to buy home insurance, take time to study the types and amounts of coverage available. Then find an informed, reputable insurance agent or broker who can advise you on the type and amount of coverage you need. Ask friends and business associates about their experience with insurance agents and companies. A. M. Best & Co. rates insurers for financial stability. The ratings are published in *Best's Insurance Reports: Property-Casualty*. This publication is available in the reference section of most public libraries. Your state insurance department may also help you evaluate a company's service and complaint record. See 11-15. In addition, you can find information on home insurance coverage, companies, and rates online.

Moving Your Possessions

Buying or renting a new or different home involves moving your belongings. Your first move may be easy. As you accumulate furniture and possessions, moving becomes more

Guidelines for Buying Home Insurance

1. Determine the cost of rebuilding or replacing your home based on local construction costs and the type of home you own.
2. Insure your home for 100 percent of the cost of rebuilding it to avoid being underinsured.
3. Consider adding an "inflation guard clause" to your policy to automatically adjust policy limits to reflect current building costs in your area.
4. Make an inventory of personal possessions and include estimated values at current prices.
5. Determine the amount of coverage your homeowner's insurance provides for the contents of your home. Generally it will be 50 percent of the amount of insurance you carry on the home. Compare the limits in coverage to the total value of possessions listed in your inventory. Find out how to increase protection for your possessions if necessary.
6. Consider replacement cost insurance for personal posessions rather than actual cash value coverage. It will pay the dollar cost of replacing a damaged item with one of similar kind and quality without deductions for depreciation.
7. Consider special coverage in the form of a floater or endorsement to protect possessions not fully covered by your homeowner's or renter's policy.
8. Keep your inventory of possessions up-to-date and file it with receipts, photos of rooms and contents, and other records in a safe place.
9. Increase the deductible amount on your coverage to reduce premiums. The higher the deductible, the lower the premium.
10. Shop carefully for a competent insurance agent with a reliable insurance company.

Filing a Home Insurance Claim

Follow these steps to file a claim on your home insurance.

1. Report any burglary or theft to the police immediately.
2. Notify your insurance agent or company promptly by phone with a written follow-up report. Determine exact coverage your policy provides and find out whether the loss exceeds the deductible. Ask about details of filing a claim and about records and estimates you may need to file a claim for repairs or replacements.
3. Make temporary repairs and take necessary steps to prevent further damage. Keep receipts and records of expenses involved for reimbursement.
4. Make a list of lost or damaged articles with estimated replacement costs and confirming records of purchase and replacement prices.
5. Keep records and receipts for living expenses if damage to your property requires you to find a place to live while repairs are being made.
6. Provide your insurance agent or company with the necessary receipts, records, and information required to handle and settle your claim.
7. Check your policy to find out what steps are involved in settling a claim. If you are dissatisfied or have questions concerning the final settlement, discuss matters with your agent or the claims adjuster.
8. If you find a settlement unsatisfactory or have a complaint that has not been handled to your liking by your insurance company, you may want to contact your state insurance department or call the National Insurance Consumer Helpline for assistance.

Insurance Information Institute

11-15
These guidelines can help you choose the home insurance coverage you need and file a claim.

complicated and expensive. The following guidelines can help you move easily and efficiently.

Before the Move

Becoming organized can help a move go more smoothly. Other items to consider before a move include:

Consider Your Options

Can you move yourself or will you need professional movers? Are you moving a short distance that can be handled by local movers? Are you moving to another state that requires a national carrier? Consider all the possibilities before deciding how to move your belongings, 11-16.

Time It Right

If you have a choice, try to move between mid-October and mid-April. During this time, you often get better service and lower rates than you would in the peak moving months of summer. For the same reasons, the middle of a month is better than the first or last of a month.

Get Rid of Excess Baggage

The more items you move, the more you pay. Getting rid of items you don't need or want can save you big money. By selling unwanted items at a garage sale, you can earn money at the same time you reduce moving costs.

Evaluate Different Movers

Recommendations from other people who have recently moved can be very helpful. The Better Business Bureau or a consumer protection agency can tell you if any complaints have been filed against the movers you are considering.

Get Several Estimates

Be sure estimators see and know about everything that is to be moved. Find out what services are included in the estimates and the cost of extra services. Rates for interstate moves are regulated by state and federal laws. Rates are based on the weight of the shipment and the distance moved. Packing and other services you require add to the cost. Movers may also charge travel and loading time.

Collect Information to Help You Move

Most major carriers offer helpful publications for planning a move and settling in a new area. They are required to provide you with a copy of the Interstate Commerce Commission pamphlet, *When You Move: Your Rights and Responsibilities*. Carriers should also provide you with information about filing claims in case of loss or damage to your possessions.

U-Haul

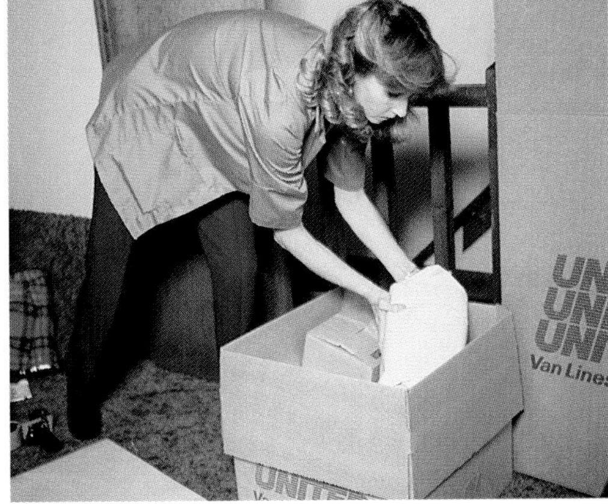

United Van Lines

11-16
Choices for moving your possessions range from do-it-yourself to professional movers and packers.

Check Insurance Coverage

A mover's liability for your possessions is limited to an amount per unit of weight. This often is less than replacement value for most items. Find out what added protection is available through the mover or through your homeowner's or renter's policy. Make sure your possessions are adequately insured before you move.

During the Move

Take an inventory of your possessions. Include descriptions of major items. An inventory can help you in checking to make sure all your belongings are packed and moved. It also helps you file claims if any of your possessions are damaged or lost.

Label Moving Cartons as You Pack

A label of contents on the outside of each carton will help you during unloading and unpacking. Label each carton with its room location so kitchen items do not end up in the bathroom.

Supervise Both Pickup and Delivery

Movers also take an inventory of all the items they load, and they make a note of any flaws or damage to furnishings prior to packing and loading. It pays to be on hand to see that their inventory is accurate. When your possessions are delivered, check the condition of furnishings as they are unloaded. Also check your own inventory for losses or damages, 11-17.

Read the Paperwork

Read the shipping order and bill of lading carefully. A *bill of lading* is a receipt listing the goods shipped in a moving van. Make sure these forms accurately state pickup and delivery dates, estimated charges, and services to be performed. They should also state any special agreements or arrangements between you and the mover.

Arrange for Payment Upon Delivery

Generally, you cannot move today and pay tomorrow. Be ready to pay with cash or a certified check. Make sure you receive an itemized receipt of the delivery that lists the moving charges, the distance traveled, and the weight.

File Claims for Damages and Losses Promptly

Keep in mind that movers are liable for any damage they may cause to real estate, too. Make a note of claims you intend to make on the delivery receipt and on the mover's inventory. Include nicks, mars, or breakages that occurred during the moving process. To file a claim, list losses and damages along with estimated replacement or repair costs. In all claims and correspondence, include the details of the move, such as dates, charges, and order numbers.

U.S. West

11-17
After your move, check all boxes against your inventory and report losses or damages immediatedly.

Summary

Home means different things to different people, but it is important space for almost everyone. Finding a place to live and making it your own is an exciting adventure. This calls for much thought and careful planning. Location is one of the first considerations. Deciding where to call home may depend on educational and job opportunities. Other factors to consider include the cost of living, climate, and your lifestyle. Look for an environment that appeals to you.

Types of housing include apartments and houses. Apartments may be rentals, condominiums, or cooperatives. These are usually multi-family buildings. Single-family housing includes custom-built homes, tract houses, town houses, and modular or manufactured houses. Choices will depend on the amount you can spend for a home and on housing needs. These needs change with different stages of the life cycle.

Before making any decisions on your first and later homes, set up a budget for housing costs. This involves determining how much you can spend on home and related costs, such as utilities, insurance, and taxes. Since most housing costs are paid on a monthly basis, it is helpful to figure out a monthly housing allowance. When buying a home, it will be important to arrive at both monthly costs and a purchase price you can afford.

Renting a home usually involves signing a lease. It will state the rights and obligations of both landlord and tenant. Since this is a legal document that can be enforced in a court of law, it is important to fully understand all of the terms before signing.

When buying a home, a number of legal documents must be signed. To protect your interests, study these carefully. The mortgage will be one of the most important commitments. Shop carefully for the best mortgage terms and the best type of mortgage for your situation. Compare interest rates and other terms of different mortgages and compare the closing costs charged by different lenders.

Once you have a home of your own, you will need insurance to protect what is yours. There are several types of policies. A reliable insurance agent can help you select the type and amount of coverage you need. Costs will depend on the type and amount of coverage you buy, the amount of the deductible, the risk factors where you live, and the insurance company.

Moving your possessions from one home to another is another housing expense. First moves are often simple. As you accumulate more furniture and possessions, moves can become complicated and expensive. Successful, relatively painless moves call for careful planning.

To Review

1. Name four factors to consider when deciding where to live.
2. What is the main difference that separates rental apartments from condominiums and cooperatives?
3. If you were considering a manufactured home, name six guidelines to follow in making a choice.
4. What percent of gross monthly income do most lenders allow for a mortgage commitment?
5. Name three circumstances that could require home buyers to keep the purchase price at a minimum.
6. List three factors that might permit a buyer to lean toward the upper limit on the purchase price of a home.
7. Why do lenders require a survey of property?
8. What happens when a buyer assumes an existing mortgage?
9. Name five factors to consider when shopping for a mortgage and comparing lenders.
10. What four major factors determine the cost of home insurance?

11. Why is it important to take an inventory of your possessions
    A. When buying homeowner's insurance?
    B. Before you move?

To Think Critically

1. How does a person's lifestyle tend to influence housing location? Give examples.
2. What sources of information can help you find a place to live?
3. What questions should you investigate before buying a condominium or a cooperative?
4. When can you usually spend more than guidelines suggest for rental housing?
5. What are the advantages of renting?
6. What should you find out before you sign a lease?
7. What are the advantages and disadvantages of the following methods of financing a home:
   A. Fixed-rate mortgage.
   B. Adjustable rate mortgage.
   C. Graduated payment mortgage.
   D. Contract sale.
8. How would you prefer to finance a home if you were buying today? Why?
9. Explain the types of coverage home insurance policies provide.
10. What guidelines would you follow to make your move as easy and efficient as possible?

To Do

1. List at least five important items to consider before renting or buying each of the following:
   A. Rental apartment.
   B. Condominium or cooperative.
   C. Manufactured home.
   D. Single-family house.
2. Survey a number of realtors and home mortgage lenders. Find out the range of current interest rates and what forms of financing most buyers are using to purchase homes.
3. Interview at least three insurance agents that sell renter's insurance. Find out how much you would pay a year for the least expensive renter's policy for a one-bedroom apartment in a given area. Investigate the claims record and reputation of each company. Which company appears to offer the best coverage and service for the least amount of money?
4. Investigate housing issues in your area to learn what is being done about housing for low- and middle-income families, problems of the homeless, and zoning for different types of housing. Check out the role of the local and state government, federal government, community organizations, and private business interests in each of these areas.
5. Develop a chart to illustrate how shelter and housing needs change with different stages in the life cycle including young singles, young marrieds, young families with children, families with teenage children, families without children, older individuals, or couples.
6. Develop a checklist to use in evaluating a neighborhood and community in which to live.
7. Take an inventory of your family's personal possessions for insurance purposes.
8. Find information on the Internet about apartments for rent and homes for sale in your area. Describe to the class what type of information you find.

Families should select housing that suits their lifestyle.

CHAPTER 12

Inside Your Home

scale floor plan
traffic patterns
case goods
hardwoods
softwoods
solid wood
veneered wood
EnergyGuide label
ENERGY STAR label
service contract

After studying this chapter, you will be able to

- decorate and choose furnishings to fit your tastes, lifestyle, and budget.
- demonstrate effective ways to choose and arrange furniture in creating the living space and atmosphere you want.
- evaluate furniture, floor coverings, lighting fixtures, and window treatments in terms of quality, design, and price.
- compare features, safety, energy efficiency, and warranties of home appliances and equipment.

You wouldn't consider empty rooms much of a home. Only when you fill space with furnishings and possessions you like and enjoy do you create a home. Understanding a few basics on decorating and furniture selection can help you turn empty rooms into a place you want to live. You also need to learn how to select electronic products, floor coverings, window treatments, and home appliances to meet your needs.

Furnishing and decorating a home can be frustrating, time-consuming, and costly for consumers who have not learned a few basics and planned purchases carefully. It can be a challenging, exciting, and satisfying adventure for the knowledgeable consumer and decorator.

Decorating Decisions

Basically, decorating is making decisions. It starts with asking the right questions and finding the right answers. Here are seven basic questions to guide your home decorating decisions.

How Do You Use Your Living Space?

Activities influence decorating choices. For studying and reading you need quiet, comfortable, well-lit space. Entertaining at home requires flexible furniture arrangements and traffic patterns. Try to decorate and furnish living space to make what you do more fun and convenient.

How Do You Like to Live?

Your lifestyle influences decorating choices. A casual lifestyle calls for a comfortable, informal atmosphere. A busy lifestyle calls for carefree furnishings that require little upkeep. Single people decorate around personal tastes. Couples usually choose furnishings that please both of them. Families with small children make different decorating decisions than families with older or no children. Take time to analyze your living pattern and to decide what type of decorating and furnishings will work best for you.

What Do You Like to See Around You?

Color and style preferences play an important role in any decorating plan. Think about your likes and dislikes. Do you prefer strong color contrasts or subtle combinations? Do you have a favorite color or two you would want to use when decorating? What types of furniture appeal to you—contemporary or traditional? Do you like rooms formal or casual? Make an effort to fill your living space with the colors and styles you really like, 12-1.

American Lighting Association

12-1
This furniture and decorating scheme gives a casual, informal feeling that is appealing to consumers of different ages with different lifestyles.

What Resources Do You Have for Decorating?

Plan the best ways to use your money, time, and talents to achieve the results you want. If you are short on money, then time for bargain hunting and talents for do-it-yourself jobs become more important. Do you have time to shop at house sales, secondhand stores, and warehouses as well as at furniture stores? Can you paint, wallpaper, sew, or upholster? Put your money, time, and talents to work in creating a home to enjoy.

What Furniture and Decorative Items Do You Already Own?

Make a list of usable items you own. Incorporate them into your plans. Many decorating decisions involve adding to or working with what you have on hand.

What Sources of Information Are Available to You?

Look for decorating ideas in magazines, newspapers, decorating books, and catalogs. Furniture manufacturers

Furnishing the Home

All at Once

Carmen is moving to Kansas City to begin her first full-time job in the public relations department of a downtown bank. Carmen is a do-it-now person. She goes to Kansas City a week early to decorate and furnish her apartment before starting her new job.

Carmen has $1,000 saved from part-time jobs and graduation gifts. She plans to spend most of it and borrow whatever more she needs to get her apartment in shape. There will be no step-by-step decorating for Carmen. She wants to get her home in shape so she can give full attention to her job and to making new friends in Kansas City.

The apartment has a bedroom, living room, kitchen, and bath. The floors are in good condition, and the walls have recently been painted. Kitchen appliances come with the apartment. Carmen already has a few items including a bed, vacuum cleaner, TV, clock, two lamps, and some books and pictures. She also has dishes, linens, and kitchen utensils. Unfortunately, the list of items she needs and wants is much longer.

With her checkbook and credit cards in hand, Carmen begins shopping and decorating. Since she is new to Kansas City, she goes to one of the leading downtown stores instead of shopping around. The prices are pretty high, but the store is reputable. It also offers credit, delivery service, and free decorating advice that Carmen finds very helpful.

When shopping, she takes along a floor plan of the apartment and a list of the items she wants to buy. She plans to decorate with her favorite colorsógreen and yellow. She wants contemporary furnishings. Besides color and style, the most important thing on Carmenís mind is prompt delivery. She passes up several good buys because they arenít in stock and delivery could take up to six months. Here is a list of Carmenís major purchases:

- ❑ Two bamboo chairs.
- ❑ Wicker desk.
- ❑ Sleeper sofa.
- ❑ Wicker chest.
- ❑ Wall unit of shelves.
- ❑ Reading lamp.
- ❑ Two area rugs.
- ❑ Mirror.
- ❑ Draperies.
- ❑ Sound system.
- ❑ Drop-leaf table.

Carmen finishes her apartment in record time and is pleased with her selections. However, she spends her $1,000 savings and charges hundreds of dollars. In addition to rent and other monthly obligations, Carmen will also be making monthly credit card payments. It will take her almost three years to pay all her decorating bills. The finance charges on her credit card purchases will reach a sizable amount, but Carmen doesnít seem to mind. She is happily settled in her own place.

Case Review

1. If you were Carmen, how would you go about furnishing a place of your own?
2. How important would it be to you to decorate all at once?
3. How would you feel about making big charges on your credit cards and then having large debts to pay?
4. How would you feel about the extra money you would have to pay in finance charges if you used credit cards to buy your furnishings?

and associations also publish booklets with decorating information and ideas. Touring model homes and looking at displays in furniture stores may give you ideas you can use when decorating your own home. You may find it helpful to start a decorating resource file. Include both pictures and articles on decorating suggestions and furnishings you especially like. Then you will have your own source of ideas on hand when you begin a decorating job.

What Are Your Most Important and Immediate Needs?

Very few people can buy all the furnishings they need in one big buying spree. Even when the money is there, it is usually a good idea to decorate one step at a time rather than make all the choices at once. Try a two- to five-year decorating plan starting with the most important items. Items you will need first include a bed, light for reading, clock, radio, and anything else you cannot live without. Add other furnishings as you can afford them.

Color as a Decorating Tool

Color offers unlimited opportunities for creative decorating without great expense. A simple coat of paint can transform a dark, dreary room into a cheerful space. Carefully chosen color combinations and designs can also do wonders. Color choices can make a room seem larger or smaller, a ceiling seem higher, or a narrow space seem wider. It can make space seem warm or cool, cozy or sophisticated, restful or stimulating. Take time to discover your favorite colors and find ways to use them effectively in decorating your living spaces.

Room Plans

Planning one room at a time is a way to break a big decorating job into pieces you can handle with ease. As you plan and decorate a home, keep future needs in mind. Your first home probably will be temporary. You can save money, time, and energy by decorating your first apartment or house with furnishings you will be able to use later in other homes.

Before spending any money, it is a good idea to set up a chart for each room you plan to decorate, 12-2. On the chart, describe the room and list the furnishings you own and those you need for the space. List the decorating and furnishings you will need. Then draw a scale floor plan of the room, like the plan in 12-3. A ***scale floor plan*** is a drawing that shows the size and shape of a room. Next, draw furniture patterns to represent the furniture you expect to place in the room. Follow the same scale as your floor plan.

Arranging furniture patterns on a scale floor plan can help you visualize different room arrangements. This makes it easier to decide what size and style of furniture to buy. It can also save you from buying furniture that will not fit the room. When arranging furniture in a room, consider traffic patterns, room characteristics, and activity areas.

Traffic patterns are the paths people normally follow as they walk through a room. Good traffic patterns allow easy passage into, through, and out of rooms without cutting through furniture groupings. TV viewers do not want people walking in front of the set. Readers do not want people blocking their light. Carefully planned furniture arrangements can help create convenient traffic patterns and activity centers.

Good traffic patterns also allow access to light switches, windows, bookshelves, and storage areas. They provide adequate space for opening doors and drawers.

A room's characteristics, especially its size and shape, influence furniture arrangement. The features of a room very often dictate the best furniture arrangement for a room. These include placement of windows and doors, built-in furnishings, and special features, such as a fireplace. Light fixtures and electrical outlets can also be major factors to consider.

The activities planned for a room influence what furnishings will be most appropriate and how they should be arranged. You may want to set apart areas for talking, studying, or working on hobbies. Each activity will require

Individual Room Chart

Room Description

Use(s) ______ Windows—number ______
Size ______ sizes ______
Exposure ______ placement ______
Walls ______ Doors—number ______
Ceiling ______ sizes ______
Floor ______ placement ______
Special Features ______

Usable Furnishings Now Owned	Description		
	Color/Pattern	Material	Style
Furnishings Needed	Color/Pattern	Material	Style

Decorating Needed	Materials	Services

Household International

12-2
This chart can help you plan the furnishings and decorating of one room at a time.

adequate space. For instance, a dining area needs enough space to seat people comfortably and to serve them easily.

When shopping for furniture and accessories, take your room chart and room floor plan with you. Also take along any fabric and color samples you have for the room. Then let the chart, floor plan, and samples be your buying guides. Also carry a tape measure to check dimensions of furniture before buying.

Furniture Selection

Much of what you need to know about furniture selection will come from shopping experience. Even so,

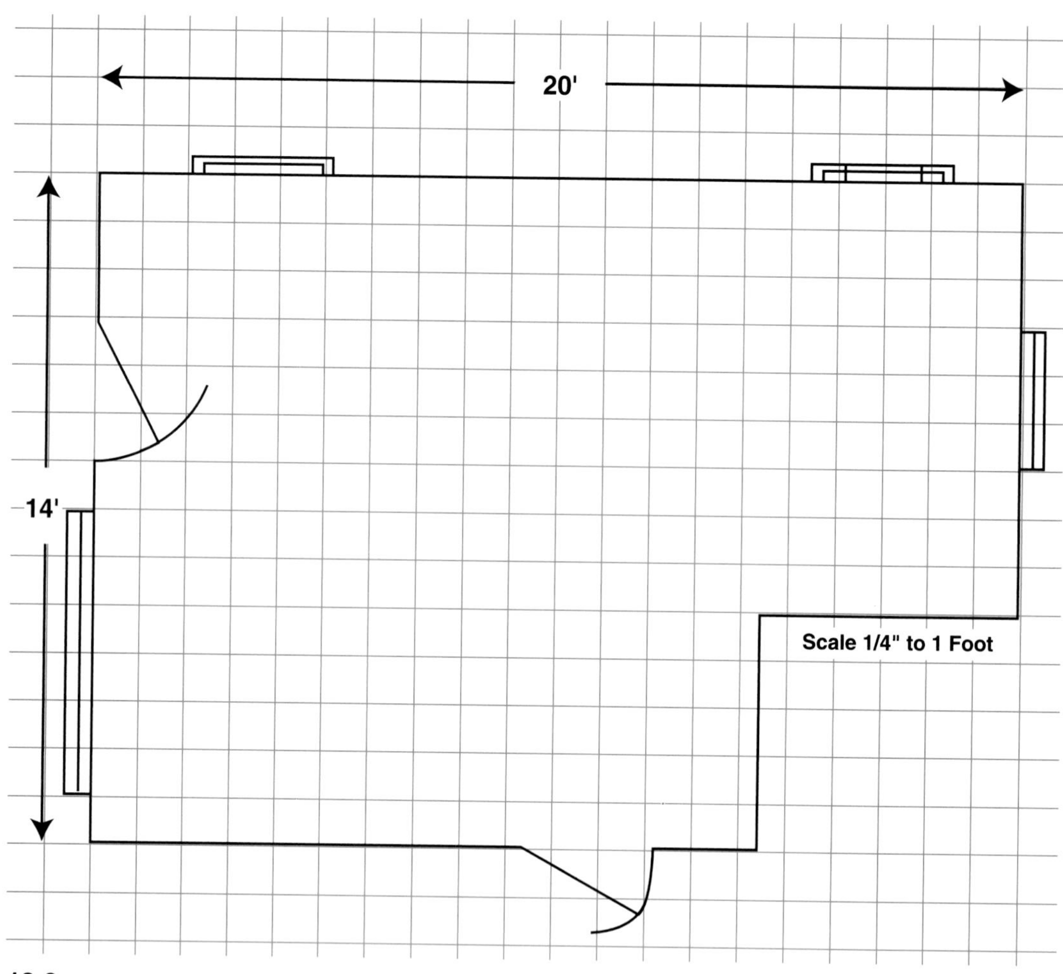

12-3 Household International
Drawing a scale floor plan can help you visualize the space you have available for decorating.

you stand to lose a lot if you enter the marketplace with no background information. Therefore, it is helpful to learn the basic facts about furniture selection before you begin shopping.

Personal needs are a primary concern. Decide what pieces of furniture you most need and want. Then consider how and where you will use them. Which pieces will you use only temporarily and which will you want on a long-term basis? Look for new items that go well with furnishings you already have.

Quality and durability are important factors in furniture selection, too. The more use a piece of furniture receives, the more durable it needs to be. For example, a bed in a guest room does not need to be the same quality as the bed you use nightly. A table you use for both family and guest meals should be sturdy and durable. An occasional table in a corner of a room may be of a lower quality or of less durable construction.

Style and appearance will be important if you want furniture to look attractive in your home and appeal to your tastes. Choose sizes, shapes, styles, and colors that fit your space and decorating theme. You also want the furniture you choose to be functional. For example, the chair you often use for relaxing and reading needs to be comfortable as well as attractive. However, an extra chair that is seldom used need not be the most comfortable chair in the room.

Furnishing the Home
One Step at a Time

Richard and Maxine are newly married. They are both in their mid-20s. Richard is an engineer working on a solar energy research project. Maxine is a paralegal for a large law firm. For a young couple getting started, they are doing well financially.

Richard and Maxine want a nice place to live, but they don't want to spend a lot of money furnishing an apartment where they may live only a year or two. They have plans for traveling, buying a house, and having children in the future. They can achieve these goals only if they spend and save wisely.

In order to reach their goals for the future, Richard and Maxine agree to spend no more than $1,000 to furnish and decorate their first apartment. They decide to decorate slowly, shop carefully, and spend their free time on do-it-yourself projects. Although Richard and Maxine have good salaries, they have no money saved. Between the two of them, they have just finished paying a college loan, buying a car, and paying wedding expenses. They do have a few possessions—a TV, stereo, clock radio, bed and bath linens, a few accessories, several small kitchen appliances, cookware, and dishes. That's it!

First, Richard and Maxine make a list of their immediate needs. A bed is at the top of their list, followed by a chest, two comfortable side chairs, a good reading lamp, and a dining table. Later, they will shop for good buys on other items such as:

- ❑ Sofa.
- ❑ Pictures.
- ❑ End tables.
- ❑ Draperies.
- ❑ Coffee table.
- ❑ Three lamps.
- ❑ Bookcases.
- ❑ Piano.
- ❑ Desk.
- ❑ Two area rugs.

Richard and Maxine shop carefully and find some real values. They spend many hours pouring over want ads, watching for special sales, and shopping at house sales, warehouses, and secondhand stores. They also spend lots of time refinishing furniture and making draperies.

Although Richard and Maxine have spent slightly more than they had planned, they are very pleased with their decorating results. The best part is the vacation they will be able to take with their savings. Richard and Maxine feel good about their achievements.

Case Review

1. If you were Richard and Maxine, how would you go about furnishing and decorating your first home?
2. How much time would you be willing to spend looking for just the right item at just the right price?
3. How would you feel about buying furnishings at a secondhand store or at a house sale? What are some of the advantages and disadvantages of buying used furniture?
4. What would be on your list of needs for a first home? How much do you think it would cost to buy all the items on your list?

Price is a key determining factor in deciding what furniture to buy. Work out a spending plan before you shop. Buy the best furniture you can afford, especially when buying major pieces you will use often and for many years. Once you decide on a piece of furniture you want, shop at several stores to compare prices.

The reputations of furniture manufacturers and sellers may affect your buying decisions. Find out about store policies on returns, exchanges, and warranties. Shopping in reliable furniture or department stores for brand-name furnishings is a safe, fast way to furnish a home. It also is expensive. With a little time, imagination, and legwork, you may be able to save money by shopping around. See 12-4. As you gain experience, you will begin to learn where to shop for different types of furniture and decorating needs.

Where to Shop for Home Furnishings

Places to Shop	Merchandise Available	Characteristics
Furniture stores and large department stores	All types of furniture, lamps and lighting equipment, floor coverings, upholstery and drapery fabrics, and decorative accessories.	Established reputation. Wide range of prices. Decorator services. Custom orders. Credit plans. Deliveries and installations. Warranties. Long wait on items not in stock.
Speciality stores that sell floor coverings, window treatments, accessories, or antiques	Broad selection within the speciality. Related merchandise and equipment.	Established reputation. Customs orders. Credit plans. Warranties. Deliveries and installations. Related services. Long wait on items not in stock.
Unfinished furniture stores	Unfinished case goods. Hardware and accessories. Supplies and equipment needed for finishing. Instruction and idea books.	Lower prices than similar quality furniture that has been finished. Usually in stock; no waiting period. Instruction and advice on techniques and supplies needed to finish furniture. Deliveries.
Outdoor furniture stores	Furniture suitable for indoor as well as outdoor use. Canvas, wicker, rattan, bamboo, and plastic furniture. Wrought iron furniture. Redwood furniture. Outdoor accessories.	Often less expensive than similar quality indoor items. Credit plans. Deliveries. Warranties.
Secondhand stores Salvation Army Thrift shops House sales Garage sales Auctions	Almost anything. Auctions may be limited to certain items, such as antiques and art objects.	Condition and quality of items vary. Guarantees, deliveries, credit, and other services seldom available. Prices may be negotiable. Prices considerably lower than those of comparable new items. May offer excellent values. Immediate availability.
Rentals with option to buy	Most types of furniture and accessories.	Wide selection. Deliveries. Credit plans. Prompt availability. Contract required.

12-4
When you shop for furniture, look in different outlets to find the best buys.

Services like credit plans and deliveries are other factors to consider as you shop. Ask the price of each service you need. Get a commitment on a delivery date if you need the furniture by a certain time. Delay on delivery is one of the most common consumer complaints related to the purchase of furniture.

Buying a table is different from buying a sofa or a bed. The following section covers specific guidelines for different types of furniture—case goods, upholstered pieces, and sleep furniture.

Case Goods

Case goods generally refers to furniture with no upholstered parts. It includes pieces that provide storage space, such as bookcases, desks, chests, and cabinets. It also includes most dining room and bedroom furniture, 12-5.

Pier 1

12-5
Dining room furniture is usually made of wood and comes in a wide range of styles, colors, and prices. This set fits a casual decorating plan and a limited budget.

Case goods may be made from a variety of woods, plastics, metals, and glass. When shopping for this type of furniture, pay attention to construction and finish as well as to size and style.

Wooden case goods may be made from several different types of wood. These include solid wood and veneered wood or wood products. Both hardwoods and softwoods are used. Any of these woods, as well as combinations of them, may be used in good quality furniture. When you shop, it is important to know how the woods differ.

Hardwoods include mahogany, maple, walnut, pecan, oak, fruit woods, and any other woods made from deciduous trees. (These are the trees that lose their leaves each year.) Hardwoods have beautiful, distinctive grains. They are generally stronger and more expensive than comparable softwood pieces.

Softwoods are made from evergreen trees, such as cedar, spruce, redwood, and pine. These woods generally are used for casual furniture. They may be less expensive than hardwoods, but they show mars and scratches more easily.

In ***solid wood*** furniture, all visible parts are made from whole pieces of wood that have been cut and carved to shape. Solid wood furniture is generally heavier and more expensive than veneered wood furniture. However, it may warp, swell, or crack under certain conditions.

Veneered wood is made of several thin layers of wood bonded together. Generally, the inside layers are made of inexpensive woods, while one or both of the outside layers are made of finer woods. Veneered wood makes strong, durable furniture. The veneer process gives furniture the look of costly woods at a reasonable price. It accounts for more than 75 percent of the furniture manufactured today. The core of veneered furniture may be solid wood, particleboard, or plywood.

Labels on wood furniture should state what type of wood is used and whether the furniture is solid or veneered wood. When a surface is not what it appears to be, the label must say what it is or that it is an imitation. For example, if a pine table looks like walnut, the label should say "pine" or "walnut finish." If furniture is labeled "genuine mahogany," the piece is made entirely from mahogany, but may be a mahogany veneer and solid wood combination. Labels may also give important care and maintenance information.

Overall, try to select case goods that are attractive and sturdy in a style you like and that fits your decorating plan. One way to judge the quality of wood furniture is to look carefully at construction details and features. Joints and joining methods are particularly important. Common methods of wood joinery are described in 12-6. Other construction features to look for are listed below.

- ❑ Doors are fitted well. They should be easy to open and shut with sturdy magnetic or other catches.
- ❑ Drawers are well fitted and smooth to operate.
- ❑ Legs are firmly attached and smoothly finished. They should stand squarely on the floor and be of a style suited to the furniture.
- ❑ Knobs and hardware on drawers and doors should be attractive, firmly attached, and easy to grasp.
- ❑ Surfaces are smoothly finished and free of defects. Select wood

Wood Joinery

Mortise-and-Tenon forms a strong union by fitting a notch made in a solid piece of wood tightly into a hole cut in an adjoining piece of wood. No nails or screws are used, only glue, to achieve one of the best methods of joining.

Double Dowel joinery is the most commonly used and the second best type of construction. Dowels are wooden pins that are fitted into holes drilled into both adjoining pieces of wood and glued.

Corner Blocks are triangular pieces of wood, screwed and glued to support and reinforce the frame. They are used in the construction of tables, case goods, and seating pieces to keep one side from pulling away from the other.

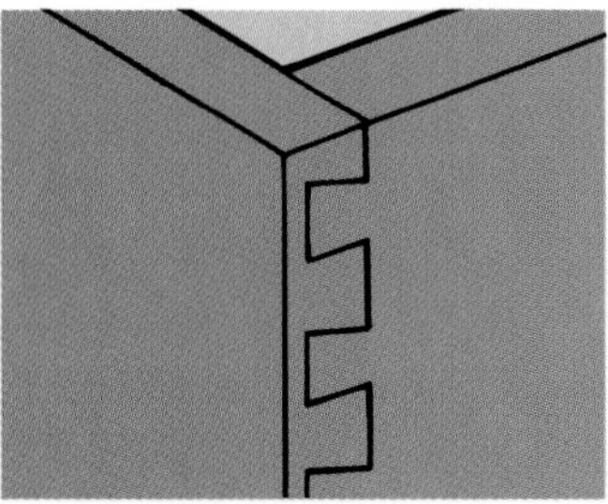

Dovetail joinery is a method of attaching boards at right angles as in the sides of a drawer. Each board has interlocking tenons that are cut in the form of a dovetail. It is almost standard construction for all drawers.

Tongue and Groove joints, if done skillfully, are invisible. An example is where several boards are joined to form a tabletop. One board will have a projecting tongue that fits into a groove on a corresponding board.

Butt Joint construction is one in which one board is glued or nailed flush to another board. It is the least desirable of all joint constructions.

12-6
The way furniture pieces are joined together determines their strength and durability.

finishes that will withstand the use you will give them. Laminated and plastic finishes resist water, scuffs, burns, and scratches. They may be desirable for furniture that will receive hard use.
- ❑ All sides of the furniture (not just the front) should be finished.

Although wood is used for most case goods, plastic is gaining popularity. Plastic can be attractive and functional. It often sells at lower prices than comparable wood pieces. It comes in a variety of colors, shapes, and styles. When shopping for plastic furniture, look for durable and sturdy pieces. They should have smooth finishes and edges and uniform color and gloss.

Wicker, rattan, and bamboo have always been popular alternatives to wood, 12-7. They are made from various parts of tropical vines. These types of furniture are versatile, durable, and suited to many different decorating plans. They are attractive, easy to care for, and often less expensive than wood furniture. When buying, check for smooth finishes and sturdiness. Chairs and upholstered pieces should be comfortable.

Some contemporary-styled case goods are made from metal and glass. When buying metal and glass furniture, look for smooth finishes, tempered glass, rustproof metals, and sturdy designs, 12-8.

Pier 1

12-7
Wicker and bamboo furniture fit into a variety of decorating plans and often offer a relatively inexpensive way to meet furnishing needs.

Upholstered Pieces

Upholstered furniture includes primarily chairs and sofas. Since much of the construction is hidden, it is important to read labels, ask questions, and buy from reliable sellers.

Labels on upholstered furniture should provide the information listed below.

- ❑ Fiber content of the upholstery fabric.
- ❑ Finishes applied to the fabric and their purposes.
- ❑ Care instructions.
- ❑ Flammability standards.
- ❑ Filling and cushioning materials used.

Pier 1

12-8
Metal often appears in outdoor furniture, such as this collection.

- ❏ Spring construction used.
- ❏ Type of wood or other material used in the frame.

The durability of upholstery fabric is determined largely by its fiber content and fabric construction. Nylon and olefin fibers and tightly woven fabrics provide the best durability. Protective finishes may be applied to some upholstery fabrics to improve wearability. Finishes produce resistance to soil, stains, and fading. Other finishes may add body and luster.

Upholstery of leather or vinyl is durable and easy to maintain. Leather is very expensive and luxurious. Good vinyl may serve as a less expensive substitute. When shopping, look for soft, pliable vinyl or leather that has uniform color.

When choosing upholstery fabrics, look for colors and designs that fit your overall decorating plan. Some fabrics produce a casual feeling; others are more formal. Some are more durable and practical than others. Look for fabrics that meet your needs and the way you will use the furniture.

Cushioning and filling materials are made primarily of down, fiberfill, latex foam, urethane foam, or a combination of these materials. Down (feathers) is the most expensive filling material. It gives soft "sink-in" comfort. Fiberfill is the closest manufactured substitute for down. It is less expensive and more durable. Latex and foam are firmer. They give cushions a more tailored look.

Springs in upholstered furniture may be zigzag or coil, 12-9. *Zig-zag springs* are generally less expensive than coil springs. They feel firmer and look less bulky. This makes them good for lightweight, sleek-looking furniture. *Coil springs* are softer and have more "bounce." They are used for larger, bulkier pieces. Both springs are covered with padding, which is usually made of foam or cotton.

Sears, Roebuck & Co.

12-9
Upholstered pieces with zig-zag springs usually are firmer and less expensive than those with coil springs.

The frame of upholstered furniture may be made of wood, plastic, metal, or a combination of materials. When it is not visible, look at the label or ask the salesperson about the frame material and construction. Look carefully at what is visible and check the same construction features you would check if buying case goods. Be sure the furniture rests squarely on the floor and that it is sturdy and strong at points of strain.

Pay attention to other visible features, too. Look for smooth, straight seams and for smooth, even hems on skirts and pleats. Any patterns, stripes, or plaids in upholstery fabrics should match. Any designs should be centered. Reversible cushions are a practical feature that can help furniture look nice longer. Cushion covers should fit snugly and have zipper closures. As a final test, sit on the chair or sofa. Does it feel comfortable in terms of size and firmness? Try it two or three times to test the height, depth, and shape for your comfort.

Sleep Furniture

Sleep furniture includes beds and dual-purpose sleeper chairs, sofas, or futons. When you buy a bed, comfort is the most important feature, 12-10.

Crate and Barrel

12-10
Comfort is the most important feature of sleep furniture.

A mattress and springs sold together as a set generally give the best wear and comfort. Look for size and degree of firmness to suit your preferences.

King- and queen-size beds are more expensive than the standard twin or double beds. Bedding is also more expensive for larger beds. However, if you find a larger bed more comfortable, paying the extra cost for a bed you will use for many years may be a wise investment.

The two most common types of mattresses are innerspring and foam. An *innerspring mattress* is constructed of steel wire coils with layers of insulation and cushioning materials and a sturdy fabric covering. The type and number of coils and the amount of padding that covers the springs determine the firmness and comfort of the mattress. Ask for any consumer information that comes with the mattress and look at the sample cross section of the mattress, which is commonly available where bedding is sold.

A *foam mattress* is usually made of polyurethane or latex foam. It is molded and then cut into mattress sizes. Foam mattresses are resilient, lightweight, and usually lower in cost than innerspring. They also resist dust, moths, and mold. The thickness of the foam will determine the firmness, comfort, and support of the mattress. It should be at least six inches thick. Look for the manufacturer's grade of density expressed in weight as a key to firmness.

Bedsprings are needed to support a mattress. The three common types of bedsprings are box, open coil, and flat springs. *Box springs* are the most popular. They are covered, usually padded, and enclosed in a covering to match the mattress. *Open coil springs* are also enclosed, but are not padded or covered. They are less expensive than box springs. *Flat springs* are neither covered nor enclosed. They are the least expensive and are not generally sold in a set with a mattress. Flat springs are not recommended for constant use.

When shopping for mattresses, read the labels to find out:

- ❑ The fiber content of the cover.
- ❑ The filler materials used.
- ❑ The type of spring construction.
- ❑ The special finishes and treatments applied.
- ❑ The flammability standards.

The bed frame holds the mattress and springs. Frames usually are made of steel and can be adjusted to fit different size mattresses. A frame with a center support is recommended for queen- and king-size mattresses and springs. The headboard attaches to the frame. Frames with casters or rollers make beds easier to move. Casters usually can be locked in place to prevent unintentional movement.

Waterbeds are another type of sleep furniture. A waterbed consists of a heavy duty vinyl water bag and a sturdy bed frame. A vinyl liner is usually between the mattress and frame to hold moisture in the event of leak. Some waterbeds include a thermostatically controlled heater for added comfort.

As with any bed, comfort is the most important feature to consider when selecting a waterbed. The construction of the mattress will determine how wavy it is. If you prefer a firmer mattress, choose one with fiber filling or with baffle strips to slow the surge of water in the mattress and reduce water shifting.

Since waterbeds are very heavy, they require a firm floor for support. Some landlords do not permit tenants to use them because of their weight and the danger of leakage.

Sleeper sofas and chairs are designed for sitting and sleeping. If you need extra sleeping space now and then, this type of furniture may be a good choice.

Sleeper sofas can also serve well in studio apartments where space is limited. If the sofa will be used mainly for sitting, comfort and appearance will be the most important factors to consider. If it will be used nightly for sleeping, look first for sleeping comfort.

When buying a sleeper sofa, check the construction and quality of the upholstery and mattress. Check to see how easily it converts to a sleeper. It should be easy to open out the mattress and fold it away. There should be no protruding parts when the sofa is open for sleeping or closed for sitting. Once again, check for both sitting and sleeping comfort.

Futons also serve both sleeping and sitting needs. These can be an inexpensive answer to furnishing a first apartment or providing extra sleeping space in a home. The *futon* is made up of frame, futon or mattress-like piece, and cover. The covers are relatively inexpensive. This makes it easy to change color and decorating schemes from time to time. This type of furniture is versatile, relatively inexpensive, and easy to assemble and move from place to place.

Floor Treatments

Floors and floor coverings are major items to consider when furnishing a home. The type and quality you select will depend on the following factors:

Use

How long do you expect to use it? Will it be in light or heavy traffic areas? Will it be subjected to light or heavy soiling? A floor that will receive a lot of wear will need to be as durable as possible.

Price Range

What can you afford? How do the costs of different floors and floor coverings compare? What are the costs of installation and maintenance?

Decorating Needs

What color, design, and texture would be most appropriate and appealing? Which type of floor or floor covering would look the best? Must the floor covering serve a particular purpose—to cover an unattractive floor or to create an illusion of greater space?

Comfort

Is there a need for warmth or sound insulation? Is resilience important for standing comfortably in areas such as the kitchen?

The three basic types of floors and floor coverings are hard floors, resilient floor coverings, and soft floor coverings.

Hard Floors

Types of hard floors include ceramic tile, clay tile, brick, concrete, stone, and wood. Hard floors are durable and attractive. However, they may be colder, noisier, and less comfortable than other floorings. In addition, they are more difficult and costly to install. Most hard floors are installed when a structure is being built. Unless you are building or remodeling a home, you are not likely to choose hard floors.

Resilient Floor Coverings

Vinyl, asphalt tile, and cork tile are the major types of resilient floor coverings. Resilient means the flooring has some "give" to it, but that it keeps its original shape. The major advantages of resilient floor coverings are their walking comfort and noise control. Most are durable, easy to clean, and fairly inexpensive, 12-11. A number of designs and colors are available in resilient floor coverings. Some patterns are designed to look like hard floors, such as stone, brick, and wood.

Soft Floor Coverings

Carpeting and rugs are the two basic types of soft floor coverings. Both come in a variety of patterns, colors, and prices. Carpeting can help insulate rooms, absorb sounds, and make rooms seem more spacious. Rugs can help define activity centers in a room. Since rugs are not attached to floors, they can be easily sent out for professional cleaning and moved from one location to another.

The quality of rugs and carpets depends in large part on the fiber content and the density of the pile. Nylon is the most common synthetic carpet fiber. It is durable, resilient, soil-resistant, but will stain easily unless treated. Most carpets are or can be treated with stain- and soil-resistant finishes. Wool is the most common natural carpet fiber. It is luxurious, wears well, and cleans easily, but is very expensive. Polyester is less expensive than nylon and wool. It is stain- and fade-resistant, durable, and offers soft texture and exceptional color clarity. Polypropylene (Olefin) is stain-, fade-, moisture-, and abrasion-resistant. It is also durable and colorfast. It is used for both indoor and outdoor carpeting and for carpet backing. Rugs made of sisal, coir, jute, or cotton rags

White Westinghouse

12-11
Because they are easy to clean, resilient floor coverings are often used in kitchens.

are relatively inexpensive and may be suited to certain uses and decorating needs. Be sure to consider the fiber content and its characteristics when buying soft floor coverings.

The "pile" of a carpet or rug refers to the surface yarns. When the yarns are close together, the pile is said to be dense or thick. A dense pile is a sign of high quality and durability. To check pile density, bend back a corner of the carpet or rug wrong side toward wrong side. The more backing you can see between yarns, the lower the density and the lower the quality is. Lower quality carpets and rugs may be suitable for rooms that have little traffic, but they cannot withstand heavy wear.

Another sign of quality is a carpet or rug backing that is sturdy enough to hold surface yarns in place. A sturdy backing prevents stretching and shrinking. Most backings are made of jute, cotton, or a synthetic material.

Shop for padding at the same time you look at rugs and carpets. Padding improves durability, warmth, and resiliency or bounce. It also helps absorb sound. Padding is fairly inexpensive and pays for itself in comfort and greater durability. Jute and foam rubber are common padding materials. Ask for padding recommendations when you buy carpeting or rugs.

Be sure to read carpeting and rug labels carefully. They should list the fiber content, construction method, care instructions, backing materials, and style and color numbers. When you find carpeting or a rug you are seriously considering, ask to see it on the floor and if possible take a sample home to try with your furnishings. Shop several stores. Prices for the same carpet can vary greatly. To compare prices accurately, be sure to ask for total prices that include the carpeting, padding, installation, and delivery. When making a major investment in wall-to-wall carpeting, it may pay to have the seller come to your home to measure rooms, halls, and stairs to be carpeted.

When you make a final choice and place an order, ask for the following items in writing:

- ❑ Style and color numbers.
- ❑ Size ordered.
- ❑ Price per square foot and total price.
- ❑ Fiber content and care instructions.
- ❑ Manufacturer's name.
- ❑ Type and price of padding.
- ❑ Delivery and installation charges and dates.

This will give you the information you need in writing to verify what you actually ordered. This is very important if you should be sent the wrong carpet or rug. Make a point of being at home when carpet is delivered to check the color and quality against your order. It also is a good idea to ask for any carpet leftovers of a useful size.

Lamps and Lighting Fixtures

Lighting is another important aspect of decorating. Most homes have ceiling and wall fixtures to provide general lighting. Table and floor lamps provide local lighting for reading and work areas, 12-12. Accent lighting may be used to highlight interesting objects or to provide special decorative effects. When you shop for a lamp or lighting fixture, consider the following questions.

- ❑ Is the type, size, style, and color of the lamp or lighting fixture appropriate for the place you plan to use it?
- ❑ Is the amount and type of light provided appropriate for the way you intend to use the lamp or fixture?
- ❑ Do the lamp base and shade go well together in terms of size, shape, and color?

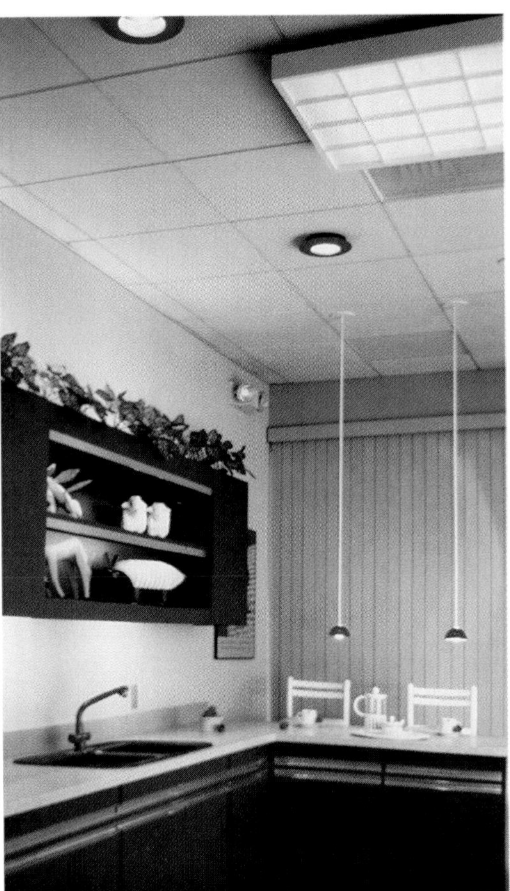

American Lighting Association

12-12
Lamps and lighting fixtures are both decorative and functional. Lighting for this area is designed to provide adequate light for specific tasks.

- ❑ Will special bulbs be needed? If so, will they be easy to buy at a reasonable price?
- ❑ Will installation of fixtures require an electrician? If so, find out the cost of installation.
- ❑ Does the lamp or lighting fixture carry the Underwriters Laboratories (UL) seal indicating that it meets electrical safety standards?

Window Treatments

Window treatments are both functional and decorative. They provide light, privacy, and insulation. They also affect the overall design of a room. Curtains, draperies, shades, blinds, and shutters are common window treatments. These treatments may be varied or combined to create a wide range of design effects, 12-13. Your choice will depend on the windows in your home, your decorating plan, and your budget. The following questions may help you choose treatments appropriate for the windows in a room you are decorating.

- ❑ Will the window treatment create the effect you want?
- ❑ Can it be adapted to fit any problem windows you have, such as corner windows, bay windows, and odd sizes?
- ❑ Will it let in enough light but still provide privacy?
- ❑ Will it permit convenient use of the windows?
- ❑ Will it be easy to install and operate?
- ❑ Does the price of the window treatment include fees for measuring, installation, or any other services required? If not, what will these services cost?
- ❑ Can necessary hardware be conveniently and properly installed around the windows in the rooms?
- ❑ Can you use ready-made window treatments or will you need custom-made treatments to fit your windows?
- ❑ Is the material used in window treatments easy to clean?
- ❑ Is it durable, sun-resistant, and soil-resistant?

Furniture and Appliance Rentals

In most major cities and suburbs, it is possible to rent furniture for an apartment or house. For those who move frequently or who haven't enough money to adequately furnish a first home, this may be an alternative worth considering. Often it is possible to rent with an option to buy. This would enable you to apply the rent to

Kirsch Division, Cooper Industries, Inc.

12-13
Window treatments also serve a function while they decorate.

the purchase price. Furniture rental companies may also be a source of used furniture at attractive prices if they sell used rented pieces.

You will find a wide variety of rental furnishings from which to choose. You can rent at different quality levels from budget to luxury. You can rent individual pieces or furnish an entire home. You can rent dishes, linens, microwave ovens, TV sets, and pictures. Usually you can furnish an apartment, home, or office within three or four days of making your selections.

Furniture rentals often involve applying for credit, signing a lease agreement, and paying a security deposit and delivery charges. Usually the shortest-term lease available runs six months. Longer terms are available and encouraged. The amount per month normally will be less for a longer-term lease. As with other contracts, read carefully and be sure you understand all the terms of the agreement before signing.

Do not confuse furniture rental agreements with aggressive Rent-to-own (RTO) plans that require no credit checks or down payments. RTO plans are not regulated under the Truth in Lending Act or state credit laws. This is because they are not technically "credit sales." The fees are not "interest charges." They are fees for "convenience and service."

Those fees typically add up to much more than the rental items are worth and more than they would cost if purchased with credit. For example, a television selling for $200 to $500 might be offered at $44 to $60 per month for an 18 month lease. This comes to a total cost of $792 to $1,080!

Protect yourself if you consider renting furniture or appliances. Determine the total cost of the purchase by multiplying the amount of each rental payment by the number of payments required in the contract. Compare this total with the cash price and the credit price of similar merchandise at reputable stores. It is important to find out what will happen if you miss a payment. Also find out whether you can buy the merchandise outright at a lower cost at any time during the contract period. Check out provisions for servicing or repairs on rented appliances, insurance requirements and fees, and penalties imposed if you cannot carry out the contract.

Buying Home Appliances

The number of large and small appliances in American homes continues to increase each year. To get an idea of the money your family spends on appliances, make a quick room-by-room count and cost estimate of appliances throughout your home. The total investment may startle you. Over a lifetime, you can make the most of the many dollars you spend on equipment by making wise choices. Careful planning can help you select the appliances you really need and can afford.

Before buying any appliances, determine your home equipment needs. What jobs do you need an appliance to perform for you? What size appliance do you need? What special features are important to you? What safety and economy features do you want? Will gas or electric equipment work better for you? What space do you have for storage of small appliances when not in use? See 12-14.

Decide how much you can spend for each appliance you want to purchase. Many people buy major home appliances on credit. If this is your choice, how much can you afford to pay in monthly installments? What are the total finance charges? How much more

12-14
This washer and dryer are part of a well-planned laundry area. It is important to choose appliances designed for your lifestyle and housing needs.

Whirlpool

is the credit price than the cash price? Is it worth the difference? How much money will you need for installation, servicing, and operating costs?

The time to obtain information on appliances is before you buy. Sources of information include consumer publications and materials from manufacturers, retailers, government, trade associations, utility companies, and consumer groups. Look for newspaper and magazine articles that give general and specific guides on buying, using, and servicing appliances. The Internet is also a good source of information on appliances, features, and prices. Be sure to read the labels, seals, and instruction booklets that accompany equipment and appliances. They provide facts and directions on use, care, performance, safety, energy efficiency, and capacity.

Shop around before you buy. Identical appliances vary in price from store to store. Shopping is essential to get the best values. As you shop and compare prices of different appliances, also consider appliance safety and performance features, energy efficiency, warranties, and servicing.

Appliance Features

One of the most important factors to consider when buying an appliance is its features. Begin with a careful check of construction features. Appliances should be sturdy, well built, and evenly balanced. Look for hard, durable finishes that will not scratch or dent easily. Ovens and refrigerators should have sturdy shelves with shelf supports. Supports prevent shelves from falling and from being pulled out accidentally. Handles and legs on all appliances should be firmly attached.

Check for seals that show that appliances meet safety standards. Electric appliances should carry the UL seal of Underwriters Laboratories. Built-in safety features are also a plus in home appliances. Look for automatic switches on washers, dryers, dishwashers, trash compactors, and microwave ovens. This type of switch automatically stops operation when the appliance door is opened. Doors on refrigerators, freezers, and dryers should have safety locks. These locks prevent children from being trapped inside these appliances accidentally.

The best appliances are not only well built and safe, they are also easy to use. Choose appliances with controls that are easy for you to read, understand, and operate. Look for the operating cycles and functions you need.

Easy care and cleaning features are helpful, too. Portable appliances that can be immersed in water are easier to clean than nonimmersible ones. For major appliances, such features as self-cleaning ovens and frost-free refrigerators make cleaning jobs easier.

The easier it is for you to use and clean an appliance, the more you will use it. The more durable an appliance is, the longer it will last. The safer an appliance is, the more protection it provides against accidents and injury. Of course, the more features an appliance has, the higher its purchase price and operating costs will be. Features that lengthen the life of an appliance or make it safer and more convenient to use may be well worth the extra cost. You need to be aware of your options and make decisions according to your personal needs and finances.

Energy Efficiency

Energy efficiency is another important factor to consider when selecting a major appliance. As you shop, look for the EnergyGuide labels that appear on these appliances: refrigerators, refrigerator-freezers, freezers, dishwashers, clothes washers, water heaters, room air conditioners, and furnaces. The ***EnergyGuide label*** shows the estimated annual cost of operating an appliance. By comparing the average cost estimates for similar appliances, you can determine which would be the most energy-efficient and least costly to own and operate. There are three types of EnergyGuide labels: energy use labels, energy efficiency rating labels, and generic labels.

Energy use labels are used on refrigerators, freezers, refrigerator-freezers, dishwashers, clothes washers, and water heaters. See 12-15. These labels tell you the estimated yearly energy used in operating an appliance based on a national average electricity rate. The lower part of the label gives a cost estimate for a certain utility rate. Your utility company can tell you local rates. Then you can figure operating costs for an appliance in your home.

Energy efficiency rating labels are used on room air conditioners, 12-16. These labels show the range of efficiency ratings for competing room air conditioners of the same cooling capacity. The labels also provide an estimated yearly energy cost of the appliance based on local electricity rates.

Generic labels are required on all furnaces. They give general tips for conserving energy in the home. They also direct consumers to ask for energy fact sheets, which manufacturers must prepare for their furnaces. The fact sheets give information on system components and overall efficiency. They also give estimated energy costs of heating systems for different geographic locations and utility rates.

The ***ENERGY STAR label*** is another indicator of energy-efficient products. This program, launched in 1996, is a voluntary partnership of the U.S. Department of Energy and the Environmental Protection Agency, product manufacturers, local utilities,

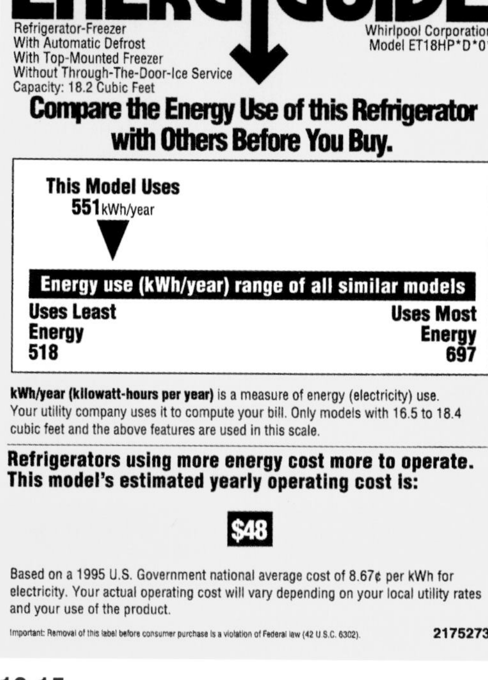

12-15
The EnergyGuide energy use label can help you compare yearly operating costs for similar appliances.

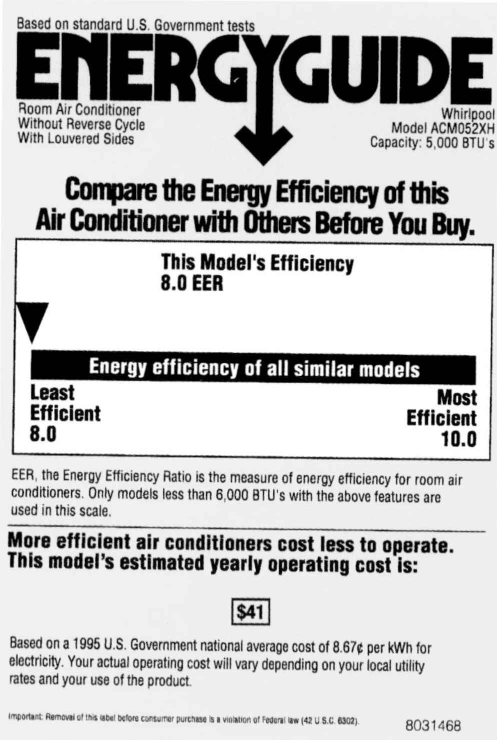

12-16
The EnergyGuide energy efficiency rating labels give an efficiency rating for climate control appliances, such as room air conditioners.

and retailers. Its purpose is to encourage the purchase of energy-efficient consumer electronics and appliances. Energy-efficient products are labeled with the ENERGY STAR, shown in 12-17. To qualify for the label, products must exceed federal minimum efficiency standards by specific percentages that vary with the appliance or product. ENERGY STAR labels appear only on the most energy-efficient household appliances, consumer electronics, heating and cooling equipment, and other products. You can conserve energy and keep your utility bills down by choosing products labeled with the ENERGY STAR.

When you buy appliances, it pays to consider energy efficiency and operating costs. This is especially true for appliances that you expect to use often for a number of years. Appliances that are more energy efficient will cost less to operate. Over time, even if the purchase price of an energy efficient appliance is high, it may still be a bargain. It can save you a lot of money in the form of lower utility bills.

Warranties

Warranties are particularly important when buying appliances that may require service or repairs from time to time. When you shop, compare warranties just as you compare other features.

An appliance may carry a full or a limited warranty. A *full warranty* provides for free repair or replacement of the warranted item or part if any defect occurs while the warranty is in effect. The warrantor decides whether to repair or replace the item. The buyer may not be asked to do anything unreasonable in order to receive performance promised by a full warranty.

A *limited warranty* provides service, repairs, and replacements only under certain conditions. It may or may not cover charges for labor and for returning the item to the manufacturer for repairs.

As you study the warranty for an appliance, check first to see whether it is a full or limited warranty. Does it cover the entire product or only certain parts? Read carefully to find out how long the warranty is in effect. Know what you must do to receive warranty servicing and to keep the warranty in effect. Also find out exactly what services the warranty provides. Does it promise repairs or replacement? Who performs the promised service and repair? Will servicing be done in the home, or must the item be returned to the seller, manufacturer, or authorized service center? If it must be returned, who pays for shipping, pick up, and redelivery?

12-17
By choosing appliances and electronic equipment with the ENERGY STAR label, you can conserve energy and save money on utility bills.

Service Contracts

The service contract is another item you may be asked to consider when you buy a major appliance. It begins where the warranty ends. With a ***service contract***, the seller guarantees servicing of the appliance if it is needed during the term of the contract. A set fee is paid at the time of purchase for this contract.

If you use appliances carefully and buy from reputable manufacturers and dealers, warranty servicing may be adequate. A service contract may be worth considering for consumers who:

- ❑ Move frequently and need installations and follow-up services with each move.
- ❑ Expect to give an appliance maximum use (such as a clothes washer would get in a household of five or more members).
- ❑ Expect the appliance to be used frequently and by several family members, including children.

When considering a service contract, make sure you find out exactly what you get for the price you pay. Find out if you can wait until the warranty expires to purchase the service contract. Ask questions before signing on for this type of protection. What will it cost? How long will it be in effect? Who is responsible for fulfilling the terms of the contract? Where do you call for service and repairs? Will you get prompt service? Is coverage good if you move to another location or sell the appliance while the contract is in effect? Does the agreement cover parts and labor? What does it exclude? What do you have to do to get service under the terms of the contract? What expenses must you pay, such as a deductible amount or fee per call?

Using Appliances Safely

Buying well-built, safe, and convenient appliances is only half the job. You also have to install, use, and care for them safely and properly. Reading the directions is the first and most important safety practice to follow. Appliances perform better, last longer, and require less servicing if you follow directions carefully. Review the instruction booklet before you buy an appliance and read it carefully before you use it. Then keep the booklet in a convenient place so you can find it as needed.

When installing major appliances, insist upon qualified and reliable service persons to make gas, electrical, and plumbing connections. Do-it-yourself installations and servicing may be risky unless you are trained to do these jobs. Nonauthorized service people may also jeopardize warranty coverage.

When using small electric appliances, select a space that is large enough for working, close enough to electrical outlets, away from the sink area, and out of the reach of small children. You can prevent many home accidents by following these simple precautions.

Before using an electric appliance, make sure the appliance and the cord are in good condition. Use extension cords only for low-wattage appliances. They are not safe for high-wattage appliances, such as irons, toasters, and coffeemakers. Turn off appliances before connecting or disconnecting them at outlets. Be sure to avoid using several electric appliances on a single circuit. Overloading circuits can blow a fuse and create a fire hazard.

If you have gas appliances, promptly call the gas company if you ever smell gas and suspect a leak. Since gas leaks are very dangerous, most gas utility companies will check your home free of charge or for a small fee.

Appliance Servicing

Most appliances require service or repair at some point, and it is generally expensive. You can reduce the need for repairs by buying well-built appliances and carefully following use-and-care directions. Another way to reduce service costs is to take advantage of warranty services to which you are entitled.

Finding a reliable service facility is the key to getting the most for the service dollars you must spend. Look for a service facility that is authorized to work on specific appliances you own and that has well-trained service technicians.

Ask in advance about charges for basic repair services, house calls, pickups, and deliveries. Compare fees of several service centers. Find out which facilities provide emergency service, give prompt regular service, and guarantee their work.

Check service facilities you are considering with the local Better Business Bureau or consumer protection agency. If complaints have been filed against a facility and not resolved to the customer's satisfaction, it may be best to look for servicing elsewhere. Ask friends, neighbors, and appliance dealers for recommendations. It is a good idea to do your shopping in advance so you know just where to call for prompt, reliable service when you need it.

One sure way to trim costs for appliance repairs is to avoid unnecessary service calls. An estimated 30 percent of all calls for service are unnecessary. Often the appliance is unplugged, not set properly for operation, or not running because of a blown fuse. In most cases, when a service person comes to your home, you pay even if there is nothing wrong with the appliance. To avoid unnecessary calls, read the checklist in 12-18 before you call for service. Also look to the owner's manual for items to check before calling for service.

When servicing is necessary, make sure you understand what caused the problem and what was done to correct it. It is a good idea to keep receipts of appliance purchases, copies of warranties, and records of servicing with dates and charges. Keep these materials filed and ready for reference as you need them.

The "Before You Dial for Service" Checklist

Is the appliance plugged in and turned on?

Did you check fuses and circuit breakers?

Are water, gas, or electric connections turned on and feeding into the appliance properly?

Are the controls set properly for the job you are doing?

Did you follow all operating instructions?

Did you check the owner's manual for a possible explanation of the difficulty?

Did you check the warranty to see if it covers service or parts that may be required?

Do you have all the data handy to give the service facility—the appliance make, model number, date purchased, and a brief description of the problem?

12-18
You may be able to avoid unnecessary service calls if you run through this checklist before calling for service.

Consumer Electronics

Most of today's homes are equipped with a variety of electronic products. These range from audio-video equipment to personal computers to telephone answering machines. Today over 1,000 companies are producing electronic products for the home. Over 15,000 products are now available. Rapid new developments in this industry make it impossible to present guidelines for buying individual products. Still, since most consumers spend a sizable amount of money on electronics, a few general guidelines may be useful.

Purchasing Electronic Products

When you are considering the purchase of an electronic product, research the following:

- Specific brands. Most manufacturers provide descriptive data on their products. This includes sizes, functions, features, installation requirements, warranties, use, and care. Collecting and comparing this information on different brands can help you make a wise choice.
- New developments. Both manufacturers and industry sources provide information on new product developments. Significant improvements and new features will often be featured in newspapers and magazines. You can go online to learn what is new in consumer electronics. It pays to find out what is new before you shop. This is particularly true when you will be buying costly products you expect to enjoy for a long time, 12-19.
- Features and accessories. Almost every type of electronic product offers a variety of features. Many products can be used with several accessories to enhance their usefulness. To learn more about these extras refer to manufacturers, publications, consumer magazines, and specialty magazines covering specific products.
- Installation, use, and care. Instruction manuals and warranty literature will tell you essential information on installing and using the products you buy. Knowledgeable salespersons can also be one of your best sources of information. Ask for demonstrations before you buy. Be sure you understand what you need to know about the installation, use, and care of any product you purchase. General care of electronic products calls for keeping them dry, clean, and cool. It is also important not to drop them. Specific care tips appear in the instruction book

Zenith

12-19
When buying costly items, such as televisions, be sure to check out new product development.

that comes with each product.

- ❑ Energy efficiency. Look for the ENERGY STAR label that indicates products surpass minimum national standards for energy efficiency set by the Environmental Protection Agency and the Department of Energy.
- ❑ Warranties and service contracts. Electronic products are sensitive, complex equipment. They occasionally require servicing and repairs by manufacturer-authorized technicians. Warranty protection and the service contract offer two ways to minimize the costs of servicing electronics. It pays to study warranty coverage carefully before buying any product that could require costly attention later. Service contracts usually offer extended coverage on parts and labor for a period of time after the warranty expires. You pay extra for a service contract.
- ❑ Reliable retail outlets for electronics. Look for a reliable retailer when buying electronic products. It is costly to buy a mistake. Have a clear idea of what you need and want in a product. Then look for a knowledgeable salesperson. Ask the salesperson to help you find the product that will best meet your needs. Take care to buy the right product. Keep in mind that promotions and sales offer advantages to you only if you can match the product to your specific needs.

Use electronic products in a safe manner. You may not think yourself at risk as you watch TV, listen to your stereo, or take off with your mobile phone. However, abuse and misuse of these products can be hazardous to your health and property. For example, if you alter the polarized plug on your TV set, you risk the danger of electric shock and create a fire hazard. If you listen to your sound system or earphones at high volume, you can incur permanent hearing damage. If you use a mobile phone while driving, you take a chance on a serious accident and injury. Read instruction books carefully and follow any safety rules on the use and care of equipment you buy.

A Note on Batteries

If you count them up, you would be surprised at how many battery-dependent products you use routinely. Today's consumers need to know a few basics about the purchase, use, care, and disposal of batteries.

Battery Selection

Batteries come in several sizes. You can buy disposable batteries that you throw away when the power is used up or rechargeable batteries to recharge and use again. Disposables include general purpose, heavy-duty, and alkaline or premium. Rechargeables may be nickel-cadmium or lead/acid.

For heavy usage, the alkaline or premium battery may cost less per hour of use than the less expensive, general-purpose battery. It discharges power more efficiently. Rechargeables may be your best buy if you find yourself replacing the batteries in a product frequently. However, they do cost more and you need to buy a charger as well. Generally, disposable batteries have a longer shelf life than rechargeables. This makes them a good choice for products used infrequently, such as a flashlight or smoke alarm.

Battery Care

For both safety and longer life of batteries, it is important to follow a few simple guidelines. Keep batteries dry and store at moderate temperatures. Keep them away from metal objects, such as coins or keys, and out of reach of children. Do not mix one type with another. Do not take batteries apart. Do not try to charge a disposable battery in a recharger designed for rechargeable batteries.

Battery Disposal

Both mercury and cadmium used in batteries are toxic substances that need to be disposed of with care. Learn and follow any guidelines your community or state has established for disposal of batteries. Do not toss them out with other waste or dispose of them in fire. Follow safe disposal instructions provided by manufacturers on labels or packaging materials.

Help with Problems and Complaints

The vast majority of manufacturers, retailers, and service people want to satisfy you, the consumer. Even so, there may be times when you have problems with appliances, furniture, electronics, and other home products. When you do, the first places to seek help include the manufacturer and the dealer or retailer where you bought the product. Most manufacturers operate toll-free numbers and Web sites to deal promptly with consumer inquiries and problems. The operator's manual or other printed material that comes with products will usually list these consumer contacts along with troubleshooting information. If you fail to obtain satisfaction from the retailer or the manufacturer, you may want to contact one of the following associations, depending on the product:

- Association of Home Appliances Manufacturers (AHAM)
- Consumer Electronics Manufacturers Association (CEMA)
- National Association of Furniture Manufacturers (NAFM)
- Carpet and Rug Institute

To find current addresses, phone numbers, and Web sites of these and other helpful associations and consumer organizations, consult the *Gale's Encyclopedia of Associations* at your library or search online.

Summary

Decorating a place to live involves more than consumer and financial considerations. It also affects your outlook on life. An attractive, comfortable home prepares you for the other things that are important to you. When you begin to make decorating decisions, consider the ways you use space, the items you like around you, the resources you can use, and your most immediate needs.

Individual room plans can guide furniture choices. It is important to plan workable traffic patterns and to work around the characteristics in each room. When selecting furnishings, consider overall needs, quality, durability, style, appearance, and prices. Different buying guides apply to different types of furniture. At some point in time, most consumers will be looking to buy case goods, upholstered pieces, sleep furniture, and possibly dual-purpose sleeper sofas or chairs. It pays to learn the marks of quality in each type.

Floor treatments are important in a decorating plan. They can be a major expense. Choices will depend on the use floor coverings will receive, prices, decorating needs, and comfort. Quality of soft floor coverings or carpets and rugs depends largely on fiber and construction. Labels provide important information on both.

Lamps and lighting fixtures, along with window treatments, play a major role in furnishing a place to live. Those used will depend on personal preferences and on the space to be decorated. Function and price will also be important factors.

Home appliances and consumer electronics represent a major investment for most consumers. Making the best choices will call for attention to performance, operating and safety features, energy efficiency, warranties, and servicing. Comparison shopping is absolutely essential to learn about new appliances and electronics on the market.

To Review

1. To guide your furnishing and decorating decisions in the years ahead, what seven basic questions should you ask yourself?
2. How can a floor plan and furniture patterns help you with furniture selection and arrangements?
3. Name six factors to consider when shopping for furniture.
4. Case goods can be made from a variety of woods including hard, soft, solid, and _____.
5. What is one of the most important construction features to check when buying wood furniture?
6. What information appears on labels of upholstered furniture?
7. What largely determines the quality of carpets and rugs?
8. What are five questions to consider before selecting lamps or lighting fixtures?
9. How does a service contract differ from a warranty?
10. True or false. Electronic products should be kept dry, clean, and cool.

To Think Critically

1. How might your lifestyle influence your decorating choices in future years?
2. Name several places you can buy furniture. Discuss the advantages and disadvantages of each.
3. What are your furniture and decorating preferences?
4. What are some ways to save money when decorating and furnishing a home?
5. What are the important features to consider when choosing:
   Sleep furniture, Dual-purpose furniture, Case goods, Upholstered furniture, Major appliances, Consumer electronics.
6. When you place a rug or carpeting order, why is it important to have a

written copy of what you ordered?

7. What small appliances would you most like to have in your home that you don't own now? What small appliance would you find most difficult not to have? Why do you want or need these appliances? If you had them, how often would you use them? What home appliances and consumer electronic products would you consider absolute necessities in your first home?
8. What are some of the important safety practices to follow when using home appliances? in using consumer electronic equipment?
9. If you have a valid complaint about home appliances or electronics that you cannot settle with the seller or manufacturer, where can you go for help?

To Do

1. Find pictures in home furnishings magazines that show:
   Casual rooms, Formal settings, Dual-purpose furniture, First home choices.
2. Write a description of the furniture and decorating you would like for your first home or apartment. Include types and style of furniture, colors, and decorating touches.
3. Develop a plan for furnishing a one-bedroom apartment. Use 12-2 to help you organize your ideas on paper. Draw up a floor plan and furniture patterns to show space and furniture arrangements. In planning, consider the resources you have available and the color, style, and design of furnishings you like. Then visit furniture stores and retail outlets to determine how much money you would need to complete your furnishing plans. Itemize the expenses you would have and discuss possible ways to reduce home furnishings costs.
4. As an individual or class, arrange to visit a furniture buyer of a large department store or furniture store. Ask the buyer to explain and show quality construction features in different pieces of furniture. Find out how quality affects the life and price of furniture. Find out what influences the buyer's decisions and choices of what to buy and show in the store.
5. Develop consumer buying guides for one of the following:
   Case goods, Upholstered furniture, Carpets and rugs, Decorative accessories.
6. Compare features, energy efficiency, warranty coverage, servicing provisions, and prices of at least four models of one of the following major home appliances:
   Clothes washer, Dishwasher, Refrigerator/freezer, Room air-conditioner.

   Report to the class about which appliance you would choose for your home and why.
7. Compare features, functions, warranties, servicing provisions, and prices of four models of one of the following consumer electronic products:
   Personal computer, Printer/scanner, Fax machine, Answring machine, Sound system, Television/VCR.

   Report to the class about which electronic product you would choose for your own use and why.
8. Conduct a survey and report the results on the safety hazards created by the abuse, misuse, and carelessness in the use and care of a specific appliance or electronic product.
9. Research and write a report on significant developments in the consumer electronics industry since 1980.
10. Investigate and report on ways to dispose of appliances, electronics, and batteries that are no longer useful.

UNIT 5

T A SAFE PLACE FOR
ST VALUABLE ASSETS
REGISTERED
voids
DEPOSIT
ATM

Finance

Managing your credit, using financial institutions and services, making investments, and buying life insurance are ways you can achieve financial security. Achieving financial security requires lifetime planning.

With a solid base of savings and insurance, investments can help you accumulate more money. Another component of achieving financial security is learning to deal with crises by using prevention, preparation, and coping methods. Finding services of qualified legal and financial professionals to manage your affairs is another aspect of achieving financial security.

CHAPTER 13

Managing Credit

credit
repossession
sales credit
cash credit
unsecured loan
secured loan
cosigner
credit rating
credit report
grace period

After studying this chapter, you will be able to

- ❑ identify the different types of consumer credit.
- ❑ explain the advantages and disadvantages of using credit.
- ❑ describe how to establish a sound credit rating.
- ❑ define the key terms in credit contracts and agreements.
- ❑ summarize the laws that govern the use of credit.
- ❑ outline the steps involved in managing credit power.
- ❑ compare credit terms and charges.
- ❑ identify steps to take in resolving credit problems.

"Buy now, pay later" has become a way of life for many consumers in our economy. People who are good credit risks can charge almost anything. They can use credit for big expenses like vacations, college tuition, and cars. They also can charge meals, clothes, and gasoline for their cars. ***Credit*** is an arrangement that allows consumers to buy goods or services now and pay for them later.

Consumer credit not only serves individuals, it plays an important role in our economy. It provides the extra buying power needed to support mass production and distribution of goods and services. Therefore, credit helps make more goods and services available to consumers at lower prices.

Consumer credit can also help launch a new product. For example, when personal computers first hit the market, prices were high and sales were low. In 1981, around 750 thousand personal computers were being used in homes across the country. By 1991, the number had increased to almost 28 million. Approximately 50 million households are equipped with personal computers and about 40 million are online. Since 1980, personal computers improved dramatically. They became more powerful, efficient, and user-friendly. They were also smaller and less expensive. A vast array of software has been developed to enhance the use of personal computers both for serious purposes and for fun and games, 13-1.

Most buyers used some form of consumer credit to pay for their personal computers in the early 80s. The use of credit made it possible for more people to buy. The increased consumer demand supported mass production and distribution. This lowered unit production costs. Manufacturers passed on these savings to consumers in the form of lower prices. Growth in the computer industry also financed research and development. This continues to bring innovation and improvements to the computer and software industry.

Radio Shack

13-1
Educational software for computers makes learning fun.

Lower prices sparked even more sales. The industry grew rapidly, bringing exciting job opportunities. More people were hired to produce, sell, and service personal computers. New businesses emerged to produce, sell, and rent software and accessories for these computers.

In the case of personal computers, credit stimulated consumer demand and business growth. It helped maintain a healthy balance between supply and demand. Without consumer credit, the industry would have grown less rapidly. Prices would have stayed higher and sales lower. Fewer jobs would have been created and fewer people employed.

This example shows a positive side to consumer credit in the economy and in one industry. On the down side, excessive use of credit can throw the economy off balance and foster inflation. When consumers use credit to buy goods and services, it increases the demand for whatever they are buying. If the demand increases faster than the supply, prices will increase. When government and business join consumers in the excessive use of credit, demand surpasses supply and inflation results. The economy is weakened and fewer job opportunities exist.

Credit also plays an important role in personal economics. Used carefully and wisely, it can help people get more of the things they need when they need them. Misused credit can lead to financial disaster. It is important for your own financial well-being to learn how to manage your credit dollars.

Understanding Consumer Credit

Credit is a medium of exchange similar to cash but with a different time frame. In a cash transaction, you hand over money in exchange for goods or services. That's the end of it. With credit, you promise to pay later in exchange for goods or services now, but that's just the start. When you borrow now and pay later, the transaction is not complete until you pay.

Credit is the present use of future income. Consumer credit simply refers to the credit that consumers use for personal needs. This does not refer to credit used for business or for home mortgages. Consumer credit is based on trust. The credit grantor must believe the credit user can and will pay what is owed, 13-2. That trust applies to everything from a car loan to a small loan between friends.

For example, suppose you are eating out with friends. When the bill comes, you find you are short $2.50. You ask a friend to loan you $2.50. If your friend trusts you and can spare the money, you will be able to borrow the $2.50. Although a car loan is more complicated, it also depends on the creditor's trust in your ability and will to pay.

The Cost of Credit

When you borrow $2.50 from a friend, you probably repay the friend an even $2.50. If you charge purchases or borrow cash in the marketplace, you usually pay finance charges. You pay these charges because it costs businesses money to grant you credit.

> *"Creditors have better memories than debtors."*
>
> *Benjamin Franklin*

Whether you borrow cash or charge purchases, it costs creditors money to extend credit. The creditors who do not have cash on hand borrow the money they need to make credit available. When they borrow, they have to pay finance charges just like you. Creditors who do have cash on hand lose the chance to invest it when they use their money to give you credit. In a sense, they are investing in you and the interest you pay is their return on investment.

Creditors must also pay the costs of opening and servicing credit accounts. These costs include employees, facilities, and materials needed to check credit ratings of consumers, open accounts, send out bills, and record payments. When consumers fail to pay on time or in full, the creditors' costs go up. The expenses of collecting overdue debts and absorbing the losses of unpaid accounts add up quickly. As a result, the price of credit goes up for all consumers, even those who pay on time.

When you apply for credit, the actual amount of finance charges you pay depends primarily on three factors.

Club Med

13-2
Credit is based on trust. If you borrow to take a vacation, the lender trusts you to pay what you owe.

These factors are the amount of credit used, the annual percentage rate, and the length of the repayment period. Here's how these factors work to determine the cost of credit.

The Amount of Credit Used

The more you charge or borrow, the more interest you will pay. For example, the interest on a loan repaid in 12 monthly payments at an annual percentage rate of 18 percent would cost:

- $50.08 for a $500 loan.
- $110.01 for a $1,000 loan.
- $220.02 for a $2,000 loan.

The Annual Percentage Rate

The higher the rate of interest, the more you will pay in finance charges. For example, the interest on a $500 loan repaid in 12 monthly payments would cost:

- $50.08 at 18 percent.
- $58.72 at 21 percent.
- $67.36 at 24 percent.

The Length of the Repayment Period

The more time you take to repay the money you borrow, the more interest you will pay. For example, the interest on a $500 loan at 1.5 percent per month (18 percent per year) would cost:

- $50.08 if repaid in 12 monthly payments.
- $99.44 if repaid in 24 monthly payments.
- $150.88 if repaid in 36 monthly payments.

Any time you use credit, it is important to know how much it will cost and to compare finance charges. This is easy to do since creditors are required to tell you the cost of credit. Creditors must state finance charges as a *dollar amount* and as an *annual percentage rate.* For example, suppose you want to borrow $500 to repay in 12 monthly payments at a monthly rate of 1.5 percent. The creditor must state in writing the dollar cost of credit as $50.08 and the annual percentage rate as 18 percent.

Knowing the exact cost of credit can help you compare finance charges and find the best deal. It also helps you decide how much credit you can afford to use. You can decide if buying now and paying later is worth the extra cost.

Pros and Cons of Using Credit

What benefits can credit offer you? What risks does it present? You need to carefully weigh the advantages and disadvantages of having now and paying later. You will find it smart to use credit in some situations but not in others.

Several advantages and disadvantages of using credit are listed below. You may think of others, depending on the situations you face.

- *Advantage #1: The use of goods and services as you pay for them.* Being able to wear a coat or drive a car as you pay for it can be a big plus, 13-3. This is a common reason for using credit.
- *Advantage #2: The opportunity to buy costly items that you might not be able to buy with cash.* Many people find it difficult or impossible to save enough in advance to pay for a car, a vacation, education, or a big medical bill.
- *Advantage #3: A source of cash for emergency or unexpected expenses.* Even the best money managers can be thrown by the unexpected. Credit can offer temporary help, 13-4.
- *Advantage #4: Convenience.* Credit is the only practical way to pay for telephone and utility services. When used for shopping, credit eliminates the need to carry large amounts of cash. It provides a record of purchases. Also, it usually simplifies exchanges, returns, telephone orders, and mail orders.

13-3
Having the use of this truck while paying for it can be an advantage worth the cost of credit.

Ford Motor Company

To use credit wisely, you need to be aware of its drawbacks as well as its benefits. Consider the following negatives when you are deciding how and when to use credit.

- *Disadvantage #1: The reduction of future income.* By using credit, you spend future income and reduce the amount of money you will have to spend later.
- *Disadvantage #2: Expense.* Using credit usually costs money. The more credit you use and the more time you take to repay, the more you will pay in finance charges. This reduces the amount you will have to spend for other goods and services.
- *Disadvantage #3: Temptation.* Credit makes it easy to spend money you do not have. It can be difficult to resist buying what you cannot afford when you have ready credit.
- *Disadvantage #4: The risk of serious consequences if you misuse credit.* Failure to pay debts on time and in full can cause serious problems. You could go bankrupt. You could lose your right to obtain credit

13-4
Families recovering from flood or drought, from serious illness or accident, or from other major losses often need credit to get back on their feet.

USDA

from reputable creditors. Items bought with credit could be repossessed. ***Repossession*** is the process of a lender/creditor taking back an item because the borrower/buyer fails to pay for it.

Types of Consumer Credit

Sales credit and cash credit are the two basic types of consumer credit. You use ***sales credit*** when you buy goods and services with a credit card or a charge account. You use ***cash credit*** when you borrow money. Each type comes in different forms and from different sources to meet different consumer needs. Many credit cards can be used for both.

Sales Credit

Sales credit is granted by retailers and merchants who sell goods and services on credit. It is also granted by banks, credit agencies, and other businesses that issue credit cards to consumers. There are three basic forms of sales credit. They may differ slightly with different creditors and in different states.

The *regular charge account* lets you charge goods and services in exchange for your promise to pay in full within 25 days of the billing date. You receive a bill or statement each month. If you pay on time, there is no finance charge. This type of account generally is available from retailers.

The *installment account* lets you charge expensive items like furniture or a stereo system. You pay according to a set schedule of monthly payments. Finance charges usually range from 18 to 24 percent annually and are included in the repayment schedule. Normally, the creditor holds title to or "owns" the merchandise until you complete the payments. You usually sign a written contract for each purchase, and you may be asked to make a cash down payment. This too is generally available through retailers.

The *revolving credit account* offers you a choice of paying in full each month or spreading payments over a period of time. If you choose not to pay in full, there is a finance charge. This is usually 1.5 to 1.8 percent per month on the unpaid balance. You must make at least the minimum payment each month. For small balances, the minimum payment is usually a set amount, such as $10. For larger amounts of credit, the minimum payment is usually a percentage of the unpaid balance.

A typical revolving charge account places a limit on the amount you may owe at any one time. You may make any number of purchases at any time as long as you do not exceed your credit limit. This type of credit is available through many retailers and through issuers of credit cards, such as Visa, MasterCard, and Discover. The cards differ from the retailer's plan in that they are not limited to a single retail outlet. They can be used to buy a wide variety of goods and services from any seller who honors the card you carry.

Cash Credit

Cash credit is granted by financial institutions, such as commercial banks, savings and loan associations, credit unions, finance companies, insurance companies, and credit card agencies. Cash loans may be unsecured or secured.

Unsecured loans are made on the strength of your signature alone. You sign a contract and promise to repay according to terms of the agreement. It is difficult to obtain a loan of this type unless you have a strong credit rating.

A ***secured loan*** requires collateral. *Collateral* is a pledge of some kind of property. For an auto loan, the car serves as collateral. If you fail to pay as agreed, the creditor may take the property to settle the claim against you. You may pay lower finance charges on a secured loan because the creditor takes less risk when collateral is pledged.

If you have nothing to pledge as collateral, you still may be able to get a loan if you have a cosigner. A ***cosigner*** is a responsible person who signs the loan with you. By signing the loan, the cosigner promises to repay the loan if you fail to pay.

The three basic forms of cash credit are the installment loan, the single payment loan, and the credit card or check credit loan.

The *installment loan* lets you borrow a given amount of money and repay it with interest in regular monthly installments. The finance charges vary with the amount of the loan, the interest rate, and the length of the repayment period. The interest rate may vary depending on the lender and whether or not you pledge collateral.

The *single payment loan* lets you borrow a given amount of money and repay it in a single payment at a given time. The finance charges may be subtracted from the amount you borrow or added to the amount you repay. As a simple example, suppose you borrowed $100 for which you will owe $15 in finance charges. You might be given just $85 and have to repay $100; you might be given $100 and have to repay $115. Usually a single payment loan requires collateral. Finance charges vary with the size of the loan, the interest rate, and the repayment period. Interest rates vary with different lenders and with the collateral pledged.

A *credit card* or *check credit loan* lets you borrow up to a set amount by using your credit card or by writing a check the bank will cover. This type of cash credit involves an agreement between you and the lender on the amount you can borrow and the repayment plan. It works much like a revolving charge account. Finance charges on the unpaid balance normally run 1.5 to 1.8 percent per month.

Credit Cards

Credit cards are most often used to buy goods and services on time. Some may be used to obtain cash. There are three common types of credit cards: travel and entertainment cards, company or retail store cards, and general purpose cards issued by financial institutions, 13-5. Here's how they work.

Travel and entertainment cards, such as American Express and Diner's Club, generally have no credit limit, but you are expected to pay the entire bill each month except for travel- and vacation-related expenses such as air fare, tours, cruises, or hotel bills, which you can pay off over a longer period. On these balances, you pay interest of 18 percent or more and you must make minimum monthly payments.

Company or retail store cards, issued by service stations, local merchants, or chain stores, permit you to charge

Lynn Hellmuth

13-5
These credit cards can be used at all of the stores and outlets that accept them around the world.

purchases only with the merchant issuing the card. Normally, you have a credit limit and are required to repay a minimum amount each month. Credit charges vary.

General purpose cards, such as Visa or MasterCard, are issued by banks, credit unions, and other financial institutions. You can use these cards around the world at any of the many places where they are accepted. Very often, you can also obtain cash at automated teller machines using these cards. They carry a credit limit and require minimum monthly payments. Credit charges and other fees vary.

Here's how a typical credit card works. Valerie opens a revolving charge account at a local department store. She is issued a credit card. In May, she charges $85 on her credit card. This amount is more than she wants to pay in June when the bill comes. She decides to pay the minimum payment of $10. During June, she charges another $15 worth of merchandise.

In July, the bill totals $91.13. This includes the $75 unpaid balance from June, a 1.5 percent finance charge of $1.13, and $15 for new purchases. Now Valerie can continue to make minimum payments or pay her account in full.

Since Valerie's credit limit is $1,000, she can continue to charge merchandise until her unpaid balance reaches that limit. As her unpaid balance goes up, so will the minimum monthly payment and the finance charge.

Before accepting and using any of these cards, you need to know the interest rate charged on unpaid balances. This will be stated both as a monthly and an annual percentage rate (APR). The issuing companies often offer an attractive "introductory rate" that lasts only three to six months after which you pay the regular rate that usually is considerably higher. In this case, it is important to check how long the introductory rate lasts and what the regular rate is. You also need to know what fees are connected with the use of the card. These may include fees for late payments, for exceeding your credit limit, for cash advances, and even a fee just for receiving the card. It pays to shop around for the best credit card deal. You can compare cards, interest rates, fees, and features online as well as by contacting individual credit card issuers. Finally, if you use credit cards, it is important to keep track of your charges and control your credit spending. It can be easy to overspend when you use a credit card.

Lost or Stolen Cards

If a person's credit cards are lost or stolen, the law offers some protection. The cardholder is responsible for only $50 in charges per card if the cards are used by someone else. However, if a cardholder notifies the companies that issued the cards before someone else uses them, the cardholder cannot be held responsible for any charges. To protect yourself, report credit card thefts or losses as soon as possible by phone and follow up with a letter.

Establishing Credit

How do you get credit? You may find it difficult to get credit the first time you try. This is because creditors want evidence that you can and will pay your debts before they grant you credit.

Creditors decide whether or not to grant people credit based on their credit ratings. A ***credit rating*** is the creditor's evaluation of a person's willingness and ability to pay debts. It is measured by the three C's: character, capacity, and capital. *Character* is based on a person's reputation for honesty and financial history. The person who has a record of paying bills on time and of assuming financial responsibility will rate high on character. *Capacity* is a person's ability to earn money and pay debts. It is measured by a person's earning power and employment history. *Capital* is a person's financial worth. People with land, a home, cars, savings, or anything of value have capital. Capital gives a person a more favorable credit rating.

When you apply for credit, you will be asked to fill out a credit application form like the one in 13-6. This form helps creditors evaluate your financial standing and credit rating.

If you have never used credit, you will need to establish a credit rating from scratch. Here are some steps you can take to build a sound financial reputation.

1. Start with a job. Prove that you can hold a job and earn money.
2. Open a savings account and save regularly. A savings record shows a responsible attitude toward financial matters. Your savings also may serve as collateral for a loan.
3. Open a checking account and manage it carefully. A well-managed checking account shows you have experience in handling money.
4. Apply to a local department store or a gasoline company for a credit card. If you are granted credit, make small purchases. Then pay promptly when the bills come. This will give you a record of steady payments of debt.

Credit Reporting Agencies

Once you use credit, you automatically establish a credit record at the local credit reporting agency. These agencies, often called credit bureaus, keep records on individual consumers. Your ***credit report*** provides a history or record of whether you paid as agreed. Your file will tell about your income, employment history, financial worth, and record of paying debts. If you make late payments or fail to pay, this will be noted on your report.

The information in credit records is valuable to companies who grant credit. Your credit report largely determines whether or not you can get credit when you need it. With a poor report, you will have trouble getting credit and may have to pay higher finance charges.

To maintain a sound credit rating:

- ❑ Use only as much credit as you can comfortably repay.
- ❑ Meet all the terms of credit contracts and agreements.
- ❑ Pay bills on time.
- ❑ Keep accurate records of charges, statements, and payments.
- ❑ Consult creditors immediately if you cannot pay on time.
- ❑ Resolve billing errors promptly.

Credit Contracts and Agreements

Using credit involves certain responsibilities for you and the creditor. These are spelled out in credit contracts and agreements, 13-7. The terms outlined in a written agreement are legally binding. They can be enforced in courts of law if you or the creditor fail to carry out the terms of the contract. It is very important to understand exactly what you are agreeing to do before you sign any contract.

Read the contract thoroughly. Be sure all blank spaces have been filled. Nothing should be left open to fill in later. Make sure the annual percentage rate and the dollar cost are stated clearly and accurately.

Study the contract to find out what action the creditor can take if you pay late or fail to make a payment. Also find out if you can pay in advance. If so, check to see if part of the finance charges will be refunded.

The monthly statement is another form you need to study and understand, 13-8. It pays to check the statement each month against your own record and memory of charges, payments, and credits. In addition to the date, amount, number, and description of each purchase, credit, and payment, the monthly statement should tell you:

- ❏ The date on which payments are due.

BELK CREDIT APPLICATION

EMPLOYEE NO. | DATE

I WANT ☐ REVOLVING ☐ 30-60-90 ☐ BOTH

Type of Account Requested: ☐ INDIVIDUAL ☐ JOINT

PLEASE TELL US ABOUT YOURSELF

FIRST NAME (TITLES OPTIONAL)	MIDDLE INITIAL	LAST NAME		AGE
STREET ADDRESS (IF P.O. BOX — PLEASE GIVE STREET ADDRESS)	CITY	STATE	ZIP	

☐ OWN ☐ LIVE WITH RELATIVE ☐ RENT ☐ OTHER | MONTHLY PAYMENT $ | YEARS AT PRESENT ADDRESS | HOME PHONE NO. ( ) | NO. OF DEPENDENTS

PREVIOUS ADDRESS | CITY | STATE | ZIP | HOW LONG

NAME OF NEAREST RELATIVE NOT LIVING WITH YOU | RELATIONSHIP | PHONE NO. ( )

ADDRESS | CITY | STATE

NOW TELL US ABOUT YOUR JOB

EMPLOYER OR INCOME SOURCE | POSITION/TITLE | HOW LONG EMPLOYED YRS. MOS. | MONTHLY INCOME $

EMPLOYER'S ADDRESS | CITY | STATE | TYPE OF BUSINESS | BUSINESS PHONE ( )

MILITARY RANK (IF NOW IN SERVICE) | SEPARATION DATE | UNIT AND DUTY STATION | SOCIAL SECURITY NO.

SOURCE OF OTHER INCOME (Alimony, child support, or separate maintenance need not be revealed if you do not wish to have it considered as a basis for repaying this obligation) | SOURCE | INCOME $ | ☐ MONTHLY ☐ ANNUALLY

AND YOUR CREDIT REFERENCES ARE

NAME AND ADDRESS OF BANK/SAVINGS AND LOAN ☐ CHECKING ☐ SAVINGS ☐ LOAN | PREVIOUS BELK OR LEGGETT ACCOUNT? ☐ YES ☐ NO ACCOUNT NO. HOW IS ACCOUNT LISTED?

List Bank cards, Dept. Stores, Finance Co.'s, and other accounts:	NAME	ACCOUNT NO.	BALANCE	PAYMENT
			$	$
			$	$
			$	$
			$	$

INFORMATION REGARDING JOINT APPLICANT

COMPLETE THIS AREA IF ☐ JOINT ACCOUNT IS REQUESTED ☐ YOU ARE RELYING ON SPOUSE'S INCOME OR CREDIT HISTORY TO OBTAIN CREDIT

FIRST NAME | MIDDLE INITIAL | LAST NAME | AGE | RELATIONSHIP | SOCIAL SECURITY NO.

JOINT APPLICANT'S ADDRESS IF DIFFERENT FROM APPLICANT ADDRESS | CITY | STATE | ZIP

JOINT APPLICANT'S PRESENT EMPLOYER | ADDRESS | HOW LONG EMPLOYED YRS. MOS.

BUSINESS PHONE ( ) | POSITION/TITLE | MONTHLY INCOME $

YOUR SIGNATURE PLEASE Store Stamp Below

I have read and agree to the Terms and Conditions of the Belk Retail Charge Agreement as set forth on attached. Belk is authorized to investigate my credit record and exchange credit experience with other creditors and Credit Reporting Agencies. This information is given to obtain credit, and is true and complete.

Applicant's Signature — Date

Joint Applicant's signature (required if joint applicant section completed) — Date

FOR OFFICE USE ONLY
Letter ______
CB. RPT. ______
EMP. VER ______

DATE | EMP. | #CARDS | T/C | CR/LN. | APPROVED

13-6
This application form helps creditors evaluate your credit worthiness. Note the questions that appear on the form.

KEEP THIS NOTICE FOR FUTURE USE

BELK RETAIL CHARGE AGREEMENT

1. Each time I receive the monthly statement (at about the same time each month) I will decide whether to pay the New Balance of the account in full or in part. If full payment of the New Balance shown on the statement is received, by BELK, by the Payment Due Date, No **FINANCE CHARGE** will be added to the account. Any month I choose not to pay the New Balance in full, I will make at least the minimum partial payment listed on the statement as Minimum Payment Now Due. Each month the Minimum Payment Due will be calculated according to the following schedule:

If New Balance Is	Less Than $10	$10-100	$101-150	$151-200	$201-250	$251-300	Over $300
Minimum Monthly Payment Is	Balance	$10	$15	$20	$25	$30	1/10 of account balance rounded to next highest $5 increment

2. If payment in full is not received by the Payment Due Date, I agree to pay a **FINANCE CHARGE** at the rate described below for my State of residence.

Annual Percentage Rate for Purchases	10% to 21% (see table below)		
State of Residence	Periodic Rate	Annual Percentage Rate	Portion of Average Daily Balance To Which Applied
DE., KY., VA., MS., GA., OK., MD.	1.75%	21%	ENTIRE
NC., PA., TN., FL., TX and all other states	1.50%	18%	ENTIRE
AL.	1.75%	21%	$750 or less
	1.5%	18%	over $750
WV.	1.5%	18%	$750 or less
	1.0%	12%	over $750
SC.	1.75%	21%	$650 or less
	1.5%	18%	over $650
MO.	1.5%	18%	$1,000 or less
	1.0%	12%	over $1,000
AR.	.083%	10%	ENTIRE
Grace Period:	You have until the next billing date which on average is 23 days if the balance is paid in full, before a finance charge will be imposed.		
Method of Computing the Average Daily Balance.	Average Daily Balance Method: We figure a portion of the finance charge on your account by applying the periodic rate to the "average daily balance" of your account (including current transactions). To get the "average daily balance", we take the beginning balance of your account each day, add any new purchases and subtract any payments or credits, and unpaid finance charges. This gives us the daily balance. Then, we add up all the daily balances for the billing cycle and divide the total by the number of days in the billing cycle. This gives us the "average daily balance".		

3. Credit for returned merchandise will not substitute for a payment.

4. BELK has the right to amend the terms and conditions of this agreement by advising me of its intentions to do so in a manner and to the extent required by law.

5. If any payment is not received by BELK by the Payment Due Date, the full unpaid balance of the account may, at the option of Belk, become due and payable. If the account is referred for collection by Belk to any outside agency and/or attorney, who is not a salaried employee of BELK, I will, to the extent permitted by law, pay all costs including attorney fees.

6. BELK reserves the right to charge a handling fee, not to exceed the amount permitted by law, on any check used for payment on the account that is returned by the bank for insufficient funds or otherwise unpaid.

7. If this is a joint account, both of us agree to be bound by the terms of this agreement and each of us agrees to be jointly and severally liable for payment of all purchases made under this agreement.

8. The credit card issued to me in connection with this account remains the property of BELK and I will surrender it upon request. I understand that BELK is not obligated to extend to me any credit and, without prior notice, may refuse to allow me to make any purchase or incur any other charge on my account. Such refusal will not affect my obligation to pay the balance existing on my account at the time.

9. If any provision of this agreement is found to be invalid or unenforceable, the remainder of this agreement shall not be affected thereby, and the rest of this agreement shall be valid and enforced to the fullest extent permitted by law. No delay, omission, or waiver in the enforcement of any provision of this agreement by BELK will be deemed to be a waiver of any subsequent breach of such provision or of any other provision of this agreement.

10. I hereby authorize BELK, or any credit bureau employed by BELK, to investigate references, statements, and other data contained on my application or obtained from me or any other source pertaining to my credit worthiness. I will furnish further information if requested. I authorize BELK to furnish information concerning its credit experience with me to credit reporting agencies and others who may lawfully receive such information.

11. Except as provided in paragraph 2 above, this agreement will be governed by the laws of the State of North Carolina.

13-7
This agreement spells out the rights and responsibilities of credit granter and credit user.

- ❑ The minimum payment due.
- ❑ The new balance.
- ❑ The previous balance.
- ❑ The total amount of new purchases, fees, and advances.
- ❑ The finance charges as a dollar amount, as well as the periodic and corresponding annual percentage rate.
- ❑ The total amount of payments and credits.
- ❑ The total amount of credit available on the account.

Consumer Credit Legislation

Over the years a number of federal laws have been passed to protect consumers when they use credit. The key points of the most important credit legislation are outlined in the following sections.

Truth in Lending Law

The Truth in Lending Law, passed in 1969, requires creditors to tell consumers what credit will cost them before they use it. Under this law, credit contracts and agreements must include:

- ❑ The amount financed or borrowed.
- ❑ The total number, amount, and due dates of payments.

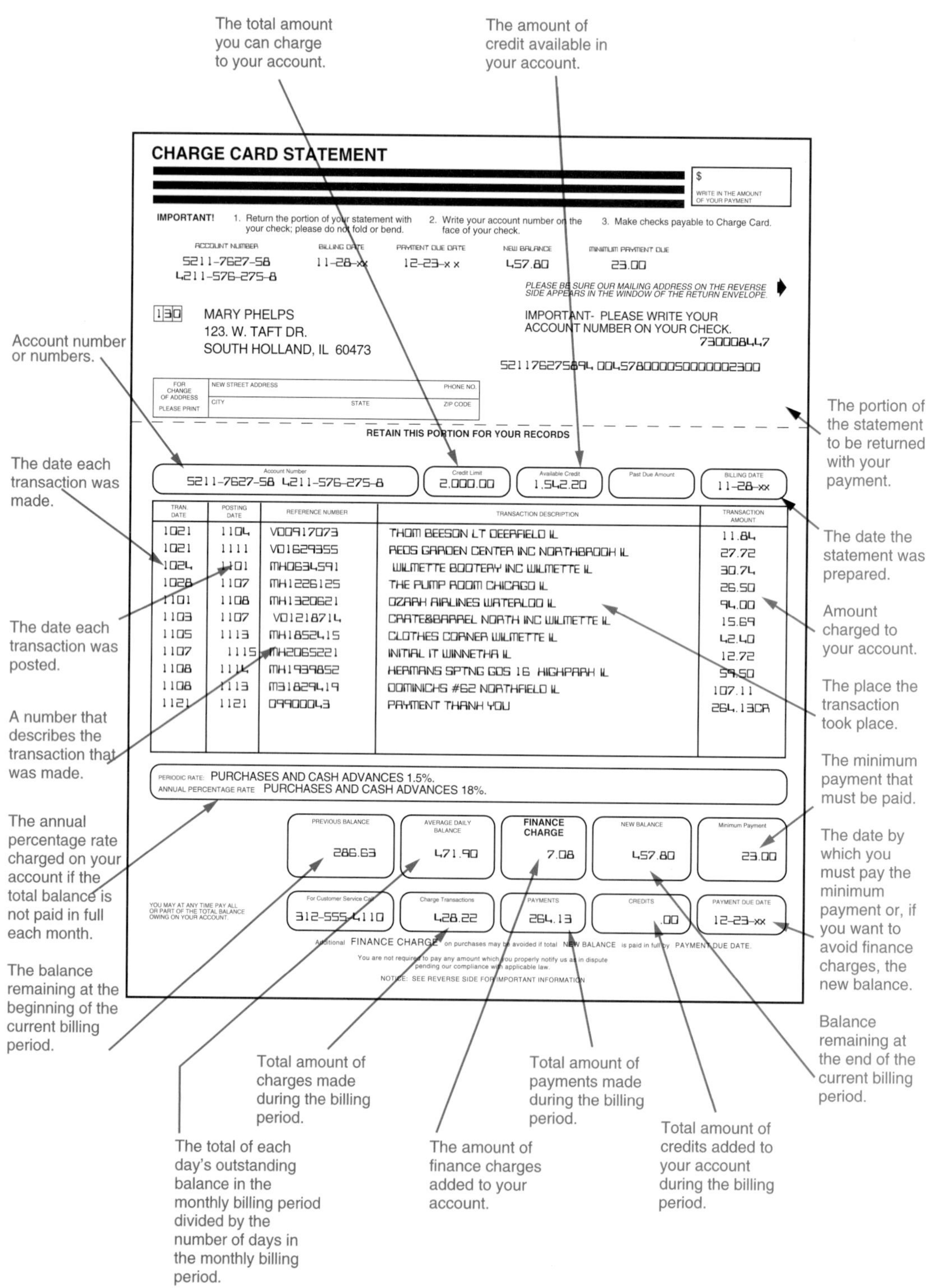

CHARGE CARD STATEMENT

$ WRITE IN THE AMOUNT OF YOUR PAYMENT

IMPORTANT! 1. Return the portion of your statement with your check; please do not fold or bend. 2. Write your account number on the face of your check. 3. Make checks payable to Charge Card.

ACCOUNT NUMBER	BILLING DATE	PAYMENT DUE DATE	NEW BALANCE	MINIMUM PAYMENT DUE
5211-7627-58 4211-576-275-8	11-28-xx	12-23-x x	457.80	23.00

PLEASE BE SURE OUR MAILING ADDRESS ON THE REVERSE SIDE APPEARS IN THE WINDOW OF THE RETURN ENVELOPE.

130 MARY PHELPS
123. W. TAFT DR.
SOUTH HOLLAND, IL 60473

IMPORTANT- PLEASE WRITE YOUR ACCOUNT NUMBER ON YOUR CHECK.
73000847

521176275894 00457800005000002300

FOR CHANGE OF ADDRESS PLEASE PRINT: NEW STREET ADDRESS / PHONE NO. / CITY / STATE / ZIP CODE

RETAIN THIS PORTION FOR YOUR RECORDS

Account Number	Credit Limit	Available Credit	Past Due Amount	BILLING DATE
5211-7627-58 4211-576-275-8	2.000.00	1.542.20		11-28-xx

TRAN. DATE	POSTING DATE	REFERENCE NUMBER	TRANSACTION DESCRIPTION	TRANSACTION AMOUNT
1021	1104	V00917073	THOM BEESON LT DEERFIELD IL	11.84
1021	1111	V01629355	REDS GARDEN CENTER INC NORTHBROOK IL	27.72
1024	1101	MK0634591	WILMETTE BOOTERY INC WILMETTE IL	30.74
1028	1107	MK1226125	THE PUMP ROOM CHICAGO IL	26.50
1101	1108	MK1320621	OZARK AIRLINES WATERLOO IL	94.00
1103	1107	V01218714	CRATE&BARREL NORTH INC WILMETTE IL	15.69
1105	1113	MK1852415	CLOTHES CORNER WILMETTE IL	42.40
1107	1115	MK2065221	INITIAL IT WINNETKA IL	12.72
1108	1114	MK1939852	HERMANS SPTNG GDS 16 HIGHPARK IL	59.50
1108	1113	M31829419	DOMINICKS #62 NORTHFIELD IL	107.11
1121	1121	09900043	PAYMENT THANK YOU	264.13CR

PERIODIC RATE: PURCHASES AND CASH ADVANCES 1.5%.
ANNUAL PERCENTAGE RATE PURCHASES AND CASH ADVANCES 18%.

PREVIOUS BALANCE	AVERAGE DAILY BALANCE	FINANCE CHARGE	NEW BALANCE	Minimum Payment
286.63	471.90	7.08	457.80	23.00

YOU MAY AT ANY TIME PAY ALL OR PART OF THE TOTAL BALANCE OWING ON YOUR ACCOUNT.

For Customer Service Call	Charge Transactions	PAYMENTS	CREDITS	PAYMENT DUE DATE
312-555-4110	428.22	264.13	.00	12-23-xx

Additional FINANCE CHARGE on purchases may be avoided if total NEW BALANCE is paid in full by PAYMENT DUE DATE.

You are not required to pay any amount which you properly notify us as in dispute pending our compliance with applicable law.

NOTICE: SEE REVERSE SIDE FOR IMPORTANT INFORMATION

13-8
This statement explains the information you will find on monthly credit card bills.

- The finance charge in dollar amount and annual percentage rate.
- All charges not included in the finance charge.
- Penalties or charges for late payment, default, or prepayment.
- A description of any security held by the creditor.

For merchandise purchased on time, creditors must provide additional information. This includes a description of the merchandise, the cash price and the deferred payment price, and the down payment or trade-in. The Truth in Lending Law also prohibits creditors from issuing unrequested credit cards.

Equal Credit Opportunity Act

The Equal Credit Opportunity Act, passed in 1975, prohibits credit granters from discriminating on the basis of sex, marital status, race, national origin, religion, age, or the receipt of public assistance. This means credit can be denied only for financial reasons, and not for any of the factors listed above. When applicants are turned down, creditors must provide a written explanation of why credit was denied.

Fair Credit Reporting Act

Passed in 1971 and revised in 1977, the Fair Credit Reporting Act requires accuracy and privacy of information contained in credit reports. If a person is refused credit because of information supplied by a credit reporting agency, this law gives the applicant the right to:

- Receive the name and address of the credit bureau or reporting agency that sent the report.
- Find out from the reporting agency what facts are on file, the source of the information, and who has received the information.
- Require a recheck of any information the applicant says is false.
- Receive a corrected report if errors are found.
- Require the agency to send the corrected report to all creditors who received false information.

Fair Credit Billing Act

The Fair Credit Billing Act, passed in 1975, protects consumers against unfair billing practices. It outlines the procedures to follow in resolving billing errors or disputes. The law requires creditors to send customers a written explanation of steps to take when questions arise concerning bills. The customer has 60 days after receiving a bill to notify the creditor of an error. The creditor must answer within 30 days. Within 90 days, the creditor must either correct the bill or explain if it is accurate. Creditors may take no collection action on amounts in question until billing disputes are resolved. However, the customer must pay any amount not in question.

Electronic Funds Transfer Act

Electronic Funds Transfer (EFT) systems use electronic impulses to activate financial transactions instead of cash, checks, or paper records. The Electronic Fund Transfer Act protects consumers in these transactions by:

- Prohibiting the distribution of unrequested EFT cards. You receive a card only if you ask for it.
- Requiring issuers of EFT cards to provide cardholders with written information outlining their rights and responsibilities for the card and its use.
- Limiting to $50 the liability for unauthorized transfer. The cardholder must notify the issuer of card loss or misuse within two business days.

- Requiring issuers to provide cardholders with printed receipts of EFT transactions.
- Requiring issuers to promptly investigate and correct EFT errors.

Fair Debt Collection Practices Act

Passed in 1978, the Fair Debt Collection Practices Act protects consumers against unfair methods of collecting debts. According to this law, debt collectors may not:

- Reveal or publicize a debtor's debt to other people.
- Contact debtors at inconvenient times (before 8:00 a.m. or after 9:00 p.m.) or places (such as work).
- Use threats or abusive language.
- Make annoying, repeated, or anonymous phone calls.
- Make false or misleading statements about the collector's identity or the consequences of nonpayment.
- Collect unauthorized fees or charge debtors for calls and telegrams.

Preservation of Consumers' Claims and Defenses Ruling

The Preservation of Consumers' Claims and Defenses Ruling was issued by the Federal Trade Commission. It protects debtors from being forced to pay for goods and services when they have a legitimate dispute with the seller of those goods or services.

> *"Money is a terrible master but an excellent servant."*
>
> *P. T. Barnum*

This applies when a retailer sells consumer credit obligations or contracts to a third party creditor. The consumer then owes the third party. If the goods or services purchased with credit are unsatisfactory, the debtor still owes the third party rather than the seller. For this reason, the seller does not feel obligated to correct any problems with the goods or services.

This ruling greatly limits the "holder-in-due-course doctrine." That doctrine says the holder of a consumer contract has a right to collect a debt regardless of any unfair practices on the part of the seller.

Here is an example to show how the rule protects you. Suppose you buy a $500 color TV from the Viewing Center. You sign an installment contract calling for 18 monthly payments. The Viewing Center offers credit through a sales finance company. Therefore, you owe the finance company rather than the seller.

After the television is delivered, you find that it does not work. You can get sound but no picture. When you complain, the seller refuses to correct the problem. You threaten nonpayment. The seller says that's not the Viewing Center's problem because you owe the finance company.

You complain to the finance company, but they tell you the television is the seller's responsibility. Legally, you owe the finance company regardless of the seller's performance.

The Preservation of Consumers' Claims and Defenses Ruling protects you in this type of situation. Under the ruling, you have a right to a legal defense in court if you refuse to pay a creditor because you have a dispute with a seller.

Managing Your Credit

Credit can make it possible for you to spend more than you earn—temporarily. With careful planning, credit can help you get more of the things you want when you want them.

Without planning, credit can create serious, long-lasting financial and legal problems. To make the most of your credit power, you need to know when to use credit and how to compare credit terms and charges.

When to Use Credit

A close look at your financial personality can help you decide when and if you can use credit safely. Your financial personality is a combination of your attitudes about money and your spending patterns. You express your financial personality by the way you handle cash and credit.

Financial personalities vary greatly. Some people spend money freely. Others find it hard to part with a dollar. Some think through each purchase while others buy on impulse. What are your money attitudes and habits? If you can answer "yes" to most of the questions in the next paragraph, credit probably will be a safe tool for you to use.

Do you find it easy to control spending? Do you save regularly? Do you follow a spending plan? Do you consider purchases carefully, particularly major purchases? Do you pay debts promptly? Do you buy only what you can afford? Do you make long-range financial plans? Do you handle financial matters with confidence? Do you see credit as a tool to use with care and caution?

People use credit for many different reasons. Here are some reasons that make good financial sense:

- To buy expensive items you need right away, such as a car or a major appliance.
- To take advantage of sale prices on goods or services you need when you don't have enough cash at sale time.
- To make a purchase that is part of a long-range financial plan, such as paying for education, furniture, or a vacation, 13-9.
- To deal with emergency needs or temporary cash shortages.

Club Med

13-9
Taking a scuba trip with your friends may be worth the cost of borrowing.

Consumers may also use credit for the wrong reasons. Here are some credit uses that can lead to financial problems:

- Buying on time what you really cannot afford.
- Buying what you could easily do without or postpone.
- Charging something you either would not or could not buy with cash.
- Living beyond your income.

> *"What some people mistake for the high cost of living is actually the cost of living high."*
>
> ***Doug Larson***

Alternatives to Using Credit

Usually you have three alternatives to using credit. You may choose not to buy. You may pay with your savings. You may also postpone buying, save your money, and buy later with cash. The choice you make will depend on what you want to buy and what you want to achieve with your cash and your credit. Here are some questions to help you evaluate your choices.

How important is it for you to make the purchase? If you can do without something, you might be wise not to buy it. Having what you want when you want it is not always worth the extra price you pay for credit.

Are you willing to use all or some of your savings to buy now? Unless you have planned to use money you have saved to make the purchase, reducing or eliminating your savings could be risky. Often it is difficult to replace the savings you use for unplanned purchases. Using your savings may leave you unprepared for unexpected emergencies or financial difficulties.

Can you save your money and buy later? This will depend on how long you can wait to make the purchase. It will also depend on your ability to save money. Many people find it easier to make monthly credit payments than to put money in savings.

By waiting and saving, you may miss the satisfaction or pleasure of having what you want now. For example, suppose you want to take a vacation with friends. They are leaving next month for a week at an ocean resort. According to your savings plan, you need three more months to save enough money for the trip. If you wait three months, you won't be able to share the vacation with your friends. In this case, you may decide to use credit to help you finance the vacation.

On the other hand, waiting may help you get more satisfaction from a purchase. Suppose you want to buy a pool table. You want it now, but you don't have enough money. You also aren't sure what type of pool table you want. You decide to wait and save. As you are saving, you do some comparison shopping. You find out what features you want and where you can get the best deal. When you finally buy the pool table, your satisfaction is greater than if you had rushed out to buy it immediately with credit. The waiting period made the purchase more valuable to you.

Shopping for Credit

Shopping for credit is as important as shopping for the goods and services you buy with it. The case study about Ed's experience shows you why.

When you want to borrow cash or use credit to finance a purchase, shop around for the best credit terms. Three factors that affect how much you will pay for credit are: the amount of credit you use, the annual percentage rate, and the length of time you take to repay. The more you borrow, the more you pay. The higher the annual percentage rate, the more you pay. The longer you take to repay, the more you pay in credit charges.

When using credit to buy merchandise, you also want to compare the price of your purchase at different stores and outlets. Compare the total cost of the purchase including the finance charges. Sellers with low prices on merchandise can more than make up the difference with high finance charges.

Other important factors to consider include:

- ❑ Dollar cost of credit.
- ❑ Down payment requirements.
- ❑ Amount, number, and due dates of monthly payments.
- ❑ Collateral required, if any.
- ❑ Charges for late payment.
- ❑ Penalties or rebates for prepayment.
- ❑ Reputation of the creditor.
- ❑ Ease and speed of obtaining credit.

If you are shopping for and using credit cards or other forms of revolving

Shopping for Credit: *Ed's "Deal"*

Ed wanted to buy a motorcycle. Since this was going to be his first big purchase, Ed was determined to find the best bike at the best price. He had already saved enough money for a down payment. He planned to pay the rest by the month.

Ed shopped at every cycle shop in the area and investigated the want ads in local newspapers. In a few weeks, Ed decided what model he wanted. Then he went to the dealer who had offered him the lowest price for that model. Ed paid the down payment, and the dealer started figuring the monthly payments and credit terms. Here's how the deal looked on paper.

Cash price of the motorcycle:	$2,250.00
Down payment:	250.00
Amount financed:	2,000.00
Finance charge:	312.48
Monthly payment for 24 months:	96.35
Total paid:	$2,562.40
Annual percentage rate:	15 percent

Ed had not expected the credit to cost so much, but he did get a good price on the bike. He rode away on his new bike feeling great until he ran into his friend Tammy. As Tammy admired the new cycle, she asked Ed where he bought it. Ed told her what a good deal he had gotten. When Ed mentioned the credit charges, Tammy shook her head.

Tammy had learned all about credit the year before when she bought a used car. She explained to Ed how credit charges differ from lender to lender. She told him that the credit charges might have been much lower at other places. She certainly was right. The chart below shows the credit charges from three other credit sources for a $2,000 loan financed over a 24-month period. Failing to shop for credit was an expensive lesson for Ed. He could have saved over $145 with a different lender.

Case Review

1. What should Ed have done before financing through the seller of the motorcycle?
2. How much money could Ed have saved by financing at a 10 percent annual rate?
3. How many months would you take to pay off a loan of this type? How would this affect your finance charges?
4. How much time would you be willing to spend looking for the best loan terms?
5. How would you have handled Ed's situation differently?

Comparing Credit Sources for Ed's Purchase

$2,000 Financed for 24 Months			
	Source 1	Source 2	Source 3
Annual Rate	8 percent	10 percent	12 percent
Monthly Payment	$ 90.28	$ 92.01	$ 93.75
Total Payments (monthly x 24)	$2,166.72	$2,208.24	$2,250.00
Down Payment	$ 250.00	$ 250.00	$ 250.00
Total Paid	$2,416.72	$2,458.24	$2,500.00
Finance Charges (total payments less $2,000)	$ 166.72	$ 208.24	$ 250.00

credit, here are important considerations. Find out whether you must pay an annual fee for the privilege of using the card. A few banks make credit cards available without annual fees; others charge from $20 to as high as $60 each year.

Check the annual percentage rate charged on unpaid balances. This can vary greatly among the financial institutions offering credit cards. Find out whether the credit card offers a ***grace period***. This is a period between the date of a purchase and the date interest charges begin. You have that many days to pay the amount due interest-free. In a few states, a grace period is mandatory on any new charges made each month. Interest may only be figured on outstanding balances from the prior month. There are no interest charges on credit card balances that are paid in full by the due date each month.

Transaction fees and other charges can also add to the cost of using credit cards. Find out about any charges for using the card to obtain cash, for late payments, or for exceeding the credit limit on the card. Ask if there is a flat monthly fee whether or not you use the card.

Finally, it is important to understand how interest is calculated. If you pay less than the full amount owed each month, you will pay interest on the unpaid balance. Most likely, you will also be charged interest on new purchases you make during the next month. Creditors compute interest charges in different ways. Their methods can result in very different actual finance charges, 13-10.

You need to read the fine print on credit agreements and monthly statements to learn what methods are used to calculate interest. Creditors are required by law to provide an explanation of how they determine interest charges. As you read, look to

Interest will be calculated in one of the following ways:

❏ **On the average daily balance including new purchases.**

The card issuer totals the beginning balance for each day in the billing period. Any payments or credits on the account and any purchases made are included on the day they are received. The resulting daily balances are totaled and divided by the number of days in the billing period to determine the average daily balance.

❏ **On the average daily balance not including new purchases.**

This method is the same as above except that new purchases are not added to arrive at the average daily balance.

❏ **On a two-cycle average daily balance.**

Figuring on balances owed over a two-month billing period means that you may end up paying interest charges on purchases from the previous statement that you may have paid off immediately. This method can result in higher interest charges.

❏ **On the adjusted balance.**

This balance is figured by subtracting payments and credits during the present billing period from the balance owed at the end of the previous billing period. The credit balance on which you pay interest does not include new purchases. You have until the end of the billing cycle to pay part or all of your balance and avoid interest charges on the amount paid.

❏ **On the previous balance.**

This is the amount you owed at the end of the previous billing period. It does not include payments, credits, or new purchases made during the current billing period.

13-10
Actual finance charges can vary depending on the method used to calculate interest.

see if there are penalties or fees for late payment, for exceeding the credit limit on your account, or for using your card to get cash advances. Extra charges can add up to a significant amount. It pays to know what extras can be charged to your account and how you can avoid these charges.

Credit Problems

Used unwisely, credit can lead to serious financial difficulties. Since many credit problems result from poor money management, the development of good management skills outlined in Chapter Five can help you avoid serious credit problems.

The quicker you realize you are having financial problems, the quicker and easier it will be to correct them. Chart 13-11 lists some of the danger signals that warn credit users of trouble ahead. It pays to tackle these problems before they get out of hand or beyond control.

If you have trouble paying your bills, notify creditors promptly. Many reputable creditors will work with you to set up a repayment program you can handle. They may be willing to extend your repayment schedules to decrease the size of your monthly payments. Of course this will cost you more in credit charges in the long run, but it may help you get through a difficult period.

Not all creditors will be cooperative in delaying payments or extending repayment periods. When you are in deep financial trouble that you cannot work out with individual creditors, you may need to consider a debt consolidation loan. This is one loan large enough to pay existing debts. It is written with a long repayment schedule and reduces the amount of monthly payments.

With a sound financial spending and savings plan, some people can correct their own financial problems. However, when financial problems get out of control, it is time to look for outside help. Following are some possible options. Be cautious of "credit doctors" and for-profit credit repair clinics that promise to fix your credit rating for a fee. These companies promise what no one can deliver. Read on for more reliable options.

> *"Money has wings."*
>
> *French Proverb*

Credit Counseling

One source of help for people with credit problems is a Consumer Credit Counseling Service. The National Foundation for Consumer Credit sponsors several hundred credit

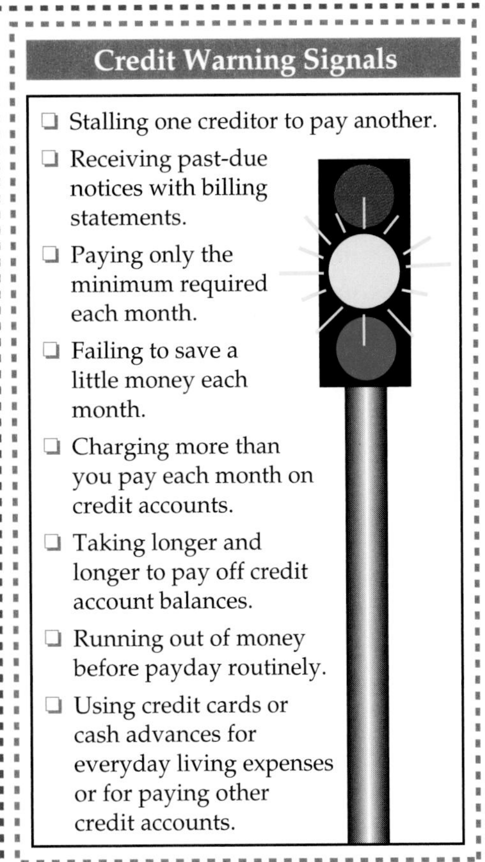

13-11
Beware of these warning signals when using credit.

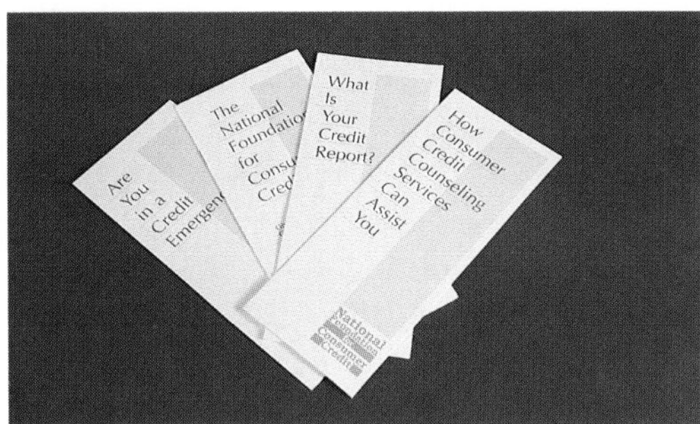

National Foundation for Consumer Credit / Jack Klasey

13-12
Consumer Credit Counseling Services can help you manage your money and handle credit wisely.

counseling services throughout the United States and Canada, 13-12. These nonprofit organizations advise and help debt-troubled individuals and families. The credit counseling services, with the support of local merchants and financial institutions, offer aid in two forms.

The service helps a debtor with a stable income work out a practical financial program for repaying debts. The service also helps the debtor plan and control current expenses to avoid further debts.

When debtors are very deep in debt, the counseling service offers another alternative. It tries to arrange new repayment plans with creditors. If creditors agree, the debtor gives the counseling service a set amount from each paycheck, and the service pays the creditors.

Credit counseling services of this type help about five out of every six applicants. Debtors pay little or nothing for the help they receive. These nonprofit credit counseling services should not be confused with debt pooling or debt adjusting businesses that charge high fees. To locate the nearest Consumer Credit Counseling Service, look in the white pages of the local telephone book.

Bankruptcy

When financial circumstances are desperate, some debtors have little choice but to go bankrupt. The *Bankruptcy Act* allows debtors to file "Chapter 7" or "Chapter 13" bankruptcy.

With *Chapter 7* bankruptcy, the court declares the person unable to meet financial obligations. This is also referred to as straight bankruptcy. The court then takes and sells the debtor's property and possessions. Proceeds from the sale are divided among the creditors. Certain assets and possessions are exempted by law. These include a small equity in a home, an inexpensive car, and limited personal property. The debtor then stands free and clear of debt.

Once a debtor files a petition for straight bankruptcy, that petition becomes part of the debtor's credit record. People who have declared bankruptcy may find it difficult to obtain credit in the future.

Chapter 13 of the Bankruptcy Act offers an alternative to straight bankruptcy. This plan permits debtors with regular incomes to pay all or a portion of their debts under the protection and supervision of the court. The court sets up a three- to five-year repayment schedule. It also establishes the monthly amount to be paid toward debts. Once the debtor's petition is accepted by the court, creditors may not take action against the debtor.

Filing under Chapter 13 has three advantages over straight bankruptcy. The debtor fulfills credit obligations, keeps most of his or her own property and possessions, and maintains a reasonably sound credit rating.

Summary

When you shop for credit carefully and use it wisely, you can usually avoid credit problems. Here are 12 pointers to guide you in your use of credit.

- ❑ Deal only with reputable creditors.
- ❑ Read credit contracts and agreements before signing. Sign only when you are sure you understand and can fulfill all terms and obligations.
- ❑ Try to pay off balances on revolving charge accounts each month to avoid finance charges.
- ❑ Establish your credit limit and do not exceed it.
- ❑ Keep complete and accurate records of credit purchases and transactions. Keep receipts, monthly statements, payments, contract agreements, inquiries, and correspondence.
- ❑ Report and correct billing errors promptly.
- ❑ Protect your credit rating by paying promptly and fulfilling your obligations as stated in credit contracts.
- ❑ Shop for the best credit deals just as you shop for the best prices for goods and services.
- ❑ Notify creditors without delay if you cannot pay as agreed. Try to work out an arrangement with creditors for fulfilling your obligations.
- ❑ Report lost or stolen credit cards immediately by phone and follow up with a letter. Keep a handy list of credit cards, their numbers, issuers, and phone numbers so you can act quickly.
- ❑ Prevent fraudulent use of your credit cards. Destroy carbons of receipts you sign and do not give your account number to an unknown caller.
- ❑ Know your rights and responsibilities when using credit. Keep up with consumer legislation that may change your legal rights.

To Review

1. How does a credit transaction differ from a cash transaction?
2. What costs are involved in granting credit?
3. What three factors determine the amount you pay in finance charges?
4. How are creditors required to state finance charges to consumers?
5. What are the two basic types of consumer credit? How are they used?
6. Name the three basic forms of sales credit and the three basic forms of cash credit.
7. What steps can you take to build a sound credit rating?
8. What is the function of a credit reporting agency?
9. What is the purpose of the Equal Credit Opportunity Act?
10. Give four sound reasons for using credit.
11. How can credit counseling services help debt-troubled individuals and families?
12. What are the advantages of filing bankruptcy under Chapter 13 bankruptcy instead of filing Chapter 7 bankruptcy?

To Think Critically

1. How can the use of credit have a positive influence on the economy?
2. How can the use of too much credit contribute to inflation?
3. What are the advantages and disadvantages of using credit?
4. How does a creditor evaluate a person's credit rating?
5. How can you establish and maintain a strong credit rating?

6. How can your financial personality help you decide when and if you can use credit safely? How would you describe your financial personality?
7. Under what circumstances is it best not to use credit?
8. What are some of the alternatives to using credit?
9. What questions should you ask yourself to decide if you should use credit?
10. Why is it important to shop for credit? What factors should you consider when shopping for credit?
11. What should you do if you have a problem paying your bills?
12. How do creditors use credit reporting agencies?

To Do

1. Suppose you want to buy a $300 television on credit. Find out what the credit terms would be if you bought the television at a department store, at a television shop, or with a bank credit card. Find out about finance charges, annual percentage rate, monthly payments, length of the repayment period, and late payment charges. Where would you get the best deal?
2. Suppose you buy a 10-speed bike and charge it. After two weeks, the bike only runs on five speeds. Although the bike has a two-year warranty, the seller refuses to do anything about the problem. Your credit contract has been sold to a finance company and the seller has been paid. Describe your rights if you refuse to pay the creditor.
3. Ask a representative from a credit counseling agency to speak to your class about how to use credit wisely. Prepare a list of questions to ask the speaker. You may want to include some of the following:
   A. What are the most common problems connected with the use of consumer credit?
   B. What are the most common causes of credit problems?
   C. How can consumers avoid credit problems?
   D. How can credit counseling help consumers with financial problems?
4. Pick up an application for a credit card or charge account from a local bank or store. Fill it out and explain why creditors require the information requested on the application.

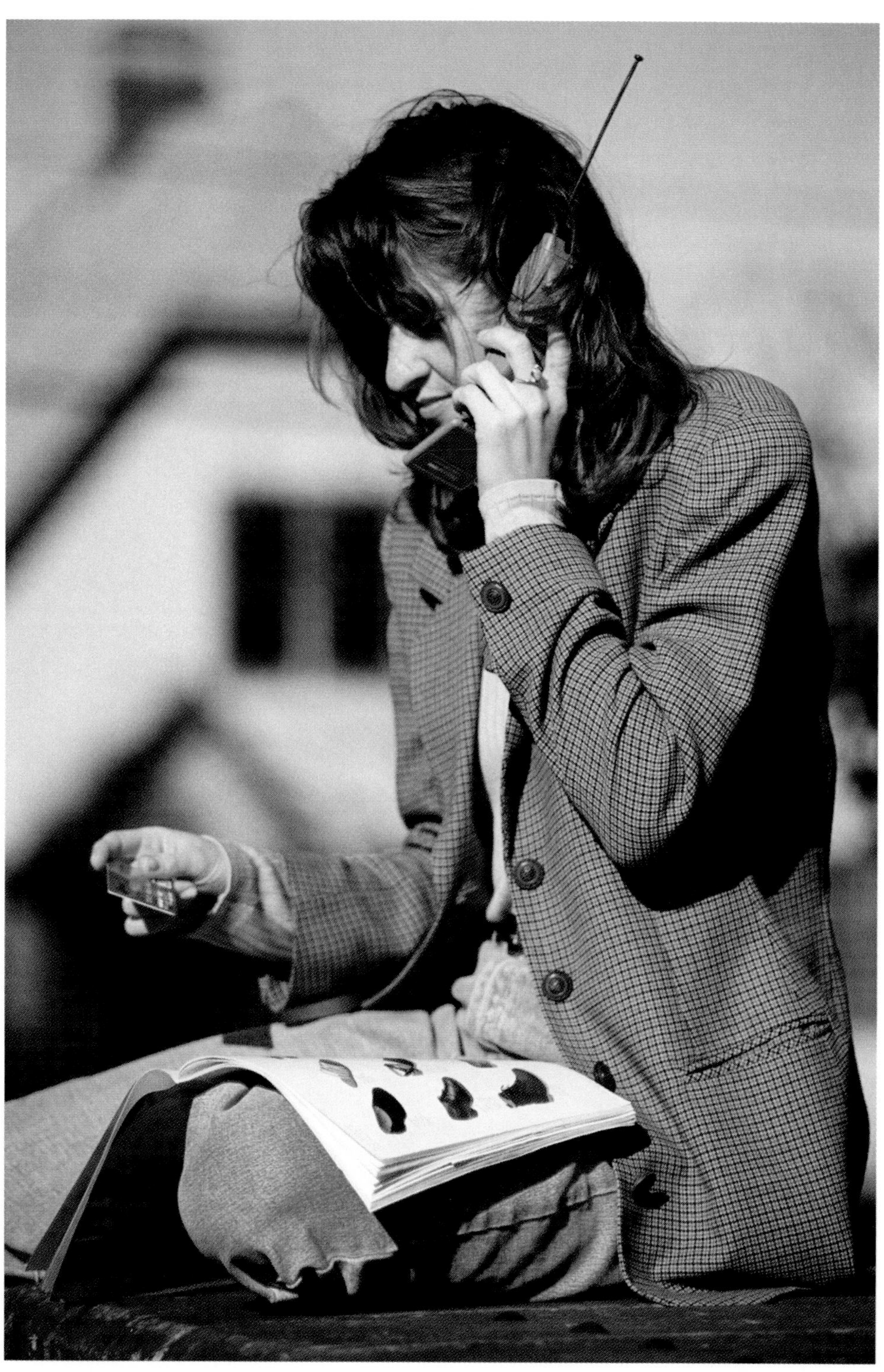

Managed wisely, credit can be a tool to make shopping more convenient for consumers.

CHAPTER 14

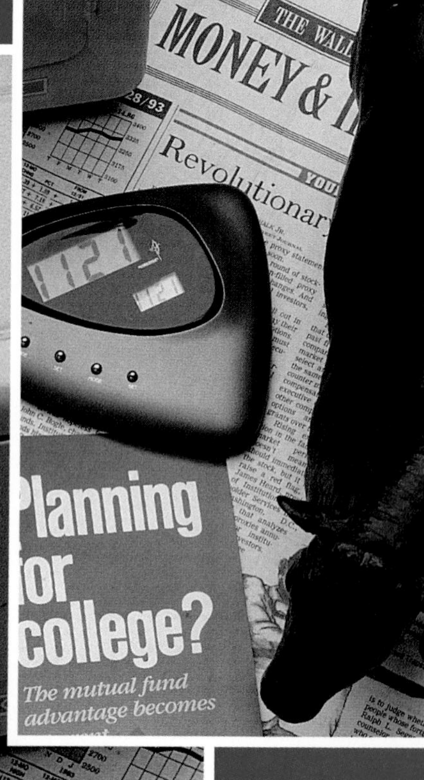

Planning for college?
The mutual fund advantage becomes

SAFE PLACE FOR
VALUABLE ASSETS

REGISTERED
10000

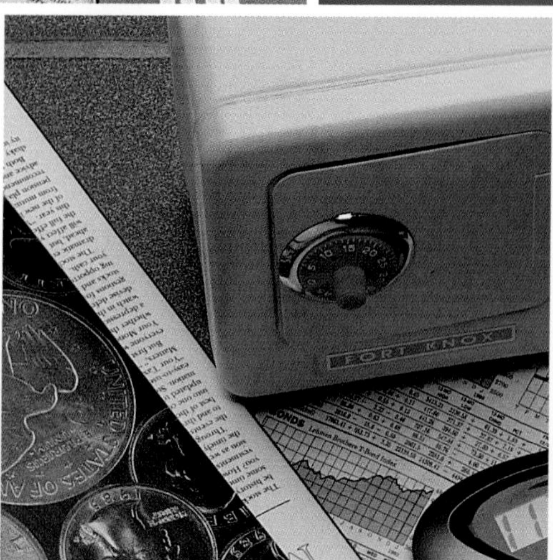

FORT KNOX

Planning for Financial Security

life cycle
tax-deferred
estate
estate planning
executor
will
beneficiaries
trustee
living will
trust

After studying this chapter, you will be able to

- ❑ Outline the steps involved in achieving financial security.
- ❑ Establish appropriate financial goals for different stages in the life cycle.
- ❑ Describe the role of a savings and an insurance program in financial planning.
- ❑ Describe ways to deal with a financial crisis.
- ❑ Explain the importance of sound investments in providing financial security.
- ❑ Outline steps to take when planning for retirement.
- ❑ Explore the basics of estate planning including wills and trusts.
- ❑ Evaluate professional services related to financial planning.

Achieving financial security requires mastering a certain body of financial and legal knowledge. It is an ongoing process of making plans to meet changing needs, goals, and income over the life cycle. Financial security begins with a savings program and adequate insurance protection against financial risks. Investment and retirement planning play important roles along the way. Learning to cope with financial crisis will help you carry out your plans. Financial security also includes a formal plan to divide your assets upon your death. Legal and financial professionals can assist you in achieving your goals.

Lifetime Financial Planning

Financial security goes beyond day-to-day, month-to-month accounting and bill paying. Achieving a sense of security and reaching certain goals involves some way of accumulating money. This starts with a savings program, 14-1.

A personalized savings program can be tailored to your situation and stage in the life cycle. A close look at where you are, your current needs and expenses, and your goals can guide you in creating a map to your financial future. Your career and income progression is one key to planning for the years ahead. Your place in the life cycle is another indicator of changing goals, needs, and expenditures.

Life cycle refers to the stages people pass through as life unfolds from birth to old age. The *family life cycle* is made up of stages from beginning to aging. Different financial responsibilities and concerns surface with each new stage. Earning and spending patterns also change with each stage of the life cycle.

14-1 Union Camp Corporation
It pays to plant your money tree early in life.

Although the family life cycle is a typical model, all individuals and families do not fit into a single mold. The number of single-parent households is increasing. The number of singles living alone and couples without children have also risen dramatically. Financial planning for these varying life situations is both similar to and different from planning for the typical family life cycle.

Certain career changes, expenses, and financial activities occur during different stages in the life cycle. Becoming familiar with this information can provide you with a framework for financial planning. See 14-2.

Young Adults

From age 18 to the late 20s, young people are getting established on the job and in life. Those who marry will begin the first stage of the family life cycle, called the *beginning stage.*

Income for most young adults starts low. This will gradually increase with time on the job. Those who marry and become two-income couples will enjoy the benefits of combined incomes and expenses.

Possible expenses at this time include education, college loans, home furnishings, and insurance. Some may decide to purchase an auto, begin savings, or make contributions to a retirement fund. Married couples may revise their current savings and investment programs to meet their changing needs. See 14-3.

Middle Adults

From the young adult stage up to age 40, life is often characterized by advancement on the job, rising incomes, and more responsibilities. Beginning with the birth of the first child, couples enter the *expanding stage.* If one spouse leaves the workforce to raise children, income will decline. At the same time, expenses will increase.

Financial Aspects of the Family Life Cycle

Stage in the Family Life Cycle	Career and Income Characteristics	Typical Expenses
Beginning Marriage. Getting started as a couple. Establishing a home.	Finishing education. Entering workforce. No or low income, gradually increasing.	Education. Educational loans. Home furnishings. Insurance. Auto. Savings. IRA contributions. Income tax.
Expanding Birth of first child. Infant and toddler years. Preschool and elementary school years.	Increasing income with increased responsibilities. One spouse may leave workforce for childrearing. Income may decrease if one spouse leaves workforce.	Child care and equipment. Educational fund. More living space. Increased insurance coverage.
Developing Children entering adolescence. High school years.	Advancement. Possible job or career change. Spouse who stayed home with children may return to workforce. Increased income. Improved benefits. Earnings may level off. Possible decline in income with a career change.	Larger home. Additional furnishings. Savings. Investments. Charitable contributions. Travel. Education. Extras.
Launching Children leaving home. Grandchildren arriving. Care for elderly parents.	Peak performance years. Increased responsibility. Income may peak. Investment income. More benefits.	Home improvements or new home. Replaced furnishings. Travel. More contributions to retirement plans. College costs. Care for aging parents.
Aging New interests and hobbies. More leisure time. Death of one spouse.	Retirement. May seek part-time or volunteer employment. Income declines. Social Security payments. Retirement benefits.	Health insurance. Health care. Retirement costs. Travel.

14-2
Your occupation, job advancement, income ups and downs, and employment benefits all play an important role in plans for financial security.

14-3
Age and life situations tend to generate common spending patterns you want to consider in financial planning.

Child-related expenses will include child care, children's clothing, baby equipment, and medical expenses. With children may come the decision to move to larger living quarters. This is a good time to review and expand insurance protection. An educational fund for the children may be started. It is important to draw up a will at this stage of the life cycle.

Singles and childless couples may also begin savings and investment programs. For some, this is a time for some self-indulgence. Some may choose to travel, spend on hobbies, or move to better housing.

Later Adults

From ages 40 through 50, individuals and couples share another set of common experiences. Families have generally had all their children. They enter the *developing stage* of the family life cycle. Job advancements usually occur along with higher incomes. Earnings may peak and level off. During this time, some may seek a job or career change. Earnings may rise or decline as a result of a job change.

For those with children, education costs are likely to peak. Parents who left the workforce earlier may choose to return now. They may need the extra income to help pay for college expenses and contribute to retirement plans.

More money will be put into savings and investments. Retirement planning becomes critical for everyone at this stage. Funds should grow as they begin more serious planning for the years ahead. Many will seek reliable financial and legal advisers as needed.

For some adults, this is a time when aging parents become a concern. These years have often been called the "sandwich generation" for those with children. Adults find themselves "sandwiched" between college-bound youngsters and aging parents. Both financial and emotional demands are great.

Older Adults

From age 50 into early retirement years, older adults adjust to new events in their lives. For families with children, this is often called the *launching stage.* Children leave home for college or work. At this time, some are enjoying grandchildren. Married couples often renew their focus on each other.

Couples may contribute more to retirement plans. They may choose to move to a smaller home and simplify their lives to prepare for retirement. Those caring for elderly parents may face heavy health and nursing care costs.

At this stage, estate planning becomes important. It is the time to review and revise wills.

Retired Adults

The *aging stage* brings about formal retirement. Some retirees may seek part-time or volunteer opportunities. Most tend to live more simply and to conserve both energy and income. For many, more free time is a welcome luxury.

Income and most expenses usually decline during retirement years. Comfort during these years will depend on the financial planning that occurred in earlier stages. Costs that will increase during this time include health care, health insurance, and other retirement costs. Those in good health may travel more. Retired adults should review their will and estate plans at this stage, 14-4.

Other Situations

Many situations call for financial planning that differs from the typical family life cycle. These include single individuals, childless couples, single-parent families, and divorced or separated people.

Singles and childless couples will have similar income and earning patterns. Though there are some similarities, financial patterns will generally differ from the family life cycle. Early on in the life cycle, single people will probably pay more for living expenses. They will be establishing and furnishing a home on one paycheck. Singles and couples with no dependents will not have the expenses related to childrearing, such as college costs and a larger home. Both groups may spend more throughout the life cycle on travel, leisure, and other extras. Some may choose to give more to charitable causes or needy relatives.

Single-parent families also have special financial circumstances. These families are often led by females. Income is typically less than two-parent families. Their expenses are often greater. Saving and planning for future security is sometimes difficult as these families struggle to meet current expenses. Government and community-sponsored assistance can be very helpful for single-parent families.

Separated or divorced people also face a unique set of financial concerns.

14-4
At retirement, financial responsibilities and activities change.

They may face the following onetime or ongoing expenses: legal fees, alimony, child support, and property settlement costs. The costs of establishing and maintaining two homes rather than one is another expense, especially if there are children. A divorce or separation may require additional furnishings and moving costs.

No matter what your situation, it is wise to begin a savings program and insure against financial risks early in the life cycle. These two steps are the foundation of financial security. Savings can cover unexpected expenses and emergencies and help to reach goals. Insurance protects against major disasters. With both, you can feel reasonably comfortable with your financial situation. Start with a personal savings plan.

> *"Money is flat and meant to be piled up."*
>
> *Scottish Proverb*

A Savings Plan

A regular savings program is the first step toward financial security. It involves a careful look at current finances, important objectives, and realistic steps to take toward reaching financial goals.

Review the money management section in Chapter 5 of this text. Follow the steps outlined to create a simple, workable budget. This will give you an in-depth look at current finances. It will also tell you how much money you can count on to start a savings program.

Early on, it will be important to save for unexpected expenses and emergencies. As income grows, you can put money aside to pay for costly goods and services you want. These may include a car, education, and travel.

> *"Money is a guarantee that we may have what we want in the future. Though we need nothing at the moment, it insures the possibility of satisfying a new desire when it arises."*
>
> *Aristotle*

Set Goals for Saving

It is easier to save if you have clearly defined goals. Begin with a list of what you want to achieve with your money. What do you want enough to make you give up spending now in order to save for the future? Here are three points to consider in setting personal goals for saving.

Goals Need to Be Realistic

Consider your income and expenses, your life situation, and any likely changes. Based on these realities, set up financial goals that are achievable. For example, suppose you could save $100 monthly and you want to buy a car within two years. A good used car is realistic while a new luxury car is not.

Goals Need to Be Specific and Measurable

Outline your goals in exact terms. "Putting together $500 for a ski trip next winter" is more specific than "saving money to travel sometime in the future." Likewise, "saving $150 per month to buy a computer next summer" is more specific than "putting money aside in case you need it next year."

Goals Need to Be Time Related

Put your goals and objectives into a time frame. When will you need your savings? This will vary for different goals. You can divide saving goals into three time frames. *Short-term goals* are to be reached within a year or two. *Mid-term goals* are to be reached in two to five years. *Long-term goals* are to be reached in five years or more.

Increasing the Value of Savings

The money you save for goals not only accumulates, it can grow. If you put money to work, it will earn more money over time. This concept is the *time value* of money. For example, if you receive $100 today, it can be worth more than $100 one year from today. This is because the money you receive today can earn interest over time. The $100 saved at a rate of eight percent will be worth $108 in one year.

The future value of today's savings is measured by the interest earned on amounts saved. Suppose you save $25 monthly for five years and earn interest at a rate of 5 percent. You will accumulate $1,707.24. This comes to $207.24 more than you saved. If you save $5 weekly for 10 years, you will accumulate $3,363. That's $763 more than you saved. The present and future value of money are important concepts to consider when saving for future goals, 14-5.

Savings Decisions

There are numerous ways and places to save your money. As you decide just how to handle the money you save, consider liquidity, safety, rate of return, and taxes. Following is a brief description of these factors. More about ways and places to save appears later in the book.

Liquidity refers to the availability of your funds on short notice. You may want part of your savings to be "ready money" for emergencies or other needs. However, you often earn more interest on money you leave on deposit for longer periods of time.

Safety refers to the security of your savings. Deposits in many financial institutions are insured by the federal government. Deposits of up to $100,000 are insured. This protects depositors if the financial institution

14-5
This chart shows how savings can accumulate at different interest rates over time.

Watch Your Savings Grow

Weekly Savings at Different Interest Rates, Compounded Monthly

Weekly Amount:	Rate	10 Years	20 Years	30 Years
$10	4.5%	$ 6,550	$ 16,814	$ 32,897
25		16,375	42,035	82,243
50		32,750	84,069	164,486
$10	5.5%	$ 6,910	$ 18,871	$ 39,576
25		17,274	47,176	98,940
50		34,548	94,353	197,880
$10	6.6%	$ 7,294	$21,243	$ 47,914
25		18,236	53,107	119,786
50		36,472	106,214	239,572
$10	7.7%	$ 7,707	$23,984	$ 58,361
25		19,267	59,959	145,903
50		38,533	119,918	291,807
$10	8.8%	$ 8,148	$27,155	$ 71,491
25		20,371	67,888	178,729
50		40,741	135,776	357,459
Original Amounts Saved:				
$10		$ 5,200	$10,400	$ 15,600
25		13,000	26,000	39,000
50		26,000	52,000	78,000

fails. Be sure to choose a sound institution that is covered by this type of insurance.

Rate of return is another key factor in deciding where to save your money. Generally, you should look for the highest rate of return in combination with the liquidity and degree of safety you want.

Tax factors related to savings come into play mostly for high-income savers. When tax rates are above 25 percent, it pays to consider putting savings into tax-exempt or tax-deferred savings plans. ***Tax-deferred*** means the money is not taxed until withdrawn from the account.

Insurance Protection

Financial security depends in part on managing and reducing financial risks. When you earn income, own property, and accumulate savings, you have something to lose. Insurance offers protection. A sound insurance program begins by assessing the risks you face. Consider the losses that could damage or destroy your financial security. Take steps to protect yourself with appropriate insurance.

Events that could put your finances at risk include illness, accidents, disability, death, and property losses. The purpose of insurance is to pay for losses that would be difficult or impossible for you to cover. The amount of insurance needed will vary from person to person. It will depend on the risks being covered, the amount available to pay for losses, and the financial obligations of the persons being insured. For example, single persons with no children will need less coverage than a head of a family with several children. Protection needs increase with each new dependent and with increased assets.

The types of insurance that protect against financial risks include life, disability, health, property, and liability. These are discussed in different sections of this book. A careful look at the risks you face and a plan for managing them with insurance and other resources are basic steps in any financial plan. See 14-6.

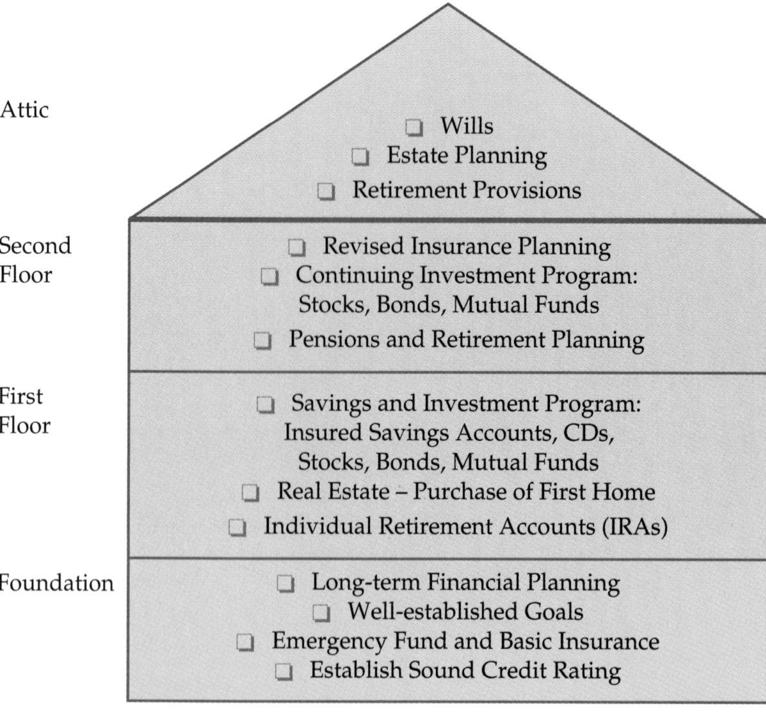

14-6
Financial planning is like building a house. It starts with a sound foundation on which everything rests.

Investments

After establishing a solid base of savings and insurance protection, investing income becomes important. Normally, savings bring a specific rate of return stated in advance. Investments offer chances for greater returns. However, they also involve some risk. When you put money in stocks, bonds, mutual funds, or other investments, there is no guaranteed return. There is generally the possibility of loss. As a rule, the greater the risk, the greater the possible return. The lower the risk, the lower the return.

Investing income takes you a step beyond saving. It calls for careful homework. In plans for financial security, investments play an important role in creating wealth. For example, if you want to retire at an early age and have enough income to cover your living expenses, you will need to invest and save wisely. Investing offers a chance to gain more than savings can provide. However, you also face the risk of losing part or all of the amount you invest.

Factors to consider when investing include timing, risk tolerance, income, growth, marketability, and diversification. These factors and other details of investing are covered in detail in Chapter 16.

Certain investments also offer tax advantages for those in high tax brackets. Tax incentives vary greatly from investor to investor and from year to year as tax laws change. It pays to look for a competent tax accountant, lawyer, or financial planner for advice in this area.

Dealing with Financial Crises

Any number of financial crises can shatter a person's sense and reality of security. Examples of crises include a job loss, a burden of debt well beyond the ability to pay, a major illness, or a serious disability. Consider the outcomes of these events. Here are some steps to take in facing the chance of financial crises in your life.

Prevention, when possible, is the most painless and effective way to deal with potential disasters. Obviously you cannot always prevent financial hardship. However, staying out of trouble is easier than getting out of trouble. Good savings habits will help you prevent financial crises. Practice sound money management and practical credit controls. Start a regular savings program. Buy enough insurance protection, and use reasonable caution in financial matters.

Preparation will go a long way toward getting you through a crisis situation. Getting the best education and job training possible is one way to be prepared. With a good education and job skills, you are better able to find work and advance on the job. It also helps to stay current in your field through continuing education and training programs. This will mean higher earnings and greater job security. These can be a great help in times of financial crisis.

Another way to be prepared is to establish an emergency fund equal to several months pay. In the event of big losses, this will give you time to assess your situation and take necessary action. Insurance protection is another form of preparation. Finally, detaching yourself from your current level of living may prepare you for the possibility of lower living standards.

> ***"Security depends not so much upon how much you have, as upon how much you can do without."***
>
> *Joseph Wood Krutch*

Coping with disaster when it strikes is a major ingredient of dealing with financial crises. Depending on the

Making Plans

A Death in the Family

Robb Williams' father died suddenly in March during Robb's senior year in high school. The death left Robb, his mother, and two younger sisters in a state of emotional and financial shock.

Mr. Williams was only 42 years old. He had been in fine health most of his life. There was no forewarning. He worked as a manufacturer's representative selling building materials. His income was good, but benefits were limited. He did participate in a pension plan that left the family $30,000. They also received $25,000 from a life insurance policy. He had two savings accounts amounting to a total of $7,500. That was it. It wasn't enough for a family of four with no regular income and three teenagers to educate.

The family has lived in the same home for 12 years. The mortgage payments come to more than they can afford without Mr. Williams' monthly income. They will have to sell the family home and look for cheaper housing. Robb hoped to go to college in the fall and had been accepted by the school. However, with no scholarship, the tuition and other costs cannot be paid. He will have to delay college plans for now.

Mrs. Williams was a teacher before the children were born and does some substitute teaching from time to time. She plans to go back to teaching full time but will have to take some additional courses. Robb figures he will have to go to work full time after graduation. He plans to save as much as possible in hopes to attend college someday. His sisters, Sue and Amy, ages 12 and 15, will have to babysit and look for other jobs if they hope to go on to school.

Case Review

1. How could the Williams family have planned better to minimize or eliminate some of these financial problems? Name at least five steps they could have taken.
2. Given the situation, what can the family do at this point to meet and overcome the financial hardships they face?
3. What government and community agencies and programs could be helpful to a family in this situation?
4. What Social Security benefits might be available to the Williams' in this situation?

crisis and the resources available, coping can involve any or all of the following steps:

- Accept and acknowledge the fact there is a crisis.
- If debt is a part of the crisis, contact creditors promptly.
- Avoid making any new credit purchases.
- Find free or affordable credit and financial counseling.
- Adjust spending habits and cut expenses.
- Look for every possible source of income.
- Have additional family members seek employment.
- Check out availability of assistance from employers, insurance, government programs, and community and charitable organizations.
- Sell some assets, such as real estate, investments, autos, and valuable possessions.
- As a last resort, consider bankruptcy.

Planning for Retirement

Retirement and estate planning are key elements of financial security. Recent trends indicate more and more people are retiring earlier and living longer. Early retirees could need income for as long as 20 to 30 years.

Providing income for this many years requires early planning, periodic review, and proper adjustments to meet changing needs.

Starting early is the most effective way to provide enough money on which to live after retiring. The chart in 14-7 shows how your money will grow beginning at different ages and saving for different lengths of time. The higher the interest rate on your savings, the greater growth you will enjoy. As you can see, it pays to begin saving as early as possible. The earlier you begin, the more you accumulate.

You may be able to draw on a variety of income sources for later years. These include Social Security, retirement programs offered by employers, individual retirement accounts, insurance, annuities, and investments. Following is a brief description of these key income sources. Most are discussed in more detail in other chapters.

Social Security

Social Security is designed to provide a floor or foundation on which to build financial security for later years. This program covers most of the U.S. population. In addition to retirement income payments, it includes health care benefits under the medicare section of the program. While Social Security benefits are not intended to be enough to live on in comfort, they will be an important piece of your retirement picture.

Employer-Sponsored Retirement Plans

Employer-sponsored retirement programs are offered by most companies and employers. While these programs vary greatly, they must meet the standards of the Employee Retirement Income Security Act. This law, passed in 1974, sets minimum standards for pension and retirement plans. The primary purpose of the act is to guarantee that workers receive the benefits they earn. Vesting requirements are an important part of this act. *Vesting* gives the worker a legal right to money an employer has put into a company pension fund in the worker's name. It is particularly important in the event of a job change.

There are two basic types of employer-sponsored plans. These are defined contribution and defined

14-7
You can see the advantages of beginning an IRA savings plan early in life.

Early Beginnings with Savings

(Three approaches all assuming 5 percent interest compounded monthly)	
From age 25 to 35 (10 years) you save each year	$ 2,000
By age 35 savings will grow to	26,587
Left in account to age 65 (30 years) it grows to	123,823
Less your original savings (10 x $2,000)	20,000
You gain	103,823
From age 35 to 65 (30 years) you save each year	$ 2,000
By age 65 savings will grow to	146,774
Less your original savings (30 x $2,000)	60,000
You gain	86,774
From age 25 to 65 (40 years) you save each year	$ 2,000
By age 65 savings will grow to	270,597
Less your original savings (40 x $2,000)	80,000
You gain	190,597

benefit. Both types provide for saving pretax dollars, which are allowed to grow on a tax-deferred basis. The money is not taxed until withdrawn at retirement.

The *defined contribution plan* describes what the employer will give toward a worker's retirement income. These contributions can take several forms. Examples include employee stock ownership, profit sharing, and deferred-compensation plans. The *defined benefit plan* describes the benefits a worker will receive at normal retirement age. It tells what the retiree will get from the plan.

Both of these plans can vary greatly from employer to employer. They can also be affected by changing tax laws. For these reasons, it is important to check out available retirement provisions with an employer. Also ask for a detailed explanation of your options.

Personal Retirement Plans

Many people place part of their earnings in their own personal retirement fund. They may begin an individual retirement account (IRA) or a Keogh plan. These programs allow savings to accumulate on a tax-deferred basis. In certain cases, annual contributions to these plans may be deducted from income for tax purposes.

The annuity is another form of personal retirement planning. This is a contract with an insurance company that provides regular income for a set period of time, usually for life. In some cases, the compound interest on money invested in an annuity builds up on a tax-deferred basis.

Estate Planning

Your ***estate,*** in simple terms, is everything you own. It includes property, savings, investments, and insurance benefits. ***Estate planning*** includes active management of your property and assets with a plan for their distribution at your death. An estate plan lets you distribute your assets according to your wishes. It requires a certain amount of record keeping and decision making as you go along. The primary objectives of estate planning include:

- Providing for any dependents.
- Deciding how your estate will be divided upon your death.
- Minimizing tax liabilities.
- Naming an ***executor*** who will oversee the management of your affairs upon your death.

Wills

A ***will*** is a legal document stating what a person wants done with his or her assets after death. When people die without a will, their property is divided according to state laws. The government may not distribute your estate the way you would choose.

A will guarantees disposal of your estate according to your wishes. This makes life much simpler for your beneficiaries. ***Beneficiaries*** are those who are to receive property under the will. The best type of will to use depends on the size of the estate, ages of any dependents, and personal goals.

Generally, it is wise to ask a lawyer to advise you on what to include in your will and to draw up the document. See 14-8. A will should clearly outline your wishes for the transfer of your property. It should also name an executor to carry out your intentions.

If there are young children, the will should name a guardian to be responsible for them. Include specific plans and instructions for their care. A guardian may also manage your estate on behalf of your dependents, or you may name a trustee to do this. A ***trustee*** is a person or institution named to manage an estate on behalf of the beneficiaries.

Jack Klasey

14-8
A lawyer or financial adviser can assist you in preparing a will.

The Living Will

The ***living will*** is a statement of instructions you wish to be followed if you become unable to make decisions on your own behalf. For instance, you might become physically or mentally disabled. The primary purpose of this is to make known what medical treatments you do or do not wish to receive in the face of terminal injury or illness. It outlines your desires about the artificial prolonging of your life. This is a serious and very personal step to take. It needs to be discussed with family members, loved ones, and your physician.

Trusts

In addition to a will, you may need one or more trust agreements if your estate is complicated or large. A ***trust*** is a legal agreement where assets and property are managed by a trustee on behalf of the beneficiaries. There are several types of trusts. Each achieves different goals. You can use a trust to

- ❑ Provide regular income during your lifetime.
- ❑ Gain professional management services.
- ❑ Minimize estate (inheritance) taxes.
- ❑ Provide income and asset management for beneficiaries.

Normally, drawing up a trust agreement calls for the services of a competent lawyer who is familiar with estate planning.

Making Plans

Looking Ahead

Maria and Tony plan to be married in six months. Maria is a nursery school teacher, and Tony is a welder. Their combined annual income will come to almost $35,000. They expect to be a two-income family for four to five years. Then they hope to start a family. Maria wants to work only on a substitute basis until their children reach school age. By then, Tony's income may be larger. His work benefits include fairly complete health care coverage and life insurance with a generous disability provision.

During their first two or three years of marriage, Maria and Tony plan to save enough money for a down payment on a house. They also plan to buy whatever furniture they still need after combining what they both now own. Tony already owns a car and the couple does not anticipate any other major expenditures in the near future. They both use credit cards, but have not incurred large debts.

Case Review

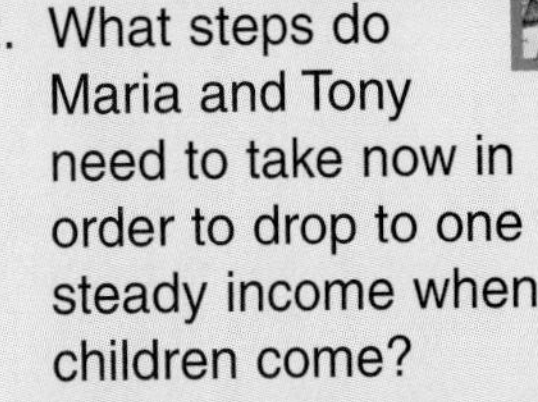

1. What expenses can you think of that this couple is likely to have in the first year or two of marriage?
2. What steps do Maria and Tony need to take now in order to drop to one steady income when children come?
3. What big expenses are likely to come with the purchase of a home? with their first child? with later children?
4. What provisions should Maria and Tony make for unexpected emergencies and expenditures?

Making Plans

Expecting the Unexpected

Myra, age 28, is a dedicated career person with no plans to marry and no children. Myra is a top-notch photographer employed by the mayor's office in a major city. She earns $38,000 annually and enjoys outstanding fringe benefits. These include health, disability, and life insurance. Myra's parents are in good health and both work. Her two brothers are married with jobs and families of their own.

Myra lives alone in a rented apartment that she has furnished very much to her own liking. Now, she is beginning to think about buying a place of her own both for the joy of ownership and for the tax advantages. Her taxes, with no dependents and few other deductions, are relatively high.

Case Review

1. What changes in Myra's situation could alter her financial needs and plans?
2. Suppose one of Myra's parents becomes ill and this causes her parents a financial setback. How could this affect Myra's financial plans?
3. If one of Myra's brothers and his wife are killed in a car crash and Myra is named guardian of their children, how might this change her financial plans?
4. What are some financial steps Myra should take before considering the purchase of a home? What steps will she need to take after becoming a homeowner? What additional expenses will home ownership bring?
5. What are some key differences you would recommend in financial planning for those with and without dependents?
6. How does an individual's age relate to financial planning and decisions?

Using Financial and Legal Professionals

Financial planning and management often involves complex decisions related to legal matters, investments, taxes, and retirement and estate planning. In addition, the laws governing these matters, as well as the economic climate, constantly change. Professionals can help in areas where you do not feel confident and competent on your own.

Following is a description of the experts you can call on in managing financial and legal matters.

Accountants keep, audit, and inspect financial records of individuals and businesses. They also prepare financial and tax reports. The initials *CPA* stand for Certified Public Accountant. This indicates an accountant has been certified by the American Institute of Certified Public Accountants.

Attorneys represent individuals and businesses in legal and business matters. Their areas of specialty include taxes, estate planning, contracts, real estate, divorce, and adoption. You also need a lawyer if you have to sue someone, if you are being sued, or if you face criminal charges. For those who cannot afford to pay an attorney, legal services may be available at low or no cost through Legal Aid. Offices are listed in local phone directories.

Bankers provide a host of financial services for regular customers. Services may include credit, savings plans, and investments. Trust management, real estate mortgages, small business loans, and financial planning may also be offered. Different banks will differ in the type of services extended.

Credit and debt counselors assist consumers who are overextended. Counselors can help in drawing up budgets, negotiating with creditors,

Making Plans

Time to Recline

Pete and Mimi Chun are in their early forties. They have two children in high school. The children are excellent students and plan to attend college. Both Pete and Mimi have worked full time and long hours over the years. Mimi's mother has lived with them and cared for the children when they were small.

Pete is a successful lawyer. However, he routinely works 50 to 60 hours a week. Mimi is a musician. She plays the violin in the symphony orchestra and gives music lessons at the local school of music.

Recently Pete suffered a minor heart attack—a "warning" the doctor said. The experience jolted Pete and Mimi. Certainly they had enough money at this point and adequate savings to send both children to college. Why were they still working so hard? Maybe it was time to taper off—travel a little, enjoy life, and spend more time with the kids before college.

The Chuns decided to begin arranging an easier life for themselves. They began planning for an early retirement so they could have more time to enjoy life and each other. While they have accumulated some savings and done well with a few investments, they have no master financial plan.

Case Review

1. What are some of the financial steps the Chuns need to take now if they wish to retire early?
2. What are some steps they could have taken years ago to make early retirement easier to achieve?
3. Who are some of the financial and legal advisers the Chuns might turn to for advice on their planning?
4. What are some of the key factors to consider and plan for when arranging for retirement?

overcoming debt problems, and controlling credit spending. Consumer Credit Counseling Services offer debt counseling at little or no cost to the consumer. These nonprofit organizations are located in most urban areas across the country. Beware of debt counselors and firms who offer to consolidate debts for high fees.

Financial planners assist consumers in forming an ongoing financial program designed to reach specific goals. They coordinate personal, financial, business, and legal affairs. Financial planners give advice on insurance, savings, investments, taxes, retirement, and estate planning.

Financial planners are not required by law to be certified or licensed. However, the Certified Financial Planner Board of Standards, Inc. (CFP Board) certifies and licenses financial planners who complete its training programs and pass CFP Certification Examinations. CFP financial planners also meet certain educational, experience, and ethics requirements. Only financial planners who meet these standards may use the designation CFP. The designation Chartered Financial Consultant (ChFC) may be used by those who have completed a 10-course curriculum on financial planning at The American College. Chartered Financial Consultants also must meet specific experience requirements and agree to comply with The American College's Code of Ethics and Procedures and its continuing education requirements.

Insurance agents offer advice on risk management. See 14-9. They also plan, coordinate, and sell insurance protection. Signs of an agent's qualifications include the *CPCU* for Chartered Property Casualty Underwriters and *CLU* for Chartered Life Underwriters.

14-9 State Farm Insurance Companies
Insurance agents can help you plan for risk management.

Investment advisers and brokers provide information and advice on different types of securities. They also handle buy and sell orders. The initials *RIA* mean Registered Investment Adviser. This indicates a person is registered with the state securities agency or the Securities and Exchange Commission. *REG REP* indicates a registered representative of the National Association of Securities Dealers.

The following questions may help you find professionals to help you manage your financial affairs.

- ❑ What areas of expertise are really important to you in managing your affairs?

Making Plans

Final Decisions

Maude and Gus Wilks were in their mid sixties. They have three adult children and six grandchildren. The Wilks had a very successful office supply business. Both Maude and Gus worked at the business over the years and made enough money to buy a house, educate their kids, travel a bit, and retire in comfort. They had been retired several years and were enjoying life in a warm climate.

Not long after the Wilks celebrated their 42nd wedding anniversary, Gus became ill with an inoperable cancer. He died shortly after his diagnosis. Maude was devastated. Not only had she lost her husband and life-long companion, she faced a sea of red tape and financial confusion. In all of their good fortune, neither Gus nor Maude had looked ahead to the day one of them would die. They just couldn't face the thought. Now Maude was facing it alone, unprepared, and burdened with complications.

Since there was no will, Gus' estate was divided according to state law. Two-thirds of his property went to their children, the other third to Maude. Unfortunately, one-third was not enough for her to live comfortably for long. She had no legal right to the money the children inherited. In addition, the court had to appoint an executor of the estate. This person was not very helpful or sympathetic to Maude's needs. The executor did not take time to explain the existing options to Maude. She ended up with an insurance payout that did not meet her needs in the best way.

Maude and Gus had paid no attention to tax planning either. Therefore, the estate tax bill came to several thousand dollars more than it would have been with proper planning.

Case Review

1. When does it become important to draw a will and look to estate planning?
2. Why is a will important even to those who do not have large amounts of money or property?
3. What are some estate planning steps that can ease financial burdens following the death of a loved one?
4. What are some consequences of dying without a will when one leaves young children behind?

- ❑ Is the service you need the primary activity of the person you are considering? For example, if you need tax advice, look for a tax accountant or a tax attorney.
- ❑ What education, training, and experience does the professional bring to the job?
- ❑ Is the person certified or licensed and qualified to perform the services you require?
- ❑ Do you feel confident in and comfortable with the persons you are considering?
- ❑ How are fees and charges figured? It pays to be clear ahead of time about hourly fees, commissions, and the approximate total cost you can expect to pay for different services.
- ❑ Will the professionals you use be able to work well with each other when it is in your interest?
- ❑ Will members of your family feel comfortable working with these professionals when necessary?

Summary

Achieving financial security requires lifetime planning. The key is to start early. Steps to financial security begin with adequate insurance protection and a savings program. These plans will vary with different individuals and different stages in life.

With a solid base of savings and insurance, investments will become important as a way of accumulating more money. Investing money offers the possibility of higher returns than saving.

Another component of achieving financial security is learning to deal with crises. Prevention, preparation, and coping methods are vital tools to use in the face of unexpected events.

Planning for retirement is a key to living comfortably in the later years. Today, people are living longer and retiring early, which makes retirement planning even more important. Estate planning is another step that requires careful consideration. This includes drawing up a will to direct the distribution of your assets upon your death.

Over the years, most people need the services of legal and financial professionals in managing their affairs. Achieving financial security depends on finding qualified professionals who will suit your personal needs.

To Review

1. What are the five stages of the family life cycle?
2. Name three life situations that exist outside the typical family life cycle.
3. What are three factors to consider in establishing goals for saving?
4. Name five financial risks that can be covered by insurance.
5. What are four key factors to consider when investing your income?
6. Name four ways to prevent financial crises.
7. What three steps can individuals and families take to cope with financial disaster if it occurs?
8. What are the three key sources of retirement income?
9. Name the four primary objectives of estate planning.
10. Which experts represent individuals and businesses in legal and business matters?

To Think Critically

1. What are the advantages of beginning savings and investment programs at an early age? What are the consequences of putting off these matters until middle thirties, forties, or fifties?
2. Why do you think people often delay serious financial planning?
3. What are some possible consequences of dying without a valid will?
4. How do you think financial security or insecurity affects
   A. Single individuals with no dependents and no sources of income other than their own earnings?
   B. Married couples?
   C. Families with dependent children?
5. How might financial crises affect those in the above categories?
6. How would a financial crisis in your family affect you personally?
7. Discuss the concept of risk as it relates to insurance, savings, and investments.
8. If you were to write a will today, what would it contain? How might it change if you were 30 years old, single, and earning $30,000 to $40,000 annually? if you were 30, earning the same amount, and married? with children? What other factors might influence the provisions you would make in a will?

To Do

1. Investigate the laws in your state regarding persons dying without a will. Report on the laws related to distribution of assets, naming of an executor, naming of a guardian, taxation of assets, and other specifics stated in the law.
2. Contact two of the following professionals for an interview:
   - ❑ Accountant
   - ❑ Attorney
   - ❑ Debt counselor
   - ❑ Financial planner
   - ❑ Insurance agent
   - ❑ Investment adviser or broker

   Find out about:
   - ❑ Services the individual offers.
   - ❑ Qualifications he or she possesses.
   - ❑ Certification or licensing requirements.
   - ❑ Charges for services and how they are determined.
   - ❑ Areas of expertise.

   Report findings in a written or oral report.
3. Check out any local organizations that offer assistance to individuals and families who are facing financial hardships. Look for government and community organizations. Develop a brief directory of available services.
4. Choose one of the following topics. Write a three-page report using at least five reliable sources of information.
   - ❑ The role of savings in achieving financial security.
   - ❑ Financial risks insurance covers.
   - ❑ Investing for the young, middle-aged, and older investor.
   - ❑ Dealing with financial crises.
   - ❑ Retirement planning.
   - ❑ The living will.
   - ❑ Wills and trusts in estate planning.

CHAPTER 15

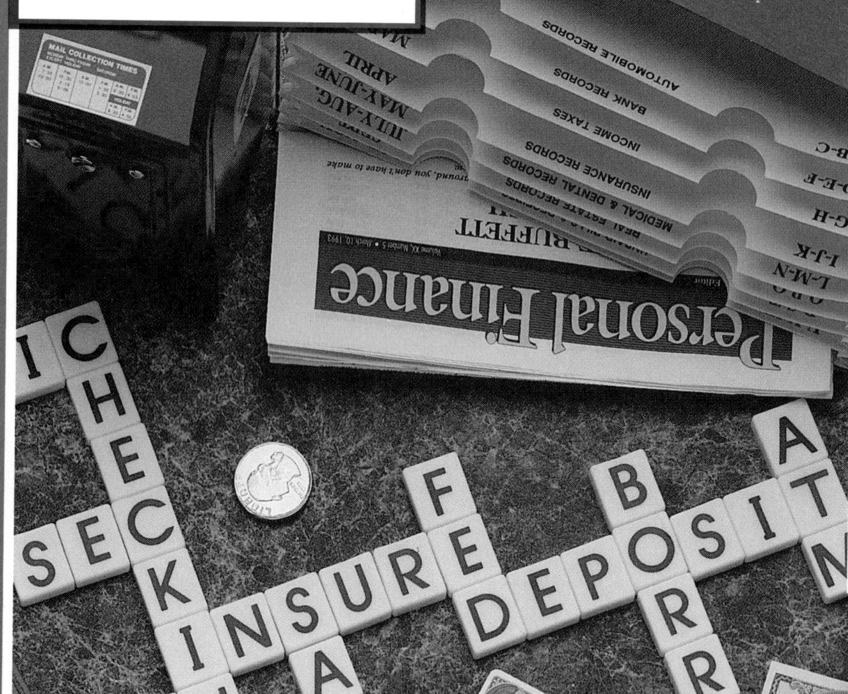

Using Financial Institutions and Services

commercial bank
Federal Deposit Insurance Corporation (FDIC)
savings and loan association
Savings Association Insurance Fund (SAIF)
credit union
National Credit Union Association (NCUA)
mutual savings bank
joint account
debit cards
ATM card
endorse
bank statement
cashier's check
certified check
money order
traveler's checks
regular savings account
compounding interest
annual percentage yield (APY)
certificate of deposit (CD)
money market account
Truth in Savings Act
Individual Retirement Account (IRA)
Keogh Plan
electronic funds transfer (EFT)

After studying this chapter, you will be able to
- select the financial institutions and services that will best meet your financial needs.
- write and endorse checks correctly.
- balance a checkbook.
- compare different types of savings plans.
- describe the two main types of personal retirement accounts.
- identify different types of financial services and select those that meet personal needs.

During your lifetime, you may earn as much as a million dollars—maybe even more. As you manage this income, you will come to rely on a number of financial institutions and services. Commercial banks, savings and loan associations, credit unions, and mutual savings banks are all financial institutions. They offer a variety of financial services to individual consumers.

Financial institutions are very important to the economy. Their primary function is to aid the flow of money between consumers, businesses, and governments. These institutions are financial go-betweens. They transfer money from one consumer, business, or government to another. They keep money moving and in use.

For example, when you deposit money in a bank, the bank lends your money to other consumers and businesses. You earn interest and your money becomes someone else's source of credit. Your dollars may be used to help finance consumer loans for new cars, homes, and vacations. It may be used to help finance commercial loans for business equipment and expansion. It may go into government and municipal loans for new highways, schools, and hospitals. The interaction that financial institutions create between consumers, businesses, and governments keeps our economy alive, 15-1.

Without financial institutions, consumers would probably have to keep their cash under a mattress or locked in a safe. Money could not circulate easily. The nation's money supply would shrink. Funds would not be available for consumer spending. Demand for goods and services would fall. Businesses could not get the money to modernize plants and develop new products. The economy would slow down. Jobs would become scarce. As you can see, our economy depends on the flow of money and the services financial institutions provide.

Types of Financial Institutions

The financial institutions offering the broadest range of services are commercial banks, savings and loan associations, credit unions, and mutual savings banks. In the past, laws and market conditions separated one type from the other in obvious ways. Each type of institution offered a distinct set of services to a specific set of

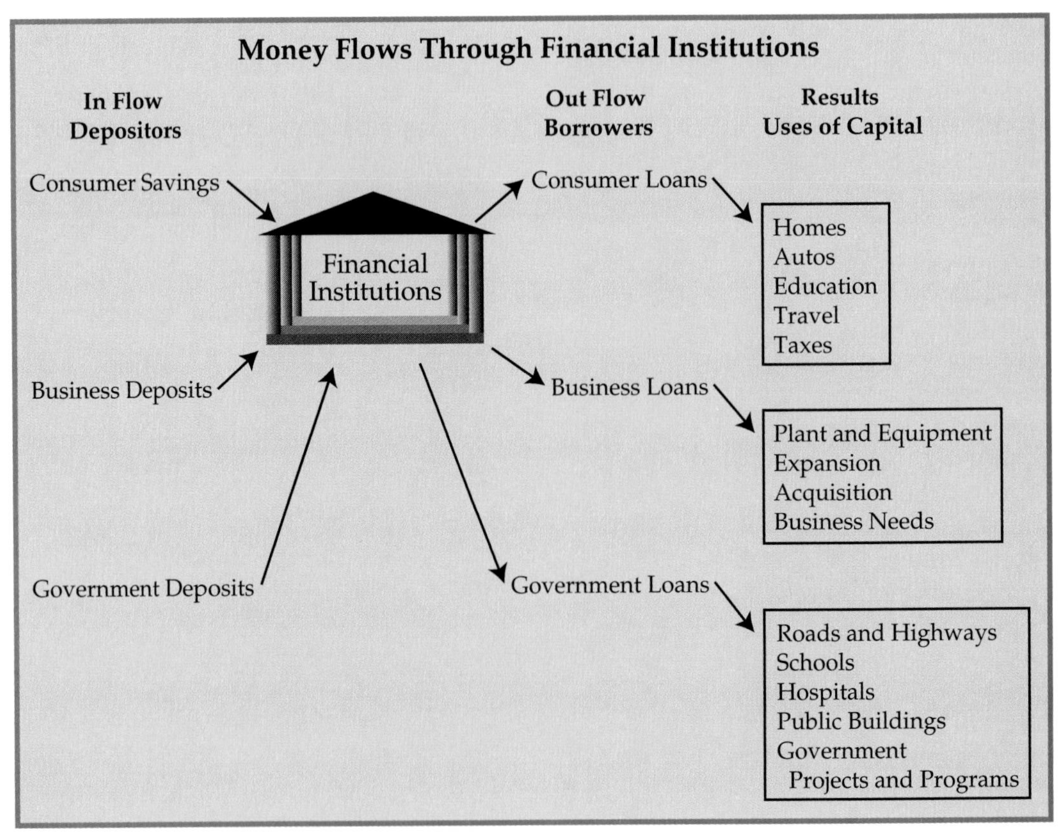

15-1
Financial institutions keep money flowing through the economy among consumers, businesses, and government.

customers. However, deregulation and recent economic conditions have made these institutions more similar to one another. In addition, other companies now offer a wider range of financial services. Examples of these companies include brokerage firms, insurance companies and the so-called "financial supermarkets." Following is a brief description of these types of institutions and the services they offer.

Commercial Banks

A ***commercial bank*** is owned by stockholders and operated for profit. Its primary functions are to receive, transfer, and lend money to individuals, businesses, and governments. Commercial banks are often called full-service banks. They offer a wide variety of services.

Commercial banks may be chartered by the federal government or by a state government. Federally chartered banks are called national banks. These banks may use the word *national* in their names. These banks must comply with federal banking regulations. State chartered banks are regulated by state banking commissions.

In most commercial banks, deposits are insured by the ***Federal Deposit Insurance Corporation (FDIC).*** The FDIC is a U.S. government agency that protects bank customers and helps maintain confidence in the banking system. It insures bank deposits up to $100,000. This means the money in a depositor's account (if $100,000 or less) will be protected. If the bank goes bankrupt or suffers serious financial losses, only amounts over $100,000 would be at risk. For example, if your savings total $25,000, the entire amount is insured. If your savings total $125,000, only the first $100,000 is insured.

Savings and Loan Associations

A ***savings and loan association*** also may offer a wide variety of financial services to consumers. These associations may be either mutual or stock companies. Mutual savings and loan associations are owned by and operated for the benefit of their depositors. These depositors receive dividends on their savings. Stock companies are owned by stockholders. Like commercial banks, these companies operate for profit. In the past, these associations had two major functions. First, they received and paid dividends on depositors' savings. Second, they made home mortgage and improvement loans. Today, they offer most of the same services as commercial banks.

Savings and loan associations are like commercial banks in other ways. They, too, must be chartered by federal or state governments. In all federally chartered associations, deposits are insured up to $100,000 by the ***Savings Association Insurance Fund (SAIF).*** This fund is administered by the FDIC. The same is true of most state chartered associations.

Credit Unions

A ***credit union*** is a nonprofit financial institution owned by and operated for the benefit of its members. Membership is limited to people who share a common bond. For instance, a credit union might serve all employees of a company. It might also serve members of a union or professional organization.

Since credit unions are not-for-profit organizations, they pay no taxes. They are often run by their members. Their operating costs may be relatively low. For these reasons, successful credit unions may be able to lend funds at slightly lower rates. They may also pay slightly higher rates on savings than many other financial institutions.

Credit unions may be either federally or state chartered. The ***National Credit Union Administration (NCUA)*** grants federal charters to qualified groups and supervises credit unions across the country. The NCUA insures accounts up to $100,000 in all federal credit unions. If state credit unions request and qualify for such coverage, the NCUA can insure these accounts as well.

State Farm Insurance Companies

15-2
Life insurance companies offer services related to money management.

Mutual Savings Banks

A ***mutual savings bank*** is owned by its depositors. After deducting operating costs and cash for reserves, earnings are divided among depositors. These earnings are dispersed in the form of dividends. Traditionally, mutual savings banks received and paid dividends on deposits and made home mortgage and improvement loans. Now, they too offer a wider variety of financial services.

Mutual savings banks are chartered only by state governments. They exist in only 17 states—mostly in the northeast. Accounts in these banks are insured up to $100,000 by the FDIC or by state-sponsored insurance.

Other Financial Institutions

Other financial institutions also offer services related to money management. These include:

- *Life insurance companies,* whose main purpose is to provide financial security for the dependents of an insured individual. Today many insurance companies offer a variety of savings and investment features as part of life insurance coverage, 15-2.
- *Investment companies* or *mutual funds,* who primarily invest the pooled funds of investors for them. These companies invest in stocks, bonds, and other financial instruments. They also offer interest on savings and often provide limited check-writing privileges. Investment companies are not protected by the FDIC. They may charge management and commission fees for their services.
- *Finance or loan companies,* whose first function is to make loans to consumers and businesses. These companies are beginning to move into financial planning and other services related to money management.
- *Financial supermarkets,* who strive to offer a complete range of financial services under one roof. These companies may offer savings, investment, checking and credit accounts. They may also handle bill payment, money transfers, insurance coverage, mortgage

loans, real estate transactions, financial advice, and estate planning. Financial supermarkets may send consumers a single monthly statement listing activity in all their accounts. These companies do have some disadvantages. They may not offer competitive rates and service fees. Most are not insured by the FDIC. Sometimes personal service may get lost in these supermarkets of financial transactions. However, it can be convenient to do all your personal financial business in one place.

Personal Checking Accounts

When you earn a regular income, you will likely need the services of financial institutions to manage your money effectively. The first financial service used by many people when they start earning money is a checking account. It offers a safe place to keep cash. It provides a convenient way to buy goods and services and pay bills. It provides a record of spending and receipts of payments, 15-3.

Jack Klasey

15-3
A personal checking account is a convenient way to track your spending.

Four basic types of checking accounts exist. The best choice will depend on the amount you can deposit. It will also depend on the number of checks you expect to write each month. For interest-bearing accounts, your choice will also depend on the interest rate deposits earn.

A *regular* or *minimum-balance account* may have different names in different banks. This type of account requires a minimum amount of money in the account at all times to avoid service charges. If you fall below this minimum, you will be charged a set service charge. This amount varies from one financial institution to another. A regular account may be a good choice if you write lots of checks and can keep the minimum balance.

A *budget* or *economy account* requires no minimum balance. However, you pay a fee for every check you write. You may also pay a monthly service charge for the account. Charges vary from bank to bank. This account is a good choice if you write few checks and keep a low balance in the account. A budget account usually works well for people with relatively small earnings and few financial obligations.

A *check credit account* permits you to write checks on credit up to a set limit. You pay finance charges on the amount you borrow. This type of account is a convenient way to get credit when you need it. However, the ease of using a check credit account tempts many to spend beyond their ability to pay. A check credit account is available only to customers with an approved credit rating. It is an advantage only for those with the self-control to avoid overusing it.

An *interest-bearing checking account* is a combination savings and checking account. Your money earns interest, and you can write checks on the account. In credit unions, these accounts are called "share drafts."

In banks and savings and loan associations, they are called "negotiable orders of withdrawal" or "NOW accounts."

Financial institutions offer variations of the interest-bearing checking account. They may differ in interest rates, minimum balance requirements, and service charges. Compare these accounts carefully to see which one best meets your savings and checking needs.

When you shop for a checking account, the following questions may help you make the best choice:

- ❑ What is the minimum balance required for a regular account?
- ❑ What are the charges if the balance drops below the minimum?
- ❑ What are the charges per check or per month for a budget account?
- ❑ Does the institution offer a check credit account? If so, what is the charge for this service?
- ❑ Does the institution offer an interest-bearing checking account? If so, what is the interest rate?
- ❑ What is the minimum deposit requirement?
- ❑ What is the penalty for failing to maintain the minimum balance?
- ❑ What other services does the institution offer in connection with different types of checking accounts?
- ❑ What fees are charged for different services and accounts?

Opening a Checking Account

Whether you bank in a large city or small neighborhood, opening a checking account requires only a few simple steps. Certain policies may apply if you are under 18 years of age at the time you open the account. For instance, some banks may require you have a parent or guardian on the account with you. Others may allow you to open the account by yourself.

When you open an account, you will be asked to sign a signature card. This will be the only signature the financial institution will honor on checks and withdrawal slips. You should sign the card the way you intend to sign your name for all your financial transactions. Over the years, you will use your signature on contracts, Social Security forms, tax forms, and other documents. Sign your name the same way on all these documents to avoid confusion.

You may want someone else to have check-cashing privileges on your account. If so, that person will also need to sign a signature card. This is helpful if you are out of town often and want someone to access your account in your absence. When you share an account with someone, it becomes a ***joint account.*** When a teen's parent is on his or her account, this would be a joint account. Husbands and wives also often share joint accounts. This requires a clear understanding of who will write checks and how records of transactions will be kept.

When you open a checking account, you will receive a small book of starter checks. These checks are blank except for your account number. You can use these starter checks while you wait for your personalized checks to arrive. You will need to order personalized checks for your account. You can do this through your bank. Checks will be printed with your name, address, and account number on them, 15-4. The checkbook will include a register for keeping track of your transactions, 15-5.

Managing the Cards Related to Your Account

You may be offered personal credit, debit, and automated teller

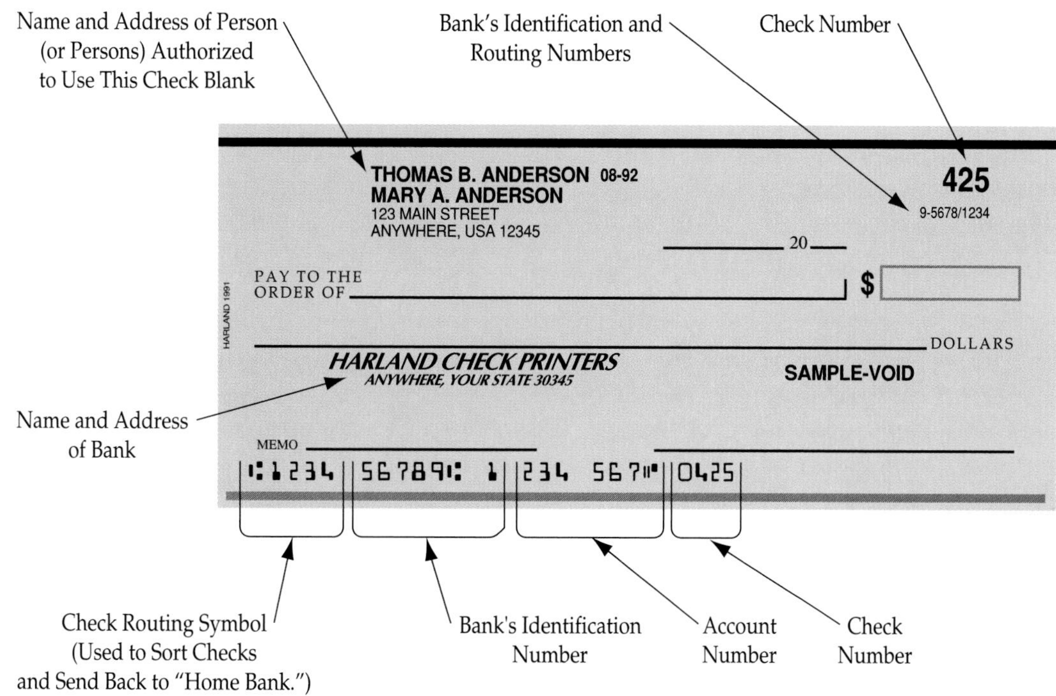

15-4
Your personalized checks include information financial institutions need to process checks correctly.

15-5
Make a point of recording all your checks, debits, ATM transactions, and deposits in the checkbook register.

RECORD ALL CHARGES OR CREDITS THAT AFFECT YOUR ACCOUNT

NUMBER	DATE	CODE	DESCRIPTION OF TRANSACTION	PAYMENT/DEBIT (−)	√ T	FEE (IF ANY) (−)	PAYMENT/CREDIT (+)	$ BALANCE
	3/1		Opening Balance				100 00	100 00
								100 00
101	3/2		Lee's Grocery	15 32				15 32
			Groceries					84 68
	3/3	ATM	Cash Withdrawal	20 00				20 00
								64 68
102	3/4		The Book Shelf	11 75				11 75
			Calender					52 93
	3/6	DC	No Limits	35 13				35 13
			Jeans					17 80
	3/8	D	Deposit				130 00	130 00
								147 80
103	3/9		Lee's Grocery	18 35				18 35
			Groceries					129 45
	3/11	AP	Unified Utilities	23 07				23 07
			Electric Bill					106 38
	3/14	DC	Mary's Dept. Store	34 60				34 60
			Navy Shirt					71 78
104	3/16		Richard's Records	21 20				21 20
			CD					50 58
	3/22	D	Deposit				130 00	130 00
								180 58
105	3/26		Lee's Grocery	47 58				47 58
			Groceries					133 00
	3/29	ATM	Cash Withdrawal	30 00				30 00
								103 00
106	3/30		Dr. Harvey	65 00				65 00
			Dental Checkup					38 00
	4/1	D	Deposit				130 00	130 00
								168 00
			Service Charge	5 00				5 00
								163 00

*USE THESE CODES WHEN RECORDING YOUR NON-CHECK TRANSACTIONS

D = DEPOSIT DC = DEBIT CARD ATM = TELLER MACHINE AP = AUTOMATIC PAYMENT TT = TELEPHONE TRANSFER T = TAX DEDUCTIBLE O = OTHER

machine cards when you open a checking account. Credit and credit cards are described in more detail in Chapter 13. Some checking accounts offer credit cards with overdraft protection for your account. If the account is overdrawn, the bank might automatically charge your credit card the amount needed to cover the overdraft. An overdraft fee would apply and might be charged to the card as well.

Debit cards, also called *check cards*, are cards used to pay for goods and services. When you make a purchase, you present the card. The merchant scans the card electronically. Then you will be asked to enter your *personal identification number* or *PIN*, which will activate the card. The purchase is then subtracted immediately from your checking account. In this way, using a debit card is similar to writing a check. Both types of payment come directly from your account. You will then keep your receipt and record the purchase in your checkbook register.

You may also receive an ATM card in connection with your checking account. An ***ATM card*** allows you to access your account using an automated teller machine (ATM). An *ATM* is a machine that allows you to deposit, withdraw, or transfer money from one account to another electronically. ATMs are located at banks, and other places, such as convenience stores, malls, airports, and grocery stores.

An ATM card allows you to access your account 24 hours a day from locations other than your bank's lobby. ATM cards can also be used at machines in other cities and states. This allows you to access your money while traveling. Generally, you may use an ATM owned by your bank at no charge. There is usually a charge, however, for any transactions you make at an ATM not owned by your bank. Fees charged for using an ATM card vary by bank.

If you obtain an ATM card, you will receive a PIN number for this card. To use the card, go to an ATM and insert the card. The machine will ask you to enter the PIN number. Then it will ask you to enter information about the transaction you want to make. With the push of a few buttons, the ATM can process your request. If you are depositing money, place it in an envelope and insert it into the machine as directed. If you are withdrawing money, the money will come out of the machine and you can remove it as directed. Safety tips for using an ATM appear in 15-6.

Some banks offer a combined debit and ATM card. This card can be used to access an ATM machine. It can also be used to pay for goods and services. In the future, more banks may provide this type of card.

Credit cards, debit cards, and ATM cards offer several advantages. They eliminate the need to carry large amounts of cash. They allow you to access your money any time of day or night. They let you purchase goods and services in places where checks are not accepted.

If used wisely, these cards can provide you greater financial flexibility. They will only benefit you if you use them responsibly, however. Safeguard you cards and your PINs so no one else can gain access to your account. Inquire about the service fees associated with using your cards and any limits that apply to their use.

Remember to record all transactions and fees in your checkbook register. This will help you avoid errors in your account balance. Keeping your receipts will also help. It is your responsibility to know how much money you have. Do *not* withdraw more than is in your account. Some ATMs will allow you to withdraw more money than is in your account. Some merchants will allow you to make a purchase with your credit or

- ❏ Memorize your personal identification number (PIN). Do not tell anyone your PIN. Do not write your PIN down and carry it with you. If anyone stole both your card and PIN, this person would have complete access to your account.
- ❏ Select your machine carefully. Do not use a machine in an unsafe or isolated area. Criminals may target ATMs as an easy place to rob people of their money. Watch carefully before approaching the ATM. If you see anyone lurking around the ATM, use another machine or come back later.
- ❏ Avoid using the ATM at night. If you must use an ATM at night, choose a well-lit machine in a populated area. For instance, consider using an ATM inside a grocery or convenience store over using an outdoor walk-up machine at a bank. If you must use a machine at a bank at night, choose a drive-up rather than walk-up machine if possible.
- ❏ Protect your privacy. Do not let anyone see you enter your PIN. If someone is standing too close to you as you make your transaction, you might politely ask the person to step back or consider using the ATM at another time. This is true for people you know as well as strangers.
- ❏ Make your transaction quickly. Spend as little time at the ATM as possible to conduct your business. For instance, when you approach the ATM, have your card out and ready. Wait to count your money until later so you can leave the area immediately.

15-6
Money is withdrawn at ATMs, making them a target for crime. Follow these tips to use ATMs safely.

debit card that exceeds your account balance. If your account is overdrawn, you will be charged a fee.

Making Deposits

To deposit money in your account, fill out a deposit slip as a record of the transaction. A deposit slip states what is being deposited—currency, coins, or checks—and the amount of each item, 15-7. Follow these steps when filling out a deposit slip:

1. Write in the date.
2. Enter the amount of money being deposited. Write the amount of cash being deposited beside the word *Currency*. Write the amount of coins to be deposited beside the word *Coin*. Write the amount of each check being deposited beside the word *Checks*. If you need more room, you may continue listing checks on the back of the deposit slip.
3. Add the total amount of currency, coins, and checks to be deposited. Write this number after the word *Sub-total*.
4. If you want to withdraw cash at the same time you make a deposit, enter the amount after the words *Less cash received*. You must sign on the line under the date if you want cash back from your deposit.
5. Subtract the amount in *Less cash received* from the amount written in the *Sub-total* box.
6. Enter the actual amount deposited after *Total deposit*.
7. Record the amount deposited in your checkbook register.

When you make a deposit in person, you will receive a receipt. If you deposit by mail, the bank will send you a receipt. When you make deposits at an ATM, insert your card and enter your PIN and the amount you are depositing. You will receive a receipt detailing the transaction and showing the current balance in your account. Save your receipts to assist you in balancing your checkbook.

Endorsing Checks

Before you can cash or deposit a check made out in your name, you must endorse it. To ***endorse*** a check, sign your name on the back of the check at the left end. The endorsement lets you cash the check or deposit it into your account. There are three ways to endorse a check. See 15-8.

A *blank endorsement* requires only the signature of the payee. The *payee* is the person to whom the check is written. A check endorsed this way may be cashed by anyone. For your protection, use this type of endorsement only at the time and place you cash or deposit a check.

A *restrictive endorsement* states what is to be done with the check. *For deposit only* is a common restrictive endorsement. A check with this type of endorsement may be used only for the specific purpose stated in the endorsement. This endorsement is often used when banking by mail or depositing at an ATM.

A *special endorsement* is used to transfer a check to another party. Only

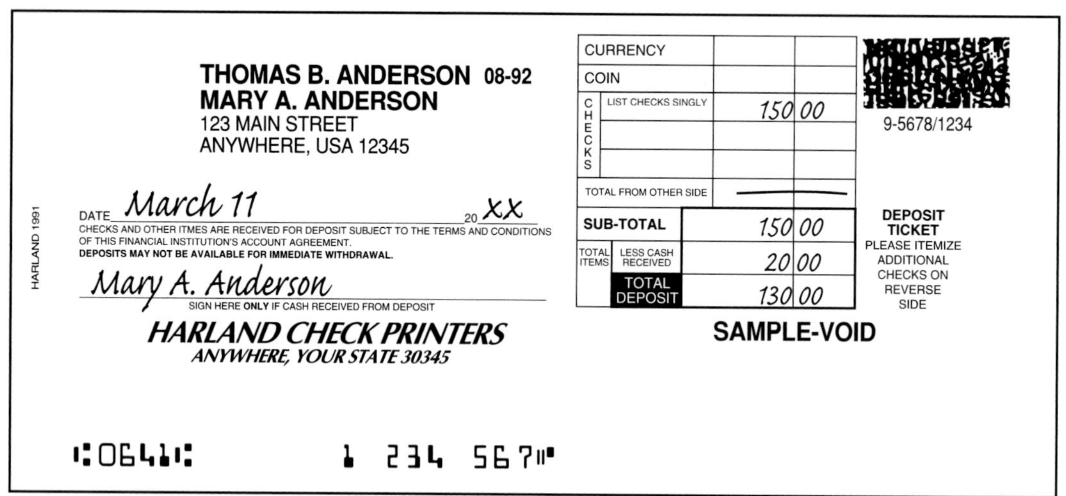

15-7
A deposit slip is a record of money you put into your account.

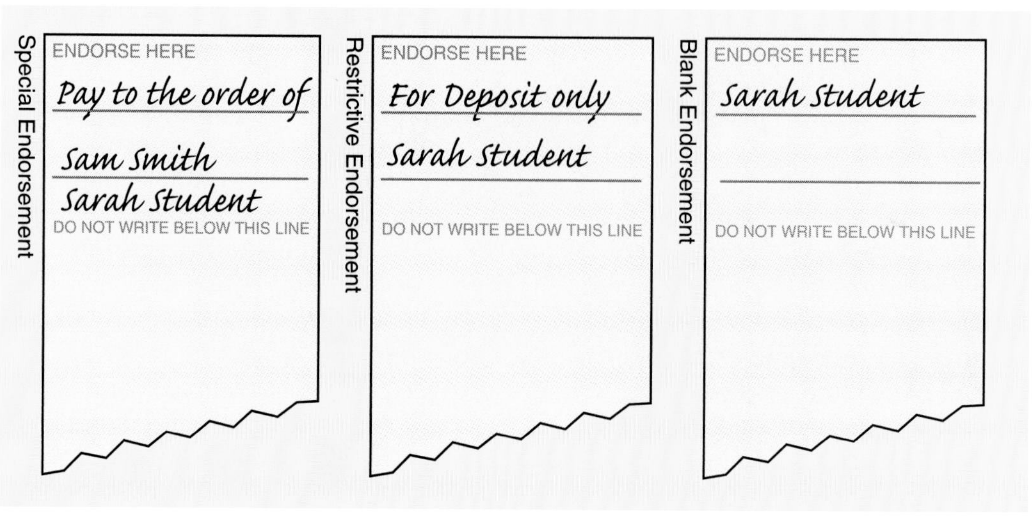

15-8
Before you deposit or cash a check made out to you, it is necessary to endorse it.

the person named in the endorsement can cash the check. To use a special endorsement, write *Pay to the order of* _____ (the name of the party to receive the check). Sign your name as it appears on the check.

Writing Checks

A blank check has important information on it. This information helps financial institutions process checks correctly. For checks to be processed, they must also be written correctly. When writing a check, you need to enter the following items in the correct spaces. See 15-9.

1. The date.
2. The name of the payee—the person, business, or organization receiving the check.
3. The amount of the check in numbers.
4. The amount of the check in words, starting at the far left. After the amount of dollars, write the amount of cents in numbers as a fraction. Draw a line through the remaining space.
5. The reason for writing the check, after the word *Memo*, if you want a record.
6. Your signature. Use the same signature you used on the bank signature card.

For your own protection, write checks in ink. Pencil could be easily erased, which means someone could alter your check after you have written it. If you make a mistake, destroy the check and start over on a new check. Do not make corrections on the check.

When you write a check, record the check number, date, payee, and amount in your checkbook register. Subtract the amount of each check from your existing balance. Also record the date and amount of each deposit you make. Add the amount of each deposit to your existing balance. If you follow these guidelines, you will always know how much money is in your account. With an up-to-date record of checks and deposits, it will be easy to balance your account each month.

Balancing Your Checkbook

Once you open a checking account, you will generally receive a bank statement each month. A ***bank statement*** is a record of checks, ATM transactions, deposits, and charges on your account. Some banks do not send a statement

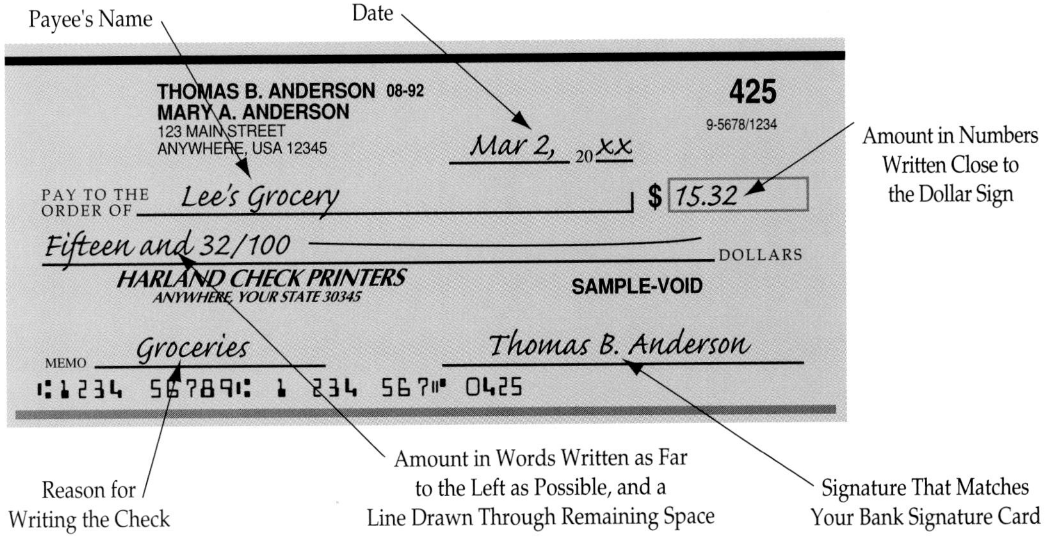

15-9
Write checks neatly and carefully to avoid mistakes.

every month. Instead, they might send a statement every quarter. For some accounts, the customer can choose whether to have monthly statements sent. Inquire about this when opening an account.

Each time you receive a bank statement, it is important to make sure your record agrees with the bank's record. This is called *reconciling* your bank statement. The bank statement will give a summary of the activity in your account, 15-10. It will usually include these items:

- Opening balance—the amount of money in your account at the beginning of the bank statement period.
- Deposits received—the date and amount of each deposit received during the statement period.
- Checks paid—the date and amount of each check paid out of your account during the statement period.
- ATM transactions—the date and amount of any withdrawals or deposits made at an ATM during the statement period.
- Other charges—the date and amount charged for checks, overdrafts, and service fees.
- Closing balance—the amount of money in your account at the end of the statement period.

Below the summary is a detailed record of each check, deposit, and ATM transaction, as well as a running balance of your account. Canceled

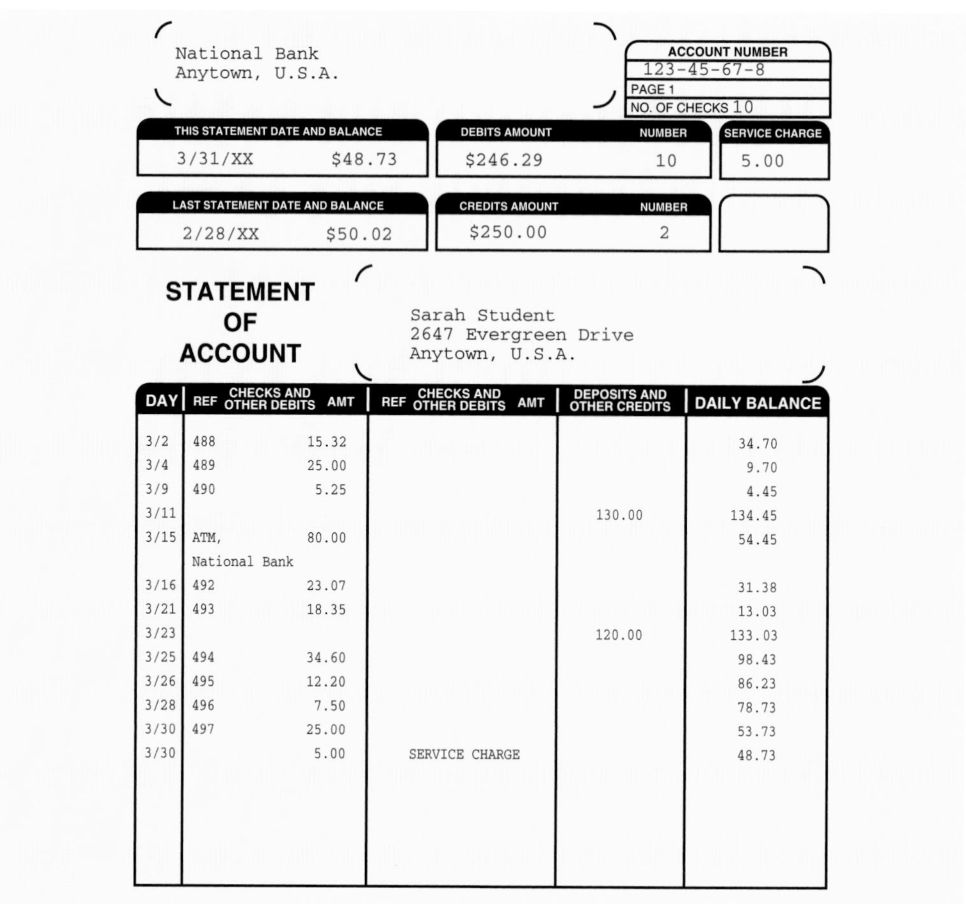

National Bank
Anytown, U.S.A.

ACCOUNT NUMBER 123-45-67-8
PAGE 1
NO. OF CHECKS 10

THIS STATEMENT DATE AND BALANCE		DEBITS AMOUNT	NUMBER	SERVICE CHARGE
3/31/XX	$48.73	$246.29	10	5.00
LAST STATEMENT DATE AND BALANCE		**CREDITS AMOUNT**	**NUMBER**	
2/28/XX	$50.02	$250.00	2	

STATEMENT OF ACCOUNT

Sarah Student
2647 Evergreen Drive
Anytown, U.S.A.

DAY	REF	CHECKS AND OTHER DEBITS AMT	REF	CHECKS AND OTHER DEBITS AMT	DEPOSITS AND OTHER CREDITS	DAILY BALANCE
3/2	488	15.32				34.70
3/4	489	25.00				9.70
3/9	490	5.25				4.45
3/11					130.00	134.45
3/15	ATM, National Bank	80.00				54.45
3/16	492	23.07				31.38
3/21	493	18.35				13.03
3/23					120.00	133.03
3/25	494	34.60				98.43
3/26	495	12.20				86.23
3/28	496	7.50				78.73
3/30	497	25.00				53.73
3/30		5.00	SERVICE CHARGE			48.73

15-10
A bank statement is a record of all deposits, checks, charges, and other transactions involving your account during the statement period.

checks paid from your account may or may not be enclosed with the statement. This may depend upon your wishes and the type of checking account you have. Some banks store their customers' canceled checks for safekeeping rather than returning them to the customer. If so, you can usually obtain copies of your canceled checks by calling the bank.

The first step in balancing your checkbook is to compare the canceled checks with the checks listed on the statement. Then compare the canceled checks with those recorded in your checkbook register. Compare the deposits in your register with those on the statement and any receipts you may have. Check ATM transactions and fees recorded in your register against those on the statement. If the statement shows any service charges, subtract these from the balance shown in your register.

Now you need to account for the checks, ATM transactions, and deposits that do not appear on the statement. On the back of most bank statements, there is a worksheet provided for this, 15-11. On the worksheet, follow these steps:

1. On the first line, write the closing balance as shown on the bank statement.
2. List all deposits you have made that are not included on the statement.
3. Add the amounts from steps 1 and 2, and write down the total.
4. List by number and amount any checks and ATM withdrawals that are not included on the statement. Add these amounts together and enter the total where it says *Checks outstanding*.
5. Subtract the amount in step 4 from the amount in step 3. Write this number by the word *Balance*.

The balance on your worksheet should match the current balance in your checkbook register. If these two do not agree, go through the above steps one more time very carefully to check your math. If the figures still do not agree, you may want to contact your bank for help.

Using Other Types of Checks

In addition to personal checks, other types of checks can be used to transfer funds from payer to payee. These include cashier's checks, certified checks, money orders, and traveler's checks. Each serves a special purpose. They are available from most financial institutions, usually for a fee.

A ***cashier's check*** is drawn by a bank on its own funds and signed by an authorized officer of the bank, often the cashier. A person may buy a cashier's check to make a large payment to another person instead of paying with a personal check. A cashier's check is a more acceptable form of payment than a personal check when the payer is not well known by the payee.

A ***certified check*** is a personal check with a bank's guarantee the

BALANCING WORKSHEET

MONTH *March --*, 20 *XX*

BANK BALANCE shown on this statement $ *48.73*

ADD+

$ *125.00*

DEPOSITS made but not shown on statement because made or received after date of this statement.

TOTAL $ *173.73*

SUBTRACT−

CHECKS OUTSTANDING .... $ *68.40*

BALANCE .... $ *105.33*

The above balance should be same as the up-to-date balance in your checkbook.

CHECKS AND DEBITS OUTSTANDING
(Written but not shown on statement because not yet received by Bank.)

NO.		
498	*28*	*40*
499	*15*	*00*
ATM	*25*	*00*
TOTAL	*68*	*40*

15-11
This type of worksheet and directions for balancing an account will appear on the back of most bank statements.

check will be paid. When a bank certifies a check, the amount of the check is immediately subtracted from the payer's account. A certified check is used to make a payment to someone who does not want to accept a personal check. It is required for certain types of transactions.

A ***money order*** is an order for a specific amount of money payable to a specific payee. People who do not have checking accounts may use money orders to send payments safely by mail. Money orders are sold in a number of places. It is wise to buy them only from reputable sellers, such as insured financial institutions and post offices.

Traveler's checks are often used by people who travel and don't want to carry large amounts of cash. They can be cashed most places around the world. If the checks are lost or stolen, they can be replaced at the nearest bank or agency that sells them. When using these checks, keep a record of the check numbers separate from the checks. *This is very important.* You need identifying numbers to replace lost or stolen checks. It is also important to sign the checks only at the time and place you cash them.

> ***"Plan ahead—it wasn't raining when Noah built the ark."***
>
> *General Features Corporation*

Savings Accounts

Saving money in a financial institution offers many advantages. It provides a safe place to keep money and a way to earn interest or dividends. Beginning a savings program can also encourage you to save regularly and help you establish a good credit rating.

Most financial institutions offer a variety of savings plans. These include regular savings accounts, money market accounts, and different types of certificates of deposit (CDs). At credit unions, savings accounts are called share accounts and CDs are called certificates of shares.

Regular Savings Accounts

A ***regular savings account*** allows you to make deposits and withdrawals in varying amounts as you wish. The two most common regular savings accounts are passbook savings and statement savings. Many financial institutions may offer other savings plans with special features for young people and senior citizens. These vary from one bank to another.

With *passbook savings,* you receive a book to record deposits and withdrawals. You would access your account in the lobby of your bank with a bank teller. Some consider this a disadvantage, because it restricts consumers from accessing their accounts outside their bank's days and hours of operation.

With *statement savings,* you receive regular statements of deposits, withdrawals, and balances. As with a passbook account, you could access your account personally at your bank. In addition, you might also use a debit card, an ATM card, or online banking with a statement savings account.

Being able to accumulate your money in a savings account is an advantage. This can help you meet financial goals and plan to meet future expenses. In addition, most savings accounts earn interest. The money you deposit does not simply sit in storage. The bank uses that money for many purposes, including loans to customers and investing in the community. For the privilege of using your money, the bank pays you an additional percentage of your earnings as interest.

How much interest you earn on savings will depend several factors. First, it is based on the annual interest rate, the frequency of compounding interest, and the annual percentage yield (APY).

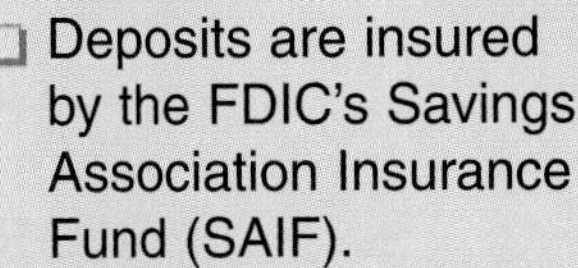

Using Dollars and Sense

A Savings Comparison

Dean and Sally are both high school juniors. Dean works as a part-time cook at a local restaurant. Sally works after school and on Saturdays at a bakery. Both want to put some money aside for the future. After studying saving and investing in their consumer education class, Dean and Sally each decided to open a savings account. At the end of a year, they will compare results.

Before beginning, they set some guidelines. Both agree to open a savings account with $100 and deposit $10 in the account each week for one year.

After shopping carefully for an account, Dean decides to open a passbook savings account at a local bank. He chooses the account for the following reasons:

- He can open the account with a small amount of money, and add to it at any time in any amount.
- The interest rate is 4 percent, compounded daily. This makes the annual percentage yield (APY) 4.08 percent, which compares favorably with other similar accounts Dean has researched. The APY is the total amount of interest paid on a $100 deposit left in an account for one year.
- Dean's bank will calculate interest from the day of deposit to the day of withdrawal. This will let him deposit and withdraw money as he chooses without loss of interest.
- His bank computes interest daily. Dean figures that, as his savings grow over a long period of time, this frequent compounding of interest will increase his earnings.
- Dean's bank gives special consideration to savings account customers who apply for auto loans. Dean plans to buy a car after graduation. A savings account with a record of regular savings would make it easier for him to get a car loan.
- His deposits are insured by the FDIC.
- The bank is in a convenient location with convenient business hours. The employees are very friendly and helpful.

While Dean chose a commercial bank, Sally decided to open her savings account at a savings and loan association. Here are the reasons for her choice:

- Sally's account has an interest rate of 4 percent, compounded quarterly. This make the APY on her account 4.06 percent, which is about average for this type of account.
- Sally has a checking account at the same savings and loan association. She can arrange to have her $10 weekly savings automatically transferred from checking to savings.
- Sally's savings and loan offers premiums for new accounts. Sally will get two free tickets to the local theater for opening an account.
- Deposits are insured by the FDIC's Savings Association Insurance Fund (SAIF).
- Drive-up ATM services are available.

At the end of one year, Dean's and Sally's earnings will differ only by a few cents. However, over a longer period of time and for a larger amount of savings, Dean's account (compounded daily at an APY of 4.08 percent) would earn slightly more than Sally's account (compounded quarterly at an APY of 4.06 percent). When rates are so close, other factors often become more important in deciding where to save.

Case Review

1. What do you think of Dean's reasons for choosing a passbook savings account at a commercial bank?
2. What do you think of Sally's reasons for choosing a savings account at a savings and loan association?
3. What would you consider most important when opening a savings account?
4. When two different accounts (like Dean's and Sally's accounts) quote almost the same annual percentage yield, how would you decide which account to choose?
5. What information could you find online to help you find a savings account to meet your needs?

Compounding interest means the interest previously earned is included in the total before any new interest earnings are computed. The more often interest is compounded, the more interest you will earn. Compounding may be done on a daily, monthly, quarterly, or yearly basis.

The ***annual percentage yield (APY)*** is the total amount of interest that would be paid on a $100 deposit based on the annual interest rate and the frequency of compounding. Financial institutions must state the APY when describing earnings on savings. This allows consumers to compare accounts at various institutions.

Figure 15-12 shows how the frequency of compounding affects the annual percentage yield (APY) and interest earnings. This example is based on a $1000 deposit at an annual interest rate of 5.0 percent over a one year period.

At first glance, the differences shown in 15-12 may seem quite small. Remember, however, this example involves only $1000 and one year of saving. The differences grow more significant when saving larger amounts of money over longer periods of time.

How often interest and dividends are credited to your account also makes a difference, 15-13. Earnings are credited to savings accounts periodically—monthly, quarterly, semiannually, or annually. For example, your savings may earn interest that is compounded daily, but those earnings may only be credited to your account once a month or once a quarter.

The way interest is calculated can also be important. For instance, you will benefit if interest and dividends are calculated from the day of deposit to the day of withdrawal. This means your money earns interest for the entire time it is on deposit.

How interest is calculated and credited to your account matters little unless you withdraw money just before the crediting date. In this case, you may not receive the uncredited earnings. To combat this problem, some institutions offer a *grace period.* During this time, you can receive full earnings on deposits or withdrawals. The grace period often extends from five days before to five days after the crediting date. You could withdraw or deposit money during the grace period and still receive interest for the entire month.

When deciding where to open a regular savings account, ask about any fees, penalties, and restrictions. These

Frequency of Compounding Interest

Frequency of Compounding	APY	Interest Earnings
No compounding (Simple interest)	5.0%	$50.00
Quarterly compounding	5.0945%	$50.95
Monthly compounding	5.1162%	$51.16
Daily compounding	5.1267%	$51.27

15-12
How often interest is compounded can make a difference in your overall earnings.

Jack Klasey

15-13
Find out exactly how your bank calculates interest before opening a savings account.

can affect both your earnings and your use of the account. Savings accounts may involve fees, minimum deposit or balance requirements, or limitations on the number of withdrawals per month. For example, you might need to deposit and maintain $50 in your account to avoid a monthly maintenance fee of $2.00. These are important considerations. In addition, there are other qualities to look for when opening a regular savings account, 15-14.

Searching for a Savings Account

For top earnings on your savings, look for:

- ❑ The highest annual interest rate.
- ❑ The highest annual percentage yield (APY).
- ❑ The most frequent compounding of interest.
- ❑ Earnings to be calculated from the day of deposit to the day of withdrawal.
- ❑ The most frequent crediting of earnings to your account.
- ❑ The lowest fees and fewest restrictions on the account.

15-14
You must look carefully to find the savings account that will make the most money for you.

Certificates of Deposit

A ***certificate of deposit (CD)*** is sometimes called a savings certificate, time deposit, or time account. A certificate of deposit requires you to deposit a given amount of money for a set period of time. It earns a set annual rate of interest. A minimum deposit is usually required.

CDs require you to commit your money for a period of time. For this reason, they pay a higher rate of interest than regular savings accounts. The longer you agree to hold a CD, the higher the rate of interest you can earn. A six-year CD will yield a higher annual rate of interest than a two-year CD.

Some certificates of deposit may offer a variable or floating interest rate. The rate moves up and down with market rates. Usually it is tied to a specific market rate, such as the rate on U.S. Treasury Bills. Normally, a variable rate will have a lowest limit on the interest rate. For example, you might buy a three-year variable rate CD with a current APY of 4.5 percent. The rate can rise as the market rate rises, but would be guaranteed to pay no less than 3.5 percent. Certificates of deposits sold by banks are covered by the FDIC and are insured for amounts up to $100,000. Most credit union CDs offer the same protection through the National Credit Union Administration.

Although most CDs can be cashed before the time period is over, a significant amount of interest would be lost. For example, suppose you buy a four-year certificate for $1,000 at an annual interest rate of 7.5 percent, compounded daily. If you hold it until maturity, you would earn $355.45 interest. If you cash it at the end of two years, you would lose two years' interest. You would also receive less interest for the two years you held the certificate. The interest would be computed at the rate of a regular savings account. If the regular account rate is 5.5 percent annually, you would only receive $117.98 interest.

Money Market Accounts and Funds

Many financial institutions offer money market accounts. A ***money market account*** is a type of mutual fund that deals only in high interest, short-term investments. These include U.S. Treasury Bills, CDs, and commercial paper. Earnings go up and down with current market interest rates. These accounts usually require minimum balances and may offer limited check-writing privileges. A money market account that is covered by the FDIC is insured for amounts up to $100,000.

Money Market Mutual Funds

You also can put your savings to work in a money market mutual fund. This type of mutual fund may be available through banks, credit unions and investment brokers. These funds "pool" the savings of many depositors. This pool is used to buy short-term debt instruments such as U. S. Treasury securities or certificates of deposit.

> *"A penny saved is a penny earned."*
>
> *Benjamin Franklin*

The interest earned, minus the expenses of operating the fund, is passed along to the depositors. This form of saving is relatively safe and convenient. However, these accounts are not covered by the FDIC. Funds are easy to convert to cash, and savings earn current market rates. Check-writing privileges are usually available. No interest penalties apply for early withdrawals.

A Personal Savings Plan

Opening a savings account or buying a CD at a financial institution is a fairly simple task. A harder task may be deciding which institution will bring you the highest earnings for your savings. The more money you save, the more important it is to shop for the best savings plan.

The ***Truth in Savings Act,*** passed in 1991, is designed to help consumers compare savings plans and interest rates. This law requires depository institutions to state earnings on deposits in uniform terms. The purpose of the Truth in Savings Act is to help consumers compare savings plans and make informed decisions. According to this Act, advertising and other materials describing savings plans should include:

- The *annual percentage rate (APR),* which is the rate of simple annual interest paid without compounding.
- The annual percentage yield (APY) and the period during which that APY is in effect.
- The minimum deposit, time requirements, and other terms the saver must meet to earn the stated APY.
- The minimum amount required to open the account.
- A description of any fees, conditions, and penalties that could lower the yield.

Using Dollars and Sense

A Closer Look at Earnings

Devan has $2,500 in a savings account that earns 5.5 percent interest. He had been saving for a down payment on a new car. When the new car models came out in September, he decided to order the model he wanted because he had enough money. On October 20, the car dealer called to tell Devan his car had arrived. Devan hurried to the bank to take out his savings for the down payment. That's when he was unpleasantly surprised.

Since the interest on his account is computed daily, Devan thought he would receive another interest payment when he withdrew his money. However, the bank applies interest on this type of account only twice a year. The last interest payment was made June 30. The next one will not be made until December 31. If Devan withdraws his savings now, he will not receive any interest for July through October.

Devan was expecting to receive interest for the entire time his money was in savings. This would have given him about $50 more in interest. However, Devan needs his money right away for the car. He will just have to lose out on the interest.

Case Review

1. How could Devan have avoided this problem?
2. Would Devan lose less if he took out a 90-day loan for the down payment instead of withdrawing his savings before the end of the interest period? How would the amount of finance charges he would pay for a 90-day loan compare with the amount of interest he would earn on his savings?

To decide which form of saving is best for you, first outline your savings plans and goals. Following are a few questions to consider:

- ❑ How much can you save regularly each week or month?
- ❑ When and how often do you expect to deposit money?
- ❑ When and how often do you expect to withdraw savings?
- ❑ Are you willing and able to deposit $1,000 or more for 90 days or longer?
- ❑ Do you have a specific goal, such as an amount you want to save within a given length of time?
- ❑ Are you saving for a specific purpose or purchase?
- ❑ Is it important to be able to convert savings to cash quickly and conveniently?

Once you determine your savings goals and needs, you are ready to shop for a savings plan. When choosing a financial institution, make sure its deposits are insured. Also find out what services each institution offers in connection with savings accounts and CDs. Look for services that will be convenient and helpful to you. Then compare various types of savings plans.

You may want to start your search online. The Internet offers hundreds of links to financial institutions. Many of these institutions offer savings plans with different rates, terms, fees, and services. The Internet is a good place to research current interest rates paid on different types of savings by various institutions.

Before you open an account, ask the following questions.

- ❑ What are the APR and APY for the account? The higher these are, the more interest your money will earn.
- ❑ What method is used to calculate interest? Suppose you make a lot of deposits and withdrawals during the interest period. The amount of interest you earn will vary with the calculating method used.

- How often is interest compounded? The more frequently interest is compounded, the more interest your savings will earn, 15-15.
- How often is interest paid or credited to your account? Interest periods may be monthly, quarterly, semiannually, or annually. Generally, shorter interest periods offer more flexibility for depositing and withdrawing money without loss of interest.
- What are the policies on deposits and withdrawals? Can you put money in or take money out as you choose without losing any interest?
- Is there a grace period? Can you withdraw or deposit money during the grace period without losing interest for that period?

Earning Power—Rate of Interest

Compound	4%	5%	6%	7%	8%	9%
Daily	$2,879.33	$2,955.26	$3,033.82	$3,115.11	$3,199.25	$3,286.33
Quarterly	$2,871.29	$2,944.48	$3,019.97	$3,097.83	$3,178.14	$3,260.97

15-15
If you deposit $10 per week over a period of three years, the growth of your savings will depend on the rate of interest and the frequency of compounding.

Using Dollars and Sense

Checking As Savings?

Cody, a high school senior, has been pumping gas at a local service station for the past two years. Although he only works part-time, he earns good pay.

Now that he has money, Cody is fascinated with the idea of letting money work for him. At a savings and loan last year, he bought a $1,000 certificate of deposit for a two-and-a-half-year term. This CD earns 5 percent interest annually.

Cody also has a checking account at a commercial bank. He usually keeps $200 to $300 in the account. Cody heard the savings and loan association is offering a checking account that earns 5.25 percent interest. He wondered if he should change accounts. Although the account wouldn't earn much more, something more would be better than nothing, right? That's not true in this case.

Unlike his regular checking account at the bank, the NOW account calls for a minimum balance of $500. If his balance fell below this minimum, there would be a $5 monthly service charge and a charge of 20 cents per check. Cody could probably manage $500 most of the time, but it wouldn't be easy. If his balance did fall below the minimum, he would lose money. Therefore, Cody decides it will be smarter for him to keep his savings separate from his checking account.

Case Review

1. What do you think of Cody's decision?
2. When would it be to your advantage to have a NOW account?
3. How do NOW accounts compare at financial institutions in your area?
4. Find out the current yields at financial institutions in your area for $1000 deposited in a regular savings account, a CD, and a money market account.

Before buying a certificate of deposit, or CD, ask these questions.

- What are the current APY and maturity date?
- What is the dollar amount of earnings if you hold the certificate to maturity?
- Can you cash the CD before maturity? If so, what are the penalties for cashing it early?
- What happens to the CD at maturity? Will your money earn interest at the regular savings account rate? Will it be automatically reinvested in another CD? Will the financial institution hold it with no interest until hearing from you? Will you receive notice of the maturity in advance? This would give you time to decide how to put the money to work again.

Personal Retirement Accounts

Personal retirement accounts help people establish financial security for their retirement years. These accounts may be opened at banks, savings and loan associations, credit unions, brokerage firms, mutual savings banks, or insurance companies. Many employers also offer retirement plans and programs. These are discussed in Chapter 14.

A person deposits money into his or her personal retirement account. This money and the interest earned on it accumulate until after a person is 59½ years old. At that time, the person can begin to withdraw the money invested. This is one way that people can put back money to pay expenses in their later years.

Personal retirement accounts may also offer tax advantages. A portion of the contributions to a retirement account may be tax deductible. This means savings accumulate tax free.

The Individual Retirement Account (IRA) and the Keogh Plan are the two main types of personal retirement accounts.

Individual Retirement Accounts

An ***Individual Retirement Account (IRA)*** is a saving account in which employed people can make annual contributions up to a set amount. The funds in an IRA accumulate and earn interest. The interest earned on amounts deposited will not be taxed until it is withdrawn at age 59½ or later. Generally, the funds may not be withdrawn before retirement without penalty. However, penalty-free withdrawal of up to $10,000 is allowed for the purchase of a first home or to pay for qualified higher education costs. The advantage of tax-free accumulation of savings can be very impressive.

IRA contributions are limited by law. Single taxpayers may contribute up to $2,000 annually to an IRA. Married couples with only one wage earner may contribute $2,250 annually. Two-income couples may contribute $4,000 annually. Those who meet specific requirements may be able to deduct IRA contributions from income to reduce current taxes. These regulations change often. They are explained in forms sent to taxpayers each year by the Internal Revenue Service.

Most taxpayers may open an IRA by making the required deposit with any responsible financial institution. IRA funds may be invested in a variety of CDs, securities, and other investment vehicles. It is possible to open more than one IRA account and spread retirement funds among different types of investments.

Consumers can shift IRA funds from one investment to another with only a few restrictions. There are also few restrictions on shifting funds from one account to another. In most cases, withdrawing funds early results in stiff tax penalties and loss of interest.

The Keogh Plan

The *Keogh Plan* is a retirement plan for self-employed persons. A self-employed person can contribute $30,000 or 20 percent of earnings, whichever is less, annually to a Keogh account. This amount can be claimed as a tax deduction. Like IRAs, the interest earned on Keogh accounts is not taxed until retirement. Retirement may begin as early as 59½.

Keogh funds may be invested in a number of ways. When opening a Keogh account or an IRA, it is important to choose a sound and reputable financial institution. This institution should be able to meet your specific investment goals.

Other Services of Financial Institutions

Financial institutions may offer many services in addition to checking accounts, special checks, savings plans, and retirement accounts. You may find some of these services helpful in managing your money over the years.

Electronic Banking Services

Electronic funds transfer (EFT) is a system of carrying out financial transactions by computer rather than using checks and cash, 15-16. Services may include:

Automated Teller Machines

An ATM is an electronic terminal at which you can make deposits, withdraw cash, or transfer funds between accounts 24 hours a day. To access your account at an ATM, use your ATM card, which is specially coded with your account information. Terminals are located at your financial institution and other convenient locations.

Direct Deposits or Withdrawals

This service lets you arrange for paychecks, social security payments, and other checks to be deposited directly into your account. You would do this by completing a form provided by your bank, employer, or other party. Then your money would be deposited directly into your account rather than given to you as a check. Direct deposits into your account should appear on your bank statement.

You can also arrange automatic payment of recurring bills from your account. Car payments, insurance premiums, utility bills, and mortgage payments are the bills most commonly paid by direct withdrawal. This allows you to pay bills without having to take the time to write checks. Direct withdrawals from your account should appear on your bank statement.

You can also have a set amount of money transferred each month from checking to savings. Using EFT in these ways can make managing your money more convenient.

15-16
ATM cards let you deposit and withdraw money from your account at all times of day and night and at a variety of locations.

Using Dollars and Sense

What About Online Banking?

For her birthday, Alyssa received a computer with all the accessories. She was eager to start using it. Alyssa marveled at the Internet and the world it opens up to people. She has had both a checking and a savings account at a local bank for several years. The idea of banking at home from her new computer sounded very tempting. How nice it would be to pay her bills and track her accounts from her own desk at home.

Alyssa visited her bank's Web site on the Net to research the bank's online services. After reading about the banking tasks she can handle at home, Alyssa is eager to sign up for this new service. She went to her bank the next day to sign up for the online service. The bank gave her a software package—a disc to install in her computer and a booklet describing what she could access online.

At home, Alyssa installed the program on her computer. She selected her user ID and security code and accessed her account online. Alyssa set up a list of merchants to pay online. Among these, she directed her rent and insurance premiums to be paid automatically. She would pay her other bills as she received them.

Alyssa also decided to have her paycheck deposited directly to her account. In addition, she arranged an automatic transfer of $50.00 from checking to savings each month. All in all, Alyssa felt she had gained a new control over her financial affairs.

Case Review

1. How would you feel about conducting your financial business online?
2. What questions would you ask when signing up for online banking services?
3. What are some of the advantages of online banking? Can you identify any disadvantages?

Pay-by-Phone Transfers

A *pay-by-phone transfer* is a service in which you handle transactions with your financial institution over the telephone. This service allows you to have your institution pay bills from your account in amounts and on dates you designate. You can also request by phone the bank transfer funds from one account to another. Ask your financial institution whether this service is available and what fees apply.

Point-of-Sale Transfers

A *point-of-sale transfer* occurs when a debit card is used. First, the merchant scans your debit card. Then the amount of the purchase will be immediately transferred from your account to the merchant's account. This allows you to purchase merchandise without checks or cash.

Online Banking Services

Many of today's consumers find online banking more convenient than traditional banking. With this service, they no longer have to go to the bank during business hours to handle their financial transactions. They can conduct banking business from their homes 24 hours a day.

If you use online banking, your bank will assign you a user identification and security code. You will need this information to gain access to your account online. Keep these codes confidential so no one else can use your account. With these codes, you can go online to do the following:

- ❑ Check your account balance.
- ❑ Review your account history.
- ❑ Arrange electronic bill payment.
- ❑ Set up direct deposits, withdrawals, and transfers.

Even if you bank online, you must still visit the bank or an ATM to make deposits or withdrawals, however. You may need to visit your bank for other special services as well.

If you are interested in online banking, ask your financial institution whether this is an option for you. This electronic service requires a computer with a modem, a checking account, and an online banking software package. Financial institutions that offer online services often give consumers the software they need to get started.

Overdraft Protection

With this service, a financial institution will honor checks you have written even if they exceed your account balance. You pay a fee for each overdraft. This differs from a check credit account. Here the protection is not set up formally, and overdrafts are not encouraged. You can ask your bank to learn what fees or charges may apply for this service.

Drive-Up and Mail-In Services

Many financial institutions offer the convenience of being able to make deposits and withdrawals by mail or at drive-up windows. Drive-up banking may even be available at times when the lobby is closed. This can be very convenient.

Safe-Deposit Boxes

Some financial institutions rent boxes in their vaults for the storage of valuables. Jewelry, wills, birth records, insurance policies, and other important items are often kept in safe-deposit boxes. This can be an important feature if you have valuable items you wish to store in a safe location. Rental charges for these boxes vary.

Stop Payment

Upon your request, a financial institution will refuse to honor a check you have written if it has not already been cashed. This service is useful if a check is lost and you want to prevent anyone from cashing it. You can also order a stop payment if you have a grievance concerning goods or services you paid for by check. A charge generally applies for this service but, depending upon the circumstance, it may be well worth the cost.

Financial Counseling and Special Programs

Find out what types of special financial services are offered. These may include a trust department, assistance with tax returns, financial planning, money market funds, mortgage loans, and other specialized services. Also inquire about the fees associated with any special services that interest you.

Choosing a Financial Institution

Before selecting a financial institution, identify your needs and match them to the services available to you. A broad range of financial services is available to consumers today. This is largely a result of deregulation, computer technology, and growing economic sophistication, 15-17. The services a financial institution offers depend primarily on its size and the needs of its customers.

When choosing a financial institution, consumers generally look for checking, savings, and borrowing facilities. There are many factors to consider when evaluating the institutions that offer these services. You can learn about different financial institutions and their services online. Before you open an account, however, it may be wise to visit the institution that interests you in person. This way you can learn where it is located. You should also be able to sense whether it appears to be a reputable business with friendly and helpful staff.

Financial Services

- ❑ Checking accounts.
- ❑ Savings accounts.
- ❑ Credit card accounts.
- ❑ Certificates of deposit.
- ❑ Personal loans.
- ❑ Home mortgages and home improvement loans.
- ❑ Farm and business loans.
- ❑ Auto loans.
- ❑ Retirement accounts.
- ❑ Money orders, cashier's checks, certified checks, and traveler's checks.
- ❑ Sale and redemption of U.S. Savings Bonds.
- ❑ Trust, investment, and estate management.
- ❑ Online banking.
- ❑ Overdraft protection.
- ❑ Automated teller machines.
- ❑ Direct deposits, withdrawals, and transfers.
- ❑ Safe-deposit boxes.
- ❑ Financial counseling and planning.

15-17
This is a brief listing of the types of services financial institutions may offer.

Types of Checking, Savings, and Credit Accounts

This chapter described different types of checking and savings accounts. Chapter 13 covers forms of consumer credit. As you identify your needs in these areas, look for financial institutions that offer the accounts and services that will work best for you.

Interest Rates

Compare the interest rates you will earn on your savings from one institution to another. Also, examine the rates you will pay to use credit. Look for high yields on savings and low rates for credit.

Restrictions and Penalties

Ask about minimum balance requirements, withdrawal limitations, and penalties for overdrafts or late payments on credit accounts. These items can increase the cost of services and create inconveniences in managing your money.

Fees and Charges

Ask about all the fees and charges associated with the type of account you want to open. These fees and charges can make it more costly to have an account. Charges may exist for check writing or having less than a minimum balance in your account. Also inquire about fees for ATM transactions, overdrafts, overdraft protection, retirement accounts, and other services.

Safety

Check to see if accounts are insured by a federal government agency. You will not want to put your money into a place where it is not protected. Also, investigate the overall soundness of the institution. You can ask others about the reputation of financial institutions you are researching.

Convenient Location, Hours, and Services

Look for financial institutions that make banking and other financial transactions easy for you. This may mean choosing hours that work well for you, a location that is easy to reach, and services that save you time and effort.

Compare the banks, credit unions, savings and loan associations, and other providers of financial services. Find the place that can best serve your current and ongoing financial needs. Once you choose a financial institution, establish a good working relationship. Make your financial needs known and learn how the institution can help you manage your money.

Summary

Financial institutions aid the flow of money in the economy. For consumers they provide key money management services. These include checking, savings, and credit accounts. The institutions that provide these services include commercial banks, savings and loan associations, credit unions, and mutual savings banks.

A checking account is the first financial service needed by most consumers. Types of checking accounts include regular accounts, budget or economy accounts, check credit accounts, and interest-bearing checking accounts. Each of these meets different consumer needs. Shop around and ask questions before choosing a specific account and financial institution.

Managing a checking account involves certain basic skills—making deposits, writing and endorsing checks, and balancing your account each month. Responsible use of checking accounts aids in money management. It also helps you build a sound credit rating.

Several types of savings accounts are also available. Key factors to consider when deciding when and where to save include the annual percentage rate (APR), the annual percentage yield (APY), the frequency of compounding interest, lowest fees, and fewest restrictions on savings accounts. Savings are also offered in the form of CDs, money market accounts, and IRAs. These types of savings are usually a part of an overall financial plan. Setting personal savings goals will help you decide where and how to save your money.

You may also want to look into the variety of other financial services designed to help consumers manage their money. It pays to shop around for a financial institution that offers the services and personal attention you need.

To Review

1. What is the primary function of financial institutions in the economy?
2. Name at least four services offered by each of the following financial institutions:
   A. commercial banks
   B. savings and loan associations
   C. credit unions
   D. mutual savings banks
3. True or false. Credit unions often charge lower interest rates on loans and pay higher interest rates on savings than commercial banks and savings and loan associations.
4. A _____ checking account requires no minimum balance, but there may be a fee per check or a monthly service charge.
5. What is an interest-bearing checking account usually called at credit unions? At banks and savings and loan associations?
6. What is the purpose of endorsing a check?
7. How can you keep track of the checks you write?
8. What determines the amount of interest you earn from a regular savings account?
9. Explain what the APY is and how it is used in reference to savings accounts.
10. An account earning 5.50 percent annual interest will earn the most if it is compounded:
    A. quarterly
    B. monthly
    C. daily
11. Which law requires depository institutions to state earnings on deposits in uniform terms?
12. The _____ is a retirement plan for self-employed persons.

To Think Critically

1. How do the FDIC and the NCUA protect depositors?

2. What are the four basic types of checking accounts? Name the advantages and disadvantages of each.
3. What are some key questions to ask when shopping for a checking account? What are some fees and charges commonly attached to checking accounts?
4. Explain how to balance a checking account using the monthly statement and checkbook register.
5. How does a cashier's check differ from a certified check?
6. When are traveler's checks often used?
7. What should you consider before buying a certificate of deposit?
8. Why does a $1,000 CD usually earn a greater yield than $1,000 deposited in a regular savings account?
9. How does an IRA differ from a Keogh Plan?
10. What is the advantage of having overdraft protection at a financial institution?

To Do

1. Survey local financial institutions to learn the types of financial services each provides. Then make a chart showing the services provided by each institution.
2. Prepare a bulletin board showing how to write and endorse checks.
3. Assume you have $1,000 you can save for one to three years. Compare savings options at three or more financial institutions. Determine which institution will pay the highest rate of interest for your money. Also find out how much you could expect to earn in one, two, and three years. In a short report, explain which savings plan you would choose and why.
4. Interview an officer in a financial institution about retirement accounts. Find out the advantages and disadvantages of opening a retirement account when you're in your twenties. Report your findings to the class.
5. Develop a checklist for comparing financial institutions to find one that best meets individual needs for checking, saving, and credit accounts.
6. Research and give a written or oral report on electronic funds transfer systems. Explain how electronic transfers work, how they have changed the financial services industry, and how they benefit consumers.
7. Go online to gather information about financial institutions. Select five institutions and compare the financial services they provide. Include consumer loans and mortgages, online banking services, savings plans, fees and charges for services, interest paid on savings, and interest charged on loans and credit cards. Report and discuss your findings in class.

CHAPTER 16

Investments and Life Insurance

investment portfolio
risk tolerance
dividend
liquidity
marketability
security
prospectus
stock
common stock
preferred stock
bond
face value
maturity date
yield
corporate bonds
municipal bonds
government bonds
investment club
mutual fund
money market fund
term life insurance
renewable term
convertible term
whole life insurance
cash value
endowment insurance
annuity

After studying this chapter, you will be able to

- ❑ explain the role of investments and life insurance in overall financial planning.
- ❑ establish goals and objectives to be achieved through a sound insurance and investment program.
- ❑ identify the various types of investment choices.
- ❑ read and understand investment listings in financial papers.
- ❑ explain the role of real estate in an investment plan.
- ❑ distinguish between the various types of life insurance.
- ❑ select appropriate life insurance coverage for different stages of the life cycle.
- ❑ access investment and life insurance information online.

Using money to make money is called *investing*. Unfortunately, investing involves risk. The degree of risk varies. High-risk investments usually offer the possibility of big gains—and big losses. Low-risk investments usually offer less profit and less chance of major losses.

Historically, investors who financed new products, such as the automobile, fountain pen, and rubber band, came away with handsome profits. Those who invested in products that didn't succeed lost their money. Most investors fall somewhere between high profits and big losses. If you want to invest and come out ahead, now is the time to learn a few basic investment facts.

Investment Goals and Strategies

When you spend money to make money, several factors are important to consider. Begin by determining your investment goals. These will differ for each individual. Investment goals will also vary for the same person at different times during the life cycle.

People often invest to achieve certain financial objectives. These may include saving money to pay for college, start a business, buy a home, travel, or retire.

In establishing your investment goals, decide what you want to achieve. Consider when you hope to reach your goal, and how much money you will require. See 16-1. Consider how much you are willing to sacrifice now to meet future investment goals. Then take a look at the amount you can invest now and as you go along. When you know what you hope to achieve with your money, it's time to develop your investment strategies. Several factors should be considered. These include the following:

Building an Investment Portfolio

First, you need to clarify your investment goals and form an investment strategy. Then you will be ready to build a *portfolio* of securities that will meet your objectives. An ***investment portfolio*** is the collection of stocks, bonds, and other securities a person or

Establishing Financial Goals

Investment objective ______________________
Target date ______________
Target amount $______________
Amount on hand $______________
Amount available to save or invest
______________ weekly
$______________ monthly
$______________ quarterly
$______________ annually

Type of Investment	Specific Objectives	Estimated Earning Potential	Estimated Risk Potential
Stocks			
Bonds			
Mutual Funds			

Choice of listed options: ______________________

Periodic evaluations and comments: ______________________

16-1
This form can help you plan and invest to meet specific investment objectives.

group owns. The selection of securities for a portfolio is generally based on several factors. Most importantly is the investor's objectives. Attention is also paid to important factors such as risk, diversity, growth and income potential, and timing. Buying, selling, and trading decisions all become part of the plan for the investment portfolio.

Risk Versus Safety

The amount of uncertainty you can bear is your ***risk tolerance.*** It is connected to the amount you can afford to lose and your comfort level with the possibility of loss. If you can take high risks, you may be rewarded with big gains. You may also suffer big losses. Conservative investors and those who cannot afford big losses will want to look for safer investments. *Safety* refers to a small risk of loss in an investment. Investments range from very safe to high risk or *speculative.* Each person needs to determine his or her own emotional tolerance for risk.

Diversification for Risk Reduction

Diversification refers to spreading risk by putting money in a variety of investments. When you invest in several types of securities, you lower your risks. One or two may disappoint you but others will bring rewards.

Growth Potential

Growth, or *appreciation,* refers to an increase in the value of an investment. Various types of investments grow at different rates. Some offer greater and faster growth possibilities than others.

Income Potential

Income from investments comes in the form of dividends or interest. A ***dividend*** is the money paid to stockholders from a company's earnings. Very often investments that emphasize current income offer limited growth potential.

Timing of Investment Decisions

Timing refers to finding the best time to buy or sell different types of investments. Ideally, you will buy at the lowest price and sell at the highest price. This does not always happen, however. Proper timing requires careful study.

Consider the time frame for your goals, the length of time you can leave cash invested, your stage in the life cycle, and the economic climate. If you hope to reach your goals soon, you will need to invest more and receive higher returns. Generally, the longer your money can be invested, the better it will be. This will give you more choices, and you are likely to earn more money.

> *"To get profit without risk, experience without danger, and reward without work, is as impossible as it is to live without being born."*
>
> *A. P. Gouthey*

Your stage in the life cycle and your earning power determine how much you can invest. These factors also influence what degree of risk you can afford to take. Young investors with years of earning power ahead can usually take greater risks than those closer to retirement. Older investors may need more security and current income from their investments.

Economic conditions, such as current interest rates, growth rates, inflation, or recession, can influence which types of investments are the best choices at different times.

Liquidity

If you want to keep cash readily available, you will need liquid assets.

Liquidity is the ease with which you can convert an asset to cash without serious loss. Assets with the highest liquidity include cash in savings accounts, money market funds, and the cash value of life insurance.

Marketability

Marketability refers to the ease of trading an investment. Securities actively traded in large numbers on major stock exchanges are highly marketable, 16-2. Stock exchanges make most stocks and bonds marketable, or easy to trade. Less marketable investments include antiques, coins, gold, and real estate. Marketability can be important to investors who may need to quickly turn their investments to cash.

United Airlines

16-2
What happens on Wall Street influences financial and investment decisions all around the world.

Tax Considerations

If you qualify to invest in an IRA, investing your money in this type of account offers substantial tax benefits. (See Chapter 15 for a review of IRAs.) Your savings accumulate tax free until you withdraw them at age 59½ or later. You can direct the investment of funds in the account. The tax-free accumulation is a substantial benefit.

Investors in high tax brackets may also want to consider municipal bonds. The interest earned on these bonds is exempt from federal income tax. Taxpayers in high-income brackets also may need to look at a variety of other tax considerations related to investing.

Investment Choices

Stocks, bonds, and mutual funds are key ways to invest your money. These are three types of securities. A ***security*** is issued by a corporation or government to raise money to operate and expand. Each security has advantages and disadvantages. Varying degrees of risk and earning potential exist for each type as well. The best choice for you will depend upon your goals, financial status, and personal preferences.

A company or government agency issues securities. When you buy a security, you become an owner or a creditor of its issuer. For instance, shares of stock are a form of ownership in a company. The stockholder is part owner of the company. Bonds represent a loan of money to the issuer of the bond. If you buy bonds, you are a creditor—the issuer owes you money. Mutual funds represent ownership in the investment company that sells shares of the fund to the public.

When securities are sold, the issuer must provide a ***prospectus***. This is a detailed description of the security. It includes financial facts, a listing of officers, business history and operations,

Life Plans

A Giving Uncle

Alia and DJ are married. They are in their early twenties and are expecting their first child. Both work, but Alia wants to work part-time after the baby is born. This will reduce their combined income by almost 25 percent. Their savings consist of an emergency fund equal to about two month's income. They had always planned to start a savings program for their child at birth. However, at this time they have no extra money.

Alia's uncle, Will, has been very successful in his own business. He has no children and Alia has been like a daughter to him. Will decides to fund a savings plan for Alia's new baby. He plans to invest $1,000 annually in the baby's name from birth through age 21. This should provide a good start on education, training, or another important goal.

Uncle Will, true to his word, puts $1,000 into a fund for the child every year. The investment earns 5.5 percent annually, compounded monthly. At the end of 21 years, it amounts to $40,558. If left in the account at 5.5 percent for another five years, it will accumulate to $59,275. In ten years, it would grow to $83,900.

Case Review

1. What is the advantage of steady saving and investing at an early age?
2. What are some ways parents can start a savings and investment program for children at birth or soon after?
3. What restrictions might parents, or in this case Uncle Will, want to place on the use of money saved in a child's name?
4. Under what circumstances would it be financially sound to use Uncle Will's fund at age 21? In five years? In ten years?

and plans. The prospectus contains information an investor would need to make an informed decision about buying the security. It is important to study the prospectus before buying. This is especially true if you invest without the advice of an investment professional.

Stocks

A ***stock*** is a share in the ownership of a corporation. Companies sell stocks to pay the costs of business start-up, continuing operations, and expansion. When you buy stock in a corporation, you become part owner of that company. Stockholders share in the profits of the company after debts, taxes, and operating expenses are paid. Two types of stock are common and preferred.

Owners of ***common stock*** may earn a share of the profits in dividends declared by the company. Dividends are paid when declared by the company's board of directors. Owners of common stock can vote on company directors and other matters. The price of common stock usually moves up and down in the market more than that of preferred stock. Prices are affected by overall economic conditions, company sales, earnings, and future outlook.

Owners of ***preferred stock*** receive regular dividends at a set rate. They do not have to wait for the board of directors to declare them. However, preferred stock owners do not have voting privileges. If a corporation goes bankrupt or is dissolved, claims on the company's assets go first to creditors. Next, preferred stockholders' claims are met. Only then are the claims of common stockholders met. Since it is paid first, preferred stock is a more conservative, safer investment with less risk than common stock. However, the price of preferred stock does not typically increase as much as common stock in companies that do well.

Bonds

A ***bond*** is a certificate of debt issued by a corporation or government. Until the bond matures, the bondholder is a creditor. He or she is entitled to a set rate of interest on the bond's face value. ***Face value*** is the amount for which a bond is issued and on which interest payments are figured. At maturity, the bondholder receives the face value. The ***maturity date*** is the day a bond or other obligation is due to be paid. Other important terms relating to bonds follow:

The ***yield*** is the percentage of a return on an investment.

Coupon rate is the annual interest the issuer promises to pay on the face value.

Market value is the amount for which a bond sells. It may be more, less, or the same as the face value.

Current yield is the annual interest or coupon rate divided by the market price of a bond.

Here's how a bond transaction works: Corporation X issues a $1,000 bond (face value) with a 9 percent coupon rate. The bond will pay $90 annual interest (9 percent × $1,000). If it sells for $1,000, the face value and the market value are the same. The coupon rate and yield are the same also—$90. However, if the bond sells for $900 (market value), the yield goes up to 10 percent ($90 annual interest ÷ $900). If the bond sells for $1,200 (market price), the yield drops to 8 percent ($90 ÷ $1,200).

Generally, $1,000 is the lowest face value for a bond. Bond prices or market values tend to move away from market interest rates. For example, as interest rates go up, bond prices fall. As interest rates fall, bond prices increase.

The safety of bonds depends on the credit rating of the issuer. Rating agencies classify and rate bonds according to risk. Two such agencies

Life Plans

Money from the Keyboard

Cotelia is thirteen years old. She is already an outstanding pianist. She studies on scholarship at a local music center and attends a music camp in the summers. She plans to become a concert pianist and play with symphony orchestras around the world.

When she is not seriously practicing her music, Cotelia raps with several friends who play other instruments. The group is pretty good. They play for school dances and other functions. Cotelia also solos frequently for parties and other events. In the past year, she has been paid for many performances. Her earnings came close to $1,800.

Cotelia and her friends want to form a musical group called "The Funky Friends" to play concerts, dances, and parties. They will charge for their performances. They could earn a considerable amount over the next few years.

Cotelia wants to earn and save as much as possible to pay for studying music in Europe. She wants to take lessons with the best music teachers there. She knows this will be necessary to reach her potential as a serious pianist.

Case Review

1. How would you advise Cotelia to save and invest her earnings over the next five years?
2. What might she be inclined to do with her money if she did not have these objectives—or if her family could afford to pay for her future study?
3. How do objectives like Cotelia's influence earning efforts, and savings and investment decisions?
4. What are some ways young people with other interests and talents can earn, save, and invest for future goals?

are Moody's and Standard and Poor's. The soundest, high-quality debt with the least risk receives a triple A rating. As the risk increases, the ratings decline, 16-3. Coupon rates generally are higher on lower quality bonds to reward buyers for taking greater risks. The three major issuers of bonds are corporations, municipalities, and the federal government.

Moody's Bond Ratings		Standard and Poor's Bond Ratings	
Aaa	B	AAA	B
Aa	Caa	AA	CCC
A	Ca	A	C
Baa	C	BBB	D
Ba		BB	

16-3
Bond ratings help buyers evaluate risks. Both Moody's and Standard & Poor's ratings are available in public libraries.

Corporate bonds are issued by businesses that need money to operate and expand. The quality, coupon rates, and yields of these bonds vary with the financial soundness of the issuing corporation. Yields and market prices move up and down as market interest rates change, 16-4.

Municipal bonds are issued by state, county, and city governments, 16-5. Coupon rates and yields depend on market rates and the financial soundness of the issuing municipality. Interest on these bonds is exempt from federal income tax. In some states, interest is also exempt from local and

Understanding Bond Quotations

1	1a	1b	2	3	4	5
Bonds			Cur Yld	Vol	Close	Net Chg
AT&T	4½	05	4.5	13	99¾	+½
Amoco	7⅜	13	6.3	6	117½	—
CmwE	7⅝	06	7.5	10	101½	—

1. The bond listing includes the name of the issuing corporation, the coupon or interest rate (1a), and the maturity date (1b). The coupon rate is stated in ten-dollar increments. To get the dollar amount, multiply the number by ten. For example, 4½ would equal $40 (4 X 10) plus $5.00 (½ X 10), or $45. The AT&T bondholder will receive $45 in interest annually until the bond matures in 2005. The Amoco bondholder will receive $73.75 annually until maturity in 2013. The CmwE bondholder will receive $76.25 annually until 2006.
2. The current yield is the amount the bondholder receives for every $100 invested. This amount is calculated by dividing the coupon rate, or annual interest, by the closing price. For AT&T, 4.5 divided by 99.75 equals 4.5 percent current yield. Amoco's 7.375 divided by 117.5 equals 6.3 percent current yield. For CmwE, 7.625 divided by 101.5 equals 7.5 percent current yield.
3. The volume shows the number of bonds traded for the day. In this example, the volume is listed in tens of thousands. Therefore, on the day of the quote, AT&T traded 130,000 bonds. Amoco traded 60,000 bonds, and CmwE traded 100,000 bonds.
4. The close is the final price for the trading day. Since the bond is issued at $1,000, these prices are a percentage of the face value. AT&T closed at 99¾ percent or $997.50 (.9975 X 1,000): Amoco closed at 117½ percent or $1175 (1.175 X 1,000); CmwE closed at 101½ percent or $101.50 (1.015 X 1,000).
5. The net change is the difference in the close and the final price of the previous trading day.

16-4
Understanding bond quotations is important when following bonds and their price changes in the marketplace.

Terry Jenkins/Evanston Chamber of Commerce

16-5
Hospitals, schools, and other public buildings are often financed by municipal bonds.

state taxes. This makes municipal bonds attractive to upper income investors in high tax brackets.

Government bonds are issued by the U.S. Treasury. They are the safest bonds you can buy. When you buy Treasury securities, you are lending your money to the federal government. Treasury bills, notes, and bonds are the major types of federal government debt. Each of these sells for a minimum of $1,000, and bids must be made in multiples of $1,000.

Treasury bills (T-bills) are short-term debts, ranging from 3 to 12 months. They are the most actively traded government debt. Treasury bills sell for less than the face value. They do not pay interest before maturity. You pay less than $1,000 for a T-bill and receive the full $1,000 at maturity. The difference between the price you pay and the amount you receive at maturity is the interest.

Treasury notes and *Treasury bonds* are sold at a stated interest rate. Buyers receive semiannual interest payments. Treasury notes have a term of one to ten years. Bonds are long-term investments—ten years or more. The interest rates on these securities depend upon the market rates at the time they are issued. For example, interest rates on federal long-term bonds was as high as 10.8 percent in 1980. In 1997, they stood at 6.67 percent. Generally, treasury securities cannot be redeemed before their maturity date.

Series EE savings bonds are also issued by the Treasury. These bonds are purchased at half their face value. For example, a $100 savings bond costs $50. If it is held until maturity, this bond will pay $100. Savings bonds earn 90 percent of the average market rate on five-year Treasury notes. These rates change periodically. Interest is credited to savings bonds monthly.

The *I-bond* is a relatively new Treasury offering. This savings bond is designed to protect the buyer from high inflation. It sells at face value in denominations ranging from $50 to $10,000. In other words, a $50 I-bond sells for $50. It pays a fixed interest rate plus a semiannual inflation add-on rate. The add-on rate will be based on changes in the consumer price index. When interest rates are low and inflation is not a threat, the return on I-bonds will be relatively low. However, they are good insurance against inflation.

Both Series EE bonds and I-bonds carry a three-month interest penalty if redeemed within the first five years. Savings bonds are exempt from state and local income taxes. If they are used to pay for education, they may also be exempt from federal income tax. To learn more about U.S. savings bonds, contact a Federal Reserve Bank or the Bonds Division of the Bureau of Public Debt. You can also check out government bonds at your bank or online.

Buying Stocks and Bonds

Stocks and bonds are bought and sold on security exchanges and other markets. Two of the major exchanges are the *New York Stock Exchange (NYSE)* and the *American Stock Exchange (AMEX).* Both are located in the financial district of New York City. See 16-6.

The *National Association of Securities Dealers Automated Quotations (NASDAQ)* is a computer network for trading securities. It quotes prices for the securities it lists. Through the NASDAQ, dealers can execute trades electronically. Over 5,400 companies are listed on the NASDAQ.

When buying stocks and bonds, you should consider current market conditions. These conditions influence the price of securities. *Bull* and *bear* are terms often used to describe the strength of the market. A bull market exists when investors are confident in the economy and stock prices are rising. A bear market exists when investors feel insecure and uncertain about the economy and stock prices begin to fall.

Since the object of investing is to make money, you want to buy low and sell high if possible. You can learn the prices of securities by reading financial publications, such as *The Wall Street Journal.* Securities transactions and investment news also appear daily in the financial pages of major newspapers. You will also find useful information on specific investments from

Alan Rosenberg

16-6
The stocks, bonds, and mutual funds of more than 1,000 companies are traded daily on the American Stock Exchange floor. Listed securities are highly marketable.

annual reports, investment firms, stock advisory services, and stockbrokers. The Internet is another valuable source. You can research and follow securities online. Investment-related Web sites provide current data on individual stocks, bonds, and mutual funds. They also give a good picture of market activity.

As you make investment decisions, look for companies in industries that are financially stable. Industries refer to groups of companies in similar businesses. Categories of industry groups include consumer, energy, financial, industrial, technology, and utilities. You no doubt can think of individual companies in each category. Look for those companies that do well within their industries. A company that does well has growth potential and a fair share of the market for its products or services.

In evaluating a company, look for a steady increase in earnings over the past several years. The *P/E ratio* or *price/earnings ratio* can be used to evaluate a company. You find this ratio by dividing the current price of one share of stock by the current earnings per share. The P/E ratios usually range from 5 to 20. Speculative stock P/E ratios are often much higher. These ratios are listed in stock quotations each business day. See 16-7. Generally, low P/E ratios indicate a good time to buy a stock. High ratios may indicate that a stock is overpriced. As a rule, you should be wary of stocks with P/E ratios at either the high or low extreme.

If current income from investments is important to you, look for stocks that pay steady dividends and show high yields. If growth is more important, choose companies that put earnings

Understanding Stock Exchange Quotes

1		2	3	4	5	6	7	8	9	10
52 Weeks		**Stocks**	**Div**	**Yld %**	**PE**	**Vol 100s**	**Hi**	**Lo**	**Close**	**Net Chg**
Hi	**Lo**									
19	13	Maytag	.50	3.0	38	19409	17⅛	16	16½	-¼

1. **The 52-week high and low** columns show the highest and lowest price paid per share of stock over the past year.
2. The **stock** column shows the full or abbreviated name of the company. It may be followed by the trading symbol used by the corporation.
3. The **dividend** column shows the distribution rates or dividends paid per share over the past 12 months.
4. The **yield percentage** column shows dividends paid by the company as a percentage of the price per share.
5. The **price/earnings** column shows the price of a share of stock divided by the earnings per share over the past year.
6. The **volume or sales** column shows the daily total of shares traded, quoted in hundreds. (For the above listing, sales totaled 1,940,900.)
7. The **high** column shows the highest price paid per share for the day.
8. The **low** column shows the lowest price paid for the day.
9. The **last or close** column shows the price paid for the last trade of the day.
10. The **net change** column shows the difference between the price paid for the last trade of the day and the price paid for the last trade on the previous day.

16-7
Stock quotations provide essential information for investing in securities and following those you own.

back into research, development, and expansion rather than paying dividends. Finally, look for companies with enough assets to cover liabilities and operating expenses. All this information should be readily available from stock reports, annual reports, and stockbrokers. Stock quotations in daily papers provide current information on individual stocks.

Investment Clubs

Basically, an ***investment club*** is a group of 12 to 18 people who work together to learn about securities and invest their pooled funds. An investment company is usually a legal partnership, largely to meet income tax requirements. Officers of the club generally include a president, vice president, secretary, and treasurer. Members attend regular meetings (usually monthly) and pay dues. The members decide by vote the amount of the dues each person will pay per month. Members research and follow stocks under consideration or in the club's portfolio. They also buy and sell securities by vote of the majority.

An investment club can be a good way to start investing. It offers the opportunity to invest on a small scale while learning. If you can find at least 11 friends who are interested in learning to invest, you may want to consider forming an investment club. The National Association of Investors Corporation is a good place to get information on starting and running a successful club. You can check this organization out online.

Mutual Funds

A ***mutual fund*** is an investment offered by a company that uses the money it receives from investors to buy securities from corporations and governments. In other words, a mutual fund is a package of several securities. They may also be called investment trusts. Mutual funds may be bought and sold through an investment company or on a stock exchange. If you buy shares in a mutual fund, you automatically become part owner in all the companies in the fund. The two basic types of mutual funds are open-end funds and closed-end funds.

A *closed-end fund* has a fixed number of outstanding shares. These shares are traded like stocks on the New York and American Stock Exchanges. They are bought and sold through investment brokers, not through an investment company.

The *open-end mutual fund* has a floating number of shares. It sells these shares and redeems them at their current market or net asset value. Open-end mutual funds may be considered *load* or *no-load funds*. Load funds are sold by broker-dealers in the open market. A sales commission of up to eight percent of the amount invested will apply. A no-load fund is purchased directly from the company that sponsors the fund. There is no sales commission for this type of fund. A redemption fee may apply, however, if the shares are sold within a set number of years.

Both closed- and open-ended mutual funds charge management fees to pay for their research, administration, sales, and other expenses. These fees normally range from one-half to two percent of the investment. Other fees may also be involved.

Mutual funds differ in their goals and the types of securities they buy. *Income funds* buy conservative bonds and stocks that pay regular dividends. Their primary goal is to provide current income. *Balanced funds* invest in common stock, preferred stock, and bonds. Their goal is to provide a low-risk investment opportunity with moderate growth and dividend income. *Growth funds* invest in securities that are expected to increase in value. They emphasize growth over income. *Specialized funds* invest in securities of certain industries, such as all computer companies. They may also invest in certain types of securities, such as all municipal bonds or common stock. Some concentrate on foreign securities.

Mutual funds offer three advantages—professional management, diversification, and marketability. They are managed by professional investors who follow the markets carefully and are assisted by a team of researchers. Mutual funds offer variety in a single investment. As mentioned earlier, when you invest in several securities, you spread your risks. Shares are easy to buy and sell at any time on exchanges or through authorized agents. See 16-8.

Money Market Funds

A ***money market fund*** is a type of mutual fund that deals only in high interest, short-term investments. These investments include U.S. Treasury Bills, certificates of deposit, and commercial paper. (Commercial paper is a short-term note issued by a major corporation.) Interest rates on money market funds go up and down with money market rates. The funds are managed and sold by investment companies, brokerage firms, and other financial institutions.

Investing in money market funds has many advantages. These funds can provide small savers with high yields when interest rates are high. They can be liquidated (cashed in) at any time since they have no term or maturity

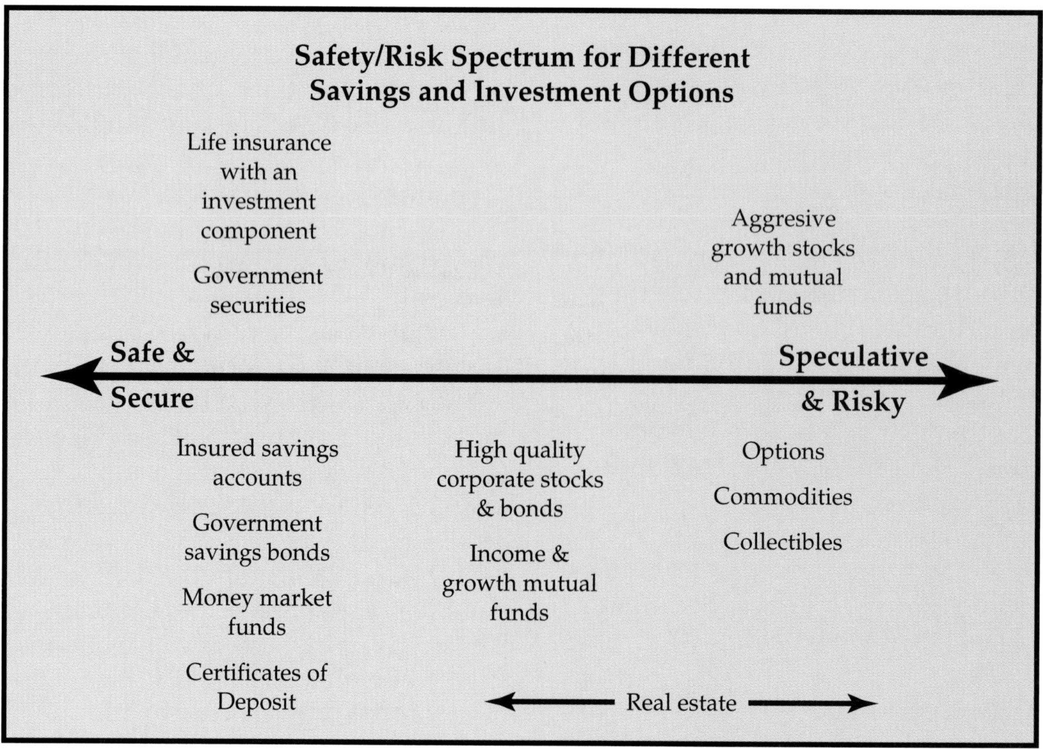

16-8
This chart shows the typical safety range for different types of investment alternatives.

date. They can be used as collateral for loans. Most money market funds offer check-cashing privileges.

Money market funds have some disadvantages, too. The rate paid on money market funds changes daily. If money market rates drop, so does the rate of return. Money market funds are not federally insured. A minimum investment of $1,000 or more is usually required. If the funds are not purchased through the firm or company operating the fund, fees are usually charged for making deposits and withdrawals.

Investing in Mutual Funds and Money Market Funds

Investigate before you invest in mutual or money market funds. As with any investment, a certain amount of risk is involved, 16-9. Begin by reading the prospectus of any fund that interests you. Look for answers to questions in the following key areas.

Management

What are the qualifications and experience of the fund managers? What are the investment policies and overall philosophy?

Objectives

What are the fund's primary goals? Does the fund seek to provide income, growth, balance, or speculative opportunities? Do the fund's goals and objectives match yours?

Performance

How has the fund performed? How does its performance compare with other funds and the market as a whole? Has performance been steady over a number of years?

Services

What services are offered by the fund? These may include check-cashing privileges, automatic reinvestment of dividends, and ease of transfer from one company fund to another.

Manufactured Housing Institute

16-9
Buying a home is a common first-time real estate investment.

Costs

What is the current net asset value per share? What management and other fees must you pay? Is there a commission or loading fee? Must you pay a fee when selling or redeeming shares?

Market information on mutual funds appears in the financial section of *The Wall Street Journal* and other major newspapers. The mutual funds section is divided into families of funds. It lists the names of individual funds within each family group. For example, the Franklin group of funds includes 72 different mutual funds. Each has its own name and investment objectives. *The Wall Street Journal* established 27 categories of investment objectives. Beside each fund is an abbreviation of its objectives. Look in the financial pages where mutual fund quotes appear for an explanation of the information in the listings.

Real Estate

Buying *real estate* (land or buildings) is another way to invest for future profit. This type of investment usually requires enough money for a down payment plus a long-term mortgage commitment. The investment may bring big returns. On the other hand, considerable risk may be involved.

For most people, buying a home is their first experience in real estate, 16-10. Owning your home increases your net worth and serves as a hedge against inflation. The property may also increase in value over time. Still, most financial experts advise thinking of a home first in terms of a place to live and second as an investment.

Buying real estate for investment purposes is not for amateurs. Before investing in real estate for profit, buyers need to know about property values and property management.

16-10
Some people buy apartments as an investment and then lease them to renters.

They also need to learn about mortgages, down payments, taxes, titles, insurance, and the legal aspects of leases and property ownership. Those who invest large amounts of money for long periods of time may find carefully selected real estate very profitable. Here are some guidelines to consider before buying.

- *Learn about property values in the area.* Is the value of the property likely to remain stable or increase? Is the area economically sound? Do zoning laws permit the use you want to make of the land?
- *Estimate the costs of buying and owning.* What is the purchase price? What must you pay for the down payment, mortgage, taxes, insurance, and maintenance? Figure the initial expenses as well as the ongoing monthly and yearly costs.
- *Estimate the income from the property.* If you buy rental property, what rental income can you expect? What is the outlook for steady rental? What tax advantages can you expect? What ongoing time and money input will be required? See 16-11.
- *Find reliable professionals to assist you.* In most cases, you will need a real estate agent and a lawyer when investing in property. Be sure both are honest, experienced, and willing to look after your best interests. The real estate agent will help you

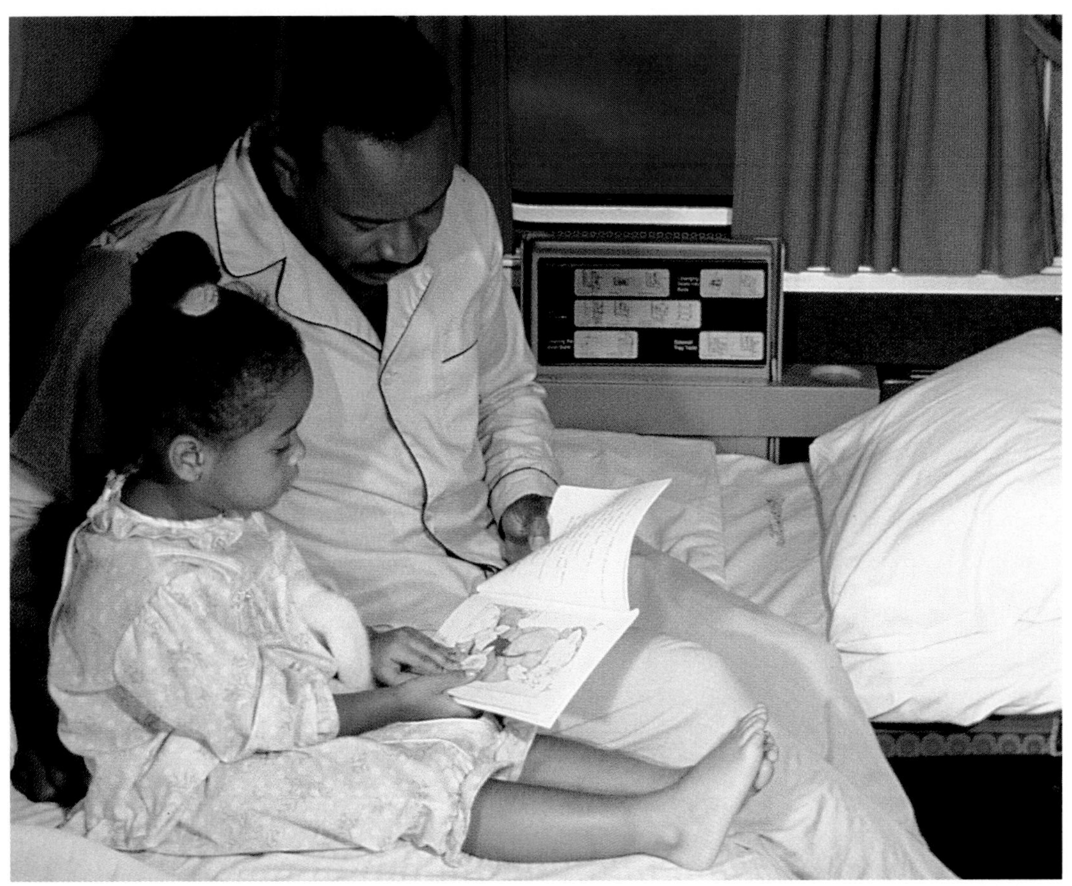

Amtrak

16-11

When people have children or other dependents to consider, life insurance becomes more important to them.

find suitable investment property and arrange for the purchase. Some agents also offer management services for rental property. A lawyer will review the legal documents involved and make sure the transaction is carried out according to the law. A lawyer will also represent you at the closing of the purchase. You may also need a tax lawyer or accountant to advise you on tax aspects of income properties.

Brokerage Firms

To buy stocks, bonds, and other securities, you may open an account with a brokerage or securities firm. First, you will make an application to open an account. Once your application is accepted, you would simply call your broker with your orders to buy and sell. The brokerage keeps a record of your transactions. You should receive a statement outlining your account activity periodically, usually every month. The fee you pay for the services of a brokerage is called a *commission*.

You can invest through a full-service or a discount broker. You can also trade with a broker online. *Full-service brokerage firms* maintain research departments to follow market trends and individual securities. Their main mission is to execute buy and sell orders for their customers. In addition, they provide investment advice, portfolio management, and other services. The commission you pay covers the cost of trading and support services provided by the firm. Both experienced and beginning investors can benefit from the expertise of full-service brokerage firms.

Discount brokerage firms execute orders to buy and sell securities but offer few, if any, other services. For instance, a discount brokerage does not offer investment advice. The commission is considerably lower than that of a full-service broker. However, you will need to do your own research and investment planning when buying from a discount broker. Experienced investors may prefer to use discount brokers to save money on commissions. They have the time and knowledge required to follow and manage their investment portfolios. They may not need the level of services a brokerage provides.

Online Trading

Today's technology allows you to use the Internet to view important investment information. In the past, this type of information was available only to brokerage firms and investment analysts. Web sites can provide useful information about individual securities and market movements. It is a good idea to research before investing. This will teach you more about securities and help you talk intelligently with your broker.

Investing online has become a fairly simple matter. Hundreds of online brokers are available to help consumers buy and sell securities. From home, you can visit the Web sites of these brokers. Here, you can indicate which securities you wish to buy or sell. Online trading is not risk free, however. Here are some guidelines for protecting your financial security if you consider investing online:

- ❑ Check out online brokers carefully before becoming involved. Make sure the people you deal with are reputable and legitimate. You can check out brokers and securities firms with your state securities regulator or the nearest Securities Exchange Commission office.
- ❑ Download hard-copy data on any investment you are considering. Before you buy, get other written material, too. This should include a prospectus, an

annual report, and recent company news. Study this information carefully. Before placing an order, know exactly what you are buying and what risks are involved.

- ❑ Obtain and keep written confirmations of your buy-and-sell orders and their completion. Store all your investment records and information in a file. This way you can locate these records easily.
- ❑ Stay on top of your investments. Prices can rise and fall swiftly in active markets. When you invest online, no one will be supervising your account. This makes it essential to follow market trends and prices of securities. You want to buy and sell at the most advantageous times.

When you buy online or by phone, you will need to use certain types of orders to conduct your trades. A *market order* instructs your broker to buy or sell a stock at the best price available. The broker will fill your order and buy or sell as you requested. The sale may be at a higher or lower price than when you placed the order. Stock prices can change between the time you place an order and the time it is executed by your broker.

One way to protect yourself against losing money to these price changes is to issue a restricted order. For example, you can place a *limit order.* This type of order instructs your broker to buy or sell a certain stock at a set price or better. If the broker cannot make the sale or purchase at the price you request, the order will not be executed. A *stop order* instructs your broker to buy or sell a stock when and if it reaches a specific price. It will be carried out whenever the stock reaches the target price. As you gain experience in investing, you will learn about these and other types of orders used in online trading.

Buying Life Insurance

Your financial security in later years will depend largely on the planning you do early in life. The right life insurance choices can help provide financial security for you and your family. These choices can protect you at all stages of the life cycle.

The main purpose of insurance is to provide protection against financial losses. Life policies protect against the loss of income due to death. The more financial responsibilities you have, the more important it is for you to have adequate coverage. Life insurance is especially important if you have a spouse, children, or elderly parents who depend on your income.

When you buy an insurance policy, you become a *policyholder.* You pay a set amount of money, called a *premium*, to the insurance company on a regular basis. The premiums you and other policyholders pay are invested by the company to earn money. The money that is earned is used to pay insurance claims. When an insured person dies, the face value of his or her policy is paid to the beneficiary. The *face value* is the amount for which the policy is written. The *beneficiary* is the person named by the policyholder to receive the death benefit.

Types of Life Insurance

The three traditional types of life insurance are term, whole life, and endowment. Each is available in slightly different forms and with different features. New types of life insurance have been developed in recent years to meet current needs and demands. These new types of coverage include variable life, adjustable life, and universal life. Each comes with different features. The following descriptions include the advantages and disadvantages of each type of life insurance.

Life Plans

Life Insurance for Peggy

When Peggy was 23, she started a new job as an assistant editor. She was single with no dependents and no plans for marriage. Both Peggy's parents were living. She owed $150 on a credit card and $1,500 on a car loan. These were her only major financial obligations other than her apartment lease.

When Peggy turned 25, her father died. His retirement funds left just enough money for her mother to make ends meet. Peggy realized her mother could become dependent upon her if she outlived her source of income.

Peggy's situation changed again at age 28. She married Tim, a thirty-year-old computer programmer. Tim also had no dependents. Peggy was worried because her mother's situation remained the same. That year, Peggy was promoted to senior editor in the same company. Peggy and Tim decided to wait to have children. They decided Peggy would continue working when the time came.

At age 30, Peggy had a baby girl. Two years later, she had a boy. She worked part-time until the children reached school age. This reduced her income temporarily. Peggy and Tim always wanted the best of everything for their children. They started setting aside money for the children's college costs. Peggy and Tim wanted all their children to afford college even if something should happen to one or both of them.

When Peggy and Tim reached their mid-forties, the children were in high school. They would start college in three and five years. Peggy's mother was in a nursing home, and Peggy was paying most of the bills. Both Peggy and Tim were working and at the peak of their careers. They expected their salaries to remain fairly stable during the remaining 20 years of work.

Now Peggy and Tim are in their mid-fifties. Both children have graduated from college. Peggy's mother has died. Peggy and Tim are beginning to turn their attention to travel and retirement.

Case Review

1. When Peggy was single and both her parents were alive, do you think she needed life insurance? Explain. Would you have advised her to make other investments? Why or why not?
2. When Peggy's father died, what changes should she have made in her insurance and investment program? Why?
3. What type of insurance and investment program would you have recommended for Peggy and Tim upon marriage? Why?
4. What insurance and other financial planning would be suitable for a couple with young children?
5. How would Peggy and Tim's financial planning change when they reached their forties?
6. What changes do you think they should make in their insurance and investment program now? Why?

Term Life Insurance

Term life insurance provides protection only for a specific period of time. This may be one, five, ten, or twenty years or until a specified age. When the term ends, so does the protection. The policy no longer has cash value. Term policies often include a renewable option. ***Renewable term*** coverage allows you to renew the coverage at the end of the term. You would pay a higher premium, but you would not need a medical exam. Some policies also may have a convertible clause. ***Convertible term*** coverage permits the insured to exchange the policy. For instance, a person might choose whole-life protection. The person could convert his or her policy without new evidence of insurability.

The advantage of term insurance is that it offers the most protection for your insurance dollar. Its pure protection costs less than policies with savings features. For those who really need insurance and cannot afford high premiums, term coverage may be the best choice.

Whole Life Insurance

Whole life insurance provides basic lifetime protection so long as premiums are paid. Whole life insurance is also called *straight life insurance.* The face amount is paid to the beneficiaries upon death of the insured. The coverage builds cash value over the years. ***Cash value*** is the amount of money a policyholder would receive if the policy were surrendered before death or maturity. The insured often can borrow against the cash value of their whole life insurance at a relatively low interest rate. However, until repaid, benefits are reduced by the amount of the loan. The policy also may be surrendered for its cash value if the insured wants to change or eliminate coverage.

The *limited payment policy* also offers lifetime protection. It calls for premium payments over a stated period of time, such as 20 years, or until you reach a certain age. During the payment period, premiums are higher and cash value builds faster than for standard whole life coverage.

Variable life insurance is another form of whole life protection. The premiums are fixed. The face amount varies with the performance of a fund in which the premiums are invested. However, the face amount may not fall below the original amount of the insurance. These policies have a guaranteed minimum death benefit. The benefit may be higher than the guarantee, depending on the earnings of the premium dollars invested. The advantage of this type of life insurance is the possibility of gaining when the value of the fund rises. Your insurance protection is combined with an investment feature. The main disadvantage is it may not offer the best of either insurance or investment opportunities.

Adjustable life insurance is a form of whole life policy. It allows the insured to alter the coverage. You can revise the policy as your needs change. Within limits, the policyholder may raise or lower the premiums, face value, and premium payment period. Coverage may start with term insurance for a given amount, premium, and term. All these may change as needed. Flexibility is the key advantage of adjustable life coverage. The need to constantly monitor coverage may be a disadvantage.

Universal life insurance permits adjustment of premium, face value, and level of protection. In addition, it offers an investment feature. The cash value is invested to earn interest at current market rates. The policyholder receives an annual statement showing the current level of protection, cash value, and interest earned. The statement also includes a breakdown of how the premiums have been allocated to protection, investment, and expenses.

An advantage of universal life is flexibility, both in the amount of the premiums and in the level of protection. Earnings also keep pace with current market rates. If interest rates go down, however, your earnings will decrease. You pay no taxes on the accumulated interest until you cash in your policy. This can be an advantage for persons in high income tax brackets.

Endowment Insurance

Endowment insurance pays the face value of the policy to beneficiaries if the insured dies before the endowment period ends. It pays the face amount to the insured if he or she lives beyond the endowment period. The advantage of endowment insurance is the combination of protection and savings. It is a type of investment. Disadvantages are the high premiums and possible tax consequences.

Annuities

An ***annuity*** is a contract that provides income for a set period of time or for life. Normally, the policyholder uses the annuity to provide retirement income. The contract can be purchased with monthly payments over time or with a lump sum. The payout usually begins at retirement and continues for a set number of years or until the death of the policyholder.

An annuity may also be written to cover more than one life. Payments then continue until the death of all persons named in the contract. This is called a joint and survivor annuity. It is used primarily by a policyholder and spouse or other dependent.

It is also possible to buy an annuity with a guaranteed number of payments. If the policyholder dies before receiving the guaranteed amount, payments continue to the beneficiary or to the annuitant's estate.

Selecting the Protection You Need

Each person's needs are unique. The life insurance coverage that is right for one person or family may be wrong for another. Finding the type and amount of protection that will work best for you requires careful planning. Consider the following factors when you are ready to shop for life insurance.

How Much Protection Should You Buy?

How much life insurance you need depends on two key factors:

- the present and future earning power of the insured.
- the financial responsibilities and obligation of the insured.

Protection often is keyed to the amount of earnings that would be lost if the insured died prematurely. It is also matched to the needs of survivors for whom the insured is financially responsible. These needs will depend upon the number of survivors, their marital status, their earning power, and their lifestyles.

Other factors to consider include the share of family income provided by the insured and income available from other sources. Each unique situation calls for careful analysis to determine the amount of protection to buy. Consider the following factors to determine how much coverage you need.

- *The people who depend on your income.* Dependents may include aging parents or invalid relatives as well as a spouse and young children. Consider the ages and financial needs of those who depend on you when determining what type and amount of insurance to buy. See 16-12.
- *The amount of money your dependents would need to maintain their standard of living without your income.* How long would they need the money? When others depend on your income, it is desirable, if possible, to leave enough money to meet their needs. Ideally, money would be left to cover a home mortgage, and everyday living expenses. It might also cover major future expenses such as college education for children.
- *Other sources of income that would be available for dependents.* Would dependents be able to draw on Social Security benefits, savings, employee benefits, or their own earnings? You want enough coverage to fill the gap between what is available from other sources and what your dependents would need.
- *The amount of cash needed to pay burial costs and unpaid debts.* Even if you are single with no dependents, you need enough life insurance to take care of these costs. Then your financial obligations will not burden your parents or other relatives.

What Types of Protection Should You Buy?

You can buy life insurance in a variety of forms and with many special benefits. The decision will depend on how much coverage you need, what you can afford to spend, and the special features you want.

Group insurance may be available through your employer, union, or another group to which you belong. As a rule, group coverage costs less than an individual policy for the same amount of coverage. Very often, group coverage is provided as a fringe benefit to employees. The employer may pay all or part of the premium. If you rely on group protection, look for a *conversion clause*. This will permit you to convert to an individual policy without proof of insurability if you should leave the group.

Individual policies, though more expensive, generally can be tailored to the policyholder's needs. Features to consider when choosing life insurance protection include the following:

- *Guaranteed renewability,* which allows the insured to keep coverage in force at the end of a term without new evidence of insurability. Premium rates increase with each new term.
- *Double indemnity,* which provides for double benefits if death is the result of an accident. This is also called an accidental death benefit.
- *Disability benefit,* which provides for a waiver of premiums if the insured becomes permanently and totally disabled. While this provision often is available as a feature on a life insurance policy, more comprehensive separate disability coverage is usually desirable.
- *Convertible provision,* which permits a policyholder to convert or exchange a term policy for another form of protection without new evidence of insurability.

Finally, consider how life insurance fits into your overall plan for future security and eventual retirement. Future financial security depends on the right mix of savings, insurance, and investments. Some people plan to use insurance as a form of savings. In this case, be sure the earnings on your insurance will match or exceed those on other forms of savings and investments.

Choosing a Company and an Agent

In the United States, there are over 2,000 life insurance companies and thousands of agents. Finding the right company and agent requires more than "a walk through the classified pages."

Choose a company that is respected within the insurance industry, by its policyholders, and by people in the financial field. Check whether the company has a reputation for settling claims fairly and promptly. Also be sure the company is licensed to operate in your state.

Research the financial soundness of insurance companies by reading *Best's Insurance Guide.* This can be found in most public libraries. Companies that are rated "most substantial" and "very substantial" are financially stronger than others. Annual reports can also reveal an insurance company's financial strength. You can check out an insurance company through your state insurance department. This should be listed under *Government Agencies* in the phone book. Additional information on buying life insurance is available from a number of online sites.

Take a close look at policies from various companies. Buy from a company that offers policies with the benefits and options important to you.

Be sure to compare the premiums charged by different companies for the same types and amounts of coverage. If you are considering whole life insurance, compare the cash value accumulation rates.

Choosing a life insurance agent is also important. Very often, the agent is the key to the quality of service you will receive. All states require licensing to sell life insurance. Initials following an agent's name indicate completion of specific studies in the insurance field. *CLU* indicates a Chartered Life Underwriter. *ChFC* indicates a Chartered Financial Consultant. *LUTCF* indicates a Life Underwriters' Training Council Fellow. Membership in the National Association of Life Underwriters shows an agent subscribes to the ethical standards of that group.

Choose an agent who can clearly explain the different types of coverage and benefits available. A good agent will advise you honestly about the type and amount of coverage you need. He or she will also help you evaluate your coverage as your needs and finances change. A responsible agent will handle policy revisions and claims promptly.

Once you have chosen a company and an agent, you are ready to select a policy. Talk honestly with your agent as you discuss your needs. After you buy a policy and it is delivered to you, review it carefully. Be sure the policy you are given is the one you chose. If the policy does not meet your expectations, most companies will allow you to return it within ten days without obligation. As you review the policy, check to see that it states the following:

- ❑ Name of the company.
- ❑ Name of the insured and the beneficiaries.
- ❑ Type of coverage.
- ❑ Amount of coverage and benefits.
- ❑ Amount and due dates of premiums.
- ❑ Terms for borrowing money against accumulated cash value, if applicable.
- ❑ Schedule of cash value accumulation, if applicable.
- ❑ Benefits and options of the policy.

Be sure to ask questions about any terms, provisions, or sections you do not understand. Once you are insured, inform your family and beneficiaries of the coverage and the location of the policy.

Summary

Investing involves using money to make money. It begins with choosing specific investment goals and making plans for reaching those goals. Sound investment planning calls for a clear look at several factors. These include risk versus safety, diversification, and specific goals, such as growth or income. Liquidity and marketability are important factors for investors concerned with converting investments to cash with ease.

Timing is another factor to consider when investing. When to buy and sell is important in terms of economic conditions and market prices. The goal is to buy low and sell high. Timing will also be a factor in terms of one's personal financial position.

Investment choices include stocks, bonds, and mutual funds. Government bonds are among the safest investments. Corporate stocks and bonds range from safe to risky depending on the financial soundness of the corporation. No matter where you put your money, it is smart to investigate before you invest.

Real estate is another way to invest. It can bring handsome profits but also involves considerable risks. Investing in real estate is not for amateurs. You need to do your homework and seek the advice of reliable professionals.

Buying life insurance can offer both financial protection and investment opportunities. Term life and whole life insurance provide protection against the losses of income from the death of a wage earner. In recent years, other forms of life insurance have begun to offer investment features along with protection. Your financial security will depend on insurance protection as well as appropriate investment choices.

To Review

1. Name four typical investment goals.
2. What are five important factors to consider in developing a personal investment strategy?
3. When buying securities, you either become an owner or _____.
4. What is the main difference between a bond and a stock?
5. If you buy a bond for less than its face value, will your yield be higher or lower than the stated rate?
6. Name the three main types of bonds.
7. Why do mutual funds offer more diversity than buying individual stocks and bonds?
8. Name four guidelines to consider before investing in real estate.
9. True or false. The more financial responsibility you have, the more important it is for you to have life insurance.
10. What are the differences between whole life insurance, term insurance, and endowment insurance?
11. Why might renewable term coverage be important?
12. What are the two key factors that determine the amount of life insurance to buy?

To Think Critically

1. If you were going to invest in stocks, would you buy common or preferred stock? Why? Which is more likely to increase in value? Which is considered a safer investment? Why?
2. Compare the three types of bonds. Which type of bond would you prefer to buy? Why?
3. What are the advantages of investing in a mutual fund?
4. What should you consider before buying shares in a mutual fund?

5. What are five reliable sources of information on stocks, bonds, and mutual funds?
6. Name and describe some of the benefits and features that can be added to a basic whole life insurance policy.
7. List four factors you should consider when selecting a life insurance company and agent.
8. What information should be stated clearly on a life insurance policy?
9. How do life insurance needs change with each of the following?
   A. increased income
   B. marriage
   C. dependents
   D. age
   E. increased financial obligations
   F. retirement

To Do

1. Form a small group of classmates and develop a plan for investing $5,000. Use the Internet, current financial publications, and books on financial planning for information on developing your plan. Factors to identify and consider include the following:
   - ❑ investment goals
   - ❑ degree of risk
   - ❑ growth and income objectives
   - ❑ liquidity and marketability
   - ❑ timing considerations
   - ❑ diversification

   Describe your plan in terms of these factors. Compare your group's plans with those of other groups in the class.
2. Describe the life insurance needs of the following family. The husband is 30 years old and earns $38,000 a year. The wife is 29 years old and earns $29,000 a year. Both have secure jobs, excellent health, and health insurance coverage through their employment. The couple has two children, ages four and two, and no other dependents. Their financial goals include a larger home, an education for their children, and a comfortable retirement income.

   Talk to three life insurance agents in your community. Ask what type of life insurance they would recommend for this family and why. Describe how life insurance decisions relate to investment and other financial decisions. Report your findings to the class.
3. Assume you have $2,500 to invest in any way you choose. Establish goals and objectives for your investments. Interview a stockbroker or an investment adviser for information on the types of securities and investment strategies available. Choose the securities you would buy. Find them on the stock, bond, or mutual fund quotations in a current paper. Develop a system for charting their ups and downs in the market. Explain your choices in terms of your objectives and follow your "investments" for at least six months. At the end of that period, evaluate your choices in terms of performance and meeting your investment goals.
4. Go online to investigate one of the following topics. Give an oral or written report on what you are able to learn.
   - ❑ Security exchanges—NYSE, AMEX, NASDAQ
   - ❑ Investment clubs
   - ❑ Government bonds
   - ❑ Mutual funds
   - ❑ Life insurance

Real estate developers often invest in newly constructed homes, which they hope to sell for a profit.

UNIT

6

SCHOOL BUS
STATE PATROL
APRIL

umanity Confront
io delegates plan
talks on preservin
the web of life.
INFORMATION PLEASE
U.S. GREEN CITY RANKINGS
STATE OF THE PLANET
FOOD
ENERGY
WATER
WASTES

THE MIGHTY
RAINFORES
Demands of People:
The Widening Impact

Citizenship

Chapter 17
Your Role As a Citizen

Chapter 18
Your Role in the Environment

As a citizen of this country, you have many responsibilities. As a citizen and taxpayer, you can influence government spending and taxing policies by participating in the political system and making yourself heard.

As a consumer and citizen of this country and the world, you can take an active role in protecting the environment. By keeping informed about environmental issues, you can help to preserve and protect the earth we share.

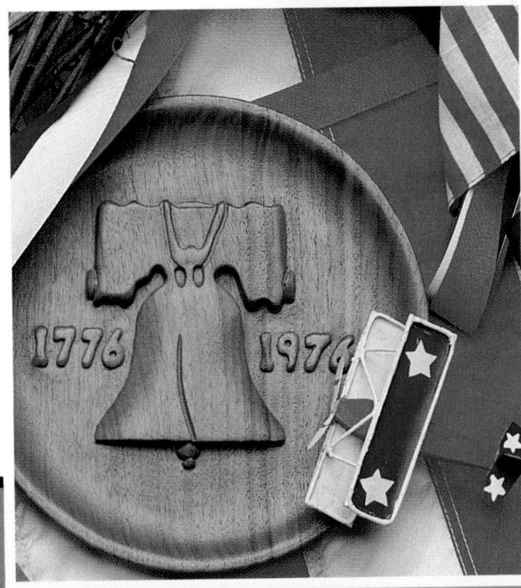

CHAPTER 17

Your Role As a Citizen

citizen
ethical behavior
social responsibility
volunteerism
community service learning
tax
progressive tax
regressive tax
Social Security
personal income tax
sales tax
excise tax
real estate tax
personal property tax
estate tax
gift tax
standard deduction
tax liability
mandatory expense item
entitlements
deficit spending
discretionary expenditures
W-4 Form
W-2 Form
exemption
tax avoidance
tax evasion
tax audit
disability

After studying this chapter, you will be able to

- ❑ define your role as a citizen.
- ❑ identify different types of taxes.
- ❑ relate taxation to government spending and budgeting decisions.
- ❑ list the various records and receipts needed for tax purposes.
- ❑ describe basic procedures for filing a tax return.
- ❑ identify different types of tax forms.
- ❑ locate reliable sources of information and assistance on personal tax matters.
- ❑ explain the overall purposes and structure of the Social Security program.
- ❑ identify problems facing the Social Security system.

This book focuses upon you as a consumer. The confident consumer plays many roles—family member, student, worker, homemaker, shopper, money manager, saver, borrower, spender, investor. Now we come to a bigger picture—your role as a citizen. What does this mean?

Citizenship

A ***citizen*** is a born or naturalized member of place, such as a country. A citizen owes allegiance to his or her country's government. In return, the citizen is entitled to protection and given certain rights. Citizens also have important responsibilities, 17-1.

In the past, the role of the citizen seemed fairly clear to everyone. The good citizen knew the basics of U.S. history and government, respected the laws of the land, voted in every election, paid taxes, served on juries when summoned, and served in the military if called.

Today the call to citizenship is a broader call. It demands more than political knowledge and voter turnout. Good citizens are asked to participate, volunteer, accept responsibility for self and others, behave ethically, and live beyond self-interest. Citizens play these expanded roles at home, in the community, on the job, in grass-roots organizations, in places of worship, and in many other places where they can make a positive difference.

> *"Ask not what your country can do for you, but what you can do for your country."*
>
> *John F. Kennedy*

Model citizenship calls for ***ethical behavior,*** or conduct that conforms to accepted standards of right and wrong. Ethical behavior is expected from businesses and government, as well as from individuals. It involves honesty, fairness, reliability, respect, courage, tolerance, civility, and compassion. These and other qualities make our lives with each other peaceful and safe. Whatever greatness we achieve as a nation comes from the people. It rests on the ethical behavior exhibited by our citizens.

17-1
Being a good citizen can begin early in life. As this girl grows, she will learn about her rights and responsibilities as a citizen of the United States.

The "golden rule" is one of the oldest and simplest guides to ethical behavior. It says "Do unto others as you would have them do unto you." How would you apply this quotation to your actions as a citizen? How would you apply it to the actions of business and government?

Another part of citizenship is ***social responsibility,*** or a general sense of concern for the needs of individuals, community, country, and world. It is about our individual and collective duty to take care of each other and the world we share. It is about finding constructive approaches to current social issues and needs. It is about providing relief for disaster victims, housing the homeless, creating jobs for the unemployed, controlling crime and violence, improving health care, and strengthening families. It is about protecting and conserving natural resources and the environment.

Today religious groups, community organizations, business, and government are beginning to focus on social responsibility. They are working to identify and meet the needs of individuals, groups, and society as a whole. Businesses are accepting responsibility in a variety of ways. For instance, they sponsor literacy programs, adopt schools, and create corporate volunteer programs. Government plays its role through the allocation of tax dollars into programs that help the public. These include Social Security, medicare, medicaid, food stamps, and other assistance programs designed to meet the needs of citizens.

Volunteerism is a component of being a responsible, ethical, and socially responsible person. ***Volunteerism*** means service given without payment. It is a gift of self. It is returning something to family, community, and country. Volunteerism covers a wide range of activities. On an individual level, it can mean taking food to a sick neighbor, helping a sibling with homework, visiting an elderly friend in a nursing home, or lending a hand where it is needed. You could also volunteer your services with a community group or agency. For instance, you might serve meals for the hungry, collect clothing for victims of disaster, or spend time with patients in a hospital, 17-2. You might give your time on projects at your school or church, in a political campaign, or in the interest of a cause that matters to you. Volunteerism is a way of living beyond yourself, and its rewards are many.

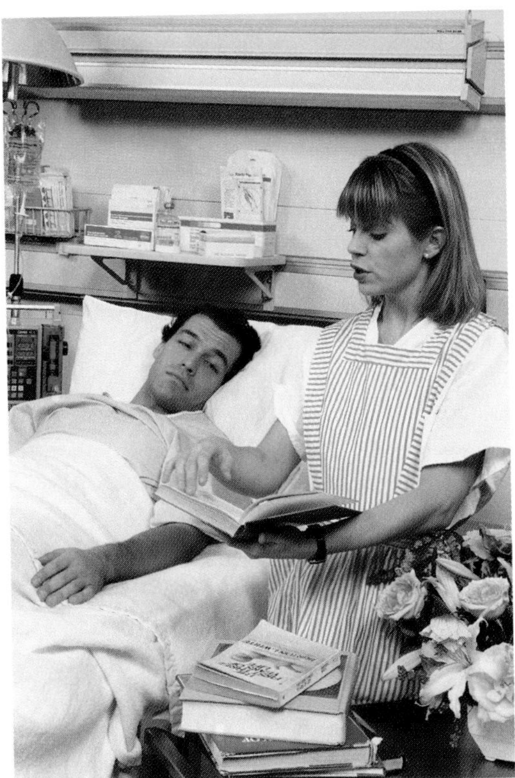

17-2
This young woman volunteers in a hospital. One of her tasks is reading to a patient to keep him company. Volunteers make a difference by doing for others.

One type of volunteerism that is growing more common among teens is ***community service learning,*** which combines classroom learning with service in the community. It involves students in course-related activities that address real needs of their communities. In many high schools and colleges, community service learning is offered to help students grow and become better citizens. It may be a mandatory part of the curriculum, an elective, or an extracurricular activity. Community service learning is intended to help students form lasting connections with their communities. The students, those they serve, and the community as a whole benefit from community service learning. This combined emphasis on learning and social responsibility makes community service learning an important tool in fostering citizenship.

Obviously, your role as a citizen goes far beyond voting and serving on juries. It involves behaving ethically and responsibly. It includes caring for others and giving of yourself. The main economic responsibility of a citizen, however, is to pay taxes. These taxes support goods and services needed by your community, state, and nation. As a citizen, it is your duty to do your part by paying your share of taxes.

Taxation

Many would agree the government provides a host of essential public goods and services. At the federal level, government pays for Social Security and medicare. It pays interest on the national debt and funds the national defense and many important programs. At the state and local levels, government pays for schools, highways, public welfare, hospitals, and health care. State and local governments also provide police and fire protection, sanitation and sewage, environmental protection, parks and recreation, and other public services.

Tax revenues pay for all these government operations and services. If you work, you pay taxes. As a taxpayer and future voter, remember the government cannot give what it does not first take away. Indirectly, the people decide what services they want from government and how much they will pay for them. At present, most taxpayers spend a sizable share of their dollars to pay their income, Social Security, and other taxes. It is to your advantage to know what your tax dollars buy and how the tax system works. Find out how you can influence tax policies and minimize your own tax liabilities.

> *"Taxes are what we pay for a civilized society."*
>
> *Oliver Wendell Holmes*

A ***tax*** is a mandatory payment made by an individual or organization to government to pay for public needs. Federal, state, and local taxes account for more than 35 percent of the average family's expenses, 17-3. For many workers, taxes are their largest single annual expense—more than shelter, food, transportation, education, medical care, or recreation.

The average person works about two hours out of every eight hours on the job to pay for government. Each year, employed persons work from January to May just to pay federal, state, and local taxes. The Tax Foundation has declared "Tax Freedom Day" as the date on which the average worker stops working just to pay his or her taxes. In recent years, that date has come in early May.

Types of Taxes

Taxes can be described as progressive or regressive. ***Progressive taxes*** take a higher percentage from the rich than from the poor. They increase at the same rate the taxed item increases. For example, income tax is a progressive tax. As a person's income increases, that person's tax rate increases. In 1999, tax rates ranged from 15 to 39.6 percent. Progressive tax rates change with new tax laws. However, lower rates always apply to lower incomes, and rates increase along with incomes.

Regressive taxes are just the opposite. ***Regressive taxes*** take a lower percentage of income from the rich and a higher percentage of income from the poor. The rates decrease as the amount being taxed increases. Sales tax is a form of regressive tax. Suppose two people have different incomes. If they buy the same item at the same price, both will pay the same amount of sales tax on this item. This amount is a higher percentage of the total income for the person with the lower income. The tax represents a smaller percentage of the total income for the person with the higher income.

Different types of taxes apply to different taxable items including income, purchases, property, and wealth. The same item can be taxed by more than one government body. For example, all levels of government have the power to tax personal income.

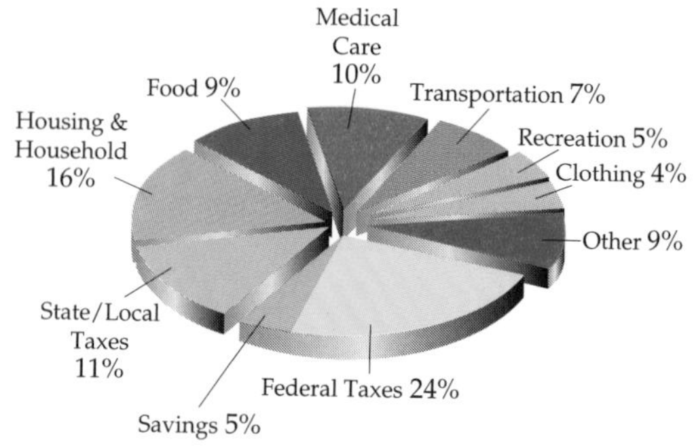

17-3 Tax Foundation
This chart shows a breakdown of a typical American family's expenses.

Payroll Taxes

You pay two types of taxes on money you earn—Social Security and income taxes. ***Social Security*** is the federal government's basic program for providing income when earnings are reduced or stopped because of retirement, disability, or death. Social Security and medicare tax is usually paid through payroll deductions. These deductions are labeled *FICA*, which stands for the *Federal Insurance Contributions Act*.

Personal income tax is a tax on money a person receives from wages, tips, bonuses, interest, and dividends. Income tax is also deducted from payroll. However, many taxpayers owe more at tax time in April than has been deducted during the year. Income tax pays for government services and operations. It may be levied by state and local governments as well as the federal government.

Purchase Taxes

Taxes on items you buy include sales tax and excise tax. ***Sales tax*** is levied by state and local governments on retail sales of certain goods and services. All but five states have a general sales tax on the goods and services people buy. In many states, food and drugs are exempt from this tax. This eases the burden of sales tax on the poor. ***Excise tax*** is levied by federal and state governments on the sale and transfer of certain items. Examples include cigarettes, alcoholic beverages, air travel, telephone services, gasoline, firearms, and certain luxury items.

Property Taxes

Taxation of property you own includes real estate property tax and personal property tax. ***Real estate tax*** is based on the value of land and buildings owned by taxpayers. This is an important source of revenue for local and state governments. Rates vary greatly from area to area and state to state. ***Personal property taxes*** are assessed in some states on such items as cars, boats, and furniture.

Wealth Taxes

The main types of taxes on one's wealth include estate tax and gift tax. Estates worth a certain amount are subject to ***estate tax.*** This is a tax imposed by the federal government on assets and life insurance left by an individual at the time of his or her death. It must be paid out of the estate before assets are distributed. ***Gift tax*** is levied by the federal government on donors or givers who transfer assets to others. Here's how it works. Suppose you have a wealthy aunt who wants to give you a $15,000 cash gift. She may give you $10,000 tax free each year. Any amount over $10,000 in a given year could be taxed. In this case, $5,000 could be taxable to your aunt's estate when she dies, depending on the total value of her estate and her lifetime total of gifts to you in excess of $10,000 annually. A state gift tax might also be imposed.

The Purposes of Taxes

The primary purpose of taxes has always been to pay for government operations, facilities, and services, 17-4. These include

- ❑ National defense.
- ❑ Social insurance.
- ❑ Schools.
- ❑ Highways.
- ❑ Airports.
- ❑ Parks.
- ❑ Fire and police protection.
- ❑ Health care.
- ❑ Interest on the national debt.
- ❑ Law enforcement.

These items are called *public goods and services.*

The main purpose of taxes is to raise money to run the government. Over the years, legislators have also

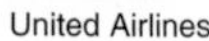

United Airlines

Nicole LaMotte

17-4 USDA

Taxes pay for the maintenance of government buildings, parks, school lunch programs, and more.

used taxes to achieve a variety of other goals. For instance, the government may either raise or lower taxes to promote economic stability, fight inflation, or stop a recession.

Taxes can be used to spread wealth from upper-income to lower-income groups. This is done largely through *transfer payments.* These are cash or service benefits distributed by the government. Examples include food stamps, medicaid, housing subsidies, and veterans' programs. These benefits are available at little or no cost to those who need them. Transfer payments are paid by taxpayers. Most citizens at one time or another receive some form of benefit from government that is paid for by tax dollars.

Taxes may also be used to influence behavior. For example, certain charitable donations can be deducted from income. This lowers taxes paid and encourages giving. The deduction allowed on mortgage interest encourages home ownership. The tax on alcohol, tobacco, and gasoline discourages their use while raising government revenues. A tax on imported goods is called a *tariff.* Tariffs tend to discourage buying imports and encourage buying domestic or American-made products. The purpose of tariffs is to protect American businesses or improve an unfavorable balance of trade with other nations.

Tax Laws and Regulations

The U.S. Tax Code contains thousands of pages of complex rules and provisions. There are also 50 state tax systems and over 80,000 local taxing agencies. Each has its own set of laws and regulations. Taxes continue to increase, and the tax system becomes more and more complex. In recent years, tax reform legislation has occupied both state and federal legislatures.

In 1978, California citizens were concerned about rising taxes. They organized and pushed a bill called Proposition 13 through their state legislature. This law limits real estate taxes and requires voter approval to levy any new taxes. Other states have followed with various forms of tax reduction or limitation.

The federal tax code changes periodically. Congress struggles to meet the need for revenues with a level of taxation voters will accept. Legislators present tax reform bills every year. The first purpose for tax reform is to raise revenues. Tax reforms are also intended to make the tax burden fairer, simplify the tax system, and achieve desired economic outcomes.

Tax rates and allowable deductions tend to change with each new tax law. Provisions in the 1999 tax code that apply to personal income tax are listed below.

One provision sets up a *five-bracket tax rate* of 15, 28, 31, 36, and 39.6 percent of taxable income. Single individuals are taxed at a rate of 15 percent on taxable income up to $23,350; 28 percent on taxable income from $23,350 to $61,400; 31 percent on taxable income from $61,400 to $128,100; 36 percent on taxable income from $128,100 to $278,450; and 39.6 percent on taxable income over $278,450. The rates are the same but the taxable income levels differ for married people and heads of households.

Taxpayers who choose not to itemize, or list, their deductions may take a standard deduction. A ***standard deduction*** is the set amount taxpayers may deduct from adjusted gross income before determining tax. The deduction amount is set by law and varies according to the taxpayer's filing status (single, married, head of household). This helps to reduce ***tax liability,*** or the amount of tax that must be paid.

In 1998, the standard deduction allowed for single taxpayers was $4,750. Heads of households could deduct $6,250. Married couples filing separately could deduct $6,250. Married couples filing jointly could deduct $7,100.

Taxpayers may take a personal exemption for themselves as well as an exemption for each of their dependents. A *tax exemption* is an amount of income on which no tax is imposed. Exemptions are indexed to the rate of inflation. In 1998, the amount was $2,700. The exemption is phased out when income exceeds a certain amount.

> ***"People want just taxes more than they want lower taxes. They want to know that every man is paying his proportionate share according to his wealth."***
>
> *Will Rogers*

Tax Legislation

Since major changes in tax policies can cause major changes in the economy, any new tax legislation needs to be thought out carefully. See 17-5. Here are some questions to consider when you want to evaluate tax proposals and policies.

Will a New Tax or Change in Tax Laws Produce Adequate Revenues?

Tax revenues should be great enough to achieve the goals of the tax proposal. Ideally, revenues should be considerably higher than the cost of administering, enforcing, and collecting the taxes. The federal income tax system spends approximately 50 cents for every $100 collected.

Is the Tax Fair?

To be fair, a tax must fit the taxpayer's ability to pay. Tax rates should be no greater than required for essential government services and operations. In addition, the burden should be distributed fairly among taxpayers. Generally, those with similar incomes and resources should be taxed at the same rate.

Fairness in taxation is not a new issue. It has been a concern for centuries. Plato said in his time, 427-347 B.C., "When there is an income tax, the just man will pay more and the unjust less on the same amount of income."

Is the Economic Impact of Tax Legislation Minimal or Beneficial?

Almost all tax legislation interferes with the operation of the economy to some degree. Tax laws should achieve positive economic goals or at least keep negative results to a minimum. For example, a tax on gasoline can lower demand and reduce dependence on foreign oil. This may discourage unnecessary driving, which will reduce auto pollution. Since it is spread among many taxpayers, a gasoline tax achieves a reasonable degree of fairness.

Tax laws should not cause major economic problems or seriously interfere with the forces of supply and demand. For example, an increase in federal income tax during a recession would lower consumer demand at a time when the economy needs the stimulus of greater demand. Eliminating the tax advantages of Individual Retirement Accounts could reduce savings rates at a time when savings are needed for business growth and expansion. An increase in Social Security taxes can result in job cutbacks and greater unemployment as employers try to control tax liabilities.

Jack Klasey

17-5
An accountant can help you more clearly understand tax legislation.

Government Taxing and Spending

Government taxing and spending may seem like an area of little concern to you. As you listen to the news, you may not feel interested in legislators negotiating new tax bills. Government taxing and spending should concern you, however. How the government uses your tax dollars affects you personally. Government taxing laws determine how much of your paycheck you can spend and how much will be taken for taxes. Policies on government spending determine what services and programs the federal government is able to provide. The following sections describe government taxing and spending in terms of federal government revenues and expenditures.

Federal Government Revenues

Taxation is the primary source of revenue for both federal and state governments. Of all tax dollars, approximately 57 percent goes to the federal government. Individual income taxes and social insurance payroll taxes are the two largest sources of federal revenues. Corporate income taxes, excise taxes, estate and gift taxes, and other taxes are also considered revenue. Other sources include customs duties, Federal Reserve earnings, fines, and penalties. Borrowing becomes a major source of revenue in those years when the government spends more than it collects.

Federal Government Expenditures

In 1999, the federal government spent 79 percent of its total budget on mandatory expense items. A ***mandatory expense item*** is a commitment the federal government has made and cannot change, even if there are not enough revenues to support it. In this case, the government would have to borrow enough money to meet these mandatory expense items. See 17-6.

> *"Collecting more taxes than absolutely necessary is legalized robbery."*
>
> *Calvin Coolidge*

Of these mandatory expenditures, 65 percent went to ***entitlements***, which are benefits promised by law to eligible citizens by the government. The largest entitlement program is Social Security, followed by medicare. Other entitlement programs include federal employee retirement benefits, the federal government's share of medicaid, veteran's pensions, food stamps, child nutrition, unemployment compensation, and housing assistance. Any reductions or changes in these programs require new legislation. As the national debt grows, it becomes even more important for law makers to take a hard look at this spending and make some hard choices in the allocation of federal dollars.

Interest on the national debt is also a mandatory expense item. This interest must be paid, even if the government has to borrow the money to pay it. The interest is paid to financial institutions and individuals who buy and own government securities. In essence, these institutions and individuals lend money to the federal government and taxpayers pay the interest. When the government spends more money than it collects in a given year, this is called ***deficit spending***. The national debt on which taxpayers pay interest is the result of years of deficit spending. The grand total of the national debt exceeds five and one-half trillion dollars.

Discretionary expenditures are expense items that can be adjusted according to needs and revenues. National defense and nondefense

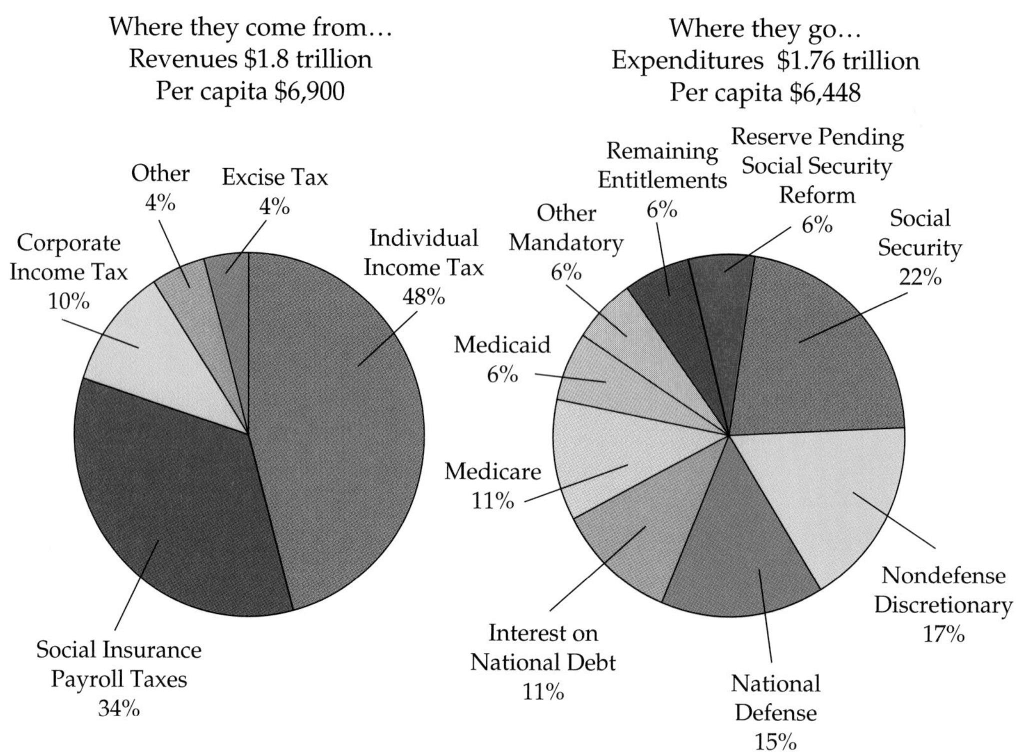

17-6
This chart shows where federal government revenues come from and where they go.

discretionary spending are the two main categories. Money for national defense is used to equip the armed forces and pay for military personnel, research, and technology. National defense accounted for 15 percent of the 1999 budget. However, when the United States becomes involved with war or military conflicts around the world, it becomes necessary to increase spending on national defense.

Nondefense discretionary spending includes the cost of government operations and a wide array of programs. Chief among these expenditures are the costs of natural resources and environmental protection, transportation, education and training, science and technology, international affairs, and administration of justice. The federal government also provides funds to state and local governments for certain programs.

> *"Blessed are the young for they shall inherit the national debt."*
>
> ***Herbert Hoover***

State and Local Government Finances

Both taxation and government spending vary widely from state to state and city to city. However, the sources of revenues and categories of expenditures are similar, 17-7. Sales taxes, personal and corporate income taxes, and property taxes pay for most state and local government spending. These taxes are used mainly to pay for public education, highways, and public welfare programs run by the state. They also pay for government operations, hospitals, public transportation, police and fire protection, parks and recreation services, and the interest on state and municipal bonds.

The State and Local Dollar

Where it came from...

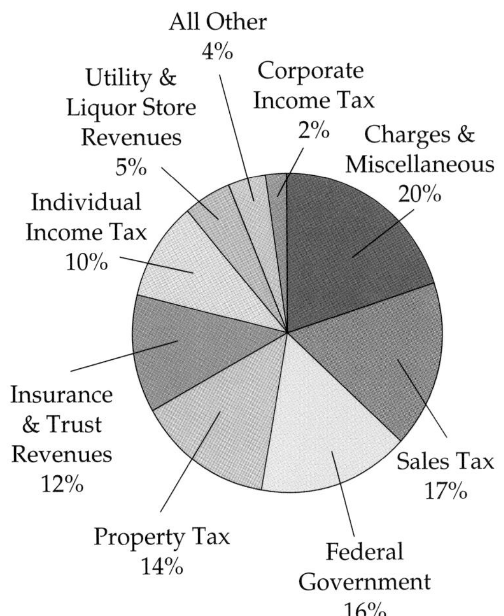

Where it went...

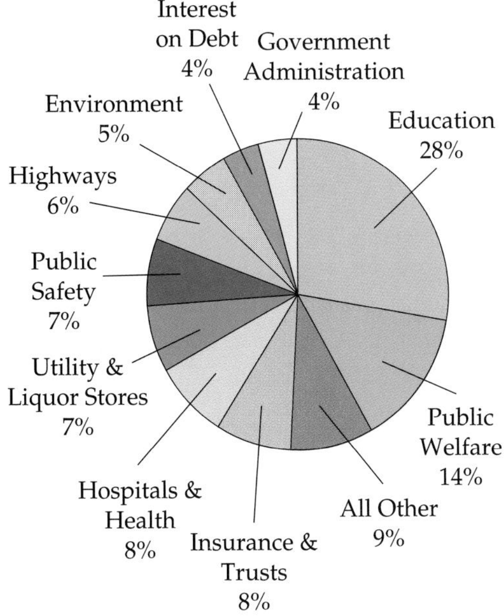

17-7
This chart gives you some idea of where money comes from and where it goes at the state and local levels.

Balancing Taxation and Spending

In 1997, two laws were passed that were intended to address federal spending and taxing issues. The *Balanced Budget Act of 1997* was intended to eliminate deficit spending. It called for a balanced budget by the year 2002 and nearly $130 billion in spending cuts. It also gave medicare recipients more choice in their health care. A fourth feature of this act was to establish a $24 billion program of health care for uninsured children. The *Taxpayer Relief Act of 1997* provided tax credits for families with dependent children and offered tax incentives for higher education. This act also reduced *capital gains tax rates*, which is the tax rate on income earned from an investment beyond its purchase price. Critics say neither law was adequate to create significant debt reduction or taxpayer relief.

As government spending and debt increase, revenues and taxes must also increase, 17-8. In recent years the growing national debt has alarmed both legislators and taxpayers. The national debt includes money owed by the government to Social Security, Civil Service Retirement, Military Retirement, medicare and other trust funds. It also includes debt held by the public in the form of government securities. In May 1999, the national debt was close to $5.6 trillion. This comes to a total of $20,498 per citizen. Annual interest on the debt is about $365 billion dollars.

Across the country, citizens are calling for controls on government taxing and spending. At the same time, they demand more government services and programs. Often the same people who want less spending and lower taxes also want more benefits. They want more Social Security benefits, broader health care coverage, better schools, safer streets, and increased national security.

Government Revenues, Expenditures, and Debt

	Revenues 1980	Revenues 1995	Expenditures 1980	Expenditures 1995	Debt 1980	Debt 1995
Federal						
Total (billions)	$565	$1,573	$617	$1,705	$914	$5,001
Per Capita	$2,496	$5,985	$2,724	$6,491	$4,036	$19,033
State and Local Combined						
Total (billions)	$452	$1,419	$434	$1,351	$336	$1,115
Per Capita	$1,993	$5,396	$1,916	$5,143	$1,481	$4,243
Total Per Capita (All levels combined)	$4,489	$10,500	$4,640	$11,650	$5,517	$23,276

17-8
These figures show the trend in government taxation, spending, and borrowing at all levels. The total per capita (person) figures show all levels combined.

Deficit reduction is particularly important to you, the young citizens of the nation. It is in your best interest to follow developments in government spending, borrowing, and taxing. Reducing the national debt requires both spending cuts and tax increases. It means establishing a reasonable level of government spending and services. It means having a tax system that produces adequate revenues, is fair to taxpayers, and is simple for both taxpayers and administrators.

Income Tax Returns

The federal income tax system is built on a pay-as-you-earn concept. This means a working person pays taxes paycheck-by-paycheck instead of in one lump sum. State and local income taxes usually work this way, too. When you begin a job, your employer will ask you to fill out a ***W-4 Form.*** This form is called the Employee's Withholding Allowance Certificate, 17-9. It tells your employer how much tax to withhold from your paychecks. Income, Social Security, and medicare taxes are withheld from your pay.

At the start of each year, you will receive a ***W-2 Form*** from your employer. This is called a Wage and Tax Statement, 17-10. It states the amount you were paid during the previous year. It also gives the amounts of income, Social Security, and medicare taxes that were withheld from your income during the year.

The amount of tax withheld from your paycheck depends on how much you earn and the number of exemptions you are allowed. An ***exemption*** is a tax benefit that reduces the amount of income on which you must pay taxes. An exemption is allowed for each taxpayer and each of the taxpayer's dependents. A spouse on a joint return, dependent children, and others who meet the definition may be claimed as dependents. The amount of money allowed for each exemption follows the rate of inflation.

The three common forms for filing a federal tax return are the *1040EZ, 1040A,* and the *1040.* Form 1040EZ and Form 1040A are short forms that are

Cut here and give the certificate to your employer. Keep the top part for your records.

Form **W-4** Department of the Treasury Internal Revenue Service

Employee's Withholding Allowance Certificate

OMB No. 1545-0010

▶ For Privacy Act and Paperwork Reduction Act Notice, see page 2.

1 Type or print your first name and middle initial — Last name — 2 Your social security number

Home address (number and street or rural route) — 3 ☐ Single ☐ Married ☐ Married, but withhold at higher Single rate.
Note: If married, but legally separated, or spouse is a nonresident alien, check the Single box.

City or town, state, and ZIP code — 4 If your last name differs from that on your social security card, check here. **You** must call 1-800-772-1213 for a new card . . . ▶ ☐

5 Total number of allowances you are claiming (from line H above or from the worksheets on page 2 if they apply) . — 5

6 Additional amount, if any, you want withheld from each paycheck . . . . — 6 $

7 I claim exemption from withholding for 1999, and I certify that I meet **BOTH** of the following conditions for exemption:

- Last year I had a right to a refund of **ALL** Federal income tax withheld because I had **NO** tax liability **AND**
- This year I expect a refund of **ALL** Federal income tax withheld because I expect to have **NO** tax liability.

If you meet both conditions, write "EXEMPT" here . . . . ▶ 7

Under penalties of perjury, I certify that I am entitled to the number of withholding allowances claimed on this certificate, or I am entitled to claim exempt status.
Employee's signature
(Form is not valid unless you sign it) ▶ — **Date** ▶

8 Employer's name and address (Employer: Complete 8 and 10 only if sending to the IRS) — 9 Office code (optional) — 10 Employer identification number

Cat. No. 10220Q

17-9
A W-4 Form, completed by employees, provides information employers need to determine how much to withhold for federal income tax.

A Taxing Situation

Our Woman in Washington

Leslie is a new congresswoman from a mid-western state. She ran on campaign promises to fight crime, improve schools, and reform the health care system. However, her emphasis was on putting an end to deficit spending by the federal government. She was convinced that control of the national debt had to come before anything else could rest on solid ground. There would be no safe social programs if the government was bankrupt.

Leslie knew ending deficit spending would require both higher taxes and less spending. Neither would be popular with all the voters. Still, she had good ideas for both. Certainly it should be easy to cut spending from a $1.7 trillion budget. Everyone knew the $5.5 trillion debt had to be trimmed. Leslie could not believe how much over-spending Congress had allowed over the years. She was eager to get to Washington where she could do something about it.

When she arrived in the Capital, it took her several months to find her way around and learn how the "system" worked. She managed to be named to one or two important committees. Leslie began to speak out on spending at every opportunity. However, she met opposition at every turn. This was not as easy as she anticipated. Here are some of her ideas for increasing revenues and the opposition she faced.

- ☐ Seek a two percent tax increase across the board on all households and corporations. Advocates for low-income groups called this an unfair, regressive tax that would be hardest on low-income taxpayers. Economists claimed increasing taxes would slow economic activity and result in fewer jobs, more unemployment, and finally lower total tax revenues. Supporters of lower spending rather than higher taxing called for spending cuts before tax increases.

(Continued)

(Continued)

- Impose a 25 cent-per-gallon increase in gasoline taxes. This, too, was seen as unfair to low-income taxpayers. It also was opposed by the trucking and transportation industries. Such a tax would increase their operating costs considerably.
- Impose higher taxes on alcohol, tobacco, and firearms. This proposal was opposed by the alcohol, tobacco, and firearms industries. Many users of these products also opposed higher taxes.
- Leslie also proposed several ideas for spending cuts.
- Cap the cost of living increases on Social Security benefits for a two-year period. Recipients of Social Security benefits, represented by the American Association of Retired Persons (AARP), strongly objected to this proposal. They claimed it was unfair to older Americans who had paid into the Social Security system all their working years and now depended on these benefits.
- Cut spending for all government agencies by five percent. Almost every agency objected to spending cuts or even caps. They all claimed costs keep going up and they needed more money, not less.
- Reduce spending for national defense by five percent. The military and the supporters of U.S. military might and readiness objected to weakening American defenses. Others, located in areas where military bases would have to close, feared the economic cost of losing these facilities in their areas. Still others opposed cuts in defense spending because it would mean unemployment of thousands who work in defense industries.
- Increase the retirement age for Social Security benefits. AARP and many older Americans opposed this proposal. They felt it was unfair to those who have earned their retirement and feel entitled to retire with full benefits at age 65 as always.

Case Review

1. What does Leslie's experience tell you about the problems involved in trying to control government spending?
2. What ideas can you propose for increasing government revenues? What opposition do you think your ideas would meet?
3. What government services would you be willing to give up in order to help reduce deficit spending?
4. What do you see as the consequences of continued deficit spending to yourself and your family? To continuing government services and programs? To business and industry? To the United States and its position in the world politically and economically?

relatively easy to complete and file, 17-11. These two forms may only be used by taxpayers whose income falls within certain limits and who choose not to *itemize*, or list, deductions. Form 1040EZ can only be filed by taxpayers who are single or married and filing a joint return. Other restrictions for using the short forms are outlined in the instruction package taxpayers receive each year from the Internal Revenue Service.

Form 1040 must be used by taxpayers with itemized deductions or with an income over a certain amount annually. In 1999, that amount was $50,000. Others must use the long form because of the sources of their income

a Control number | Void ☐

b Employer's identification number

c Employer's name, address, and ZIP code

d Employee's social security number

e Employee's name, address, and ZIP code

1 Wages, tips, other compensation | 2 Federal income tax withheld

3 Social security wages | 4 Social security tax withheld

5 Medicare wages and tips | 6 Medicare tax withheld

7 Social security tips | 8 Allocated tips

9 Advance EIC payment | 10 Dependent care benefits

11 Nonqualified plans | 12 Benefits included in Box 1

13 See Instrs. for Box 13 | 14 Other

15 Statutory employee ☐ | Deceased ☐ | Pension plan ☐ | Legal rep. ☐ | 942 emp. ☐ | Subtotal ☐ | Deferred compensation ☐

16 State | Employer's state I.D. No. | 17 State wages, tips, etc. | 18 State income tax | 19 Locality name | 20 Local wages, tips, etc. | 21 Local income tax

Department of the Treasury—Internal Revenue Service

Form **W-2** Wage and Tax Statement

This information is being furnished to the Internal Revenue Service.

Copy B To Be Filed With Employee's FEDERAL Tax Return

OMB No. 1545-0008

17-10
A W-2 Form shows how much an employee was paid and what deductions were taken.

or because of their deductions, adjustments to income, and tax credits. The tax instruction booklet tells who should use which tax forms.

Record Keeping for Tax Purposes

You need certain records, receipts, and documents to help you fill out tax return forms. Accurate, detailed records are particularly important to claim itemized deductions, adjustments to income, and tax credits. Here are some of the items you may need for tax purposes.

- ❑ Social Security numbers for yourself and household members.
- ❑ W-2 Forms reporting wages, salary, and withholding.
- ❑ Records of income, including wages, tips, and taxable benefits.
- ❑ Records of interest earned and dividends received.
- ❑ Canceled checks and receipts for expenses entered on tax returns as deductions or credits.
- ❑ Itemized bills and receipts for deductible expenses.
- ❑ Bills and receipts for permanent home improvements.
- ❑ Records of interest paid on home mortgages.
- ❑ Real estate closing statements.
- ❑ Investment transactions including purchase and sale dates, prices, gains, losses, and commissions.
- ❑ Past tax returns.

Preparing Income Tax Returns

When preparing your tax return, you will need your Social Security number, the W-2 Form provided by your employer, and the tax packet of forms and instructions which you receive from the IRS. Follow the steps outlined on the tax form you are using. If you owe taxes, write your check or money order for the amount payable to the Internal Revenue Service. Be sure your check or money order gives your name, address, Social Security number, and daytime phone number. Whether you owe or not, sign your return and mail it to the Internal Revenue office for your area.

It will be to your advantage to use Form 1040A or Form 1040 when adjustments to income, itemized deductions, and tax credits can reduce your taxes. When using these forms, you may want to consult a tax specialist to help you complete the forms and determine what expenses you can claim as deductions. Following are some of the items that may be deducted from income for tax purposes.

- Medical and dental expenses when the total comes to more than 7.5 percent of your adjusted gross income.

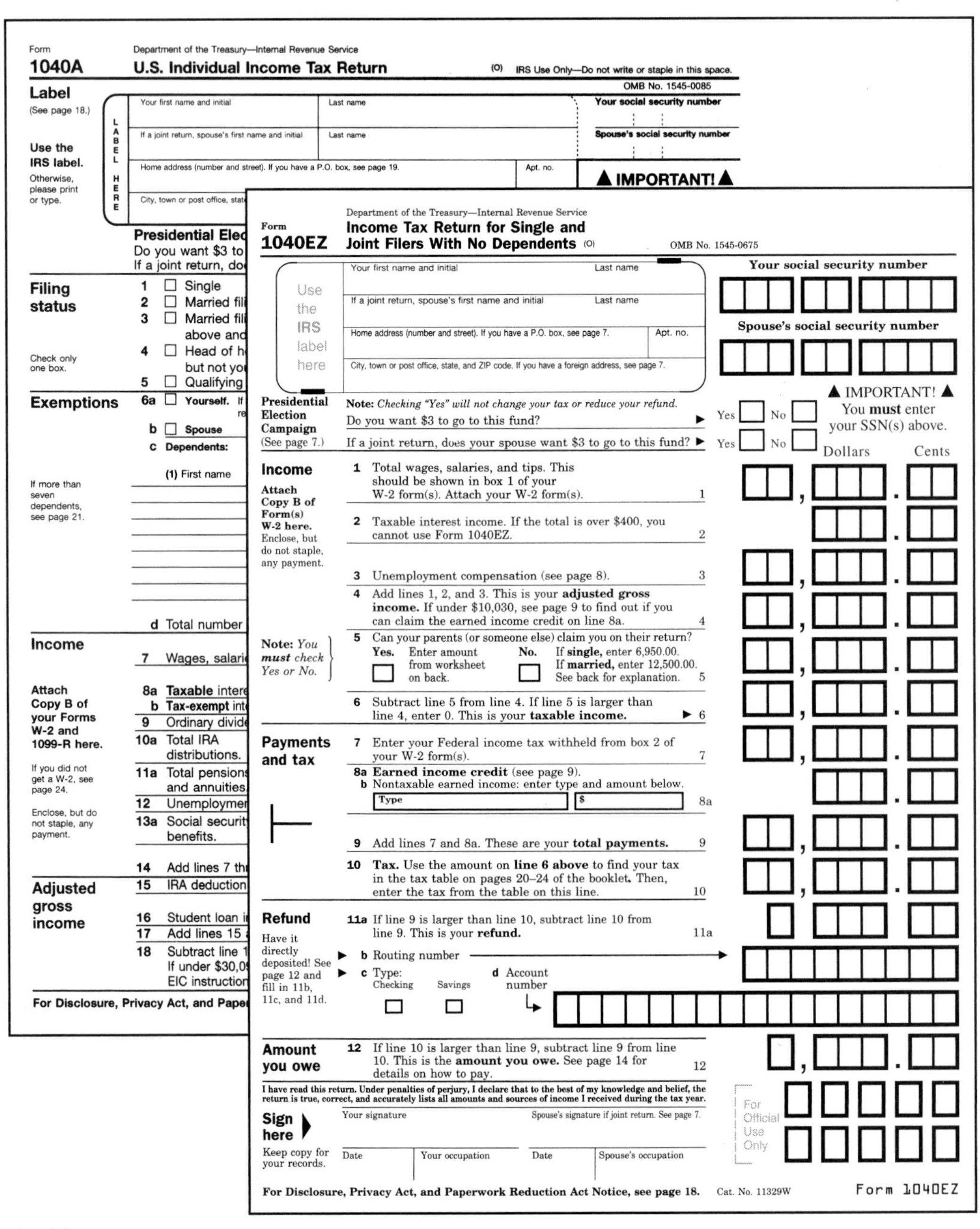

Form **1040A** Department of the Treasury—Internal Revenue Service
U.S. Individual Income Tax Return (O) IRS Use Only—Do not write or staple in this space.
OMB No. 1545-0085

Label (See page 18.)
LABEL HERE
Use the IRS label. Otherwise, please print or type.
Your first name and initial | Last name | Your social security number
If a joint return, spouse's first name and initial | Last name | Spouse's social security number
Home address (number and street). If you have a P.O. box, see page 19. | Apt. no. | ▲ IMPORTANT! ▲
City, town or post office, stat

Presidential Elec
Do you want $3 to
If a joint return, do

Filing status
Check only one box.
1 ☐ Single
2 ☐ Married fili
3 ☐ Married fili
above and
4 ☐ Head of h
but not yo
5 ☐ Qualifying

Exemptions
6a ☐ **Yourself.** If
b ☐ **Spouse**
c **Dependents:**
(1) First name
If more than seven dependents, see page 21.
d Total number

Income
Attach Copy B of your Forms W-2 and 1099-R here.
If you did not get a W-2, see page 24.
Enclose, but do not staple, any payment.
7 Wages, salari
8a **Taxable** intere
b **Tax-exempt** int
9 Ordinary divid
10a Total IRA distributions.
11a Total pension and annuities
12 Unemploymen
13a Social securit benefits.
14 Add lines 7 th

Adjusted gross income
15 IRA deduction
16 Student loan i
17 Add lines 15
18 Subtract line 1 If under $30,0 EIC instruction

For Disclosure, Privacy Act, and Pape

Form **1040EZ** Department of the Treasury—Internal Revenue Service
Income Tax Return for Single and Joint Filers With No Dependents (O) OMB No. 1545-0675

Use the IRS label here
Your first name and initial | Last name | **Your social security number**
If a joint return, spouse's first name and initial | Last name | **Spouse's social security number**
Home address (number and street). If you have a P.O. box, see page 7. | Apt. no.
City, town or post office, state, and ZIP code. If you have a foreign address, see page 7.

▲ IMPORTANT! ▲ You **must** enter your SSN(s) above.

Presidential Election Campaign (See page 7.)
Note: *Checking "Yes" will not change your tax or reduce your refund.*
Do you want $3 to go to this fund? ▶ Yes ☐ No ☐
If a joint return, does your spouse want $3 to go to this fund? ▶ Yes ☐ No ☐

Dollars Cents

Income
Attach Copy B of Form(s) W-2 here. Enclose, but do not staple, any payment.
1 Total wages, salaries, and tips. This should be shown in box 1 of your W-2 form(s). Attach your W-2 form(s). 1
2 Taxable interest income. If the total is over $400, you cannot use Form 1040EZ. 2
3 Unemployment compensation (see page 8). 3
4 Add lines 1, 2, and 3. This is your **adjusted gross income.** If under $10,030, see page 9 to find out if you can claim the earned income credit on line 8a. 4
Note: *You* ***must*** *check Yes or No.*
5 Can your parents (or someone else) claim you on their return?
Yes. Enter amount from worksheet on back. ☐ **No.** If **single,** enter 6,950.00. If **married,** enter 12,500.00. See back for explanation. ☐ 5
6 Subtract line 5 from line 4. If line 5 is larger than line 4, enter 0. This is your **taxable income.** ▶ 6

Payments and tax
7 Enter your Federal income tax withheld from box 2 of your W-2 form(s). 7
8a **Earned income credit** (see page 9).
b Nontaxable earned income: enter type and amount below.
Type $ 8a
9 Add lines 7 and 8a. These are your **total payments.** 9
10 **Tax.** Use the amount on **line 6 above** to find your tax in the tax table on pages 20–24 of the booklet. Then, enter the tax from the table on this line. 10

Refund
Have it directly deposited! See page 12 and fill in 11b, 11c, and 11d.
11a If line 9 is larger than line 10, subtract line 10 from line 9. This is your **refund.** 11a
▶ b Routing number
▶ c Type: Checking ☐ Savings ☐ d Account number

Amount you owe
12 If line 10 is larger than line 9, subtract line 9 from line 10. This is the **amount you owe.** See page 14 for details on how to pay. 12

I have read this return. Under penalties of perjury, I declare that to the best of my knowledge and belief, the return is true, correct, and accurately lists all amounts and sources of income I received during the tax year.

Sign here ▶ Keep copy for your records.
Your signature | Spouse's signature if joint return. See page 7.
Date | Your occupation | Date | Spouse's occupation

For Official Use Only

For Disclosure, Privacy Act, and Paperwork Reduction Act Notice, see page 18. Cat. No. 11329W Form 1040EZ

17-11
The 1040EZ is the simplest income tax return form. Form 1040A will be required if your financial situation becomes more complicated.

- State and local income, real estate, and property taxes.
- Home mortgage interest payments.
- Charitable contributions.
- Casualty and theft losses greater than 10 percent of adjusted gross income that were not reimbursed by insurance, minus $100.
- Job- and business-related expenses not paid for by employer and totaling more than two percent of adjusted gross income.

Reducing your taxes by claiming legitimate adjustments, deductions, and credits is called ***tax avoidance.*** It is a legal way to avoid paying unnecessary taxes. Failing to declare all income and falsifying deductions, adjustments, and credits are forms of ***tax evasion.*** This is a criminal offense that can carry heavy penalties.

The final date for filing federal taxes for the previous year is April 15. If that date falls on a Saturday, Sunday, or legal holiday, taxes are due on the next business day. Returns must be postmarked no later than the due date. Late payment may result in penalties.

Sources of Tax Information and Assistance

Many places offer help in tax planning and filing your return. As income increases, finances become more complicated. You may want to find professionals to advise you on tax matters. Several sources of assistance are listed below.

Internal Revenue Service

Tax rates and laws change from year to year. The IRS publishes new instruction booklets each year. These booklets give up-to-date details on who must file a federal income tax

A Taxing Situation

Unmet Expectations

Alvira is a high school junior. She just landed the summer job of her dreams. She loves animals and hopes someday to live in the country and breed dogs for a living. Her interest in the animal world led her to a local veterinarian. Luckily, the vet was looking for an assistant in the office. She needed someone good with animals to help at the receiving desk and assist in handling the animals that came in for treatment, grooming, and boarding.

Alvira was thrilled to get the job. She would be getting paid to do what she loved. How lucky could you be? She would earn $8 an hour for six-hour days and five-day weeks. Alvira would work 30 hours and earn $240 per week. The vet said she would get paid every two weeks.

At the end of two weeks, Alvira's first paycheck was considerably less than the $480 she expected. In fact, it was more than $100 less than she expected! Her paycheck stub showed the following deductions from her wages: $29.76 for FICA or Social Security tax, $6.96 for medicare tax, $62.10 for federal withholding tax, and $28.80 for state income tax. Alvira was shocked and disappointed to receive only $352.38. Still, she had the job she wanted and felt it was pretty good money anyway.

Case Review

1. Do these figures surprise you? What has been your experience with jobs and paycheck deductions?
2. Do you think it is fair for Alvira to pay so much in taxes? Why or why not?
3. What benefits does Alvira receive from the money she pays in taxes? Does she receive any direct benefits? What services that she enjoys are paid for by tax dollars?
4. What information from her paycheck stub will be important when Alvira files her income tax return?

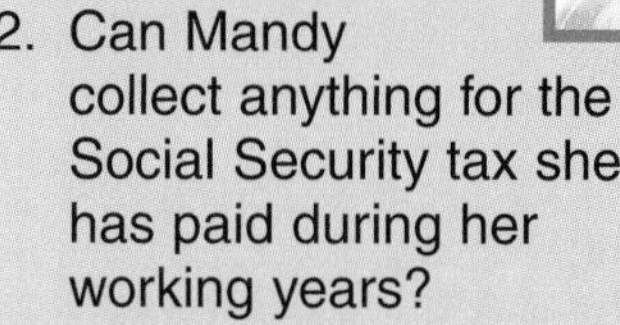

A Taxing Situation

A Time to Collect

Horace and Mandy Khan have raised a family of four. Their youngest child left home last year. Horace is just turning 65, and Mandy is 62. Horace worked 42 years for the same company and can now retire with full pension. Mandy worked part-time when the kids were young and full-time for the last ten years. The Khans always paid Social Security taxes when they were working. With retirement near, the Khans look to their Social Security benefits for part of their retirement income.

Horace Khan's earnings over the past five years have been between $40,000 and $50,000 annually. Mandy earns between $25,000 and $30,000 each year. Horace's pension will pay him $2,500 each month. Mandy has no retirement plan where she works.

Case Review

(Contact your local Social Security office for information and publications you need to answer the questions that follow.)

1. Approximately how much can the Khans expect in Social Security retirement benefits each month?
2. Can Mandy collect anything for the Social Security tax she has paid during her working years?
3. Will the Khans be required to pay income tax on their Social Security benefits?
4. How will monthly payments change if Horace dies? If Mandy dies?

return, what form to use, and how to file. They are available at your nearest IRS office. These materials can also be obtained at your local library or post office. Once you file a return, you will receive a tax package at the beginning of each year from the IRS. It will provide instructions for filing.

The IRS also publishes hundreds of other free materials related to tax laws and regulations. Check your local phone directory for the IRS number to call for information on publications and for advice on specific tax questions. The IRS operates a system of recorded phone messages that provide tax information on a variety of questions. They also offer a Web site and a toll-free hot line for specific questions. Walk-in service is also available at some 500 IRS offices located across the country.

Nongovernment Publications and Computer Programs

Each year, a number of tax guides are published and available for sale. They may also be available at public libraries. Some well-known guides include *American Express Tax Guide, The Ernst & Young Tax Guide, H&R Block Income Tax Guide, J.K. Lasser's Your Income Tax, Taxes for Dummies,* and *The Complete Idiot's Guide to Doing Your Income Tax.* Most news and financial periodicals also run articles on tax filing and regulations. These appear in the weeks and months before April 15 each year.

A variety of computer programs provide tax information and advice. They can help reduce the time required to complete your return. After the first year, you simply update the figures and details on your return. This simplifies record keeping. It also helps maintain accurate and up-to-date tax information. Reliable computer tax programs usually provide annual updates covering changes in the tax laws. You will find a variety of programs for sale at your local bookstore or computer outlet. Three of the well known software tax packages are *Kiplinger TaxCut, Simply Tax,* and *Turbo Tax.*

Tax Preparation Services

Taxes can be complicated by unusual investment transactions, deductions, income sources, or financial circumstances. If this becomes the case for you, it may be desirable to call on a professional to assist with or prepare your tax return. Services of this type range from one-person offices to nationwide firms specializing in tax preparation.

Tax attorneys and certified public accountants who specialize in tax matters are among the experts who can advise you on tax questions, 17-12. They may also prepare your tax return for your signature, based on records and receipts you provide. Some tax preparers guarantee to pay penalties resulting from errors they've made on tax returns. However, the taxpayer has the ultimate legal responsibility for any errors and any penalties for late payment.

Tax Return Audits

A ***tax audit*** is a detailed examination of your tax return by the IRS. In 1996, the IRS examined 1.67 percent or 1.9 million of the 116 million personal income tax returns filed. If your return is audited by the IRS, you will need to prove the accuracy of your reported income, deductions, adjustments, credits, and other details on your tax return. This is when your good record keeping practices will come in handy.

The Internal Revenue Service Reform Act of 1998 was passed to ensure taxpayers receive due process in their dealings with the IRS when tax liabilities are in question. It pays to know your rights as a taxpayer if your return is audited. The IRS must provide a detailed statement of your rights and the IRS's obligations during the audit, appeals, refund, and collection process. You have the right to make an audio recording of any audit interview conducted by the IRS. You are guaranteed the right to be represented by an attorney currently licensed to practice before the IRS.

You will be expected to answer the IRS agent's questions honestly and completely, providing documentation when necessary. You may take an accountant, attorney, or tax preparer

17-12
Many people call on certified public accountants to assist them with tax filing.

Jack Klasey

with you to the audit session. If you disagree with the outcome of a tax audit, you have the right to a conference at the Regional Appeals Office. From there, you can take your case to a U.S. tax court, U.S. claims court, U.S. district court, and even to the U.S. Supreme Court. At the final outcome, you will be required to pay any additional taxes, interest, and penalties if they are assigned.

State and Local Taxation

Sales, real estate, and personal property taxes make up a large part of state and local revenues. Most states and localities also rely on personal and corporate income tax for a large share of their revenues. Forty-three states collect personal income tax. Rates vary from state to state and are usually based on adjusted gross income, taxable income, or some other figure taken from federal returns. Filing deadlines usually correspond with filing of federal returns. The departments of revenue for your state and municipality can provide the information you need on state and local income, property, and other taxes.

Social Security Taxes

The Social Security Act was signed into law in 1935 by Franklin Roosevelt. This federal program provides income when earnings are reduced or stopped because of retirement, disability, or death. Social Security also provides hospital and medical insurance to the elderly and the disabled through medicare. Medicare became part of the law in 1965.

The Social Security Administration of the Department of Health and Human Services manages the Social Security program. Today, the program covers almost everyone who works except for federal government employees hired before 1984, railroad workers, and some state and local government employees. These groups are covered by other forms of insurance.

Workers and employers share payments of the Social Security taxes that cover Social Security and hospital insurance. The tax is figured as a percentage of an employee's income. Employees and employers each pay equal amounts in Social Security taxes. Each pays 7.65 percent—6.2 percent for Social Security and 1.45 percent for medicare. Self-employed workers pay the entire 15.3 percent. The percentage is figured on income up to a cap of $72,600 for Social Security and on all income for medicare. Both the rates and the cap on earnings are likely to continue upward as the cost of benefits increases.

Employers deduct Social Security tax from each employee's paycheck. They send this amount, along with the employer's share, to the IRS under the employee's name and Social Security number. The amount of Social Security tax deducted appears on an employee's paycheck. It will be identified as Social Security or FICA. Income tax will also be deducted from your paycheck, 17-13.

Your Social Security Number

The Tax Reform Act of 1986 requires a taxpayer claiming an exemption for a dependent age five or older to include that dependent's Social Security number on the tax form. The taxpayer can obtain a Social Security number for the dependent by completing a simple form. Since this is the law, you probably already have a Social Security number.

A Social Security number serves two major purposes. The Social Security Administration uses this number to keep a record of your covered earnings. These earnings determine the amount you will eventually receive in retirement or

Earnings	Hours	Amount	Deduction	Current	Year to Date
Regular Overtime Total	70.00 14.75 84.75	846.16 267.57 1, 113.73	FICA Tax Medicare Tax Federal Tax NY State Tax NY City Tax Disability LTD	69.06 16.15 116.17 52.40 27.05 1.20 1.00	494.17 115.58 880.89 347.68 183.34 9.60
Year to Date Gross		$7,970.53	Total	$283.03	
			Net Pay	$830.70	

17-13
This paycheck stub shows how withholding amounts may appear on your paychecks.

disability benefits and benefits to your survivors should you die. The Internal Revenue Service uses your Social Security number as a taxpayer identification number. The number must be used on all returns and forms filed with the IRS.

No two Social Security numbers are alike. Your number is yours alone. It prevents your records from getting mixed up with the records of someone else who may have the same name. If you lose your card or change your name, contact the nearest Social Security office for a new card, 17-14.

Social Security Benefits

When you begin working, your Social Security taxes pay for the benefits others receive. When you retire, become disabled, or die, other workers pay Social Security taxes to cover benefits to you and your family. Before a worker or a worker's family can receive benefits, the worker must have paid Social Security taxes a certain length of time.

As you work, you earn Social Security credits—usually four per year. Workers received one credit for every $700 earned in 1999 up to a maximum of four credits per year. The amount you must earn to receive a credit has been increased several times. The number of credits required to receive Social Security benefits varies. Most workers need 40 credits or ten years of work to qualify for benefits. Younger workers who become disabled may require fewer credits to qualify for benefits.

The amount of the benefits depends on the worker's age and average earnings over a period of years. Here are the types of benefits the Social Security program provides.

Retirement Benefits

In the past, workers became eligible for full retirement benefits at age 65. They could retire as early as age 62, but received only about 80 percent of retirement benefit payments. The eligibility age will gradually increase to 67. Benefits may also be made to a retired worker's

- ❑ Unmarried children under 18 (under 19 if full-time high school students) or over 18 if severely disabled with a disability beginning before age 22.
- ❑ Spouse who is age 62 or over.
- ❑ Spouse of any age if caring for a disabled or retired worker's child who is under 16 or disabled.

17-14
After an application form is completed, the Social Security office will issue you a Social Security number and card.

SOCIAL SECURITY ADMINISTRATION
Application for a Social Security Card
Form Approved OMB No. 0960-0066

1 NAME TO BE SHOWN ON CARD — First, Full Middle Name, Last
FULL NAME AT BIRTH IF OTHER THAN ABOVE — First, Full Middle Name, Last
OTHER NAMES USED
2 MAILING ADDRESS Do Not Abbreviate — Street Address, Apt. No., PO Box, Rural Route No.; City, State, Zip Code
3 CITIZENSHIP (Check One) — U.S. Citizen; Legal Alien Allowed To Work; Legal Alien Not Allowed To Work; Other (See Instructions On Page 1)
4 SEX — Male; Female
RACE/ETHNIC — Asian, Asian-American or Pacific Islander; Hispanic; Black (Not Hispanic); North American Indian or Alaskan Native; White (Not Hispanic)
7 PLACE OF BIRTH (Do Not Abbreviate) — City, State or Foreign Country, FCI; Office Use Only
First, Full Middle Name, Last Name At Her Birth
...RITY ...for a child under age 18.) ☐☐☐-☐☐-☐☐☐☐
First, Full Middle Name, Last
...RITY ...for a child under age 18.) ☐☐☐-☐☐-☐☐☐☐
...ng on his/her behalf ever filed for or received a Social Security
No (If "no", go on to question 14.) Don't Know (If "don't know", go on to question 14.)
...r previously ...tem 1. ☐☐☐-☐☐-☐☐☐☐
...ost ...ed for the person listed in item 1. — First, Middle, Last
13 Enter any different date of birth if used on an earlier application for a card. — Month, Day, Year
14 TODAY'S DATE — Month, Day, Year
15 DAYTIME PHONE NUMBER ( ) — Area Code, Number
DELIBERATELY FURNISHING (OR CAUSING TO BE FURNISHED) FALSE INFORMATION ON THIS APPLICATION IS A CRIME PUNISHABLE BY FINE OR IMPRISONMENT, OR BOTH.
16 YOUR SIGNATURE
17 YOUR RELATIONSHIP TO THE PERSON IN ITEM 1 IS: Self; Natural or Adoptive Parent; Legal Guardian; Other (Specify)

DO NOT WRITE BELOW THIS LINE (FOR SSA USE ONLY)							
NPN			DOC	NTI	CAN		ITV
PBC	EVI	EVA	EVC	PRA	NWR	DNR	UNIT
EVIDENCE SUBMITTED					SIGNATURE AND TITLE OF EMPLOYEE(S) REVIEWING EVIDENCE AND/OR CONDUCTING INTERVIEW		
					DATE		
					DCL	DATE	

Form SS-5 (2-98) Destroy Prior Editions Page 5

SOCIAL SECURITY
987-65-4321
THIS NUMBER HAS BEEN ESTABLISHED FOR
DEPARTMENT OF HEALTH & HUMAN SERVICES · USA
SIGNATURE

Disability Benefits

A worker who becomes disabled before retirement age may receive disability benefits. A ***disability*** is a severe physical or mental condition that prevents a person from working. Monthly disability benefits may also be paid to a disabled worker's family members under the same terms described under retirement benefits.

Survivors' Benefits

If a worker dies, benefits may be paid to certain members of the worker's family. A single, lump-sum payment may also be made when a worker dies. This payment usually goes to the surviving spouse. Monthly benefits may be paid to a deceased worker's

- ❑ Unmarried children under 18 (19 if full-time high school students) or over 18 if severely disabled with disability occurring before age 22.
- ❑ Spouse 60 or older (50 if disabled).
- ❑ Spouse at any age who is caring for a worker's child under age 16 or disabled.
- ❑ Spouse 50 or older who becomes disabled.
- ❑ Parents who depend on the worker for half or more of their support.

Benefits for Divorced People

An ex-spouse can be eligible for benefits on a worker's record under certain circumstances. This eligibility does not affect the amount of benefits the worker and the worker's family are entitled to receive. To qualify for benefits, an ex-spouse must

- Have been married to the worker at least 10 years.
- Be 62 years old.
- Not be eligible on his or her own or someone else's Social Security record.

Social Security benefits do not start automatically. When a person becomes eligible, he or she must apply for them at the nearest Social Security office. The Social Security administration calculates benefits and issues monthly payments. The administration also will calculate possible future benefits based on current earnings. However, calculations cannot be exact for young workers far from retirement age. It is a good idea to check your Social Security record every few years to make sure your earnings are being credited to your record. You can get a free postcard form at any Social Security office for this purpose.

Retirees need to contact the Social Security office in their area several months before retirement. This will give the office plenty of time to calculate benefits and begin payments as soon as retiring workers are eligible.

A Look Ahead

The sound future of Social Security depends upon responsible fiscal action today. Today people are living longer, healthier lives, 7-15. By 2030, there will be almost twice as many older Americans as there were in 1999. Presently, about three workers pay Social Security taxes for every beneficiary. By 2030, there will be only two workers to every beneficiary. While the system has some reserves, benefit payments will begin to exceed tax collection around 2013 unless Social Security reforms are enacted soon.

If a time comes when benefit payments do exceed tax collection, the Social Security trust fund will be depleted. At this time, there will be no money in the fund to support all the persons who have paid into it. Dealing with this problem will require increasing taxes, decreasing benefits, or both. In the 1980s, Congress called for taxing some retirees' benefits and raising the retirement age. This was not enough. Among the other solutions proposed are plans to

- Reduce automatic cost-of-living allowance increases in benefits.
- Raise taxes on benefits to higher-income recipients.
- Cut benefits for higher-income recipients.
- Raise the retirement age again.
- Increase Social Security tax contributions.
- Invest Social Security trust fund surpluses in the stock market.

17-15
As the population ages, more money is going out of the Social Security system than is going into it.

- ❑ Privatize part of the Social Security program by permitting individuals to invest a portion of their Social Security taxes in personal retirement accounts.

As policy makers work to achieve meaningful Social Security reform, their primary goals will be to strengthen and protect the future of the Social Security system. They will strive to maintain the universality and fairness of the system. It will be important to provide benefits people can count on regardless of changes in the economy and financial markets. It will be necessary to continue benefits for disabled and low-income beneficiaries who currently receive payments, since one of every three beneficiaries of the current system are *not* retirees. Finally, any reform of the system needs to preserve and promote fiscal discipline with regard to both the Social Security system and the federal budget.

No satisfactory solution can be found through increased deficit spending and a growing national debt. It will be in your best interest to keep up with new developments in Social Security reform as it relates to both taxes and benefits. It is your money at both ends—paying and receiving.

Summary

Taxation is the primary source of government revenues. It pays for government operations and services. Both citizens and businesses pay taxes. The federal tax code changes frequently as Congress struggles to meet the need for revenues with a level of taxation voters will accept. The law allows certain income tax deductions, exemptions, and credits that reduce the taxes owed.

Government spending and taxation are closely related. The more government spends, the more taxes people must pay. When government spends more than it receives, deficit spending results. The recurring deficits each year add up to the national debt that currently amounts to more than five and one-half trillion dollars. Interest on the debt is one of the largest annual expenditures of the federal government.

Citizens can influence government spending and taxing policies by voting and participating in the political system—by making themselves heard. This is one of the key roles of the taxpayer and citizen. Filing a federal income tax return each year is the other key responsibility of the taxpayer. This involves keeping necessary records and receipts and mastering the income tax forms. As a person's financial situation grows more complex, filing the annual return can become very complicated. It may be necessary for some taxpayers to call on professionals to assist with filing requirements.

Social Security and medicare taxes are generally deducted from paychecks. Social Security provides income when earnings stop for certain reasons. Medicare pays certain hospital and medical costs for the elderly and disabled. Generally, employers and employees each pay half of the Social Security tax on total income. The rates increase periodically. Self-employed persons must pay the entire tax since they have no employer to pay half.

As tax rates increase and government spending continues to rise, it will become necessary to make difficult choices in the future. Citizens may want to take a harder look at what government should provide and who should pay how much of the cost.

To Review

1. Explain how ethical behavior and social responsibility relate to citizenship.
2. Give three reasons volunteerism is an important part of citizenship.
3. What is the primary purpose of taxes?
4. List the five current tax rates as they are applied to different levels of income for federal income taxes.
5. What are the two largest sources of federal revenues?
6. What are the three greatest federal government expenditures?
7. Name the four major types of taxes that provide most state and local government revenues.
8. How does government spending relate to taxation?
9. When you become employed, your employer will ask you to fill out a _____ Form for tax withholding purposes.
10. What are the three common forms for filing taxes?
11. Which tax form is the simplest to file?
12. Name three items that can be deducted from income for tax purposes.
13. True or false. The IRS typically audits about 25 percent of all personal income tax returns.
14. What are the two major purposes of Social Security numbers?
15. What actions are being considered in reforming the Social Security system?

To Think Critically

1. Compare and contrast progressive and regressive taxes.
2. What government services would you be willing to pay higher taxes to support? Why?
3. If you had the task of reducing federal government spending, what programs or services would you cut or eliminate and why?
4. What records are important to keep for tax purposes?
5. Why is Social Security reform necessary?
6. What actions would you recommend for strengthening the Social Security program? Why?

To Do

1. How would you describe your role as a citizen as it relates to each of the following?
   - ❑ national history, the constitution, the laws of the land
   - ❑ family, neighbors, and community
   - ❑ your state, your nation, and the world
   - ❑ ethics, character, volunteerism
   - ❑ the environment, natural resources
   - ❑ commitment, participation, involvement
   - ❑ local, state, and federal government
2. The Center for Civic Education outlines the following fundamental values and principles, which are the foundation of your American citizenship.
   - ❑ individual rights
   - ❑ liberty
   - ❑ the public good
   - ❑ self-government
   - ❑ equality
   - ❑ diversity
   - ❑ openness and free inquiry
   - ❑ truth
   - ❑ patriotism

   These civic values were written in the Declaration of Independence and the Constitution. Discuss how they relate to your role as a citizen. Give examples of citizen behavior related to each of these.
3. If your school offers community service learning as part of the curriculum, interview the faculty advisor in charge to learn about the following:
   - ❑ Services being performed.
   - ❑ Learning outcomes expected.
   - ❑ Benefits for service providers, recipients, and the community.
   - ❑ Evaluation procedures for services and learning.
   - ❑ Recognition given for accomplishments of community service.
4. Find out the current amount of the national debt and the per capita amount. Prepare a brief report discussing how the national debt affects the economy and you as a citizen.
5. Interview a representative in the nearest Internal Revenue Service office on the following:
   - ❑ Services the IRS provides for taxpayers.
   - ❑ Questions and problems taxpayers most frequently bring to the IRS.
   - ❑ Available advice and publications on filing federal tax returns.
   - ❑ Recent and pending legislation that affects individual and corporate income taxes.
   - ❑ Tax audits—reasons returns are audited and the procedure.

   Write a two-page summary of your interview.

6. Obtain copies of tax Forms 1040EZ, 1040A, and 1040. Compare the three forms. Learn the meaning of any terms appearing on the forms you do not understand. Complete Forms 1040EZ and 1040A using various income and expense figures.
7. Visit your local Social Security office and obtain pamphlets about Social Security and medicare. Using this information, prepare a three-page written report describing the purposes of Social Security and medicare and the benefits they provide.
8. Visit the Web sites of the IRS and the Social Security administration. Report to the class on the information and publications available from each agency.

CHAPTER 18

Humanity Confronts
Rio delegates plan talks on preserving the web of life
Demands of People: The Widening Impact
THE RAIN
IN ASSOCIATI
INFORMATION PLEASE
U.S. GREEN CITY RANKINGS
COMPILED BY WORLD RESOURCES INSTITUTE
STATE OF THE PLANET
FOOD
ENERGY
WATER
WASTES
FORESTS & WETLANDS
AIR POLLUTION
RECREATION & ECOTRAVEL
GREEN CITIES
STATE COMPARISONS
•FACTS TO GUIDE YOUR DAILY ACTIONS
•STATE, NATIONAL, GLOBAL STATISTICS
•WASTE AND CLEAN-UP INFORMATION
•RATINGS OF "GREEN" U.S. CITIES
ENVIRONMENTAL ACTION
You Can Build An Environmentally Sound Economy
Co-op America's
How to Make the World a Better Place
A Guide to
How You Can Effect Positive
SOUTH AMERICA
6,879,450 Sq. Miles
Mt. Aconcagua, 22,834 Ft.
Valdez Peninsula, -131 Ft.
EUROPE

Your Role in the Environment

sustainable development
environmental impact statement (EIS)
environmental audit
ecology
conservation
environmentalists
global warming
fossil fuels
urban sprawl
Better America Bonds
landfill
recycle
composting
green products
renewable energy sources
nonrenewable energy sources

After studying this chapter, you will be able to

- outline major environmental and ecological issues facing the nation and the world today.
- explain steps individuals, citizen groups, and governments can take to conserve energy and other natural resources and to protect the environment.
- describe the major environmental problems related to the production and use of energy.
- identify the costs, benefits, and trade-offs related to environmental protection regulations and activities.
- identify reliable sources of information on environmental and ecological problems and issues.

People around the world have used and misused our planet and natural resources in ways that will affect the quality of life for generations to come. We are finally beginning to see the long-term results of our actions and the way we live. We are starting to grasp the importance of developing a healthy relationship with our world, 18-1.

In recent years, a new term has evolved to describe the goal of long-term economic and environmental planning. ***Sustainable development*** is meeting present needs without

> *"The frog does not drink up the pond in which it lives."*
>
> *Chinese Proverb*

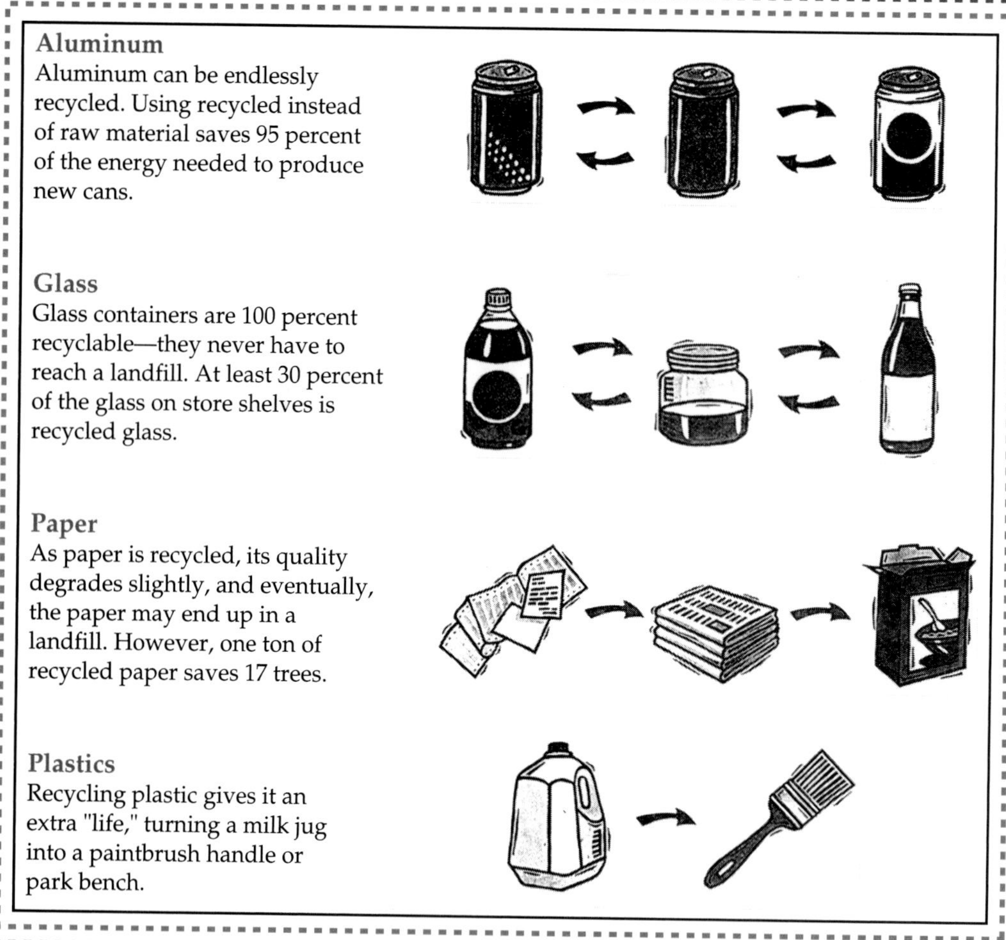

18-1
Everyone can participate in recycling glass, cans, newspapers, most plastics, and other materials.

compromising the ability of future generations to meet their own needs. This term was defined and used by the United Nations World Commission on Environment and Development. The ***environmental impact statement (EIS)*** and the ***environmental audit*** are two tools that can assist in meeting the goals of sustainable development. The EIS is an assessment of potential environmental outcomes of government regulations or of government and government-approved projects such as airports, public buildings, military complexes, highways, etc. The National Environmental Policy Act requires an EIS from federal agencies for any major projects or legislative proposals which could have a significant effect on the environment. These statements are published in the *Federal Register* and are available to the public from the issuing agencies. The *environmental audit* is a similar assessment conducted on a voluntary basis by businesses who strive to meet environmental performance targets and to comply with environmental regulations.

Sustainable development is not really a new idea. In the early 1900's, Theodore Roosevelt wrote, "The nation behaves well if it treats the natural resources as assets which it must turn over to the next generation, increased and not impaired in value."

Protecting the world around you is one of your most critical duties as a consumer, citizen, and taxpayer. The future belongs to you. You vote for the policymakers who decide how we will use natural resources. You, with your tax dollars and consumer spending, pay for environmental mishaps and mistakes. You pay for the research required to find earth-friendly ways of meeting basic human needs. You will pay the costs of protecting the planet and solving environmental problems far into the future. Learning how your money is being spent and what environmental choices you have is important.

Current Environmental Issues

Ecology is the study of the relationship between living things and their environment. A host of ecological issues trouble the informed citizens of planet earth. Each day, people awake somewhere to severe shortages of food, water, and fuel. Citizens are becoming aware of problems with the air they breathe, the water they drink, and the food they eat. Newspapers carry headlines on global warming, deforestation, holes in the ozone layer, and disappearing wetlands. Each day, we learn more about the challenges of solid waste management, the dangers of hazardous substances and toxic waste, and the perils of overpopulation.

> *"Then I say the earth belongs to each generation during its course, fully and in its own right, no generation can contract debts greater than may be paid during the course of its own existence."*
>
> *Thomas Jefferson, 1789*

Finally, we are learning more about actions we can take to help solve some of these problems. We are learning to act individually and in groups. We are finding out that lifestyle changes will be needed to save our planet. ***Conservation*** means acting to save and preserve our environment and natural resources. We are slowly becoming aware of the need to conserve—to reduce, reuse, and recycle. See 18-2. We are recognizing

Waste Management of North America

18-2
Recycling and disposal facilities are being developed across the country.

the need for worldwide cooperation and a sensible approach to environmental concerns.

Environmentalists are people who are concerned with issues related to maintaining quality of life. These issues include land use; water, air, and noise pollution; depletion of natural resources; global warming; and endangered species and habitats. Scientists conduct studies and make suggestions for solving these problems. Here are brief descriptions of current environmental issues.

> *"The first law of ecology is that everything is related to everything else."*
>
> *Barry Commoner*

Energy-Related Problems

Both the production and use of fuel damage the planet. Oil spills foul the waters. Strip-mining causes long-lasting damage to the land. Fumes from burning fuels pollute the air. Nuclear waste, improperly handled, could cause environmental damage beyond any we have known in the past. That's why it is vital to evaluate energy-related threats to the environment. We must find earth-friendly ways of producing and using energy to meet basic needs.

Global Warming

Also called the greenhouse effect, ***global warming*** is a warming near the earth's surface. It results when the earth's atmosphere traps the sun's heat. The amount of carbon dioxide in the air contributes to global warming.

Unless we find ways to reduce it, the amount of carbon dioxide in the air is predicted to double by 2050. This is caused by the burning of the fossil fuels—coal, oil, and natural gas. (***Fossil fuels*** are nonrenewable energy sources derived from the partly decayed bodies of animals and plants that lived long ago.) This could cause average temperatures of earth to rise by three to eight degrees Fahrenheit. The potential outcome of changes in global climate is an important environmental concern today.

Steps we can take to reduce the release of carbon dioxide into the atmosphere include:

- ❑ Developing more fuel-efficient and low-emission autos, planes, and trains.
- ❑ Developing and using more energy-efficient home appliances and equipment.
- ❑ Developing alternative, safe, and renewable energy sources.
- ❑ Establishing sound fuel-efficiency and conservation programs.
- ❑ Reducing or eliminating unnecessary driving.

Air Pollution

The Environmental Protection Agency monitors air quality at close to 3,000 sites around the nation. Air pollutants of greatest concern include particulate matter, such as ash, dirt, dust, smoke, and soot. These can cause respiratory problems. Smog, sulfur dioxide, acid rain, and carbon monoxide are also of great concern. These pollutants are produced largely by transportation, fuel combustion, and industry. Stricter air quality standards have reduced pollution, but the problem remains and is severe in some areas.

Solid Waste Disposal

A ***landfill*** is a permanent waste disposal site for most solid and nonhazardous wastes. Existing landfill capacity is running out. Building new landfills is costly, 18-3. Also, because few communities are willing to permit landfills in their area, they are being located further and further from the areas they serve. This makes it necessary to transport waste long distances at considerable cost.

Reducing waste is the most economical and practical way to lessen this problem. However, it requires a team effort on the part of individuals, businesses, communities, and

Waste Management of North America

18-3
This recycling and disposal facility meets environmental standards with sound landfill practices and technology.

government. Reducing trash involves buying less, using less, reusing, recycling—an overall sense of economy. To ***recycle*** means to reprocess resources so they can be used again. This will not only ease the landfill problem, it can also help conserve resources, save energy, and reduce industrial pollution.

Hazardous Waste

Hazardous chemicals and nuclear waste are serious problems in certain areas. We must assess the danger posed by hazardous waste sites and learn how to clean them up. This will be among the greatest and costliest challenges in the future of environmental protection.

Urban Sprawl

Urban sprawl is defined as "dispersed development outside of compact urban and village centers along highways and in rural countrysides." This type of random, unplanned, and uncontrolled development creates and aggravates a number of environmental and economic problems. See 18-4. According to the Sierra Club's sprawl fact sheet, the negatives of unplanned sprawl include:

- ❑ higher taxes to cover the increased costs of providing public services.
- ❑ accelerated decline of cities and towns.
- ❑ increased environmental pollution—water, air, and noise.
- ❑ destruction of open space, farmlands, rivers, and lakes.
- ❑ greater dependence on cars.
- ❑ increased commuting for greater distances.
- ❑ heavy traffic and congestion.

How does your community deal with growth and new development? Find out about your local planning and zoning laws. Communities across the country need to begin promoting smart, compact growth as opposed to sprawl. Zoning boards and plan commissions have been effective in some areas. ***Better America Bonds*** offer

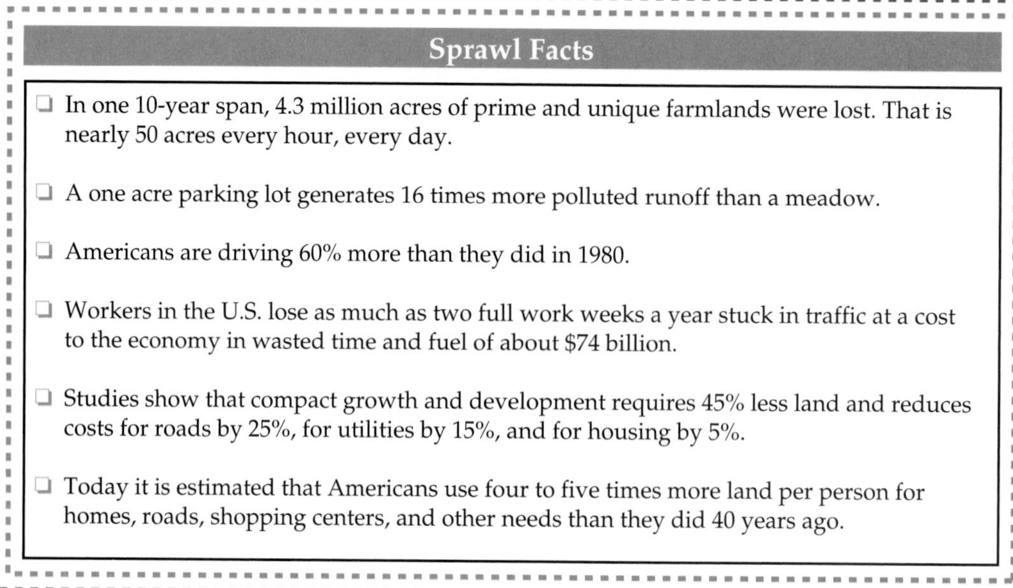

Sprawl Facts

- In one 10-year span, 4.3 million acres of prime and unique farmlands were lost. That is nearly 50 acres every hour, every day.
- A one acre parking lot generates 16 times more polluted runoff than a meadow.
- Americans are driving 60% more than they did in 1980.
- Workers in the U.S. lose as much as two full work weeks a year stuck in traffic at a cost to the economy in wasted time and fuel of about $74 billion.
- Studies show that compact growth and development requires 45% less land and reduces costs for roads by 25%, for utilities by 15%, and for housing by 5%.
- Today it is estimated that Americans use four to five times more land per person for homes, roads, shopping centers, and other needs than they did 40 years ago.

18-4
Urban sprawl is a threat to the environment.

one incentive for states and local communities to protect open space and enhance the quality of life. These bonds are a $9.5 billion credit program sponsored by the Environmental Protection Agency for the purpose of helping local communities fight urban sprawl. With EPA approval, states and local communities can issue Better America Bonds to acquire land, set up parks and greenbelts, protect water and farmland, and attack traffic congestion. This financing tool enables states and local communities to control their own smart growth initiatives and programs.

What You Can Do

These are but a few of the current environmental concerns. As a consumer, citizen, and taxpayer, you have a large stake in promoting a healthy, caring relationship with the world we share. Among the many questions, one fact is clear—the burden for a clean, wholesome environment belongs to all of us. There are many ways to accept that challenge, as individuals and group members. Following are some general guidelines.

Keep Yourself Informed About Local Environmental Issues

Watch for activities in your community that could alter the environment. Take whatever steps you can to protect the air you breathe, water you drink, and parks and open spaces you enjoy. Be ready to act when pollution, urban sprawl, and other environmental problems arise in your community. Local action is the speediest, most direct way to deal with problems in and near your community.

Recognize the Cumulative Effect of Small Acts

Some environmental problems can be traced to careless litter and waste. For example, a single can or wrapper tossed aside, a single dripping faucet, or a single car running on leaded fuel is no cause for concern. However, millions of littered cans, dripping faucets, and cars burning leaded fuel create big problems. Just as little acts can create big problems, little acts can often solve big problems. There are many small steps you can take in your home, community, and marketplace to improve and protect your world.

Town Meeting

When the Landfill Is Full

Chris Webb was recently elected president of the town council. He has inherited a number of community problems including a local landfill almost filled to capacity. A sanitation department report calls for closing the existing landfill facility within two to three years.

Chris and the town council want to extend use of the existing facility as long as possible. They must find another place to dispose of solid waste in the meantime. In educating himself on the issues, Chris learns that transporting solid waste to a distant landfill will be very costly. The town will have to pay both fees to use the landfill and transportation costs. These will be in addition to the present costs of curbside pickup. Cost increases may run as much as $200 to $300 annually per household.

Chris knows the townspeople will not be happy with this situation. He decides to write a list of the possible approaches to the problem. He wrote down the following suggestions:

- ❑ Promote voluntary recycling with curbside pickup of recyclable materials.
- ❑ Establish mandatory recycling with curbside pickup and fines for failure to recycle.
- ❑ Charge a fee per pound of waste over a specified minimum to encourage recycling and compost of yard wastes. Yard waste accounts for a high percentage of overall waste.
- ❑ Establish a community-based compost program for yard wastes.
- ❑ Assist with individual composting of both yard and food waste per household.
- ❑ Designate convenient drop-off centers for all recyclable waste, including papers, magazines, glass, aluminum, plastics, and cardboard.
- ❑ Levy a special tax per household to pay for solid waste disposal.
- ❑ Pass a law requiring local merchants to recycle packing materials and other recyclable waste.
- ❑ Organize an awareness campaign to encourage residents and merchants to reduce, reuse, and recycle solid waste materials.

Case Review

1. Which three ideas would you favor most? Explain.
2. Which three ideas would you favor least? Explain.
3. What other actions can you think of for reducing, recycling, and disposing of solid waste?
4. Which of the above would be the most and least costly for individuals, businesses, and the town government? the most and least convenient?
5. Choose one of the alternatives and prepare a report describing the environmental pros and cons of the action and the costs for individuals, merchants, and the local government.
6. Which of any of the described actions have been carried out in your area and how well do they work?

Make Conservation a Way of Life

Avoid wasting water, gas, electricity, and food. Recycle newspapers, bottles, plastics, magazines, and cans. Buy reusable rather than disposable products when possible. Contact local government offices to learn about recycling programs, landfill policies, regulations on water usage, and other local ecological issues. Some communities encourage composting as a method of reducing and recycling yard and other organic waste. ***Composting*** is a natural process that transforms materials like food waste, leaves, and grass into useful soil-like products. Find out whether your local government sponsors a composting project or offers information on home compost measures.

Reduce Noise Pollution

Noise frequently comes from sources that are beyond direct individual control, such as jet aircraft, industrial machinery, and heavy traffic. However, in the home and community, individuals can control noise levels with relative ease. Set the volume controls at moderate levels on stereos, radios, and televisions. Limit the use of noisy yard equipment to reasonable hours. Local noise ordinances exist in many communities.

Participate in Community Pollution Control, Recycling Programs, and Beautification Projects

Many communities sponsor a variety of programs to protect and enhance the environment. These may include recycling programs; composting plans; restrictions on water, fuel, and land use; emission controls; tree planting policies; and environmental education and awareness programs, 18-5.

18-5 Ashland Oil Inc.
This river sweep project is one example of community action working to beautify the environment.

Avoid Unnecessary and Careless Use of Pesticides and Harsh Chemicals

In caring for your yard and garden, limit the use of pesticides. In household cleaning, look for biodegradable, nontoxic products with low or no phosphate and chlorine content. When you must use potentially hazardous substances, carefully follow directions for proper use, storage, and disposal. Motor oil is one of the chemicals frequently disposed of improperly.

> *"Each year, 20 times the amount of oil spilled by the tanker Exxon Valdez in Alaska is improperly dumped into America's environment by do-it-yourselfers changing their own motor oil."*
>
> *Automotive Information Council*

Look for Opportunities in the Marketplace to Make Environmentally Sound and Safe Choices

Buy products that can be recycled and avoid over-packaged products. Support businesses that take responsible positions on environmental issues, 18-6. Buy energy-efficient autos, appliances, furnaces, air conditioners, and other equipment. Shop at stores that provide for convenient recycling of packaging materials. Look for *green products*—those that are environmentally safe according to objective, authoritative testing. See 18-7 for more information on identifying green products through environmental labeling.

FUTONAIR

18-6
This futon is being marketed as an environmentally friendly product.

What Citizen Groups Can Do

At the local level, citizen action is often the driving force that protects a community's environment. For example, some communities have managed to turn solid waste into an asset. About 100 landfills have developed a way to harness the methane gas built up by the decomposition of organic waste and use it to produce energy. A mountain of solid waste in one area has become a center of recreational activity. In another area, trash is processed together with coal and used to generate electrical power. In still another, the landfill has been developed as a golf course. See 18-8.

To reduce air pollution from cars, some communities are restricting

Environmental Labeling

Spending your dollars with environmental awareness calls for careful shopping. "Green Marketing" has become a promotional tool for a number of companies who have learned that it sells—and pays. Among the labels used in green marketing are the *Cross and Globe* and *Green Seal.*

Scientific Certification Systems (SCS) started a consumer product labeling program in 1989. The program has two main goals. The first is to verify environmental claims made by manufacturers about their products. *The Cross and Globe* emblem appears on certified products along with a brief description of specific claims that have been verified.

The second goal is to conduct a thorough study of the environmental burdens associated with each stage in the life cycle of a product and its packaging. SCS issues an *Environmental Performance Statement* that may be printed on the product label. This report card tells the consumer how the labeled product performed in up to 25 separate environmental burden areas.

Green Seal, founded in 1990, is a nonprofit organization located in Washinton, DC. It, too, evaluates the environmental impact of products through their life cycle. Products that create the least environmental damage in a given category may carry the Green Seal. This is intended to be a guide for the consumer and a marketing advantage for the producer. Ultimately, the advantages of the seal as a selling tool will motivate more companies to produce earth-friendly products.

To carry the Green Seal, products must first pass objective, scientific tests and meet specific standards. Testing is conducted by Underwriters Laboratories Inc. (UL). A brief explanation of the basis for certification appears with the seal.

18-7
Product labeling gives consumers a way of measuring the environmental impact of different products.

downtown parking, banning auto traffic in certain parts of the city, and improving public transportation. Other areas have established express lanes on highways for cars with two or more passengers to encourage carpooling.

Waste Management of North America

18-8
This golf course is part of a landfill project.

Citizen groups have also been active in establishing local air and water quality standards. They have established recycling and composting centers and provided pickup services for recyclable items.

What Government Can Do

Government actions to protect the environment can take a variety of forms ranging from simple leadership to a vast network of regulation and legislation. Government frequently pursues environmental interests at the international level as well as national, state, and local levels. Following is an outline of possible government action to help clean up and protect the planet.

Taxation

While tax dollars do pay for government activities in protecting the environment, the use of taxes as a tool in fighting pollution is a recent concept. The so-called "green tax" offers a way to charge the cost of pollution to the polluter, whether producer

Town Meeting

One Can Make a Difference

Maxine is a high school junior. Maxine is always concerned about the state of the world at large and her piece of it in particular.

Recently, her town council president, Chris Webb, organized a town meeting. Chris invited a highly informed and effective environmentalist to speak on "Survival on Planet Earth." Maxine and several of her friends from school attended the meeting. The speaker outlined five critical environmental issues:

- ❑ Solid Waste Disposal
- ❑ Energy Conservation
- ❑ Global Warming
- ❑ Water Purity and Conservation
- ❑ Hazardous Waste Disposal

The speaker also shared powerful "what you can do" directives. Maxine was highly motivated by the speech. She immediately started recruiting students to form a "Mother Earth" action group. The response was quick and positive. Within a week's time, Maxine had 40 enthusiastic members. The group wants to take steps in each of the five areas. They hope to gain both individual and community participation.

Case Review

1. Choose two environmental issues and outline at least three actions Maxine's Mother Earth group could take in each area. Include individual and community projects.
2. What environmental protection and conservation projects might work in your home, school, and community?

or consumer. Examples of possible items subject to a green tax include the carbon generated by burning fossil fuels, sulfur dioxide, excess household garbage, auto emissions, and heavy traffic. A carbon tax could help pay to correct the undesirable effects of burning carbon, discourage use of fuels that release carbon, and encourage conservation.

Green taxes could take the form of direct tax, fines, or user fees. Advantages of this type of taxation include not only furthering environmental goals but also producing cash revenues. These revenues could be used to help clean up pollution and reduce the deficit. Side benefits could include reduced commuter traffic congestion, less air pollution, less demand for foreign fuels, and ultimately a cleaner environment. Green taxes would provide greater incentive and pressure on manufacturers, producers, and consumers to find cost-effective ways of reducing and controlling pollution. If the polluters were required to pay directly for clean-up costs, they would soon find ways to reduce the pollution and save money.

Regulation and Legislation

Federal, state, and local governments have passed a host of laws and regulations to protect the environment. In 1970, the federal government passed legislation creating the Environmental Protection Agency (EPA). The EPA was created to serve as the national watchdog and coordinating bureau for the environment. The EPA proposes and enforces regulations and laws concerning air and water quality, noise, solid waste, hazardous waste, toxic substances, and other environmental issues. See 18-9 for a list of some of the environmental legislation from the past 30 years.

Earth-Friendly Legislation

Major laws which form the basis for the programs of the Environmental Protection Agency (EPA) include:

- *The National Environmental Policy Act* establishes a national charter for the protection of the environment.
- *The Clean Air Act* authorizes funding for local, state, and federal air pollution control. Amendments establish regulations to control smog, airborne toxins, and acid rain.
- *The Clean Water Act* prohibits discharging pollutants into navigable waters.
- *Comprehensive Environmental Response, Compensation, and Liability Act* established a "superfund" to help pay for the clean up of hazardous waste sites.
- *The Emergency Planning & Community Right-to-Know Act* requires industry to reveal publicly its discharges of wastes.
- *The Endangered Species Act* gives broad based protection to both living things and habitats.
- *The Federal Insecticide, Fungicide, and Rodenticide Act* authorizes federal control of pesticide distribution, sale, and use.
- *The Pollution Prevention Act* identifies measurable goals for reducing industrial pollution.
- *The Toxic Substances Control Act* provides for the federal control of hazardous industrial chemicals.
- *The Safe Drinking Water Act* authorizes the EPA to establish safe standards of purity and to require all owners or operators of public water systems to comply with primary (health-related) standards.
- *The Resource Conservation and Recovery Act* gives the EPA the authority to control the generation, transportation, treatment, storage, and disposal of hazardous waste.

18-9
Legislators have taken steps to improve the environment by passing acts such as these.

Add to these federal laws countless state and local regulations and you end up with a substantial body of law governing environmental activities. Some legislation has been effective; some has not. All of it has been costly. The costs of just administering the EPA runs several billion dollars annually.

Businesses spent billions more to meet government regulations. The total costs of water pollution control rose from $10 billion in 1972 to approximately $55 billion in 1992. The EPA estimates that the cost of environmental regulatory programs over the period from 1991 to 2000 will total $1.6 trillion. This amounts to about $9,000 per person.

All of the environmental legislation has been costly—but not necessarily cost-effective. Obviously, regulations are needed to safeguard people and the environment. However, government, environmentalists, industries, and individuals need to weigh the benefits and costs of laws and regulations. Goals need to focus not only on environmental protection, but also on achieving the most protection possible per dollar.

Considering the Choices

Zero-risk in the environmental arena is as impossible as it is in health care, traffic safety, or crime control. There will always be health problems, traffic accidents, and crime—and there will always be some measure of environmental pollution. The problem becomes one of cost effectiveness and trade-offs. There needs to be accurate, scientific risk assessment followed by assigning top priority for action and regulation to the highest risk problems.

We need to decide which risks are the greatest and set priorities. We must also decide what trade-offs we are willing to make for a cleaner, safer world, 18-10. How many dollar and nondollar sacrifices are we willing to

USDA

18-10
Pesticide use is one area that calls for careful investigation to determine what is necessary and safe.

make to reduce risk? What environmental risks are we willing to accept? How do we identify the most critical risks? In thinking through legislative and other actions, many factors should be considered.

Environmental problems need to be addressed at different levels. For example, global warming, deforestation, and ozone depletion are all international in scope. Community-based problems, such as the town landfill, urban sprawl, and safe drinking water, call for local action and involvement. This will be more direct and cost effective than state or federal action. "Think globally and act locally" is the best guideline to follow.

No matter who makes the choices or what they may be, *you* need to become involved in the process. *You* will make the sacrifices and pay the costs. The costs will come as higher taxes, higher prices, and possible changes in the way you live and the consumer choices you make. It may mean driving smaller cars, living in smaller homes, and buying less "stuff."

Vote for a cleaner environment through consumer spending. Today, businesses recognize the sales appeal of environmentally-safe products and policies. Companies are producing more earth-friendly products. Look for them when you shop.

View natural resources as economic assets. Wealth declines as they are used up just as it does when money is spent. Natural resources include land, water, forests, fuel, wildlife—even wilderness, 18-11. What if we measured the value of these resources in economic terms and included them in the national wealth (gross domestic product)? Proper conservation and management policies would very likely follow. This approach would serve both economic and ecological interests, 18-12.

Energy: Where Are Tomorrow's Sources?

At present, the United States does not meet its energy needs with its own resources. The country depends on

FINA

18-11
Protecting wildlife involves preserving the natural habitat of various forms of animal and plant life.

The Nature Conservancy

18-12
These natural resources are a significant part of our national wealth. They call for responsible guardians.

foreign sources for close to 46 percent of its petroleum. This dependence is of concern for two reasons. First, we have little or no control over the supply or price of fuel imports. Second, fuel imports, which have been totaling close to $53 billion annually, worsen the nation's trade deficit. Reducing dependence on fuel imports would help reduce the trade deficit and strengthen the economy.

Achieving energy independence for the United States will require greater fuel efficiency, conservation, and development of our own energy resources. It will mean reducing energy waste and finding new, affordable, environmentally-safe sources of power.

Energy Sources

Energy sources can be classified as renewable or nonrenewable. ***Renewable energy sources*** are those that keep coming or can be replenished. Wind, water, and the sun are renewable energy sources. ***Nonrenewable energy sources*** are those that can be used up or that cannot be used again. Fossil fuels are nonrenewable energy sources. The petroleum, natural gas, and coal used today were produced over a period of millions of years. These fuels are nonrenewable because once used they are gone and cannot be replaced.

Petroleum and natural gas are the main forms of energy used in the

United States today. Since the nation is not self-sufficient in this resource, oil companies search for new sources of petroleum to increase domestic production. Although these new sources may not produce enough fuel to meet current demand, they will help reduce dependence on imports. New petroleum sources will also help meet fuel needs until other energy sources can be developed.

Coal is the most plentiful source of energy in the United States and one of our major exports. Unfortunately, it has several drawbacks. Coal is difficult to transport. Mining and burning coal damage the environment and add to global warming. Converting coal to a gaseous or liquid form is a costly process. Even with these drawbacks, coal is likely to be a major source of energy well into the future.

Nuclear energy could replace petroleum for many of the nation's energy needs. This energy source now produces 22 percent of our electric power. It accounts for almost 10 percent of our total energy production. Nuclear power could provide more energy, but questions about plant safety and waste disposal have slowed its development. Predicting the future role of nuclear energy is difficult since its use remains controversial.

Solar energy (energy from the sun) is the most desirable source of energy from an environmental standpoint. It produces almost no undesirable side effects. Unfortunately, there are economic and technological problems. At present, it is impossible to concentrate solar energy into high-grade, usable fuel in quantities that will begin to meet the country's energy needs. The storage of solar energy is also a problem. Because of the lack of sunshine at night and on cloudy days, storage systems are needed to provide continuous solar power.

Solar heating systems and water heaters are used most often and most effectively in warm climates. In cooler areas, solar energy systems are sometimes used along with other forms of power. More research is needed before solar energy can become a practical source of power for meeting residential, industrial, and transportation needs.

Other sources of energy for the future may include hydropower, wind, and biofuels. *Biofuels* are made of biological matter that can be converted to energy, such as wood and ethanol. It is not yet possible to produce large quantities of usable energy from any of these sources. However, research is being done to find out the potential, problems, and costs involved in developing these renewable energy sources.

Energy Conservation

Conservation is one of the most effective tools available for addressing energy-related environmental problems. Consider its many advantages. It is cheap, particularly when compared with producing more fuel, importing oil, and developing new sources of energy. It is immediate, which means a reduction in imports now and more time to develop new energy sources. Conservation is environmentally desirable. It poses no threats and reduces some existing environmental problems. Finally, conservation can involve everyone. It can help save you money by reducing the amount of energy you need in the home and on the road.

Most individuals can conserve a considerable amount of energy without major inconvenience. In many senses, it simply involves a new mindset, an habitual tendency to use less, to economize, to save. Following are some ways to reduce personal and family energy use.

In the Home

Space heating and cooling consumes by far the greatest share of

Town Meeting

Cold Weather Fuel Crisis

Chris Webb has had a busy time as town council president. Now he is faced with another crisis. Chris lives in a community where the winters are quite severe. Most homes, businesses, and public buildings in his community are heated with oil, which is scarce and expensive. In recent years, the community has experienced oil shortages during severe cold weather. This year, serious shortages are expected to occur for four or five weeks unless an alternate energy source can be used.

The community generating system could use coal as a source of energy and relieve the fuel shortage. Coal is plentiful in the area and relatively inexpensive. However, the generating facilities do not meet EPA standards for burning coal. Without special generating equipment, the burning of coal could be hazardous to the environment.

Installing the necessary equipment to meet EPA regulations would cost several million dollars. Chris knows the local government could not pay for the new equipment. They would have to pass the costs on to the residents in the form of special fees, higher taxes, or higher utility rates.

Chris met with the town council to discuss the problem. The following ideas were suggested:

- ❑ Close schools and public buildings during severe cold periods to reduce fuel consumption.
- ❑ Open stores, schools, and other public buildings an hour later and close an hour earlier to reduce heating needs.
- ❑ Pass a law requiring that thermostats be set no higher than 65°F.
- ❑ Double fuel prices when demand exceeds supply.
- ❑ Seek special permission from the EPA to permit the burning of coal during peak demand periods.
- ❑ Install the equipment that conforms to EPA standards.

Case Review

1. What should the community do in this case and why?
2. What other alternatives can you suggest for the town council?
3. How might your solutions to this problem differ if this type of situation existed across the country rather than in one community?
4. How might your solutions to this problem differ if the shortage lasted as long as four months each year instead of a few weeks?

energy used in the home. It also offers the greatest room for saving. The better insulated a home is, the less energy it will require for heating and cooling. Insulation is a material used to slow the movement of hot or cool air. It is usually installed in attics, ceilings, walls, and floors to reduce the amount of energy needed for heating and cooling. In winter, heat often escapes through poorly insulated attics. Adequate attic insulation reduces the heat loss and lowers heating bills. Although insulating a home can be costly, over time, it can more than pay for itself in lower fuel costs.

Weather-stripping doors and windows and using well-fitted storm doors and windows also prevents heat from escaping. Closing off rooms that are not in use and keeping all outside doors and windows tightly closed are other ways to conserve energy.

Thermostats can also be set to conserve energy. Set them no higher than 68°F during cold weather and no lower than 78°F during hot weather. Use heating and cooling equipment efficiently. For example, you conserve energy by keeping equipment clean and in good working order. Change or clean filters regularly. Also, use heating and cooling units of the proper size and capacity for the space to be heated or cooled.

The water heater is another major energy eater in the home. Set the temperature no higher than 140°F. A well-insulated hot water storage tank reduces energy use. Less heat will escape and less energy is needed to keep the water hot.

Be water conscious. Try to use less water when bathing and washing dishes by hand. Use warm or cold water instead of hot water for laundering. Heating the water accounts for almost 90 percent of the energy used in washing clothes. Avoid running hot water unnecessarily. Repair leaky faucets promptly.

Electrical appliances and equipment account for approximately 23 percent of energy used in the home. To conserve in this area, turn off the television, radio, stereo, lights, and other electrical equipment when not in use. Keep appliances and equipment in good working condition. Use the appliance that takes the least amount of energy for the job. For example, toasting bread in the oven uses three times more energy than using a toaster. Use your microwave if you have one. It uses approximately one-third of the energy of a conventional oven. Also, look for energy efficiency and energy-saving features when buying appliances, 18-13.

To use less energy when cooking, remove pan lids and open oven doors only when needed. Plan meals so more than one food can be cooked in the oven at the same time. Avoid heating the entire oven for a small job that can be done with a smaller appliance.

To operate refrigerators and freezers efficiently, set refrigerators at 38°F and freezers at 0°F. Periodically check and clean door seals to make sure they fit tightly. Open doors only when necessary. Remember to defrost a freezer before the frost becomes more than ¼-inch thick. To use less energy, keep the freezer filled to near capacity. When buying a refrigerator or freezer, keep in mind that manually defrosted models use less energy than automatics, if they are defrosted regularly. Look also to EnergyGuide labels to find the most efficient models.

Try to use dishwashers, clothes washers, and clothes dryers in the early

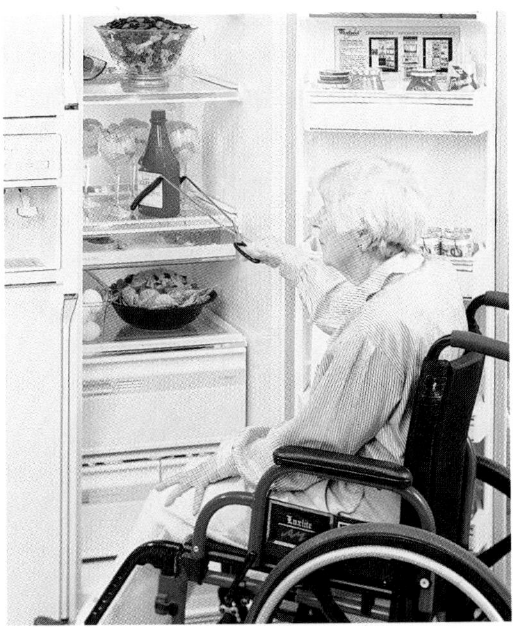

Whirlpool

18-13
Look for energy-saving features when buying appliances and learn to use those appliances efficiently.

morning or late evening. This will help ease the demand for electricity during peak energy usage times. Use these appliances only for full loads. Select the shortest cycle that will do a good job. For greater efficiency with a clothes dryer, clean the filter after each use.

The amounts of electricity and gas you use each month are measured by your electric meter and gas meter. To find out how much energy you use monthly, learn to read your electric and gas meters. Take readings once a month for several months to find out how much fuel you are using and to be sure billing is accurate.

On the Road

Transportation accounts for almost two-thirds of the petroleum used in the United States. There is lots of room for energy conservation and pollution control in this area. The most dramatic difference you can make is switching from car to pollution-free bike or foot. This will cut 100 percent of your fuel usage. By changing from car to bus, you save 42 percent; from car to commuter train, you save 52 percent. If you must drive, you can conserve fuel and cut down driving costs by eliminating unnecessary driving, driving more efficiently, and maintaining your car properly.

To eliminate unnecessary driving, plan trips carefully. Combine errands when possible. Walk or bike when possible. Drive only when there is no other choice. Share rides with friends and neighbors when you can. Carpooling saves energy and money.

To improve driving economy, lower your driving speed, 18-14. Most cars get about 20 percent better fuel economy on the highway at 55 miles per hour than they do at 70 miles per hour. Driving habits also affect fuel consumption. The more you accelerate and decelerate, the more gas you use. When you accelerate smoothly, drive at a moderate speed, and brake gradually, you burn less fuel. When you will be stopped for several minutes, turn the motor off rather than letting the car idle. It takes less gasoline to restart the car than to let it idle for an extended period.

When you are ready to buy a new car, consider its environmental impact. You can save on fuel and cut down on pollution by driving smaller cars. Buy only as much car as you need. Look too for fuel-efficient and low-emission autos. For detailed environmental information on car choices, see the annual *Green Guide to Cars and Trucks* published by the American Council for an Energy-Efficient Economy.

18-14
Most cars use less fuel at lower speeds.

Ford Motor Company

> *"Every 10 days motorists who drive with under-inflated tires and poorly maintained engines waste 70 million gallons of gasoline."*
>
> *Car Care Council*

Have your car tuned regularly. This will extend engine life and improve performance. A poorly-tuned car can use as much as three to nine percent more gasoline than a well-tuned one. Also keep the engine filters clean. Clogged filters waste gasoline. Be sure to use the gasoline and grade of oil recommended for your car and check tire pressures regularly. Underinflated tires increase fuel consumption.

The Government's Role

What individuals and families can do to conserve energy is fairly easy to see. However, this nation's energy policy involves a number of hard choices and controversial issues. For example, should emphasis fall on conservation or finding new sources of energy? Will voluntary conservation work, or should government ration fuel? Should government tax fuel and permit rising fuel prices to discourage use or should it maintain the current lower-than-market prices?

At present, United States gasoline consumption per person is the highest in the world. Annual consumption per capita is more than twice that of any other nation. Low prices encourage that consumption and discourage exploration and development of new fuel sources. Higher gasoline prices would certainly promote greater fuel efficiency and lower consumption.

Should government compromise environmental standards to produce more energy, or should we do with less fuel to protect the environment? To what extent should government encourage and fund the development of renewable sources of energy? What role should government play in helping to determine the real risks and benefits of nuclear power?

Considering energy and the environment, what steps can government take to reduce the use of fossil fuels that contribute so significantly to global warming? More efficient use of fuel alone could cut fossil fuel usage by as much as 50 percent without major sacrifices in the way we live. How can government encourage this efficiency?

It's next to impossible for anyone to grasp all aspects of the energy situation. Geologists can study our untapped energy resources. They cannot estimate how much potential fuel is available or what it would cost to make it usable. Engineers can develop new technologies for producing solar, geothermal, and other forms of energy. They cannot tell how much energy a new technology will produce, how soon, or how much it would cost. Environmentalists and scientists can point out health and ecological threats connected with energy use. They cannot tell how to balance these threats with the need for energy.

Making energy choices is difficult. The decisions we make today will affect the quality of life now and in the future. Energy policies and choices can affect jobs, prices, industries, the environment, and lifestyles here and around the world. Chart 18-15 lists 10 actions governments could take on energy issues.

You may think of additional government actions. Consider the costs, benefits, and consequences of each action. How would each affect you? How would each affect taxpayers, persons at different income levels, and consumers in general? How would your community be affected? What would be the impact on energy-producing industries and other industries, such as transportation, housing, clothing, food, travel, and entertainment? How could each action affect employment, prices, and the environment? What impact might each action make on the supply, demand, and cost of energy and on other goods and services? How might international trade be affected? How might future generations gain or lose from each of these government actions?

Possible Government Action

- ❑ Restrict fuel imports.
- ❑ Set reasonable environmental standards for the exploration, production, distribution, and use of energy sources.
- ❑ Develop and enforce uniform safety standards for the use of nuclear power.
- ❑ Lower environmental standards to permit greater use of coal, which is a plentiful resource.
- ❑ Tax fossil fuels to encourage greater efficiency, to discourage excessive consumption, and to help pay for their negative environmental impact.
- ❑ Mandate energy conservation by such measures as gas rationing, requiring special permits to own a car, raising the legal driving age, and other restrictions.
- ❑ Encourage conservation with incentives, such as tax credits for the purchase of the most fuel efficient cars and home energy efficiency projects.
- ❑ Provide government funding for research and development of renewable, environmentally-safe energy sources.
- ❑ Provide incentives for industry to set up comprehensive research programs to uncover and develop new safe energy sources.
- ❑ Work out a cooperative policy with other nations for the development, allocation, and efficient safe use of world energy resources.
- ❑ Charge fines for environmental abuse.

18-15
Here are some measures government can take on energy issues. Which of these actions would you favor?

Water Resources—Present and Future

Most people in the United States take fresh, pure water for granted. In most parts of the country, water is plentiful and relatively cheap. Water use per person is higher in the United States than in any other nation. However, in recent years both the availability and the quality of water have become serious environmental issues. Water scarcity creates severe problems in some areas.

Actually, water is the most common substance on the earth. It covers 71 percent of the earth's surface. Unfortunately, only about one percent of that water is fresh. Two percent is ice, and 97 percent is saltwater. This substance, which is vital to all forms of life, is becoming more and more precious. While water is a renewable resource recycled through sun and rain, demands for fresh water increase dramatically with population growth. In the years ahead, conserving water will become vitally important, 18-16.

Conserving Water: Your Role

There are many ways to cut down on water usage without seriously disturbing your routine. It pays to do so both to save on your water bill and to conserve a valuable resource. In certain areas, water shortages make conservation crucial and it has become a way of life.

Much of the water usage by individuals is in the bathroom. To conserve, shorten showers and install a low-flow showerhead. Flush less and investigate using a toilet dam to reduce the amount of water used per flush. When installing new toilets, buy low-flow models. This is required by law in some communities for new installations. Use only as much water as necessary for tub bathing. Do not let water run while shaving and brushing teeth.

Kitchen and laundry are other places where water tends to flow too freely. Do not let it run constantly while washing dishes or cleaning vegetables and fruits, 18-17. Throughout the house, take care to repair leaky faucets promptly. Use the dishwasher and clothes washer only for full loads. When buying appliances, look for models with water-saving features. For example, front-loading washers use less water than top-loading machines.

USDA

18-16
This photo shows the impact of severe drought on farmland.

Peerless

18-17
To conserve water in the kitchen, rinse fresh vegetables just enough to remove soil and pesticide residues.

In the yard, you can conserve by watering in the early evening to prevent evaporation by the sunlight. A soak hose uses water more efficiently than sprinklers. During dry spells, use scarce water resources mostly for trees and plantings rather than grass. Lawns normally will recover after a drought, while big trees suffer permanent damage.

Sources of Additional Information

No one can begin to keep up with the ever-increasing numbers of environmental action groups, organizations, government agencies, books, and articles. The danger is not that we may be uninformed or underinformed, but rather, that we may be misinformed. Finding accurate coverage of environmental issues and reasonable solutions to problems is a major challenge for anyone who wants to be informed and involved.

Sources of information on the environment include daily newspapers, news magazines, and government agencies. The EPA, the Department of Energy (DOE), the Department of Agriculture (USDA), and the Department of the Interior are all sources of environmental information. State and local governments also provide information on environmental issues and regulations at those levels.

Contact local water and electric utilities to learn what conservation devices, services, and information they may provide. Contact local government offices to learn about policies and ordinances pertaining to solid and toxic waste management, zoning, water and air quality, water and energy use and conservation, and other environmental issues.

A number of magazines cover conservation and ecology. These include *Audubon, National Wildlife, Natural History*, and *Sierra*. Your local and school libraries will no doubt offer

Town Meeting

The Well Runs Dry

Two summers after Chris began his five-year term as town council president, a drought hit the area and the water table dropped substantially. Water shortages hit agriculture, gardening, and manufacturing. It became necessary to reduce water usage and to limit the use of water for even the most essential purposes. Chris and the town council faced hard choices.

The council called a special meeting to brainstorm ideas for dealing with the water shortage. Chris suggested that they raise water rates by 20 percent. Another member of the council, Alicia Baxter, recommended a ban on watering lawns. Hayden Lupe agreed with Alicia and even suggested limiting watering of trees, shrubs, and gardens. Sherise Garrett advised limiting watering in yards to evening and early morning to get the most efficient results.

Patrick Mendibles thought it would be good to encourage limited use of water-using appliances. People could take shorter showers, shallow baths, and find other ways to cut back their use of water. Another idea of the council was to mandate low-flow toilets, showerheads, and appliances in new and remodeled bathroom and kitchen units. Installing a system of water rationing to limit the amount of water going to each household was also discussed.

As each idea was presented, Chris wrote them on a poster at the front of the room. The council ended up with a pretty lengthy list. They decided to list advantages and disadvantages of each suggestion.

Case Review

1. What other steps can you think of for conserving water?
2. How would each of the council's suggestions affect you and your family?
3. Which idea do you think would be most effective? Why?
4. How would you be willing to change your own habits to help conserve water and other resources in a crisis situation?
5. What are some important considerations for government bodies to think about when passing laws and policies to deal with shortages of resources?

a wide variety of books and other reading material on conservation. Look for environmental Web sites online.

Follow these guidelines when evaluating printed material, organizations, and proposed action:

- ❑ Read two or three accounts of major issues—preferably conflicting accounts. Compare what you learn and research further if you are confused or need to know more.
- ❑ Consider the source of the information. Does the producer have anything to gain in convincing you or motivating you to certain action? Could there be a hidden reason for specific statements and positions on environmental issues?
- ❑ Think through the total impact of potential actions, regulations, and laws to protect the environment. How cost-effective are proposals? How practical are they? How will they affect jobs? living standards? people at different income levels? different industries? other nations?
- ❑ Try to find the most responsible, least hysterical approach to environmental problems and challenges.

It is your world and your future. What can you do now to preserve it?

> *"Woodsman spare that tree!*
> *Touch not a single bough!*
> *In youth it sheltered me,*
> *And I'll protect it now."*
>
> *George Pope Morris*

Summary

Protecting the environment is one of your most important duties as consumer, citizen, and taxpayer. You can take an active role in protecting the earth. Stay informed about current environmental issues. Learn to conserve resources. Lastly, participate in community environmental protection programs.

Conservation is one of the least expensive and most effective ways to protect the environment and stretch natural resources. Community and government programs often encourage conservation. Tools governments can use to benefit and protect the environment include taxation, regulation, and economic incentives to do the right thing.

Both the production and use of various forms of energy create environmental threats. The challenge of the future will be to find earth-friendly sources of energy. Conservation is effective in addressing energy-related environmental concerns. Numerous ways for individuals to conserve exist in both the home and on the road. Government can use policies and laws to encourage conservation and the development of efficient and safe forms of energy.

Protecting water sources is another important issue to consider. Many parts of the country and world face water shortages. Steps should be taken to conserve water resources.

Environmental issues will continue to be important in the years ahead. New issues will most likely surface. It is important to stay informed and take action on these matters. We must all work to preserve and protect the earth we share.

To Review

1. What are six key environmental issues facing the United States and the world today?
2. List four items in your home you could be recycling.
3. What is a "green product?"
4. Which government agency was created to serve as the national watchdog and coordinating bureau for the environment?
5. What are the two main forms of energy used in the United States?
6. What are some consequences of depending too heavily on foreign sources for petroleum?
7. Name three renewable energy sources.
8. What are three drawbacks of using coal as an energy source?
9. List four ways to cut water heating costs.
10. What are three ways to use less gasoline in your car?
11. Name at least three ways to conserve water use in the kitchen and laundry.
12. Name five sources of information on environmental issues.

To Think Critically

1. Why is it important for you to be informed about threats to the environment?
2. What are some of the problems that concern environmentalists today? What environmental problems concern you the most?
3. Why is it difficult to determine what we as a nation should do about energy and water shortages and environmental problems?
4. Give examples of ways the production and use of fuel can damage the environment.
5. Name several steps you as an individual can take to improve and protect our planet.
6. What are some ways to measure the cost effectiveness of environmental protection laws and regulations?
7. How can consumer spending habits and decisions serve as an environmental protection tool?

8. What are some environmental problems that exist in your community? How might they be solved?

To Do

1. Divide into research teams to investigate one of the following sources or types of energy: nuclear, natural gas, coal, solar, geothermal, petroleum, wind, water, or underwater technology. Prepare a report on its use, cost, safety, effectiveness, availability, and impact on the environment.
2. Conduct a survey in your community to learn what specific steps individuals, businesses, and government have taken to protect the environment and conserve resources.
3. Consider the different ways people contribute to environmental problems by their use and disposal of products. Then design a poster or bulletin board to illustrate "Common Consumer Attacks on the Environment."
4. Select one of the current laws or pending bills designed to protect the environment. Study it carefully to find out:
   A. Its main objectives and key provisions.
   B. Its costs and benefits.
   C. Its impact on different segments of society.
   D. Its effectiveness in achieving its purpose.
   E. The ease of enforcing it.

   Present your findings to the class in an oral report or a written report.
5. Debate the pros and cons of an energy tax to reduce pollution, conserve energy, and generate government revenues.
6. Develop a model organization or project for a specific environmental protection goal that could be launched in your community.
7. Investigate to find out where water shortages have been a serious problem in the United States. Find out how affected communities coped with the problem. Report findings.
8. Go online or contact the Environmental Protection Agency, the Department of Energy, or one of the other organizations listed under "sources of additional information" for facts and data you need to prepare a written or an oral report on one of the following:
   - ❑ global warming
   - ❑ ecosystems
   - ❑ urban sprawl
   - ❑ air quality
   - ❑ water quality
   - ❑ Earth Day
   - ❑ recycling
   - ❑ pollution control regulations and costs
   - ❑ an environmental topic of your choice

   Make an effort to present a balanced view covering both sides of controversial issues. Site specific authorities, events, dates, figures, pros, and cons.
9. Investigate environmental industries such as solid waste management, water treatment, hazardous waste management, pollution control equipment, etc. What has been the growth rate of these industries? What employment opportunities do they offer?
10. Write an essay on one of the following:
    - ❑ living car-free
    - ❑ alternatives to driving
    - ❑ cold showers
    - ❑ green-minded shopping
    - ❑ environmentally-friendly life styles.
11. Go online to play "The Great Green Web Game" produced by the Union of Concerned Scientists, www.ucsusa.org.

12. As a class, identify and research a local environmental issue such as urban sprawl, poor water quality, water shortages, power outages, or abandoned property. Outline action citizens could take to help resolve the problem.
13. Write a letter to an appropriate government agency, representative, or official at the federal, state, or local level regarding an environmental issue of concern to you. Define the issue, suggest possible solutions, and express your opinion with supporting arguments. Cite authorities and relevant publications or studies, if available.
14. Write a letter to a corporate president or officer to:
    - ❑ congratulate the company on environmentally friendly products or policies
    - ❑ complain about products or policies that damage the environment
    - ❑ suggest ways the company can improve its environmental record.

Reusing and recycling can help reduce the amount of solid waste that must be put into landfills.

Glossary

A

ATM card. A card that allows you to access your account using an automated teller machine (ATM). (15)

abilities. Physical and mental skills developed through learning, training, and practice. (3)

abstract of title. A summary of the public records or history of the ownership of a particular piece of property. (11)

adjustable rate mortgage. A mortgage in which the interest rate is adjusted up or down periodically according to a national interest rate index causing monthly payments to vary throughout the life of the mortgage. (11)

amortization. The process by which loan payments are applied to the principal, or amount borrowed, as well as to the interest on a loan according to a set schedule. (11)

annual percentage rate (APR). The actual rate of interest figured on a yearly basis. (10)

annual percentage yield (APY). The total amount of interest that would be paid on a $100 deposit based on the annual rate of simple interest and the frequency of compounding over a 365-day period. (15)

annuity. A contract that provides income for a set period of time or for life. (16)

anti-trust laws. Laws and legal actions designed to ensure fair trade and competition and to prevent monopolies in trade. (1)

appraisal. A written estimate of the value of a certain property, such as real estate. (11)

apprenticeship. A type of education that combines on-the-job training, work experience, and classroom-type instruction. (3)

aptitudes. Natural physical and mental talents. (3)

assets. Items that a person owns, such as cash, stocks, bonds, real estate, and personal possessions. (5)

B

bait and switch. A technique that involves advertising an item at a very attractive price to attract customers. When the customer comes to buy, the seller claims to be out of that item. Instead, the seller presents a more expensive substitute. (6)

balance of payments. An account of the flow of goods, services, and money coming into and going out of the country. (1)

bank statement. A record of checks, deposits, and charges on a checking account. (15)

beneficiaries. The people designated to receive property under the terms of a will. (14)

Better America Bonds. An incentive for states and local communities to protect open space and enhance the quality of life. These bonds are a $9.5 billion credit program sponsored by the Environmental Protection Agency for the purpose of helping local communities fight urban sprawl. (18)

binding arbitration. A method of settling disputes outside of court in which the parties involved agree to accept the decision of a third party. (4)

blend. A yarn made by combining two or more fibers. (8)

bond. A certificate of debt issued by a corporation or government that entitles the bondholder to a set rate of interest on the face value of the bond until it matures. (16)

bonus. An amount added to base pay either as a reward for performance or as a share of business profits. (3)

budget. A plan for the use or management of money based on goals and expected income and expenditures. (5)

buying incentives. Trading stamps, coupons, store games, and prizes offered by sellers to help sell goods and services. (6)

C

case goods. Furniture with no upholstered parts. (12)

cash credit. Borrowed money used to purchase goods and services. (13)

cash value. The replacement cost of one's personal property minus depreciation. (11) The amount of money a policyholder would receive if the policy were surrendered before death or maturity. (16)

cashier's check. A check drawn by a bank on its own funds and signed by an authorized officer of the bank, often the cashier. (15)

certificate of deposit. Money deposited for a set period of time that earns a set annual rate of interest (also called CD, savings certificate, time deposit, or time account). (15)

certified check. A personal check with a bank's guarantee the check will be paid. (15)

Chapter 7. Straight bankruptcy in which the court declares a person unable to meet financial obligations and then takes and sells the debtor's property and possessions. Proceeds from the sale are divided among the creditors. (13)

Chapter 13. A legal proceeding that permits debtors with regular incomes to pay all or a portion of their debts under the protection and supervision of the court. The debtor usually keeps all property and possessions. (13)

citizen. A born or naturalized member of a place, such as a country. (17)

claim. A formal demand for payment of a loss covered under the terms of an insurance policy. (2)

class action lawsuits. Legal actions in courts of law brought by a group of individuals who have been similarly wronged. (4)

clearance sale. A reduction from previous prices on merchandise the seller wants to clear or sell, usually to make room for new merchandise. (6)

closeout sale. A discount by suppliers or manufacturers on products that are no longer being produced. (6)

closing costs. Fees that must be paid before the sale of a home can be made final. (11)

co-insurance. The amount of each claim that an insured person must pay, usually 20 percent of costs up to a stated maximum. (9)

collateral. A pledge of some kind of property as security for a loan. (10) (13)

command economy. An economy in which the state or other central authority decides how to use and distribute resources. (2)

commercial bank. A bank owned by stockholders and organized to receive, transfer, and lend money to individuals, businesses, and governments. (15)

commissions. Income paid as a percentage of sales made by a salesperson. (3)

common stock. Stock that pays dividends based on company earnings and economic conditions. (16)

community service learning. Program that combines classroom learning with service in the community. (17)

composting. A natural process that transforms materials like food waste, leaves, and grass into useful soil-like products. (18)

compounding interest. A way of calculating interest where interest previously earned is included in the total before new interest earnings are computed. (15)

compulsory auto insurance laws. A law that requires proof of insurance prior to the occurrence of an accident. (10)

condominium. A form of home ownership in which an individual owns his or her own unit and shares ownership and expenses of maintaining common areas such as halls, stairs, lobby, and grounds. (11)

conservation. The preservation and protection of the environment and natural resources. (18)

consumer advocates. Individuals or groups who promote consumer interests in areas such as health and safety, education, redress, truthful advertising, fairness in the marketplace, and environmental protection. (4)

consumer cooperative. A nonretail association that offers limited goods and services at lower prices than retail stores. (6)

consumer price index (CPI). A measurement of changes in the prices of selected consumer goods and services. (1)

convenience foods. Foods that are partially prepared or ready-to-eat. (7)

conventional home mortgage. A mortgage in which the lender decides the maximum amount of the loan, the amount of the down payment, the interest rate, and other terms of the agreement. (11)

convertible term. Life insurance coverage that permits the insured to exchange the policy without needing new evidence of insurability. (16)

co-payment. A stated amount the policyholder will have to pay for certain expenses. (9)

cooperative. A form of home ownership in which an individual buys shares in a corporation that owns the property. In return, the buyer becomes a resident in a designated unit and a member of the cooperative. (11)

corporate bond. Certificate of debt issued by businesses when they need money to operate and expand. (16)

cosigner. A responsible person who signs a loan along with a borrower thereby agreeing to pay the obligation if the borrower fails to do so. (13)

credit. An arrangement that allows consumers to buy goods or services now and pay for them later. (13)

credit rating. A creditor's evaluation of a person's willingness and ability to pay debts as judged by character, capacity, and capital. (13)

credit report. A history or record of a person's financial and credit practices. (13)

credit union. A nonprofit financial association owned by and operated for the benefit of its members. It accepts deposits and makes loans. (15)

D

debit cards. Cards used to pay for goods and services directly from a checking account, also called *check cards.* (15)

deductible. The amount an insured person must pay before an insurance company pays on a claim. (9)

deduction. An expense that can be subtracted from a person's gross pay before figuring taxes on Form 1040. (3)

deficit spending. The process of spending more money than is available. (17)

depreciation. A decrease in the value of an item over a period of time due to age, wear, and use — applies particularly in valuing property for tax purposes and insurance claims. (10)

Dietary Guidelines for Americans. Seven healthy eating guidelines developed by the U.S. Department of Agriculture. (7)

disability. A severe physical or mental condition that prevents a person from working. (17)

discount rate. The interest rate Federal Reserve banks charge commercial banks for credit when they borrow. (1)

discretionary expenditures. Expense items that can be adjusted according to needs and revenues. (17)

dividend. The money paid to stockholders out of a company's earnings—usually represents a share of profits paid in proportion to the share of ownership. (16)

durable goods. Products that have lasting value, such as furniture, appliances, and cars. (2)

E

ecology. The study of the relationship between living things and their environment. (18)

economic competition. Two or more sellers offer similar goods and services for sale. Each seller tries to attract more customers and sales, and reap financial gain. (1)

economy. The structure of production, distribution, and consumption of goods and services. (1)

electronic funds transfer (EFT). A part of a system of carrying out financial transactions by computer rather than using checks and cash. (15)

endorse. To sign one's name on the back of a check at the left end in order to cash or deposit the check. (15)

endowment insurance. Insurance that pays the face amount of the policy to beneficiaries if the insured dies before the endowment period ends. It also pays the face amount to the insured if he or she lives beyond the endowment period. (16)

EnergyGuide label. A label that lists the estimated annual cost of operating an appliance. (12)

ENERGY STAR label. A program that is a voluntary partnership of the U.S. Department of Energy and the Environmental Protection Agency, product manufacturers, local utilities, and retailers. Its purpose is to encourage the purchase of energy-efficient consumer electronics and appliances. (12)

entitlements. Payments and programs promised by the federal government, such as Social Security and medicare benefits, unemployment benefits, welfare payments, veterans' services, food stamps, and housing subsidies. (17)

entrepreneur. A person who owns and operates his or her own business. (3)

environmental audit. An assessment conducted on a voluntary basis by businesses that strive to meet environmental performance targets and to comply with environmental regulations. (18)

environmental impact statement (EIS). An assessment of potential environmental outcomes of government regulations or of government and government-approved projects such as airports, public buildings, military complexes, highways, etc. (18)

environmentalists. People who are concerned with issues related to maintaining quality of life. (18)

estate. The possessions, such as property, savings, investments, and insurance benefits, a person leaves when he or she dies. (14)

estate planning. Active management of a person's property and assets with a plan for their disposal at his or her death. (14)

estate tax. A tax imposed by the federal government on assets and life insurance left by an individual at the time of his or her death. (17)

ethical behavior. Conduct that conforms to accepted standards of right and wrong. (17)

euro. A common currency used in Europe among the nations participating in the *economic and monetary union (EMU).* (1)

exchange rate. The value of one currency compared to another. (1)

excise tax. A tax levied by federal and state governments on the sale and transfer of certain items, such as cigarettes, gasoline, and alcoholic beverages. (17)

executor. A person who will oversee the management of a person's affairs upon his or her death. (14)

exemption. A tax benefit that reduces the amount of income on which a person must pay taxes. (17)

expiration date. The last day a product should be used. (7)

exporting. Selling products to other nations. (1)

F

fabric finish. A treatment applied to a fabric to achieve certain characteristics. (8)

face value. The amount for which a bond is issued and on which interest payments are figured. (16)

fad. A fashion style that stays popular for only a short time. (8)

family life cycle. The stages of change people pass through as life unfolds from birth to old age. (4)

Federal Deposit Insurance Corporation (FDIC). A U.S. government agency that insures bank deposits up to $100,000. (15)

fee-for-service. Plans, also called indemnity insurance, that pay their share of covered medical services after treatment is provided. (9)

FHA-insured loan. A loan in which the Federal Housing Administration insures the lender against the borrowers' possible default or failure to pay. (11)

finance charge. The total amount a purchaser must pay for the use of credit, including interest charges and any other fees. (10)

financial responsibility laws. A law that requires drivers to show proof of their ability to pay stated minimum amounts in damages after an accident. (10)

financial statement. A written record of a person's financial condition. It states what a person is worth at a given time. (5)

fiscal policies. Government policies related to taxing and spending. (1)

fixed expenses. A set amount of money due on a set date. (5)

fixed-rate mortgage. A mortgage that requires a down payment and fixed monthly payments over an extended period of time. The monthly payments include interest figured at a set rate throughout the life of the loan. (11)

flexible expenses. Varying amounts of money due regularly that can be reduced or shifted to fit the amount of cash available. (5)

food grades. An indication of how well a food meets quality standards. (7)

fossil fuels. Nonrenewable energy sources derived from the partly decayed bodies of animals and plants that lived long ago. (18)

freshness date. The last day a product should be sold. (7)

fringe benefit. Any of a variety of nonwage compensation that offers important financial advantages to workers. (3)

full warranty. A guarantee that provides free repair or replacement of defective products or parts within a reasonable time, places no unreasonable demands on the customer as a condition of receiving repairs or replacement, replaces products or parts if a number of attempts at repair fail, and transfers coverage to a new owner if the product changes hands during the warranty period. (6)

G

generic drug. A drug sold by its common name, chemical composition, or class. Generally costs considerably less than a similar brand-name drug. (9)

generic products. Items that do not carry brand names or trademarks; they usually sell for less than similar brand-name items. (6)

gift tax. A tax levied by the federal government on donors or givers who transfer assets to others. (17)

global warming. A warming near the earth's surface that results when the earth's atmosphere traps the sun's heat. (18)

goals. The specific achievements or objectives that a person wants to reach. (3)

going-out-of-business sale. A deduction from prices by sellers who are attempting to hasten the closing of their business. (6)

government bond. Certificate of debt issued by the U.S. Treasury. (16)

grace period. A period a borrower has between the date of a purchase and the date interest charges begin during which he or she can pay the amount due interest-free. (13)

graduated payment mortgage. A mortgage that allows the buyer to pay low monthly payments at first and higher payments in the future. It is based on the idea the buyer's income will increase as the monthly payments increase. (11)

green products. Products that are environmentally safe according to objective, authoritative testing. (18)

gross domestic product (GDP). The total value of goods and services produced within a country in one year. (1)

gross pay. The amount of income a person earns before deductions. (3)

H

hardwoods. Strong wood from deciduous trees, such as mahogany, maple, walnut, pecan, oak, and fruit woods. They have beautiful, distinctive grains. (12)

health maintenance organization (HMO). Programs that provide a variety of health care services to members for a set prepaid fee. (9)

human resources. Resources a person has within themselves. (5)

hypoallergenic. A type of product that does not contain ingredients that are likely to cause allergic reactions. (9)

I

implied fitness. An unwritten warranty that guarantees a product is fit for any performance or purpose promised by the seller. (6)

implied merchantability. An unwritten warranty that guarantees a product is what it is called and does what its name implies. (6)

importing. Buying products from other nations. (1)

import quota. A limitation on the number or quantity of imports allowed in a country. (1)

impulse spending. Unplanned or "spur of the moment" purchases. (7)

indemnifies. Payment of either the actual cash value of a loss or an amount that will return an insured person to his or her financial position before the loss, whichever is less. (2)

Individual Retirement Account (IRA). An account to which taxpayers may make annual, tax-deductible contributions up to a set amount. The funds in the account accumulate, earn interest, and may not be withdrawn before retirement without penalty. (15)

inflation. An increase in prices or decrease in the value of money resulting from an increase in the amount of money in circulation relative to the amount of goods and services available. (1)

inspection stamps. Stamps indicating foods are wholesome and safe to eat. (7)

insurance. A way to protect yourself against certain financial losses by paying a fee. (2)

international trade. The buying and selling of products and services between nations. (1)

Internet. A network that allows access to millions of different resources around the globe. (3)

internship. A short-term position with a sponsoring organization to gain experience in a certain field of study. (3)

interview. A meeting in which a prospective employer or an admissions officer of a school talks with an applicant. (3)

introductory offer. A promotion in which new merchandise is sold at a lower price that will increase after the initial offer. (6)

investment portfolio. The collection of stocks, bonds, and other securities a person or group owns. (16)

J

joint account. A type of checking account in which more than one person has access to the account. (15)

K

Keogh Plan. A retirement account for self-employed persons that allows tax-deductible contributions up to $30,000 or 20 percent of self-employment earnings, whichever is less, to be made to the account annually and claimed as a tax deduction. The funds in the account accumulate, earn interest, and may not be withdrawn before retirement without penalty. (15)

knit fabrics. Fabrics made by looping yarns together. (8)

L

landfill. A permanent waste disposal site for most solid and nonhazardous wastes. (18)

law of supply and demand. Price and supply tend to follow demand. (1)

law of scarcity. Resources are scarce while the needs they must satisfy are never ending. (1)

lease (car). A legal rental agreement between the car dealer and the lessee, where the lessee pays an initial cost, which usually includes the first monthly payment, a security deposit, and a *capitalized cost reduction*. Monthly payments are made for a set period of time, however, the lessee does not own the car at the end of the lease, though there may be an option to buy it. (10)

lease (housing). A legal rental agreement between the tenant (lessee) and the landlord (lessor) that outlines the terms and conditions under which the tenant occupies the property. (11)

liabilities. Amounts a person owes, such as unpaid bills, credit card charges, personal loans, and taxes. (5)

limited warranty. A guarantee that may require the customer to pay labor costs or handling charges. (6)

life cycle. The stages people pass through as life unfolds from birth to old age. (14)

liquidation. The sale of merchandise at reduced prices in order to aid in converting stock to cash. (6)

liquidity. The ease with which a person can convert an asset to cash without serious loss. (16)

living will. A statement of instructions a person wishes to be followed if he or she becomes unable to make decisions on his or her own behalf. (14)

loss leader. Sales tactic where an item is priced at below cost to attract buyers who will then purchase other merchandise. (6)

M

managed care plan. Health care plans that contract with specific doctors and other health care providers, hospitals, and clinics to provide a range of medical services and preventive care to members of the plan at reduced cost. (9)

management. The process of organizing and utilizing resources to accomplish predetermined objectives. (5)

mandatory expense item. A commitment the federal government has made and cannot change, even if there are not enough revenues to support it. (17)

manufactured fibers. Fibers, such as polyester, nylon, and rayon, that are produced artificially from chemicals. (8)

marketability. The ease of trading an investment. (16)

market economy. An economy designed to respond to the people and reflect the decisions and choices of the people. (2)

maturity date. The day a bond or other obligation is due to be paid. (16)

medicaid. A medical assistance program administered and financed by the states with matching funds from the federal government that helps pay the cost of certain health care services for low-income persons. (9)

medicare. A federal government health insurance program that helps people 65 and older and certain disabled individuals under 65 pay for many health care services. (9)

medigap insurance. Supplemental insurance coverage used to pay for health care not covered by medicare such as deductibles, co-payments, and other out-of-pocket costs. (9)

minimum wage. The lowest amount an employer can pay by law. (3)

monetary policies. Government policies that control the amount of money in circulation by controlling interest rates and credit terms. (1)

money market account. A type of savings account that requires minimum balances and offers limited check-writing privileges. Interest is based on U.S. Treasury Bill rates and fluctuates with current market interest rates. (15)

money market fund. A type of mutual fund that deals only in high interest, short-term investments such as U.S. Treasury Bills, certificates of deposit, and commercial paper. (16)

money order. An order for a specific amount of money payable to a specific payee. (15)

monopoly. A market situation in which only one seller produces the entire output of an industry or sells a product or service for which there is no substitute. (1)

mortgage. A home loan. (11)

mortgage lock-in. Sometimes called a rate-lock or rate commitment, this is a promise from the lender to honor the quoted rates and terms while a loan application is being processed. (11)

municipal bonds. A certificate of debt issued by state, county, and city governments. (16)

mutual fund. An investment offered by a company that uses the money it receives from investors to buy securities from corporations and governments. (16)

mutual savings bank. A saving depository owned by the depositors that divides the profits among depositors in the form of dividends. (15)

N

National Credit Union Association (NCUA). An agency that grants federal charters to qualified groups, supervises credit unions, and insures accounts up to $100,000 in all federal credit unions and in state credit unions that request and qualify for such coverage. (15)

natural fibers. Fibers made from natural sources, such as cotton, linen, silk, and wool. (8)

needs. Items a person must have in order to survive. (4)

net pay. The amount of income a person has left after deductions. (3)

net worth. The difference between total assets and total liabilities. (5)

nonhuman resources. External resources, such as money, time, and equipment. (5)

nonrenewable energy sources. Sources of energy that can be used up or that cannot be used again, such as petroleum, natural gas, and coal. (18)

nonstore sellers. Also called direct marketers, they sell goods and services in different ways and from different locations. They include door-to-door salespersons, catalogs, telemarketers, electronic sales via television or Internet, and consumer cooperatives. (6)

nonwoven fabrics. Cloth, such as felt, artificial suede, lace, and net, made from construction methods other than weaving or knitting. (8)

nutrients. Chemical substances found in foods. (7)

O

occasional expenses. Varying amounts of money due periodically. (5)

open dates. A date on food that indicates when it should be used for best quality, flavor, and nutritive value. (7)

open market operations. The buying or selling of Treasury securities and other government debt instruments in the marketplace by the Federal Reserve. (1)

opportunity costs. The resource a person uses to satisfy one goal that cannot be used for another; essentially, the weighing of one alternative against another rather than merely considering the cash price or value of a specific good or service. (5)

options. Features available at extra cost. (10)

osteopathic medicine. A type of medicine that emphasizes the relationship among nerves, muscles, bones, and organs in treating the whole person. (9)

over-the-counter drugs. Nonprescription medications considered safe for consumers to use by following label directions and warnings. (9)

P

pack date. The day the product was processed or packaged. (7)

personal income tax. A tax on the amount of money a person receives from wages, tips, bonuses, interest on savings and investments, and dividends. (17)

personal property tax. A tax assessed on such items as cars, boats, and furniture. (17)

piecework income. When an employee is paid per piece of work done. (3)

point-of-sale. Shopping aids that save the consumer time and money and help him or her make appropriate selections. (7)

point-of-service plan. A health care plan that connects members with a primary care doctor who participates in the plan. That doctor supervises member care and makes referrals as necessary to participating or nonparticipating specialists. Members may choose specialists outside the plan on their own as well. (9)

points. A one-time charge by lenders at closing to increase the return on a loan. A point is one percent of the amount of the loan. (11)

preferred provider organization (PPO). An arrangement between employers or insurers and doctors and/or hospitals whereby employees receive reduced fees for medical services. (9)

preferred stock. Stock that pays set dividends (profits) at set rates regardless of the amount of profits the company earns. (16)

premium. A certain amount of money or fee a person pays regularly to an insurance company for protection. (2)

prescription drug. Medications prescribed by a doctor and available only by prescription. (9)

primary care physician. A doctor trained to diagnose and treat a variety of illnesses in all phases of medicine. (9)

priorities. The importance a person places on different values and goals. (4)

private ownership. Refers to property and resources individuals own and control. (1)

producers. Those who make and sell goods and services to satisfy consumer needs and wants. (1)

productive resources. All the resources—such as labor, land, factories, machinery, capital, and management skills—that are used to provide and produce goods and services. (1)

productivity. The amount of goods and services created for each hour on the job. (2)

progressive tax. A higher percentage tax is placed on the rich rather than on the poor. (17)

protectionism. A policy of discouraging imports through trade barriers such as tariffs or import quotas, in order to protect American businesses and jobs from foreign competition and to reduce the trade deficit. (1)

public goods. Property and resources owned and controlled by the government. (1)

pull date. The last day a product should be sold. (7)

purchase agreement. A contract between a home buyer and a seller that includes a description of the real estate, its location, the purchase price, the possession date, and any other conditions and terms of the sale. (11)

pyramid schemes. Scams calling for each participant to buy into the plan for a given amount of money and to sign up a certain number of additional participants to do the same. The only way you can move up the pyramid and collect the promised profits is to recruit new participants who in return will recruit other participants. The many participants at the bottom of the pyramid end up paying money to the few at the top. The promises almost always are exaggerated and false. (6)

R

real estate tax. A tax based on the value of land and buildings owned by taxpayers. Rates vary greatly from area to area and state to state. (17)

rebate. A deduction in price that is returned after a product has been purchased. (6)

recession. A phase in the business cycle in which economic activity declines and unemployment increases. (1)

Recommended Dietary Allowances (RDA). A guideline detailing the necessary daily nutrients for people of different sexes, ages, and weights. (7)

recycle. To reprocess resources so they can be used again. (18)

reference. A person who has direct knowledge of a person and his or her past work record. (3)

regressive tax. A tax that taxes a lower percentage of income from the rich and a higher percentage from the poor. (17)

regular savings account. A savings account that allows deposits and withdrawals to be made in varying amounts at any time. (15)

renewable energy sources. Sources of energy that are unending or can be replenished, such as wind, water, and the sun. (18)

renewable term. Type of life insurance coverage that allows you to renew your coverage at the end of the term. (16)

repossession. A lender regains possession of an item because the buyer fails to make payments. (13)

resources. Any means a person uses to reach his or her goals. (5)

resume. A summary of a person's skills, training and education, and past work experiences. (3)

retail stores. Stores that sell goods or services directly to consumers. (6)

risk tolerance. The amount of uncertainty or possibility of loss that a person can bear. (16)

S

salary. Income paid as a set amount for a period of time. (3)

sales credit. The use of a credit card or a charge account to buy goods and services. (13)

sales tax. A tax levied by state and local governments on retail sales of certain goods and services. (17)

savings and loan association. A cooperative association that receives and pays dividends on depositors' savings, makes home mortgage or improvement loans, and offers most of the services commercial banks offer. (15)

Savings Association Insurance Fund (SAIF). A fund administered by the FDIC that insures deposits up to $100,000. (15)

scale floor plan. A drawing that shows the size and shape of a room. (12)

secured loan. A loan for which some kind of asset must be pledged as collateral. (13)

security. A stock, bond, mutual fund, or other investment issued by corporations and governments to raise money to operate and expand. (16)

security deposit. Amount of money a renter pays a landlord to insure against financial losses if the renter damages the dwelling or fails to pay rent. (11)

service contract. Contract that provides for the servicing of an appliance if it is needed during the term of the contract. (12)

small claims court. A simple, inexpensive way to settle minor differences involving small amounts of money. (4)

social responsibility. A general sense of concern for the needs of individuals, community, country, and world. (17)

Social Security. The federal government's basic program for providing income when earnings are reduced or stopped because of retirement, disability, or death. (17)

softwoods. Woods made from evergreen, such as cedar, spruce, redwood, and pine trees, that are used for casual furniture. (12)

solid wood. Furniture in which all exposed parts are made of whole pieces of wood that are cut and carved to shape. (12)

specialist. A physician who has had further education and training in a specific branch of medicine. (9)

standard deduction. An amount fixed by law and based on filing status and age, which taxpayers may deduct from adjusted gross income before determining tax. (17)

standard of identity. Common foods that contain ingredients in preset amounts and have standard names, such as ice cream, catsup, and mayonnaise. (7)

standards. Established measures of quality or excellence. (4)

standard of living. The total amount and quality of goods and services you can afford. (2)

stock. A share in ownership of a corporation. (16)

survey. The map of a property showing the measurements, boundaries, and characteristics of the property. It is often required by a lender granting a mortgage to make sure the property conforms to its legal description. (11)

sustainable development. Meeting present needs without compromising the ability of future generations to meet their own needs. (18)

T

tariff. A tax on imported products. (1)

tax. A mandatory payment made by an individual or organization to government for public needs. (17)

tax audit. A thorough detailed examination of a person's tax return by the IRS. (17)

tax avoidance. A legal means of reducing taxes by claiming legitimate adjustments, deductions, and credits. (17)

tax-deferred. The money that is not taxed until withdrawn from an account. (14)

tax evasion. An illegal means of reducing taxes by failing to declare all income and falsifying deductions, adjustments, and credits. (17)

tax liability. The amount of tax that must be paid. (17)

term life insurance. Insurance that covers the policyholder for a specific period of time—5, 10, or 20 years or until a specified age. (16)

tip. Income in the form of money that a customer gives to a worker for services provided. (3)

title. A document that gives proof of the rights of ownership and possession of a particular piece of property. (11)

trade barrier. Any action taken to control or limit imports. (1)

trade deficit. The loss of economic power due to a country importing more than it is exporting over a period of time. (1)

traffic patterns. The paths people normally follow as they walk through a room. (12)

traveler's checks. Checks that can be cashed in most places around the world. They are often used by people who travel and don't want to carry large amounts of cash. (15)

trust. A legal agreement where assets and property are managed by a trustee on behalf of the beneficiaries. (14)

trustee. A person or institution named to manage an estate on behalf of the beneficiaries. (14)

Truth in Lending Law. A law requiring creditors to provide borrowers with a complete written account of credit terms and costs. (10)

Truth in Savings Act. A law that requires depository institutions to state earnings on deposits in uniform terms. (15)

U

unit price. The price of an item based on the cost per unit, weight, or measure. (7)

universal product code (UPC). A series of black lines, bars, and numbers that appear on products to facilitate computerized checkout and inventory control in stores. (7)

unsecured loan. Generally a loan that only requires a signature promising to repay the loan as stated in the contract; not backed by collateral or pledge of valuables. (13)

urban sprawl. Dispersed development outside of compact urban and village centers along highways and in rural countrysides. This type of random, unplanned, and uncontrolled development creates and aggravates a number of environmental and economic problems. (18)

V

VA-guaranteed loan. A long-term, fixed-rate mortgage insured by the Veterans Administration for veterans of the U.S. Armed Forces. (11)

values. The ideals and principles that are important to a person. (3)

value system. A system that guides a person's behavior and provides a sense of direction in his or her life. (4)

veneered wood. Strong, durable wood made of several thin layers of wood bonded together. Fine wood is often used for the top layer. (12)

volunteerism. Service given without payment. (17)

W

W-2 Form. A Wage and Tax Statement that states the amount an employee was paid in the previous year. It also gives the amounts of income, Social Security, and medicare taxes that were withheld from an employee's income during the year. (17)

W-4 Form. The Employee's Withholding Allowance Certificate that tells the employer how much tax to withhold from an employee's paycheck. (17)

wages. Income paid by the hour in exchange for labor. (3)

wants. Items that a person would like to have but are not essential for life. (4)

wardrobe inventory. A list of all the clothes, shoes, and accessories a person owns. (8)

warranty. A guarantee made by a manufacturer or seller of a product or service concerning the responsibility for quality, characteristics, and performance of the product or service. (6)

whole life insurance. Insurance that provides the policyholder with basic lifetime protection so long as premiums are paid. (16)

will. A legal document stating what a person wants done with his or her assets after death. (14)

woven fabrics. Cloth made by interlacing two or more sets of yarn at right angles. (8)

Y

yield. The percentage of a return on an investment. (16)

Index

D

E

F

G

H

I

N

O

P

R

S

T

U

V

W

Y